TABLE OF CONTENTS

Preface v
List of Nutshell Titles and Abbreviations vii
General Index Index-1
Table of Nutshell/Am Jur 2d Correlations Tables-1
Table of Nutshell/Key Number System Correlations . . . Tables-11

PREFACE

West Group is pleased to provide this **Nutshell Series Fast Finder.** This pamphlet contains a General Index which provides easy access to all current Nutshell Series titles published as of June, 1998. Among the features of this Fast Finder are:

- A list of titles in the Nutshell Series, along with the abbreviations used to represent those titles in this Fast Finder;
- An alphabetical subject index to legal and factual words and concepts, leading cases, and statutory popular names;
- A table correlating the titles of the Nutshell Series to the articles in Am Jur 2d for additional research; and
- A table correlating the Nutshell Series to the topics in the West Digest Key Number system.

For references to Nutshell titles published subsequent to this Fast Finder, please consult the indexes contained in those pamphlets.

LIST OF NUTSHELL TITLES AND ABBREVIATIONS

The following table shows the titles of all current publications in the Nutshell Series as of June, 1998, and the abbreviated titles by which they are referred in the General Index. For references to Nutshell titles published after June, 1998, consult the indexes contained in the back of those titles.

TITLE	ABBREVIATION
Accounting and Finance for Lawyers	Acctg & Fin Attys
Administrative Law	Admin Law
Admiralty	Admiralty
Agency - Partnership	Agency-Partn
Agency, Partnership, and the LLC	Partn & LLC
Agriculture Law	Agric
AIDS Law	AIDS
Alternative Dispute Resolution	Alt Disp Resol
American Indian Law	Am Indian
Anglo-American Law	Anglo-Am
Antitrust Law and Economics	Antitrust & Econ
Appellate Advocacy	App Adv
Art Law	Art
Banking and Financial Institutions Law	Bank & Fin
Bankruptcy and Other Debtor-Creditor Law	Bankr
California Civil Procedure	Cal Civ Proc
Civil Procedure	Civ Proc
Coastal and Ocean Management	Coastal and Ocean
Community Property	Comm Prop

TITLES AND ABBREVIATIONS

TITLE	ABBREVIATION
Comparative Legal Traditions	Comp Legal Trad
Conflicts	Conflicts
Constitutional Analysis	Const Analysis
Constitutional Civil Rights	Civ Rts
Constitutional Federalism	Const Federalism
Constitutional Law	Const Law
Consumer Law	Consumer
Contract Remedies	Contract Rem
Contracts	Contracts
Corporations, The Law of	Corp Law
Criminal Law	Crim
Criminal Procedure-Constitutional Limitations	Crim Proc-Const. Lim.
Elder Law	Elder
Employee Benefit Plans	Emp Bene Plans
Energy and Natural Resources Law	Energy
Environmental Law	Environ
Estate Planning, Intro to	Est Plan
Estates in Land and Future Interests	Est in Land
European Union Law	Euro Union
Evidence, State and Federal Rules	Evid
Family Law	Fam Law
Federal Disability Law	Fed Disab
Federal Estate and Gift Taxation	Fed Est & Gift Tax
Federal Income Taxation of Corporations and Stockholders	Fed Corp Tax
Federal Income Taxation of Individuals	Fed Income Tax, Ind
Federal Income Taxation of Partners and Partnerships	Fed Income Tax, Partn
Federal Jurisdiction	Fed Jurisd
Federal Law of Employment Discrimination	Emp Discrim
Federal Rules of Evidence	Fed Rules Evid
First Amendment Law	First Amd
First Trial, The	First Trial

TITLES AND ABBREVIATIONS

TITLE	ABBREVIATION
Government Contracts	Govt Contracts
Hazardous Wastes and Toxic Substances, The Law of	Haz Waste & Toxic Sub
Health Care Law and Ethics	Health Care
Immigration Law and Procedure	Immigration
Individual Employee Rights	Indiv Employee Rts
Injunctions	Inj
Insurance Law	Insur
Intellectual Property	Intell Prop
International Business Transactions	Intn'l Bus
International Environmental Law	Intn'l Environ
International Human Rights	Intn'l Human Rts
International Taxation	Intn'l Tax
International Trade and Investment	Intn'l Trade & Invest
Judicial Process	Judicial Proc
Jurisprudence - Legal Philosophy	Jurispr
Labor and Employment Arbitration	Labor Arb
Labor Law	Labor
Land Use	Land Use
Landlord and Tenant	L&T
Law, The Study and Practice of	Law Study & Prac
Law and Economics	Law & Eco
Legal Drafting	Legal Draft
Legal Interviewing and Counseling	Legal Interview
Legal Negotiation	Legal Nego
Legal Research	Legal Research
Legal Writing	Legal Writing
Legislative Law and Process	Legis Law & Proc
Local Government Law	Loc Govt
Mass Communications Law	Mass Comm
Medical Liability, The Law of	Med Liab
Mental Health and Disability Law	Mental Health & Disab
Military Law	Mil

TITLES AND ABBREVIATIONS

TITLE	ABBREVIATION
Negotiable Instruments and Check Collection	Neg Inst
Oil and Gas Law	Oil & Gas
Personal Property	Pers Prop
Pretrial Litigation	Pretr Lit
Products Liability	Prod Liab
Professional Responsibility	Prof Resp
Public International Law	Pub Intn'l Law
Public Land Law, Modern	Pub Land
Real Estate Finance	Real Est Fin
Real Property	Real Prop
Regulated Industries	Reg Indus
Religion, The State and	Relig
Remedies	Remedies
Sales and Leases of Goods	Sales & Leases Goods
Schools, Students & Teachers, The Law of	Schools
Sea, The Law of the	Law of the Sea
Section 1983 Litigation	Sec 1983 Lit
Secured Transactions	Secur Trans
Securities Regulation	Securities Reg
Sentencing, Corrections, and Prisoners' Rights, Law of	Sentencing
Sex Discrimination	Sex Discrim
Sports Law	Sports
State & Local Taxation & Finance	State & Loc Tax & Fin
State Constitutional Law	State Const
Study Law and Take Law Exams, How to	Study Law & Exams
Tax Procedure & Tax Fraud	Tax Proc & Fraud
Torts	Torts
Toxic Torts	Toxic
Trial Advocacy	Trial Adv
Trial and Practice Skills	Trial & Prac
Unfair Trade Practices	Unfair Trade
Uniform Commercial Code	UCC

TITLES AND ABBREVIATIONS

TITLE	ABBREVIATION
Uniform Probate Code	Unif Probate
Water Law	Water
White Collar Crime	White Collar Crim
Wills and Trusts	Wills
Workers' Compensation and Employee Protection Laws	Work Comp

GENERAL INDEX

References are to Titles and Pages

ACCEPTANCE
Contracts (this index)
Uniform Commercial Code (this index)

ACCOUNTING AND FINANCE FOR LAWYERS
Accounting principles board defined, **Acctg & Fin Attys 49**
Accounts, generally, **Acctg & Fin Attys 39-42**
Accrual method of accounting, **Acctg & Fin Attys 25, 60**
Accrued expenses, **Acctg & Fin Attys 27, 28, 189, 190**
Accrued liabilities, **Acctg & Fin Attys 103, 104**
Accrued revenues, **Acctg & Fin Attys 26**
Additional paid-in-capital, **Acctg & Fin Attys 22**
Adjusting entries defined, **Acctg & Fin Attys 24**
AICPA, **Acctg & Fin Attys 50**
Allowance for doubtful accounts, **Acctg & Fin Attys 89-92**
American Institute of Certified Public Accountants, **Acctg & Fin Attys 50**
Amortization, **Acctg & Fin Attys 155, 156, 164-170**
Assets, **Acctg & Fin Attys 2, 3, 332-335**
Audits, reports, **Acctg & Fin Attys 14, 15**
Bad debts, **Acctg & Fin Attys 89-92**
Balance sheet, **Acctg & Fin Attys 1, 2, 6, 45**
Balance sheet equation defined, **Acctg & Fin Attys 5**
Bonds, **Acctg & Fin Attys 161-172, 193, 194, 354-359**
Bulletins, accounting research bulletins, **Acctg & Fin Attys 50**
Capital and capitalization, **Acctg & Fin Attys 22, 35, 136-138, 149-151, 209-217, 367-369, 371-372**

ACCOUNTING AND FINANCE FOR LAWYERS —Cont'd

Cash, **Acctg & Fin Attys 73, 74, 82-88**
Changes in accounting principles, **Acctg & Fin Attys 341-344**
Closing the books, **Acctg & Fin Attys 42-44**
Combinations, business combinations, **Acctg & Fin Attys 298-300, 311-314**
Common stock, valuation, **Acctg & Fin Attys 362-369**
Completed contract method of accounting, **Acctg & Fin Attys 71, 72**
Computer software costs, **Acctg & Fin Attys 157, 158**
Conservatism, **Acctg & Fin Attys 61-63**
Consolidated financial statements, generally, **Acctg & Fin Attys 179-183**
Contingent liabilities, **Acctg & Fin Attys 4, 62, 108-111**
Contra accounts, **Acctg & Fin Attys 36, 90, 139, 140**
Contributions to capital, cash, **Acctg & Fin Attys 257-250**
Convertible debt, **Acctg & Fin Attys 201-204, 322-326**
Copyrights, **Acctg & Fin Attys 154**
Corporations, stock and stockholders, **Acctg & Fin Attys 172-183, 204, 205, 257-273, 275-281, 320-322, 359-369**
Cost-benefit analysis, **Acctg & Fin Attys 64**
Cost defined, **Acctg & Fin Attys 77**
Cost method, accounting for investments in stock, **Acctg & Fin Attys 172-176**
Cost of capital, **Acctg & Fin Attys 369-372**
Cost of goods sold, **Acctg & Fin Attys 37, 38, 114-118, 127, 128**
Credits, journals, **Acctg & Fin Attys 17-21**
Current assets, **Acctg & Fin Attys 6, 33-35, 37, 38, 54, 62, 73, 74, 81-97, 112-129, 333, 334**
Current liabilities defined, **Acctg & Fin Attys 6, 81, 82**
Current ratio, **Acctg & Fin Attys 328, 329**
Customers, reporting on major customers, **Acctg & Fin Attys 349, 350**
Debits, journals, **Acctg & Fin Attys 17-21**
Debt equity ratio, **Acctg & Fin Attys 330**

ACCOUNTING AND FINANCE FOR LAWYERS —Cont'd

Debt securities, **Acctg & Fin Attys 101-103, 161-172, 186-205, 354-359**
Deferred expenses, generally, **Acctg & Fin Attys 3**
Deferred revenues, **Acctg & Fin Attys 4, 31-33, 104**
Deferred taxes, income tax accounting, **Acctg & Fin Attys 223-237**
Defined benefit pension plans, **Acctg & Fin Attys 244-253**
Defined contribution pension plans, **Acctg & Fin Attys 241-243**
Depletion, **Acctg & Fin Attys 147, 148**
Deposits, **Acctg & Fin Attys 105, 106**
Depreciation, **Acctg & Fin Attys 35, 36, 138-147**
Discontinued operations, **Acctg & Fin Attys 340, 341**
Dividends, **Acctg & Fin Attys 173, 177, 178, 263-269, 337**
Double-entry bookkeeping, **Acctg & Fin Attys 18**
Earnings per share, generally, **Acctg & Fin Attys 10, 336**
Equity method, accounting for investments in stock, **Acctg & Fin Attys 176-178**
Errors, **Acctg & Fin Attys 269**
Exchanges of assets, **Acctg & Fin Attys 132-135**
Expenses defined, **Acctg & Fin Attys 8, 77, 78**
Extraordinary items, **Acctg & Fin Attys 339**
Financial accounting, **Acctg & Fin Attys 1**
Financial accounting standards boards, **Acctg & Fin Attys 48, 55, 56**
Financial ratios, generally, **Acctg & Fin Attys 327, 328**
Financial statement analysis, **Acctg & Fin Attys 326-328**
Financial statements, generally, **Acctg & Fin Attys 1**
Fixed assets, **Acctg & Fin Attys 130-138, 149-152**
Footnotes, generally, **Acctg & Fin Attys 10, 11**
Foreign segment reporting, **Acctg & Fin Attys 348, 349**
Franchises, **Acctg & Fin Attys 154**
Fully diluted earnings per share, **Acctg & Fin Attys 320, 321, 325, 326**
Future values, computing, **Acctg & Fin Attys 385-387, 390-393**
GAAP, **Acctg & Fin Attys 46-51**

ACCOUNTING AND FINANCE FOR LAWYERS—Cont'd

Gains defined, **Acctg & Fin Attys 7**
Generally accepted accounting principles, **Acctg & Fin Attys 46-51**
Going concerning assumption, **Acctg & Fin Attys 58, 59**
Goodwill, generally, **Acctg & Fin Attys 59**
Historical cost, **Acctg & Fin Attys 58, 57, 131**
Income statement, **Acctg & Fin Attys 7, 9, 45, 339-345**
Income tax accounting, generally, **Acctg & Fin Attys 53, 54**
Induced conversions, **Acctg & Fin Attys 203, 204**
Industry segment reporting, **Acctg & Fin Attys 346-348**
Inflation, accounting for, **Acctg & Fin Attys 58**
Intangible assets, **Acctg & Fin Attys 153-159**
Interest rates, determinants, **Acctg & Fin Attys 95, 96, 100, 136-138, 162-172, 188-193, 356-358**
Interim financial statements, **Acctg & Fin Attys 350-352**
Internal controls, **Acctg & Fin Attys 84, 85**
Inventory, **Acctg & Fin Attys 37, 38, 54, 62, 112-129, 333, 334**
Investments, generally, **Acctg & Fin Attys 183-185**
Journals, **Acctg & Fin Attys 17-21**
Land held for investment, **Acctg & Fin Attys 183, 184**
Last in, last out (LIFO) method. Inventory, supra
Leases, generally, **Acctg & Fin Attys 206-209, 217-221**
Ledgers defined, **Acctg & Fin Attys 19, 20**
Leveraged leases, **Acctg & Fin Attys 217, 218**
Liabilities, **Acctg & Fin Attys 3, 4, 6, 81, 82, 101-103, 106-111, 186-205**
Life insurance, cash value as an investment, **Acctg & Fin Attys 184, 185**
Long term contracts, **Acctg & Fin Attys 71, 72**
Long term debt, **Acctg & Fin Attys 101-103, 186-205**
Losses defined, **Acctg & Fin Attys 8**
Marketable securities, accounting for, **Acctg & Fin Attys 85, 86**
Market values, recognizing revenues based on changes, **Acctg & Fin Attys 74-76**
Matching concept, **Acctg & Fin Attys 61, 78-80**

ACCOUNTING AND FINANCE FOR LAWYERS —Cont'd

Materiality, effect on accounting methods, **Acctg & Fin Attys 63, 64**
Natural resources, depletion, **Acctg & Fin Attys 147, 148**
Notes, **Acctg & Fin Attys 94-96, 100, 101**
Operating cycle defined, **Acctg & Fin Attys 81**
Operating leases, **Acctg & Fin Attys 210, 211, 214, 215**
Organization costs, corporations, **Acctg & Fin Attys 261**
Owner's equity, **Acctg & Fin Attys 4, 5, 10, 39-41**
Partnerships, **Acctg & Fin Attys 282, 283, 288-294**
Patents, **Acctg & Fin Attys 153, 154**
Payable, accounts payable, **Acctg & Fin Attys 98-100**
Payout ratio, **Acctg & Fin Attys 337**
Percentage of completion method accounting, long term contracts, **Acctg & Fin Attys 71, 72**
Posting, **Acctg & Fin Attys 20, 21**
Preferred stock, valuation, **Acctg & Fin Attys 359-362**
Prepaid expenses, **Acctg & Fin Attys 33-35, 96, 97**
Present value, **Acctg & Fin Attys 355, 356, 363-366, 375-378, 388-390, 393-398, 401, 402, 405, 406**
Price earnings (p/e) ratio, **Acctg & Fin Attys 336**
Primary earnings per share, **Acctg & Fin Attys 319, 321, 324-326**
Prior period adjustments, **Acctg & Fin Attys 269**
Profit margin, **Acctg & Fin Attys 334**
Property, plant, and equipment, **Acctg & Fin Attys 130-138, 149-152**
Purchase discounts, accounts payable, **Acctg & Fin Attys 98, 99**
Quick ratio, **Acctg & Fin Attys 329**
Real estate, leases, **Acctg & Fin Attys 218**
Realization requirement, generally, **Acctg & Fin Attys 61**
Receivables, **Acctg & Fin Attys 86-96, 333**
Regulatory agencies, financial statements filed with, **Acctg & Fin Attys 52, 53**
Repairs, related to fixed assets, **Acctg & Fin Attys 149, 150**
Research and development, **Acctg & Fin Attys 157**
Restructuring of long term debt, **Acctg & Fin Attys 197-201**

ACCOUNTING AND FINANCE FOR LAWYERS —Cont'd

Retained earnings, **Acctg & Fin Attys 262-270**
Retirement of long term debt, **Acctg & Fin Attys 194-197, 241-255**
Return on assets, **Acctg & Fin Attys 334, 335**
Return on equity, **Acctg & Fin Attys 335**
Revenue recognition principle, generally, **Acctg & Fin Attys 61**
Revenues defined, **Acctg & Fin Attys 7**
Reversing entries, **Acctg & Fin Attys 29, 30**
Sales, **Acctg & Fin Attys 68, 69, 151, 152, 218-220**
SEC, regulation of accounting standards, **Acctg & Fin Attys 51, 52**
Securities and Exchange Commission, regulation of accounting standards, **Acctg & Fin Attys 51, 52**
Segment reporting, **Acctg & Fin Attys 346-350**
Service marks, **Acctg & Fin Attys 154**
Sinking funds, investment in, **Acctg & Fin Attys 185**
Software costs, **Acctg & Fin Attys 157, 158**
Source documents, **Acctg & Fin Attys 16, 17**
Statements, **Acctg & Fin Attys 1, 2, 6, 7, 9-13, 45, 339-345**
Stock and stockholders, **Acctg & Fin Attys 172-183, 204, 205, 257-273, 275-281, 320-322, 359-369**
Subsidiaries, in consolidated financial statements, **Acctg & Fin Attys 179-183**
T-accounts, **Acctg & Fin Attys 20**
Times fixed charges earned, **Acctg & Fin Attys 331, 332**
Times interest earned, **Acctg & Fin Attys 331**
Trademarks, **Acctg & Fin Attys 154**
Trade names, **Acctg & Fin Attys 154**
Treasury stock, **Acctg & Fin Attys 270-273**
Trial balance, **Acctg & Fin Attys 42, 43**
Valuation, **Acctg & Fin Attys 353-369, 372-381**
Warrants, stock warrants, **Acctg & Fin Attys 204, 205**
Work-in-process inventory, **Acctg & Fin Attys 128, 129**
Writedowns of assets, generally, **Acctg & Fin Attys 76**

GENERAL INDEX

References are to Titles and Pages

ADMIRALTY

Abandoned Shipwreck Act of 1987, **Admiralty 131**

Access, **Law of the Sea 79-85, 129-131, 228**

Admiralty Extension Act, **Admiralty 33, 353**

Aircraft, **Law of the Sea 107, 110, 121**

Air defense identification zone, jurisdiction of coastal state, **Law of the Sea 233**

Air routes, archipelagic, **Law of the Sea 110**

Air space, **Law of the Sea 56-58, 79, 97, 105, 122, 123, 161**

Allowable catch, **Law of the Sea 124, 125**

Amalfi, Tablets of, **Admiralty 2**

American Maritime Law, development, **Admiralty 3**

Anadromous species, **Law of the Sea 132-134, 139**

Arbitration, **Law of the Sea 77, 78, 123, 128, 144, 182, 184, 237-246**

Archipelagic states, **Law of the Sea 56-58, 79, 110, 111**

Arrest, **Law of the Sea 18-27, 31-34, 85-90, 92, 93, 102, 133, 134, 221-224, 231**

Articles of confederation, **Admiralty 2**

Artificial islands and installations, **Law of the Sea 144-149, 161, 205, 206, 236**

Assistance, **Law of the Sea 97, 184**

Atmosphere, pollution from or through, **Law of the Sea 208**

Atolls, baseline of islands situated on, **Law of the Sea 50**

Austral charter, **Admiralty 1**

Baselines, **Law of the Sea 37-58**

Bays, **Law of the Sea 41-46, 58, 59**

Benedict's doubt, **Admiralty 31**

Benefits review board, **Admiralty 242**

Bills of lading, **Admiralty 54**

Boarding of ships, **Law of the Sea 19-27, 85-92, 101, 102, 113, 114, 133, 134, 221-223**

Bonds, **Law of the Sea 92, 133, 223**

Bottomry and respondentia bonds, **Admiralty 81**

Boundaries, **Law of the Sea 37-79, 243**

Breadth, **Law of the Sea 95, 113, 121, 157, 158**

ADMIRALTY—Cont'd
Cables and pipelines (submarine), **Law of the Sea 100, 161, 235, 236**
Carriage of goods, generally, **Admiralty 44**
Catadromous species, conservation of, **Law of the Sea 132**
Certificates, **Law of the Sea 8-12, 83**
Cesser clause, **Admiralty 52**
Charter parties, **Admiralty 44, 45, 47-49, 51, 53**
Choice of law, **Admiralty 150, 214, 320**
Clause paramount, **Admiralty 52**
Coastal state, **Law of the Sea 28, 85-93, 99-105, 113, 114, 123-128, 133, 134, 141-143, 145, 159-165, 191, 198-202, 221-224, 235, 236**
Collisions, **Admiralty 18, 19, 151-162, 164-166**
Commission on the limits of the continental shelf, **Law of the Sea 158**
Common heritage of mankind, deep seabed mineral resources, **Law of the Sea 172, 180**
Connally amendment, effect on settlement of disputes, **Law of the Sea 239, 240**
Conservation and management of living resources, **Law of the Sea 100, 120, 123-141, 163-165, 233-235, 243**
Contiguous zone, **Law of the Sea 113, 114**
Continental shelf, **Law of the Sea 64-76, 133, 150-171, 205, 206**
Contracts, **Law of the Sea 25-29, 181-183**
Contributions, **Law of the Sea 183, 189, 190**
Damages, **Admiralty 30, 37, 137, 140, 144, 145, 164, 189, 201, 269, 270, 272, 273-281**
Death on the High Seas Act, **Admiralty 30, 37, 269**
Deep seabed mining, **Law of the Sea 172-190, 196, 207, 208**
Delimitation, **Law of the Sea 58-79, 243**
Delta, baseline, **Law of the Sea 40**
Developing states, **Law of the Sea 126, 181, 182, 184, 195-198**
Drug trade, **Law of the Sea 19, 21, 26**
Energy, **Law of the Sea 141, 142**
Exclusive economic zone, **Law of the Sea 57, 64-76, 115-131, 133-149, 199-202, 221-223, 243**

GENERAL INDEX

References are to Titles and Pages

ADMIRALTY—Cont'd

Federal Employers' Liability Act, **Admiralty 175**

Federal Tort Claims Act, **Admiralty 294**

Finds, **Admiralty 130**

Fire statute, **Admiralty 64**

Fishing, **Law of the Sea 120, 125, 126, 129-134, 139, 163-165, 233-235**

Flag, **Law of the Sea 3, 6-9, 22, 31**

Flag state, **Law of the Sea 1, 15-19, 90, 91, 134, 219-221**

Force majeure, **Law of the Sea 90, 97, 149**

Fragile ecosystems, protection of, **Law of the Sea 208, 209**

Gencom charter, **Admiralty 51**

General average, **Admiralty 132-135**

General Maritime Law, development, **Admiralty 1**

General Maritime Tort Law, **Admiralty 136-145, 149, 269, 298, 300, 301, 303**

Geographically disadvantaged states, **Law of the Sea 125, 129-131**

Government commercial ships, **Law of the Sea 32-37, 231**

Great Lakes Rule, **Admiralty 154**

Harter Act, **Admiralty 44**

Held covered clause, **Admiralty 69**

Highly migratory species, **Law of the Sea 131, 243**

High seas, **Law of the Sea 18-21, 232, 228-237**

Himalaya clause, **Admiralty 75**

Honor policy, **Admiralty 109**

Hot pursuit, **Law of the Sea 23, 134**

Inland rules, **Admiralty 154**

Innocent passage, **Law of the Sea 53, 54, 97-106, 109, 111, 198**

Inspection of ships, **Law of the Sea 92, 93, 133, 221, 223**

Insurance Act of 1906, **Admiralty 108**

Internal waters, **Law of the Sea 10, 28, 38, 41, 56-58, 79-90, 148, 149, 198, 199**

International Environmental Law (this index)

International rules, **Admiralty 154**

International tribunal for the law of the sea, **Law of the Sea 133, 184, 241, 242, 245**

ADMIRALTY—Cont'd
Islands, **Law of the Sea 46-49, 51-54, 56-79, 110, 111, 144-149, 161, 205, 206, 236, 243**
Jason clause, **Admiralty 135**
Joint and several liability, **Admiralty 298**
Jones Act, seamen, **Admiralty 175, 203, 205-208, 210, 212, 213**
Judicial competence, **Admiralty 10**
Jurisdiction and procedure, generally, **Admiralty 4**
Land-locked states, **Law of the Sea 81, 125, 129-131, 228**
Law of the sea, generally, **Law of the Sea 1-246**
Legislative competence, **Admiralty 12**
Liability, **Law of the Sea 20, 108, 210-218, 225, 226, 232, 235**
Liens, generally, **Admiralty 78**
Limitation of liability, **Admiralty 304-309, 314, 316, 320**
Longshore and Harbor Workers' Compensation Act, generally, **Admiralty 42**
Low-tide elevation, **Law of the Sea 49, 50**
Maintenance and cure, seamen, **Admiralty 173, 181-183, 185-191**
Marine environment, protection and preservation of, **Law of the Sea 144, 191-228**
Marine Insurance, **Admiralty 26, 107, 109-112**
Marine mammals, **Law of the Sea 132, 235**
Marine pollution, **Admiralty 168, 169**
Marine scientific research, **Law of the Sea 108, 142-144, 165, 237, 243**
Maritime common law, **Admiralty 6**
Maritime contracts, **Law of the Sea 25-29, 181-183**
Maritime flavor (nexus), **Admiralty 13**
Maritime Lien Act, **Admiralty 88, 91**
Nationality of ships, **Law of the Sea 1-12, 15-19, 22, 31, 90, 91, 134, 219-221**
Navigable waters, **Admiralty 18, 21**
Navigation, right of, **Law of the Sea 231-233**
New Jason clause, **Admiralty 135**
Nuclear weapons, testing, **Law of the Sea 230, 231**
Ocean dumping, **Law of the Sea 202-205**

ADMIRALTY—Cont'd

Ocean thermal energy, **Law of the Sea 141, 142**
Oil pollution, **Law of the Sea 191, 192, 197, 200, 212-214, 220**
Oleron, rules of, **Admiralty 2**
Outer Continental Shelf Lands Act, **Admiralty 169**
Overflight, **Law of the Sea 10, 107, 121, 228**
Pennsylvania rule, **Admiralty 161**
Pilotage, **Admiralty 118, 119**
Pipelines (submarine), **Law of the Sea 100, 161, 235, 236**
Piracy, **Law of the Sea 19, 20**
Plan of work, generally, **Law of the Sea 181**
Platform injuries, **Admiralty 283, 284, 285, 287-290**
Pomerone Act, **Admiralty 55**
Ports, **Law of the Sea 10, 28, 79-90, 148, 149, 198, 199**
Port state, **Law of the Sea 91-93, 233, 234**
Preemption of state law, **Admiralty 7**
Prize, **Admiralty 131**
Production charge, generally, **Law of the Sea 182, 183**
Property, **Admiralty 43**
Public Vessels Act, **Admiralty 293, 328**
Reefs, baseline, **Law of the Sea 50**
Rivers and harbors, **Admiralty 166, 168; Law of the Sea 39-41**
Roadsted, **Law of the Sea 51**
Rocks, **Law of the Sea 47**
Rule 9(H) declaration, **Admiralty 342**
Safety zones, artificial islands and installations, **Law of the Sea 145**
Salvage, **Admiralty 120-124, 126-128, 130, 131**
Saving to suitors clause, **Admiralty 4, 326**
Seabed disputes chamber, generally, **Law of the Sea 184, 245**
Sea lanes, **Law of the Sea 100, 101, 108, 110**
Seamen, generally, **Admiralty 42, 172**
Seaplanes, **Admiralty 16**
Sedentary species, **Law of the Sea 133, 160, 163-165**
Settlement of disputes, **Law of the Sea 77, 78, 123, 128, 144, 184, 237-246**

ADMIRALTY—Cont'd

Ship Mortgage Act, **Admiralty 81**
Ships, **Law of the Sea 1-27, 30, 31, 85-92, 101, 102, 113, 114, 133, 134, 196-200, 219-223**
Ship's agent, **Admiralty 26**
Ship's husband, **Admiralty 26**
Sieracki seamen, **Admiralty 196, 244**
Slave trade, **Law of the Sea 20**
Sovereign immunity, **Admiralty 293, 294, 296, 297, 328**
Straddling species, **Law of the Sea 131, 134**
Straits, **Law of the Sea 106-110**
Submarines, **Law of the Sea 10, 105, 107**
Suits in Admiralty Act, **Admiralty 294, 328**
Technology transfer, deep seabed mining, **Law of the Sea 182**
Territorial sea, **Law of the Sea 37-58, 94, 99-105, 111-113, 191, 198, 199**
Torts, **Admiralty 136-145, 149, 151-162, 164-166, 269, 298, 300, 301, 303**
Towage, **Admiralty 115-118**
Transit passage, **Law of the Sea 106-110**
UNCLOS (United Nations Convention on the Law of the Sea). **International Environmental Law** (this index)
Unseaworthiness, **Admiralty 173, 193, 194, 196, 197, 199-201, 244**
Vessels, generally, **Admiralty 14, 16, 17**
Warranty of workmanlike performance, **Admiralty 300**
Warships, **Law of the Sea 31, 32, 104, 227, 231**
Western rivers rules, **Admiralty 154**
Worker injury (compensation) claims, generally, **Admiralty 171, 247**
Wreck Act, **Admiralty 166**
Wrongful death, **Admiralty 30, 37, 269, 270, 272, 273-281**
York-Antwerp Rules, **Admiralty 135**

ADVERTISING

First Amendment (this index)
Lanham Act, **Unfair Trade 354 et seq.**

GENERAL INDEX

References are to Titles and Pages

AGED PERSONS

Elder Law (this index)

AGENCY-PARTNERSHIP

Accounting, winding up, **Agency-Partn 267-269**

Agency relationship, **Agency-Partn 3 et seq., 26, 28 et seq., 33 et seq., 45 et seq., 67-69, 142**

Agent, generally, **Agency-Partn 7 et seq., 18, 24-28, 80**

Apparent authority, generally, **Agency-Partn 128 et seq.**

Assumption of risk, generally, **Agency-Partn 56 et seq.**

Authority (actual), **Agency-Partn 20 et seq., 125 et seq., 131, 133-135, 149, 150**

Bankruptcy of partnership, distribution, **Agency-Partn 275**

Business trust, generally, **Agency-Partn 241 et seq.**

Capital contributions, partnership property, **Agency-Partn 251 et seq.**

Common name statutes, generally, **Agency-Partn 246 et seq.**

Consent, agency relationship, **Agency-Partn 3, 8, 26, 28 et seq.**

Contract integration, **Agency-Partn 174 et seq.**

Contribution for loss, generally, **Agency-Partn 54 et seq.**

Corporate officers, generally, **Agency-Partn 131 et seq.**

Custom, **Agency-Partn 51, 129-131**

Directors, generally, **Agency-Partn 19 et seq.**

Dissolution of partnership, **Agency-Partn 36, 37, 257 et seq., 260 et seq.**

Distribution, generally, **Agency-Partn 271 et seq.**

Dormant partners, generally, **Agency-Partn 235 et seq.**

Election, undisclosed principal, **Agency-Partn 195 et seq.**

Exoneration, against undisclosed principal, **Agency-Partn 198**

Factor, **Agency-Partn 24, 119, 120, 137-139**

FELA, personal injury losses, **Agency-Partn 58, 59, 68, 69**

Fellow servant rule, personal injury losses, **Agency-Partn 57, 58**

Fictitious name statutes, generally, **Agency-Partn 199 et seq.**

Fiduciary duties, generally, **Agency-Partn 45 et seq.**

Fraud and false representation, generally, **Agency-Partn 107 et seq., 112 et seq.**

General agent, apparent authority compared, **Agency-Partn 130**

AGENCY-PARTNERSHIP—Cont'd

Guest, **Agency-Partn 93, 194**
Incoming partner, dissolution, **Agency-Partn 257 et seq.**
Indemnity (agent's), generally, **Agency-Partn 49 et seq.**
Indemnity (employer's), generally, **Agency-Partn 100 et seq.**
Independent contractor, generally, **Agency-Partn 14 et seq., 115 et seq.**
Intermediate agent, respondeat superior, **Agency-Partn 78-81**
Irrevocable agencies, **Agency-Partn 42-45**
Joint enterprise, generally, **Agency-Partn 214 et seq.**
Joint principals, nonprofit associations, **Agency-Partn 227, 228**
Joint stock associations, generally, **Agency-Partn 239 et seq.**
Joint venture, generally, **Agency-Partn 210 et seq.**
Jury instructions, apparent authority, **Agency-Partn 131**
Labor union, **Agency-Partn 248, 249**
Lent servant, **Agency-Partn 16 et seq.**
Limitations and revocation, generally, **Agency-Partn 141 et seq.**
Limited liability company. **Partnership and LLC** (this index)
Limited partnership, generally, **Agency-Partn 12 et seq., 233-235, 252**
Negative covenants, **Agency-Partn 38 et seq., 142**
Negligence compared, respondeat superior, **Agency-Partn 6**
Nonfeasance, generally, **Agency-Partn 95 et seq.**
Nonprofit associations, generally, **Agency-Partn 226 et seq.**
Notice, generally, **Agency-Partn 153 et seq.**
Organization, **Agency-Partn 18, 154, 160**
Outgoing partner, dissolution of partnership, **Agency-Partn 260 et seq.**
Partnership, generally, **Agency-Partn 12 et seq., 206 et seq.**
Personal injury losses, generally, **Agency-Partn 56 et seq.**
Personal relationship, **Agency-Partn 3 et seq., 26, 28 et seq., 33 et seq., 45 et seq., 67-69, 142**
Principal, **Agency-Partn 26, 27, 183 et seq.**
Promoters, generally, **Agency-Partn 179 et seq.**
Property of partnership, generally, **Agency-Partn 251 et seq.**
Ratification, generally, **Agency-Partn 162 et seq.**

AGENCY-PARTNERSHIP—Cont'd
Realty agents or brokers, **Agency-Partn 113, 114, 118, 149, 150**
Respondeat superior, generally, **Agency-Partn 72 et seq.**
Restatement of agency, references to, **Agency-Partn Appx D**
Restitution, generally, **Agency-Partn 168 et seq.**
Restraint of trade, **Agency-Partn 23, 24, 40, 41, 221, 222**
Sale, agency distinguished, **Agency-Partn 23, 24**
Servant defined, **Agency-Partn 9 et seq.**
Statute of frauds, **Agency-Partn 152, 201, 202**
Strict liability, generally, **Agency-Partn 122 et seq.**
Termination of authority, generally, **Agency-Partn 145 et seq.**
Ultra vires doctrine, **Agency-Partn 144**
Unauthorized agent, generally, **Agency-Partn 170 et seq.**
Undisclosed principal, **Agency-Partn 183 et seq.**
Uniform laws, generally, **Agency-Partn 199, 200**
Winding up, generally, **Agency-Partn 267 et seq.**
Workmen's compensation, generally, **Agency-Partn 60 et seq.**

AGREEMENTS
Contracts (this index)

AGRICULTURE
Administrative agencies, see lines throughout this topic
Agricultural Act of 1949, **Agric 9, 15**
Agricultural Acts, generally, **Agric 11-14**
Agricultural Adjustment Act of 1933, **Agric 7, 8, 40**
Agricultural Adjustment Act of 1938, **Agric 7, 9, 15**
Agricultural districts, **Agric 233, 352, 361, 362, 365, 369-373, 386, 387, 404-418**
Agricultural Fair Practices Act of 1967, **Agric 308**
Agricultural Marketing Agreement Act of 1937 (AMAA), **Agric 24, 25, 27, 28, 308**
Agriculture Stabilization and Conservation Service (ASCS), **Agric iii, 8, 10, 32, 34-36, 47, 119, 172, 191, 192, 394, 423**
Aliens, **Agric 47, 48, 329, 330, 335-339**
Animal and Plant Health Inspection Service (APHIS), **Agric 268, 271**

AGRICULTURE—Cont'd

Bankruptcy, **Agric 52, 81, 86-95, 103, 127, 128, 203, 217, 218, 221, 222, 224-227, 249, 266, 282**
Bureau of Reclamation, **Agric 3, 420-422**
Casualty to crops, **Agric 30, 31, 75, 76, 143-145**
Commerce clause issues, **Agric 8, 9, 28, 29, 121, 122, 183, 268, 418, 419**
Commodity credit corporation (CCC), generally, **Agric 9-12**
Commodity futures contracts, **Agric 145-151**
Commodity Futures Trading Commission (CFTC), **Agric 146**
Consolidated Farm Service Agency (CFSA), **Agric iii, 8, 30-32, 34, 44, 47, 49, 51, 52, 68-73, 75-80, 82-87, 91, 119, 178, 382, 394, 395, 406, 423**
Cooperatives, generally, **Agric 50, 274-308**
Corporate farming, **Agric 45-47**
Corps of Engineers, U.S. Army, **Agric 407-409**
Crop insurance, **Agric iii, 30, 31**
Dairies, **Agric 16, 17, 24, 26-30, 32, 39, 49, 157, 166, 228-232, 236-245, 268-271, 274, 306-308, 398**
Disaster Assistance Act of 1988, **Agric 30**
Disaster payments, **Agric 29-31, 33**
Emblements, doctrine of, **Agric 115, 116**
Emergency Livestock Feed Assistance Act of 1988, **Agric 29**
Employment, **Agric 310-349, 346**
Employment and Training Administration (ETA), **Agric 326, 327**
Environmental Protection Agency (EPA), **Agric 318, 343-345, 398-404, 408, 409, 411**
Equal protection challenges, **Agric 34, 46-48, 233, 234, 325, 326, 353, 365, 366**
Experiment stations, **Agric 3, 50**
Farm credit system generally, **Agric 4, 51, 52, 54, 55**
Farmers Home Administration, generally, **Agric 44, 49, 51, 52**
Farmland Protection Policy Act of 1981 (FPPA), **Agric 380, 381**
Farm products rule, **Agric 179-191, 205, 206**
Farm programs (USDA), generally, **Agric 11-15**
Farm sales, generally, **Agric 11**
Farms for the Future Act of 1990, **Agric 381**

AGRICULTURE—Cont'd

Federal Crop Insurance Corporation (FCIC), **Agric iii, 31, 170**
Federal Crop Insurance Reform Act of 1994, **Agric 30, 31**
Federal Grain Inspection Service (FGIS), **Agric 125**
Federal Trade Commission (FTC), **Agric 247, 262, 307**
Feedlots, **Agric 159-162, 164, 165, 253, 254, 256, 257, 316, 358-360, 396, 398, 399**
Field crop production and marketing, generally, **Agric 4 et seq.**
Food, Agriculture Conservation and Trade Act of 1990 (1990 farm bill), **Agric 9, 15, 16, 21, 23, 24, 29, 37, 38, 383, 393, 410**
Food Security Act of 1985 (1985 farm bill), **Agric 9, 15, 16, 21, 23, 24, 37, 38, 182, 381, 383, 392, 393, 395**
Foreign Agricultural Service (FAS), **Agric 38**
Frauds, statute of, **Agric 100-102, 138-143**
Fruit and vegetable production and marketing, generally, **Agric 4, 9**
Grain dealers, **Agric 121, 122, 125, 133-145, 220-225**
Immigration and Naturalization Service (INS), **Agric 338**
Insolvent buyers of farm products, **Agric 220-228**
International agricultural trade, generally, **Agric 12, 13, 19, 37**
International Trade and Investment (this index)
Irrigation, **Agric 3 et seq.**
Land grant colleges, **Agric 2**
Leases, **Agric 45-48, 63, 82, 83, 96-120, 157, 158, 203-206, 383, 421**
Livestock production and marketing, generally, **Agric 4 et seq.**
National Labor Relations Board (NLRB), **Agric 314, 315, 346**
Natural Resources Conservation Service (NCRS), **Agric iii, 24, 31, 389, 390, 392-394, 407, 408, 423, 424**
Occupational Safety and Health Administration (OSHA), **Agric 331, 339-344**
Packers and Stockyards Administration, **Agric 246, 250, 251**
Patent and Trademark Office (PTO), **Agric 2, 272, 273**
Payment limitations, **Agric 14, 19, 23, 30, 32-36, 49**
Pesticides, **Agric 29, 102, 318, 319, 342-345, 349, 356, 359, 360, 396, 397, 400-405**
Poultry production, **Agric 16, 43, 45, 162, 165, 166, 225, 228, 261-272, 304, 305, 313-315, 340, 341, 398, 400**

AGRICULTURE—Cont'd

Railroads, **Agric 2, 219**

Reclamation law, **Agric 3, 44, 49, 420-422**

Regulatory takings, allegations of, **Agric 58, 59, 270-272, 364-368 et seq.**

Right-to-farm laws, **Agric 356-360**

Rural Housing and Community Development Service (RHCDS), **Agric iii, 68**

Secured transactions, generally, **Agric 152-206**

Securities and Exchange Commission (SEC), **Agric 296**

Sherman Antitrust Act, **Agric 231, 232, 246, 299, 306, 307**

Soil and Water Resources Conservation Act of 1977 (RCA), **Agric 391, 411**

Soil Conservation Act of 1935, **Agric 389**

Soil Conservation and Domestic Allotment Act of 1936, **Agric 8, 389**

Soil Conservation Service (SCS), **Agric 24, 31, 36, 381, 389, 390, 392-394, 409, 409, 423, 424**

Soil erosion, generally, **Agric iii, 7-9 et seq.**

Taxation, **Agric 118, 119, 136, 137, 277, 287-296, 319-323, 336, 351-354, 370, 371, 377, 378, 382, 391**

United States Department of Agriculture, generally, **Agric 2**

U.S. Department of Labor (USDOL), **Agric 328, 329, 331, 334, 339**

U.S. Employment Service (USES), **Agric 326**

U.S. Fish & Wildlife Service (USF&WS), **Agric 408**

U.S. Forest Service (USFS), **Agric 393**

Vertical integration, **Agric 43-45, 54, 262-267, 304, 305, 314, 315, 340, 341**

Warehouses, **Agric 3, 4, 121-145, 194-200, 207-225, 292, 343**

Water, **Agric 3 et seq.**

Wetlands, **Agric 23, 24, 31, 36, 366, 367, 390, 391, 405-411, 424, 425**

Zoning, generally, **Agric 360-369, 372, 375, 376**

AIDS LAW

Abortion, use to avoid birth of child with AIDS, **AIDS 96**

AIDS LAW—Cont'd

Adoption, **AIDS 86, 87, 96-98**
Aliens, **AIDS 289-295, 299, 301**
Americans with Disabilities Act (ADA), **AIDS 46-61, 81**
Blood banks, liability for supplying AIDS-infected blood, **AIDS 176-185, 202, 203**
Children, right to sue for transmission of AIDS, **AIDS 95, 97, 98, 202-206**
Comparison to other diseases, **AIDS 1, 2**
Couples, generally, **AIDS 83, 84, 89-92, 100, 101, 186-190**
Criminal law, **AIDS 92-94, 142-175, 240, 241, 247, 258; AIDS 247, 258**
Discovery, **AIDS 4, 5**
Dispute over who discovered, **AIDS 299, 300**
Divorce, **AIDS 101-104**
Drugs, development of new AIDS drugs, generally, **AIDS 225, 226**
Education, **AIDS 27-29, 69, 99, 226-230**
Effects, **AIDS 2, 3**
Estate planning, **AIDS 66, 105-114, 259**
Financial costs, **AIDS 45, 105**
Funerals, **AIDS 66, 112-114, 259**
Health care workers, **AIDS 46, 59, 65, 66, 72-77, 92, 140, 185, 186, 207-210, 237, 238**
Hospitals, **AIDS 67, 72-74, 76, 77, 176-185, 202, 203**
Housing, **AIDS 45, 47, 48, 52, 79-81**
Human Immunodeficiency Virus (HIV), **AIDS 5, 6, 25, 299, 300**
Illegal drugs, generally, **AIDS 230, 231**
Immigration, **AIDS 289-295, 299, 301**
Insurance, **AIDS 6-8, 92, 106, 114, 115, 123-141, 275, 295**
International law, **AIDS 276-286**
Marriage, **AIDS 84-86, 88, 89, 101-104, 106, 238-240**
Modes of transmission, **AIDS 8-10, 94, 95**
Nursing homes, duty to accept persons with AIDs, **AIDS 66**
Origins, **AIDS 10-15**
Parents, **AIDS 95, 97-100, 202-206**
Political aspects, **AIDS 29-44, 290-293**

AIDS LAW—Cont'd
Prisoners, **AIDS 92-94, 173, 174, 240, 241**
Prostitutes, **AIDS 163, 170, 173, 174, 261**
Public safety officers, right to learn AIDS status of others, **AIDS 247, 258**
Quarantine, **AIDS 259-264, 293**
Reporting, **AIDS 252-259**
Restaurants, **AIDS 46, 59, 70, 71**
Schools, **AIDS 62-64**
Sexual relations, **AIDS 83, 89-92, 101, 186-190, 264-266**
Symptoms, **AIDS 15-18, 104, 105, 266-274**
Teachers, right to continue working after being diagnosed with AIDS, **AIDS 49-51**
Testing, **AIDS 18-20, 173, 174, 231-252**
Tort law, **AIDS 176, 186-201, 210, 212-219**
Treatment regimens, **AIDS 20-25**
Workplaces, **AIDS 45, 48, 60, 61, 68-72, 77-79**
World Health Organization (WHO), **AIDS 295-299, 301**

ALIENS
Immigration Law and Procedure (this index)

ALTERATION
Change or Modification (this index)

ALTERNATIVE DISPUTE RESOLUTION
Generally, **Alt Disp Resol 1, 2**
Active listening, **Alt Disp Resol 29, 32, 33, 71-73**
Adhesion contracts, **Alt Disp Resol 148, 149**
Adjudication, **Alt Disp Resol 6, 113**
Administrative Dispute Resolution Act, **Alt Disp Resol 8**
Adversarial, negotiation approach, **Alt Disp Resol 19-22, 25**
Age Discrimination in Employment Act, compulsory arbitration, **Alt Disp Resol 136-138**
Agreements, **Alt Disp Resol 36, 43-47, 50-52, 223-226**
American Arbitration Association (AAA), **Alt Disp Resol 98, 99, 196-199**

ALTERNATIVE DISPUTE RESOLUTION—Cont'd

American Bar Association, **Alt Disp Resol 5, 9, 12, 30, 36, 40, 43, 66, 80-82, 214-222**
Arbitrability, generally, **Alt Disp Resol 131-140**
Arbitration, generally, **Alt Disp Resol 119-169**
Arbitration Act of 1888, **Alt Disp Resol 55**
Arbitration award, **Alt Disp Resol 156-159**
Arbitrators, generally, **Alt Disp Resol 152, 153, 155, 156, 265-283**
Bargaining, generally, **Alt Disp Resol 11-53**
Board of Mediation and Conciliation, **Alt Disp Resol 55**
Body language, **Alt Disp Resol 76**
Boulwarism, **Alt Disp Resol 34**
Caucus, **Alt Disp Resol 106-108**
Center for Public Resources (CPR), **Alt Disp Resol 97, 98, 195, 196**
Civil justice expense and delay reduction plan (EDRP), **Alt Disp Resol 7**
Civil Justice Reform Act, **Alt Disp Resol 7, 171**
Claim preclusion, res judicata, **Alt Disp Resol 161-166**
Code of Ethics for Arbitrators in Commercial Disputes, **Alt Disp Resol 153, 265-283**
Code of Professional Responsibility for Arbitrators of Labor-Management Disputes, **Alt Disp Resol 153**
Collateral estoppel, **Alt Disp Resol 161-166**
Confidentiality, **Alt Disp Resol 47-49, 90-101, 206**
Contract liability, generally, **Alt Disp Resol 49-41**
Contracts, **Alt Disp Resol 43-47, 50-52, 148, 149, 223-226**
Counseling, lawyers and clients, **Alt Disp Resol 2, 3, 85, 112, 115, 116**
Court-annexed arbitration, generally, **Alt Disp Resol 127-129**
Court system, **Alt Disp Resol 170-189, 223-226**
Disclosure, negotiation, **Alt Disp Resol 39**
Distributive bargaining, **Alt Disp Resol 15, 16**
Early neutral evaluation, generally, **Alt Disp Resol 180-183**
Erdman Act of 1898, **Alt Disp Resol 55**

ALTERNATIVE DISPUTE RESOLUTION—Cont'd

Ethical Standards of professional Responsibility of the Society of Professionals in Dispute Resolution (SPIDR), **Alt Disp Resol 105, 227-233**
Ethics, **Alt Disp Resol 36-43, 79-82, 105, 110, 111, 227-233, 265-283**
Evidentiary exclusionary rules, **Alt Disp Resol 47-49, 91, 92**
Exchanging information, **Alt Disp Resol 32-35, 65, 66, 193**
Fact investigation, **Alt Disp Resol 29**
Federal Arbitration Act (FAA), **Alt Disp Resol 120, 121, 136-138, 142-147, 150, 246-261**
Federal Magistrates Act, **Alt Disp Resol 184**
Federal Rules of Civil Procedure, **Alt Disp Resol 49, 50-52, 185, 188, 189, 207-213**
Federal Rules of Evidence, **Alt Disp Resol 48, 49, 91, 206, 408**
First offer, **Alt Disp Resol 33, 34**
Getting to Yes, **Alt Disp Resol 33, 34**
Guaranteed verdict agreements, **Alt Disp Resol 46**
Historical aspects of ADR, **Alt Disp Resol 4, 5**
Hybrid dispute resolution procedures, **Alt Disp Resol 199-201**
Immunity, **Alt Disp Resol 153, 154**
Information acquisition, **Alt Disp Resol 32-35, 65, 66, 75, 193**
Injunctions, **Alt Disp Resol 149-151**
Institutionalization, justice system methods of dispute resolution, **Alt Disp Resol 170-190**
International chamber of commerce, arbitration rules, **Alt Disp Resol 166, 167**
Interviewing and counseling, **Alt Disp Resol 29**
Judicial settlement conferences, **Alt Disp Resol 49, 50**
Labor-Management Relations Act, **Alt Disp Resol 121**
Law, **Alt Disp Resol 54, 83-85, 87, 155, 156**
Lawyers and lawyering, generally, **Alt Disp Resol 9, 10, 19, 20**
Lax and Sebenius, **Alt Disp Resol 20, 22-24**
Listening, **Alt Disp Resol 32, 70-74**
Logrolling, **Alt Disp Resol 35, 36**
Magistrates, generally, **Alt Disp Resol 184, 185**
Mary Carter Agreements, **Alt Disp Resol 46**

ALTERNATIVE DISPUTE RESOLUTION—Cont'd
Masters, generally, **Alt Disp Resol 185-188**
Med-arb, **Alt Disp Resol 200, 201**
Mediation, generally, **Alt Disp Resol 54-118**
Mediators, **Alt Disp Resol 49, 50, 68-78, 104-111**
Minitrial, generally, **Alt Disp Resol 191-200**
Misrepresentation, negotiation, **Alt Disp Resol 39-42**
Multidoor courthouse, **Alt Disp Resol 6**
National Labor Relations Board, **Alt Disp Resol 121**
National Mediation Board, **Alt Disp Resol 55**
Negotiated rulemaking, **Alt Disp Resol 202, 203**
Negotiated Rulemaking Act of 1990, **Alt Disp Resol 202, 203**
Negotiation, generally, **Alt Disp Resol 11-53**
Neutral experts, **Alt Disp Resol 188, 189**
Newlands Act of 1913, **Alt Disp Resol 55**
New York Convention, **Alt Disp Resol 167**
Ombudsperson, **Alt Disp Resol 204**
Polycentric problem, **Alt Disp Resol 6**
Pound Conference, **Alt Disp Resol 5**
Puffing, **Alt Disp Resol 40**
Punitive damages, **Alt Disp Resol 159-161**
Railway Labor Act of 1926, **Alt Disp Resol 55**
References procedures, **Alt Disp Resol 199, 200**
Rent-a-judge, **Alt Disp Resol 199**
Res judicata, **Alt Disp Resol 161-166**
Separability, **Alt Disp Resol 140, 141**
Settlement agreement, **Alt Disp Resol 43-47, 50-52, 223-226**
Society of Professionals in Dispute Resolution (SPIDR), **Alt Disp Resol 223-233**
Standards, **Alt Disp Resol 214-222, 227-233**
Strategic planning, **Alt Disp Resol 14**
Summary jury trial (SJT), generally, **Alt Disp Resol 171-180**
Tactics, negotiation, **Alt Disp Resol 21, 22, 37**
Taft-Hartley Act, **Alt Disp Resol 121**
Threats, **Alt Disp Resol 42, 43**
Tort liability, **Alt Disp Resol 39, 40**

ALTERNATIVE DISPUTE RESOLUTION—Cont'd
Transactional negotiation, generally, **Alt Disp Resol 11-53**
Truthfulness, **Alt Disp Resol 38-41**
Unauthorized practice of law, **Alt Disp Resol 110, 111**
Uncitral, **Alt Disp Resol 166, 168**
Uniform Arbitration Act (UAA), **Alt Disp Resol 120, 234-245**
Value-claimer, **Alt Disp Resol 20**
Value-creators, **Alt Disp Resol 22**
Zero-sum, **Alt Disp Resol 15, 16**

AMERICAN INDIAN LAW
Generally, **Am Indian 1 et seq.**

AMERICANS WITH DISABILITIES ACT
Individual Employee Rights (this index)

ANALYSIS
Constitutional Analysis (this index)
Legal Writing (this index)

ANGLO-AMERICAN LAW
Bill in equity, **Anglo-Am 40**
Bills of exchange, **Anglo-Am 223, 261-277**
Cases, **Anglo-Am 99, 100, 101, 104**
Civil law, **Anglo-Am 13-15, 17, 18**
Coke, Sir Edward, **Anglo-Am 92, 124**
Commercial law, **Anglo-Am 27, 98, 255-259, 265, 276**
Contracts, **Anglo-Am 210-240, 242-254, 268, 269**
Corporations, **Anglo-Am 250, 251, 254, 257, 278-295, 301, 302**
Courts
  admiralty, **Anglo-Am 264**
  baron, **Anglo-Am 26**
  borough, **Anglo-Am 27, 173, 265, 266**
  chancery, **Anglo-Am 18-20, 37-39, 45, 46, 173, 174**
  church, **Anglo-Am 10, 42, 162, 173, 211, 212**
  Colonial American, **Anglo-Am 44-46**
  common pleas, **Anglo-Am 33, 235**

ANGLO-AMERICAN LAW—Cont'd
Courts—Cont'd
curia regis, **Anglo-Am 9, 26**
definition, **Anglo-Am 20**
Exchequer Chamber, informal, **Anglo-Am 239**
Exchequer of Pleas origin, **Anglo-Am 35, 36**
High Court of Parliament, **Anglo-Am 42, 43**
honors, **Anglo-Am 26**
hundred, **Anglo-Am 23, 24**
judicial review of legislation, **Anglo-Am 16, 17**
King's Bench, **Anglo-Am 34, 35, 184, 235**
leet, **Anglo-Am 23**
manorial, **Anglo-Am 26, 27**
modern English, **Anglo-Am 44**
piepowder, **Anglo-Am 265**
seignorial, **Anglo-Am 25-27**
shire, **Anglo-Am 23-25**
star chamber, **Anglo-Am 18, 40, 41**
suitors, **Anglo-Am 22, 23**
trial and appellate defined, **Anglo-Am 20, 21**
Criminal law, **Anglo-Am 12, 17, 18, 24, 25, 29, 30, 63, 64, 182-184**
Custom, **Anglo-Am 11, 12, 95-98**
Definitions
absolute liability, **Anglo-Am 182**
active trust, **Anglo-Am 178**
advocacy, **Anglo-Am 75**
Agnati, **Anglo-Am 169**
aids, **Anglo-Am 136, 137**
alienation, **Anglo-Am 143**
appellate court, **Anglo-Am 21**
attaint of jurors, **Anglo-Am 64, 65**
barrister, **Anglo-Am 63**
beneficiary, **Anglo-Am 173, 174**
bill distinguished from writ, **Anglo-Am 40**
bookland, **Anglo-Am 130, 131**
borough English, **Anglo-Am 98**
Bot, **Anglo-Am 12**
cestui que use, **Anglo-Am 174**
civil law system, **Anglo-Am 13-15**

ANGLO-AMERICAN LAW—Cont'd
Definitions—Cont'd
code, **Anglo-Am 112**
common law, **Anglo-Am 13-15, 18-20**
community property, **Anglo-Am 161**
contingent fees of lawyers, **Anglo-Am 77**
contract, **Anglo-Am 214**
contract to sell and of sale, **Anglo-Am 210**
copyhold, **Anglo-Am 97**
court, **Anglo-Am 20**
Cwide, **Anglo-Am 170**
determination of an estate in land, **Anglo-Am 152**
dry, or passive, trust, **Anglo-Am 178**
equitable principles, **Anglo-Am 18**
escheat, **Anglo-Am 56, 137**
estoppel, **Anglo-Am 251**
fee estate in land, **Anglo-Am 129**
feoffor and feoffee to uses, **Anglo-Am 173, 174**
feudalism, **Anglo-Am 10**
folkland, **Anglo-Am 129, 130**
forfeiture, **Anglo-Am 137**
formal and informal contracts, **Anglo-Am 210, 211**
frankmarriage, **Anglo-Am 155**
frankpledge, view of, **Anglo-Am 24**
freehold estate, **Anglo-Am 138**
Gage, **Anglo-Am 213**
gavelkind, **Anglo-Am 142**
Gens, **Anglo-Am 169**
hundred, **Anglo-Am 8, 9**
information, distinguished from indictment, **Anglo-Am 72**
judge, **Anglo-Am 89**
judgment by peers, **Anglo-Am 42, 65, 66**
Judicium Die, **Anglo-Am 58**
jury, **Anglo-Am 54**
laen land, **Anglo-Am 131, 132**
legal history, **Anglo-Am 5**
legislation, **Anglo-Am 108, 109**
leviation, **Anglo-Am 286, 287**
livery of seisin, **Anglo-Am 56, 176**
marriage right, **Anglo-Am 136**

ANGLO-AMERICAN LAW—Cont'd
Definitions—Cont'd
ordeal, **Anglo-Am 58-60**
parage, **Anglo-Am 140, 141**
particular estate, **Anglo-Am 152**
patrimonium, **Anglo-Am 170**
peine forte et dure, **Anglo-Am 63**
possibility of reverter, **Anglo-Am 154**
post obit gift, **Anglo-Am 171**
prerogative powers, **Anglo-Am 39**
primogeniture, **Anglo-Am 141, 142**
quid pro quo, **Anglo-Am 243**
recognizance, **Anglo-Am 218**
relief, **Anglo-Am 135, 136**
responsalis, **Anglo-Am 78**
scutage (escuage), **Anglo-Am 135**
seisin, **Anglo-Am 142, 143**
sergeants-at-law, **Anglo-Am 79**
sergeanty, tenancy in, **Anglo-Am 137**
servientes regis, **Anglo-Am 79**
settlor, in trusts, **Anglo-Am 174**
solicitor, **Anglo-Am 76**
special verdict, **Anglo-Am 238**
stare decisis, **Anglo-Am 14, 15, 102**
subinfeudation, **Anglo-Am 26, 134**
succession, **Anglo-Am 168**
sui juris, **Anglo-Am 151**
suitors, **Anglo-Am 22, 23**
tenants in demesne and in service, **Anglo-Am 26**
testament, **Anglo-Am 168**
tithing, **Anglo-Am 24**
tort, **Anglo-Am 180**
trespass, **Anglo-Am 183**
trial court, **Anglo-Am 20, 21**
trustee, **Anglo-Am 174**
trusts, active and passive, **Anglo-Am 178**
universitas, **Anglo-Am 281**
usufruct, **Anglo-Am 165**
wardship right, **Anglo-Am 136**
wed, **Anglo-Am 191**

ANGLO-AMERICAN LAW—Cont'd
Definitions—Cont'd
wer and wite, **Anglo-Am 12**
writ, **Anglo-Am 31**
writs, infra
Doctrinal writings, **Anglo-Am 81, 82, 90, 103, 120-127**
Domesday Book, use of inquest, **Anglo-Am 55**
Dower and curtesy, **Anglo-Am 160-163, 181**
Equity, **Anglo-Am 17-19, 52, 67, 68**
Feudalism, **Anglo-Am 10, 26, 134, 135, 137-149, 151-153, 172**
Great council, **Anglo-Am 9, 28**
Judges, **Anglo-Am 29, 30, 38, 44-46, 71, 89-93**
Jury and other means of finding facts, **Anglo-Am 32, 38, 48-72, 167, 241, 265, 266**
Lawyers, **Anglo-Am 74-88, 206**
Legislation, **Anglo-Am 9, 61, 62, 108-119**
Negotiable instruments, **Anglo-Am 223, 261-277**
Partnerships, **Anglo-Am 295-302**
Possessory assizes, **Anglo-Am 32, 56-58, 167**
Real property, **Anglo-Am 27, 56, 97, 98, 129-132, 143-147, 149-168, 175-177**
Shires, **Anglo-Am 8-10, 28, 29**
Stare decisis, **Anglo-Am 13, 14, 102-107, 186, 187**
Statutes, generally, **Anglo-Am 14-16**
Torts, **Anglo-Am 166, 167, 181-209, 223-227, 255**
Uses and trusts, **Anglo-Am 153, 154, 173-175, 177, 178**
Wills, **Anglo-Am 11-13, 168-175, 178, 179**
Writs, generally, **Anglo-Am 31 et seq.**

ANTITRUST LAW AND ECONOMICS
Generally, **Antitrust & Eco 15-41; Law & Eco 183-218**
Antitrust injury, generally, **Antitrust & Eco 34, 35, 302-304, 464, 465, 470, 471**
Appeals to government, **Antitrust & Eco 40, 153-155, 277, 278, 480-496**
Boycotts, **Antitrust & Eco 146-152, 204-218, 260, 261, 318-325**
Cartels, **Antitrust & Eco 157-164, 227, 228, 268-271**

ANTITRUST LAW AND ECONOMICS—Cont'd
Celler-Kefauver Act, **Antitrust & Eco 29, 33, 34, 364-366**
Clayton Act
- generally, **Antitrust & Eco 27-29, 326-328, 363-366**
- background, **Antitrust & Eco 27-29**
- Celler-Kefauver Act, **Antitrust & Eco 29, 33, 34, 364-366**
- exclusive dealing, **Antitrust & Eco 340-347**
- mergers, **Antitrust & Eco 27-29, 363-366**
- price discrimination, **Antitrust & Eco 432-434**
- Robinson-Patman Act, **Antitrust & Eco 433, 434**
- Section 7, amendment of, **Antitrust & Eco 364-366**
- tying arrangements, **Antitrust & Eco 326-340**

Common law, **Antitrust & Eco 1-20**
Competition, **Antitrust & Eco 52-58, 66-78, 268-271**
Conspiracy, **Antitrust & Eco 12, 13, 164, 195, 223-239, 271-277, 281-283, 318-325, 456**
Criticism of antitrust laws, **Antitrust & Eco 19, 20, 38-41**
Deconcentration, **Antitrust & Eco 77, 78, 95, 134-136, 274, 280, 284, 285**
Department of Justice, generally, **Antitrust & Eco 29, 449-456**
Economics, generally, **Antitrust & Eco 42-90**
Enforcement, generally, **Antitrust & Eco 13, 14**
Exemptions, **Antitrust & Eco 40, 480-496**
Export Trading Company Act, **Antitrust & Eco 479**
Federal Trade Commission Act, **Antitrust & Eco 27-30, 278-282, 343, 344, 452, 453**
Foreign Trade Antitrust Improvements Act, **Antitrust & Eco 475, 476**
Goals of antitrust laws, **Antitrust & Eco 21, 22, 31-36, 86, 87, 126, 127, 288, 289, 352, 353, 365, 366, 433**
Hart-Scott-Rodino Antitrust Improvements Act, **Antitrust & Eco 400-402**
Herfindahl-Hirschman Index, mergers, **Antitrust & Eco 396, 397**
Historical background, **Antitrust & Eco 15-20, 27, 28, 38-41, 363-366, 432-434**
Horizontal restraints, generally, **Antitrust & Eco 3-10**
Joint ventures, **Antitrust & Eco 202, 203, 252-265, 389-391**
Judiciary, **Antitrust & Eco 22-24, 30, 31, 468-472, 501-505**

ANTITRUST LAW AND ECONOMICS—Cont'd
Jurisdiction, **Antitrust & Eco 475-480**
Local Government Antitrust Act, **Antitrust & Eco 492**
Market allocations and divisions, generally, **Antitrust & Eco 196-204**
Market definition, **Antitrust & Eco 72, 73, 97-112, 114-116, 376-379, 395, 396, 402, 403**
Market power, **Antitrust & Eco 63-65, 84, 85, 94-120, 169, 213-217, 258, 260, 261, 316, 317, 336-340, 344-347, 387, 388, 396, 397**
Mergers, generally, **Antitrust & Eco 348-408**
Monopoly, generally, **Antitrust & Eco 91-155**
Monopsony, generally, **Antitrust & Eco 65, 66, 186, 187, 404**
National Cooperative Research Act, **Antitrust & Eco 264, 501**
National Cooperative Research and Production Act, **Antitrust & Eco 264, 265**
Oligopoly, generally, **Antitrust & Eco 74-81, 266-285**
Patents, generally, **Antitrust & Eco 409-430**
Per se rule, **Antitrust & Eco 165-204, 206-222, 288, 292-304, 311, 312, 326-340, 504**
Predatory practices, generally, **Antitrust & Eco 136-153**
Price discrimination, generally, **Antitrust & Eco 431-448**
Price fixing, generally, **Antitrust & Eco 170-196, 292-304**
Private enforcement, generally, **Antitrust & Eco 23, 24, 34-37, 461-468**
Remedies, generally, **Antitrust & Eco 23, 24, 134-136, 449-468**
Resale price maintenance, generally, **Antitrust & Eco 292-304, 318-325**
Robinson-Patman Act, generally, **Antitrust & Eco 29, 431-448**
Rule of reason, generally, **Antitrust & Eco 165-179, 190-196, 219-222, 504**
Sherman Act, generally, **Antitrust & Eco 20-27, 360-362**
Standing, generally, **Antitrust & Eco 465, 466**
Summary judgment, generally, **Antitrust & Eco 233, 234, 469-471**
Sylvania case, generally, **Antitrust & Eco 287-287, 312-318**
Trade associations, **Antitrust & Eco 240-247**

ANTITRUST LAW AND ECONOMICS—Cont'd
Tying arrangements, generally, **Antitrust & Eco 326-340**
Vertical restraints, generally, **Antitrust & Eco 286-347**
Webb-Pomerene Export Trade Act, antitrust laws, **Antitrust & Eco 479**

APPEAL AND ERROR
Energy and Natural Resources Law (this index)
Federal Jurisdiction (this index)
Injunctions (this index)
Labor Law (this index)
Land Use (this index)

APPELLATE ADVOCACY
Generally, **App Adv 1 et seq.**

APPRAISAL
Insurance Law (this index)

APPROVAL
Consent (this index)

ARBITRATION
Labor Arbitration Law and Practice (this index)
Medical Liability (this index)
Public International Law (this index)

ARMED FORCES
Military Law (this index)

ART LAW
AAM Code of Ethics for Museums, **Art 312, 3113**
Aid to the arts, **Art 154-170**
Alternative space, **Art 139**
American Association of Museums, **Art 300, 301**
Angkor Wat Shrine, **Art 30, 31**
Archaeological Resources Protection Act of 1979, **Art 25**

ART LAW—Cont'd
Art advisory service, **Art 51**
Art and the law program, **Art 162, 163**
Art Dealers Association of America, **Art 99**
Art-defined, **Art 1-8**
Art in public places program, **Art 255, 256**
Artist's Authorship Rights Act, **Art 248-250**
Artist's equity association, **Art 152**
Artist v. artisan, **Art 5, 6**
Art registry systems, **Art 96, 97**
Association of Art Museum Directors (AAMD), **Art 300, 312**
Auctions, **Art 53-65**
Authentication
  art experts, **Art 71-77**
  certificate of authenticity, **Art 69**
  forgeries, fakes and frauds, infra
Berne Convention, **Art 206, 207, 236-238**
Bird in Flight (Brancusi), **Art 2, 3**
Blind bidding, **Art 188, 189**
Bronzed sculptures, **Art 307**
Brooklyn Museum, labor relations, **Art 310**
Buenos Aires Convention, **Art 205**
California Arts Preservation Act, **Art 248-250**
California Non-Profit Corporation Code, **Art 296**
California Resale Royalties Act, **Art 254-257**
California State Arts Council, **Art 255**
Censorship
  freedom of expression, infra
  obscenity, infra
Charitable donations for tax purposes, **Art 123-127, 129, 130, 135, 136, 179, 180**
Chicago Civic Center, **Art 202**
Chicago's Harding Museum, mismanagement, **Art 290, 291**
Chicago's Public Building Commission, **Art 202**
Civil Works Administration (CWA), **Art 155**
Coin collections, **Art 111**
Collectors, **Art 115-137**

ART LAW—Cont'd
Comprehensive Employment and Training Act, **Art 163**
Conventions, **Art 20-23, 31, 34, 39, 40, 205-207, 236, 300**
Cooperative galleries, **Art 139, 140**
Copyright
  Berne Convention Implementation Act, **Art 206, 207**
  common law copyright, **Art 186, 187**
  constitutional basis, **Art 186**
  Copyright Act of 1909, **Art 186, 201, 208, 256**
  Copyright Law of 1790, **Art 186**
  creative component required, **Art 195**
  independent createaion of identical work, **Art 194, 195**
  infringement, **Art 207, 209-217, 240**
  innocent infringement of copyright, **Art 207, 212**
  international protection, **Art 205-207**
  parody, **Art 214-217**
  publication, **Art 201-204**
  register of copyright, **Art 208, 209, 254**
  Revision Act of 1976, **Art 187-198, 200-209, 211-217, 241, 251**
Cottage industries, **Art 150, 151**
Council of Fine Arts, **Art 155**
Crafts, **Art 150**
Customs, **Art 1-8, 18, 19, 276, 277**
Deaccessions, **Art 305-309**
Dealers, **Art 99, 115-137, 142-148**
Deceptive trade practices, **Art 188**
Defamation, **Art 72-74, 188, 244, 252, 253**
Defenses, **Art 33, 70-77, 81, 82, 207-212-214**
Definition of art, **Art 1-8**
De Groot collection, **Art 307, 308**
Denver Art Museum, **Art 13**
Department of Labor, **Art 150, 1551**
Dumbarton Oaks Museum, **Art 15**
Dutch bid, descending bid, **Art 55, 56**
Economic rights, **Art 253-257**
Elginism, **Art 13**
Elgin marbles episode, **Art 12, 13**

ART LAW—Cont'd
English bid, ascending bid, **Art 55, 56**
Erotic art, Kronhausen collection, **Art 277**
Estate planning, **Art 127-131, 180-184**
Etruscan horse, **Art 307**
European art, removal of internal borders, **Art 12**
Expert testimony as to valuation, **Art 110, 111**
Exportation, **Art 9, 10, 15-19**
Fair use doctrine, **Art 212-214**
Federal assistance, **Art 154-163**
Federal Council on the Arts and the Humanities, **Art 157, 158**
Fine prints and editioned sculptures, **Art 93-96, 237**
Finger printing of art, **Art 97**
Flag Protection Act of 1989, **Art 272, 273**
Forgeries, fakes and frauds
  art registry systems, **Art 97, 98**
  attempted legal solutions, **Art 44-46, 68, 91-96**
  certification marks, **Art 98**
  deaccessioning, fakes and forgeries, **Art 306-309**
  forgers, **Art 67, 68**
  fraud, generally, **Art 51, 52, 66-69**
  prevention of fraud, **Art 96-99**
  purchaser's remedies, **Art 78-82**
  reducing the purchaser's risk, **Art 51, 52, 68-71, 96-99**
Freedom of expression
  First Amendment rights, **Art 71-74, 252, 253, 261-273, 280**
  history, **Art 258, 259**
  political criticism, **Art 260, 272, 273**
Free exercise of religion, **Art 169**
Frick Collection, **Art 302, 303**
Galleries, **Art 139-147, 273-281**
General Services Administration, **Art 156, 163**
Generation skipping trust, **Art 131**
Grand Central Terminal episode, **Art 167, 168**
Graphic section of war services program, **Art 156**
Historic preservation, Art Grand Central Terminal episode, **Art 167, 168**
Holy Crown of St. Stephen, **Art 38**

ART LAW—Cont'd

Immunity of art experts, **Art 76, 77**
Import restrictions, **Art 9, 10, 18, 19**
Indian arts and crafts, **Art 14, 15, 25, 98, 99, 300, 301**
Insurance
  generally, **Art 100**
  contracts/policies, **Art 103, 105-114**
  traveling exhibits, **Art 101**
  trustee responsibility, **Art 102**
International Art Registry, **Art 97**
International Association of Art, **Art 24**
International Centre for the Study and Preservation Restoration of Cultural Property, **Art 24**
International council of monuments and sites, **Art 25**
International council of museums, **Art 25, 300, 312**
International movement of art, **Art 9-13, 15-29**
Invasion of privacy, **Art 250**
Investing in art, **Art 42-52**
Japanese bid-simultaneous bid, **Art 55, 56**
Joint professional policy on museum acquisitions, **Art 300, 213, 313**
Kansas City Art Museum, **Art 72**
Kronhausen collection of erotic art, **Art 277**
Kumluca silver treasures, **Art 15**
Labeling of Hazardous Art Materials Act, **Art 151, 152**
Lanham Act, **Art 78, 218, 244, 250, 251**
Library of Congress, **Art 209**
Lieber Code, **Art 31**
Louvre, **Art 72, 306, 307**
Maryhill Museum, **Art 290**
Metropolitan Arts Commission of Portland, **Art 165**
Metropolitan Museum of Art, **Art 74, 307**
Mexican antiquities laws, **Art 21, 26-28**
Moral rights, **Art 235-253**
Museum of Modern Art, **Art 51, 179, 310**
Museum organization
  generally, **Art 284**

ART LAW—Cont'd
Museum organization—Cont'd
legal structure, **Art 284, 285**
taxation, **Art 286-289**
trustee-director duties and liabilities, **Art 289-299**
Museum policies
acquisitions, **Art 299-302, 312, 313**
deaccessions, **Art 305-309**
ethics code, **Art 312, 313**
labor relations, **Art 309-311**
loans, **Art 303, 304**
National Commission for Fine Arts Act, **Art 155**
National Commission of Fine Arts, **Art 154**
National Council on the Arts, **Art 159, 160**
National endowment for the arts, **Art 157-163, 254**
National Endowment for the Humanities, **Art 157**
National Fine Arts Inventory of New Deal Art, **Art 156**
National Labor Relations Board, **Art 311, 312**
National Stolen Property Act, **Art 26-28**
Native American Graves Protection and Repatriation Act, **Art 14, 15, 25, 300, 301**
New York City Landmarks Preservation Commission, **Art 167**
Obscenity
generally, **Art 273**
alternative regulatory approaches, **Art 281, 282**
child pornography, **Art 278-281**
content or viewpoint restrictions, **Art 267**
defined, **Art 274**
Kronhausen Collection of Erotic Art, **Art 277**
NEA controversy, **Art 160-162**
RICO statutes, alternative regulatory approaches, **Art 282**
standards, **Art 274-277**
transmittal through U.S. mail, **Art 277, 278**
Patent and Trademark Office, **Art 218**
Perls Gallery, **Art 33**
Plagiarism, **Art 210, 211**
Plunder, **Art 30-32, 34, 37-41**
Pornography. Obscenity, supra
Protection of art in wartime, **Art 31, 32, 34**

ART LAW—Cont'd
Publishing contracts, **Art 242**
Purchaser's remedies, **Art 78-82**
Queens Museum, **Art 310**
Racketeer Influenced and Corrupt Organizations Act, **Art 46, 282**
Ransoms, **Art 109**
Remedies, **Art 32-39, 78-82 et seq., 207**
Right of first refusal, **Art 143**
Right of privacy, **Art 241, 243, 244**
San Salvadore Convention, **Art 20, 21**
Securities Act of 1933, **Art 44, 45**
Securities and Exchange Act of 1934, **Art 45, 46**
Securities and Exchange Commission (SEC), **Art 44**
Slander of title, **Art 74, 75**
Smithsonian Institution, **Art 295**
Society of American Archaeology, **Art 24**
St. Louis Mercantile Libraary, **Art 308, 309**
Taxation
  artist, **Art 171-184**
  business deductions, **Art 118-123, 177-179**
  capital gains, **Art 116, 117**
  characterizing income, **Art 115-127, 171-177**
  charitable deductions, **Art 123-127, 179, 180**
  dealers and collectors, **Art 115-137**
  estate planning, **Art 127-131, 180-184**
  hobby, **Art 118, 119, 177**
  income defined, **Art 115, 116**
  incorporation by the artist, **Art 174-177, 183, 184**
  installment method of accounting, **Art 172, 173**
  tax shelters, **Art 132-137**
Tax shelters, **Art 132-137**
Theft/conversion statutes, **Art 24-29**
Trademark
  generally, **Art 218**
  commerce use, requirement, **Art 221**
  confusing marks, **Art 222**
  copyright, supra
  definition, **Art 219**

ART LAW—Cont'd
Trademark—Cont'd
enforcement, **Art 219**
false description of origin, **Art 222, 231**
federal common laws, **Art 219-224**
generic and descriptive marks, **Art 220**
infringement, **Art 227-230**
loss of rights, **Art 223, 224**
official registers, **Art 225-227**
personal names, **Art 222, 223**
principal register, **Art 225, 226**
renewal, **Art 224**
service marks, **Art 218, 219**
state laws, **Art 230, 231**
supplemental register, **Art 227**
symbols, **Art 224, 225, 228**
trade dress protection of style, **Art 233-235**
unregistered marks, **Art 221**
words, symbols and shapes, **Art 220**
Trademark Law Revision Act of 1988, **Art 218, 224**
Treasures of the Wawal castle, **Art 38**
Trustees, liability for breach of fiduciary duties, **Art 289-299**
UNESCO, **Art 12, 21-23, 40, 300**
Unfair competition, **Art 244, 250**
Uniform Commercial Code, **Art 57, 60, 63, 82-91, 144**
Union of artistic property, **Art 254**
Universal Copyright Convention, **Art 205**
Valazquez, Metropolitan Museum Acquisition, **Art 307, 308**
Visual Artists Rights Act (VARA), **Art 237, 238, 243, 247, 248, 254**
Volunteer lawyers for the arts, **Art 152**
Warranties, **Art 61, 62, 82-93**
Weimer art collection, **Art 35, 36**
West's Art and Law Program, **Art 162, 163**
Working artists, **Art 138-148, 151-153**
Works Progress Administration (WPA), **Art 155, 156**

GENERAL INDEX

References are to Titles and Pages

ASSAULT AND BATTERY

Medical Liability (this index)

ASSIGNMENTS

Insurance Law (this index)

ASYLUM

Immigration Law and Procedure (this index)

ATHLETICS

Sports Law (this index)

ATTORNEYS

Interest on Lawyers' Trust Account (IOLTA) Funds. **Professional Responsibility** (this index)

Legal Interviewing and Counseling (this index)

Legal Negotiation (this index)

White Collar Crime (this index)

AUTHENTICATION

Art Law (this index)

BAILMENT

Sales and Leases of Goods (this index)

BANKING AND FINANCIAL INSTITUTIONS LAW

Accord of 1951, **Bank & Fin 19, 38, 65**

Accounting, **Bank & Fin 54, 117, 126-155, 231-235, 254, 271-283, 289, 295, 296, 305, 309, 329, 359-367, 411-414, 437**

Automated Tell Machines (ATMs), **Bank & Fin 186, 187, 211**

Balanced budget amendment, **Bank & Fin 114-116, 432-435**

Balance of payments and exchange rate oriented policies, **Bank & Fin 82-84, 88, 89, 91, 92, 95-97, 434-436, 439, 440**

Bank affiliate transactions (firewalls), **Bank & Fin 158-160, 169, 170, 323, 453**

Bank for International Settlements (BIS), **Bank & Fin 232-234, 459, 460**

BANKING AND FINANCIAL INSTITUTIONS LAW —Cont'd

Bank Holding Company Act (BHCA), **Bank & Fin 191-197**

Bank insurance, FDIC, **Bank & Fin 16, 31, 54, 55, 118, 119, 131-138, 279**

Bank mergers, **Bank & Fin 184-189, 192, 193, 197-210**

Bank money and it's creation, **Bank & Fin 3-8**

Bank of Commerce and Credit International (BCCI), **Bank & Fin 160, 233-234, 459**

Bank of North American, **Bank & Fin 34**

Bank of U.S., **Bank & Fin 8, 9, 32, 35-39**

Banks, corporate, **Bank & Fin 6, 8**

Banks, defined, **Bank & Fin 3-6**

Banks, private and partnership, **Bank & Fin 3-6**

Basle Concordats, **Bank & Fin 232-234, 459, 460**

Borrowing limits, banks, **Bank & Fin 162, 163**

Branching, **Bank & Fin 36, 43, 185-191, 211, 216-218, 222-224, 444-456**

Bribery, **Bank & Fin 163, 164**

Bush policies, **Bank & Fin 84-88**

CAMEL, **Bank & Fin 141, 142**

Capital requirements, capital adequacy, **Bank & Fin 126-131, 151-155, 232, 233, 271-273, 276-281, 297, 328-330, 359-363, 459, 460**

Carter policies, **Bank & Fin 75-77**

Casualty insurance, **Bank & Fin 344-355**

Central banks, **Bank & Fin 5, 30, 31, 36-39, 46, 47, 50, 51, 65-107, 429-440, 459, 460**

Chartering and entry, **Bank & Fin 120-126, 242-244, 250-255, 259, 260, 271-273, 283-294, 307-323, 356-359**

Clayton Act, **Bank & Fin 197-203**

Clinton policies, **Bank & Fin 88-92**

Closure and deposit payoff, **Bank & Fin 133, 134, 137, 138, 142-154**

Colonial Finance, **Bank & Fin 33**

Commodity monies, **Bank & Fin 3, 5, 10, 33, 35, 39, 41, 45, 54, 57, 72, 73**

BANKING AND FINANCIAL INSTITUTIONS LAW —Cont'd

Community Reinvestment Act (CRA), **Bank & Fin 183**
Competitive Equality Banking Act (CEBA), **Bank & Fin 278**
Comptroller of the Currency (OCC), **Bank & Fin 31, 42, 46, 47, 118-126, 168, 279**
Concentration, **Bank & Fin 190, 199-210, 444-456**
Continental-Illinois Bank, **Bank & Fin 135, 151**
Council of Economic Advisors, **Bank & Fin 29**
Credit cards, **Bank & Fin 176, 177, 210-213**
Credit controls, **Bank & Fin 77, 107-110**
Credit unions, **Bank & Fin 238, 239, 283-298**
Currency, **Bank & Fin 5, 6, 13, 41, 47**
Debt policies, **Bank & Fin 34, 35, 41, 57, 60-65, 71, 74, 75, 78-91, 93-97, 110-116, 431-436**
Deposit insurance, **Bank & Fin 16, 27, 31, 54, 55, 118, 119, 131-138, 239-241, 258, 259, 270-283, 289, 290**
Depressions, **Bank & Fin 15, 16, 39, 44, 45, 51-54**
Devaluations, **Bank & Fin 54, 57, 72, 73, 76, 77, 83, 91, 92**
Discount rates, **Bank & Fin 105-107**
Discriminatoin in credit, **Bank & Fin 180-183**
Disintermediation, **Bank & Fin 265-269**
Douglas Amendment (BHCA of 1956), **Bank & Fin 187, 188**
Edge Act Corporations, **Bank & Fin 218, 220, 222**
Eisenhower policies, **Bank & Fin 69, 70**
Electronic funds transfer, **Bank & Fin 25-27, 210-213**
Electronic Funds Transfer Act, **Bank & Fin 177**
Employee Retirement Income Security Act (ERISA), **Bank & Fin 403-415**
Employment Act of 1946, **Bank & Fin 62, 98, 132**
Equal Credit Opportunity Act (ECOA), **Bank & Fin 180-182**
Exchange rate and trade balance oriented policies, **Bank & Fin 82-84, 88, 89, 91, 92, 95-97, 434-436, 439, 440**
Expedited Funds Availability Act, **Bank & Fin 212**
Extortion, **Bank & Fin 164**
Failing and failure, **Bank & Fin 130-154, 232-2324, 269-280, 329-332, 356, 359-363, 411-414, 459, 460**

BANKING AND FINANCIAL INSTITUTIONS LAW —Cont'd

Failures, **Bank & Fin 27, 52, 54, 84, 85, 117, 126-155, 231-235, 254, 271-283, 289, 295, 296, 329-332, 359-367, 411-414**

Fair Credit Billing Act, **Bank & Fin 176, 177**

Fair Credit Reporting Act, **Bank & Fin 178**

False statements to obtain loans, **Bank & Fin 164**

FDIC Improvement Act (FDICIA), **Bank & Fin 131, 147, 153, 163, 282**

Federal Assets Disposal Administraation (FADA), **Bank & Fin 280**

Federal Deposit Insurance Corporation (FDIC), **Bank & Fin 16, 31, 54, 55, 118, 119, 131-138, 279**

Federal Emergency Management Agency (FEMA), **Bank & Fin 378, 379**

Federal Home Loan Bank Board (FHLBB), **Bank & Fin 52, 244, 245, 255-259, 271-280**

Federal Insurance Administration (FIA), **Bank & Fin 376-381**

Federal insurance regulation, **Bank & Fin 373-428**

Federal Reserve, **Bank & Fin 13-20, 25-27, 30, 31, 45-53, 57-110, 431-440**

Federal Reserve Open Market Committee (FOMC), **Bank & Fin 30, 50, 98-107**

Federal Savings and Loan Insurance Corporation (FSLIC), **Bank & Fin 27, 54, 55, 239-241, 258, 259, 270-283**

Financial Institutions Reform, Recovery, and Enforcement Act (FIRREA), **Bank & Fin 27, 85, 130, 147, 151, 153, 163, 164, 239, 270, 271, 279-283, 458**

Financial Institutions Regulatory and Rate Control Act (FIRA), **Bank & Fin 146, 161**

Financial Institutions Supervisory Act (FISA), **Bank & Fin 146**

Financial Service Holding Companies (FSHC's), **Bank & Fin 168-170, 196, 197, 209, 210, 382-386, 445, 456**

Fire insurance, **Bank & Fin 54, 117, 126-155, 158-160, 169, 170, 231-235, 254, 271-283, 289, 295, 296, 323, 329-332, 359-367, 411-414, 453**

Fiscal policies, **Bank & Fin 15, 17-20, 25-27, 30, 31, 34, 35, 41, 49-53, 57-116, 431-440**

BANKING AND FINANCIAL INSTITUTIONS LAW —Cont'd

Ford policies, **Bank & Fin 74, 75**

Foreign banks in U.S.ford policies, **Bank & Fin 221-224**

Fraud, **Bank & Fin 163, 164**

Free banking, **Bank & Fin 10, 11, 40**

Garn-St. Germain Act, **Bank & Fin 23, 157, 167, 270-272**

Glass-Steagall Act, **Bank & Fin 56, 164-171, 193, 196, 219, 382-386, 444-456**

Gold, specie money, **Bank & Fin 3, 5, 10, 33, 35, 39, 41, 45, 54, 57, 72, 73**

Graft, **Bank & Fin 163, 164**

Gramm-Rudman Act, **Bank & Fin 82-87**

Home Mortgage Disclosure Act, **Bank & Fin 175, 182, 183**

Hoover policies, **Bank & Fin 50-53**

Individual Retirement Accounts (IRSs), **Bank & Fin 391, 415-419**

Inflation, monetary policy, **Bank & Fin 15, 17-20, 25-27, 30, 31, 49-53, 57-110, 431-440**

Insider lending, **Bank & Fin 160-163**

Insolvency, **Bank & Fin 130-154, 232-2324, 269-280, 329-332, 356, 359-363, 411-414, 459, 460**

Insurance, **Bank & Fin 16, 27, 31, 54, 55, 118, 119, 131-138, 239-241, 258, 259, 270-283, 289, 290, 328-387, 411-414, 419-428**

Interest on demand deposits, NOW accounts, **Bank & Fin 174, 241, 248, 249**

Interest on Deposits, Regulation Q, **Bank & Fin 172, 173**

International banking, **Bank & Fin 24, 26, 91, 92, 95, 96, 127-131, 213-236, 436-440, 459, 460**

International Banking Act, **Bank & Fin 222-224**

International banking controversy, **Bank & Fin 91, 92, 95, 96, 224-235, 436-440, 459, 460**

International banking facilities, **Bank & Fin 220**

Interstate banking, **Bank & Fin 36, 42-48, 185-191, 445, 447-456**

Interstate Banking and Branching Efficiency Act of 1994, Reigle-Neal, **Bank & Fin 186, 189-191**

BANKING AND FINANCIAL INSTITUTIONS LAW —Cont'd

Investment banking, **Bank & Fin 56, 164-171, 193, 196, 219, 299-341, 382-386, 444-456**
Investment companies, **Bank & Fin 304, 332-341**
Investment Company Act, **Bank & Fin 333-338**
Johnson policies, **Bank & Fin 70, 71**
Kennedy policies, **Bank & Fin 70, 71**
Keogh (H.R. 10) Plans for Self Employed retirement, **Bank & Fin 391, 415-419**
Keynesian policies, **Bank & Fin 15, 17-20, 25-27, 30, 31, 34, 35, 41, 49-53, 57-116, 431-436**
Lending limits, **Bank & Fin 156-158**
Life insurance, **Bank & Fin 346-356, 365, 366**
Macro economic policies, **Bank & Fin 59-116, 431-440**
Margin regulations, **Bank & Fin 314-317**
Marine insurance, **Bank & Fin 344-347, 366**
McFadden Act, **Bank & Fin 21, 43, 186, 188-190, 444-453**
Merger guidelines, **Bank & Fin 202, 205-208**
Mergers, bank mergers, **Bank & Fin 184-189, 192, 193, 197-210**
Monetarism, **Bank & Fin 15, 17-20, 25-27, 30, 31, 49-53, 57-110, 431-440**
Monetary policy, **Bank & Fin 15, 17-20, 25-27, 30, 31, 49-53, 57-110, 431-440**
Money, banks defined, **Bank & Fin 3-6**
Money laundering, **Bank & Fin 234**
Money market funds, accounts, **Bank & Fin 22-24, 166, 167, 304**
Multinational banks, international banking, **Bank & Fin 24, 26, 91, 92, 95, 96, 127-131, 213-236, 436-440, 459, 460**
Municipal bonds and securities, **Bank & Fin 308, 309**
Mutual funds, **Bank & Fin 304, 332-341**
Mutual savings banks (MSBs), **Bank & Fin 242-250**
National Association of Insurance Commissioners (NAIC), **Bank & Fin 356, 358, 363, 368, 381**
National Bank Act, **Bank & Fin 11, 12, 41, 42, 54-57**
National banks, **Bank & Fin 12, 32, 41-43, 118, 120-126**

BANKING AND FINANCIAL INSTITUTIONS LAW —Cont'd

National Credit Union Administraator, **Bank & Fin 289, 290, 293, 297**

National Credit Union Share Insurance Fund (NCUSIF), **Bank & Fin 132, 289, 290**

National market system, **Bank & Fin 316, 317, 320**

New Deal, **Bank & Fin 16, 53**

Nixon policies, **Bank & Fin 71-75**

NOW accounts, **Bank & Fin 174, 241, 248, 249**

OCC, Comptroller of the Currency, **Bank & Fin 31, 42, 46, 47, 118-126, 168, 279**

Office of Management and Budget (OMB), **Bank & Fin 29**

Office of Thrift Supervision (OTS), **Bank & Fin 85, 239, 279, 282**

Open market operations, **Bank & Fin 15, 17-20, 25-27, 30, 31, 49-53, 57-110, 238, 279, 282, 431-440**

Panics and depressions, **Bank & Fin 36, 39, 44, 51, 61, 305, 306, 316, 317**

Pension Benefit Guaranty Corpooration (PBGC), **Bank & Fin 411-414**

Pension funds and plans, **Bank & Fin 388-414**

Pension regulation, **Bank & Fin 388-428**

Privacy, **Bank & Fin 178-180, 234**

Problem institutions, supervision, **Bank & Fin 54, 117, 126-155, 231-235, 254, 271-283, 289, 295, 296, 329-332, 359-367, 411-414**

Property insurance, **Bank & Fin 342-356, 364, 365**

Purchase and assumption (P&A) transactions, **Bank & Fin 131-133, 137, 138, 152-154**

Rate-making insurance, **Bank & Fin 363-366**

Reagan policies, **Bank & Fin 77-84**

Real Estate Investment Trust (REIT), **Bank & Fin 334**

Real Estate Settlement Procedures Act (RESPA), **Bank & Fin 176**

Reconstruction Finance Corporation (RFC), **Bank & Fin 52, 54, 241, 260, 278-280**

BANKING AND FINANCIAL INSTITUTIONS LAW —Cont'd

Regulation Q, **Bank & Fin 22, 23, 59, 71, 72, 77, 172, 173, 266-269**

Regulatory organization and framework, **Bank & Fin 456-460**

Rescheduling problems, **Bank & Fin 436-440**

Reserves, **Bank & Fin 4, 11, 14, 17, 36, 40, 42, 47, 48, 58, 103-105, 139, 226**

Resolution Trust Corporation (RTC), **Bank & Fin 280**

Restructuring financial markets, **Bank & Fin 440-456**

Riegle-Neal Insterstate Banking and Branching Efficiency Act of 1994, **Bank & Fin 186-191**

Right to Financial Privacy Act, **Bank & Fin 178-180, 234**

Risk-based capital requirements, **Bank & Fin 126-131, 151-155, 232, 233, 271-273, 276-281, 297, 328-330, 359-363, 459, 460**

Risk-based deposit insurance, **Bank & Fin 127-131, 142, 151**

Roosevelt, Franklin, **Bank & Fin 16, 53**

Savings and loan associations (S&Ls), **Bank & Fin 238, 239, 250-283**

Savings Association Insurance Funds (SAIF), **Bank & Fin 279, 283**

Savings banks, **Bank & Fin 238, 239, 242-250, 273, 274**

Secret bank accounts, **Bank & Fin 178-180, 219-227, 233, 234**

Section 20 affiliates, **Bank & Fin 56, 164-171, 193, 196, 219, 323, 382-386, 444-456**

Securities exchanges, **Bank & Fin 303, 304, 316-321**

Securities Investor Protection Corporation (SIPC), **Bank & Fin 329-332**

Securities marketing and commercial banking, Glass-Steagall Act, **Bank & Fin 56, 164-171, 193, 196, 219, 382-386, 444-456**

Securities markets, **Bank & Fin 299-307**

Securities regulation, **Bank & Fin 299-341**

Self-Employed Individuals Tax Retirement Act (H.R. 10 or Keogh Act), **Bank & Fin 391, 415-419**

Silver, specie money, **Bank & Fin 3, 5, 10, 33, 35, 39, 41, 45, 54, 57, 72, 73**

Socialized insurance, **Bank & Fin 369-373, 386, 387, 419-428**

Social security, **Bank & Fin 419-428**

BANKING AND FINANCIAL INSTITUTIONS LAW —Cont'd

Specie money, gold and silver, **Bank & Fin 3, 5, 10, 33, 35, 39, 41, 45, 54, 57, 72, 73**
St. Germain, Garn-St. Germain Act, **Bank & Fin 23, 157, 167, 270-272**
State Banking Commissioners or Departments, **Bank & Fin 12, 13, 32, 36-40, 42, 43**
State banks, **Bank & Fin 12, 13, 32, 36-40, 42, 43**
Supervision, **Bank & Fin 54, 117, 126-155, 231-235, 254, 271-283, 289, 295, 296, 329-332, 359-367, 411-414**
Tax havens, **Bank & Fin 24, 178-180, 219-221, 225, 226, 234**
Thrift institution regulation, **Bank & Fin 236-298**
Too big to fail, **Bank & Fin 126-131, 137, 138, 151-154**
Trade balance and exchange rate oriented policies, **Bank & Fin 82-84, 88, 89, 91, 92, 95-97, 434-436, 439, 440**
Treasury Department, **Bank & Fin 9, 18, 19, 29, 34, 47, 54, 66, 67, 110**
Truman policies, **Bank & Fin 62-65, 69, 70**
Trust accounts, **Bank & Fin 56, 164-172, 193, 196, 219, 382-386, 444-456**
Truth-In-Lending, **Bank & Fin 175, 176**
Underwriters, **Bank & Fin 56, 164-171, 175, 176, 193, 196, 219, 299-341, 382-386, 444-456**
Uniform Interagecy Bank Rating System (UIBRS), **Bank & Fin 141-143**
Wage-price controls, **Bank & Fin 61, 64, 67, 74-76**
Williams Act, **Bank & Fin 312, 313**
World Debt Crisis, **Bank & Fin 126-129, 229-233, 436-440**
World War II finance, **Bank & Fin 18, 61-63**

BANKRUPTCY AND OTHER DEBTOR-CREDITOR LAWS

Abstention, **Bankr 396**
Adequate protection, **Bankr 163**
After-acquired property, **Bankr 338**
Alias writ, **Bankr 49**

BANKRUPTCY AND OTHER DEBTOR-CREDITOR LAWS—Cont'd
Allowance of claim, **Bankr 277**
Appraisal statute, **Bankr 57**
Assignment for benefit of creditors, **Bankr 117**
Assuming lease or executory contract, **Bankr 294**
Assumption and assignment of lease or executory contract, **Bankr 303**
Attachment, **Bankr 19**
Automatic stay, **Bankr 155**
Avoidance of prebankruptcy transfers, **Bankr 183**
Badges of fraud, **Bankr 65**
Bankruptcy Act of 1898, **Bankr 6, 130, 136, 386**
Bankruptcy Code, **Bankr 6, 130**
Bankruptcy court jurisdiction, **Bankr 393**
Bankruptcy estate, **Bankr 171**
Bankruptcy judges, **Bankr 137**
Bankruptcy jurisdiction, **Bankr 137**
Bankruptcy law, **Bankr 5, 130**
Bankruptcy referees, **Bankr 136**
Bankruptcy Reform Act of 1944, **Bankr 6**
Bankruptcy Reform Act of 1978, **Bankr 6, 130**
Bankruptcy rules, **Bankr 133**
Bankruptcy trustee, **Bankr 139**
Breach of peace, **Bankr 84**
Capias ad staisfaciendum, **Bankr 47, 48**
Cash collateral, **Bankr 339**
Caveat emptor, **Bankr 58**
Chapter 7, **Bankr 134**
Chapter 11, **Bankr 135, 331, 344**
Chapter 13, **Bankr 135, 367, 370, 371**
Choate lien doctrine, **Bankr 103**
Circuity of priority, **Bankr 113**
Claims in bankruptcy, **Bankr 253, 271**
Codebtor, **Bankr 158, 368**
Cognovit judgment, **Bankr 40**

BANKRUPTCY AND OTHER DEBTOR-CREDITOR LAWS—Cont'd

Collective creditors' remedies, **Bankr 117**
Commencement of involuntary bankruptcy cases, **Bankr 173**
Commencement of voluntary bankruptcy cases, **Bankr 143**
Commencing Chapter 13 bankruptcy case, **Bankr 367**
Commencing Chapter 11 case, **Bankr 333**
Commercially reasonable, **Bankr 87**
Commission on Bankruptcy Laws of the United States, **Bankr 6**
Common-law liens, **Bankr 91**
Compositions, **Bankr 125**
Confirmation of Chapter 13 plan, **Bankr 373**
Confirmation of plan, **Bankr 354**
Consensual lien, **Bankr 3, 79**
Constructively fraudulent transfer, **Bankr 213**
Conversion of bankruptcy case, **Bankr 151**
Cram down, **Bankr 356**
Creditor's bill, **Bankr 52**
Customarily sold in recognized market, **Bankr 86**
Debt, **Bankr 315**
Debt collector, **Bankr 13, 40**
Debts affected by discharge, **Bankr 316**
Defamation, **Bankr 10**
Default, **Bankr 82**
Default judgment, **Bankr 39**
Deficiency judgment, **Bankr 88**
Delivery bond, **Bankr 27**
Discharge in bankruptcy, **Bankr 307**
Discharge in Chapter 13 case, **Bankr 376**
Discharging bond, **Bankr 27**
Discrimination due to bankruptcy, **Bankr 328**
Dismissing bankruptcy case, **Bankr 151**
Dismiss or convert Chapter 13 case, **Bankr 378**
Dissolution bond, **Bankr 27**
Distraint, **Bankr 30**
District court jurisdiction in bankruptcy, **Bankr 392**

BANKRUPTCY AND OTHER DEBTOR-CREDITOR LAWS—Cont'd

Docketing, **Bankr 43**
Dormancy, **Bankr 50**
Effect of bankruptcy discharge, **Bankr 327**
Elegit, **Bankr 47**
1111(b) elections, **Bankr 351**
Enabling loans, **Bankr 197**
Equality of distribution, **Bankr 283**
Equitable liens, **Bankr 93**
Exceptions to discharge, **Bankr 315**
Exclusivity period, **Bankr 344**
Ex contractu, **Bankr 20**
Ex delicto, **Bankr 20**
Execution, **Bankr 48**
Execution lien, **Bankr 47**
Execution sale, **Bankr 57**
Executory contracts, **Bankr 293, 304**
Exemption, **Bankr 15**
Exempt property, **Bankr 15**
Exempt property in bankruptcy, **Bankr 175**
Extensions, **Bankr 125**
Extrajudicial collection, **Bankr 9**
Extraordinary situations, **Bankr 24**
Extreme and outrageous, **Bankr 12**
Fair and equitable, **Bankr 356**
Fair Debt Collection Practices Act (FDCPA), **Bankr 12**
FDCPA, **Bankr 12**
Federal claims, **Bankr 94, 114**
Federal priority provision, **Bankr 95**
Federal tax lien, **Bankr 98**
Federal Tax Lien Act, **Bankr 98**
Field code, **Bankr 32**
Fieri facias, **Bankr 47**
Fieri facias (fi-fa), **Bankr 48**
Floating lien, **Bankr 199, 258**

BANKRUPTCY AND OTHER DEBTOR-CREDITOR LAWS—Cont'd

Foreclosure, **Bankr 89, 213**
Foreign debtor, **Bankr 150**
Forthcoming bond, **Bankr 27**
Fraudulent conveyance, **Bankr 62**
Fraudulent conveyance law in bankruptcy, **Bankr 212**
Garnishment, **Bankr 28**
Guarantors, **Bankr 158**
Hardship discharge, **Bankr 314, 378**
Homestead law, **Bankr 17**
Impairment of claims, **Bankr 351**
Improvement in position, **Bankr 188, 209**
Indemnity bonds, **Bankr 26**
Indirect preferences, **Bankr 191**
Individual with regular income, **Bankr 367**
Indubitable equivalent, **Bankr 165**
In personam jurisdiction, **Bankr 25**
Insider, **Bankr 187**
Insolvent, **Bankr 67, 72**
Intercoroprate guarantees, **Bankr 214**
Interests of debtor in property, **Bankr 173**
Invasion of privacy, **Bankr 11**
Involuntary bankruptcy, **Bankr 143**
Involuntary relief, **Bankr 148**
Judgment by confession, **Bankr 40**
Judgment lien, **Bankr 42, 105**
Judicial lien, **Bankr 4**
Judicial power and jurisdiction in bankruptcy, **Bankr 385**
Judicial sale to enforce mortgage, **Bankr 89**
Jury trials in bankruptcy, **Bankr 398**
Landlord's lien in bankrtupcy, **Bankr 241**
Leases, **Bankr 293**
Levari facias, **Bankr 47, 48**
Leveraged buyouts, **Bankr 215**
Levy, **Bankr 22**

BANKRUPTCY AND OTHER DEBTOR-CREDITOR LAWS—Cont'd

Lien, **Bankr 2**
Liquidation, **Bankr 134**
Mortgage, **Bankr 4, 88**
Mutual debt, **Bankr 206**
Nulla bona writ, **Bankr 49**
Objection to discharge, **Bankr 309**
1111(b) elections, **Bankr 351**
Opt out legislation, **Bankr 176**
Order of paying unsecured claims, **Bankr 283**
Ordinary course, **Bankr 196**
Partial assigment for benefit of creditors, **Bankr 120**
Perfecting security interest, **Bankr 80**
Pluries writ, **Bankr 49**
Post-bankruptcy transfers, **Bankr 247**
Postjudgment garnishment, **Bankr 59**
Postponing tax liens in bankruptcy, **Bankr 267**
Preference, **Bankr 185, 186**
Prejudgment matters, **Bankr 19, 28**
Prepackaged plans, **Bankr 361**
Prepetition transfers that are not timely recorded or perfected, **Bankr 221**
Priorities, **Bankr 4, 242, 285**
Proof of claim, **Bankr 275**
Property of estate, **Bankr 171, 172**
Provisional collection remedy, **Bankr 20**
Quasi in rem jurisdiction, **Bankr 25**
Reaffirmation agreement, **Bankr 328**
Reasonably equivalent value, **Bankr 71**
Receiver and receivership, **Bankr 31, 32**
Redemption, **Bankr 57, 85, 89**
Rehabilitation, **Bankr 134**
Rejecting lease or executory contract, **Bankr 294**
Relief from automatic stay, **Bankr 160**
Renewal of judgment lien, **Bankr 46**

BANKRUPTCY AND OTHER DEBTOR-CREDITOR LAWS—Cont'd
Reorganization, **Bankr 134**
Replevin, **Bankr 30**
Revival of judgment lien, **Bankr 46**
Sale pursuant to power of sale in mortgage, **Bankr 89**
Scire facias, **Bankr 46**
Section 105 injunction, **Bankr 158**
Secured claims in bankruptcy, **Bankr 253**
Secured party, **Bankr 80**
Security agreement, **Bankr 80**
Security interest, **Bankr 3, 80, 180**
Seller's rights of reclamation and return, **Bankr 242**
Setoff, **Bankr 205**
Sewer service, **Bankr 39**
Single asset real estate, **Bankr 168, 363**
Small business election, **Bankr 362**
State collection law, **Bankr 5**
Statute of Elizabeth, **Bankr 63**
Statutory liens, **Bankr 4, 94**
Strict foreclosure, **Bankr 89**
Subordination, **Bankr 290**
Substantially contemporaneous exchange, **Bankr 195**
Supplementary proceedings, **Bankr 54**
Title III of Consumer Credit Protection Act, **Bankr 18**
Trustee process, **Bankr 28**
Uniform Commercial Code Article 9, **Bankr 3, 81**
Uniform Enforcement of Foreign Judgments Act, **Bankr 44**
Uniform Fraudulent Conveyances Act (UFCA), **Bankr 66**
Uniform Fraudulent Transfer Act (UFTA), **Bankr 66, 71**
United States trustee, **Bankr 141**
Unsecured claims, **Bankr 271, 272**
Waiver of discharge, **Bankr 311**
Workouts, **Bankr 124**
Wrongful attachment, **Bankr 26**

BANKRUPTCY OR INSOLVENCY
Insurance Law (this index)

BANKS AND BANKING
Negotiable Instruments and Check Collection (this index)

BASIS ALLOCATION
Federal Income Taxation of Partners and Partnerships (this index)

BENEFITS
Employee Benefit Plans (this index)

BIDS AND BIDDING
Government Contracts (this index)

BILLS OF LADING
Uniform Commercial Code (this index)

BOOK/TAX DISPARITIES
Federal Income Taxation of Partners and Partnerships (this index)

BOYCOTTS
Labor Law (this index)

BRIEFS
How to Study Law and Take Law Exams (this index)

BROADCASTING
Generally, **Mass Comm 1 et seq.**

BUILDING AND CONSTRUCTION
Real Estate Finance (this index)

BUSINESSES AND INDUSTRIES
International Business Transactions (this index)

BUSINESSES AND INDUSTRIES—Cont'd
Regulated Industries (this index)

BUYER'S REMEDIES, UCC, SUPRA

CABLE TELEVISION
Generally, **Mass Comm 450 et seq.**

CALIFORNIA CIVIL PROCEDURE
Additur, **Cal Civ Proc 8, 150**
Admissions, in answer, **Cal Civ Proc 47**
Affirmative defenses, **Cal Civ Proc 49**
Alternate jurors, **Cal Civ Proc 41**
Amendments, **Cal Civ Proc 53-56**
Amount in controversy, **Cal Civ Proc 17-19**
Answer, **Cal Civ Proc 47-49**
Appeal, **Cal Civ Proc 4, 6, 67, 175, 181, 183-186, 190-192**
Arbitration, **Cal Civ Proc 119, 120, 122, 123, 134**
At issue memorandum, **Cal Civ Proc 134**
Attachment, **Cal Civ Proc 160-162**
Attorney-client, **Cal Civ Proc 78, 80**
Attorney's fees, **Cal Civ Proc 177-179**
Book of approved jury instructions (BAJI), **Cal Civ Proc 152**
Brown-Lockyer Civil Liability Reform Act, **Cal Civ Proc 102**
California Constitution, **Cal Civ Proc 10, 16, 20, 126, 135, 138, 154, 192**
California Economical Litigation Project, **Cal Civ Proc 88**
California Judicial Council, **Cal Civ Proc 126**
Charts, **Cal Civ Proc 6, 38, 58, 69, 151**
Choice/conflict of laws, **Cal Civ Proc 32-35**
Choice of forum, **Cal Civ Proc 2, 15**
Civil active list, **Cal Civ Proc 134**
Civil Justice Reform Act (federal), **Cal Civ Proc 129**
Claim and delivery, **Cal Civ Proc 160**
Claim preclusion, **Cal Civ Proc 199, 200, 207**
Class actions, **Cal Civ Proc 65**

CALIFORNIA CIVIL PROCEDURE—Cont'd

Closing argument, **Cal Civ Proc 146**
Collateral orders, **Cal Civ Proc 183, 184**
Complaint nomenclature, **Cal Civ Proc 37**
Compulsory cross-complaint, **Cal Civ Proc 51**
Consolidation, **Cal Civ Proc 62**
Constitution (federal), **Cal Civ Proc 7, 20, 136**
Consultants, **Cal Civ Proc 79,96**
Contempt, **Cal Civ Proc 172, 173**
Continuing discovery, **Cal Civ Proc 88**
Contractual arbitration, **Cal Civ Proc 119**
Contribution, **Cal Civ Proc 117, 118**
Coordination, **Cal Civ Proc 4**
Costs, **Cal Civ Proc 175, 176**
Counterclaims, **Cal Civ Proc 38**
Cross-claim, **Cal Civ Proc 38**
Cross-complaints, **Cal Civ Proc 38, 50-53**
Damages, **Cal Civ Proc 102, 111**
Default judgment, **Cal Civ Proc 110, 112**
Demurrers, **Cal Civ Proc 44-46**
Depositions, **Cal Civ Proc 89**
Diligent prosecution, **Cal Civ Proc 71, 72, 132**
Directed verdict, **Cal Civ Proc 49**
Discovery, **Cal Civ Proc 54, 76, 78-81, 84, 86-99, 102**
Disposition without trial, **Cal Civ Proc 105**
Distance for travel, **Cal Civ Proc 90**
District Court of Appeal, **Cal Civ Proc 4, 6**
Doe defendants, **Cal Civ Proc 54**
Entry on land/property, **Cal Civ Proc 91**
Equitable indemnity, **Cal Civ Proc 60**
Equitable tolling, **Cal Civ Proc 70**
Exchange of experts, **Cal Civ Proc 97**
Execution, **Cal Civ Proc 169**
Ex parte injunctions, **Cal Civ Proc 165**
Experts, **Cal Civ Proc 96-98**
Extraordinary writs, **Cal Civ Proc 188**

CALIFORNIA CIVIL PROCEDURE—Cont'd

Fact pleading, **Cal Civ Proc 40**
Failure to admit, **Cal Civ Proc 95, 96**
Fast track, **Cal Civ Proc 71, 127-129**
Federal courts, **Cal Civ Proc 5**
Federal notice pleading, **Cal Civ Proc 41**
Federal preemption, **Cal Civ Proc 124**
Fishing expeditions, **Cal Civ Proc 86**
Form pleading, **Cal Civ Proc 42**
Forum non conveniens, **Cal Civ Proc 29-31**
Full faith and credit, **Cal Civ Proc 207**
General appearance, **Cal Civ Proc 21**
General denial, **Cal Civ Proc 47**
General verdict, **Cal Civ Proc 154**
Good faith, **Cal Civ Proc 116-118**
Harmless error rule, **Cal Civ Proc 192**
Immunity from service, **Cal Civ Proc 24**
Indemnity, **Cal Civ Proc 57-60**
Injunctions, **Cal Civ Proc 164, 165, 167**
Inspection demands, **Cal Civ Proc 91**
Instructions, **Cal Civ Proc 152, 153**
Insurance discovery, **Cal Civ Proc 84**
Interpleader, **Cal Civ Proc 63**
Interrogatories, **Cal Civ Proc 88**
Intervention, **Cal Civ Proc 64**
Issue preclusion, **Cal Civ Proc 202-204**
Joinder, **Cal Civ Proc 61**
Judgments, **Cal Civ Proc 109, 110, 113, 150, 156, 159, 172, 198, 202, 205-207**
Judicial arbitration, **Cal Civ Proc 120**
Judicial districts, **Cal Civ Proc 16**
Jury, **Cal Civ Proc 135-145, 152-155**
Justice court system, **Cal Civ Proc 6**
Lis pendens, **Cal Civ Proc 162**
Local policies, **Cal Civ Proc 12**
Local rules, **Cal Civ Proc 11**

CALIFORNIA CIVIL PROCEDURE—Cont'd

Mandatory settlement conference, **Cal Civ Proc 135**
Medical examinations, **Cal Civ Proc 92, 94**
Misconduct of jury, **Cal Civ Proc 155**
Mixed venue action, **Cal Civ Proc 26**
Motions, **Cal Civ Proc 6, 12, 21, 28, 29, 46, 72-74, 105, 107, 145, 147-150, 154, 165, 186, 205**
Offer of judgment, **Cal Civ Proc 114, 115**
Opening statement, **Cal Civ Proc 146**
Oral depositions, **Cal Civ Proc 89**
Order of trial proceedings, **Cal Civ Proc 146**
Orders, **Cal Civ Proc 73**
Parallel court systems, **Cal Civ Proc 2, 7**
Peremptory challenges, **Cal Civ Proc 145**
Permissive cross-complaint, **Cal Civ Proc 50**
Personal jurisdiction, **Cal Civ Proc 21, 22**
Personal service, **Cal Civ Proc 22-24**
Physical evidence, **Cal Civ Proc 91**
Physical examinations, **Cal Civ Proc 93**
Pleading, **Cal Civ Proc 40, 41, 43, 44, 46, 47, 53, 61, 63-66**
Practice publications, **Cal Civ Proc 40, 42, 152**
Prayer for relief, **Cal Civ Proc 43**
Preemption, **Cal Civ Proc 124**
Presentation of evidence, **Cal Civ Proc 146**
Pretrial conference, **Cal Civ Proc 135**
Pretrial injunctions, **Cal Civ Proc 164**
Prevailing party, **Cal Civ Proc 175**
Prior adjudication, **Cal Civ Proc 195**
Privilege, **Cal Civ Proc 78-80, 82**
Process defined, **Cal Civ Proc 22**
Protective orders, **Cal Civ Proc 92, 95, 102**
Proveup hearing, **Cal Civ Proc 111**
Punitive damages, **Cal Civ Proc 102, 103**
Reasonable diligence, **Cal Civ Proc 22**
Receivership, **Cal Civ Proc 167**
Relationback, **Cal Civ Proc 55**

CALIFORNIA CIVIL PROCEDURE—Cont'd
Relation between state and federal courts, **Cal Civ Proc 5**
Relevance to subject matter, **Cal Civ Proc 83**
Relief from judgment, **Cal Civ Proc 156, 157**
Remedies, **Cal Civ Proc 159, 160, 162, 164, 165, 167, 169, 170, 178-180, 188**
Remittitur, **Cal Civ Proc 150**
Request for admissions, **Cal Civ Proc 91, 95**
Res judicta, **Cal Civ Proc 195, 197**
Rule of 35, **Cal Civ Proc 88, 95**
Rules of court, **Cal Civ Proc 11**
Sanctions, **Cal Civ Proc 66, 98-102, 128, 173, 185**
Service, **Cal Civ Proc 22-24, 71, 73**
Small claims court, **Cal Civ Proc 4, 6**
Sources of procedural law, **Cal Civ Proc 10-13**
Special appearance, **Cal Civ Proc 21**
Special denial, **Cal Civ Proc 48**
Special verdicts, **Cal Civ Proc 154**
Stare decisis, **Cal Civ Proc 7, 196**
State court system, **Cal Civ Proc 3**
State/federal court relationship, **Cal Civ Proc 5**
Statute of limitations, **Cal Civ Proc 54, 68-71**
Subject matter jurisdiction, **Cal Civ Proc 8, 16-18, 52**
Substantial evidence rule, **Cal Civ Proc 192**
Summary judgment, **Cal Civ Proc 105-108**
Summons, **Cal Civ Proc 22**
Superior court system, **Cal Civ Proc 6, 16**
Supplemental complaint, **Cal Civ Proc 42**
Supplementary proceedings, **Cal Civ Proc 170**
Temporary restraining orders, **Cal Civ Proc 164**
Third-party complaint, **Cal Civ Proc 38**
Transfer, **Cal Civ Proc 18, 28**
Travel distance, **Cal Civ Proc 90, 94**
Trial, **Cal Civ Proc 4, 55, 67, 96, 125, 131, 134, 135, 146-150, 152, 154, 175**
Truth in pleading, **Cal Civ Proc 66**

CALIFORNIA CIVIL PROCEDURE—Cont'd
Venire, **Cal Civ Proc 141**
Venue, **Cal Civ Proc 25-29**
Verdicts, **Cal Civ Proc 154**
Verification, **Cal Civ Proc 49**
Voir dire, **Cal Civ Proc 142**
Work product, **Cal Civ Proc 80-83, 89, 96**

CANADA
United States/Canada. **International Environmental Law** (this index)

CAPACITY OR INCAPACITY
Negotiable Instruments and Check Collection (this index)

CAPITAL AND CAPITAL ACCOUNTS
Federal Income Taxation of Partners and Partnerships (this index)
International Taxation (this index)

CAPS
Medical Liability (this index)

CARRIERS
Uniform Commercial Code (this index)

CASE LAW
Legal Research (this index)
Legal Writing (this index)

CASE METHOD
How to Study Law and Take Law Exams (this index)

CASUALTY INSURANCE
Insurance Law (this index)

CEILINGS
Medical Liability (this index)

CENSORSHIP
Art Law (this index)

CERCLA (COMPREHENSIVE ENVIRONMENTAL RESPONSE, COMPENSATION, AND LIABILITY ACT)
Hazardous Wastes and Toxic Substances, Law of (this index)

CHANGE OR MODIFICATION
Injunctions (this index)
Landlord and Tenant (this index)
Negotiable Instruments and Check Collection (this index)

CHARACTER OR CHARACTERIZATION
Federal Income Taxation of Partners and Partnerships (this index)

CHARTERS
International Human Rights (this index)

CHECKS
Negotiable Instruments and Check Collection (this index)

CHILDREN AND MINORS
Family Law (this index)

CITIZENSHIP
Immigration Law and Procedure (this index)

CIVIL CONTEMPT
Injunctions (this index)

GENERAL INDEX

References are to Titles and Pages

CIVIL PROCEDURE

Generally, **Civ Proc 1 et seq.**

California Civil Procedure (this index)

How to Study Law and Take Law Exams (this index)

CIVIL RIGHTS

Abortion, **Civ Rts 15-17, 29-39**

Access to the courts, **Civ Rts 159-164**

Actions under 42 USC § 1983, generally, **Civ Rts 252 et seq.**

Aliens, **Civ Rts 134-137**

Badges of slavery, **Civ Rts 224, 225**

Bill of Rights, **Civ Rts 3-6, 10-13**

Bona fide occupational qualifications, **Civ Rts 232-235**

Civil Rights Act of 1964, commerce clause, **Const Law 68**

Compensatory treatment of racial minorities, **Civ Rts 96-113**

Congressional implementation of constitutional rights, **Civ Rts 212-216**

Congressional modification of constitutional rights, **Civ Rts 216-221**

Congressional power over private discrimination, **Civ Rts 211, 222-225**

Counsel, right to, **Civ Rts 161, 162, 164**

Desegregation, **Civ Rts 75-77, 80-93**

Discrimination, generally, **Civ Rts 64 et seq., 185 et seq., 211 et seq., 252 et seq.**

Distinction between personal and economic freedoms, **Civ Rts 17-19**

Due process, generally, **Civ Rts 7 et seq., 40 et seq.**

Education, **Civ Rts 57-60, 70-77, 80-96, 137, 166, 167, 169, 170, 201-203**

Employment discrimination, **Civ Rts 229-246**

Employment Discrimination (this index)

Entitlement doctrine, **Civ Rts 41-45**

Equal protection, **Civ Rts 64 et seq., 129-131, 145 et seq.**

Fundamental interests, **Civ Rts 164-170**

Health Care Law and Ethics (this index)

Hearing, right to, **Civ Rts 41-63**

CIVIL RIGHTS—Cont'd
Housing, **Civ Rts 164-166, 194-198, 223, 224, 226, 248, 249**
Illegitimacy, **Civ Rts 138-144**
Indians, **Civ Rts 131**
Individual Employee Rights (this index)
International Human Rights (this index)
International Taxation (this index)
Irrebuttable presumptions, **Civ Rts 60-63**
Judicial enforcement of discrimination, **Civ Rts 194-198**
Legislative apportionment, **Civ Rts 68, 100, 101, 177-183**
Ninth Amendment, **Civ Rts 13-15**
Political parties, **Civ Rts 150-154, 186, 187**
Post-Brown statutes, **Civ Rts 226-229**
Privacy, right to, **Civ Rts 15-17, 21-39**
Privileges and immunities, **Civ Rts 1-3**
Public employment, **Civ Rts 44-46, 54-56**
Public Function Doctrine, **Civ Rts 186-194**
Racial classifications, **Civ Rts 65-72, 75-77, 80-93, 96-113, 230, 231**
Rationality test, **Civ Rts 64, 65, 68, 100, 101, 164, 165, 171, 172, 175-183, 194-198**
Reconstruction statutes, **Civ Rts 244-251**
Segregation, **Civ Rts 70-77, 80-96**
Seizure of property, **Civ Rts 46-51**
Sex discrimination, **Civ Rts 113-131**
Sex Discrimination (this index)
Significant state involvement, **Civ Rts 198, 199-202, 205-209**
State action, generally, **Civ Rts 184 et seq.**
Suspect classifications, generally, **Civ Rts 64 et seq.**
Travel, right to, **Civ Rts 154-158**
Wealth classifications, **Civ Rts 132-134, 146, 155-167, 170**

CLAYTON ACT
Antitrust Law and Economics (this index)

CLEANUP
Hazardous Wastes and Toxic Substances, Law of (this index)

GENERAL INDEX

References are to Titles and Pages

CLOSING OF TAXABLE YEAR

Federal Income Taxation of Partners and Partnerships (this index)

COAL

Energy and Natural Resources Law (this index)

COASTAL MANAGEMENT

Generally, **Coastal and Ocean 1 et seq.**

COLLECTION

Negotiable Instruments and Check Collection (this index)

COLLECTIVE BARGAINING

Labor Law (this index)

COMMON LAW

Individual Employee Rights (this index)
Judicial Process (this index)

COMMON MARKET

European Union (this index)

COMMUNICATIONS

Generally, **Mass Comm 1 et seq.**

COMMUNITY PROPERTY

Acquisition, **Comm Prop 3, 30-32, 39-41, 44-46, 64, 138, 139**
Alimony, **Comm Prop 278, 310, 311**
All-or-nothing, characterization approach, **Comm Prop 149, 192, 193, 199, 215, 217**
Analogies
  fault, commingling, **Comm Prop 153**
  metric conversion, **Comm Prop 406**
  New Mexico borders, **Comm Prop 16**
Annuities, retirement plans, **Comm Prop 180-189**
Annulment of marriage, **Comm Prop 366**

COMMUNITY PROPERTY—Cont'd
Apportionment, character, **Comm Prop 144-150, 182-185, 195-199**
Bigamist, division among spouses, **Comm Prop 372-374**
Character, exchanges, **Comm Prop 39**
Characterization, defined, **Comm Prop 1**
Civil law, **Comm Prop 1, 39, 44-49**
Commingling, **Comm Prop 140-143, 150-153**
Community, civil law definition, **Comm Prop 30**
Community labor, separate business, **Comm Prop 189-199**
Community purpose, expense, **Comm Prop 274, 275**
Concubinage, meretricious relationship, **Comm Prop 370**
Confidential relationship, **Comm Prop 22**
Conflict of laws, **Comm Prop 38, 94, 398-402**
Confused, characters, **Comm Prop 140-150**
Constitutional basis, sexual distinctions, **Comm Prop 25**
Contract issues, transmutations, **Comm Prop 19-23**
Contracts, postmarital or premarital, **Comm Prop 22, 23**
Convenience title, joint tenancy, **Comm Prop 114, 115**
Credit, acquisitions, **Comm Prop 160, 172**
Death, community division, **Comm Prop 5**
Decedent's estate, **Comm Prop 344-347**
Defense, community property, **Comm Prop 51**
Deferred compensation, generally, **Comm Prop 179-189**
Depleting property, character, **Comm Prop 47**
Depreciating property, character, **Comm Prop 47**
Disability payment, character, **Comm Prop 56**
Disability plans, deferred compensation, **Comm Prop 179-189**
Divorce, **Comm Prop 6, 23, 304-333**
Domiciled, definition element, **Comm Prop 4**
Education assistance, deferred compensation, **Comm Prop 179**
Election, decedent's estate, **Comm Prop 344-347**
Emigrants, **Comm Prop 405-407**
End, **Comm Prop 407**
Exchanges, character, **Comm Prop 39**
Exercise, drill, **Comm Prop 80-82, 160-166**

COMMUNITY PROPERTY—Cont'd
Fault, divorce, **Comm Prop 42, 43**
Federal supremacy, **Comm Prop 19, 39, 116, 128, 186-189, 299, 384-388**
Footnotes, location, **Comm Prop 407**
Forced share, decedent's estate, **Comm Prop 344-347**
Fruits, natural and civil, **Comm Prop 62-66**
Future earnings, **Comm Prop 37**
Ganancial, system, **Comm Prop 10, 31**
Gifts, **Comm Prop 23-25, 34, 64, 137**
Gratuitous, **Comm Prop 4, 30, 33-35**
Guadalupe Hildalgo, treaty, **Comm Prop 14**
Historic, **Comm Prop 38**
History, systems, **Comm Prop 8-11**
Homesteads, survivorship, **Comm Prop 111**
How acquired, community, **Comm Prop 30, 31**
Humor, **Comm Prop 3, 11, 12, 38, 62, 65, 337**
Immunity, interspousal, **Comm Prop 50**
Improvements, **Comm Prop 153-160**
Inception of title, generally, **Comm Prop 41, 144-150, 175, 176, 182-185**
Income, rents, issues and profits, **Comm Prop 61**
Interest, as rent, **Comm Prop 31**
Interlocutory divorce decree, **Comm Prop 42**
Interspousal immunity, **Comm Prop 50**
Intestacy, statutes, **Comm Prop 338, 347-364**
Inventory, separate property, **Comm Prop 91-93**
Joint bank accounts, generally, **Comm Prop 115-118**
Joint safe deposit box, generally, **Comm Prop 118, 119, 122**
Joint tenancy, **Comm Prop 106-136**
Labor and capital, character, **Comm Prop 47**
Legal separation, described, **Comm Prop 305, 306**
Liabilities, generally, **Comm Prop 269-303**
Life insurance, **Comm Prop 172-179, 314, 386**
Litigation issues, **Comm Prop 36, 49-52**
Lucrative, acquisition, **Comm Prop 30**

COMMUNITY PROPERTY—Cont'd

Management and control, **Comm Prop 8, 23-25, 49, 50, 232-303**
Maps, community states, **Comm Prop 2, 36**
Marital property, Texas and Wisconsin usage, **Comm Prop 2, 13**
Marriage, contracts, **Comm Prop 19-23**
Marriage agreement, Louisiana form, **Comm Prop 26**
Married, definition element, **Comm Prop 3, 4**
Marshaling, assets and liabilities, **Comm Prop 273, 274**
Medical expenses, reimbursement, **Comm Prop 37, 55, 56**
Medical plans, deferred compensation, **Comm Prop 180**
Meretricious, spouse, **Comm Prop 4, 369-371**
Metaphors, **Comm Prop 13, 18, 40, 61, 168, 224, 310, 311, 374**
Multistate, immigration problems, **Comm Prop 402-407**
National service, life insurance, **Comm Prop 179, 386**
Natural increase, property, **Comm Prop 48**
Nominal title, joint tenancy, **Comm Prop 114, 115**
Nothing at all, **Comm Prop 408**
Onerously, definition element, **Comm Prop 4**
Pain and suffering, **Comm Prop 38, 56**
Part-gift, part sale, **Comm Prop 34**
Party, proper, **Comm Prop 49, 50**
Pensions, generally, **Comm Prop 179-189**
Personal injury, recovery, character, **Comm Prop 36, 37, 55, 56**
Premarital, contracts, **Comm Prop 19-23**
Presumptions, **Comm Prop 32, 85-90, 95**
Probate administration, decedent's estate, **Comm Prop 339-344**
Property, definition elements, **Comm Prop 3**
Public policy, postmarital contracts, **Comm Prop 23**
Puns, **Comm Prop 3, 65, 270**
Putative, **Comm Prop 4, 51, 366-369, 372-378**
Quasi-community, **Comm Prop 94, 95, 317, 349-353, 404, 405**
Quasi-marital property, **Comm Prop 368**
Railroad Retirement Act, federal supremacy, **Comm Prop 384-388**
Rationale, community system, **Comm Prop 6-8**
Record title, **Comm Prop 87-89**

COMMUNITY PROPERTY—Cont'd

Regime, community, **Comm Prop 9, 172**
Relationship, confidential, **Comm Prop 22**
Rent, as sale, **Comm Prop 31**
Rents, issues and profits, character, **Comm Prop 31, 35, 36, 39, 44-49**
Residence, domicile distinguished, **Comm Prop 4**
Restitution, restatement, **Comm Prop 151-153**
Retirement, **Comm Prop 56, 179-189, 315**
Retroactive, application, **Comm Prop 13, 14, 392-397**
Roman Dutch, system, **Comm Prop 10, 31**
Savings bonds, federal provisions, **Comm Prop 384, 385**
Separate and apart, living, **Comm Prop 42-44**
Separate business, community labor, **Comm Prop 189-199**
Separate property, **Comm Prop 4, 91-93**
Separations, **Comm Prop 32, 33, 42-44, 317, 318**
Sole trader, statutes, **Comm Prop 18**
State constitutions, generally, **Comm Prop 388-392**
Statute, basic community, **Comm Prop 83, 84**
Statute of frauds, transmutations, **Comm Prop 20, 21**
Stock options, deferred compensation, **Comm Prop 179**
Support, liability, **Comm Prop 282**
Supremacy, federal, **Comm Prop 19, 39, 384-388**
Temporary, community status, **Comm Prop 12**
Tenancy by entirety, nonexistent, **Comm Prop 109**
Third party, protective statutes, **Comm Prop 89, 90**
Thrift plans, deferred compensation, **Comm Prop 179**
Title, **Comm Prop 41, 137, 144-150, 175, 176**
Tracing, property, **Comm Prop 86, 137, 138, 143, 144**
Transmutations, **Comm Prop 18-29**
Uniform Disposition of Community Property Rights at Death Act, generally, **Comm Prop 406**
Uniform Divorce Act, Kentucky modification, **Comm Prop 12**
Uniform Marital Property Act, generally, **Comm Prop 2**
Uniform Probate Code, **Comm Prop 334, 340, 343, 347, 352, 357**
U.S. Savings Bonds, "or" registration, **Comm Prop 116**

COMMUNITY PROPERTY—Cont'd

Usufruct, rents, issues and profits, **Comm Prop 44-49, 64, 65**
Visigoth, origins, **Comm Prop 11**
Wedding gifts, community character, **Comm Prop 24, 26, 34, 35**
When acquired, community, **Comm Prop 31-34**
Widow's election, decedent's estate, **Comm Prop 344-347**

COMPARATIVE LEGAL TRADITIONS

Administration of Justice Act, 1969, England, **Comp Legal Trad 186**
Administrative courts, **Comp Legal Trad 56, 306-308**
Administrative law, civil law, **Comp Legal Trad 103-106, 117**
Anglo-Saxon Law, **Comp Legal Trad 144**
Appellate Jurisdiction Act 1876, England, **Comp Legal Trad 157**
Appellate review, **Comp Legal Trad 96, 226-232, 341, 354-358, 362, 369**
Australia, effect of common law in, **Comp Legal Trad 159, 161-169, 187**
Barons, English, **Comp Legal Trad 145, 147**
Barristers, England, **Comp Legal Trad 192-207**
Bill of Rights 1689, England, **Comp Legal Trad 155, 248**
Bills of Exchange Act 1882, England, **Comp Legal Trad 256**
Bologna, Roman law revival, **Comp Legal Trad 15, 17, 20, 194**
British North American Act 1867, **Comp Legal Trad 164**
Caesar, Julius, **Comp Legal Trad 143**
Cambridge University, **Comp Legal Trad 153, 193, 253**
Canada, effect of common law, **Comp Legal Trad 162, 164, 165, 187**
Canon Law, **Comp Legal Trad 19, 22, 149, 150**
Central Criminal Courts Act 1934, England, **Comp Legal Trad 182**
Chancellor, England, **Comp Legal Trad 150**
Civil law, classification into subjects, **Comp Legal Trad 106-110**
Civil law tradition, **Comp Legal Trad 6, 13, 39, 40, 43-46**
Civil procedure, **Comp Legal Trad 91-93, 211-217, 259, 261, 272, 328, 336, 340, 341, 375, 380**
Civil War, England, **Comp Legal Trad 154, 155**

COMPARATIVE LEGAL TRADITIONS—Cont'd
Clergy, English, **Comp Legal Trad 148-150**
Codification, **Comp Legal Trad 27, 28, 47-50, 86, 116, 139, 261-267, 272, 378, 384**
Commercial law, **Comp Legal Trad 19, 23, 106, 107, 112, 113**
Common law tradition, **Comp Legal Trad 7, 161-167**
Communist Party, constitution of C.P.S.U., **Comp Legal Trad 288, 290**
Conventions. Sources of law, infra
Corpus juris civilis, Justinian compilations, **Comp Legal Trad 15, 16, 19, 21, 27, 29, 194**
County Court Act 1846, England, **Comp Legal Trad 176**
County Court Act 1959, England, **Comp Legal Trad 176**
Court for Crown Cases Act 1848, England, **Comp Legal Trad 228**
Court's Act 1971, England, **Comp Legal Trad 158, 173, 180, 182, 183**
Court systems
- civil law, **Comp Legal Trad 58, 59, 63-65**
- England, generally, **Comp Legal Trad 146-152**
- judiciary, infra
- socialist law, **Comp Legal Trad 275, 298, 301, 302, 304-312, 315, 318, 323, 326, 328, 334**

Criminal Appeal Act 1966, England, **Comp Legal Trad 228**
Criminal investigator, socialist law, **Comp Legal Trad 275, 313, 324, 347**
Criminal Justice Act 1967, England, **Comp Legal Trad 224**
Criminal law, civil law, **Comp Legal Trad 104**
Criminal procedure
- civil law, **Comp Legal Trad 94-96**
- England, generally, **Comp Legal Trad 217-226**
- socialist law, **Comp Legal Trad 259, 261, 272, 313, 328, 338, 343, 347, 349, 350, 354, 355**

Crown Proceedings Act 1947, England, **Comp Legal Trad 144**
Crusades, effect on England, **Comp Legal Trad 151, 177**
Curia regis, King's council, **Comp Legal Trad 146, 152, 185, 186**
Custom. Sources of law, infra

COMPARATIVE LEGAL TRADITIONS—Cont'd

Customary law, **Comp Legal Trad 18, 20, 24, 25, 32**
Devolution, England, **Comp Legal Trad 161, 171**
Domesday survey, **Comp Legal Trad 145**
Double jeopardy, socialist law, **Comp Legal Trad 312**
English law, definition, **Comp Legal Trad 159**
Equity, **Comp Legal Trad 101, 109, 150, 151, 158, 254, 255, 260, 301**
European Communities, England and, **Comp Legal Trad 171, 174, 189-201, 212, 228, 248, 250-252**
European Communities Act 1972, England, **Comp Legal Trad 189, 247, 248, 250-252**
European institutions, **Comp Legal Trad 47, 66, 67-69, 120, 174, 189-191, 228, 238, 251**
Executive branch, socialist system, **Comp Legal Trad 287, 294, 296, 299, 304, 307, 309, 314, 322, 324, 367, 368, 379**
Family law, civil law, **Comp Legal Trad 108**
Fictions, **Comp Legal Trad 148**
Forms of action, England, **Comp Legal Trad 147, 150, 158**
Franks Committee 1957, England, **Comp Legal Trad 174**
French civil code, **Comp Legal Trad 29, 31, 32, 39, 40, 266**
French Revolution, compared to England, **Comp Legal Trad 155**
German civil code, **Comp Legal Trad 29, 33, 35, 36, 41, 266**
Gloucester, Statute of, 1278, England, **Comp Legal Trad 149**
Goikhbarg, **Comp Legal Trad 266, 267**
Government lawyers, civil law, **Comp Legal Trad 83**
Habeas Corpus Act 1679, England, **Comp Legal Trad 248**
Hastings, **Comp Legal Trad 142, 144**
India, effect of common law, **Comp Legal Trad 159, 161, 166, 167, 187**
Industrial Relations Act 1971, England, **Comp Legal Trad 171**
Injunctive relief, England, **Comp Legal Trad 151**
Inns of Court, England, **Comp Legal Trad 193-195, 197, 198, 204**
Judicature Act 1873, England, **Comp Legal Trad 157, 158, 173, 179, 212, 254**
Judicial process, civil law, **Comp Legal Trad 119, 124, 136, 138, 139, 218, 129, 133, 136**

COMPARATIVE LEGAL TRADITIONS—Cont'd

Judicial review, **Comp Legal Trad 55, 57, 273, 366, 368**
Judiciary
  civil law, **Comp Legal Trad 56, 78**
  England, generally, **Comp Legal Trad 157, 169**
  France, **Comp Legal Trad 97, 99**
  Germany, **Comp Legal Trad 25, 26, 97, 99, 131, 132**
  socialist law, **Comp Legal Trad 259, 261, 263-265, 272-275, 287, 294, 298, 299, 322, 350, 354, 359, 367**
Jurisconsults, **Comp Legal Trad 14, 15, 82, 321, 330, 331**
Jus commune, **Comp Legal Trad 22, 24, 26, 28, 32, 33, 37**
Justices of the peace, England, **Comp Legal Trad 152, 177, 178, 183**
Justices of the Peace Act 1361, England, **Comp Legal Trad 152, 177**
Justinian compilations, **Comp Legal Trad 15, 16, 19, 21, 27, 29, 194**
Keepers of the peace, England, **Comp Legal Trad 151**
Labor courts, socialist law, **Comp Legal Trad 306**
Labor law, civil law, **Comp Legal Trad 114**
Law society, England, **Comp Legal Trad 193**
Legal aid, England, **Comp Legal Trad 204**
Legal Aid Act 1974, England, **Comp Legal Trad 204**
Legal Aid and Advice Act 1949, England, **Comp Legal Trad 204**
Legal education, **Comp Legal Trad 70, 87, 89, 102, 153, 156, 192-197, 204**
Legal professions, **Comp Legal Trad 9, 73, 75-77, 192-207, 321, 325-330**
Legal scholars
  civil law, **Comp Legal Trad 26, 27, 33, 34, 38, 82, 85, 87, 88, 129, 130, 137, 138**
  Roman, **Comp Legal Trad 14, 21**
  socialist, **Comp Legal Trad 321, 334, 377, 382, 384**
Legislation, England, **Comp Legal Trad 146, 170**
Legislature, **Comp Legal Trad 260, 264, 265, 279, 287, 291, 294-297, 299, 300, 304, 314, 322, 367-369, 378-380**
Life Peerages Act 1958, England, **Comp Legal Trad 171**

COMPARATIVE LEGAL TRADITIONS—Cont'd
Lord Chancellor, England, **Comp Legal Trad 157, 169, 176, 177, 185, 186**
Lords of Appeal in Ordinary, England, **Comp Legal Trad 157**
Magna Carta, **Comp Legal Trad 148, 149, 154, 155, 243**
Marxism-Leninism, **Comp Legal Trad 258, 259, 261, 277, 278, 280, 282, 317**
Norman Conquest, **Comp Legal Trad 142, 143, 149, 173**
Notaries, **Comp Legal Trad 76, 77, 314, 315, 331-334**
Oath, trial by, England, **Comp Legal Trad 147**
Obligations, civil law, **Comp Legal Trad 111**
Oral tradition, law as an, **Comp Legal Trad 143**
Ordeal, trial by, England, **Comp Legal Trad 147**
Oxford University, **Comp Legal Trad 153, 156, 193, 253**
Parliamentary government
- civil law tradition, **Comp Legal Trad 52**
- England, **Comp Legal Trad 153-159, 168-171, 173**
- executive, civil law, **Comp Legal Trad 53**
- legislature, civil law, **Comp Legal Trad 52, 55, 56**

Partnership Act 1890, England, **Comp Legal Trad 256**
Persons, civil law, **Comp Legal Trad 107**
Petition of Right Act 1628, England, **Comp Legal Trad 154**
Plantagenet period, England, **Comp Legal Trad 150**
Poor law system, England, **Comp Legal Trad 157**
Precedent. Sources of law, infra
Private law, civil law, **Comp Legal Trad 45, 46, 102, 106, 115**
Privy council, England, **Comp Legal Trad 160, 165, 244**
Procurator, socialist law, **Comp Legal Trad 275, 309, 313, 318, 322, 323, 336, 337, 347, 349, 350, 358, 361-364, 367, 368, 374**
Program of the C.P.S.U., **Comp Legal Trad 288-290**
Property law, civil law, **Comp Legal Trad 109**
Public law, **Comp Legal Trad 24, 31, 47, 102, 103, 115, 255**
Public prosecutors, civil law, **Comp Legal Trad 84**
Queen's counsel, England, **Comp Legal Trad 202-204, 207**
Reforms law, England 19th century, **Comp Legal Trad 156**
Registrar, England, **Comp Legal Trad 176**
Renaissance, **Comp Legal Trad 153**

COMPARATIVE LEGAL TRADITIONS—Cont'd

Reporting of decisions, England, **Comp Legal Trad 239, 240**
Res judicata, socialist law, **Comp Legal Trad 311, 339, 348, 349, 358, 362, 364, 365**
Resolution of 1688, England, **Comp Legal Trad 155, 168**
Roman law, **Comp Legal Trad 14-16, 17-19, 21, 23-25, 27, 29, 31, 35, 142-144, 157, 160, 163, 193, 194, 253, 254**
Royal Commission on Legal Services 1979, England, **Comp Legal Trad 193, 197, 201**
Russian Civil Code, **Comp Legal Trad 262**
Russian Criminal Code, **Comp Legal Trad 262**
Sale of Goods Act 1893, England, **Comp Legal Trad 256**
Scotland, law of, **Comp Legal Trad 160, 186**
Separation of powers, France, **Comp Legal Trad 83**
Sergeants, England, **Comp Legal Trad 192, 193**
Settlement Act of 1701, England, **Comp Legal Trad 155, 168, 248**
Sheriff, power of, England, **Comp Legal Trad 149**
Socialist law, distribution, **Comp Legal Trad 283**
Socialist legal tradition, history, **Comp Legal Trad 7, 258, 261**
Solicitors, England, **Comp Legal Trad 192-207**
Sources of law
  civil law tradition, generally, **Comp Legal Trad 119**
  England, generally, **Comp Legal Trad 233, 234**
  socialist law, **Comp Legal Trad 261, 272, 376, 377, 379-381, 384**
South Africa, effect of common law, **Comp Legal Trad 162, 165, 166, 187**
Sovereign, role of, England, **Comp Legal Trad 169, 172, 173**
Specific performance, England, **Comp Legal Trad 151**
Star chamber, **Comp Legal Trad 152, 154, 243**
Stuart Period, England, **Comp Legal Trad 152, 154-156, 243**
Succession law, civil law tradition, **Comp Legal Trad 110**
Swiss Civil Code, **Comp Legal Trad 42, 266**
Trade union organization, socialist law, **Comp Legal Trad 275, 285, 290-293, 306, 309, 323, 379**
Treaty of 1707 with Scotland, England, **Comp Legal Trad 160**

COMPARATIVE LEGAL TRADITIONS—Cont'd
Tribunals and Inquiries Act 1958, England, **Comp Legal Trad 189**
Tudor Period, England, **Comp Legal Trad 152, 153**
Union, Act of, 1707, England, **Comp Legal Trad 248**
United Kingdom, Law of, **Comp Legal Trad 159, 160, 190**
United States, effect of common law, **Comp Legal Trad 156, 159, 161**
War of the Roses, **Comp Legal Trad 152**
Westminster, **Comp Legal Trad 145**
Westminster, Statute of 1285, England, **Comp Legal Trad 148**
Westminster, Statute of 1931, England, **Comp Legal Trad 160**
Writs, England, **Comp Legal Trad 147, 148, 150**

COMPENSATION
Individual Employee Rights (this index)
Land Use (this index)
Workers' Compensation and Employee Protection Laws (this index)

COMPETITION
International Trade and Investment (this index)

COMPLIANCE FAILURE
Immigration Law and Procedure (this index)

COMPREHENSIVE ENVIRONMENTAL RESPONSE, COMPENSATION, AND LIABILITY ACT (CERCLA)
Hazardous Wastes and Toxic Substances, Law of (this index)

COMPROMISE AND SETTLEMENT
International Trade and Investment (this index)
Legal Negotiation (this index)

COMPULSORY MATTERS
First Amendment (this index)

COMPUTATION
International Taxation (this index)

COMPUTERS
How to Study Law and Take Law Exams (this index)

CONFIDENTIALITY
Health Care Law and Ethics (this index)

CONFLICT OF INTEREST
Insurance Law (this index)

CONFLICTS
Abatement, full faith and credit for judgments based on pleas in, **Conflicts 355**
Act of State Doctrine, generally, **Conflicts 310-312**
Administrative determinations, **Conflicts 369**
Admiralty, **Conflicts 96, 306-309**
Adoption, **Conflicts 408-409**
Agency, **Conflicts 53-55**
Alimony. Support and alimony, infra
Ancillary administration, **Conflicts 301**
Ancillary letters, **Conflicts 297, 299**
Annulment, choice of law, **Conflicts 377**
Antitrust laws, extraterritorial application, **Conflicts 310**
Appearance, **Conflicts 87-89, 126, 345 et seq., 381**
Appointment, power of, **Conflicts 305**
Arbitration, **Conflicts 226-229, 322, 340, 349, 369, 370**
Bar, full faith and credit for judgments based on please in, **Conflicts 355**
Better rule of law, choice of law item, **Conflicts 200, 207, 251-253, 259**
Bhopal settlement, **Conflicts 312, 343**
Bibliography, **Conflicts 12, 13**
Business disparagement, choice of law, **Conflicts 284, 285**
Center of gravity, **Conflicts 204**

CONFLICTS—Cont'd
Characterization, **Conflicts 183, 232-235**
Child custody, **Conflicts 402-408**
Choice-influencing considerations, **Conflicts 199, 237, 251, 257, 259**
Choice of law, generally, **Conflicts 25-29**
Citations, **Conflicts 2, 3**
Citizenship, **Conflicts 15, 16**
Claim preclusion, **Conflicts 358**
Class actions, full faith and credit for judgments, **Conflicts 357**
Cognovits, **Conflicts 57**
Collateral attack, **Conflicts 364**
Collateral estoppel, **Conflicts 358, 360**
Comity, **Conflicts 10, 342, 343**
Common law marriage, **Conflicts 375**
Community property, **Conflicts 393**
Comparative impairment test, choice of law, **Conflicts 249, 250, 258**
Confession of judgment, **Conflicts 57**
Conflict of laws, **Conflicts 1-4, 12**
Consent, **Conflicts 56, 57**
Consortium, loss of, choice of law, **Conflicts 243, 256, 264**
Contacts, **Conflicts 8, 59, 155, 161, 271**
Contesting jurisdiction, **Conflicts 125-127**
Continuing jurisdiction, **Conflicts 93**
Contributory negligence, **Conflicts 187, 280, 281**
Corporate securities, **Conflicts 115, 293**
Corporations, **Conflicts 20, 21; Conflicts 46, 48-51, 121; Conflicts 47, 141, 221-224**
Courts, categories of, **Conflicts 36**
Death on the High Seas Act, **Conflicts 308**
Declaratory judgment, use in matrimonial actions, **Conflicts 376**
Deeds, recognition when executed outside state, **Conflicts 367**
Defamation, **Conflicts 82, 284**
Defaults, **Conflicts 90, 91, 346, 358**
Depositions, admissibility if testimony privileged, **Conflicts 190**

CONFLICTS—Cont'd
Direct actions, **Conflicts 162, 185, 186**
Direct attack, **Conflicts 364**
Diversity cases, **Conflicts 6, 316-336, 338, 343**
Divisible divorce doctrine, **Conflicts 402**
Documents, situs of for jurisdiction, **Conflicts 114, 115**
Domestic law, extraterritorial application of, **Conflicts 310**
Domicile, **Conflicts 11, 14-26, 52, 53, 244, 377-379**
Dower and curtesy, divorce, **Conflicts 397**
Dram shop acts, choice of law, **Conflicts 235, 249**
Due process, **Conflicts 8, 41, 42, 69, 70, 122, 154, 155, 357**
Election against will, **Conflicts 394**
Election of remedies, **Conflicts 358**
Employer's claim, injury to employee, **Conflicts 250**
Equal protection, Erie doctrine, **Conflicts 327, 328**
Equitable conversion, choice of law in realty cases, **Conflicts 303**
Equity judgments, full faith and credit application to, **Conflicts 365**
Erie Doctrine, **Conflicts 6, 316-336, 338, 343**
Escheat cases, situs of property for, **Conflicts 115**
Estates, jurisdiction, **Conflicts 64**
Estate taxes, **Conflicts 24, 296, 297**
Evidence, generally, **Conflicts 186**
Ex parte divorce, generally, **Conflicts 377, 386**
Extradition, alternative to prosecution under foreign penal law, **Conflicts 133**
False conflicts, chice of law, **Conflicts 253, 260, 264**
Federal courts, **Conflicts 37-39, 118, 119, 125**
Federal Rules of Civil Procedure, **Conflicts 125, 324, 325**
Federal Tort Claims Act, choice of law, **Conflicts 282**
FELA claims, jurisdiction, **Conflicts 144**
Foreign actions, **Conflicts 144, 146**
Foreign acts, domestic law application to, **Conflicts 310-313**
Foreign national involvement, **Conflicts 310-312**
Foreign soil, conduct on, **Conflicts 310**
Foreign sovereignty, **Conflicts 310-312**

CONFLICTS—Cont'd
Forum, **Conflicts 157-159, 274, 277**
Forum-law approach, choice of law, **Conflicts 238, 257, 260, 264, 277**
Forum non conveniens, **Conflicts 138-144, 332, 333**
Forum shopping, generally, **Conflicts 274**
Fraternal benefit society, **Conflicts 164**
Fraud, **Conflicts 285, 364, 365**
Frauds, statute of, **Conflicts 195, 210, 211, 267, 275**
Full faith and credit, **Conflicts 7, 8, 10, 154, 159, 340 et seq., 402 et seq.**
Gambling, public policy in cases involving, **Conflicts 167**
Garnishee, **Conflicts 117**
Grouping of contacts, **Conflicts 204**
Guest-host statutes, choice of law, **Conflicts 193, 240-243, 251, 254-256, 265, 270**
Inconsistent judgments, **Conflicts 367**
Injunctions, **Conflicts 144, 146**
In rem jurisdiction, **Conflicts 99-101**
Instruments, choice of law in gifts of, **Conflicts 292, 293**
Insurance, **Conflicts 155, 156, 162, 163, 207, 208, 242**
Intangibles, choice of law in transfer of, **Conflicts 292**
Interest analysis, **Conflicts 204, 236, 246, 257, 259**
Internal law, **Conflicts 27, 30**
International law, **Conflicts 2**
Interstate commerce, dismissal of action for interfering with, **Conflicts 143**
Intestacy, **Conflicts 298, 301**
Issue preclusion, **Conflicts 358, 360**
Jones Act, **Conflicts 308, 309**
Judgments, generally, **Conflicts 340 et seq.**
Jurisdiction, generally, **Conflicts 4, 31**
Labeling, **Conflicts 185**
Laches, **Conflicts 176**
Lex loci delictus, **Conflicts 192, 193, 229**
Liability, imputation of, choice of law, **Conflicts 231, 232, 268**

CONFLICTS—Cont'd

Limitations, statute of, **Conflicts 155, 161-163, 169-182, 268-270, 319**
Lis pendens, **Conflicts 366**
Longarm jurisdiction, **Conflicts 56 et seq.**
Longshoremen's and Harbor Workers Compensation Act, **Conflicts 308**
Matrimonial actions, generally, **Conflicts 373**
Matrimonial res, **Conflicts 102, 377, 387**
Merger, **Conflicts 5, 385, 386**
Merits, full faith nd credit as barring relitigation of, **Conflicts 350**
Money, gift of, choice of law, **Conflicts 292**
Montreal Agreement, **Conflicts 313, 314**
Most significant relationship test, **Conflicts 198, 204, 237, 239, 257, 259, 284**
Multiparty cases, **Conflicts 312, 343, 359**
Municipal law, **Conflicts 27, 30**
Mutuality of estoppel, **Conflicts 358, 360**
Neutral case, choice of law, **Conflicts 264**
Nonresident motorist statutes, **Conflicts 55, 56**
Outcome determinative test, generally, **Conflicts 321, 325**
Partnership, service on partner as giving jurisdiction of, **Conflicts 51**
Penal laws, **Conflicts 133 et seq.**
Personal (personam) jurisdiction, generally, **Conflicts 4, 39 et seq.**
Personal property, **Conflicts 113, 291, 295-299, 392**
Personal representatives, **Conflicts 64, 296**
Plaintiff's viewpoint rule, choice of law, **Conflicts 257, 262, 271**
Pleading, burden of, **Conflicts 185, 188**
Power of appointment, **Conflicts 305, 306**
Predictability, **Conflicts 209, 210, 241**
Presumptions, **Conflicts 187**
Privacy right, choice of law, **Conflicts 284**
Privileged communications, **Conflicts 188, 189**
Privileges and immunities, **Conflicts 164, 165, 172, 179, 180**
Privity, **Conflicts 356, 358, 383**

CONFLICTS—Cont'd

Probate courts, not jurisdictional magic in, **Conflicts 64**
Procedure, **Conflicts 185, 317**
Procedure labeling, choice of law avoidance with, **Conflicts 183, 233, 267**
Process service, **Conflicts 44-46, 122-125**
Proof, burden of, **Conflicts 187, 188, 323**
Property, situs of, **Conflicts 112-117**
Public policy, **Conflicts 132, 142, 166, 167, 169, 234**
Punitive damages, choice of law, **Conflicts 266**
Quasi in rem jruisdiction, generally, **Conflicts 104-117**
Quasi-judicial determinations, recognition, **Conflicts 369**
Realty, **Conflicts 101, 102, 141, 212, 213, 266, 301 et seq.**
Rem jurisdiction, generally, **Conflicts 94 et seq.**
Renvoi, **Conflicts 26-29, 281, 283, 303**
Restrictions on jurisdiction, generally, **Conflicts 128-133**
Rules of Decision Act, generally, **Conflicts 316**
Savings to suitors clause, **Conflicts 306**
Secured transactions, choice of law, **Conflicts 218**
Security interests, **Conflicts 117, 218, 295**
Seider Doctrine, generally, **Conflicts 110, 278**
Separation agreements, incorporation or merger in divorce judgments, **Conflicts 386**
Shaffer v. Heitner, generally, **Conflicts 104-117**
Sovereign states, **Conflicts 8, 9, 310-312, 343**
Spendthrift adjudications, choice of law, **Conflicts 208, 276, 279**
Splitting, **Conflicts 358**
Spouses, **Conflicts 168, 234, 235, 394**
Stacking of insurance coverage, choice of law, **Conflicts 252, 276**
Stipulations, choice of law, **Conflicts 201, 204**
Subject matter jurisdiction, **Conflicts 33, 34, 37**
Subpoenas, extrastate service of, **Conflicts 52, 53**
Substance versus procedure niching, **Conflicts 183, 317, 318, 321**
Support and alimony, **Conflicts 273, 361, 394-401**
Supremacy clause, choice of law, **Conflicts 165**
Survival of claim issues, choice of law, **Conflicts 232, 268, 269**

CONFLICTS—Cont'd
Tax claims, **Conflicts 137, 138**
Tenth Amendment, Erie Doctrine, **Conflicts 346**
Torts, generally, **Conflicts 229 et seq.**
Transfer of actions, federal courts, **Conflicts 140**
Treaties, generally, **Conflicts 313**
True conflicts, choice of law, **Conflicts 256, 264**
Trusts, **Conflicts 294, 303-306**
Uniform Child Custody Jurisdiction Act, **Conflicts 404**
Uniform Commercial Code, **Conflicts 116, 213, 218, 293**
Uniform Reciprocal Enforcement of Support Act, **Conflicts 400**
Unprovided-for case, choice of law, **Conflicts 264**
Usury, **Conflicts 225**
Validation, rule of, **Conflicts 205, 225, 294, 304-306**
Vested rights, **Conflicts 194**
Wage assignments, choice of law, **Conflicts 206**
Warsaw Convention, **Conflicts 313**
Wills, **Conflicts 297, 301, 302, 394**
Workers' compensation, **Conflicts 160, 286-288, 291**
Wrongful death actions, choice of law on damages, **Conflicts 157, 233, 243, 244, 247, 248, 254, 270, 278**

CONFRONTATION
Trial and Practice Skills (this index)

CONGRESS
Federal Jurisdiction (this index)

CONSENT
Medical Liability (this index)
Public International Law (this index)

CONSTITUTIONAL ANALYSIS
Civil Rights Act of 1964, exceptions permitting discrimination, **Const Analysis 111**
Congress, generally, **Const Analysis 119-144**
Constitution, functions, **Const Analysis 33-36**

CONSTITUTIONAL ANALYSIS—Cont'd

Criminal law, protection of life and property, **Const Analysis 112**
Criminal procedure, genreally, **Const Analysis 278-282**
Divine or natural law, genreally, **Const Analysis 2, 3**
Due process of law, generally, **Const Analysis 3, 64-66**
Economic due process of law, generally, **Const Analysis 75-84**
Election, **Const Analysis 44, 105-110, 141, 142**
Equal protection, generally, **Const Analysis 68-72, 287-294**
Federal commerce power, generally, **Const Analysis 150-165, 314-317**
Freedom of association, generally, **Const Analysis 105-110**
Freedom of contract principle, generally, **Const Analysis 147, 148, 284, 285**
Freedom of expression, generally, **Const Analysis 85-90, 296-308**
Freedom of press, generally, **Const Analysis 302-304**
Freedom of religion, generally, **Const Analysis 308-313**
Freedom of speech, generally, **Const Analysis 85-90, 296-308**
Governmental relationships, generally, **Const Analysis 241-263**
Judicial review, generally, **Const Analysis 1-32, 265**
Jury's role, **Const Analysis 1, 102**
Libel, generally, **Const Analysis 300, 301**
Liberty, generally, **Const Analysis 36-52**
National powers, generally, **Const Analysis 145-182, 313-320**
National power to tax and spend for general welfare, generally, **Const Analysis 169-176, 318**
Naturalization, state powers, **Const Analysis 158-164**
Obscenity, **Const Analysis 90-104, 307, 308**
Political questions, generally, **Const Analysis 27-32, 268**
Privilege or immunity clause, not applicable to states, **Const Analysis 61-63**
Procedural due process, generally, **Const Analysis 75-85**
Racial discrimination, **Const Analysis 136-138, 158-164, 278-282**
Record, judicial review involving individual liberties, **Const Analysis 227**
Right to discriminate, generally, **Const Analysis 105-110**

CONSTITUTIONAL ANALYSIS—Cont'd

Right to privacy, right of personal autonomy, **Const Analysis 285, 286**
Right to travel, generally, **Const Analysis 290**
State powers, generally, **Const Analysis 183-217, 320-332**
Substantive due process of law, generally, **Const Analysis 75-84**
Taking of property, generally, **Const Analysis 282-284**
Thirteenth Amendment, racial discrimination as badge of slavery, **Const Analysis 43, 44, 135-141**
Treaty power, generally, **Const Analysis 176-182, 319, 320**
Voting age, form of discrimination, **Const Analysis 111**
War power, generally, **Const Analysis 318, 319**
Written constitutions, development, **Const Analysis 3, 4**

CONSTITUTIONAL FEDERALISM

Administrative agencies, **Const Federalism 26, 351, 352, 404, 405**
Affecting commerce, **Const Federalism 26, 29, 122, 123**
Ancillary powers, **Const Federalism 17**
Apportionment, **Const Federalism 138-142, 308, 309, 311, 318-322, 331, 332**
Articles of commerce, **Const Federalism 101, 102**
Bills of credit, **Const Federalism 200**
Bootstrap, **Const Federalism 65-68, 198, 199, 210**
Burdens, **Const Federalism 287-292, 316, 322**
Cession of jurisdiction, **Const Federalism 215**
Class basis, **Const Federalism 32, 33, 38, 39, 238**
Collision, **Const Federalism 252**
Compacts, **Const Federalism 212, 394 et seq.**
Competition, **Const Federalism 114-117**
Concurrent powers, **Const Law 86-88**
Conflict, **Const Federalism 251, 341, 344-347**
Consent, **Const Federalism 357 et seq., 399-402**
Contract, **Const Federalism 84, 175, 185-189, 196, 197**
Contractors, **Const Federalism 377-380, 382**
Delegated powers, **Const Federalism 8, 9**
Direct, **Const Federalism 22, 23, 25, 261, 262**

CONSTITUTIONAL FEDERALISM—Cont'd

Direct taxes, **Const Federalism 138-141**
Discrimination, **Const Federalism 260, 281-287, 302, 303, 309-312, 322, 323**
Dormant power, **Const Federalism 248 et seq., 362**
Dual federalism, **Const Federalism 11, 53, 103-106, 111-113, 122, 258, 261, 278, 300, 324, 368, 387, 593**
Earmarked taxes, **Const Federalism 144**
Enclaves, **Const Federalism 213-217, 226-228**
Enumerated powers, **Const Federalism 8, 9, 11, 13, 17, 51, 53, 206, 217, 219-221, 230, 246**
Equal footing, **Const Federalism 222, 223, 231**
Exclusive power, **Const Federalism 251-254, 256, 304, 334, 336-339**
Executive agreements, **Const Federalism 213**
Exports, **Const Federalism 143, 212, 250, 326-330**
Extradition, **Const Federalism 393**
Extraneous, **Const Federalism 18, 22, 53, 59, 60, 63, 64, 77, 79, 83, 84, 97, 98, 135, 146, 170, 174-183, 202, 370-373, 375, 376, 382, 383**
Extraneous to tax needs, **Const Federalism 156-160**
Extraterritoriality, **Const Federalism 217, 227, 256, 257, 277, 303, 304, 322**
Federal common law, **Const Federalism 75, 76, 292, 293**
Filiation of necessities, **Const Federalism 21, 237**
Formal rule, **Const Federalism 279, 301, 302, 309, 323**
Free trade, **Const Federalism 277, 278, 294**
Frustration, **Const Federalism 80, 180, 344, 345, 354**
Full faith and credit, **Const Federalism 393**
General jurisdiction, **Const Federalism 10, 27, 29, 67, 68, 216, 217, 220-223, 229, 230**
General welfare, **Const Federalism 162, 164-166, 184**
Hamilton, Alexander, **Const Federalism 17, 18, 93, 108, 167-173, 184**
Home port doctrine, **Const Federalism 306**
Immunity, **Const Federalism 79, 191-195, 223, 368 et seq.**
Implied powers, **Const Federalism 17**

CONSTITUTIONAL FEDERALISM—Cont'd

Import-export clause, **Const Federalism 212, 250, 326-330**
Instrumentality, **Const Federalism 105, 369, 376, 377**
International commerce, **Const Federalism 135-137, 326-333**
Intoxicants, **Const Federalism 271, 272**
Jefferson, Thomas, **Const Federalism 17, 23, 167**
Law of the union doctrine, **Const Federalism 401-406**
Legitimate, **Const Federalism 14, 19, 61, 62, 68, 69, 77**
Madison, James, **Const Federalism 12, 93, 166, 167, 171, 184**
Madisonian democracy, **Const Law 2**
Market participant doctrine, **Const Federalism 269-271**
Marshall, John (C.J.), **Const Federalism 13, 20, 52, 94, 96, 234**
Monroe, James, **Const Federalism 168-170**
Multiple taxation, **Const Federalism 306-308, 323**
Navigable waters, **Const Federalism 128-135**
Negative implications, **Const Federalism 103, 248 et seq., 359**
New Deal, **Const Federalism 4, 22, 259, 260**
Nexus, **Const Federalism 50, 305, 307, 309, 312-315, 322**
Obstacle to accomplishment, **Const Federalism 343, 346, 347, 353, 354**
Occupation of the field, **Const Federalism 337, 338, 346, 347, 349**
Original package doctrine, **Const Federalism 117, 118, 328-330, 360**
Particularity, **Const Federalism 27-31, 49, 90-92, 157**
Penalty (distinguished from tax), **Const Federalism 147-154**
Pie-slice, **Const Federalism 11, 53, 104**
Plenary, **Const Federalism 53, 97, 127**
Police power, **Const Federalism 54, 58, 252-254, 258, 261**
Powers, **Const Federalism 8, 10-12**
Pretext, **Const Federalism 52, 56, 124, 146**
Prevention, **Const Federalism 237, 238, 240**
Private action, **Const Federalism 238**
Privileges and immunities, **Const Federalism 246, 247, 297, 298**
Probation, **Const Federalism 96**
Prophylaxis, **Const Federalism 237, 238, 247**

CONSTITUTIONAL FEDERALISM—Cont'd
Purpose, **Const Federalism 39-48, 150-154, 285**
Rational basis, **Const Federalism 35-39, 43-48, 150-154, 285**
Reciprocity, **Const Federalism 281, 365, 394**
Remedial enforcement, **Const Federalism 233, 240**
Reserved powers, **Const Federalism 9**
Scarlet letter, **Const Federalism 117-122**
Sham taxes, **Const Federalism 147-154, 160**
Situs, **Const Federalism 303-305, 307, 308**
Sovereignty, **Const Federalism 203, 204**
State regulation of commerce, **Const Law 87 et seq.**
Story, Joseph, **Const Federalism 168, 171**
Stream of commerce, **Const Federalism 109, 110**
Substantiality, **Const Federalism 34, 35**
Supremacy, **Const Federalism 74, 82-85, 185, 212, 224, 229, 334 et seq., 405**
Sweeping clause, **Const Federalism 17**
Telic, **Const Federalism 20, 24, 60, 71, 72, 235**
Tenth Amendment, **Const Federalism 9, 390**
Territories, **Const Federalism 218-222, 224, 230**
Treaties, **Const Federalism 74, 209-213, 395**
Trivial impact, **Const Federalism 34, 35**
Uniformity, **Const Federalism 141-143, 275, 290, 363**
Unitary business, **Const Federalism 313, 314, 318-320, 322, 331**
Wilson, James, **Const Federalism 7, 8, 12**

CONSTITUTIONAL LAW
Abortion, **Const Law 176-191**
Access to justice, **Const Law 282-287**
Affectation doctrine, **Const Law 66-72**
Affirmative action, **Const Law 243-249, 261-263**
Age Discrimination in Employment Act, state sovereignty, **Const Law 81, 82**
Alienage classification, **Const Law 251-254**
Analysis. **Constitutional Analysis** (this index)
Animal sacrifices, free exercise clause, **Const Law 467**

CONSTITUTIONAL LAW—Cont'd

Appellate jurisdiction, **Const Law 9, 10, 12-15**
Appointment and removal, **Const Law 128-134**
Articles of incorporation, executive power, **Const Law 116**
Balancing approach, **Const Law 89, 90, 102-105**
Ballot access, **Const Law 281, 282**
Bicameralism clause, legislative veto, **Const Law 125, 126**
Bill of rights, generally, **Const Law 3**
Busing, school desegregation, **Const Law 240, 241**
Cable television, **Const Law 417-419**
Causal relationship requirement, **Const Law 32, 35-37**
Certiorari, **Const Law 12-15**
Challenges to federal action, standing, **Const Law 41, 42**
Checks and balances, **Const Law 118, 119, 128-132**
Circuit court of appeals, review of conflicts by Supreme Court, **Const Law 15**
Civil Rights (this index)
Clear and present danger doctrine, **Const Law 310-315**
Commerce clause, **Const Law 60-72**
Commerce power, **Const Law 71, 72, 88-105; Const Law 89, 90, 101-105**
Commercial speech, **Const Law 371-380**
Common law tradition, parliamentary supremacy, **Const Law 5**
Compulsory school attendance, free exercise clause, **Const Law 461, 462**
Concentration of power, **Const Law 2**
Conclusive presumption doctrine, procedural due process, **Const Law 211, 212**
Congressional powers, generally, **Const Law 57-85**
Constitutional principles, **Const Law 1-3**
Contraception, right of privacy, **Const Law 171-176**
Criminal justice system, liberty interests, **Const Law 206, 207**
Criminal Procedure (this index)
Defamation and libel, **Const Law 380-389, 392**
Dormant commerce clause, **Const Law 33-93, 100, 101, 105-109, 115**
Dual federalism, **Const Law 63-65, 78, 79**

CONSTITUTIONAL LAW—Cont'd

Due process, generally, **Const Law 152**
Economic due process, **Const Law 155-161**
Electoral process, **Const Law 419, 420, 423, 424; Const Law 419-431**
Eminent domain, **Const Law 162-165**
Equal protection, **Const Law 218-243, 249, 264-266, 268-292**
Establishment clause, **Const Law 432-456**
Executive immunity, **Const Law 144-146**
Executive power, **Const Law 116-125, 135-144**
Executive privilege, **Const Law 9, 142-146**
Fair Labor Standards Act, **Const Law 64, 78, 80**
Federal courts, judicial review, **Const Law 1**
Federalism. **Constitutional Federalism** (this index)
Federalization of criminal law, affectation doctrine, **Const Law 70, 71**
Federal jurisdiction, **Const Law 10 et seq.**
Federal Jurisdiction (this index)
Fighting words doctrine, **Const Law 343-352**
Firearm possession, commerce power, **Const Law 71, 72**
First Amendment (this index)
Foreign relations power, **Const Law 135-139**
Fourteenth Amendment, **Const Law 503**
Fourteenth Amendment, generally, **Const Law 148-150**
Freedom of association, **Const Law 325-335, 494**
Freedom of belief, implied right, **Const Law 324**
Freedom of conscience, **Const Law 336-340**
Freedom of expression, **Const Law 293-323, 342, 343, 352-380, 393-405, 430, 431**
Freedom of religion, **Const Law 432-470**
Freedom of the press, **Const Law 405-430**
Free exercise clause, **Const Law 456-458, 460-469**
Fundamental personal rights, **Const Law 167 et seq.**
Fundamental rights equal protection, **Const Law 268-291**
Gender classification, **Const Law 255-263**
Heightened scrutiny test, commerce power, **Const Law 100, 101**

CONSTITUTIONAL LAW—Cont'd
Holmes, Oliver Wendell, Supreme Court judicial review, **Const Law 10**
Homosexual activities, privacy rights, **Const Law 189-191**
How to Study Law and Take Law Exams (this index)
Illegitimacy, **Const Law 264-267**
Impeachment, political question doctrine, **Const Law 55, 56**
Impoundment, **Const Law 122, 123**
Institutionalized persons, substantive due process, **Const Law 196, 197**
Intergovernmental immunities, **Const Law 77-85**
Interstate commerce, **Const Law 86-88**
Interstate privileges and immunities clause distinguished from Privileges and Immunities Clause of 14th Amendment, **Const Law 109-112**
Involuntary civil commitment, **Const Law 215-217, 227**
Judicial review, **Const Law 6-10, 16, 26 et seq., 48-56**
Judiciary Act of 1789, construction, **Const Law 6**
Just compensation clause, **Const Law 162-166**
Lawyer advertising, **Const Law 375-378**
Legislative veto, **Const Law 125-127**
Less burdensome alternatives test, freedom of expression, **Const Law 304**
Liberty interests, **Const Law 206-210**
Limited government, constitutional principles, **Const Law 2, 3**
Loyalty oaths, freedom of association, **Const Law 332, 333**
Madisonian democracy, **Const Law 2**
Malapportionment, **Const Law 50-54, 508**
Marital privacy, Bill of Rights, **Const Law 173-175**
Market participant doctrine, dormant commerce clause, **Const Law 105-109**
Marketplace of ideas rationale, **Const Law 294, 295, 306**
Militia clauses, congressional war powers, **Const Law 140, 141**
Minority set aside programs, affirmative action, **Const Law 246, 247**
Mootness, **Const Law 44-48**
Multi-member districting, voting rights, **Const Law 280**

CONSTITUTIONAL LAW—Cont'd

National police power, **Const Law 62-71**
Newsgathering, **Const Law 406-413**
Nondelegation doctrine, executive power, **Const Law 123, 124**
Obscenity, **Const Law 393-405**
Organizational standing, third party standing, **Const Law 44**
Overbreadth doctrine, **Const Law 302-305, 375**
Parliamentary supremacy, **Const Law 5**
Peremptory challenges, gender classification, **Const Law 258, 259**
Political patronage, freedom of expression, **Const Law 430, 431**
Political primaries, state action doctrine, **Const Law 478**
Political question doctrine, **Const Law 50-56**
Post-civil war amendments, constitutional principles, **Const Law 3**
Preemption, **Const Law 113, 114**
Presentment clause, legislative veto, **Const Law 125-127**
President, veto power, **Const Law 1**
Pretext principle, enumerated powers, **Const Law 60, 63**
Prior restraint, **Const Law 305-309**
Privileges and immunities clause, Fourteenth Amendment, **Const Law 148, 149**
Procedural due process, **Const Law 202-218**
Property interests, **Const Law 203-206**
Protectionist regulation, **Const Law 90-100**
Punitive damages, substantive due process, **Const Law 161, 162**
Racial discrimination, Thirteenth Amendment, **Const Law 493-495**
Racial gerrymandering, equal protection, **Const Law 249, 274**
Racial preferences in broadcast programming, intermediate standard of review, **Const Law 251**
Rational basis test, equal protection, **Const Law 218, 219**
Reasonable classification, equal protection, **Const Law 219, 220**
Religious Freedom Restoration Act of 1993, free exercise clause, **Const Law 466**
Reputational interests, liberty interests, **Const Law 209-211**
Residency requirements, right to travel, **Const Law 269-273**

CONSTITUTIONAL LAW—Cont'd
Resource protectionism, commerce power, **Const Law 95, 96**
Right of privacy, generally, **Const Law 171 et seq.**
Right to care and protection, institutionalized person, **Const Law 197, 198**
Right to die, liberty interests, **Const Law 200, 201**
Right to marry, child support obligations, **Const Law 273, 274**
Right to refuse treatment, **Const Law 199-201**
Right to travel, **Const Law 269-273**
Ripeness, cases or controversies requirement, **Const Law 48-50**
School prayer, **Const Law 445-448**
School segregation
  de jure versus de facto, **Const Law 236 et seq.**
Separation of powers, **Const Law 1, 35, 36, 145**
Sexual privacy, Bill of Rights, **Const Law 175**
Slavery and involuntary servitude, private action, **Const Law 493**
Sovereign immunity, **Const Law 18-22**
Spending power, **Const Law 73-77**
Standing, **Const Law 26 et seq.**
State action doctrine, **Const Law 472-481, 484-486**
State Constitutional Law (this index)
State courts, **Const Law 10**
State sovereignty, **Const Law 77-84**
Steel seizure case, executive power, **Const Law 120**
Stream of commerce, **Const Law 65, 66**
Strict scrutiny standard of review, suspect classifications, **Const Law 229 et seq.**
Subject matter jurisdiction, **Const Law 11 et seq.**
Substantive due process, **Const Law 160-162, 164, 167 et seq., 197-201**
Supremacy clause, **Const Law 10, 113, 114**
Supreme court, **Const Law 8 et seq.**
Suspect classifications, **Const Law 228, 229, 251-266**
Symbolic conduct, **Const Law 315-323**
Taxing power, **Const Law 72-77**
Taxpayer litigation, **Const Law 39-41**

CONSTITUTIONAL LAW—Cont'd
Termination of parental rights, liberty interests, **Const Law 209**
Third party standing, **Const Law 42-44**
Timing, rule against mootness, **Const Law 44-48**
Treaties, **Const Law 137-139**
Two-part conditions test, just compensation clause, **Const Law 166**
Unconstitutional conditions doctrine, freedom of association, **Const Law 331**
Vagueness doctrine, freedom of expression, **Const Law 302-305**
Vestiture clause, executive power, **Const Law 116**
Voting discrimination, equal protection, **Const Law 234**
Voting rights, **Const Law 275-282**
Voting Rights Act of 1965, **Const Law 496, 504, 505**
War powers, executive versus congressional power, **Const Law 139-142**
Watergate tapes, executive privilege, **Const Law 142-146**

CONSTRUCTION AND INTERPRETATION
Judicial Process (this index)
Labor Arbitration Law and Practice (this index)
Uniform Commercial Code (this index)

CONSUMER LAW
Acceleration, **Consumer 125-128, 404**
Advertising, **Consumer 24 et seq.**
After-acquired property clause, **Consumer 124, 125, 266-269**
Agreement waiving defenses, waiver of defenses clauses, **Consumer 298-324**
Assignment, **Consumer 169-174, 204, 205, 291-324**
Balloon payments, **Consumer 264, 265**
Bona fide error, **Consumer 177-182, 206**
Class actions, **Consumer 9-11, 183-189, 207**
Closing costs, **Consumer 102, 139, 150, 151**
Cognovit, confession of judgment, **Consumer 395-398**
Collateral, **Consumer 266-269, 398-410**
Collection torts, **Consumer 373-376**

CONSUMER LAW—Cont'd

Confession of judgment, **Consumer 395-398**
Consumer defined, **Consumer 1, 2, 284**
Convenience and advantage, **Consumer 50-52**
Cooling off period, **Consumer 36, 37, 143-146, 148**
Credit bureaus, **Consumer 53-72**
Credit cards, **Consumer 3, 324-331**
Credit insurance, **Consumer 103-105, 253-264**
Creditor remedies, **Consumer 371-410**
Credit reports, **Consumer 53-72**
Criminal sanctions, **Consumer 24, 25, 69, 161**
Damages, generally, **Consumer 69-72**
Deceptive sales practices, **Consumer 26, 27, 38, 39**
Defamation, **Consumer 373, 374**
Default, consequences, **Consumer 371-410**
Deficiency judgment, **Consumer 406-416**
Disclosure regulation, generally, **Consumer 79-211**
Discrimination, **Consumer 72-78**
Door-to-door sales, **Consumer 36, 37**
Electronic fund transfer, **Consumer 331-346**
Exemptions, **Consumer 386-389**
Express warranty, **Consumer 275-280**
Fair Credit Reporting Act, **Consumer 53-55, 58-66, 68-72**
Federal Trade Commission, **Consumer 12-21, 37, 309-332**
Finance charge, **Consumer 99-108, 212-251**
Flipping, **Consumer 358, 359**
Free entry, **Consumer 49-52**
Garnishment, **Consumer 381, 386-389**
Holder in due course, **Consumer 292-307, 309-329**
Home solicitation sales, **Consumer 36, 37**
Implied warranties, **Consumer 275-280**
Initial statement, **Consumer 131-134**
Insurance, **Consumer 99-108, 212-251, 253-264**
Interest, **Consumer 99-108, 212-251**
Interlocking loans and sales, **Consumer 307-309**
Licensing, **Consumer 50, 51**

CONSUMER LAW—Cont'd
Magnuson-Moss, **Consumer 16, 17, 282-289**
Merchantability, **Consumer 276**
Open end transactions, **Consumer 93, 129-138**
Overinsurance, **Consumer 256, 257**
Periodic statement, **Consumer 134-138**
Prepayment, **Consumer 359-371**
Prices, **Consumer 271-274**
Rate disclosure, generally, **Consumer 79-211**
Real estate, **Consumer 84, 102, 122, 138, 139, 141-146, 148, 149**
Rebate, **Consumer 126-128, 359-371**
Referral sales, described, **Consumer 38**
Regulation Z, **Consumer 81, 82**
Replevin, **Consumer 382**
Repossession, **Consumer 400-403**
Reverse competition, **Consumer 262**
Rule of 78's, **Consumer 363-371**
Secured party's remedies, **Consumer 398-410**
Security interest, limits on security in consumer credit transactions, **Consumer 266**
Small claims courts, **Consumer 7, 8**
State consumer protection acts, **Consumer 6, 7**
Third party financing, **Consumer 169-174, 292-329**
Time price doctrine, **Consumer 220-227**
Truth in Lending, **Consumer 28-34, 81-92, 97-138, 161-207**
Unconscionability, generally, **Consumer 267, 268**
Uniform small loan law, **Consumer 214**
Usury laws, **Consumer 212-215, 220-227, 229-251**
Waiver of defense clauses, **Consumer 298-324**
Warranties, **Consumer 275-289**

CONTEMPT
Injunctions (this index)

CONTRACTS
Acceptance
generally, **Contract Rem 161, 162, 194; Contracts 9 et seq.**

CONTRACTS—Cont'd
Acceptance—Cont'd
Uniform Commercial Code (this index)
Action for price, generally, **Contract Rem 179 et seq., 194 et seq.**
Assignment of rights, **Contracts 360 et seq.**
Avoidable consequences doctrine, generally, **Contract Rem 24**
Breach, **Contract Rem 17, 55, 77, 172**
Burden of proof, restitution for plaintiff in default, **Contract Rem 82**
Buyer's remedies, UCC, generally, **Contract Rem 139 et seq., 161 et seq.**
Cancellation, buyer's remedies, UCC, **Contract Rem 139**
Causation, **Contract Rem 41, 153**
Consequential damages, generally, **Contract Rem 20**
Contract implied in law, generally, **Contract Rem 89**
Cost of performance versus diminished value, **Contract Rem 11-13, 15, 17**
Cover, **Contract Rem 24, 140-143, 145**
Defenses, **Contracts 196 et seq.**
Delegation of duties, **Contracts 360 et seq.**
Diminished value, cost of performance versus, **Contract Rem 11-13, 15, 17**
Discharge, **Contracts 393 et seq.**
Divisible contract, **Contract Rem 62, 64**
Down payment, breaching vendee's inability to recover, **Contract Rem 85**
Election of remedies, **Contract Rem 70, 139, 179**
Energy and Natural Resources Law (this index)
Excuse of performance, **Contracts 383 et seq.**
Expectation of damages, generally, **Contract Rem 4 et seq.**
Foreseeability defined, **Contract Rem 38**
Frustration of purpose, **Contract Rem 11-13, 15, 17, 100**
Generally, **Contracts 1 et seq.**
Good faith and fair dealing, **Contracts 184-189**
Government Contracts (this index)
How to Study Law and Take Law Exams (this index)

CONTRACTS—Cont'd
Impossibility of performance, **Contract Rem 11-13, 15, 17, 100**
Incidental damages, **Contract Rem 149, 172, 177, 190**
Interpretation, **Contracts 158 et seq.**
Land contracts, **Contract Rem 70-72, 84, 113, 114, 251**
Limitation of remedy, generally, **Contract Rem 217 et seq.**
Liquidated damages, generally, **Contract Rem 197 et seq.**
Loss of bargain, generally, **Contract Rem 4 et seq.**
Market price, contract price differential, **Contract Rem 139 et seq., 161 et seq., 179 et seq., 194 et seq.**
Market value, **Contract Rem 7, 57, 189**
Mental suffering, when damages allowed for, **Contract Rem 21**
Mistake, generally, **Contract Rem 233 et seq., 269 et seq., 285 et seq.**
Mitigation of damages, generally, **Contract Rem 24**
Modification, **Contracts 190 et seq.**
Modification of remedy, generally, **Contract Rem 217 et seq.**
Mutual assent to bargain, **Contracts 9 et seq.**
Mutuality of remedy, **Contract Rem 131**
Negotiable Instruments and Check Collection (this index)
Nominal damages, **Contract Rem 24**
Offer, **Contracts 9 et seq.**
Parol evidence rule, **Contract Rem 277; Contracts 174-183**
Partial performance, valuation problems in action for restitution, **Contract Rem 56**
Performance, **Contracts 289 et seq.**
Promissory estoppel, **Contracts 118-125**
Punitive damages, **Contract Rem 22**
Quasi-contract, generally, **Contract Rem 89**
Real property, **Contract Rem 70-72, 84, 113, 114, 251**
Reclamation, seller's remedies, UCC, **Contract Rem 95, 96**
Recoupment, generally, **Contract Rem 139 et seq., 161 et seq.**
Reformation, generally, **Contract Rem 269 et seq.**
Rejection, generally, **Contract Rem 139 et seq., 161 et seq.**
Reliance damages, generally, **Contract Rem 99 et seq.**
Remedies, **Contract Rem 1 et seq.; Contracts 248 et seq.**

CONTRACTS—Cont'd
Replevin, generally, **Contract Rem 139 et seq., 161 et seq.**
Resale, seller's remedies, UCC, **Contract Rem 180, 181**
Rescission, generally, **Contract Rem 233 et seq.**
Restitution, generally, **Contract Rem 51 et seq., 233 et seq., 285 et seq.; Contracts 126-137**
Restoration, **Contract Rem 66-68**
Revocation of acceptance, generally, **Contract Rem 139 et seq., 161 et seq.**
Sale of goods, generally, **Contract Rem 139 et seq., 161 et seq., 179 et seq., 194 et seq.**
Seller's remedies, UCC, generally, **Contract Rem 179 et seq., 194 et seq.**
Specific performance, generally, **Contract Rem 111 et seq.**
Specific restitution, **Contract Rem 70, 251**
Statute of frauds, **Contract Rem 74, 76, 278; Contracts 138 et seq.**
Third party beneficiaries, **Contracts 347 et seq.**
Unconscionability, generally, **Contract Rem 293 et seq.**
Unenforceable contracts, **Contract Rem 74, 75, 77, 103**
Unjust enrichment, **Contract Rem 51 et seq., 233 et seq., 285 et seq.; Contracts 126-137**
Value, **Contract Rem 6-8, 10, 56-60, 97, 163, 172, 173, 189, 256**

CONTRIBUTIONS
Federal Income Taxation of Partners and Partnerships (this index)

CONVENTIONS
Comparative Legal Traditions (this index)

COOPERATION
Insurance Law (this index)

COPYRIGHT
Art Law (this index)
Generally, **Unfair Trade 212 et seq.**

CORPORATIONS

Generally, **Corp Law 1-25**
Advances for expenses, indemnification and insurance, **Corp Law 454-456**
Advantages of debt financing, **Corp Law 160-164**
Affiliated corporations, generally, **Fed Corp Tax 43, 44, 127-133**
Agreements to form corporation, **Corp Law 79-81**
Aiding and abetting provisions, class action suits, **Corp Law 494**
Alternative minimum tax, generally, **Fed Corp Tax 31-36**
Antifraud provision, duties of directors, shareholders and officers, **Corp Law 431**
Appraisal right, **Corp Law 550-554**
Approval of fundamental corporate changes, shared responsibility, **Corp Law 192, 193**
Articles of incorporation, generally, **Corp Law 47-49**
Auditor's disclosure of corporate fraud provisions, class action suits, **Corp Law 494-496**
Authorized and issued shares, definitions, **Corp Law 124, 125**
Bailouts, income tax, **Fed Corp Tax 123, 127, 158-167**
Bankruptcy, piercing the corporate veil, **Corp Law 119-121**
Basis of income tax, **Fed Corp Tax 15, 64-70, 72-74, 97, 98, 139-142, 145, 146, 156, 157, 170, 190, 191, 208, 223-225, 259, 260, 262, 263, 265-268, 289, 290**
Books and records, inspection of, **Corp Law 523-532**
Business judgment rule, duties of directors, shareholders and officers, **Corp Law 385-398, 415-418**
Bylaw amendments, shared responsibility, **Corp Law 193, 194**
Capital and capitalization, **Corp Law 36-39, 104-107, 127-135, 164, 165, 167-170, 177, 178, 352-355**
Care, duties of directors, shareholders, and officers, **Corp Law 381-385**
Cash-out mergers, **Corp Law 544, 545**
Cautionary postscript, risk of violating securities acts while raising capital, **Corp Law 177, 178**
C corporations, **Corp Law 35, 36, 164, 165**
Changes, **Corp Law 192-194, 533-538**
Chicago School of law and economics, publicly held corporations, **Corp Law 347-352**

CORPORATIONS—Cont'd

Chief Executive Officer, publicly held corporations, **Corp Law 323, 324, 340-342**
Choice of law issues, piercing the corporate veil, **Corp Law 113-115**
Circular ownership of shares, **Corp Law 177**
Claims under state law, duties of directors, shareholders and officers, **Corp Law 423-426**
Class action suits, generally, **Corp Law 481 et seq.**
Classes or classification, **Corp Law 152-160, 165, 166**
Closely held corporations, generally, **Corp Law 22-24, 286 et seq.**
Combining partnership tax treatment and limited liability, **Corp Law 37-39**
Common stock, definitions, **Corp Law 124, 125**
Compelling dividend, shareholders' rights, **Corp Law 515-517**
Compensation, **Corp Law 324-326, 405-409**
Contests, publicly held corporation proxy contests, **Corp Law 364-368**
Contracts, **Corp Law 83-89, 101-104, 514, 515**
Damage provisions, class action suits, **Corp Law 493, 494**
Debts, **Corp Law 148-152, 160-166**
Deep Rock Doctrine, **Corp Law 166, 167**
De facto doctrine, premature commencement of business and, **Corp Law 92-95**
Defenses, duties of directors, shareholders and officers, **Corp Law 420-422**
Defensive tactics, publicly held corporation, **Corp Law 373-375**
Definitions, **Corp Law 124, 125, 448**
Development of corporation law in United States, **Corp Law 12-14**
Dictionary of unincorporated business forms, **Corp Law 25-30**
Directors, generally, **Corp Law 252 et seq.**
Disclosure, **Corp Law 356-359, 482, 483, 494-496**
Discovery provisions, class action suits, **Corp Law 489**
Dissension right, **Corp Law 550-554**
Dissolution as voluntary, **Corp Law 554-556**

CORPORATIONS—Cont'd
Distress, duties of directors of financially distressed corporations, **Corp Law 427, 428**
Distribution of powers within corporation, generally, **Corp Law 179 et seq.**
Distributions and dividends, **Corp Law 498-522**
Dividends and distributions, **Corp Law 498-522**
D&O insurance, **Corp Law 456-458**
Double tax regime, economic effects of, **Corp Law 39-41**
Economic effects of double tax regime, **Corp Law 39-41**
Equalizing capital and services when forming corporation, **Corp Law 167-170**
Equity securities, **Corp Law 148, 149, 152-160**
Estoppel, corporations by, **Corp Law 95-97**
Excessive debt capitalization in C corporations, **Corp Law 164, 165**
Executive compensation, duties of directors, shareholders and officers, **Corp Law 405-409**
Exoneratory provisions, duties of directors, shareholders and officers, **Corp Law 419, 420**
Fairness, duties of directors, shareholders and officers, **Corp Law 413-418**
Federal income tax of corporations and stockholders. Income tax, infra
Federal law of piercing the corporate veil, **Corp Law 115, 116**
Federal regulations relating to proxy contests, publicly held corporation, **Corp Law 368**
Federal securities laws, **Corp Law 19, 20**
Federal taxation of business forms, **Corp Law 32-35**
Fee shifting provisions, class action suits, **Corp Law 491, 492**
Fiduciaries
  director as, **Corp Law 89, 90, 378, 379, 547, 548**
Financially distressed corporations, duties of directors of, **Corp Law 427, 428**
Financial reports for shareholders, **Corp Law 532**
Financing the corporation, generally, **Corp Law 123 et seq.**
Formation of corporations, generally, **Corp Law 42**

CORPORATIONS—Cont'd
Fraud, **Corp Law 431, 494-496**
Furtherance of public policy, piercing the corporate veil for, **Corp Law 117-119**
Going concern, issuance of shares by, **Corp Law 170-175**
Headquarters, publicly held corporations, **Corp Law 320-322**
Illegal dividends, liability of directors and shareholders for, **Corp Law 515**
Inadequate capitalization, **Corp Law 104-107**
Income tax
  accounting methods and principles, generally, **Fed Corp Tax 28, 29, 326**
  accounts receivable or payable, **Fed Corp Tax 62-64**
  accumulated earnings tax, generally, **Fed Corp Tax 39-42**
  affiliated corporations, generally, **Fed Corp Tax 43, 44, 127-133**
  allocation of income and deductions, generally, **Fed Corp Tax 29-31**
  allocation of purchase price, taxable acquisitions, **Fed Corp Tax 207-212**
  alternative minimum tax, generally, **Fed Corp Tax 31-36**
  attribution of stock ownership, generally, **Fed Corp Tax 118-122**
  bailouts, **Fed Corp Tax 58, 59, 145, 158, 159, 251, 252, 273, 274**
  basis, generally, **Fed Corp Tax 15**
  boot, **Fed Corp Tax 54-57, 72, 241-244, 253-255, 260-263, 265, 266, 287-289**
  bootstrap sales, **Fed Corp Tax 133-135**
  brother-sister corporations, redemptions through, **Fed Corp Tax 127-133**
  cancellation of indebtedness, generally, **Fed Corp Tax 27, 250, 251**
  capital structure, **Fed Corp Tax 36-39, 352-355**
  carryover of corporate attributes, generally, **Fed Corp Tax 296-315**
  choice of business entity, generally, **Fed Corp Tax 13, 14**
  classification as corporation, generally, **Fed Corp Tax 18-23**
  collapsible corporations, generally, **Fed Corp Tax 196-203**
  complete liquidations, generally, **Fed Corp Tax 168-203**

CORPORATIONS—Cont'd
Income tax—Cont'd
constructive ownership of stock, generally, **Fed Corp Tax 118-122**
corporate divisions, generally, **Fed Corp Tax 270-295**
death taxes, redemptions to pay, generally, **Fed Corp Tax 125-127**
deductions, **Fed Corp Tax 26, 27, 37, 38, 186, 187, 225-230, 326**
dividends, generally, **Fed Corp Tax 6, 7, 102-105, 133-137**
dividends-received deduction, generally, **Fed Corp Tax 99-102**
divisive reorganizations, **Fed Corp Tax 270-295**
double taxation, generally, **Fed Corp Tax 1-7**
earnings and profits, generally, **Fed Corp Tax 85-88**
estate taxes, redemptions to pay, generally, **Fed Corp Tax 125-127**
incorporations, generally, **Fed Corp Tax 45-79**
installment sale treatment, generally, **Fed Corp Tax 57, 67, 68**
integration, generally, **Fed Corp Tax 351-368**
limited liability companies, generally, **Fed Corp Tax 14, 19-21, 350**
liquidation-reincorporations, generally, **Fed Corp Tax 184, 185, 293**
mergers, generally, **Fed Corp Tax 231-269**
multiple corporations, generally, **Fed Corp Tax 43, 44**
net operating losses, generally, **Fed Corp Tax 296-315**
nonliquidating distributions, generally, **Fed Corp Tax 80-105**
organizational expenses, **Fed Corp Tax 26, 27, 37, 38, 186, 187, 225-230, 326**
parent-subsidiary corporations, generally, **Fed Corp Tax 187-196**
partial liquidations, generally, **Fed Corp Tax 122-125**
personal holding company tax, generally, **Fed Corp Tax 39, 40, 42, 43**
personal service corporations, generally, **Fed Corp Tax 28-31, 33**
recapitalizations (Type E), **Fed Corp Tax 248-252**
redemptions, generally, **Fed Corp Tax 106-143**

CORPORATIONS—Cont'd
Income tax—Cont'd
reincorporations, generally, **Fed Corp Tax 184, 185, 293**
reorganizations, generally, **Fed Corp Tax 231-269**
S corporations, generally, **Fed Corp Tax 316-350**
Section 338 election, taxable acquisitions generally, **Fed Corp Tax 213-225**
Section 306 stock, generally, **Fed Corp Tax 158-167**
stock dividends, generally, **Fed Corp Tax 144-167**
subsidiary liquidations, generally, **Fed Corp Tax 187-196**
taxable acquisitions, generally, **Fed Corp Tax 204-230**
value of loss corporation, generally, **Fed Corp Tax 307-309**
Incorporators, generally, **Corp Law 45-47**
Indebtedness of corporation, shareholder responsibility for, **Corp Law 99, 100**
Indemnification, generally, **Corp Law 448 et seq.**
Independent directors, publicly held corporations, **Corp Law 339, 340**
Inside directors, publicly held corporations, **Corp Law 339, 340**
Insider trading prohibition, duties of directors, shareholders and officers, **Corp Law 431-437**
Inspection of books and records, **Corp Law 523-532**
Institutional investors, publicly held corporations, **Corp Law 328-332**
Insurance, generally, **Corp Law 448 et seq.**
Interlocking directors, duties of, **Corp Law 404, 405**
Internal structure of large publicly held corporations, **Corp Law 315-317**
International Taxation (this index)
Investors and investments, publicly held corporations, **Corp Law 326-332**
Judicial response to increased litigation, class action suits, **Corp Law 485, 486**
Limitations or restrictions, **Corp Law 146, 147, 194-202, 450, 451, 508-513**
Limited liability, combining partnership tax treatment and, **Corp Law 37-39**
Limited role of ultra vires, generally, **Corp Law 66-68**
Lists of shareholders, inspection of, **Corp Law 530-532**

CORPORATIONS—Cont'd

Loyalty, duties of directors, shareholders and officers, **Corp Law 398**
Mechanics of creating corporation, **Corp Law 43-45**
Mergers and consolidations, generally, **Corp Law 538-542**
Model Business Corporation Act, **Corp Law 18, 19**
Modern rule of ultra vires, **Corp Law 68, 69**
Names, registration of publicly held corporations' securities in street name or in name of nominees, **Corp Law 332-335**
Nexus of contracts theory, **Corp Law 6-12**
No par shares, **Corp Law 135, 136**
Officers, generally, **Corp Law 268 et seq.**
Oppressive issuance of shares, **Corp Law 175-177**
Parent-subsidiary cases, **Corp Law 109-112**
Partnership, combining partnership tax treatment and limited liability, **Corp Law 37-39**
Par value, **Corp Law 127-136**
Personal liability and taxes, selection of business form, **Corp Law 30-32**
Piercing the corporate veil, generally, **Corp Law 98 et seq.**
Pleading provisions, class action suits, **Corp Law 492, 493**
Preemptive rights, issuance of shares by going concern, **Corp Law 170-175**
Preincorporation transactions, generally, **Corp Law 76 et seq.**
Premature commencement of business, **Corp Law 92-95**
Price of common shares, **Corp Law 126, 127**
Prices and changing body of shareholders, publicly held corporations, **Corp Law 352**
Private actions for violations of federal proxy rules, publicly held corporations, **Corp Law 362-364**
Private Securities Litigation Reform Act of 1995, class action suits, **Corp Law 486, 487**
Professional Responsibility (this index)
Profit centers, publicly held corporations, **Corp Law 317-320**
Promoters, generally, **Corp Law 81-83**
Property, shares issued for, **Corp Law 136-140**
Proportionate liability provisions, class action suits, **Corp Law 489-491**

CORPORATIONS—Cont'd

Proposals by shareholders, publicly held corporations, **Corp Law 359-362**
Proxy, publicly held corporation, **Corp Law 354-359, 362-368**
PSLRA, future of class action suits resulting from, **Corp Law 496, 497**
Publicly held corporation, generally, **Corp Law 313 et seq**
Public policy limitations on indemnification, **Corp Law 450, 451**
Purchase or sale, **Corp Law 423-426, 548-550**
Race for the button, economic analysis of, **Corp Law 16-18**
Ratification by shareholders, duties of directors, shareholders and officers, **Corp Law 418, 419**
Reacquisition of shares as distributions, **Corp Law 504-506**
Redeemable securities, **Corp Law 521, 522**
Registration of securities in street name or in name of nominees, publicly held corporations, **Corp Law 332-335**
Removal from employment or office, shareholders' powers as to removal of directors, **Corp Law 183-185**
Repurchase of own shares by corporation, **Corp Law 518-521**
Reverse piercing the corporate veil, **Corp Law 116, 117**
Rights or warrants, distributions of, **Corp Law 504**
Rule 10b-5, duties of directors, shareholders and officers, **Corp Law 428-439**
Safe harbor provisions, class action suits, **Corp Law 487-489**
Sale or purchase, **Corp Law 423-426, 548-550**
S corporations, **Corp Law 35, 36, 165, 166, 316-350**
SEC disclosure requirements, class action suits, **Corp Law 482, 483**
Second class of stock in S corporations, debt as, **Corp Law 165, 166**
Section 102(b)(7) of Delaware GCL, duties of directors, shareholders and officers, **Corp Law 391, 392**
Securities, **Corp Law 148-152, 177, 178, 203 et seq., 332-335, 481-487**
Securities Exchange Act of 1934, duties of directors, shareholders and officers, **Corp Law 439-442**
Selection of state of incorporation, **Corp Law 42**

CORPORATIONS—Cont'd
Self-dealing, duties of directors, shareholders and officers, **Corp Law 399-404**
Senior executives of publicly held corporations, compensation to, **Corp Law 324-326**
Services
  equalizing capital and services when forming corporation, **Corp Law 167-170**
  shares issued for, **Corp Law 136-140**
Settlement provisions, class action suits, **Corp Law 491**
Shared responsibility, **Corp Law 190-194**
Shareholder's suits, generally, **Corp Law 459 et seq.**
Short form mergers, **Corp Law 545, 546**
Social responsibility debate, publicly held corporation, **Corp Law 20-22**
Stated capital, **Corp Law 127-135**
State law, duties of directors, shareholders and officers as to claims under, **Corp Law 423-426**
State legislative responses to takeover movement, publicly held corporation, **Corp Law 375-377**
Statutes, generally, **Corp Law 179 et seq.**
Stock and stockholders, generally, **Corp Law 203 et seq.**
Street name, registration of securities in, **Corp Law 332-335**
Subscriptions for shares, **Corp Law 76-79**
Subsidiaries, parent-subsidiary cases, **Corp Law 109-112**
Takeover movement, **Corp Law 353, 354, 368-373, 375-377, 392-394**
Taxation
  generally, **Corp Law 30-41, 119-121, 164, 165, 517, 518**
  income tax, supra
Torts, piercing the corporate veil, **Corp Law 101-104**
Transfers of control, duties of directors, shareholders and officers, **Corp Law 442-447**
Treasury shares as device to avoid restrictions on issuance of shares, **Corp Law 146, 147**
Ultra vires, generally, **Corp Law 66-68**
Unincorporated business forms, generally, **Corp Law 25**
Upstream and downstream mergers, **Corp Law 545**

CORPORATIONS—Cont'd
Voluntary dissolution, **Corp Law 554-556**
Warrants or rights, distributions of, **Corp Law 504**
Wrongful conduct, duties of directors, shareholders and officers, **Corp Law 438, 439**

CORRECTIONS
Sentencing, Corrections, and Prisoners' Rights, Law of (this index)

CORRECTIONS LAW
Sentencing, Corrections, and Prisoners' Rights, Law of (this index)

COSTS
Hazardous Wastes and Toxic Substances, Law of (this index)

COUNSELING
Attorneys (this index)

COURTS
Comparative Legal Traditions (this index)
Federal Jurisdiction (this index)
International Environmental Law (this index)
State courts. **Federal Jurisdiction** (this index)
United States Tax Court. **Tax Procedure and Tax Fraud** (this index)

CREDITORS
Bankruptcy and Other Debtor-Creditor Laws (this index)

CREDITS
International Taxation (this index)

CRIMINAL CONTEMPT
Injunctions (this index)

GENERAL INDEX

References are to Titles and Pages

CRIMINAL LAW

Abandonment, **Crim 215-217, 247, 248, 260**
Abortion, victimless crimes, **Crim 287**
Absolute liability, generally, **Crim 123-127**
Accessories, generally, **Crim 231-234**
Accomplice, generally, **Crim 231-234**
Accountability for acts of others, **Crim 233-248**
Actus reus, generally, **Crim 140**
Addiction, intoxication, **Crim 66, 119, 120, 175-179, 186-188**
Adultery, victimless crime, **Crim 283**
Age, **Crim 174, 175**
Agent, **Crim 231-248**
Aggravated assault, **Crim 57**
Aggravated battery, generally, **Crim 57**
Agreement, generally, **Crim 249-272**
Aider and abettor, **Crim 231-248**
Alcoholism, **Crim 66, 119, 120, 175-179, 184-188**
Alteration, **Crim 104-106, 111**
American Law Institute (A.L.I.), generally, **Crim 30 et seq.**
Apprehension of criminals, **Crim 76-79**
Arrest, **Crim 74-79**
Arson, generally, **Crim 116, 117**
Asportation, **Crim 64, 82-94**
Assault, generally, **Crim 56-58**
Attempt, **Crim 104, 141, 205-213, 215-218, 221-230, 249**
Bad checks, **Crim 101, 104**
Battery, **Crim 56, 58, 59, 122, 129, 130, 215**
Belief, **Crim 98, 99, 106, 118-121, 127-139, 239-243**
Bifurcated trial, insanity, **Crim 166**
Bigamy, **Crim 131**
Blackmail, **Crim 108-110**
Breaking and entering, **Crim 113-115**
Breaking bulk, larceny, **Crim 92**
Burden of proof, **Crim 192-196, 198**
Burglary, **Crim 27, 42, 113-116, 128, 129, 220-223**
Burning, generally, **Crim 116, 117**

CRIMINAL LAW—Cont'd
But for test, causation, **Crim 50, 236, 237**
Capital punishment, **Crim 18, 20-24**
Causation, generally, **Crim 49-55**
Cheats, generally, **Crim 97-104**
Checks, bad, **Crim 101, 104**
Child, **Crim 174, 175**
Civil lawsuit, general principles of criminal law, **Crim 1**
Coercion, generally, **Crim 179-181**
Common law crimes, **Crim 281-283**
Conspiracy, generally, **Crim 249-272**
Constitutional protections, generally, **Crim 14, 15, 17, 18, 20-24**
Contempt. **Injunctions** (this index)
Contraceptives, victimless crime, **Crim 285, 286**
Conversion, generally, **Crim 94-97**
Corrupt motive, generally, **Crim 249-272**
Criminal negligence. Recklessness, infra
Cruel and unusual punishment, **Crim 17, 18, 20-24, 182-187**
Death penalty, **Crim 18, 20-24**
Defense of others (another), generally, **Crim 73, 74**
Defense of property, **Crim 66, 79, 80**
Deterrance, **Crim 1-3, 5-14, 17-24, 30, 54, 205, 206, 220, 250, 251**
Disposition of insane defendants, **Crim 166, 167**
Disproportionality of punishment to offense, **Crim 17-20**
Drunkenness, **Crim 66, 119, 120, 175-179, 186-188**
Due process, **Crim 137, 166, 167, 187-189, 237-278**
Duress, generally, **Crim 179-181**
Durham test, insanity, **Crim 158-160**
Duty to act, generally, **Crim 145-151**
Embezzlement, generally, **Crim 94-97**
Entrapment, generally, **Crim 187-189**
Equal protection, **Crim 14, 15, 166, 167**
Ex post facto laws, **Crim 135, 278-281**
Extortion, **Crim 108-110**
Failure to act. Omissions, infra

CRIMINAL LAW—Cont'd
False imprisonment, kidnapping, **Crim 64, 65**
False pretenses, generally, **Crim 97-104**
Felony murder, generally, **Crim 26, 42-46**
First Amendment, **Crim 125, 217-220, 269, 275, 276**
Forcible rape, **Crim 42, 59-64, 128-131**
Forgery, **Crim 104-106, 111**
Fornication, victimless crime, **Crim 285-287**
Fraudulent conversion, generally, **Crim 94-97**
Freedom of speech, **Crim 125, 217-220, 269, 275, 276**
Gambling, victimless crime, **Crim 283**
General intent, generally, **Crim 28-31**
General principles of criminal law, **Crim 1-9**
Gross negligence, **Crim 25-31, 35-38, 99, 116, 118-121**
Habitual offender laws, **Crim 17-20**
Hearsay, conspiracy, **Crim 226**
Heat of passion, manslaughter, **Crim 33**
Homicide, generally, **Crim 25**
Homosexuality, victimless crimes, **Crim 284**
How to Study Law and Take Law Exams (this index)
Imperfect self-defense, **Crim 25, 70-73**
Impossibility of attempt, generally, **Crim 224-230**
Indefiniteness, generally, **Crim 273-278**
Individual Employee Rights (this index)
Infancy, **Crim 174, 175**
Injunctions (this index)
Insanity, **Crim 66, 142, 152-163, 166-173**
Intent, generally, **Crim 28-31**
Intoxication, **Crim 66, 119, 120, 175-179, 186-188**
Involuntary manslaughter, **Crim 26, 38-40**
Kidnapping, **Crim 27, 42, 64, 65**
Knowledge, **Crim 98, 99, 106, 118-121, 127-139, 239-243**
Larceny, generally, **Crim 82-94**
Liability without fault, generally, **Crim 123-127**
Maim, **Crim 58, 59**
Malice aforethought, murder, **Crim 25, 26, 31, 36**

CRIMINAL LAW—Cont'd

Malum in se, offense for misdemeanor-manslaughter, **Crim 47**
Malum prohibition, offense for misdemeanor-manslaughter, **Crim 47**
Manslaughter, **Crim 25-35, 38-41, 46-48, 70-73**
Mayhem, **Crim 58, 59**
Mens rea, generally, **Crim 118-121**
Mental disease or defect, **Crim 66, 142, 152-163, 166-173**
Misappropriation of property, **Crim 81, 84, 111-113**
Misdemeanor-manslaughter, **Crim 46-48**
Misprision of felony, defined, **Crim 233**
Mistake of fact, generally, **Crim 127-133**
Mistake of law, generally, **Crim 133-139**
M'Naghten right-wrong test, **Crim 153-155**
Model Penal Code, generally, **Crim 30 et seq.**
Murder, **Crim 25-31, 35, 36, 38-46, 119, 168, 207**
Necessity, **Crim 66, 181-183**
Negative act, generally, **Crim 145-151**
Negligence defined, **Crim 120**
No retreat rule, self-defense, **Crim 68**
Omissions, generally, **Crim 145-151**
Overt act, conspiracy, **Crim 249-272**
Parties to crime, generally, **Crim 231-234**
Penalties, **Crim 1-3, 5-14, 17-24, 30, 54, 205, 206, 220, 250, 251**
Political conspiracy, **Crim 269-271**
Possession, **Crim 221, 222**
Presumptions, **Crim 192-196, 198-204**
Prevention of crime, **Crim 79**
Procedure. **Criminal Procedure** (this index)
Prostitution, victimless crimes, **Crim 284**
Protection of property, **Crim 66, 79, 80**
Provocation, manslaughter generally, **Crim 31-35**
Proximate cause, generally, **Crim 49-55**
Punishment, **Crim 1-3, 5-14, 17-24, 30, 54, 205, 206, 220, 250, 251**
Purpose of the criminal law, **Crim 1-9**

CRIMINAL LAW—Cont'd

Rape, **Crim 42, 59-64, 128-131**
Receiving stolen goods or property, generally, **Crim 106, 107**
Recklessness, **Crim 25-31, 35-38, 99, 116, 118-121**
Reformation, **Crim 1-3, 5-14, 17-24, 30, 54, 205, 206, 220, 250, 251**
Rehabilitation, **Crim 1-3, 5-14, 17-24, 30, 54, 205, 206, 220, 250, 251**
Resisting unlawful arrest, **Crim 74-76**
Restraint, **Crim 1-3, 5-14, 17-24, 30, 54, 205, 206, 220, 250, 251**
Retreat rule, self-defense, **Crim 68-70**
Retribution, **Crim 1-3, 5-14, 17-24, 30, 54, 205, 206, 220, 250, 251**
RICO, generally, **Crim 249-272**
Right-wrong test, M'Naghten right-wrong test, **Crim 153-155**
Robbery, **Crim 27, 42, 106, 107, 111, 112**
Self-defense, generally, **Crim 66-68**
Sixth Amendment, conspiracy, **Crim 266**
Solicitation, generally, **Crim 217-220**
Strict liability, generally, **Crim 123-127**
Tax Procedure and Tax Fraud (this index)
Theft, **Crim 81, 84, 111-113**
Trespass, generally, **Crim 82-94**
Unlawful arrest, resisting, **Crim 74-76**
Uttering forged instrument, **Crim 104-106, 111**
Vagrancy, generally, **Crim 222**
Vagueness, generally, **Crim 273-278**
Vicarious liability, generally, **Crim 123-127**
Victimless crimes, generally, **Crim 283-288**
Voluntary acts, generally, **Crim 140**
Voluntary manslaughter, **Crim 25, 32, 46, 47, 70-73**
White Collar Crime (this index)

CRIMINAL PROCEDURE

Acceptance of guilty plea, **Crim Proc-Const Lim 424-426**
Access, **Crim Proc-Const Lim 452-454, 460-465**

CRIMINAL PROCEDURE—Cont'd

Administrative burdens, expansive interpretations of individual guarantees, **Crim Proc-Const Lim 42-44**
Administrative proceedings, exclusionary rule, **Crim Proc-Const Lim 282, 283**
Airport inspections, **Crim Proc-Const Lim 135, 136**
Appeals, **Crim Proc-Const Lim 365-367, 474-476**
Appointed counsel, **Crim Proc-Const Lim 338-340, 350-354, 376, 377, 382-384**
Arraignment, right to counsel, **Crim Proc-Const Lim 361**
Arrest, generally, **Crim Proc-Const Lim 57-149**
Assistance of counsel, effective, **Crim Proc-Const Lim 385-400**
Automatic reversal, harmless error, **Crim Proc-Const Lim 485-488**
Automobiles, **Crim Proc-Const Lim 67, 112-118, 135**
Bill of Rights guarantees, application to states, **Crim Proc-Const Lim 10-25**
Border searches, **Crim Proc-Const Lim 133-135**
Broken bargains, guilty pleas, **Crim Proc-Const Lim 429-431**
Burden of proof, exclusionary rules, **Crim Proc-Const Lim 333-337**
Collateral challenges, guilty pleas, **Crim Proc-Const Lim 431-433**
Collateral proceedings, right to counsel, **Crim Proc-Const Lim 367-369**
Commercial premises, protected areas and interests, **Crim Proc-Const Lim 65-67**
Comparative Legal Traditions (this index)
Confessions, **Crim Proc-Const Lim 177-235, 303-310**
Confrontation of witnesses, **Crim Proc-Const Lim 239-250, 458-460**
Consent searches, **Crim Proc-Const Lim 138-149**
Constitutional limitations, generally, **Crim Proc-Const Lim 1-56**
Construction or interpretation, **Crim Proc-Const Lim 4-16, 25-44**
Continued surveillance, Title III of Crime Control Act, **Crim Proc-Const Lim 158-161**
Crime Control Act, **Crim Proc-Const Lim 153-156, 203, 204**

CRIMINAL PROCEDURE—Cont'd

Deception, consent search by, **Crim Proc-Const Lim 143**
Decision to charge, postinvestigatory process, **Crim Proc-Const Lim 404-408**
Defective appointment of counsel, **Crim Proc-Const Lim 382-384**
Defense discovery, postinvestigatory process, **Crim Proc-Const Lim 419, 420**
Defense strategy, counsel's control over, **Crim Proc-Const Lim 379, 380**
Derivative evidence, exclusionary rule, **Crim Proc-Const Lim 286-310**
Derivative right to counsel, **Crim Proc-Const Lim 349, 350**
Discovery and disclosure, **Crim Proc-Const Lim 170-173, 292-294, 418-423**
Driver's license, regulatory searches, **Crim Proc-Const Lim 135**
Due process, **Crim Proc-Const Lim 250-255, 262-264, 345-349, 403, 404**
DWI, inspections, **Crim Proc-Const Lim 135**
Effective assistance of counsel, **Crim Proc-Const Lim 385-400**
Effects, protected areas and interests, **Crim Proc-Const Lim 67-70**
Eighth Amendment, pretrial release, **Crim Proc-Const Lim 401-403**
Electronic eavesdropping, generally, **Crim Proc-Const Lim 150-176**
Employees, supervision of, **Crim Proc-Const Lim 137, 138**
Encouraging criminal conduct, use of secret agents for, **Crim Proc-Const Lim 173-176**
Entrapment, use of secret agents to encourage criminal conduct, **Crim Proc-Const Lim 173, 174**
Equal protection, **Crim Proc-Const Lim 350-354, 435-440**
Escobedo case, police interrogation and confessions, **Crim Proc-Const Lim 187-191**
Evidence, **Crim Proc-Const Lim 286-310, 314, 315, 333-337, 419-423, 460-466**
Exclusionary rules, generally, **Crim Proc-Const Lim 256-337**
Execution of search warrants, **Crim Proc-Const Lim 89-93**

CRIMINAL PROCEDURE—Cont'd
Expansive interpretations of individual guarantees, **Crim Proc-Const Lim 25-44**
Fair cross-section requirement, impartial jury and judge, **Crim Proc-Const Lim 440-442**
Fair hearing right to counsel, **Crim Proc-Const Lim 345-347**
Fair trial, postinvestigatory process, **Crim Proc-Const Lim 450-455**
Fifth Amendment, **Crim Proc-Const Lim 256-337, 314, 315**
Fourth Amendment, **Crim Proc-Const Lim 57-60, 150-176, 256-337**
Free press, postinvestigatory process, **Crim Proc-Const Lim 450-455**
Fruit of the poisonous tree doctrine, **Crim Proc-Const Lim 286-288, 296-310**
Fundamental rights interpretation, **Crim Proc-Const Lim 11-14**
Gag orders, fair trial and free press, **Crim Proc-Const Lim 450-452**
Good faith exceptions, **Crim Proc-Const Lim 274-279**
Grand jury, **Crim Proc-Const Lim 129-131, 227-235, 280, 281, 357-359, 406-408**
Guilty pleas, **Crim Proc-Const Lim 305, 306, 372, 423-433**
Habeas corpus, exclusionary rule, **Crim Proc-Const Lim 284-286**
Harmless error, **Crim Proc-Const Lim 480-488**
Hearing, protected areas and interests, **Crim Proc-Const Lim 62-64**
Historical acceptance, expansive interpretations of individual guarantees, **Crim Proc-Const Lim 32-36**
How to Study Law and Take Law Exams (this index)
Identification, **Crim Proc-Const Lim 236-259**
Illegal arrest, **Crim Proc-Const Lim 57-60, 296-301**
Immunity, self-incrimination and grand jury witness, **Crim Proc-Const Lim 233-235**
Impartial jury and judge, **Crim Proc-Const Lim 433-450**
Impeachment, **Crim Proc-Const Lim 311-320**
Imperative of judicial integrity, Fourth Amendment exclusion, **Crim Proc-Const Lim 270, 271**

CRIMINAL PROCEDURE—Cont'd

In-court identification, due process, totality of circumstances, **Crim Proc-Const Lim 255**

Incriminating statements, use of secret agents to obtain, **Crim Proc-Const Lim 165-170**

Independent source limitation, exclusionary rules, **Crim Proc-Const Lim 288-292**

Indictments, preindictment lineup identification, **Crim Proc-Const Lim 246, 247**

Inevitable discovery limitation, exclusionary rules, **Crim Proc-Const Lim 292-294**

Information, probable cause and related problems, **Crim Proc-Const Lim 77-83**

Initial appearance, right to counsel, **Crim Proc-Const Lim 359, 360**

Inspections, regulatory searches, **Crim Proc-Const Lim 131-138**

Interference, **Crim Proc-Const Lim 380-385, 454, 455**

Interpretation, **Crim Proc-Const Lim 4-16, 25-44**

Introduction, **Crim Proc-Const Lim 1-10**

Invasion of lawyer-client relationship by state, **Crim Proc-Const Lim 384, 385**

Issuance of search warrants, **Crim Proc-Const Lim 83-89**

Joinder of offenses, postinvestigatory process, **Crim Proc-Const Lim 408-412**

Joinder of parties, postinvestigatory process, **Crim Proc-Const Lim 412, 413**

Judge, impartial jury and, **Crim Proc-Const Lim 433-450**

Judicial interpretation, **Crim Proc-Const Lim 4-10**

Judicial protection of civil liberties, expansive interpretations of individual guarantees, **Crim Proc-Const Lim 26-29**

Jury and jury trial, **Crim Proc-Const Lim 129-131, 227-235, 280, 281, 357-359, 406-408, 433-450**

Knowing and intelligent requirement, waiver of counsel and right to proceed pro se, **Crim Proc-Const Lim 369-376**

Limitations upon charging decisions, postinvestigatory process, **Crim Proc-Const Lim 404-406**

Limited retroactive application doctrine, **Crim Proc-Const Lim 44-56**

CRIMINAL PROCEDURE—Cont'd

Lineups, **Crim Proc-Const Lim 236-255**

Linkletter approach, limited retroactive application doctrine, **Crim Proc-Const Lim 44-56**

Media interference, fair trial and free press, **Crim Proc-Const Lim 454, 455**

Miranda rules, **Crim Proc-Const Lim 198-227, 306-310**

Mistake or error, postinvestigatory process, **Crim Proc-Const Lim 474-476, 480-488**

Multiple confessions, exclusionary rules, **Crim Proc-Const Lim 303-305**

Negotiated guilty pleas, **Crim Proc-Const Lim 426-429**

Nontelephonic electronic eavesdropping, **Crim Proc-Const Lim 152, 153**

Notice, postinvestigatory process, **Crim Proc-Const Lim 418, 419**

Objectives, totality of circumstances test, **Crim Proc-Const Lim 181-185**

Offices, protected areas and interests, **Crim Proc-Const Lim 65-67**

One-man showups, due process, totality of circumstances, **Crim Proc-Const Lim 253-255**

Parole or probation, **Crim Proc-Const Lim 136, 137, 362-364**

Per se analysis desirable, expansive interpretations of individual guarantees, **Crim Proc-Const Lim 36-40**

Person, seizure of, generally, **Crim Proc-Const Lim 57-60**

Persons, warrantless searches and seizures, **Crim Proc-Const Lim 93-102**

Pictures, identification procedures, **Crim Proc-Const Lim 248, 249, 252, 253**

Plain view, protected areas and interests, **Crim Proc-Const Lim 62-64**

Police interrogation, generally, **Crim Proc-Const Lim 177-235**

Police investigation, right to counsel, **Crim Proc-Const Lim 357**

Police station, self-incrimination privilege, **Crim Proc-Const Lim 198-200**

Postinvestigatory process, generally, **Crim Proc-Const Lim 401-488**

CRIMINAL PROCEDURE—Cont'd

Posttrial procedures, **Crim Proc-Const Lim 470-480**

Preindictment identification, lineups, **Crim Proc-Const Lim 246, 247**

Prejudicial publicity, impartial jury and judge, **Crim Proc-Const Lim 447-449**

Preliminary hearings, **Crim Proc-Const Lim 360, 361, 406-408**

Premises, warrantless searches and seizures, **Crim Proc-Const Lim 102-112**

Presence at trial, right to, **Crim Proc-Const Lim 456, 457**

Presentation of evidence at trial, right of, **Crim Proc-Const Lim 465, 466**

Pretrial identification procedures, **Crim Proc-Const Lim 236-255**

Pretrial release, postinvestigatory process, **Crim Proc-Const Lim 401-404**

Priority of reliability guarantees, expansive interpretations of individual guarantees, **Crim Proc-Const Lim 29-32**

Prisoners, supervision of, **Crim Proc-Const Lim 136, 137**

Privacy interests versus property interests, arrest, search and seizure, **Crim Proc-Const Lim 60-62**

Probable cause, generally, **Crim Proc-Const Lim 59, 60, 71-83**

Probation or parole, **Crim Proc-Const Lim 136, 137, 362-364**

Property interests versus privacy interests, arrest, search and seizure, **Crim Proc-Const Lim 60-62**

Prophylactic requirements desirable, expansive interpretations of individual guarantees, **Crim Proc-Const Lim 40-42**

Pro se, waiver of counsel and right to proceed, **Crim Proc-Const Lim 369-376**

Prosecution discovery, postinvestigatory process, **Crim Proc-Const Lim 420-423**

Prosecutorial misconduct, **Crim Proc-Const Lim 469, 470**

Protected areas and interests, arrest, search and seizure, **Crim Proc-Const Lim 60-71**

Protective search, stop-and-frisk, **Crim Proc-Const Lim 126-128**

Publicity as prejudicial, impartial jury and judge, **Crim Proc-Const Lim 447-449**

Public right of access, fair trial and free press, **Crim Proc-Const Lim 452-454**

CRIMINAL PROCEDURE—Cont'd

Public trial, right to, **Crim Proc-Const Lim 455, 456**
Purged taint limitation, exclusionary rules, **Crim Proc-Const Lim 294-296**
Reasonable doubt standard, harmless error, **Crim Proc-Const Lim 483-485**
Records, disclosure of electronic surveillance records, **Crim Proc-Const Lim 170-173**
Rejecting Linkletter, limited retroactive application doctrine, **Crim Proc-Const Lim 52-56**
Residential premises, protected areas and interests, **Crim Proc-Const Lim 64, 65**
Retained counsel, **Crim Proc-Const Lim 338, 347-349, 377-379**
Retrials, posttrial procedures, **Crim Proc-Const Lim 476-480**
Retroactivity, limited retroactive application doctrine, **Crim Proc-Const Lim 44-56**
Right to counsel, generally, **Crim Proc-Const Lim 338-400**
Scientific methods, other identification procedures, **Crim Proc-Const Lim 249, 250**
Scope and timing of prosecution, **Crim Proc-Const Lim 408-418**
Search and seizure, generally, **Crim Proc-Const Lim 57-149**
Secret agents, use of, generally, **Crim Proc-Const Lim 150-176**
Section 605, wiretapping, electronic eavesdropping, and use of secret agents, **Crim Proc-Const Lim 151, 152**
Selection, **Crim Proc-Const Lim 376, 377, 447-449**
Selective incorporation, shift to, **Crim Proc-Const Lim 16-21**
Self-incrimination, generally, **Crim Proc-Const Lim 227-239**
Self-representation, waiver of counsel and right to proceed pro se, **Crim Proc-Const Lim 369-376**
Sentencing, **Crim Proc-Const Lim 362-364, 470-473**
Silence of defendant, impeachment, exclusionary rules, **Crim Proc-Const Lim 317-319**
Sixth Amendment, **Crim Proc-Const Lim 259-262, 338-345, 433-440**
Smell, protected areas and interests, **Crim Proc-Const Lim 62-64**
Standby counsel, waiver of counsel and right to proceed pro se, **Crim Proc-Const Lim 375-380**
Standing, exclusionary rules, **Crim Proc-Const Lim 320-333**

CRIMINAL PROCEDURE—Cont'd

Statute of limitations, disclosure of electronic surveillance records, **Crim Proc-Const Lim 172, 173**

Statutes, **Crim Proc-Const Lim 83, 172, 173, 278, 279**

Stop-and-frisk, **Crim Proc-Const Lim 118-129**

Stores, protected areas and interests, **Crim Proc-Const Lim 65-67**

Students, supervision of, **Crim Proc-Const Lim 137**

Subpoenas, **Crim Proc-Const Lim 129-131, 230-233**

Supreme Court's response, police interrogations and confessions, **Crim Proc-Const Lim 179-181**

Surveillance, generally, **Crim Proc-Const Lim 150-176**

Tainted witness, exclusionary rules, **Crim Proc-Const Lim 301-303**

Third party, **Crim Proc-Const Lim 144-149, 319, 320**

Timing of prosecution, postinvestigatory process, **Crim Proc-Const Lim 413-418**

Title II of Crime Control Act, **Crim Proc-Const Lim 153-156**

Total incorporation interpretation, **Crim Proc-Const Lim 14-16**

Totality of circumstances, **Crim Proc-Const Lim 181-187, 250-255**

Trash or garbage, protected areas and interests, **Crim Proc-Const Lim 67-70**

Trial, generally, **Crim Proc-Const Lim 455-470**

Unconstitutional statute, probable cause and related problems, **Crim Proc-Const Lim 83**

Vehicles, **Crim Proc-Const Lim 67, 112-118, 135**

Voluntariness, **Crim Proc-Const Lim 181-187, 423, 424**

Waiver of counsel, **Crim Proc-Const Lim 194-196, 241, 242, 369-376**

Warnings, consent searches, **Crim Proc-Const Lim 139, 140**

Warrant, police reliance on, good faith exceptions, **Crim Proc-Const Lim 275-278**

Warrantless searches and seizures, **Crim Proc-Const Lim 93-118**

Waste baskets, protected areas and interests, **Crim Proc-Const Lim 67-70**

Wiretapping, generally, **Crim Proc-Const Lim 150-176**

CRIMINAL PROCEDURE—Cont'd
Witnesses, **Crim Proc-Const Lim 227-250, 301-303, 458-460**

CRITICISMS
Jurisprudence (this index)

CROSS-EXAMINATION
Trial and Practice Skills (this index)

DAMAGES
Injunctions (this index)
Labor Arbitration Law and Practice (this index)
Land Use (this index)
Medical Liability (this index)
Personal Property (this index)

DEBTORS AND CREDITORS
Bankruptcy and Other Debtor-Creditor Laws (this index)

DECEDENTS' ESTATES
Federal Estate and Gift Taxation (this index)
Plans or planning. **Estate Planning** (this index)

DEDUCTIONS
Federal Estate and Gift Taxation (this index) generally
Federal Income Taxation of Partners and Partnerships (this index)
International Taxation (this index)

DEFAULT
Uniform Commercial Code (this index)

DEFENSES
Hazardous Wastes and Toxic Substances, Law of (this index)
Individual Employee Rights (this index)
Insurance Law (this index)
Negotiable Instruments and Check Collection (this index)

DEFENSES—Cont'd
Uniform Commercial Code (this index)

DEFICIENCIES
Tax Procedure and Tax Fraud (this index)

DEFINITIONS OR DISTINCTIONS
Appellate Advocacy (this index)
Individual Employee Rights (this index)
Injunctions (this index)
Insurance Law (this index)
International Taxation (this index)

DELEGATION
State Constitutional Law (this index)

DELIVERY
Personal Property (this index)
Trial and Practice Skills (this index)
Uniform Commercial Code (this index)

DEPORTATION
Immigration Law and Procedure (this index)

DEPOSITS
Negotiable Instruments and Check Collection (this index)

DEVELOPMENT
Land Use (this index)
Oil and Gas Law (this index)

DIGESTS
Legal Research (this index)

DIRECT EXAMINATION
Trial and Practice Skills (this index)

DISABLED PERSONS
Americans With Disabilities Act. **Individual Employee Rights** (this index)
Federal Disability Law (this index)
Individual Employee Rights (this index)
Mental Health and Disability Law (this index)
Workers. **Individual Employee Rights** (this index)

DISCHARGE OF LIABILITY
Negotiable Instruments and Check Collection (this index)

DISCIPLINE
Labor Law (this index)

DISCLOSURE
Medical Liability (this index)
Tax Procedure and Tax Fraud (this index)

DISCRETION
Injunctions (this index)

DISCRIMINATION
Civil Rights (this index)

DISGUISED ACTIONS
Federal Income Taxation of Partners and Partnerships (this index)

DISHONOR
Negotiable Instruments and Check Collection (this index)

DISPUTE SETTLEMENT
International Trade and Investment (this index)

DISTRIBUTIONS
Federal Income Taxation of Partners and Partnerships (this index)

DIVIDENDS
International Taxation (this index)

DRAFTING
Legal Drafting (this index)
Trial and Practice Skills (this index)

DURATION OF LEASE
Landlord and Tenant (this index)

DUTIES
Insurance Law (this index)

E

EAA (EXPORT ADMINISTRATION ACT)
International Trade and Investment (this index)

ECONOMICS
Antitrust Law and Economics (this index)
International Trade and Investment (this index)
Law and Economics (this index)

ELDER LAW
Abuse and neglect, generally, **Elder 397-415**
Accelerated benefits, **Elder 138-140**
Age Discrimination in Employment Act, generally, **Elder 384-396**
Annuities, pension plans, **Elder 347, 353, 356-362, 364, 370, 381**
Board and care homes, **Elder 163-166, 405**
Brain death, **Elder 34, 35**
Client competency, **Elder 12-16, 22-24, 227-229, 250, 251**
Continuing care retirement communities, generally, **Elder 188, 219-224**
Custodial care, **Elder 128, 141-163**
Durable powers of attorney, generally, **Elder 256-262**
Ethics, generally, **Elder 8-16**

ELDER LAW—Cont'd
Euthanasia, **Elder 54, 55**
Guardianship, generally, **Elder 227-270**
Health care decisionmaking, generally, **Elder 17-57**
Housing, generally, **Elder 168-224**
Individual Retirement Accounts (IRA), **Elder 356, 363, 364, 366, 368, 370, 372, 374, 378-383**
Insurance, **Elder 89-96, 126-140**
Joint tenancy, generally, **Elder 251-255**
Keogh plans, **Elder 356, 363, 366**
Life insurance, accelerated benefits, **Elder 138**
Living trusts, generally, **Elder 262-270**
Long-term care insurance, generally, **Elder 126-140**
Lump sum distributions, pension plans, **Elder 352, 353, 370-383**
Medicaid, generally, **Elder 97-140**
Medicare, generally, **Elder 57-89**
Medigap, generally, **Elder 89-96**
Mental capacity, health care decisionmaking, **Elder 23**
Nursing homes, generally, **Elder 141-163**
Pension plans, generally, **Elder 345-383**
Probate, **Elder 124, 251, 252, 256, 267-270**
Reverse mortgages, generally, **Elder 200-210**
Revocable trusts, generally, **Elder 262-270**
Social security, generally, **Elder 271-316**
Supplemental security income, generally, **Elder 317-327**
Taxation, **Elder 138-140, 172-194, 302, 306, 308-312, 355-380**
Veterans' benefits, generally, **Elder 328-344**

ELECTIONS
Federal Income Taxation of Partners and Partnerships (this index)
Labor Law (this index)
State Constitutional Law (this index)

ELECTRONIC RESOURCES
Legal Research (this index)

GENERAL INDEX

References are to Titles and Pages

EMPLOYEE BENEFIT PLANS

Accrued benefits, **Emp Bene Plans 80-84, 96-104, 108-111, 132**
Actuarial principles, **Emp Bene Plans 406-413**
Additional matters
  distributions, additional taxes on, **Emp Bene Plans 162-165**
  ESOPs, additional tax advantages, **Emp Bene Plans 303-305**
  limitations on contributions and benefits, **Emp Bene Plans 399-404**
Administrative exemptions, prohibited transactions, **Emp Bene Plans 282-284**
Age and service requirements, **Emp Bene Plans 360**
Age discrimination rules, **Emp Bene Plans 104**
Aggregate limitations, **Emp Bene Plans 402-404**
Amendments, **Emp Bene Plans 105-108, 395-397**
Amount of contribution or benefits, generally, **Emp Bene Plans 372-384**
Annuities, **Emp Bene Plans 112-121, 143-150, 456-458**
Anti-alienation rules, **Emp Bene Plans 135-142**
Asset transfer, prohibited fiduciary conduct, **Emp Bene Plans 274**
Attorneys' fees, **Emp Bene Plans 339-341**
Bankruptcy, personal bankruptcy, **Emp Bene Plans 137, 138**
Banks, prohibited transactions, **Emp Bene Plans 281, 282**
Business aggregation rules, **Emp Bene Plans 357, 358**
Capital gains, ESOPs, **Emp Bene Plans 304, 305**
Caselaw development, suits for benefits, **Emp Bene Plans 178-183**
Cashouts, **Emp Bene Plans 122, 123**
Civil penalties, breach of fiduciary duty, **Emp Bene Plans 266, 267**
Claims procedure, generally, **Emp Bene Plans 166-174**
Classification, **Emp Bene Plans 352-357**
Collective bargaining units, **Emp Bene Plans 359**
Combined plan, **Emp Bene Plans 383**
Common law answers, traditional frameworks for plan regulation, **Emp Bene Plans 56-63**
Compensation, **Emp Bene Plans 43-47, 345-349**
Contributions, generally, **Emp Bene Plans 405-428**

EMPLOYEE BENEFIT PLANS—Cont'd

Corporate control contests, ESOPs and, **Emp Bene Plans 305-313**
Corporate finance, **Emp Bene Plans 47-51**
Corresponding code provisions, prohibited transactions, **Emp Bene Plans 275**
Cross-testing, **Emp Bene Plans 380, 381**
Death benefits and distributions, **Emp Bene Plans 130, 131, 134, 135**
Deductions for contributions, **Emp Bene Plans 424-428**
Deferred capital gains, ESOPs, **Emp Bene Plans 304, 305**
Defined benefit plans, **Emp Bene Plans 104, 376-380, 401, 402 426, 427**
Defined contribution plans, **Emp Bene Plans 104, 373-376, 400, 401**
Definitions, employer securities, **Emp Bene Plans 288-291**
Denominated fiduciary roles, **Emp Bene Plans 219-224**
Disclosure, plan information, **Emp Bene Plans 189-207**
Disparities and integration, **Emp Bene Plans 384-394**
Distribution of benefits, generally, **Emp Bene Plans 112-142**
Dividend deduction, ESOPs, **Emp Bene Plans 303, 304**
Economic aspects of plans, **Emp Bene Plans 31-54**
Employee Retirement Income Security Act of 1974, **Emp Bene Plans 1-21**
Employee Stock Option Plans, generally, **Emp Bene Plans 288, 294-313**
Employer as fiduciary, **Emp Bene Plans 228-230**
Employer securities, **Emp Bene Plans 288-294**
Employer stock or real property, prohibited fiduciary conduct, **Emp Bene Plans 275**
ERISA, **Emp Bene Plans 1-21**
ESOPs, generally, **Emp Bene Plans 288, 294-313**
Exceptions or exemptions, **Emp Bene Plans 141, 142, 279-284, 282-284, 291-294**
Expectations, traditional frameworks for plan regulation, **Emp Bene Plans 55, 56**
Fiduciary regulation, generally, **Emp Bene Plans 217-268**
Finance, generally, **Emp Bene Plans 22-30**

EMPLOYEE BENEFIT PLANS—Cont'd

Financial markets, **Emp Bene Plans 52-54**
Forfeitures, **Emp Bene Plans 84-86**
Former employees, **Emp Bene Plans 360, 381, 382**
Funding, generally, **Emp Bene Plans 405-428**
Goods and services, prohibited fiduciary conduct, **Emp Bene Plans 274**
Group insurance, **Emp Bene Plans 325, 326**
Highly compensated employees, **Emp Bene Plans 345-349**
Incompleteness of ERISA, **Emp Bene Plans 74-76**
Information regarding plan, generally, **Emp Bene Plans 189-216**
Insurance, **Emp Bene Plans 325-330**
Insurers, prohibited transactions, **Emp Bene Plans 281, 282**
Integration and disparities, **Emp Bene Plans 384-394**
Interference or noninterference, **Emp Bene Plans 94-111**
Internal Revenue Code, termination of plan, **Emp Bene Plans 429, 430**
Jurisdiction, **Emp Bene Plans 336, 337**
Jury trial availability, suits for benefits, **Emp Bene Plans 183-185**
Kickbacks, prohibited fiduciary conduct, **Emp Bene Plans 279**
Labor law, **Emp Bene Plans 175-177, 359**
Leased employees, **Emp Bene Plans 358, 359**
Legislative background to ERISA, **Emp Bene Plans 69-76**
Leveraged ESOPs, **Emp Bene Plans 295-297**
Liabilities incidental to benefit payments, **Emp Bene Plans 185-188**
Limitation periods, **Emp Bene Plans 338, 339**
Limitations or restrictions, **Emp Bene Plans 259-263, 399-404**
Loans, **Emp Bene Plans 124-128, 273, 280, 297-299**
Lump sum distributions, **Emp Bene Plans 121, 122, 151-157**
Markets and marketing, financial markets, **Emp Bene Plans 52-54**
Minimum age and service requirements, **Emp Bene Plans 360**
Minimum participation test, **Emp Bene Plans 365-369**
Modifications of funding rules, **Emp Bene Plans 418-420**
Motivations for ERISA, legislative background to ERISA, **Emp Bene Plans 69-71**

EMPLOYEE BENEFIT PLANS—Cont'd

Multiemployer plans, **Emp Bene Plans 8, 436, 437**
Nondiscrimination, **Emp Bene Plans 344-398**
Noninterference, **Emp Bene Plans 94-111**
Nonretirement benefits, **Emp Bene Plans 128-131**
Notices, funding standards, **Emp Bene Plans 423**
Operating contracts, prohibited transactions, **Emp Bene Plans 280, 281**
Oral plans, information regarding, **Emp Bene Plans 211-216**
Participation, noninterference, **Emp Bene Plans 94, 95**
Parties in interest, prohibited transactions, **Emp Bene Plans 269, 270, 285-287**
Payment procedure, generally, **Emp Bene Plans 166-188**
PBGC and benefit guaranty program, termination of plan, **Emp Bene Plans 431-438**
Penalties, **Emp Bene Plans 266, 267, 423, 424, 427, 428**
Pension plans, generally, **Emp Bene Plans 3-6, 8-11**
Personal bankruptcy, **Emp Bene Plans 137, 138**
Preemption, generally, **Emp Bene Plans 314-335**
Present value, **Emp Bene Plans 22-24**
Privileges, **Emp Bene Plans 341, 342**
Process and venue, **Emp Bene Plans 337, 338**
Profit-sharing plans, deductions for contributions, **Emp Bene Plans 425, 426**
Prohibited transactions, generally, **Emp Bene Plans 269-287, 291-293**
Property transactions, prohibited fiduciary conduct, **Emp Bene Plans 272, 273**
Protection of benefits, generally, **Emp Bene Plans 77-93**
Qualified domestic relations orders, **Emp Bene Plans 138-140, 156, 157**
Real property of employer, prohibited fiduciary conduct, **Emp Bene Plans 275**
Remedies, **Emp Bene Plans 263-268, 285-287**
Reports and reporting, **Emp Bene Plans 189-207, 438, 439**
Restructuring of plan, **Emp Bene Plans 383, 384**
Retroactive corrections, **Emp Bene Plans 397, 398**

EMPLOYEE BENEFIT PLANS—Cont'd

Reversions, termination of plan, **Emp Bene Plans 453-456**
Rollover distributions, **Emp Bene Plans 158-161**
Securities of employer, **Emp Bene Plans 288-294**
Self-dealing, prohibited fiduciary conduct, **Emp Bene Plans 275-279**
Separate line of business rules, **Emp Bene Plans 361-365**
Service requirements, **Emp Bene Plans 360**
Services, prohibited fiduciary conduct, **Emp Bene Plans 274**
Single-employer plan benefits guaranteed, termination of plan, **Emp Bene Plans 434-436**
Single-employer plan terminations, **Emp Bene Plans 440-452**
Social security offset plans, **Emp Bene Plans 393, 394**
Spousal consent, nonannuity payments, **Emp Bene Plans 123, 124**
Standards, **Emp Bene Plans 78-89, 241-258, 413-428**
State insurance regulation, **Emp Bene Plans 326-330**
Statutory regulations before ERISA, traditional frameworks for plan regulation, **Emp Bene Plans 63-68**
Stocks, **Emp Bene Plans 275, 425, 426**
Subject matter jurisdiction, **Emp Bene Plans 336, 337**
Substantive standards, generally, **Emp Bene Plans 112-142**
Taxation, generally, **Emp Bene Plans 22-30, 143-165**
Termination of plan, **Emp Bene Plans 86-88, 429-460**
Term of fiduciary office, **Emp Bene Plans 230**
Time of distributions, **Emp Bene Plans 132, 133**
Title I, ERISA, **Emp Bene Plans 8-11, 15-17, 430**
Title II, ERISA, **Emp Bene Plans 8-11, 17-19**
Title IV, ERISA, **Emp Bene Plans 19, 20, 431**
Top-heavy plans, **Emp Bene Plans 88, 89, 104, 105**
Traditional frameworks for plan regulation, **Emp Bene Plans 55-68**
Trust and related requirements, **Emp Bene Plans 230-241**
Trusts and trustees, **Emp Bene Plans 161, 162, 177, 178**
Valuing pensions, **Emp Bene Plans 24, 25**
Venue, **Emp Bene Plans 337, 338**
Vesting, **Emp Bene Plans 77-93**

EMPLOYEE BENEFIT PLANS—Cont'd
Welfare plans, generally, **Emp Bene Plans 7-11**
Withdrawal liability, termination of plan, **Emp Bene Plans 459, 460**
Writing requirement, plan information, **Emp Bene Plans 207-216**

EMPLOYERS AND EMPLOYEES
Benefit plans. **Employee Benefit Plans** (this index)
Discrimination in employment. **Employment Discrimination** (this index)
Federal Estate and Gift Taxation (this index) generally
Immigration Law and Procedure (this index)
Individual Employee Rights (this index)
Labor Law (this index)
Services (this index)
Staffing
  Health Care Law and Ethics (this index)
Staffing. **Health Care Law and Ethics** (this index)
Workers' Compensation and Employee Protection Laws (this index)

EMPLOYMENT
First Amendment (this index)
International Trade and Investment (this index)

EMPLOYMENT DISCRIMINATION
Accommodation, **Emp Discrim 131, 134, 156**
Actuarial differences, **Emp Discrim 187, 196**
ADA, generally, **Emp Discrim 15, 153**
ADEA, generally, **Emp Discrim 14**
Adverse impact, **Emp Discrim 88, 89, 91, 95-99, 106, 117, 132, 139, 162, 193**
Advertisements, discriminatory, **Emp Discrim 39**
Affirmative action, **Emp Discrim 20, 59, 60, 62, 64-66, 224, 225**
Age, **Emp Discrim 136, 137**
Age Discrimination in Employment Act, generally, **Emp Discrim 14**

EMPLOYMENT DISCRIMINATION—Cont'd

AIDS, as disability, **Emp Discrim 154**
Airline pilots, age discrimination against, **Emp Discrim 142**
Alcoholism, as disability, **Emp Discrim 154**
Alienage, **Emp Discrim 121, 122**
American Indians, **Emp Discrim 66, 115**
Americans with Disabilities Act, generally, **Emp Discrim 15, 153**
Appellate review, motive finding, **Emp Discrim 71**
Arbitration, **Emp Discrim 10, 278**
Attorney, appointment of, **Emp Discrim 234**
Attorneys' fees, **Emp Discrim 234, 236, 238**
At-will, **Emp Discrim 1-3**
Back pay, **Emp Discrim 219-221, 226, 230, 231**
Bankruptcy Act, discrimination because of use, **Emp Discrim 46**
Bargaining, collective bargaining generally, **Emp Discrim 9-11**
Benefit plans, **Emp Discrim 45, 146, 163, 187, 189**
Bennett Amendment, **Emp Discrim 19, 45, 146, 150, 163, 171, 172, 186, 187, 189, 196**
BFOQ, generally, **Emp Discrim 51**
Bona fide occupational qualification, generally, **Emp Discrim 51**
Bottom line, impact analysis, **Emp Discrim 91**
Burdens, **Emp Discrim 75, 77, 79, 95, 171**
Business necessity, **Emp Discrim 57, 86, 95**
Cause, basis for discrimination, **Emp Discrim 49**
Charge, **Emp Discrim 258, 243, 266, 273**
Citizenship, generally, **Emp Discrim 17**
Civil Rights Act of 1866, **Emp Discrim 19, 34, 116-118, 201**
Civil Rights Act of 1991, generally, **Emp Discrim 13**
Civil service rates, Equal Pay Act defense, **Emp Discrim 184**
Class actions, **Emp Discrim 254, 270**
Clubs, bona fide membership, coverage, **Emp Discrim 26**
Colleges, as employment agencies, **Emp Discrim 30**
Color, protected by Title VII, **Emp Discrim 115**
Common law, **Emp Discrim 1-3, 5, 6**
Comparable worth, Title VII, **Emp Discrim 193**
Comparator, Equal Pay Act, **Emp Discrim 177**

EMPLOYMENT DISCRIMINATION—Cont'd

Compensation, **Emp Discrim 19, 45, 146, 150, 163, 171, 172, 186, 187, 189, 196**
Complaint, nature of, **Emp Discrim 252**
Congressional employees, Title VII, **Emp Discrim 25**
Consent decree, challenge to, **Emp Discrim 66**
Constitution, **Emp Discrim 43, 44**
Constructive discharge, Title VII, **Emp Discrim 212**
Construct validation, testing, **Emp Discrim 106**
Consumer Credit Protection Act, generally, **Emp Discrim 45**
Content validation, testing, **Emp Discrim 101**
Continuing violations, statutes of limitations, **Emp Discrim 247**
Contract, **Emp Discrim 2, 5, 18, 21**
Costs, **Emp Discrim 146, 149, 235, 238**
Counsel, appointment of under Title VII, **Emp Discrim 234**
Coverage, generally, **Emp Discrim 23**
Credibility, pretext, **Emp Discrim 78**
Credit, discrimination because of, **Emp Discrim 45**
Criminal records, impact of, **Emp Discrim 98**
Criterion validation, testing, **Emp Discrim 102**
Damages, **Emp Discrim 4-6, 218, 222, 223, 227, 228, 232, 233**
Defenses, **Emp Discrim 4, 47, 106, 110, 112, 142, 145, 174, 178, 179, 224**
Direct evidence, **Emp Discrim 67, 137**
Disability, **Emp Discrim 15, 153**
Discharge, **Emp Discrim 3, 49, 74**
Discriminatory act, identifying for statute of limitations, **Emp Discrim 247**
Disease, as disability, **Emp Discrim 154**
Disparate treatment, **Emp Discrim 70, 72, 74, 75, 77, 138, 160**
Drug addiction, **Emp Discrim 92, 154**
Due process of law, government employee protection, **Emp Discrim 43**
Education, **Emp Discrim 97, 182**
EEOC, generally, **Emp Discrim 40**
Employer, **Emp Discrim 24, 211**

EMPLOYMENT DISCRIMINATION—Cont'd

Employment agency, **Emp Discrim 29, 39**
Enforcement, **Emp Discrim 10, 241, 258, 262, 264, 272, 275**
Enterprise coverage, Equal Pay Act, **Emp Discrim 31**
Environment, **Emp Discrim 199, 209**
Equal Employment Opportunity Commission, generally, **Emp Discrim 40**
Equal Pay Act, generally, **Emp Discrim 19, 171**
Equal work, Equal Pay Act, **Emp Discrim 172**
Equity, powers of courts, **Emp Discrim 218**
ERISA, benefit plan discrimination, **Emp Discrim 45**
Establishment, Equal Pay Act defined, **Emp Discrim 175**
Executive Order 11246, generally, **Emp Discrim 20, 59**
Executives, ADEA application to, **Emp Discrim 141**
Experience, Equal Pay Act factor, **Emp Discrim 182**
Expulsion from union, common law, **Emp Discrim 2**
Extraterritorial coverage, **Emp Discrim 28**
Facial distinctions, generally, **Emp Discrim 47**
Factors other than age, ADEA, **Emp Discrim 144**
Factors other than sex, Equal Pay Act, **Emp Discrim 179**
Failing company, layoffs, **Emp Discrim 149**
Fair representation, **Emp Discrim 8, 9**
Federal employees, **Emp Discrim 258, 272, 275**
Fetal protection policies, sex discrimination, **Emp Discrim 56**
Firefighters, ADEA exemption for, **Emp Discrim 140**
Front pay, **Emp Discrim 218, 231**
Golden parachute, ADEA, voluntary retirement, **Emp Discrim 150**
Good faith, **Emp Discrim 112, 220, 227**
Good faith and fair dealing, employment contracts subject to, **Emp Discrim 2**
Governments, state and local, **Emp Discrim 25, 32, 43, 141**
Grooming rules, **Emp Discrim 202, 203, 205**
Handbooks and manuals, as common law contracts, **Emp Discrim 5**
Handicap, generally, **Emp Discrim 15, 153**

EMPLOYMENT DISCRIMINATION—Cont'd

Harassment, **Emp Discrim 6, 117, 207, 208, 211, 212**
Head of household, Equal Pay Act, **Emp Discrim 180**
Hiring and promotion, disparate treatment analysis, **Emp Discrim 72**
Hiring orders, **Emp Discrim 219, 231**
History, legislative, **Emp Discrim 12**
Homosexuality, **Emp Discrim 127, 128**
Identical treatment, violation of law, **Emp Discrim 78**
Immigration Reform and Control Act, generally, **Emp Discrim 17**
Impact analysis, **Emp Discrim 88, 91, 95-99, 106, 117, 132, 139, 162, 193**
Impairment, defined as disability, **Emp Discrim 153**
Independent contractors, coverage of, **Emp Discrim 36**
Indians, **Emp Discrim 66, 115**
Indian tribes, coverage of, **Emp Discrim 26**
Injunctions, **Emp Discrim 218, 219, 228**
Intentional, **Emp Discrim 217, 268, 269**
Interest, **Emp Discrim 222, 228, 232**
Jurisdiction of courts, **Emp Discrim 256, 270**
Jury trial, **Emp Discrim 256, 263, 270, 274**
Labor relations statutes, generally, **Emp Discrim 7**
Labor unions, **Emp Discrim 1, 28, 33, 38, 201, 229**
Landrum-Griffin Act, internal union affairs, **Emp Discrim 38**
Language, national origin discrimination, **Emp Discrim 120, 205**
Law enforcement officers, ADEA exemption for, **Emp Discrim 140**
Layoffs, ADEA, **Emp Discrim 148**
Legislation, Equal Pay Act defense, **Emp Discrim 184**
Legitimate, nondiscriminatory reason, disparate treatment analysis, **Emp Discrim 70, 75**
Licensing authorities, coverage of, as employment agencies, **Emp Discrim 30**
Lie detectors, limits on use of, **Emp Discrim 45**
Liquidated damages, **Emp Discrim 227, 232**
Major life activity, disability, **Emp Discrim 155**
Marital status, discrimination based on, as sex, **Emp Discrim 127**

EMPLOYMENT DISCRIMINATION—Cont'd
Marriage rules, discrimination based on, **Emp Discrim 214**
Matching salaries, Equal Pay Act, factor other than sex, **Emp Discrim 182**
Medical examinations, ADA, **Emp Discrim 164**
Merit systems, Equal Pay Act defense, **Emp Discrim 179**
Motive, **Emp Discrim 67, 68, 70, 78, 79, 85, 88, 112, 160, 190, 194**
Multiple regression, statistical technique, **Emp Discrim 192**
National Labor Relations Act, generally, **Emp Discrim 7**
National origin, **Emp Discrim 12, 17, 119, 120, 205**
Native Americans, **Emp Discrim 66, 115**
Nepotism, discrimination, **Emp Discrim 214**
Newspapers, coverage of as employment agencies, **Emp Discrim 30**
Older Worker Benefit Protection Act, generally, **Emp Discrim 148, 151**
Opposition, **Emp Discrim 7, 167**
Participation, protection for, **Emp Discrim 166**
Partnership, decisions covered, **Emp Discrim 37**
Parttime work, Equal Pay Act, **Emp Discrim 182**
Pattern and practice, **Emp Discrim 79, 255**
Pensions, **Emp Discrim 146, 187**
Perpetuation, **Emp Discrim 85, 192**
Physical examinations, ADA, **Emp Discrim 164**
Physical requirements, impact of, **Emp Discrim 98**
Political and social beliefs, religion, **Emp Discrim 130**
Polygraphs, limits on use of, **Emp Discrim 45**
Portal-to-Portal Act, **Emp Discrim 263, 264**
Preferential treatment, prohibition of, Section 703(j), **Emp Discrim 60**
Pregnancy, **Emp Discrim 55, 126, 189, 216**
Pretext, **Emp Discrim 71, 77, 78**
Prisoners, coverage of, **Emp Discrim 37**
Procedures, **Emp Discrim 241, 258, 264-267, 272, 275**
Professional associations, coverage of, as employment agencies, **Emp Discrim 30**

EMPLOYMENT DISCRIMINATION—Cont'd

Professors, ADEA, **Emp Discrim 141**
Profit, Equal Pay Act, **Emp Discrim 183**
Protected activity, labor relations statutes, **Emp Discrim 7**
Protective legislation, BFOQ defense, **Emp Discrim 57**
Public policy, wrongful discharge, **Emp Discrim 3**
Qualifications, **Emp Discrim 77, 145**
Qualified, **Emp Discrim 73, 74, 156**
Race, **Emp Discrim 12, 18, 51, 57, 115, 116, 207**
Race discrimination, **Emp Discrim 7, 8, 12, 18, 27, 115, 116, 205**
Railway Labor Act, generally, **Emp Discrim 7**
Ratios, affirmative action, **Emp Discrim 64**
Red circle rates, Equal Pay Act, factors other than sex, **Emp Discrim 181**
Reductions in force, ADEA, **Emp Discrim 148**
Rehabilitation Act, generally, **Emp Discrim 15, 153**
Reinstatement, remedy, **Emp Discrim 218, 230, 231**
Religion, **Emp Discrim 129, 130**
Religious discrimination, generally, **Emp Discrim 129**
Religious organizations, **Emp Discrim 26, 27, 134**
Religious practices, accommodation duty, **Emp Discrim 131**
Remedies, **Emp Discrim 60, 217-219, 222, 224, 226-228, 230-233**
Res judicata, generally, **Emp Discrim 277**
Retaliation, generally, **Emp Discrim 166**
Retirement, voluntary, ADEA, **Emp Discrim 150**
Right to sue notice, generally, **Emp Discrim 249, 251, 252**
Rule of 4/5ths, impact proof, **Emp Discrim 90**
Security clearances, title VII defense for, **Emp Discrim 119**
Segregation, generally, **Emp Discrim 200**
Seniority, **Emp Discrim 106, 110, 112, 142, 145, 179, 224**
Severance pay, ADEA violation, **Emp Discrim 150**
Sex, **Emp Discrim 12, 91, 117, 124, 125-127, 171, 203, 208, 215**
Sex-plus, discrimination concept, **Emp Discrim 48**
Shift differential, Equal Pay Act treatment of, **Emp Discrim 181**
Social relationships as discrimination, **Emp Discrim 215**

EMPLOYMENT DISCRIMINATION—Cont'd
Speech, freedom of, **Emp Discrim 43**
Standard deviation, **Emp Discrim 81, 90**
State proceedings, **Emp Discrim 243, 268, 278**
Statistics, **Emp Discrim 79, 81, 84, 90, 104, 139, 192**
Statutes of limitations, **Emp Discrim 112, 226, 243, 247, 248, 250, 253, 258, 263, 264, 266-269, 273**
Students, coverage of, **Emp Discrim 37**
Subjectivity, **Emp Discrim 76, 96**
Systemic discrimination, **Emp Discrim 79, 255**
Temporary work, Equal Pay Act defense, **Emp Discrim 182**
Testing, **Emp Discrim 64, 99-102, 104, 106**
Title VII, generally, **Emp Discrim 12**
Torts, common law, **Emp Discrim 6**
Training programs, Equal Pay Act defense, **Emp Discrim 182**
Treaties, impact of, **Emp Discrim 122**
Undue hardship, **Emp Discrim 131, 159**
Uniform guidelines, testing, **Emp Discrim 100**
Unions, **Emp Discrim 1, 28, 33, 38, 201, 229**
Vagueness, reasons, **Emp Discrim 76**
Validation, **Emp Discrim 64, 98-102, 104, 106**
Veterans, **Emp Discrim 44**
Wage rate, Equal Pay Act calculation, **Emp Discrim 176**
Waiver, ADEA rights, **Emp Discrim 151**
Whistleblower, **Emp Discrim 4**
Wilful, **Emp Discrim 263, 268, 269**
Working conditions, Equal Pay Act, **Emp Discrim 173**
Wrongful discharge, common law, **Emp Discrim 3**

ENCYCLOPEDIAS
Legal Research (this index)

ENERGY AND NATURAL RESOURCES LAW
Adequacy of impact statement, environmental assessment and NEPA, **Energy 235-242**
Administration, environmental assessment and NEPA, **Energy 219-223**

ENERGY AND NATURAL RESOURCES LAW —Cont'd

Administrative law, **Energy 40-53**
Air pollution, **Energy 152-167**
Alcohol fuels, developing energy resources, **Energy 485, 486**
Alternative fuels and policies, **Energy 430-437**
Antecedents, federal energy policy, **Energy 408-423**
Bald eagles, management of natural resources on public lands, **Energy 136, 137**
Biomass and alcohol fuels, developing energy resources, **Energy 485, 486**
Birds, management of natural resources on public lands, **Energy 137**
Burros, management of natural resources on public lands, **Energy 136**
Chemical spraying, federal timber law, **Energy 355**
Clean Water Act, federal timber law, **Energy 353-355**
Coal
  developing energy resources, **Energy 449-461**
  federal timber law, **Energy 338**
  leasable, energy minerals, **Energy 285-297**
Coastal Zone Management Act (CZMA), offshore oil and gas, **Energy 284**
Common goods, property interests in natural resources, **Energy 5, 6**
Common law and natural resources, **Energy 30-61**
Comprehensive Environmental Response, Compensation, and Liability Act (CERCLA), **Energy 202-217**
Consent or approval, cutting timber without permission, **Energy 319, 320**
Conservation, developing energy resources, **Energy 491, 492**
Constitutional law, **Energy 53-61**
Contracts
  common law, uses of, **Energy 38, 39**
  timber, contracts to log and market, **Energy 318, 319**
Controlling environmental decisionmaking of federal agencies, **Energy 147-151**

ENERGY AND NATURAL RESOURCES LAW —Cont'd

Conventional policies and conventional fuels, federal energy policy, **Energy 407-429**
Conversion and distribution of energy, **Energy 494-536**
Cost-benefit analysis, **Energy 24-28**
Cultural preservation, management of special purpose public lands, **Energy 107-109**
Cutting timber without permission, **Energy 319, 320**
Damages, private timber law, **Energy 320**
Developing energy resources, **Energy 438-493**
Discovery, hard rock minerals, **Energy 256-259**
Disposal of salable materials, **Energy 305, 306**
Dual systems, water law, **Energy 378-380**
Ecological purposes, management of special purpose public lands, **Energy 107-119**
Economically valuable resources, management of natural resources on public lands, **Energy 120**
Economics and natural resources markets, generally, **Energy 2-62**
Electricity, energy conversion and distribution, **Energy 508-521**
Endangered Species Act, management of natural resources on public lands, **Energy 129-136**
Enforcement, environmental assessment and NEPA, **Energy 219-223**
Environmental law
    generally, **Energy 139-217**
    assessment and NEPA, **Energy 218-244**
    federal timber law, environmental and preservationist values, **Energy 348-355**
Failures of the market, **Energy 19-24**
Federal and interstate water law, **Energy 390-397**
Federal energy policy, **Energy 400-536**
Federal jurisdiction, offshore oil and gas, **Energy 281, 282**
Federal power over public lands and resources, **Energy 64-90**
Federal reserved mineral rights, **Energy 306-210**
Federal timber law, **Energy 326-355**
Forests
    federal timber law, generally, **Energy 327-340**

ENERGY AND NATURAL RESOURCES LAW —Cont'd

Forests—Cont'd
- management of forests by planning, federal timber law, **Energy 340-348**

Free market and natural resources use, **Energy 6-19**

Geothermal
- developing energy resources, **Energy 486-488**
- leasable, energy minerals, **Energy 299, 300**

Geothermal Steam Act, leasable, energy minerals, **Energy 299, 300**

Groundwater pollution, **Energy 186**

Hard rock mining and minerals
- generally, **Energy 249-269**
- federal timber law, **Energy 335, 336**

Hazardous substance control, **Energy 190-217**

Hazardous waste and oil spills, pollution control, **Energy 185**

History
- development of public lands and resources policy, **Energy 77-90**
- management of special purpose public lands, **Energy 107-119**
- preservation, management of special purpose public lands, **Energy 107-109**

Horses, management of natural resources on public lands, **Energy 136**

Hydroelectric power, developing energy resources, **Energy 470-483**

Impact statement, environmental assessment and NEPA, **Energy 235-242**

International protection of wildlife species, management of natural resources on public lands, **Energy 138**

Interstate water law, **Energy 390-397**

Intervention, environmental assessment and NEPA, **Energy 221-223**

Judicial review
- agency environmental decisionmaking, judicial review of, **Energy 149-151**
- environmental assessment and NEPA, **Energy 221-223**

ENERGY AND NATURAL RESOURCES LAW —Cont'd

Leasable, energy minerals, **Energy 269-300**
Limitations on common law, **Energy 30-35**
Locatable, hard rock minerals, **Energy 249-269**
Logging, contracts to log and market timber, **Energy 318, 319**
Management and protection of resources, **Energy 63-244**
Marine mammals, management of natural resources on public lands, **Energy 137**
Markets and marketing, contracts to log and market timber, **Energy 318, 319**
Migratory birds, management of natural resources on public lands, **Energy 137**
Minerals law
  generally, **Energy 246-310**
  federal timber law, mining and minerals development, **Energy 334-338**
Moral hazard, failures of the market, **Energy 24**
National Forest Management Act of 1976, federal timber law, **Energy 342-348**
National forests
  federal timber law, generally, **Energy 327-340**
  National Forest Management Act of 1976, federal timber law, **Energy 342-348**
National parks and monuments, management of special purpose public lands, **Energy 101-105**
National Pollutant Discharge Elimination System (NPDES), **Energy 179-183**
National Wildlife Refuge System, management of natural resources on public lands, **Energy 127, 128**
Natural gas, energy conversion and distribution, **Energy 495-507**
Nuclear power, developing energy resources, **Energy 461-469**
Offshore oil and gas, leasable energy minerals, **Energy 281-285**
Oil and Gas Law (this index)
Oil shale, leasable, energy minerals, **Energy 297, 298**
Oil spills, pollution control, **Energy 185**
Outer Continental Shelf Lands Act (OCSLA), offshore oil and gas, **Energy 282, 283**

ENERGY AND NATURAL RESOURCES LAW —Cont'd

Ownership, private timber law, **Energy 314, 315**
Patented claim, locatable hard rock minerals, **Energy 268, 269**
Paternalism, failures of the market, **Energy 23, 24**
Pollution control, **Energy 152-189**
Preservation lands, management of special purpose public lands, **Energy 99-138**
Private enforcement of federal statutory violations, environmental law, **Energy 148, 149**
Private environmental law, **Energy 143-147**
Private goods, property interests in natural resources, **Energy 3, 4**
Private timber law, **Energy 314-320**
Property law
  common law, uses of, **Energy 37, 38**
  property interests in natural resources, generally, **Energy 3-6**
Public goods, property interests in natural resources, **Energy 4, 5**
Public rights, water law, **Energy 380-383**
Public utility regulation, energy conversion and distribution, **Energy 521-536**
Rangelands, management of special purpose public lands, **Energy 90-99**
Rationalization, failures of the market, **Energy 23**
Recreation, management of special purpose public lands, **Energy 101-107**
Reforestation, state forest practice acts, **Energy 321-323**
Resource Conservation and Recovery Act (RCRA), **Energy 192-202**
Resources Planning Act of 1974, federal timber law, **Energy 341, 342**
Riparian rights, water law, **Energy 358-363**
Royalties management, oil and gas leases, **Energy 271-273**
Safe Drinking Water Act (SWDA), **Energy 187, 188**
Sales
  common variety minerals, salable, **Energy 300-306**
  timber, federal timber law, **Energy 329-333**
Scarce resource allocation, **Energy 22, 23**

ENERGY AND NATURAL RESOURCES LAW —Cont'd

Scientific preservation, management of special purpose public lands, **Energy 107-109**
Synthetic fuels, developing energy resources, **Energy 488-491**
Solar power, developing energy resources, **Energy 484, 485**
State environmental law, **Energy 143-147**
State timber law, **Energy 320-325**
Thermal pollution, **Energy 185, 186**
Threshold requirements, environmental assessment and NEPA, **Energy 223-228**
Timber law, **Energy 311-355**
Timing, environmental assessment and NEPA, **Energy 233-235**
Tort law, uses of common law, **Energy 36, 37**
Toxic and hazardous substance control, **Energy 190-217**
Trespass, cutting timber without permission, **Energy 319, 320**
Unpatented mining claim, locatable hard rock minerals, **Energy 259-268**
Values
- federal timber law, environmental and preservationist values, **Energy 348-355**
- wilderness values, management of special purpose public lands, **Energy 109-115**

Water law
- generally, **Energy 356-397**
- management of special purpose public lands, water resources, **Energy 115-119**
- pollution of water, **Energy 168-189**

Wilderness, management of special purpose public lands, **Energy 107-119**
Wildlife
- federal timber law, wildlife protection, **Energy 351, 352**
- management of natural resources on public lands, **Energy 120-138**

ENFORCEMENT

Hazardous Wastes and Toxic Substances, Law of (this index)
Injunctions (this index)

ENFORCEMENT—Cont'd
International Human Rights (this index)
Labor Arbitration Law and Practice (this index)
Land Use (this index)
Negotiable Instruments and Check Collection (this index)
Uniform Commercial Code (this index)

ENTRY AND REENTRY
Immigration Law and Procedure (this index)

ENVIRONMENTAL CONCERNS
Land Use (this index)

ENVIRONMENTAL LAW
Air pollution, **Environ 97-127, 199-202**
Balancing test, federalism and the environment, **Environ 79-81**
Clean Air Act, **Environ 97-127**
Clean Water Act, **Environ 127-145**
Coastal waters, preservation of natural areas, **Environ 281-294**
Commerce clause, federalism and the environment, **Environ 73-81**
Commerce power, federalism and the environment, **Environ 59-68**
Common law remedies, control of toxic substances, **Environ 246-254**
Comprehensive Environmental Response, Compensation, and Liability Act (CERCLA), **Environ 222-245**
Contribution, Comprehensive Environmental Response, Compensation, and Liability Act (CERCLA), **Environ 238, 239**
Criminal liability, Resource Conservation and Recovery Act (RCRA), **Environ 219-222**
Damages, Comprehensive Environmental Response, Compensation, and Liability Act (CERCLA), **Environ 239-242**
Definitions, Resource Conservation and Recovery Act (RCRA), **Environ 207-212**
Discharge, marketable discharge permits, **Environ 152-156**

ENVIRONMENTAL LAW—Cont'd

Economic incentives for environmental protection, **Environ 145-156**
Effluent charges and noncompliance penalties, **Environ 148-152**
EIS (environmental impact statement), **Environ 24-56**
Endangered species, preservation of, **Environ 306-310**
Energy and Natural Resources Law (this index)
Environmental impact statement (EIS), **Environ 24-56**
Evaluation of NEPA, **Environ 54-56**
Federalism and the environment, **Environ 57-87**
Federal preemption, **Environ 81-87**
Hazardous waste defined, Resource Conservation and Recovery Act (RCRA), **Environ 207-212**
Imminent hazards, Resource Conservation and Recovery Act (RCRA), **Environ 215-219**
International Environmental Law (this index)
Judicial review of government decisions, **Environ 1-24**
Land disposal ban, Resource Conservation and Recovery Act (RCRA), **Environ 212-215**
Marketable discharge permits, **Environ 152-156**
National Environmental Policy Act (NEPA), generally, **Environ 24-56**
Natural areas, preservation of, **Environ 255-310**
Navigational servitude, preservation of natural areas, **Environ 276-281**
Penalties, effluent charges and noncompliance penalties, **Environ 148-152**
Permits, marketable discharge permits, **Environ 152-156**
Pesticide regulation, **Environ 182-189**
Pollution control, generally, **Environ 88-156**
Preemption, **Environ 81-87**
Preservation of natural areas, **Environ 255-310**
Private land, restrictions on development of, **Environ 259-281**
Public lands, preservation of natural areas, **Environ 294-306**
Public trust doctrine, preservation of natural areas, **Environ 272-275**
Reform of Comprehensive Environmental Response, Compensation, and Liability Act (CERCLA), **Environ 244, 245**

ENVIRONMENTAL LAW—Cont'd
Remedies, judicial review of government decisions, **Environ 20-24**
Resource Conservation and Recovery Act (RCRA), **Environ 202-222**
Restrictions on development of private land, preservation of natural areas, **Environ 259-281**
Risk management and scientific uncertainty, **Environ 157-181**
Sale of toxic substances, **Environ 182-195**
Scientific uncertainty, **Environ 157-181**
Settlements, Comprehensive Environmental Response, Compensation, and Liability Act (CERCLA), **Environ 242-244**
Solid waste defined, Resource Conservation and Recovery Act (RCRA), **Environ 207-212**
Toxic substances, generally, **Environ 182-254**
Toxic Substances Control Act, **Environ 190-195**
Water and water pollution, **Environ 127-145, 196-199, 281-294**

EQUITY COURT
Injunctions (this index)

ESTATE PLANNING
Abatement, **Est Plan 38, 39**
Accumulations rule against, **Est Plan 269, 270**
Ademption, **Est Plan 31**
Administration of estate, **Est Plan 13-15, 284-289**
Adoption, **Est Plan 42, 43**
Advancement, **Est Plan 38**
Annual exclusion, **Est Plan 299, 300, 302, 303**
Annuities, federal estate and gift taxes, **Est Plan 324, 325**
Appointments, **Est Plan 257-261, 326-329**
Assignment, **Est Plan 126-131**
Attestation clause, simple wills, **Est Plan 93, 94**
Avoidance of probate, survivorship interests, **Est Plan 51, 52**
Caveats, simple wills, **Est Plan 85-88**
Change of beneficiary of life insurance policy, **Est Plan 124-126**
Charitable matters, **Est Plan 234-241, 329-331**

ESTATE PLANNING—Cont'd

Children or minors, federal estate and gift taxes, **Est Plan 302, 303**
Class gifts, **Est Plan 200-204, 252-257**
Codicils, **Est Plan 32**
Community foundations, charitable trusts, **Est Plan 240, 241**
Community property, **Est Plan 22, 23, 60-73**
Conflict of laws, community property, **Est Plan 69-72**
Contract and tort liability of fiduciary, **Est Plan 271-277**
Credit, federal estate and gift taxes, **Est Plan 299, 300**
Disclaimers, **Est Plan 43, 44**
Dispositive clause, simple wills, **Est Plan 82-84**
Divorced spouse, survivorship interests, **Est Plan 57, 58**
Durable power of attorneys, trusts, **Est Plan 184, 185**
Elections, surviving spouse, **Est Plan 33, 34, 72, 73**
Exclusion, federal estate and gift taxes, **Est Plan 299-303**
Execution, simple wills, **Est Plan 95, 96**
Executors or administrators, **Est Plan 15, 16, 27, 91, 92**
Executory interest, future interests, **Est Plan 186-190**
Federal estate and gift taxes, **Est Plan 290-334**
Federal law, generally, **Est Plan 20-22**
Fiduciary administration, generally, **Est Plan 271-289**
Fire insurance, **Est Plan 130, 131**
Forced retirement, estate arising from status, **Est Plan 146, 149**
Forced share statutes, revocable trusts under, **Est Plan 232-234**
Foreign assets, **Est Plan 23, 24**
Future interests, generally, **Est Plan 186-222**
Generation-skipping transfers, federal estate and gift taxes, **Est Plan 331-334**
Gifts to minors, federal estate and gift taxes, **Est Plan 302, 303**
Gross estate, federal estate and gift taxes, **Est Plan 310, 311**
Guardianship, **Est Plan 88-90, 223-228**
Illegitimacy, **Est Plan 43**
Incorporation by reference, trusts, **Est Plan 169-171**
Individual retirement accounts, **Est Plan 228, 229**
Insurance, **Est Plan 105-131, 325, 326**

ESTATE PLANNING—Cont'd

Intervivos gifts, simple intervivos gifts of personal property, **Est Plan 5-10**
Intestacy, generally, **Est Plan 25-45**
Keogh trusts, **Est Plan 228, 229**
Lapses, **Est Plan 30, 31**
Liability insurance, **Est Plan 113, 114, 131**
Life insurance, **Est Plan 64-67, 107-112, 117-120, 124-126, 128-130, 325, 326**
Lifetime gifts, generally, **Est Plan 4, 5**
Living wills, trusts, **Est Plan 185**
Loyalty duty, fiduciaries, **Est Plan 277-280**
Marital deduction, **Est Plan 229-232, 303-310**
Mortmain Acts, **Est Plan 239, 240**
Operation of law, estate planning by, **Est Plan 27-30**
Options, insurance, **Est Plan 120-123**
Orphan's deduction, federal estate and gift taxes, **Est Plan 305, 306**
Pensions and retirement, **Est Plan 141-144, 146, 149, 228, 229**
Per capita and per stirpes, **Est Plan 39-41**
Portability, estate arising from status, **Est Plan 144-146**
Pour-over wills, trusts, **Est Plan 171-176**
Power of attorneys, trusts, **Est Plan 184, 185**
Powers of appointment, federal estate and gift taxes, **Est Plan 326-329**
Private express trusts, generally, **Est Plan 155-158, 223-241**
Probate, **Est Plan 25, 51, 52**
Property insurance, **Est Plan 113, 114**
Remainders, future interests, **Est Plan 186-190**
Retirement, **Est Plan 141-144, 146, 149, 228, 229**
Reversions, future interests, **Est Plan 186-190**
Revocable trusts, **Est Plan 163-169, 232-234**
Revocation, **Est Plan 35, 36**
Rule against perpetuities, **Est Plan 246-269**
Rule in Shelley's Case, **Est Plan 242-246**
Safeguarding will, simple wills, **Est Plan 99**

ESTATE PLANNING—Cont'd

Satisfaction, **Est Plan 38**
Self-proved wills, simple wills, **Est Plan 96-99**
Separate property, community property, **Est Plan 62-64**
Settlement, **Est Plan 16-18, 120-123**
Severability, survivorship interests, **Est Plan 48-50**
Simple intervivos gifts of personal property, **Est Plan 5-10**
Simple wills, **Est Plan 74-104**
Simultaneous death, survivorship interests, **Est Plan 54-56**
Small estates, generally, **Est Plan 16-18**
Social security, estate arising from status, **Est Plan 133-141**
Split gifts, federal estate and gift taxes, **Est Plan 303-305**
State law, generally, **Est Plan 19, 20**
Status, estate arising from, **Est Plan 132-154**
Statute of fraud, trusts, **Est Plan 158-163**
Statute of wills, trusts, **Est Plan 158-163**
Statutory wills, simple wills, **Est Plan 99**
Surviving spouse, **Est Plan 32-34, 57, 58, 72, 73**
Survivors and survivorship, **Est Plan 32-34, 36-38, 45-59, 72, 73, 307, 308, 311-316**
Taxation, **Est Plan 53, 54, 290-334**
Termination of trust, **Est Plan 180-184**
Testacy or intestacy, generally, **Est Plan 25-45**
Tort liability of fiduciary, **Est Plan 271-277**
Totten Trusts, survivorship interests, **Est Plan 56, 57**
Trusts, generally, **Est Plan 56, 57, 155-185, 223-241, 280-284**
Unified credit, federal estate and gift taxes, **Est Plan 299, 300**
United States Savings Bonds, survivorship interests, **Est Plan 50, 51**
Vesting, estate arising from status, **Est Plan 144-146**
Veterans' benefits, estate arising from status, **Est Plan 150-153**
Wills, **Est Plan 25-45, 74-104, 158-163, 171-176, 185**
Workers' compensation, estate arising from status, **Est Plan 147-150**
Worthier Title Doctrine, **Est Plan 242-246**

ESTATES
Decedents' Estates (this index)
Planning. **Estate Planning** (this index)

ESTATES IN LAND AND FUTURE INTERESTS
Age contingencies exceeding 21, perpetuity reform, **Est in Land 278**
Alienability of future interests, consequences of classification, **Est in Land 105-117**
Classification, **Est in Land 11-151**
Condition precedent, **Est in Land 83-90, 323-325**
Condition subsequent, vesting of estates, **Est in Land 83-90**
Contingent remainders, **Est in Land 77-81, 185**
Creditors' rights, involuntary alienability, **Est in Land 112-117**
Defeasible fee simple, **Est in Land 18-21**
Definitions, **Est in Land 33-35, 57, 58, 313, 314**
Destructibility, **Est in Land 119-136, 179-181**
Enforcement, possibilities of reverter and rights of entry, **Est in Land 52-54**
Evolution of worthier title doctrine from rule of law to rule of construction, **Est in Land 161-166**
Executory interests, **Est in Land 90-95, 107-111, 185, 201-203**
Federal estate tax consequences, worthier title doctrine, **Est in Land 175, 176**
Fee simple estates, **Est in Land 17-21**
Fee tail, **Est in Land 21**
Forfeiture, destruction by, **Est in Land 124-133**
Fractional interests, Rule in Shelley's Case, **Est in Land 153-156**
Fragmentation of ownership, generally, **Est in Land 1, 2**
Historical development of Rule in Shelley's Case, **Est in Land 138, 139**
Hypothetical examples used in this book, **Est in Land 5-8**
Immediate-reformation method of perpetuity reform, **Est in Land 274-276**
Importance and process of classification, **Est in Land 11-16**
Intervivos matters, **Est in Land 107-111, 124, 151, 164-166, 169**
Involuntary alienability, creditors' rights, **Est in Land 112-117**

ESTATES IN LAND AND FUTURE INTERESTS —Cont'd

Legal theory underlying destructibility rule, **Est in Land 119-122**
Life estates, **Est in Land 22, 23**
Life in being part of perpetuity period, **Est in Land 187**
Merger, **Est in Land 124-133, 151-156**
Nonreversionary future interests, **Est in Land 27-31, 33-55, 57-64**
Permissible changes in classificatin due to subsequent events, **Est in Land 97-101**
Possessory estates, **Est in Land 17-25**
Premature termination, **Est in Land 43-46, 60, 61**
Present status, **Est in Land 133-135, 158, 159**
Rebutting presumption, worthier title doctrine, **Est in Land 170-172**
Remainders and executory interests, inter vivos alienability of reversions, **Est in Land 107-111**
Reversions, generally, **Est in Land 27-31, 33-55**
Right of entry, possibility of, **Est in Land 46-55**
Rule against perpetuities, generally, **Est in Land 183-247**
Rule in Shelley's Case, generally, **Est in Land 137-160**
Rule of law to rule of construction, **Est in Land 164-169**
Shelley's Case, generally, **Est in Land 137-160**
Social policy, **Est in Land 135, 136, 159, 160, 177-179**
Specific-statutory-repair method, perpetuity reform, **Est in Land 277, 278**
Taxation, **Est in Land 175, 176, 203, 204, 221, 222, 254-267**
Technical reversions, **Est in Land 41-43**
Termination, **Est in Land 43-46, 60, 61, 173-175**
Term of years, **Est in Land 23-25**
Time or date, **Est in Land 124-133, 203-208**
Transferability at death, alienability of future interests, **Est in Land 105, 106**
Trust termination, worthier title doctrine, **Est in Land 173-175**
21-year part of perpetuity period, **Est in Land 187**
Validity or invalidity, rule against perpetuities, **Est in Land 191-203, 212-216, 325-331**

ESTATES IN LAND AND FUTURE INTERESTS —Cont'd

Vesting, future interests differentiated in terms of, **Est in Land 65-95**

Voluntary alienability during life, alienability of future interests, **Est in Land 107-112**

Worthier title doctrine, generally, **Est in Land 161-181**

ETHICS

Health Care Law and Ethics (this index)

EUROPEAN UNION

International Trade and Investment (this index)

EUROPEAN UNION LAW

Agents, external trade law, **Euro Union 264-266**

Agricultural policy, internal union policies, **Euro Union 223-229**

Antidumping duties, external trade law, **Euro Union 242-247**

Antitrust, business competition law, **Euro Union 332, 333**

Association agreements, external trade law, **Euro Union 255-258**

Attorney-client privilege, business competition law, **Euro Union 272-277**

Broadcasting, internal union policies, **Euro Union 209-212**

Business competition law, **Euro Union 267-333**

Central and Eastern Europe, external trade law, **Euro Union 255-258**

Choice of law, litigating European Union law, **Euro Union 125, 126**

COMECON, EFTA (1959) and, **Euro Union 11-13**

Commercial agents, external trade law, **Euro Union 264-266**

Common agricultural policy, internal union policies, **Euro Union 223-229**

Common customs law, external trade law, **Euro Union 232-238**

Compensation, internal union policies, **Euro Union 217-222**

Competition, **Euro Union 179-184, 267-333**

Conflicts of law, business competition law, **Euro Union 329-332**

Countervailing duties, external trade law, **Euro Union 247, 248**

EUROPEAN UNION LAW—Cont'd

Court of First Instance, litigating European Union law, **Euro Union 115-120**

Customs law, external trade law, **Euro Union 232-238**

Direct effects doctrine, litigating European Union law, **Euro Union 86-89**

Dumping, external trade law, **Euro Union 242-247**

Duty free access to common market, external trade law, **Euro Union 263**

EEC, **Euro Union 16-18**

EFTA, **Euro Union 11-18**

Enforcement of judgments of national courts, litigating European Union law, **Euro Union 126-135**

Environmental policy, internal union policies, **Euro Union 200-208**

Equal pay and equal treatment, internal union policies, **Euro Union 217-222**

Escape clause proceedings, external trade law, **Euro Union 239, 240**

Exclusive dealing agreements exemption, business competition law, **Euro Union 285**

Exemptions, business competition law, **Euro Union 280-285, 288**

External trade law, **Euro Union 231-266**

Free movement, **Euro Union 136-174**

GATT, **Euro Union 13-16**

Generalized tariff preferences, external trade law, **Euro Union 238, 239**

Government subsidies, internal union policies, **Euro Union 179-184**

Harmonizing national laws, internal union policies, **Euro Union 184-200**

History, **Euro Union 1-33**

Illegality, litigating European Union law, **Euro Union 109-112**

Intellectual property rights, **Euro Union 145-149, 297-299**

Internal union policies, **Euro Union 175-230**

Law-making in European Union, generally, **Euro Union 34-83**

Litigation, **Euro Union 84-135, 324-326**

EUROPEAN UNION LAW—Cont'd
Lome Conventions, external trade law, **Euro Union 258-262**
Maastricht, **Euro Union 29-31, 334-344**
Mediterranean Policy, external trade law, **Euro Union 255-258**
Mergers and acquisitions, business competition law, **Euro Union 311-315**
Negative clearances, business competition law, **Euro Union 280-283**
Nondistorted competition policy, **Euro Union 269, 270**
Nontariff trade barriers (NTDs), **Euro Union 149-152, 142-145**
Notices, business competition law, **Euro Union 284, 285**
Occupational safety, internal union policies, **Euro Union 212-217**
Pleas of illegality, litigating European Union law, **Euro Union 109-112**
Procurement, internal union policies, **Euro Union 184-190**
Products liability, internal union policies, **Euro Union 190-194**
Professionals, free movement of, **Euro Union 159, 160**
Remedies, business competition law, **Euro Union 324-326**
Sanctions, business competition law, **Euro Union 277-280**
Securities, internal union policies, **Euro Union 194-200**
Self-employed, free movement of, **Euro Union 155-159**
Social policy, internal union policies, **Euro Union 212-217**
Standing to challenge, litigating European Union law, **Euro Union 109-112**
Subsidies, internal union policies, **Euro Union 179-184**
Taxation, internal union policies, **Euro Union 175-179**
Treaty of Paris, **Euro Union 2-4**
Treaty of Rome, **Euro Union 4-10, 13-16**
United States-European union antitrust cooperation, business competition law, **Euro Union 332, 333**
Voluntary trade restraints, external trade law, **Euro Union 239, 240**

EVASION
Tax Procedure and Tax Fraud (this index)

EVASIVE WITNESSES
Trial and Practice Skills (this index)

EVIDENCE
Administrative hearings, **Evid 30-33**
Attorney-client privilege, **Evid 208-222**
Authentication of evidence, **Evid 618-623**
Best evidence rule, **Evid 623-628**
Bias, witness evidencing, **Evid 292-298**
Character, **Evid 104-187, 298**
Collateral matter, impeachment of witness, **Evid 289-292**
Competency of witness, **Evid 261-319**
Compulsory process clause, **Evid 468-470**
Confrontation clause, **Evid 449-468**
Confusion, counterweight to relevance, **Evid 72-89**
Credibility of witnesses, **Evid 160-177, 301-307**
Cross examination, **Evid 307-313**
Defining hearsay, **Evid 383-399**
Direct examination, **Evid 307-313**
Doctor-patient privilege, **Evid 233-240**
Due process clause, **Evid 468-470**
Examination of witness, **Evid 261-319**
Exceptions, exemptions, or exclusions, **Evid 30-42, 481-617**
Excited utterances, **Evid 518-523**
Exclusionary rules, deterrence rationales, **Evid 255, 256**
Exhibits, **Evid 613-618**
Expert and opinion evidence, **Evid 320-382**
Federal Rules of Evidence (this index)
Governmental privileges, **Evid 241-247**
Habit and routine practices, **Evid 153-156**
Hearings, administrative hearings, **Evid 30-33**
Hearsay, **Evid 383-470**
Impeachment of witness, **Evid 268-273, 298-300, 379-382**
Injunctions (this index)
Instructions to jury, **Evid 11-19**
Insurance Law (this index)

EVIDENCE—Cont'd
Interpretation of rules, **Evid 1-42**
Judicial notice, substitutes for evidence, **Evid 43-46**
Jury instructions, **Evid 11-19**
Labor Arbitration Law and Practice (this index)
Marital privilege, **Evid 223-233**
Modifications, **Evid 471-516**
Nonjury trials, **Evid 30-33**
Objections, **Evid 11-19**
Offers, **Evid 11-19**
Out-of-court statements or conduct, **Evid 429-449**
Parol evidence rule, **Evid 628, 629**
Parol evidence rule. **Insurance Law** (this index)
Prejudice, counterweight to relevance, **Evid 72-89**
Present sense impressions, **Evid 523-584**
Presumptions and burden of proof, substitutes for evidence, **Evid 47-60**
Prior inconsistent statements, **Evid 273-285, 289-292**
Privileges, **Evid 188-260**
Propensity, **Evid 104-187**
Psychotherapist-patient privilege, **Evid 233-240**
Questions of law or fact, **Evid 19-30**
Refreshing recollection, **Evid 314-319**
Rehabilitation of credibility, **Evid 301-307**
Relevancy, **Evid 61-103**
Scientific evidence, expert and opinion evidence, **Evid 347-379**
Self-incrimination privilege, **Evid 247-255**
Sexual assaults, **Evid 137-145**
Similar acts, **Evid 120-137, 145-153**
Specific contradiction, impeachment of witness by, **Evid 285-288**
Substitutes for evidence, **Evid 43-60**
Time consumption, counterweight to relevance, **Evid 72-89**
Witnesses
- bias, witness evidencing, **Evid 292-298**
- character-related impeachment, **Evid 298**
- collateral matter, impeachment of witness, **Evid 289-292**

EVIDENCE—Cont'd
Witnesses—Cont'd
competency of witness, **Evid 261-319**
credibility of witnesses, **Evid 160-177, 301-307**
cross examination, **Evid 307-313**
direct examination, **Evid 307-313**
examination of witness, **Evid 261-319**
impeachment of witness, **Evid 268-273, 298-300, 379-382**
Labor Arbitration Law and Practice (this index)
prior inconsistent statements, **Evid 273-285, 289-292**
refreshing recollection, **Evid 314-319**
rehabilitation of credibility, **Evid 301-307**
specific contradiction, impeachment of witness by, **Evid 285-288**
Trial and Practice Skills (this index)

EXAMINATION
How to Study Law and Take Law Exams (this index)

EXAMINATIONS
Professional Responsibility (this index)

EXCEPTIONS
Injunctions (this index)
International Business Transactions (this index)
Medical Liability (this index)

EXCEPTIONS, EXEMPTIONS, OR EXCLUSIONS
White Collar Crime (this index)

EXCEPTIONS, EXEMPTIONS OR EXCLUSIONS
International Taxation (this index)

EXCEPTIONS OR EXCLUSIONS
Insurance Law (this index)

EXCEPTIONS OR EXEMPTIONS
Health Care Law and Ethics (this index)

EXCEPTIONS OR EXEMPTIONS—Cont'd
Land Use (this index)

EXCLUSION
Immigration Law and Procedure (this index)

EXCLUSIONS
Uniform Commercial Code (this index)

EXEMPTIONS
State Constitutional Law (this index)

EXPORT /ADMINISTRATION ACT (EAA)
International Trade and Investment (this index)

EXTENSIONS AND RENEWALS
Landlord and Tenant (this index)

FAKES
Art Law (this index)

FALSE ADVERTISING
Generally, **Unfair Trade 354 et seq.**

FALSE STATEMENTS
Tax Procedure and Tax Fraud (this index)

FAMILY
Immigration Law and Procedure (this index)

FAMILY LAW
Generally, **Fam Law 1-17**
Abortion, husband and wife in ongoing marriage, **Fam Law 143, 144**
Abuse of child, generally, **Fam Law 274-276, 291-294, 307, 308**
Acknowledgment, parent child relationship, **Fam Law 176**
Adoption, generally, **Fam Law 195-211**

FAMILY LAW—Cont'd

Adultery, **Fam Law 150, 151, 339, 340**
Adversary process, **Fam Law 364-374**
Affinity, marriage relationship, **Fam Law 49-51**
Age, marriage relationship, **Fam Law 48, 49**
Alimony, **Fam Law 401-426, 465-468**
Annulment, **Fam Law 357-363, 378**
Anonymity of adoption, **Fam Law 208, 209**
Antenuptial contracts, **Fam Law 91-94, 101-107**
Arbitration, **Fam Law 372, 373**
Artificial insemination, **Fam Law 212-215**
Attorneys, **Fam Law 286-288, 367-369, 472**
Attorneys' fees, **Fam Law 472**
Bankruptcy, **Fam Law 460-463**
Battered wife syndrome, **Fam Law 152-155**
Best interests of child, custody of child on divorce, **Fam Law 296-298**
Blood tests, parent child relationship, **Fam Law 176, 177**
Can child divorce parents, **Fam Law 282**
Change in child custody on divorce, **Fam Law 323-325**
Children and minors. See lines throughout this topic
Child support, generally, **Fam Law 244-260, 468-470**
Cohabitation, **Fam Law 71-87, 418-420**
Collusion, divorce, **Fam Law 349, 350**
Common law marriages, **Fam Law 58-60**
Common law property rights, husband and wife in ongoing marriage, **Fam Law 115, 116**
Community property, **Fam Law 120-122, 128-130, 432-434**
Compulsory schooling and parental control, **Fam Law 233-238**
Conciliation, **Fam Law 371, 372**
Condonation, divorce, **Fam Law 347, 348**
Conflicts of laws, noncompliance with marriage regulation, **Fam Law 68-70**
Connivance, divorce, **Fam Law 348, 349**
Consent, **Fam Law 54-57, 203-205**
Consortium rights, husband and wife in ongoing marriage, **Fam Law 138**

FAMILY LAW—Cont'd

Constitutional law, generally, **Fam Law 18-40, 282-286, 376-378, 386-390**
Contracts, **Fam Law 88-108, 483-486**
Court fees, divorce reform, **Fam Law 388, 389**
Criminal prosecution, generally, **Fam Law 288-291**
Cultural diversity and family law, **Fam Law 14-16, 276-278**
Custody of child, generally, **Fam Law 225-331**
Death and death actions, **Fam Law 94, 122-124, 259, 260, 415, 416**
Defenses, **Fam Law 174, 344, 345, 359**
Definitions, **Fam Law 61, 62, 166**
Dependency of child, **Fam Law 274-276**
Desertion, divorce for, **Fam Law 340, 341**
Disability pay, division of property on divorce, **Fam Law 438, 439**
Discipline, professional ethics and discipline, **Fam Law 367**
Disclosure, separation agreements, **Fam Law 483**
Discrimination, sex-specific discrimination in family law, **Fam Law 159-161**
Divisions or divisibility, **Fam Law 427-459**
Divorce, **Fam Law 333-356, 371, 372, 385-490**
Domestic violence, **Fam Law 145-147, 310**
Due process, **Fam Law 29, 30, 282-286, 441, 442**
Duration of support obligation, **Fam Law 256, 257, 259, 260**
Economic consequences of divorce, **Fam Law 401-490**
Emancipation of child, **Fam Law 228, 229**
Embryo transfers, **Fam Law 212, 213**
Enforcement, **Fam Law 261-273, 320-322, 460-479**
Equality of spouses, **Fam Law 156-162**
Equal protection, **Fam Law 23-29, 156, 157**
Equal rights amendment, equality of spouses, **Fam Law 157-159**
Equitable adoption, **Fam Law 208**
Ethics, professional ethics and discipline, **Fam Law 367**
Eugenics, marriage relationship, **Fam Law 51, 52**
Fairness, separation agreements, **Fam Law 483**

FAMILY LAW—Cont'd

Family courts, **Fam Law 369-371**
Family support, husband and wife in ongoing marriage, **Fam Law 109-111**
Federal constitution, sources and applications of family law, **Fam Law 7-10**
Federal courts, sources and applications of family law, **Fam Law 10, 11**
Federal legislation, **Fam Law 13, 14, 165**
Federal Parental Kidnapping Act, child custody on divorce, **Fam Law 329-331**
Feeding, child custody on divorce, **Fam Law 310, 311**
Foreign state or country, **Fam Law 325-329, 375-384**
Formalities, marriage formalities, **Fam Law 54-60**
Fornication, sex crimes and marriage, **Fam Law 150, 151**
Fraud, annulment for, **Fam Law 359-361**
Full faith and credit, **Fam Law 267, 278, 376-378**
Gay lifestyles, child custody on divorce, **Fam Law 309, 310**
Gender, custody of child on divorce, **Fam Law 298-304**
Grandparents' visitation rights, child custody on divorce, **Fam Law 322, 323**
Hague Convention and International Parental Kidnapping Crime Act, child custody on divorce, **Fam Law 329-331**
Health, marriage relationship, **Fam Law 52**
Heart balm actions, **Fam Law 138-143, 232, 233**
Heterosexual marriage, **Fam Law 43-47**
Higher education, support obligation, **Fam Law 257-259**
Husband and wife, generally, **Fam Law 109-162**
Incest, **Fam Law 49-51, 149, 150**
Insanity, divorce for, **Fam Law 343, 344**
International matters, **Fam Law 14, 209-211, 325-328**
Interstate matters, **Fam Law 325-329**
Intra-family tort immunities, husband and wife in ongoing marriage, **Fam Law 135-138**
In vitro fertilization, **Fam Law 212, 213, 215**
Joint custody, child custody on divorce, **Fam Law 316-318**

FAMILY LAW—Cont'd

Joint property, husband and wife in ongoing marriage, **Fam Law 118-120**
Judge's role, child custody on divorce, **Fam Law 314-316**
Jurisdiction, **Fam Law 118-120, 375-384, 427-432**
Juvenile court's dispositional powers, **Fam Law 278, 279**
Legal effects of invalid marriages, **Fam Law 63-65**
Legitimacy or illegitimacy, **Fam Law 166-169**
Legitimate state interests in the family, **Fam Law 36-40**
Limited divorce, **Fam Law 353-356**
Marriage penalty tax, **Fam Law 472-477**
Married woman's name, **Fam Law 133-135**
Married Women's Property Acts, **Fam Law 116-118**
Mediation, **Fam Law 373, 374**
Medical care, **Fam Law 113, 114, 238-243**
Mental condition, marriage relationship, **Fam Law 52**
Mental cruelty, divorce for, **Fam Law 342, 343**
Migratory divorce, **Fam Law 376-378**
Modification of alimony, **Fam Law 413, 414**
Monogamous marriage, **Fam Law 47, 48**
Morality, custody of child on divorce, **Fam Law 307**
Names, married woman's name, **Fam Law 133-135**
Neglect of child, **Fam Law 274-276**
Negotiated fault divorce, **Fam Law 350-352**
No-fault divorce, **Fam Law 399, 400, 408, 409, 440, 441**
Noncompliance with marriage regulation, **Fam Law 61-70**
Out-of-state matters, **Fam Law 325-329, 375-384**
Ovum transplant, **Fam Law 212, 213, 215**
Parent and child relationship, generally, **Fam Law 163-331**
Paternity, generally, **Fam Law 171-173**
Pensions, divisibility of, **Fam Law 444-453**
Personal jurisdiction, **Fam Law 378-383**
Physical cruelty, divorce for, **Fam Law 341, 342**
Poverty and family law, **Fam Law 16, 17**
Presumptions, **Fam Law 65, 66, 118-120, 167-169**
Primary caretaker, custody of child on divorce, **Fam Law 298-304**

FAMILY LAW—Cont'd
Privacy doctrine, **Fam Law 30-33**
Professional ethics and discipline, **Fam Law 367**
Professional licenses, divisibility of, **Fam Law 453-458**
Property, generally, **Fam Law 109-132**
Proposal, separation agreements, **Fam Law 483-486**
Protection orders, husband and wife in ongoing marriage, **Fam Law 145-147**
Provocation, divorce, **Fam Law 346, 347**
Publication, service of process by, **Fam Law 383, 384**
Putative spouse doctrine, **Fam Law 66-68**
Race or racial matters, **Fam Law 201-203, 304-306**
Rape, sex crimes and marriage, **Fam Law 147-149**
Rebutting presumption of legitimacy, **Fam Law 167-169**
Reconciliation, **Fam Law 99, 486**
Recrimination, divorce, **Fam Law 345, 346**
Religion and religious matters, **Fam Law 199-201, 306**
Relocation right of custodial parent, child custody on divorce, **Fam Law 325-328**
Remarriage, alimony, **Fam Law 416, 417**
Residence requirements, divorce jurisdiction, **Fam Law 375-384**
Res judicata, parent child relationship, **Fam Law 175, 176**
Retirement, alimony, **Fam Law 414, 415**
Retroactivity of annulment, **Fam Law 362**
Revocation of adoption, **Fam Law 207**
Schools and education, compulsory schooling and parental control, **Fam Law 233-238**
Separate maintenance, limited divorce and, **Fam Law 353-356**
Separate property, **Fam Law 118-120, 441, 442**
Separation agreements, generally, **Fam Law 100, 101, 480-490**
Service of process by publication, **Fam Law 383, 384**
Settlements, parent child relationship, **Fam Law 175, 176**
Sex and sexual offenses, **Fam Law 147-151, 307, 308**
Sex-specific discrimination in family law, **Fam Law 159-161**
Smoking, child custody on divorce, **Fam Law 310, 311**
Social legislation, sources and applications of family law, **Fam Law 11-13**

FAMILY LAW—Cont'd

Social security, alimony, **Fam Law 420**
Solemnization of marriage, **Fam Law 57, 57**
Standard of proof in termination proceedings, **Fam Law 286-288**
States, generally, **Fam Law 5-7**
Statutes of limitation, parent child relationship, **Fam Law 174, 175**
Subject matter, variability of marriage contract, **Fam Law 99, 100**
Substantive requirements, marriage regulation, **Fam Law 41-53**
Summary divorce, **Fam Law 400**
Support, husband and wife in ongoing marriage, **Fam Law 109-132**
Surrogacy, **Fam Law 215-223**
Survivor's rights upon partner's death, husband and wife in ongoing marriage, **Fam Law 122-124**
Taxation, **Fam Law 107, 356, 452, 453, 460-479**
Tender years doctrine, custody of child on divorce, **Fam Law 298-304**
Termination of status or rights, **Fam Law 279-288, 333-400**
Testimonial privilege, husband and wife in ongoing marriage, **Fam Law 151, 152**
Third parties, antenuptial contracts, **Fam Law 106, 107**
Torts, **Fam Law 230, 261-263**
Travel rights, child custody on divorce, **Fam Law 325-328**
Treaties, international treaties for sources and applications of family law, **Fam Law 14**
Uniform Interstate Family Support replaces Uniform Reciprocal Enforcement of Support Act, **Fam Law 268-270**
Uniform Marital and Divorce Act, separation agreements, **Fam Law 488-490**
Uniform Marital Property Act (UMDA), **Fam Law 128-130, 439, 440**
Uniform Marriage and Divorce Act, **Fam Law 393, 394, 404-406, 434-438**
Uniform Parentage Act, **Fam Law 172, 173**
Uniform Premarital Agreements Act, variability of marriage contract, **Fam Law 101-106**

FAMILY LAW—Cont'd
Uniform Reciprocal Enforcement of Support Act replaced by Uniform Interstate Family Support, **Fam Law 268-270**
Unmarried father, **Fam Law 179-194, 194, 323**
Unwritten law, husband and wife in ongoing marriage, **Fam Law 152-155**
Variability of marriage contract, **Fam Law 88-108**
Variations on theme of marriage, **Fam Law 33-36**
Visitation rights, **Fam Law 194, 318-323**
Void and voidable marriages defined, **Fam Law 61, 62**
Waiting period, marriage relationship, **Fam Law 52, 53**
Wrongful death, parent and child relationship, **Fam Law 231**
Wrongful life, parent and child relationship, **Fam Law 231, 232**

FEDERAL COMMUNICATIONS COMMISSION
Generally, **Mass Comm 334 et seq.**

FEDERAL DISABILITY LAW
Generally, **Fed Disab 1-8**
Access, **Fed Disab 124-184, 358-360**
Access board guidelines for purposes of ADA Titles II and III, **Fed Disab 174-184**
Accommodations, effects of, **Fed Disab 28, 29**
ADA, generally, **Fed Disab 70**
ADA Title I enforcement and remedies, employment discrimination, **Fed Disab 73, 74**
ADA Title II, generally, **Fed Disab 158-173**
ADA Title III, **Fed Disab 131-158, 174-184, 271, 301-304**
ADA Title IV, telecommunications relay services, **Fed Disab 283-286**
Advertisements, Fair Housing Act, **Fed Disab 189, 190**
Affirmative action plans, Rehabilitation Act of 1973, **Fed Disab 65-67**
Air Carrier Access Act of 1986, **Fed Disab 273-282**
Airline transportation, **Fed Disab 272-283**
Alcoholics, **Fed Disab 19-21**

FEDERAL DISABILITY LAW—Cont'd
Alternate dispute resolution, Americans with Disabilities Act, **Fed Disab 310**
Americans with Disabilities Act, generally, **Fed Disab 70**
Appropriateness/least restrictive environment, Individuals with Disabilities Education Act (IDEA), **Fed Disab 372, 373**
Architectural and Transportation Barriers Compliance Board, **Fed Disab 113-118**
Attorneys' fees, **Fed Disab 109, 110, 286, 287, 458-464**
Brokerage services, Fair Housing Act, **Fed Disab 191**
Burden of proof, Individuals with Disabilities Education Act (IDEA), **Fed Disab 442, 443**
Change or alteration, **Fed Disab 84, 153-156, 178, 179, 484-488**
Child Abuse Amendments of 1984, newborns with disabilities, **Fed Disab 324-328**
Coercion, **Fed Disab 191, 192, 304, 305**
Collective bargaining agreements, employment discrimination, **Fed Disab 84-86**
Commercial facilities, Title III of ADA, **Fed Disab 136, 137**
Communications, Title II of ADA, **Fed Disab 166, 167**
Compensatory educational services, Individuals with Disabilities Education Act (IDEA), **Fed Disab 456-458**
Confidentiality, Individuals with Disabilities Education Act (IDEA), **Fed Disab 358-360**
Conflicting state statutes, Fair Housing Act, **Fed Disab 195, 196**
Constitutional rights, generally, **Fed Disab 9-15**
Continuum of educational options, Individuals with Disabilities Education Act (IDEA), **Fed Disab 385, 386**
Cost, Individuals with Disabilities Education Act (IDEA), **Fed Disab 383, 384**
Damages, Individuals with Disabilities Education Act (IDEA), **Fed Disab 446-450**
Devices, effects of, **Fed Disab 28, 29**
Disciplining students with disabilities, **Fed Disab 479-495**
Discrimination solely on basis of disability, Rehabilitation Act of 1973, **Fed Disab 48-52**
Disparate impact, **Fed Disab 76-78, 192**

FEDERAL DISABILITY LAW—Cont'd
Disparate treatment, employment discrimination, **Fed Disab 76-78**
Drug abusers, **Fed Disab 19-21**
Due process, generally, **Fed Disab 14**
Education, generally, **Fed Disab 7**
Elementary and secondary education, Section 504 and the ADA, **Fed Disab 465-478**
Eleventh Amendment immunity, **Fed Disab 35, 36, 286**
Eligibility criteria, postsecondary education, **Fed Disab 212, 213**
Employment, **Fed Disab 13-15, 68-110**
Enforcement and remedies, **Fed Disab 63, 73, 74, 102-110, 156-158, 167-170, 196-202, 271, 333-336, 446-464**
Equal protection, **Fed Disab 9, 10, 13**
Exhaustion of administrative remedies, **Fed Disab 34, 35, 55-57, 435-437**
Existing facilities and programs, Title II of ADA, **Fed Disab 162-165**
Expungement of records, disciplining students with disabilities, **Fed Disab 494, 495**
Extended school year, Individuals with Disabilities Education Act (IDEA), **Fed Disab 384, 385**
Extracurricular activities, Individuals with Disabilities Education Act (IDEA), **Fed Disab 360-362**
Fair Housing Act, **Fed Disab 185-202**
Federal Architectural Barriers Act, **Fed Disab 111-123**
Former employees, employment discrimination, **Fed Disab 72, 73**
Franchisors and franchisees, Title III of ADA, **Fed Disab 139, 140**
General definition of disabled, **Fed Disab 16**
Harassment free environment provided, employment discrimination, **Fed Disab 101, 102**
Health services, access to programs and services, **Fed Disab 125-127**
Historic buildings, access board guidelines for purposes of ADA Titles II and III, **Fed Disab 179, 180**
Hostile learning environment, postsecondary education, **Fed Disab 231**

FEDERAL DISABILITY LAW—Cont'd

Housing, **Fed Disab 185-203**

Impartiality of hearing officers, Individuals with Disabilities Education Act (IDEA), **Fed Disab 443-445**

Inconsistent statements, employment discrimination, **Fed Disab 87, 88**

Independent educational evaluations, Individuals with Disabilities Education Act (IDEA), **Fed Disab 425-429**

Individuals with Disabilities Education Act (IDEA), **Fed Disab 330-464, 479**

In-school discipline, disciplining students with disabilities, **Fed Disab 493, 494**

Insurance and benefit plans, Americans with Disabilities Act, **Fed Disab 287-304**

Interference, Fair Housing Act, **Fed Disab 191, 192**

Irrebuttable presumption, constitutional rights, **Fed Disab 14**

Judicial review, **Fed Disab 57, 438-442**

Jury trial right, **Fed Disab 37-39, 57, 441**

Landlords and lessees, Title III of ADA, **Fed Disab 138, 139**

Mass ground transportation, generally, **Fed Disab 239-242**

Medicaid reimbursement, Individuals with Disabilities Education Act (IDEA), **Fed Disab 433, 434**

Medical examinations and inquiries, employment discrimination, **Fed Disab 95-101**

Mental impairment, **Fed Disab 18, 19**

Misbehavior at issue, disciplining students with disabilities, **Fed Disab 492, 493**

Multifamily dwellings, Fair Housing Act, **Fed Disab 188, 189**

Newborns with disabilities, **Fed Disab 311-329**

New construction or alterations, Title II of ADA, **Fed Disab 165, 166**

Newly altered facilities, Title III of ADA, **Fed Disab 153-156, 178, 179**

Newly constructed buildings or facilities, Titles II and III of ADA, **Fed Disab 153-156, 175-178**

Notice of disability, postsecondary education, **Fed Disab 230, 231**

Parking, uniform system for disabled parking, **Fed Disab 271, 272**

FEDERAL DISABILITY LAW—Cont'd

Persons in parental role, Individuals with Disabilities Education Act (IDEA), **Fed Disab 419-421**

Physical impairment, **Fed Disab 16-18**

Post employment medical examinations and inquiries, employment discrimination, **Fed Disab 98, 99**

Post-offer medical examinations and inquiries, employment discrimination, **Fed Disab 97, 98**

Postsecondary education, **Fed Disab 204-238**

Preemployment medical examinations and inquiries, employment discrimination, **Fed Disab 95-97**

Private clubs, Title III of ADA, **Fed Disab 137, 138**

Private insurance, Individuals with Disabilities Education Act (IDEA), **Fed Disab 429-433**

Private right of action, Rehabilitation Act of 1973, **Fed Disab 32-34, 55, 62**

Private schools, **Fed Disab 405-419, 476-478**

Public service announcements, Title IV of ADA, **Fed Disab 286**

Quality of life, newborns with disabilities, **Fed Disab 311-315**

Reasonable accommodations, **Fed Disab 78-82, 214-223**

Recipients of federal financial assistance, Rehabilitation Act of 1973, **Fed Disab 40-48**

Records, **Fed Disab 21, 22, 494, 495**

Rehabilitation Act of 1973, generally, **Fed Disab 30-67**

Reimbursement, Individuals with Disabilities Education Act (IDEA), **Fed Disab 433, 434, 450-455**

Religious entities, Title III of ADA, **Fed Disab 140, 141**

Removal of barriers from existing facilities, Title III of ADA, **Fed Disab 146-150**

Rental of house, Fair Housing Act, **Fed Disab 186-190**

Residential real estate, Fair Housing Act, **Fed Disab 190**

Retaliation, **Fed Disab 231, 304, 305**

Safety, **Fed Disab 91-93, 150, 151, 223-226**

Sale of house, Fair Housing Act, **Fed Disab 186-190**

Smoking, Americans with Disabilities Act, **Fed Disab 305, 306**

Sovereign immunity, Individuals with Disabilities Education Act (IDEA), **Fed Disab 455, 456**

FEDERAL DISABILITY LAW—Cont'd

Specifically excluded criteria, **Fed Disab 19**
Standing to sue, Rehabilitation Act of 1973, **Fed Disab 39, 40**
Statutes of limitation, **Fed Disab 36, 37, 437, 438**
Substantial limitation, **Fed Disab 24-28**
Television, access to programs and services, **Fed Disab 128-130**
Terminology and concepts, Individuals with Disabilities Education Act (IDEA), **Fed Disab 336-345**
Tests and testing, **Fed Disab 93-95, 421-425**
Third parties, **Fed Disab 62, 63, 429-434**
Transportation, **Fed Disab 239-282**
Undue hardship, employment discrimination, **Fed Disab 82-84**
Uniform system for disabled parking, **Fed Disab 271, 272**
Waivers, employment discrimination, **Fed Disab 87, 88**
Zero reject principle, Individuals with Disabilities Education Act (IDEA), **Fed Disab 360**
Zoning, Fair Housing Act, **Fed Disab 192-195**

FEDERAL ESTATE AND GIFT TAXATION

Generally, **Fed Est & Gift Tax 1-40**
Administration and administrative process, generally, **Fed Est & Gift Tax 30-34**
Alteration, transfers during life, **Fed Est & Gift Tax 174-179**
Alternates and alternatives
  alternate valuation date, **Fed Est & Gift Tax 312-317**
  present transfer tax system, alternatives to, **Fed Est & Gift Tax 439-471**
Amendment, transfers during life, **Fed Est & Gift Tax 174-179**
Annuities and employees death benefits, **Fed Est & Gift Tax 269-282**
Annulment, donative intent and consideration, **Fed Est & Gift Tax 132-142**
Appointment powers, estate and gift tax consequences, **Fed Est & Gift Tax 283-300**
Charitable contribution deduction, **Fed Est & Gift Tax 353-359**
Community property, **Fed Est & Gift Tax 229-242**
Conflicts, transfers during life, **Fed Est & Gift Tax 183-190**

FEDERAL ESTATE AND GIFT TAXATION—Cont'd
Congruence, transfers during life, **Fed Est & Gift Tax 183-190**
Constitutionality of transfer taxes, generally, **Fed Est & Gift Tax 37-40**
Credits against estate and gift taxes, **Fed Est & Gift Tax 404-416**
Crummey trusts, gifts to minors, **Fed Est & Gift Tax 341-345**
Debts, deductions for, **Fed Est & Gift Tax 346-353**
Deductions
  generally, **Fed Est & Gift Tax 346-361**
  marital deductions, infra
Disallowance of charitable contribution deduction, **Fed Est & Gift Tax 359, 360**
Divorce, donative intent and consideration, **Fed Est & Gift Tax 132-142**
Donative intent and consideration, **Fed Est & Gift Tax 113-142**
Employment
  annuities and employees death benefits, **Fed Est & Gift Tax 269-282**
  transfers during life, employment affected, **Fed Est & Gift Tax 174-179**
Estate tax, generally, **Fed Est & Gift Tax 14-16, 41-51**
Exemptions and exclusions, **Fed Est & Gift Tax 330-345**
Expenses, deductions for, **Fed Est & Gift Tax 346-353**
Federal income tax, fundamentals of estate planning, **Fed Est & Gift Tax 426-433**
Generation-skipping transfer tax
  generally, **Fed Est & Gift Tax 19-26, 55-79**
  deductions in, **Fed Est & Gift Tax 361**
  fundamentals of estate planning, **Fed Est & Gift Tax 433-438**
  liability and payment of taxes, **Fed Est & Gift Tax 416**
Gift tax, generally, **Fed Est & Gift Tax 16-19, 51-55**
Husband and wife. Marital deductions, infra
Inclusion, **Fed Est & Gift Tax 301-329**
Income tax, fundamentals of estate planning, **Fed Est & Gift Tax 426-433**
Incomplete transfers, transfers during life, **Fed Est & Gift Tax 157-160, 213-228**

FEDERAL ESTATE AND GIFT TAXATION—Cont'd

Jointly owned property, **Fed Est & Gift Tax 229-242**
Judicial process and procedure, generally, **Fed Est & Gift Tax 34, 35**
Legislation and legislative process, generally, **Fed Est & Gift Tax 28-30**
Liability and payment of taxes, **Fed Est & Gift Tax 404-416**
Life, transfers during, **Fed Est & Gift Tax 143-228**
Life insurance, **Fed Est & Gift Tax 243-268**
Losses, deductions for, **Fed Est & Gift Tax 346-353**
Marital deductions
  generally, **Fed Est & Gift Tax 362-403**
  estate planning, fundamentals of, **Fed Est & Gift Tax 418-422**
Marital property, donative intent and consideration, **Fed Est & Gift Tax 125-132**
Minors, gifts to, **Fed Est & Gift Tax 341-345**
Orphans' deduction, marital deductions and split gifts, **Fed Est & Gift Tax 402, 403**
Overlaps, transfers during life, **Fed Est & Gift Tax 183-190**
Payment of taxes, **Fed Est & Gift Tax 404-416**
Planning estates, fundamentals of, **Fed Est & Gift Tax 417-438**
Proceeds of life insurance, **Fed Est & Gift Tax 243-262**
Reciprocal trusts, transfers during life, **Fed Est & Gift Tax 199-202**
Reform proposals, **Fed Est & Gift Tax 439-471**
Reporting and payment of taxes, generally, **Fed Est & Gift Tax 26-28**
Retained life estate, transfers during life, **Fed Est & Gift Tax 160-174**
Revocation, transfers during life, **Fed Est & Gift Tax 174-179**
Separation, donative intent and consideration, **Fed Est & Gift Tax 132-142**
Special valuation rules, **Fed Est & Gift Tax 307-310**
Split gifts, **Fed Est & Gift Tax 362-403**
Spouses. Marital deductions, supra
Terminable interest rule, marital deductions and split gifts, **Fed Est & Gift Tax 383-391**

FEDERAL ESTATE AND GIFT TAXATION—Cont'd

Termination, transfers during life, **Fed Est & Gift Tax 174-179**
Transfers, generally, **Fed Est & Gift Tax 80-112**
Transfer tax advantages of lifetime gifts, fundamentals of estate planning, **Fed Est & Gift Tax 422-425**
Trusts
  gifts to minors, **Fed Est & Gift Tax 341-345**
  transfers during life, **Fed Est & Gift Tax 199-202**
Unified credit, credits against estate and gift taxes, **Fed Est & Gift Tax 404-409**
Valuation, **Fed Est & Gift Tax 301-329**
Widow's election, transfers during life, **Fed Est & Gift Tax 206-213**
Wife. Marital deductions, supra

FEDERAL INCOME TAXATION

Generally, **Fed Rules Evid 1-29**
Accelerated cost recovery, **Fed Rules Evid 157-178**
Accident and health plan benefits, **Fed Rules Evid 90-97**
Accretion, **Fed Rules Evid 52-56**
Accrual method, annual accounting, **Fed Rules Evid 310-318**
Alimony, **Fed Rules Evid 384-387**
Alternative minimum tax, **Fed Rules Evid 114-117**
Amortization, **Fed Rules Evid 157-178**
Annual accounting, **Fed Rules Evid 298-355**
Annual tax periods and accounting, **Fed Rules Evid 22-24**
Annuities, **Fed Rules Evid 86-90**
Anticipatory assignments of income, **Fed Rules Evid 360-367**
Assignments of income, **Fed Rules Evid 360-367**
Bad-debt losses, **Fed Rules Evid 231-236**
Business/profit losses, **Fed Rules Evid 219-224**
Capital asset, **Fed Rules Evid 444-455, 461-467**
Capital expenditures, **Fed Rules Evid 151-157**
Capital gains or losses, **Fed Rules Evid 435-444, 476-479**
Carryovers, capital losses, **Fed Rules Evid 441-444**
Cash method, annual accounting, **Fed Rules Evid 304-310**
Casualty losses, **Fed Rules Evid 224-231**

FEDERAL INCOME TAXATION—Cont'd

Charitable contributions, **Fed Rules Evid 249-276**
Compensation, **Fed Rules Evid 90-97, 136-138, 138-141, 330-342**
Complete trusts, **Fed Rules Evid 401-410**
Compound interest, **Fed Rules Evid 24-28**
Copyrights, **Fed Rules Evid 461**
Corporation income tax, generally, **Fed Rules Evid 7, 8**
Corporations (this index)
Costs and expenses, **Fed Rules Evid 138-141, 151-178, 276-282**
Credits, **Fed Rules Evid 178-184, 287-291**
Death benefits, **Fed Rules Evid 80-86**
Decedent, income in respect of, **Fed Rules Evid 387, 388**
Deductions, **Fed Rules Evid 142-150**
Deferred compensation, annual accounting, **Fed Rules Evid 330-342**
Defined and construed, **Fed Rules Evid 30-59**
Delayed recognition of capital gain or loss, **Fed Rules Evid 476-479**
Dental expenses, **Fed Rules Evid 276-282**
Dependents, **Fed Rules Evid 238-242, 282-287**
Depletion allowances, **Fed Rules Evid 187-191**
Depreciation, **Fed Rules Evid 157-178**
Disability payments, **Fed Rules Evid 90-97**
Discounts, **Fed Rules Evid 24-28**
Employee fringe benefits, **Fed Rules Evid 48, 49, 107-114**
Estates and trusts, **Fed Rules Evid 389-410**
Exceptions, exemptions, or exclusions, **Fed Rules Evid 60-120, 133-136, 282-287 449-455**
Family partnerships, **Fed Rules Evid 410-418**
Fellowships, **Fed Rules Evid 77-79**
Gain, income as, **Fed Rules Evid 38-40**
Gifts, **Fed Rules Evid 48, 49, 61-74, 249-276, 360-381**
Graduated rates, **Fed Rules Evid 17-20**
Gross income, statutory inclusion and exclusion from, **Fed Rules Evid 60-120**
Gross receipts, **Fed Rules Evid 32-34**

FEDERAL INCOME TAXATION—Cont'd
Holding period, **Fed Rules Evid 459-461**
Household expenses necessary for gainful employment, **Fed Rules Evid 238-242**
Illegal receipts, **Fed Rules Evid 49-52**
Imputed income, **Fed Rules Evid 44-48**
Income averaging, annual accounting, **Fed Rules Evid 353, 354**
Insurance, **Fed Rules Evid 80-86, 90-97**
Interest on money, **Fed Rules Evid 17-20; Fed Rules Evid 24-28, 97-100, 200-211, 419-486**
International Taxation (this index)
Inventories, annual accounting, **Fed Rules Evid 325-330**
Investment credit, **Fed Rules Evid 178-184**
Judicial definitions of income, **Fed Rules Evid 35, 36**
Judicial procedure, **Fed Rules Evid 11, 12**
Leasing and tax allowances, **Fed Rules Evid 184-187**
Legislation and administration, **Fed Rules Evid 8-11**
Life insurance, **Fed Rules Evid 80-86**
Limitations on business deductions, **Fed Rules Evid 142-150**
Lodging and meals, **Fed Rules Evid 100-107**
Losses, generally, **Fed Rules Evid 214-219**
Mallinckrodt trusts, **Fed Rules Evid 396**
Meals and lodging, **Fed Rules Evid 100-107**
Medical expenses, **Fed Rules Evid 276-282**
Minimum tax on tax preference income, **Fed Rules Evid 482-484**
Mixed deductions, **Fed Rules Evid 195-245**
Ordinary and necessary expenses, **Fed Rules Evid 130-132**
Partners and partnerships. **Federal Income Taxation of Partners and Partnerships** (this index)
Partnerships. **Federal Income Taxation of Partners and Partnerships** (this index)
Passive losses, **Fed Rules Evid 236-238**
Patents, **Fed Rules Evid 461**
Payroll taxes, **Fed Rules Evid 20-22**
Personal deductions, **Fed Rules Evid 195-245, 246-297**
Personal exemptions, **Fed Rules Evid 282-287**

FEDERAL INCOME TAXATION—Cont'd

Personal injury and sickness compensation, **Fed Rules Evid 90-97**
Personal service income, former minimum tax on, **Fed Rules Evid 484-486**
Prizes and awards, **Fed Rules Evid 74-77**
Profit-related deductions, **Fed Rules Evid 121-194**
Progressive tax, **Fed Rules Evid 17-20**
Property settlements, **Fed Rules Evid 381-384**
Public policy exception, **Fed Rules Evid 133-136**
Quasi-capital assets, **Fed Rules Evid 461-467**
Realization, **Fed Rules Evid 40-44, 342-345**
Reasonable compensation, **Fed Rules Evid 136-138**
Recapture of depreciation, **Fed Rules Evid 467-476**
Receipts and disbursements, annual accounting, **Fed Rules Evid 304-310**
Recognition and nonrecognition, annual accounting, **Fed Rules Evid 345-353**
Retirement savings, annual accounting, **Fed Rules Evid 330-342**
Return of capital, **Fed Rules Evid 32-35**
Sales, **Fed Rules Evid 422-435, 455-459**
Scholarships, **Fed Rules Evid 77-79**
Shifting income, **Fed Rules Evid 356-418**
Significance of definition of income, **Fed Rules Evid 36-38**
Simple trusts, **Fed Rules Evid 399, 400**
Standard deduction, **Fed Rules Evid 291-296**
Statutory inclusion and exclusion from gross income, **Fed Rules Evid 60-120**
Support of person, **Fed Rules Evid 384-387**
Tax shelters, annual accounting, **Fed Rules Evid 330-342**
Terms, **Fed Rules Evid 12-17**
Time value of money, **Fed Rules Evid 24-28**
Traveling expenses, **Fed Rules Evid 138-141**
Trusts, **Fed Rules Evid 389-410**
Withholding payroll taxes, **Fed Rules Evid 20-22**
Zero-bracket amount, **Fed Rules Evid 291-296**

FEDERAL INCOME TAXATION OF PARTNERS AND PARTNERSHIPS

Generally, **Fed Income Tax, Partn 1**
Accounting, generally, **Fed Income Tax, Partn 72-111**
Accounts receivable and accounts payable, **Fed Income Tax, Partn 173-175, 244-246**
Adjustments
  death of partner, **Fed Income Tax, Partn 346-348**
  distributions, **Fed Income Tax, Partn 292-302**
  outside basis, partnership tax accounting, **Fed Income Tax, Partn 79-86**
Aggregate and entity concepts, **Fed Income Tax, Partn 1, 2**
Allocations
  generally, **Fed Income Tax, Partn 112-180**
  distributive share allocations when interests shift, **Fed Income Tax, Partn 274-277**
  Section 707 payments versus special allocations, **Fed Income Tax, Partn 220-224**
  transfers of partnership interests, **Fed Income Tax, Partn 241, 242**
  treatment of transferee partner, **Fed Income Tax, Partn 257-261**
Alternate economic effect test, allocations, **Fed Income Tax, Partn 129-134**
Amount realized, transfers of partnership interests, **Fed Income Tax, Partn 240, 241**
Ancillary consequences, Section 707(a) and 707(c), **Fed Income Tax, Partn 218**
Anti-abuse rules, recourse liabilities, **Fed Income Tax, Partn 196, 197**
Assumption, definition of, **Fed Income Tax, Partn 184, 185**
At-risk rules, partnership tax accounting, **Fed Income Tax, Partn 92-99**
Avoidance of general utilities repeal, disguised sales between partners and partnerships, **Fed Income Tax, Partn 234**
Basis allocation
  transfers of partnership interests, generally, **Fed Income Tax, Partn 241, 242**

FEDERAL INCOME TAXATION OF PARTNERS AND PARTNERSHIPS—Cont'd

Basis allocation—Cont'd
- treatment of transferee partner, **Fed Income Tax, Partn 257-261**

Book/tax disparities
- capital accounts, generally, **Fed Income Tax, Partn 17-19**
- maintenance of capital accounts, **Fed Income Tax, Partn 127, 128**

Capital accounts
- generally, **Fed Income Tax, Partn 10-19**
- allocations, capital account analysis, **Fed Income Tax, Partn 118-120**
- distributions, **Fed Income Tax, Partn 304-309**
- maintenance of capital accounts, **Fed Income Tax, Partn 126-129**
- organization of partnership, **Fed Income Tax, Partn 49-51, 55-63**
- Section 707(a) and 707(c), capital expenditures, **Fed Income Tax, Partn 217, 218**
- treatment of transferee partner, **Fed Income Tax, Partn 264-266**

Ceiling-rule distortions, Section 704(c) allocations, **Fed Income Tax, Partn 164-168**

Centralized management, partnership versus corporation, **Fed Income Tax, Partn 28, 29**

Character or characterization
- organization of partnership, character of contributed property, **Fed Income Tax, Partn 51-53**
- Section 707(a) and 707(c), **Fed Income Tax, Partn 211-214**

Closing of taxable year
- death of partner, **Fed Income Tax, Partn 340, 341**
- distributive share allocations when interests shift, **Fed Income Tax, Partn 272, 273**

Constructive liquidation, recourse liabilities, **Fed Income Tax, Partn 186-189**

Continuity of life, partnership versus corporation, **Fed Income Tax, Partn 27, 28**

FEDERAL INCOME TAXATION OF PARTNERS AND PARTNERSHIPS—Cont'd

Contributions
- capital accounts, **Fed Income Tax, Partn 10-12**
- organization of partnership, **Fed Income Tax, Partn 38-48, 51-53, 56, 57**
- transactional approach, **Fed Income Tax, Partn 4, 5**

Conversion, nonrecourse deductions, **Fed Income Tax, Partn 161**

Coownership, partnership status, **Fed Income Tax, Partn 22, 23**

Corporation, partnership versus, **Fed Income Tax, Partn 25-33**

Current distributions, **Fed Income Tax, Partn 280-284, 315-317**

Death or retirement of partner, **Fed Income Tax, Partn 319-348**

Deductions
- conversion, nonrecourse deductions, **Fed Income Tax, Partn 161**
- distributions, nonrecourse deductions, **Fed Income Tax, Partn 157-160**
- minimum gain, nonrecourse deductions, **Fed Income Tax, Partn 149-157**
- nonrecourse deductions, allocations, **Fed Income Tax, Partn 145-161**
- safe harbor, nonrecourse deductions, **Fed Income Tax, Partn 146-149**
- timing of income and deduction, Section 707(a) and 707(c), **Fed Income Tax, Partn 214-217**

Deemed-sale adjustment, capital accounts, **Fed Income Tax, Partn 19**

Definition of liability and assumption, **Fed Income Tax, Partn 184, 185**

Direct payment obligations, recourse liabilities, **Fed Income Tax, Partn 189-192**

Disguised actions
- payments for services, Section 707 payments versus special allocations, **Fed Income Tax, Partn 222-224**
- sales between partners and partnerships, **Fed Income Tax, Partn 224-234**

Distributions
- generally, **Fed Income Tax, Partn 279-318**

FEDERAL INCOME TAXATION OF PARTNERS AND PARTNERSHIPS—Cont'd

Distributions—Cont'd
- alternate economic effect test, **Fed Income Tax, Partn 131-133**
- nonrecourse deductions, **Fed Income Tax, Partn 157-160**
- Section 704(c) allocations, **Fed Income Tax, Partn 171-173**
- shifted interests, distributive share allocations, **Fed Income Tax, Partn 272-278**
- transactional approach, **Fed Income Tax, Partn 4, 5**
- treatment of transferee partner, **Fed Income Tax, Partn 266**

Economic effect, allocations, **Fed Income Tax, Partn 118-125**

Economic risk of loss, recourse liabilities, **Fed Income Tax, Partn 185, 186**

Elections
- accounting, **Fed Income Tax, Partn 77-79, 110, 111**
- distributions, **Fed Income Tax, Partn 302-304**
- status of partnership, election out, **Fed Income Tax, Partn 24, 25**
- treatment of transferee partner, **Fed Income Tax, Partn 266, 267**

Entity-level, partnership tax accounting, **Fed Income Tax, Partn 75-77**

Entrepreneurial risk, disguised sales between partners and partnerships, **Fed Income Tax, Partn 225, 226**

Estate tax inclusion and basis, death of partner, **Fed Income Tax, Partn 341**

Exchanges, transfers of partnership interests, **Fed Income Tax, Partn 251-253**

Expected distributions, alternate economic effect test, **Fed Income Tax, Partn 131-133**

Family partnerships, allocations, **Fed Income Tax, Partn 175-180**

Free transferability, partnership versus corporation, **Fed Income Tax, Partn 31, 32**

Goodwill
- death or retirement of partner, **Fed Income Tax, Partn 327-329**

FEDERAL INCOME TAXATION OF PARTNERS AND PARTNERSHIPS—Cont'd

Goodwill—Cont'd
- treatment of transferee partner, **Fed Income Tax, Partn 261, 262**

Guaranteed minimum, Section 707(a) and 707(c), **Fed Income Tax, Partn 218-220**

Incorporation of partnership, transfers of partnership interests, **Fed Income Tax, Partn 253**

Installment sales, transfers of partnership interests, **Fed Income Tax, Partn 250, 251**

Interest-only guarantee, recourse liabilities, **Fed Income Tax, Partn 198, 199**

Interim adjustments, transfers of partnership interests, **Fed Income Tax, Partn 242**

Inventory, transfers of partnership interests, **Fed Income Tax, Partn 246-250**

Investment partnerships, organization of partnership, **Fed Income Tax, Partn 53, 54**

IRD attributable to partnership interests, death of partner, **Fed Income Tax, Partn 342-346**

Joint-profit motive, partnership status, **Fed Income Tax, Partn 21, 22**

Liabilities of partnership
- generally, **Fed Income Tax, Partn 181-209**
- disguised sales between partners and partnerships, **Fed Income Tax, Partn 229-233**
- distributions, **Fed Income Tax, Partn 289-291**
- maintenance of capital accounts, **Fed Income Tax, Partn 127**

Limitations on losses, partnership tax accounting, **Fed Income Tax, Partn 86-92**

Limited liability, partnership versus corporation, **Fed Income Tax, Partn 29, 30**

Limits on flexibility, **Fed Income Tax, Partn 7, 8**

Liquidation
- death or retirement of partner, **Fed Income Tax, Partn 337-340**
- distributions, **Fed Income Tax, Partn 285-289, 310-315**

FEDERAL INCOME TAXATION OF PARTNERS AND PARTNERSHIPS—Cont'd

Liquidation—Cont'd
recourse liabilities, **Fed Income Tax, Partn 186-189**
Loans to partners, recourse liabilities, **Fed Income Tax, Partn 195, 196**
Losses
capital accounts, **Fed Income Tax, Partn 14-16**
disallowance, sales or exchanges with respect to controlled partnership, **Fed Income Tax, Partn 235-237**
Maintenance of capital accounts, **Fed Income Tax, Partn 126-129**
Minimum gain, nonrecourse deductions, **Fed Income Tax, Partn 149-157**
Nonrecourse deductions, allocations, **Fed Income Tax, Partn 145-161**
Nontax considerations, choice of business form, **Fed Income Tax, Partn 8, 9**
Optional adjustments
death of partner, **Fed Income Tax, Partn 346-348**
partnership distributions, **Fed Income Tax, Partn 292-302**
transactional approach, **Fed Income Tax, Partn 6**
treatment of transferee partner, **Fed Income Tax, Partn 253-257**
Optional revaluation, partnership distributions, **Fed Income Tax, Partn 306-309**
Ordinary income treatment, sales or exchanges with respect to controlled partnership, **Fed Income Tax, Partn 237, 238**
Organization of partnership, **Fed Income Tax, Partn 37-71**
Passive-income exception, publicly-traded partnerships, **Fed Income Tax, Partn 35**
Passive loss limitations, partnership tax accounting, **Fed Income Tax, Partn 99-105**
Pledge of property as security, recourse liabilities, **Fed Income Tax, Partn 199**
Primary test, allocations, **Fed Income Tax, Partn 118**
Profits interest, organization of partnership, **Fed Income Tax, Partn 55, 56, 63-69**

FEDERAL INCOME TAXATION OF PARTNERS AND PARTNERSHIPS—Cont'd

Proportionate or disproportionate
- distributions, **Fed Income Tax, Partn 309-318**
- loss sharing disproportionate, recourse liabilities, **Fed Income Tax, Partn 192-194**

Publicly-traded partnerships, **Fed Income Tax, Partn 33-36**

Qualified income offset, alternate economic effect test, **Fed Income Tax, Partn 133, 134**

Reallocation, family partnerships, **Fed Income Tax, Partn 177-180**

Recapture property, organization of partnership, **Fed Income Tax, Partn 53**

Receipt of partnership interest for services, organization of partnership, **Fed Income Tax, Partn 54-71**

Recourse liabilities, **Fed Income Tax, Partn 185-199**

Revaluation of property, Section 704(c) allocations, **Fed Income Tax, Partn 168-171**

Safe harbor
- nonrecourse deductions, **Fed Income Tax, Partn 146-149**
- publicly-traded partnerships, **Fed Income Tax, Partn 34, 35**

Sales
- controlled partnership, sales or exchanges with respect to, **Fed Income Tax, Partn 235-238**
- death or retirement of partner, **Fed Income Tax, Partn 337-340**
- disguised sales between partners and partnerships, **Fed Income Tax, Partn 224-234**
- transfers of partnership interests, **Fed Income Tax, Partn 250, 251**

S corporations and partnerships, choice of business form, **Fed Income Tax, Partn 9**

Section 707(a) and 707(c), generally, **Fed Income Tax, Partn 211-220**

Self-charged interest, partnership tax accounting, **Fed Income Tax, Partn 103**

Services
- disguised payments for services, Section 707 payments versus special allocations, **Fed Income Tax, Partn 222-224**

FEDERAL INCOME TAXATION OF PARTNERS AND PARTNERSHIPS—Cont'd

Services—Cont'd
- receipt of partnership interest for, **Fed Income Tax, Partn 54-71**

Shifting allocations, substantiality, **Fed Income Tax, Partn 135-137**

Special allocations, Section 707 payments versus, **Fed Income Tax, Partn 220-224**

Special partner's interest test, substantiality, **Fed Income Tax, Partn 144, 145**

Status of partnership, **Fed Income Tax, Partn 19-25**

Step-transaction doctrine, death or retirement of partner, **Fed Income Tax, Partn 338**

Subsequent dispositions, partnership distributions, **Fed Income Tax, Partn 291, 292**

Subsequent distributions, treatment of transferee partner, **Fed Income Tax, Partn 266**

Substantiality, allocations, **Fed Income Tax, Partn 135-143**

Substantially appreciated inventory, transfers of partnership interests, **Fed Income Tax, Partn 246-250**

Tax shelters, limits on flexibility, **Fed Income Tax, Partn 7, 8**

Termination of partnership, **Fed Income Tax, Partn 272-278**

Tiered partnerships
- distributive share allocations when interests shift, **Fed Income Tax, Partn 277**
- transfers of partnership interests, **Fed Income Tax, Partn 250**
- treatment of transferee partner, **Fed Income Tax, Partn 267, 268**

Time
- income and deduction timing, Section 707(a) and 707(c), **Fed Income Tax, Partn 214-217**
- payments, death or retirement of partner, **Fed Income Tax, Partn 333-337**

Time-value of money, recourse liabilities, **Fed Income Tax, Partn 197, 198**

Transactional approach, **Fed Income Tax, Partn 2-7**

Transactions, generally, **Fed Income Tax, Partn 210-238**

FEDERAL INCOME TAXATION OF PARTNERS AND PARTNERSHIPS—Cont'd

Transfer of partnership interest
 generally, **Fed Income Tax, Partn 239-278**
 maintenance of capital accounts, **Fed Income Tax, Partn 128, 129**
 transactional approach, **Fed Income Tax, Partn 6**
Transitory allocations, substantiality, **Fed Income Tax, Partn 137-141**
Two-person partnership, death or retirement of partner, **Fed Income Tax, Partn 338-340**
Unrealized receivables, transfers of partnership interests, **Fed Income Tax, Partn 244-246**
Vested capital interest, organization of partnership, **Fed Income Tax, Partn 57-63**
Vested profits interest, organization of partnership, **Fed Income Tax, Partn 63-69**

FEDERALISM

Constitutional Federalism (this index)

FEDERAL JURISDICTION

Abstention and related doctrines, **Fed Jurisd 173-183**
Administrative questions, cases and controversies, **Fed Jurisd 30, 31**
Admiralty, **Fed Jurisd 110-116**
Advisory opinions, cases and controversies, **Fed Jurisd 8-10**
Amount in controversy, **Fed Jurisd 143-147**
Ancillary jurisdiction, complete diversity, **Fed Jurisd 125, 126**
Appellate review
 generally, **Fed Jurisd 3-6, 45-90**
 three-judge courts, **Fed Jurisd 207-209**
Citizenship of corporation determined, diversity cases, **Fed Jurisd 131**
Civil rights removal, **Fed Jurisd 196-201**
Collateral review, **Fed Jurisd 45-90**
Common law, law applicable in federal courts, **Fed Jurisd 226-230**

FEDERAL JURISDICTION—Cont'd

Complete diversity, **Fed Jurisd 122-128**
Conflict of laws, law applicable in federal courts, **Fed Jurisd 223-225**
Congress
 power to regulate federal jurisdiction, **Fed Jurisd 31-44**
 sovereign immunity, **Fed Jurisd 169-171**
Constitutional law
 generally, **Fed Jurisd 3-44**
 abstention and related doctrines, **Fed Jurisd 176, 177**
 identification of federal question cases, **Fed Jurisd 91-94**
 three-judge courts, **Fed Jurisd 203-206**
Corporations and associations, diversity cases, **Fed Jurisd 129-136**
Courts, generally, **Fed Jurisd 3-44**
Damages, sovereign immunity, **Fed Jurisd 162-169**
Derivative suits, diversity cases, **Fed Jurisd 134-136**
Diversity cases, **Fed Jurisd 117-134**
Domestic relations, abstention and related doctrines, **Fed Jurisd 179-181**
Erie doctrine, law applicable in federal courts, **Fed Jurisd 217-219**
Exclusive jurisdiction, **Fed Jurisd 138, 139**
Exhaustion of state remedies, abstention and related doctrines, **Fed Jurisd 181-183**
Federal common law, law applicable in federal courts, **Fed Jurisd 226-230**
Federal law in state courts, law applicable in federal courts, **Fed Jurisd 230, 231**
Federal Rules of Civil Procedure, law applicable in federal courts, **Fed Jurisd 221, 222**
Finality, cases and controversies, **Fed Jurisd 7**
Forum, obligation of states to provide, **Fed Jurisd 141, 142**
Forum non conveniens, **Fed Jurisd 214-216**
Historical introduction, **Fed Jurisd 1, 2**
Identification of federal question cases, **Fed Jurisd 91-105**
Incorporation of federal or state law, identification of federal question cases, **Fed Jurisd 100-105**

FEDERAL JURISDICTION—Cont'd
Injunctions against suit, **Fed Jurisd 184-195**
Interpleader, complete diversity, **Fed Jurisd 123-125**
Judges, three-judge courts, **Fed Jurisd 202-209**
Judicial review, generally, **Fed Jurisd 3-6**
Jurisdictional amount, **Fed Jurisd 143-147**
Local governments, sovereign immunity, **Fed Jurisd 162-169**
Mootness, cases and controversies, **Fed Jurisd 24-26**
Multiple citizenships, diversity cases, **Fed Jurisd 133, 134**
Multiple claims, jurisdictional amount, **Fed Jurisd 145-147**
Officers of government, sovereign immunity, **Fed Jurisd 156-169, 171, 172**
Pendent jurisdiction, federal question cases, **Fed Jurisd 105-109**
Pending actions, abstention and related doctrines, **Fed Jurisd 179-181**
Place of trial, **Fed Jurisd 210-216**
Political questions, cases and controversies, **Fed Jurisd 26-30**
Postconviction review, **Fed Jurisd 54-82**
Presidential immunity, sovereign immunity, **Fed Jurisd 169-171**
Probate, abstention and related doctrines, **Fed Jurisd 179-181**
Raising jurisdictional issues, **Fed Jurisd 137, 138**
Remote federal issues, identification of federal question cases, **Fed Jurisd 94-96**
Removal
  generally, **Fed Jurisd 139, 140**
  civil rights removal, **Fed Jurisd 196-201**
Ripeness, cases and controversies, **Fed Jurisd 20-24**
Separate-claim removal, complete diversity, **Fed Jurisd 126-128**
Service of process, **Fed Jurisd 210-213**
Sovereign immunity, **Fed Jurisd 148-172**
Standing, cases and controversies, **Fed Jurisd 10-20**
State courts
  federal law in, **Fed Jurisd 230, 231**
  sovereign immunity, state court jurisdiction over federal officers, **Fed Jurisd 171, 172**
Substance and procedure, law applicable in federal courts, **Fed Jurisd 219-221**

FEDERAL JURISDICTION—Cont'd
Supreme Court review of state judgments, **Fed Jurisd 45-54**
Three-judge courts, **Fed Jurisd 202-209**
Venue, **Fed Jurisd 210-213**
Waiver, sovereign immunity, **Fed Jurisd 152-156**
Well-pleaded complaint rule, identification of federal question cases, **Fed Jurisd 96-100**

FEDERAL LAW OF EMPLOYMENT DISCRIMINATION
Employment Discrimination (this index)

FEDERAL REGULATION
Individual Employee Rights (this index)

FEDERAL RULES OF EVIDENCE
Generally, **Fed Rules Evid 1-15**
Abandonment of res gestae, exceptions to hearsay rule, **Fed Rules Evid 340-342**
Acknowledged documents, self-authentication, **Fed Rules Evid 454, 455**
Agent, hearsay, **Fed Rules Evid 324, 325**
Alcohol use, witnesses, **Fed Rules Evid 169, 187, 188**
Amendments, **Fed Rules Evid 487**
Ancient documents, **Fed Rules Evid 380, 440**
Animations, demonstrative evidence, **Fed Rules Evid 82-85**
Applicability of rules, **Fed Rules Evid 482-486**
Attorneys, **Fed Rules Evid 155-159, 324, 325**
Authentication and identification, **Fed Rules Evid 423-457**
Baptismal certificates, exceptions to hearsay rule, **Fed Rules Evid 374, 375**
Best evidence rule, contents of writings, recordings and photographs, **Fed Rules Evid 458-460**
Bias of witness, **Fed Rules Evid 188-190**
Boundaries, exceptions to hearsay rule, **Fed Rules Evid 387, 391**
Business records, **Fed Rules Evid 354-361, 462, 463**
Calling of witnesses by court, **Fed Rules Evid 244, 245**

FEDERAL RULES OF EVIDENCE—Cont'd

Certified copies of public records, self-authentication, **Fed Rules Evid 450, 451**

Chain of custody, authentication and identification, **Fed Rules Evid 426, 427**

Character and reputation, **Fed Rules Evid 96-109, 191-200, 388**

Characteristics, authentication and identification, **Fed Rules Evid 432, 433**

Charts, demonstrative evidence, **Fed Rules Evid 81**

Child molestation cases, **Fed Rules Evid 146-150**

Coercion, witness, **Fed Rules Evid 188-190**

Collateral matters, admissibility of evidence of contents, **Fed Rules Evid 473, 474**

Commercial paper, self-authentication, **Fed Rules Evid 456**

Common knowledge, expert testimony, **Fed Rules Evid 255, 256**

Competency of witness, **Fed Rules Evid 163-169**

Compromise and settlement, relevancy, **Fed Rules Evid 116-119**

Computer records, authentication and identification, **Fed Rules Evid 441-443**

Conflicting presumptions, **Fed Rules Evid 55, 56**

Confrontation clause, hearsay rule and, **Fed Rules Evid 331-335**

Confusion, exclusion of relevant evidence on grounds of, **Fed Rules Evid 91-95**

Construction, **Fed Rules Evid 2, 3**

Conviction of crime, **Fed Rules Evid 201-217, 389, 390**

Corruption, witness, **Fed Rules Evid 188-190**

Courts, generally, **Fed Rules Evid 479-481**

Credibility of witnesses, generally, **Fed Rules Evid 178-191**

Criminal cases, presumptions in, **Fed Rules Evid 67-69**

Cross examination on writing, original required, **Fed Rules Evid 468, 469**

Definitions, **Fed Rules Evid 283-330, 401-403**

Demonstrative and real evidence, **Fed Rules Evid 76-86**

Disclosure of facts or data underlying expert opinion, **Fed Rules Evid 271-275**

Documents affecting interest in property, exceptions to hearsay rule, **Fed Rules Evid 377-379**

FEDERAL RULES OF EVIDENCE—Cont'd
Domestic public documents, self-authentication, **Fed Rules Evid 446, 447**
Drawings, demonstrative evidence, **Fed Rules Evid 81**
Drug use, witnesses, **Fed Rules Evid 169, 187, 188**
Duplicates, **Fed Rules Evid 463, 469, 470**
Emotional condition, exceptions to hearsay rule, **Fed Rules Evid 343-347**
Errors, generally, **Fed Rules Evid 5-15**
Exceptions or exclusions, **Fed Rules Evid 91-105, 246-248, 282-421**
Excited utterance, exceptions to hearsay rule, **Fed Rules Evid 340-342**
Exclusions or exceptions, **Fed Rules Evid 91-105, 246-248, 282-421**
Experiments, demonstrative and real evidence, **Fed Rules Evid 86, 87**
Expert and opinion testimony, **Fed Rules Evid 249-280, 430-432**
Family records, exceptions to hearsay rule, **Fed Rules Evid 376, 385, 386, 416, 417**
Foreign public documents, self-authentication, **Fed Rules Evid 448, 449**
Guilty plea, hearsay, **Fed Rules Evid 319**
Habit, relevancy, **Fed Rules Evid 109-114**
Handwriting, authentication and identification, **Fed Rules Evid 428-430**
Hearsay, **Fed Rules Evid 282-421**
Hearsay within hearsay, **Fed Rules Evid 419, 420**
History, exceptions to hearsay rule, **Fed Rules Evid 385-387, 391, 416, 417**
Husband-wife privilege, **Fed Rules Evid 159, 160**
Identification, authentication and, **Fed Rules Evid 423-457**
Imminent death, exceptions to hearsay rule, **Fed Rules Evid 410, 411**
Impeachment, **Fed Rules Evid 178-191, 201-217**
In limine motions, **Fed Rules Evid 13, 14**
Instructions to jury, **Fed Rules Evid 56-61**

FEDERAL RULES OF EVIDENCE—Cont'd

Interpretation of definition of hearsay, **Fed Rules Evid 307-308**
Interpreters, witnesses, **Fed Rules Evid 173, 174**
Interrogation of witnesses, **Fed Rules Evid 218-232, 244, 245**
Irrelevant evidence inadmissible, **Fed Rules Evid 89-91**
Judge as witness, competency of, **Fed Rules Evid 174, 175**
Judicial notice, **Fed Rules Evid 27-40**
Jury and jury trial, **Fed Rules Evid 175-178, 479-481**
Lawyer-client privilege, **Fed Rules Evid 155-159**
Learned treatises, exceptions to hearsay rule, **Fed Rules Evid 383, 384**
Liability insurance, relevancy, **Fed Rules Evid 129, 130**
Limited admissibility, **Fed Rules Evid 21-23**
Lost or destroyed original, **Fed Rules Evid 472**
Maps, demonstrative evidence, **Fed Rules Evid 81**
Market reports, exceptions to hearsay rule, **Fed Rules Evid 381, 382**
Marriage certificates, exceptions to hearsay rule, **Fed Rules Evid 374, 375**
Medical diagnosis or treatment, exceptions to hearsay rule, **Fed Rules Evid 348-351**
Medical expenses, payment of, **Fed Rules Evid 119, 120**
Mental capacity of witness, **Fed Rules Evid 166-169**
Mental condition, exceptions to hearsay rule, **Fed Rules Evid 343-347**
Models, demonstrative evidence, **Fed Rules Evid 81**
Newspapers, self-authentication, **Fed Rules Evid 453**
Notice to produce original, **Fed Rules Evid 473**
Oath or affirmation, witnesses, **Fed Rules Evid 172, 173**
Official publications, self-authentication, **Fed Rules Evid 452**
Original required, **Fed Rules Evid 464-469**
Periodicals, self-authentication, **Fed Rules Evid 453**
Personal injuries, real evidence, **Fed Rules Evid 80, 81**
Personal knowledge, witnesses, **Fed Rules Evid 170-172, 187**
Photographs, **Fed Rules Evid 82-85, 458-481**
Physical condition, exceptions to hearsay rule, **Fed Rules Evid 343-347**

FEDERAL RULES OF EVIDENCE—Cont'd

Plain error, **Fed Rules Evid 14, 15**
Pleas, **Fed Rules Evid 121-129, 319**
Prejudice, exclusion of relevant evidence on grounds of, **Fed Rules Evid 91-95**
Preliminary questions, **Fed Rules Evid 15-21**
Presence impression, exceptions to hearsay rule, **Fed Rules Evid 339, 340**
Presentation, mode and order of, **Fed Rules Evid 218-232**
Presumptions and burden of proof, **Fed Rules Evid 41-69**
Presumptions under act of Congress, self-authentication, **Fed Rules Evid 456**
Prima facie, presumptions and burden of proof, **Fed Rules Evid 46-48, 53, 54**
Prior testimony, **Fed Rules Evid 238-244, 404-409**
Privileges, **Fed Rules Evid 151-161**
Public records, **Fed Rules Evid 364-369, 371, 372, 438, 439**
Qualification of experts, **Fed Rules Evid 254, 255**
Rape cases, **Fed Rules Evid 130-143**
Recorded recollection, exceptions to hearsay rule, **Fed Rules Evid 352, 353**
Records and recordings, **Fed Rules Evid 23-26, 354-382, 450, 451, 458-481**
Refreshing memory, **Fed Rules Evid 232-238**
Relevancy, **Fed Rules Evid 73-150**
Religious organization records, exceptions to hearsay rule, **Fed Rules Evid 373**
Res gestae, exceptions to hearsay rule, **Fed Rules Evid 340-342**
Scientific knowledge of expert, reliability of, **Fed Rules Evid 256-262**
Self-authentication, **Fed Rules Evid 444-456**
Sex offense cases, **Fed Rules Evid 130-146, 149, 150**
Sound recordings, authentication and identification, **Fed Rules Evid 434, 435**
State law, applicability of, **Fed Rules Evid 70, 71**
Statements against interest, exceptions to hearsay rule, **Fed Rules Evid 412-415**

FEDERAL RULES OF EVIDENCE—Cont'd

Subscribing witness testimony, self-authentication, **Fed Rules Evid 457**

Subsequent remedial measures, relevancy, **Fed Rules Evid 115, 116**

Technical knowledge of expert, reliability of, **Fed Rules Evid 256-262**

Telegrams, contents of, **Fed Rules Evid 462, 463**

Telephone conversations, authentication and identification, **Fed Rules Evid 436, 437**

Third person, original in possession of, **Fed Rules Evid 472, 473**

Trade inscriptions, self-authentication, **Fed Rules Evid 454**

Treatises, exceptions to hearsay rule, **Fed Rules Evid 383, 384**

Ultimate issues, opinion on, **Fed Rules Evid 267-271**

Untrustworthy partiality, witnesses, **Fed Rules Evid 188-190**

Videotapes, demonstrative evidence, **Fed Rules Evid 82-85**

Vital statistics records, exceptions to hearsay rule, **Fed Rules Evid 370, 371**

Voice identification, authentication and identification, **Fed Rules Evid 434, 435**

Waiver or estoppel, **Fed Rules Evid 5-11, 160, 161**

Waste of time, exclusion of relevant evidence on grounds of, **Fed Rules Evid 91-95**

Witnesses, generally, **Fed Rules Evid 163-348**

Writings, contents of, **Fed Rules Evid 458-481**

X-rays, demonstrative evidence, **Fed Rules Evid 85, 86**

FEDERAL TAXES

Corporations (this index)

Estate tax. **Federal Estate and Gift Taxation** (this index)

Federal Income Taxation of Partners and Partnerships (this index)

Federal Income Taxation (this index)

Gift tax. **Federal Estate and Gift Taxation** (this index)

Income tax

  Corporations (this index)

  Partners and Partnerships (this index)

FEDERAL TAXES—Cont'd
Income tax—Cont'd
stockholders. **Corporations** (this index)
Income tax. **Federal Income Taxation** (this index)
International Taxation (this index)
Partners and partnerships. **Federal Income Taxation of Partners and Partnerships** (this index)
Partners and Partnerships (this index)
Stockholders. **Corporations** (this index)

FINAL OR FINALITY
Negotiable Instruments and Check Collection (this index)
Uniform Commercial Code (this index)

FINANCES AND FUNDS
Banking and Financial Institutions Law (this index)
Negotiable Instruments and Check Collection (this index)
Real Estate Finance (this index)
State and Local Taxation and Finance (this index)

FINANCIAL INSTITUTIONS
Banking and Financial Institutions Law (this index)

FINDERS
Personal Property (this index)

FIRST AMENDMENT
Generally, **First Amd 1-19**
Access
ballot access, electoral process, **First Amd 286-290**
courtroom access, freedom of the press, **First Amd 375-387**
equal access, freedom of religion, **First Amd 425-430**
Acknowledgement of religion by government, freedom of religion, **First Amd 441-448**
Advocacy of illegal conduct, **First Amd 57-70**
Antiestablishment clause, freedom of religion, **First Amd 410-460**

FIRST AMENDMENT—Cont'd

Art law, **Art 71-74, 252,253, 261-273, 280**
Ballot access, electoral process, **First Amd 286-290**
Belief, free exercise clause, **First Amd 464-466**
Casino gambling, advertising prohibited, **First Amd 172-175**
Categorization and balancing, **First Amd 20-27**
Censorship, government sponsored environments, **First Amd 327-340**
Certification statements, lawyer advertising, **First Amd 170, 171**
Child pornography, **First Amd 99-103**
Collateral bar rule, freedom of the press, **First Amd 368, 369**
Commercial speech, generally, **First Amd 140-175**
Compulsory matters
    freedom of association and belief, compelled association, **First Amd 251-260**
    free exercise clause, compelling interest analysis, **First Amd 469-479**
Conduct, free exercise clause, **First Amd 464-466**
Confidentiality protected, freedom of the press, **First Amd 346-357**
Content-based versus content-neutral regulations, **First Amd 27-39**
Courtroom, freedom of the press, **First Amd 375-387**
Critics of special protection for free expression, **First Amd 18, 19**
Curriculum control, freedom of religion, **First Amd 438-441**
Defamation, **First Amd 116-139**
Direct or indirect burdens, free exercise clause, **First Amd 466-469**
Disclosure, freedom of association and belief, **First Amd 247-251**
Draft card burning, **First Amd 218-224**
Due process, **First Amd 112-115**
Electoral process, **First Amd 261-295**
Electronic media, freedom of the press, **First Amd 387-393**
Emotional distress, intentional infliction of, **First Amd 136-139**
Employment
    environments, government sponsored, **First Amd 309-327**
    freedom of association and belief, government employment

FIRST AMENDMENT—Cont'd
Employment—Cont'd
and benefits, **First Amd 243-247**
Equal access, freedom of religion, **First Amd 425-430**
Feminism, pornography and, **First Amd 185-190**
Fighting words, **First Amd 71-77**
Financial aid, government financial aid to religious institutions, **First Amd 417-425**
Flag burning, **First Amd 224-229**
Freedom of association and belief, generally, **First Amd 238-260**
Freedom of religion, generally, **First Amd 397-503**
Freedom of the press, generally, **First Amd 342-395**
Free exercise clause, generally, **First Amd 461-503**
Gagging the press, **First Amd 362-369**
Government employment and benefits, freedom of association and belief, **First Amd 243-247**
Government financial aid to religious institutions, freedom of religion, **First Amd 417-425**
Government sponsored environments
generally, **First Amd 296-341**
censorship, **First Amd 327-340**
employment, **First Amd 309-327**
patronage, **First Amd 321-327**
political activity, **First Amd 319-321**
political patronage, **First Amd 321-327**
religion in government sponsored environments, free exercise clause, **First Amd 480-484**
student speech, **First Amd 299-309**
Hostile audiences, **First Amd 78-81**
Illegal conduct, advocacy of, **First Amd 57-70**
Indecent speech, **First Amd 103-112**
In-person solicitation, lawyer advertising, **First Amd 163-166**
Intentional infliction of mental distress, **First Amd 136-139**
Journalist's privilege, freedom of the press, **First Amd 346-362**
Lawyer advertising, **First Amd 161-171**
Media, freedom of the press, **First Amd 387-395**
Mental distress, intentional infliction of, **First Amd 136-139**
Methodology, generally, **First Amd 20-55**

FIRST AMENDMENT—Cont'd

Nude dancing, **First Amd 229-237**
Obscenity, **First Amd 86-99**
Offensive speech, **First Amd 82-85**
Opinion, free exercise clause, **First Amd 464-466**
Overbreadth and vagueness
  generally, **First Amd 39-47**
  commercial speech, **First Amd 151, 152**
Patronage, government sponsored environments, **First Amd 321-327**
Pharmacists, commercial speech, **First Amd 145-148**
Political activity, government sponsored environments, **First Amd 319-321**
Political parties regulation, electoral process, **First Amd 290-295**
Political patronage, government sponsored environments, **First Amd 321-327**
Political speech during campaign, electoral process, **First Amd 262, 263**
Pornography
  child pornography, **First Amd 99-103**
  feminism and pornography, **First Amd 185-190**
Pretrial proceedings, freedom of the press, **First Amd 376-380**
Print media, freedom of the press, **First Amd 393-395**
Prior restraint
  generally, **First Amd 47-55**
  commercial speech, **First Amd 151, 152**
Privacy, generally, **First Amd 132-136**
Private property, nonpublic forum, **First Amd 208-214**
Public figures, **First Amd 122-129**
Public forum, generally, **First Amd 191-214**
Public speech and private speech, **First Amd 129-132**
Racist speech, **First Amd 176-185**
Rationale for differentiation, commercial speech, **First Amd 148, 149**
Registration, freedom of association and belief, **First Amd 247-251**
Released time, freedom of religion, **First Amd 425-430**

FIRST AMENDMENT—Cont'd
Religion, freedom of
  generally, **First Amd 397-503**
  see, also **Religion, the State and** (this index)
  antiestablishment clause, **First Amd 410-460**
  free exercise clause, religion in government sponsored environments, **First Amd 480-484**
  government financial aid to religious institutions, **First Amd 417-425**
  Sabbath Day observance laws, related establishment clause problems, **First Amd 452-456**
  schools, religion in, **First Amd 425-441**
  taxation and tax exemptions, related establishment clause problems, **First Amd 448-452**
Repudiation of judicial exemptions, free exercise clause, **First Amd 479-503**
Routine services, lawyer advertising, **First Amd 161-163**
Sabbath Day observance laws, related establishment clause problems, **First Amd 452-456**
Schools, religion in, **First Amd 425-441**
Self-fulfillment and autonomy, **First Amd 14, 15**
Self-government model, **First Amd 11-14**
Silencing bar and other trial participants, freedom of the press, **First Amd 370-375**
Solicitation, lawyer advertising, **First Amd 163-170**
Specialization, lawyer advertising, **First Amd 170, 171**
Spending, electoral process, **First Amd 264-286**
Standards for expressive conduct, **First Amd 216-224**
State public utility commission, banned promotional advertising, **First Amd 153-156**
Student speech, government sponsored environments, **First Amd 299-309**
Taxation and tax exemptions, related establishment clause problems, **First Amd 448-452**
Text, history and theory, **First Amd 3-8**
Truthful advertising about lawful but harmful activity, **First Amd 172-175**
Unprotected commercial speech, **First Amd 149-151**

FIRST AMENDMENT—Cont'd
Vagueness
generally, **First Amd 39-47**
commercial speech, **First Amd 151, 152**

FIRST TRIAL
Addressing jury, **First Trial 44-48**
Argument of counsel, **First Trial 88-95, 98-102, 191-209, 390-396**
Audience, **First Trial 166-179, 182-190**
Client, preparation of, **First Trial 134-137**
Closing argument, **First Trial 88-95, 390-396**
Consistency or inconsistency, impeachment by prior inconsistent statements, **First Trial 333-355**
Courtroom stage presence, **First Trial 48-59**
Cross examination, **First Trial 128-134, 213-225, 271-333**
Diagram, use of, **First Trial 39-44**
Direct examination, **First Trial 115-128, 213-270**
Evidence advocacy, lawyer's part, **First Trial 361-389**
Examination of witnesses, generally, **First Trial 210-369**
Exhibits presented by the numbers, **First Trial 26-39**
Expert witness, preparation of, **First Trial 137-145**
Impeachment by prior inconsistent statements, **First Trial 333-355**
Instructions to jury, early preparation, **First Trial 95-98**
Interrogation of witnesses, **First Trial 22-26**
Jury and jury trial, **First Trial 44-48, 95-98**
Lawyer's part, **First Trial 9-16**
Notebook, prepare the play in trial notebook, **First Trial 75-102**
Numbers or numbering, presenting exhibits by the numbers, **First Trial 26-39**
Opening statement, **First Trial 98-102, 191-209**
Order the witnesses, **First Trial 105-111**
Perspective, generally, **First Trial 4-16**
Place, where to sit, **First Trial 17-59**
Players in the woodshed, preparation of, **First Trial 103-179**
Preparation for first trial, **First Trial 71-179**

FIRST TRIAL—Cont'd
Presence, courtroom stage presence, **First Trial 48-59**
Presenting exhibits by the numbers, **First Trial 26-39**
Prior inconsistent statements, impeachment by, **First Trial 333-355**
Props, gathering of, **First Trial 146-165**
Rehabilitation of witness, **First Trial 355-360**
Script, what to say, **First Trial 60-70**
Stage, generally, **First Trial 17-59**
Testimony, **First Trial 22-26, 103-179, 210-335, 355-360**
Theater, trial is, **First Trial 9-16**
Use of diagram, **First Trial 39-44**
Voir dire, thinning the audience, **First Trial 182-190**
Witnesses, **First Trial 22-26, 103-179, 210-335, 355-360**

FOREIGN COUNTRIES
European Union Law (this index)
International Business Transactions (this index)
International Human Rights (this index)
International Matters (this index)
International Taxation (this index)
International Trade and Investment (this index)

FORESTS
Energy and Natural Resources Law (this index)

FORGERY
Art Law (this index)
Negotiable Instruments and Check Collection (this index)

FORM AND CONTENT
Legal Writing (this index)

FRAUD
Art Law (this index)
Immigration Law and Procedure (this index)

FRAUD—Cont'd
Negotiable Instruments and Check Collection (this index)
Tax Procedure and Tax Fraud (this index)

FREEDOM OF EXPRESSION
Art Law (this index)

FREEDOM OF SPEECH AND PRESS
First Amendment (this index)

FUTURE INTERESTS
Estates in Land and Future Interests (this index)

GAS AND OIL
Oil and Gas Law (this index)

GATT (GENERAL AGREEMENT ON TARIFFS AND TRADE)
International Trade and Investment (this index)

GENERAL AGREEMENT ON TARIFFS AND TRADE (GATT)
International Trade and Investment (this index)

GENERATION-SKIPPING TRANSFER TAX
Federal Estate and Gift Taxation (this index) generally

GEOTHERMAL
Energy and Natural Resources Law (this index)

GIFTS
Federal Estate and Gift Taxation (this index)

GOODWILL
Federal Income Taxation of Partners and Partnerships (this index)

GENERAL INDEX

References are to Titles and Pages

GOVERNMENT CONTRACTS

Acceptance of sealed bid, withdrawal after, **Govt Contracts 133, 134**

Acquisition planning, **Govt Contracts 58-97**

Adjustment of price, sealed bids, **Govt Contracts 132, 133**

Administration of contracts, **Govt Contracts 412-427**

Advance payments, contract financing, **Govt Contracts 224-226**

Advertising costs and bad debts, **Govt Contracts 203**

Allocations, delivery and performance of contract, **Govt Contracts 96, 97**

Allotments, contract funding, **Govt Contracts 241-243**

Allotments and allocations, delivery and performance of contract, **Govt Contracts 96, 97**

Antitrust violations, reports of, **Govt Contracts 38, 39**

Appeals, General Services Administration Board of Contract Appeals (GSBCA), **Govt Contracts 269-272**

Appeals and disputes, **Govt Contracts 284-366**

Appropriation process, **Govt Contracts 234-239**

Architect-engineering services contracts, **Govt Contracts 402-411**

Assignment of claims, contract funding, **Govt Contracts 254, 255**

Attorneys' fees, disputes and appeals, **Govt Contracts 357-366**

Audit, corporate administrative contracting officer, **Govt Contracts 414-416**

Authority, contract modifications, **Govt Contracts 428-432**

Authority, Federal acquisition regulation system, **Govt Contracts 12-30**

Authorization acts, contract funding, **Govt Contracts 239**

Backpay costs, **Govt Contracts 206, 207**

Basic and basic ordering agreements, **Govt Contracts 193, 194**

Bids and bidding

- competition requirements, **Govt Contracts 55, 56**
- damages for refusal to property consider bid and bid preparation costs, **Govt Contracts 281-284**
- reports of bids, **Govt Contracts 38, 39**
- sealed bidding, methods of contracting, **Govt Contracts 98-136**

Bids and bidding, subcontracting, **Govt Contracts 472, 473**

GOVERNMENT CONTRACTS—Cont'd

Board of Contract Appeals, appeals to, **Govt Contracts 318-347**
Bona fide need, contract funding, **Govt Contracts 239, 240**
Buy-in, improper business practices and personal conflicts of interest, **Govt Contracts 39**
Certification, disputes and appeals, **Govt Contracts 293-299**
Change of name agreements, contract administration, **Govt Contracts 425-427**
Changes clause, construction contract clauses, **Govt Contracts 395-400**
Christian Doctrine, Federal acquisition regulation system, **Govt Contracts 5, 6**
Claims Court, appeals to, **Govt Contracts 347-354**
Claims Court, preaward jurisdiction of, **Govt Contracts 272-281**
Compensation for personal services, **Govt Contracts 203-206**
Competition requirements, **Govt Contracts 50-57**
Comptroller General, contracting by negotiation, **Govt Contracts 139, 140**
Conflicts of interest, **Govt Contracts 31-46**
Congressional referrals of claims, **Govt Contracts 272**
Consent to subcontracting, **Govt Contracts 451-459**
Construction and architect-engineer contracts, **Govt Contracts 375-411**
Consultant service costs, **Govt Contracts 214-216**
Contingencies contributions and donations, **Govt Contracts 207**
Contingent fees, improper business practices and personal conflicts of interest, **Govt Contracts 39-41**
Contract cost principles, **Govt Contracts 200-221**
Contractor gratuities to government personnel, **Govt Contracts 37, 38**
Contractor qualifications, **Govt Contracts 65-92**
Contra Proferentem Doctrine, negotiated procurements, **Govt Contracts 515-523**
Contributions, contingencies contributions and donations, **Govt Contracts 207**
Cost accounting standards (CAS), **Govt Contracts 195-199**
Cost of money, **Govt Contracts 207, 208**

GOVERNMENT CONTRACTS—Cont'd

Cost plus percentage of cost (CPPC) prohibitions, contracting authority and responsibilities, **Govt Contracts 23-26**

Cost-reimbursement contracts, **Govt Contracts 176-186**

Court of Appeals for Federal Circuit (CAFC), **Govt Contracts 354-357**

Damages, delivery and performance of contract, **Govt Contracts 94-96**

Damages for refusal to property consider bid and bid preparation costs, **Govt Contracts 281-284**

Debarment, contractor qualifications, **Govt Contracts 76-80; Govt Contracts 80-90**

Debts, contract financing, **Govt Contracts 230-234**

Default, termination of government contracts for, **Govt Contracts 475-500**

Defense of fraud proceedings, **Govt Contracts 219, 220**

Defense production, loan guarantees for, **Govt Contracts 223, 224**

Delays in construction, construction contract clauses, **Govt Contracts 388-393**

Delivery

  indefinite delivery contracts, **Govt Contracts 188-191**

Delivery of contract, **Govt Contracts 93-97**

Depreciation, **Govt Contracts 208**

Differing site conditions, construction contract clauses, **Govt Contracts 393, 394**

Discounts, sealed bids, **Govt Contracts 132, 133**

Disputes and appeals, **Govt Contracts 284-366**

Dormitory costs and credits, **Govt Contracts 208, 209**

Educational institutions, contracts with, **Govt Contracts 221**

Eligibility or ineligibility, contractor qualifications, **Govt Contracts 76-80**

Engineers, construction and architect-engineer contracts, **Govt Contracts 375-411**

Ethics, **Govt Contracts 31-36**

Examination of records by Comptroller General, contracting by negotiation, **Govt Contracts 139, 140**

GOVERNMENT CONTRACTS—Cont'd

Extension of implied warranty, construction contract clauses, **Govt Contracts 383-385**

Federal acquisition regulation system, generally, **Govt Contracts 1-57**

Fees, improper business practices and personal conflicts of interest, **Govt Contracts 39-41**

Financing contracts, **Govt Contracts 222-255**

Fixed-price contracts, **Govt Contracts 172-176**

Food service, **Govt Contracts 208, 209**

Former government employees, personal conflicts of interest, **Govt Contracts 44-46**

Fraud proceedings, cost of defense of, **Govt Contracts 219, 220**

General contracting requirements, **Govt Contracts 195-366**

General Services Administration Board of Contract Appeals (GSBCA), **Govt Contracts 269-272**

Goodwill, **Govt Contracts 220**

Gratuities, contractor gratuities to government personnel, **Govt Contracts 37, 38**

Health and welfare, employees, **Govt Contracts 208, 209**

Identical bids, reports of, **Govt Contracts 38, 39**

Idle facilities, **Govt Contracts 208, 209**

Illegal contracts, contracting authority and responsibilities, **Govt Contracts 22-30**

Implied warranty, construction contract clauses, **Govt Contracts 383-385**

Impoundment, contract funding, **Govt Contracts 244-246**

Improper business practices, generally, **Govt Contracts 31-46**

Incentive contracts, **Govt Contracts 186-188**

Indefinite delivery contracts, **Govt Contracts 188-191**

Independent pricing, ethics in contracting, **Govt Contracts 35, 36**

Indirect cost rates, contract administration, **Govt Contracts 416-422**

Interest on debts, contract financing, **Govt Contracts 233, 2342**

Jurisdiction, preaward jurisdiction of Claims Court and U.S. District Courts, **Govt Contracts 272-281**

Kickbacks, improper business practices and personal conflicts of interest, **Govt Contracts 40, 41**

GOVERNMENT CONTRACTS—Cont'd
Labor-hour contracts, **Govt Contracts 191-193**
Letter contracts, **Govt Contracts 192, 193**
Limitation of cost or funds, contract funding, **Govt Contracts 247-253**
Liquidated damages, delivery and performance of contract, **Govt Contracts 94-96**
Loan guarantees for defense production, financing contracts, **Govt Contracts 223, 224**
Lobbying costs, **Govt Contracts 213**
Make-or-buy programs of prime contractors, contracting by negotiation, **Govt Contracts 157, 158**
Management of contracts, **Govt Contracts 412-511**
Material costs, **Govt Contracts 216, 217**
Methods of contracting, **Govt Contracts 98-194**
Mistakes in bids, **Govt Contracts 123-128**
Modification of bids, **Govt Contracts 111**
Modification of contract, **Govt Contracts 428-449**
Money, cost of, **Govt Contracts 207, 208**
Morale of employees, **Govt Contracts 208, 209**
Negotiation
  Contra Proferentem Doctrine, negotiated procurements, **Govt Contracts 515-523**
  price negotiation, construction contracts, **Govt Contracts 381**
Negotiation, contracting by, **Govt Contracts 137-169**
Negotiations, contract administration, **Govt Contracts 423-425**
Nonprofit organizations, contracts with, **Govt Contracts 221**
Novation, contract administration, **Govt Contracts 425-427**
Obligations and allotments, contract funding, **Govt Contracts 241-243**
Opening of bids and award of contract, **Govt Contracts 108-134**
Organizational conflicts of interest, contractor qualifications, **Govt Contracts 90, 91**
Organization costs, **Govt Contracts 213, 214**
Palpable illegal versus improper action doctrine, contracting authority and responsibilities, **Govt Contracts 26-30**
Pension costs, **Govt Contracts 206, 207**

GOVERNMENT CONTRACTS—Cont'd

Performance of contract, **Govt Contracts 93-97**
Personal conflicts of interest, **Govt Contracts 31-46**
Personal services, compensation for, **Govt Contracts 203-206**
Precontract costs, **Govt Contracts 214**
Price adjustments, sealed bids, **Govt Contracts 132, 133**
Price negotiation, **Govt Contracts 158-166**
Price negotiation, construction contracts, **Govt Contracts 381**
Priorities, delivery and performance of contract, **Govt Contracts 96, 97**
Privity, subcontracting, **Govt Contracts 460-469**
Procurement, ethics in contracting, **Govt Contracts 36**
Procurements
  Contra Proferentem Doctrine, negotiated procurements, **Govt Contracts 515-523**
Professional and consultant service costs, **Govt Contracts 214-216**
Progress payments based on costs, contract financing, **Govt Contracts 226-230**
Proposals, contracting by negotiation, **Govt Contracts 142-144; Govt Contracts 144-149**
Protests to General Accounting Office (GAO), **Govt Contracts 257-269**
Publicizing contract actions, **Govt Contracts 47-49**
Qualifications of contractor, **Govt Contracts 65-92**
Quotations solicited, contracting by negotiation, **Govt Contracts 142-144**
Ratification, contracting authority and responsibilities, **Govt Contracts 20-22**
Records, contracting by negotiation, **Govt Contracts 139, 140**
Rejection of bids, **Govt Contracts 109, 110**
Rejection of individual bids, **Govt Contracts 111-116**
Reports of identical bids and suspected antitrust violations, **Govt Contracts 38, 39**
Rescinding contracts, improper business practices and personal conflicts of interest, **Govt Contracts 46**
Research and development, **Govt Contracts 209-213**

GOVERNMENT CONTRACTS—Cont'd

Research and development contracting, **Govt Contracts 367-374**
Research and development pools, contractor qualifications, **Govt Contracts 92**
Responsibilities, Federal acquisition regulation system, **Govt Contracts 12-30**
Responsibilities, prospective contractors, **Govt Contracts 65-76**
Sealed bidding, construction contracts, **Govt Contracts 378-380**
Sealed bidding, methods of contracting, **Govt Contracts 98-136**
Sealed bids, competition requirements, **Govt Contracts 55, 56**
Selecting contract types, **Govt Contracts 170-172**
Selling costs, **Govt Contracts 216**
Services, compensation for personal services, **Govt Contracts 203-206**
Setoff of debts, contract financing, **Govt Contracts 233, 2342**
Settlement authority, disputes and appeals, **Govt Contracts 299-307**
Solicitation of proposals and quotations, contracting by negotiation, **Govt Contracts 142-144**
Solicitation provisions and contract clauses, **Govt Contracts 512-523**
Statute of frauds, contract funding, **Govt Contracts 243, 244**
Subcontracting, **Govt Contracts 450-473**
Subcontractor claims, certification of, **Govt Contracts 297-299**
Subcontractor kickbacks, improper business practices and personal conflicts of interest, **Govt Contracts 40, 41**
Suspected antitrust violations, reports of, **Govt Contracts 38, 39**
Suspension, contractor qualifications, **Govt Contracts 76-80; Govt Contracts 80-90**
Suspension of work, construction contract clauses, **Govt Contracts 386-388**
Taxes, **Govt Contracts 217, 218**
Termination cost in excess of limitation of costs (LOC), contract funding, **Govt Contracts 253, 254**
Termination costs, **Govt Contracts 218, 219**
Termination of government contracts, **Govt Contracts 474-511**
Time and materials contracts, **Govt Contracts 191-193**

GOVERNMENT CONTRACTS—Cont'd
Travel costs, **Govt Contracts 220, 221**
U.S. District Court, preaward jurisdiction of, **Govt Contracts 272-281**
Voiding contracts, improper business practices and personal conflicts of interest, **Govt Contracts 46**
Withdrawal, sealed bids, **Govt Contracts 133, 134**
Withdrawal of bids, **Govt Contracts 111**
Work and specifications, construction contract clauses, **Govt Contracts 382, 383**

GOVERNMENT SPONSORED ENVIRONMENTS
First Amendment (this index)

GRAMMAR
Legal Writing (this index)

HANDICAPPED DISABLED
Disabled Persons (this index)

HARD ROCK MINING AND MINERALS
Energy and Natural Resources Law (this index)

HAZARDOUS WASTES AND TOXIC SUBSTANCES, LAW OF
Generally, **Haz Waste & Toxic Sub 1-13**
Abandonment of facility, avoiding liability for hazardous substance cleanup costs, **Haz Waste & Toxic Sub 503, 504**
Additional hazardous waste cleanup options under RCRA and CERCLA, **Haz Waste & Toxic Sub 418-441**
Additives to food (FFDCA), regulation of use of toxic substances, **Haz Waste & Toxic Sub 83-86**
Administrative order, enforcement under CERCLA, **Haz Waste & Toxic Sub 373-378**
Apportionment, Comprehensive Environmental Response, Compensation, and Liability Act (CERCLA), **Haz Waste & Toxic Sub 406-410**

HAZARDOUS WASTES AND TOXIC SUBSTANCES, LAW OF—Cont'd

Avoiding liability for hazardous substance cleanup costs, **Haz Waste & Toxic Sub 492-504**

Bankruptcy, avoiding liability for hazardous substance cleanup costs, **Haz Waste & Toxic Sub 501-504**

Causation, common law approaches to hazardous wastes and toxic substances, **Haz Waste & Toxic Sub 461-470**

Class actions, common law approaches to hazardous wastes and toxic substances, **Haz Waste & Toxic Sub 488-491**

Clean Air Act, regulation of toxics under, **Haz Waste & Toxic Sub 124-139**

Cleanup
- additional hazardous waste cleanup options under RCRA and CERCLA, **Haz Waste & Toxic Sub 418-441**
- avoiding liability for hazardous substance cleanup costs, **Haz Waste & Toxic Sub 492-504**
- Comprehensive Environmental Response, Compensation, and Liability Act (CERCLA), **Haz Waste & Toxic Sub 282-305, 367-380, 418-441**
- mandated by government, CERCLA, **Haz Waste & Toxic Sub 367-380**
- performed by government, CERCLA, **Haz Waste & Toxic Sub 282-305**

Clean Water Act, regulation of toxics under, **Haz Waste & Toxic Sub 101-124**

Common law, risk and scientific uncertainty, **Haz Waste & Toxic Sub 17-20**

Common law approaches to hazardous wastes and toxic substances, **Haz Waste & Toxic Sub 442-492**

Comprehensive Environmental Response, Compensation, and Liability Act (CERCLA)
- generally, **Haz Waste & Toxic Sub 256-281**
- additional hazardous waste cleanup options under RCRA and CERCLA, **Haz Waste & Toxic Sub 418-441**
- administrative order, enforcement by, **Haz Waste & Toxic Sub 373-378**
- apportionment, **Haz Waste & Toxic Sub 406-410**

HAZARDOUS WASTES AND TOXIC SUBSTANCES, LAW OF—Cont'd

Comprehensive Environmental Response, Compensation, and Liability Act (CERCLA)—Cont'd
- cleanup, **Haz Waste & Toxic Sub 282-305, 367-380, 418-441**
- contribution under § 113, **Haz Waste & Toxic Sub 394-396**
- corrective actions, **Haz Waste & Toxic Sub 426-434**
- cost recovery actions brought by government, **Haz Waste & Toxic Sub 306-366**
- costs, recovery of, **Haz Waste & Toxic Sub 382-396**
- defenses, **Haz Waste & Toxic Sub 403-406**
- defenses to liability, **Haz Waste & Toxic Sub 372, 373**
- disposal of hazardous wastes, **Haz Waste & Toxic Sub 166-169**
- enforcement, **Haz Waste & Toxic Sub 373-380**
- imminent and substantial endangerment actions, **Haz Waste & Toxic Sub 419-425**
- injunction, enforcement by, **Haz Waste & Toxic Sub 373-378**
- jurisdictional overlap, **Haz Waste & Toxic Sub 435-438**
- liability standards, cleanup mandated by government, **Haz Waste & Toxic Sub 369-372**
- overlap between RCRA and CERCLA, **Haz Waste & Toxic Sub 434-441**
- private parties, actions brought by, **Haz Waste & Toxic Sub 381-417**

Comprehensive general liability insurance, avoiding liability for hazardous substance cleanup costs, **Haz Waste & Toxic Sub 495-499**

Consumer Product Safety Act (SPSA), regulation of use of toxic substances, **Haz Waste & Toxic Sub 80-82**

Consumer protection, regulation of use of toxic substances, **Haz Waste & Toxic Sub 78-87**

Contribution under § 113, Comprehensive Environmental Response, Compensation, and Liability Act (CERCLA), **Haz Waste & Toxic Sub 394-396**

Corrective actions, Comprehensive Environmental Response, Compensation, and Liability Act (CERCLA), **Haz Waste & Toxic Sub 426-434**

HAZARDOUS WASTES AND TOXIC SUBSTANCES, LAW OF—Cont'd

Cost-benefit standards, risk and scientific uncertainty, **Haz Waste & Toxic Sub 31-33**

Cost recovery actions brought by government, CERCLA, **Haz Waste & Toxic Sub 306-366**

Costs

- avoiding liability for hazardous substance cleanup costs, **Haz Waste & Toxic Sub 492-504**
- Comprehensive Environmental Response, Compensation, and Liability Act (CERCLA), **Haz Waste & Toxic Sub 382-396**

Defenses

- common law approaches to hazardous wastes and toxic substances, **Haz Waste & Toxic Sub 445-461**
- Comprehensive Environmental Response, Compensation, and Liability Act (CERCLA), **Haz Waste & Toxic Sub 346-358, 372, 373, 403-406**

Defining hazardous wastes and toxic substances, **Haz Waste & Toxic Sub 5-7**

Discharge of debtor in bankruptcy, avoiding liability for hazardous substance cleanup costs, **Haz Waste & Toxic Sub 502, 503**

Discharge restrictions and permits, regulation of toxics under Clean Water Act, **Haz Waste & Toxic Sub 109, 110**

Disposal of hazardous wastes, **Haz Waste & Toxic Sub 161-255**

Emergency Planning and Community Right-to-Know Act (EPCRTKA), regulation of use of toxic substances, **Haz Waste & Toxic Sub 91-94**

Employee protection, regulation of use of toxic substances, **Haz Waste & Toxic Sub 87-97**

Enforcement

- common features of acts, **Haz Waste & Toxic Sub 156-159**
- Comprehensive Environmental Response, Compensation, and Liability Act (CERCLA), **Haz Waste & Toxic Sub 358-366, 373-380**
- disposal of hazardous wastes, **Haz Waste & Toxic Sub 233-253**

HAZARDOUS WASTES AND TOXIC SUBSTANCES, LAW OF—Cont'd

Environmental impairment liability insurance, avoiding liability for hazardous substance cleanup costs, **Haz Waste & Toxic Sub 500, 501**

Exclusions, Comprehensive Environmental Response, Compensation, and Liability Act (CERCLA), **Haz Waste & Toxic Sub 346-358**

Feasibility standards, risk and scientific uncertainty, **Haz Waste & Toxic Sub 30, 31**

Federal and state law, relationship of, **Haz Waste & Toxic Sub 153-155**

Federal Food, Drug, and Cosmetic Act (FFDCA), regulation of use of toxic substances, **Haz Waste & Toxic Sub 82-87**

Federal Insecticide, Fungicide, and Rodenticide Act (FIFRA), **Haz Waste & Toxic Sub 38-56**

Formaldehyde saga, regulation of use of toxic substances, **Haz Waste & Toxic Sub 81, 82**

Future of Comprehensive Environmental Response, Compensation, and Liability Act (CERCLA), **Haz Waste & Toxic Sub 280, 281**

Generation regulation, disposal of hazardous wastes, **Haz Waste & Toxic Sub 199-203**

Health-based standards, risk and scientific uncertainty, **Haz Waste & Toxic Sub 28-30**

HMTA (Hazardous Materials Transportation Act), regulation of use of toxic substances, **Haz Waste & Toxic Sub 94, 95**

HSA (Hazardous Substances Act), regulation of use of toxic substances, **Haz Waste & Toxic Sub 78-80**

Imminent and substantial endangerment actions, CERCLA, **Haz Waste & Toxic Sub 419-425**

Indemnity and hold harmless agreements, avoiding liability for hazardous substance cleanup costs, **Haz Waste & Toxic Sub 493, 494**

Injunction, enforcement by under CERCLA, **Haz Waste & Toxic Sub 373-378**

Insurance, avoiding liability for hazardous substance cleanup costs, **Haz Waste & Toxic Sub 494-501**

HAZARDOUS WASTES AND TOXIC SUBSTANCES, LAW OF—Cont'd

Judicial reaction to risk regulation, risk and scientific uncertainty, **Haz Waste & Toxic Sub 33-35**

Jurisdictional overlap, CERCLA, **Haz Waste & Toxic Sub 435-438**

Land ban, disposal of hazardous wastes, **Haz Waste & Toxic Sub 205-227**

Liability

- avoiding liability for hazardous substance cleanup costs, **Haz Waste & Toxic Sub 492-504**
- cleanup mandated by government, liability standards, **Haz Waste & Toxic Sub 369-372**
- cost recovery actions brought by government under CERCLA, **Haz Waste & Toxic Sub 307-346**

Local regulation, production and sale of toxic substances, **Haz Waste & Toxic Sub 76**

Monitoring requirements, common features of acts, **Haz Waste & Toxic Sub 155, 156**

Multiple defendants, common law approaches to hazardous wastes and toxic substances, **Haz Waste & Toxic Sub 471-476**

Occupational Safety and Health Act (OSHA), regulation of use of toxic substances, **Haz Waste & Toxic Sub 87**

Outside advisory groups, common features of acts, **Haz Waste & Toxic Sub 159, 160**

Overlap between RCRA and CERCLA, **Haz Waste & Toxic Sub 434-441**

Pesticides

- FFDCA, pesticide residues, **Haz Waste & Toxic Sub 86, 87**
- regulation of production and sale of toxic substances, **Haz Waste & Toxic Sub 38-58, 86, 87**

Pollution, generally, **Haz Waste & Toxic Sub 98-160**

Preemption, relationship of federal and state law, **Haz Waste & Toxic Sub 154**

Private parties, actions brought by under CERCLA, **Haz Waste & Toxic Sub 381-417**

Procedural responses, common law approaches to hazardous wastes and toxic substances, **Haz Waste & Toxic Sub 481-491**

HAZARDOUS WASTES AND TOXIC SUBSTANCES, LAW OF—Cont'd

Production and sale of toxic substances, regulation of, **Haz Waste & Toxic Sub 33-76**

Recordkeeping requirements, common features of acts, **Haz Waste & Toxic Sub 155, 156**

Regulatory approach, risk and scientific uncertainty, **Haz Waste & Toxic Sub 20-33**

Remedies, common law approaches to hazardous wastes and toxic substances, **Haz Waste & Toxic Sub 476-481**

Reporting requirements, common features of acts, **Haz Waste & Toxic Sub 155, 156**

Research programs, common features of acts, **Haz Waste & Toxic Sub 159, 160**

Resource Conservation and Recovery Act (RCRA)
- generally, **Haz Waste & Toxic Sub 161-255**
- additional hazardous waste cleanup options under RCRA and CERCLA, **Haz Waste & Toxic Sub 418-441**
- cleanup, **Haz Waste & Toxic Sub 418-441**
- Comprehensive Environmental Response, Compensation, and Liability Act (CERCLA), **Haz Waste & Toxic Sub 418-441**
- overlap between RCRA and CERCLA, **Haz Waste & Toxic Sub 434-441**

Risk and scientific uncertainty, **Haz Waste & Toxic Sub 14-76**

Safe Drinking Water Act, regulation of toxics under Clean Air Act, **Haz Waste & Toxic Sub 139-153**

Scientific uncertainty, **Haz Waste & Toxic Sub 14-76**

Solid wastes, disposal of hazardous wastes, **Haz Waste & Toxic Sub 174-186**

State regulation
- production and sale of toxic substances, **Haz Waste & Toxic Sub 76**
- regulation of use of toxic substances, **Haz Waste & Toxic Sub 95-97**

Superfund, Comprehensive Environmental Response, Compensation, and Liability Act (CERCLA), **Haz Waste & Toxic Sub 277-280**

HAZARDOUS WASTES AND TOXIC SUBSTANCES, LAW OF—Cont'd

Title insurance, avoiding liability for hazardous substance cleanup costs, **Haz Waste & Toxic Sub 499, 500**

Transportation
  disposal of hazardous wastes, transporters regulation, **Haz Waste & Toxic Sub 203-205**
  Hazardous Materials Transportation Act, regulation of use of toxic substances, **Haz Waste & Toxic Sub 94, 95**

TSCA (Toxic Substances Control Act), **Haz Waste & Toxic Sub 58-76**

TSD facilities regulation, disposal of hazardous wastes, **Haz Waste & Toxic Sub 205-227**

Underground storage tanks (USTs), disposal of hazardous wastes, **Haz Waste & Toxic Sub 230-233**

HEALTH CARE LAW AND ETHICS

Accreditation of hospital, **Health Care 134, 135**

AIDS
  confidentiality, **Health Care 376-389**
  refusal to treat, **Health Care 81-88**

Allied health professionals, antitrust boycott law, **Health Care 208, 209**

Antitrust matters, generally, **Health Care 186-221**

Boycotts, **Health Care 187-210**

Certificate of need (CON) laws, **Health Care 124-134**

Charitable tax exemptions, **Health Care 136-147**

Children, seriously ill child, **Health Care 312-330**

Competency of patient, generally, **Health Care 259-283**

Competition, **Health Care 56-59, 184, 185**

Confidentiality
  AIDS patients, **Health Care 376-389**
  peer review confidentiality and immunity, **Health Care 169-172**

Conspiracy, boycotts, **Health Care 188-192**

Constitutional rights, access to health care, **Health Care 98, 99**

Containment of costs, **Health Care 33-38**

HEALTH CARE LAW AND ETHICS—Cont'd

Controlling medical costs while ensuring patient access, **Health Care 1-101**
Corporate practice of medicine, **Health Care 104-109**
Covenants not to compete, employment, **Health Care 184, 185**
Crisis in health care spending, generally, **Health Care 3-24**
Death defined, **Health Care 224-231**
Defining death, **Health Care 224-231**
Delivery of health care, legal structure of, **Health Care 103-221**
Discrimination
  employment discrimination, **Health Care 183**
  handicapped, discrimination against, **Health Care 81-88**
Disputes, hospital medical staff, **Health Care 151-172**
Doctors, duty to treat paying patients, **Health Care 72-78**
Do not resuscitate (DNR) orders, **Health Care 337-340**
Double effect doctrine, withholding or withdrawing medical care, **Health Care 251, 252**
Durable powers of attorney, **Health Care 287, 288**
Emergency care, duty to treat indigent patients, **Health Care 91-95**
Employment discrimination, **Health Care 183**
ERISA preemption, business of insurance, **Health Care 111-116**
Ethical issues, generally, **Health Care 222-389**
Euthanasia, **Health Care 245-251**
Exceptions or exemptions
  AIDS, confidentiality and, **Health Care 379-381**
  antitrust boycott law, state action exemption, **Health Care 206, 207**
Exclusive contract tie-ins, antitrust boycott law, **Health Care 210**
Fee-splitting prohibitions, **Health Care 116-124**
Food, withholding of, **Health Care 330-337**
Handicap discrimination, **Health Care 81-88**
Health maintenance organizations (HMOs), **Health Care 61-68**
Hospitals
  medical staff, **Health Care 148-185**
  mergers, **Health Care 218-221**
  paying patients, duty to treat, **Health Care 78-88**

HEALTH CARE LAW AND ETHICS—Cont'd
Hospitals—Cont'd
    rate regulation, **Health Care 38-42**
Indigent patients, duty to treat, **Health Care 89-97**
Institutionalized persons, treatment rights of, **Health Care 100**
Insurance and insurance companies
    AIDS, insurance coverage, **Health Care 386**
    ERISA preemption, business of insurance, **Health Care 111-116**
    monopolization, **Health Care 215-218**
    moral rights of access and problem of uninsured, **Health Care 95-97**
Interstate commerce requirement, antitrust boycott law, **Health Care 204-206**
Judicial review, medical staff disputes, **Health Care 154-169**
Labor and employment, **Health Care 172-185**
Legal structure of health care delivery, **Health Care 103-221**
Licensure of hospital, **Health Care 134, 135**
Living wills, **Health Care 284-286**
Malpractice standard, containment of costs and, **Health Care 33-38**
Mandatory testing, confidentiality and AIDS, **Health Care 385, 386**
Maternal-fetal conflict, **Health Care 355-375**
Medicaid program, access to health care under, **Health Care 99, 100**
Medicare
    prospective payment, **Health Care 24-33**
    reimbursement, **Health Care 19-24**
Mergers, hospital mergers, **Health Care 218-221**
Monopolies and restraints of trade
    boycotts, medical staff boycotts as restraints of trade, **Health Care 192-204**
    insurance company monopolization, **Health Care 215-218**
Moral rights of access and problem of uninsured, **Health Care 95-97**
Newborn children, seriously ill child, **Health Care 312-330**
Orders not to resuscitate, **Health Care 337-340**

HEALTH CARE LAW AND ETHICS—Cont'd

Ordinary versus extraordinary treatment doctrine, withholding or withdrawing medical care, **Health Care 252**
Organization and operation of health care business, **Health Care 103-147**
Organs
    procurement of organs, **Health Care 231-235**
    rationing of organ transplants, **Health Care 52-56**
Patient access to health care, generally, **Health Care 1-101**
Paying patients, duty to treat, generally, **Health Care 71-89**
Peer review confidentiality and immunity, **Health Care 169-172**
Personal autonomy and beneficence, competing principles of, **Health Care 256-259**
Powers of attorney, **Health Care 287, 288**
Preferred provider organizations (PPOs), **Health Care 68, 69, 110, 111, 210-215**
Price fixing by preferred provider organizations, **Health Care 210-215**
Private accreditation of hospital, **Health Care 134, 135**
Privileges or immunities, peer review confidentiality and immunity, **Health Care 169-172**
Professional society rules, antitrust boycott law, **Health Care 209, 210**
Quarantine, confidentiality and AIDS, **Health Care 387, 388**
Rationing health care and treatment, **Health Care 42-56**
Recapitulation, **Health Care 70**
Reimbursement, **Health Care 3-70**
Reproductive medicine, **Health Care 341-375**
Restraints of trade. Monopolies and restraints of trade, supra
Resuscitation, orders not to resuscitate, **Health Care 337-340**
Review
    certificate of need review procedure, **Health Care 129**
    medical staff disputes, **Health Care 154-172**
    peer review confidentiality and immunity, **Health Care 169-172**
Rights of patients, generally, **Health Care 100, 101**
Selection process, hospital medical staff, **Health Care 151-154**
Seriously ill child, **Health Care 312-330**

HEALTH CARE LAW AND ETHICS—Cont'd
Splitting fees prohibited, **Health Care 116-124**
Staffing
  hospital medical staff, **Health Care 148-185**
  medical staff boycotts as restraints of trade, **Health Care 192-204**
State action exemption, antitrust boycott law, **Health Care 206, 207**
Structure
  health care delivery, **Health Care 103-221**
  hospital medical staff, **Health Care 148-151**
Surrogate motherhood, **Health Care 341-355**
Tort liability for infecting others, confidentiality and AIDS, **Health Care 388, 389**
Transplants, rationing of organ transplants, **Health Care 52-56**
Uninsured, duty to treat indigent patients, **Health Care 95-97**
Water, withholding of, **Health Care 330-337**
Withdrawing medical care, **Health Care 236-340**
Withholding
  food or water, **Health Care 330-337**
  medical care, **Health Care 236-340**
Wrongful discharge, labor and employment, **Health Care 179-183**

HEARINGS
Immigration Law and Procedure (this index)
Labor Arbitration Law and Practice (this index)

HEARSAY
Labor Arbitration Law and Practice (this index)

HISTORY
Energy and Natural Resources Law (this index)

HONG KONG INHABITANTS
Immigration Law and Procedure (this index)

GENERAL INDEX

References are to Titles and Pages

HOSPITALS

Health Care Law and Ethics (this index)

HOUSING

Land Use (this index)

HOW TO STUDY LAW AND TAKE LAW EXAMS

Administrative law, law libraries, **Jurisp 84, 85**
After first year, **Jurisp 201-211**
American Law Reports, law libraries, **Jurisp 90**
American Legal System, generally, **Jurisp 15-36**
Arrival at law school, preparation for entering law school, **Jurisp 12, 13**
Athletic activities, **Jurisp 195**
Attendance, classroom experience, **Jurisp 126-130**
Briefs
  case briefs, study aids, case briefs, **Jurisp 156, 157**
  format of case brief, preparation for class, **Jurisp 106-113**
  preparation for class, briefing cases, **Jurisp 104-106**
  sample case briefs, **Jurisp 113-119**
Business career, what do lawyers do, **Jurisp 45, 46**
Caption, case brief format, **Jurisp 107**
Case digests, law libraries, **Jurisp 75-78**
Case law, law libraries, **Jurisp 68-74**
Case method
  preparation for class, **Jurisp 98-100**
  study of law, **Jurisp 50-52**
Citators, law libraries, **Jurisp 92-94**
Civil Procedure
  first year course, **Jurisp 55-57**
  sample exam questions and answers, **Jurisp 214-233**
Classroom experience, **Jurisp 120-133**
Clerkships, summer clerkships, **Jurisp 210, 211**
Clinical education, **Jurisp 203-205**
Comprehensive digests, law libraries, **Jurisp 76-78**
Computers
  preparation for entering law school, **Jurisp 13, 14**

HOW TO STUDY LAW AND TAKE LAW EXAMS —Cont'd

Computers—Cont'd
  study aids, computer-based exercises, **Jurisp 157, 158**
Concurring opinions, case brief format, **Jurisp 113**
Constitutional law
  first year course, **Jurisp 57, 58**
  law libraries, **Jurisp 79-83**
  sample exam questions and answers, **Jurisp 234-251**
Contracts
  first year course, **Jurisp 58, 59**
  sample exam questions and answers, **Jurisp 252-274**
Corporate law office, what do lawyers do, **Jurisp 43**
Course selection, **Jurisp 206-208**
Criminal law and procedure
  first year course, **Jurisp 59-61**
  sample exam questions and answers, **Jurisp 275-292**
Daily review, learning after class, **Jurisp 135, 136**
Dictionaries and thesauri, law libraries, **Jurisp 91, 92**
Digests, law libraries, **Jurisp 75-78**
Disposition, case brief format, **Jurisp 113**
Dissenting opinions, case brief format, **Jurisp 113**
Electronic research, law libraries, **Jurisp 94-97**
Employment, law school employment, **Jurisp 197, 198**
Encyclopedias, law libraries, **Jurisp 88, 89**
English roots, beginnings of common law, **Jurisp 15-23**
Exams, generally, **Jurisp 162-192**
Executive branch, modern American legal system, **Jurisp 35, 36**
Facts, case brief format, **Jurisp 107**
Federal digests, law libraries, **Jurisp 76**
Federal legislation and constitution, law libraries, **Jurisp 79-82**
Field trips, **Jurisp 196, 197**
First year curriculum, **Jurisp 53-67**
Flash cards, study aids, **Jurisp 160, 161**
Generalist training, what do lawyers do, **Jurisp 37, 38**
Government, what do lawyers do, **Jurisp 43, 44**
Grading, first year curriculum, **Jurisp 66, 67**

HOW TO STUDY LAW AND TAKE LAW EXAMS —Cont'd

Groups, learning after class in study groups, **Jurisp 147, 148**
Holdings, case brief format, **Jurisp 110, 111**
Hornbooks, study aids, **Jurisp 152, 153**
Institutions, law related, **Jurisp 44**
International programs, **Jurisp 209**
Issues, case brief format, **Jurisp 109, 110**
Joint degree programs, **Jurisp 209, 210**
Judicial branch, modern American legal system, **Jurisp 25-30**
Law, the study and practice of
  Exams, **Law Study & Prac 112-149**
Law dictionaries and thesauri, law libraries, **Jurisp 91, 92**
Law journals, **Jurisp 201-202**
Law school employment, **Jurisp 197, 198**
Law student organizations, **Jurisp 193-195**
Learning after class, **Jurisp 134-148**
Lectures and special events, **Jurisp 195, 196**
Legal encyclopedias, law libraries, **Jurisp 88, 89**
Legal periodicals, law libraries, **Jurisp 86, 87**
Legislation
  first year course, **Jurisp 61, 62**
  law libraries, legislation and constitutions, **Jurisp 79-83**
Legislative branch, modern American legal system, **Jurisp 30-34**
Legislative history, law libraries, **Jurisp 83, 84**
Libraries and librarians, law libraries, **Jurisp 68-97**
Modern American Legal System, **Jurisp 24-36**
Moot court, **Jurisp 205, 206**
Municipal legislation and constitution, law libraries, **Jurisp 82, 83**
New adventures, **Jurisp 211**
Notes, classroom experience, **Jurisp 130-133**
Organizations, law student organizations, **Jurisp 193-195**
Outlines and outlining
  learning after class, **Jurisp 136-147**
  study aids, subject outlines, **Jurisp 154-156**
Participation, classroom experience, **Jurisp 126-130**
Periodicals, law libraries, **Jurisp 86, 87**

HOW TO STUDY LAW AND TAKE LAW EXAMS —Cont'd

Post-class learning, **Jurisp 134-148**

Post-exam, **Jurisp 191, 192**

Post-first year, **Jurisp 201-211**

Preparation
- class, preparation for, **Jurisp 98-119**
- entering law school, preparation for, **Jurisp 7-14**
- exam, preparation for, **Jurisp 163-169**

Pro bono activities, **Jurisp 47, 199, 200**

Procedural history, case brief format, **Jurisp 108**

Property
- first year course, **Jurisp 62-64**
- sample exam questions and answers, **Jurisp 293-309**

Rationale, case brief format, **Jurisp 111, 112**

Readings
- class, reading cases in preparation for, **Jurisp 100-104**
- entering law school, preparation for, **Jurisp 7-10**

Regional digests, law libraries, **Jurisp 76**

Research
- electronic research, law libraries, **Jurisp 94-97**
- legal research as first year curriculum, **Jurisp 65, 66**

Restatements of the Law, law libraries, **Jurisp 90, 91**

Review of exams, study aids, **Jurisp 158, 159**

Samples
- case briefs, **Jurisp 113-119**
- exam questions and answers, **Jurisp 212-355**
- outlines, learning after class, **Jurisp 140-147**

Selection of courses, **Jurisp 206-208**

Socratic method
- classroom experience, **Jurisp 120-126**
- study of law, **Jurisp 49, 50**

Specialization, what do lawyers do, **Jurisp 39-42**

State digests, law libraries, **Jurisp 75**

State legislation and constitution, law libraries, **Jurisp 82**

Student organizations, **Jurisp 193-195**

Study aids, **Jurisp 149-161**

Study groups, learning after class, **Jurisp 147, 148**

GENERAL INDEX

References are to Titles and Pages

HOW TO STUDY LAW AND TAKE LAW EXAMS —Cont'd

Study of law, generally, **Jurisp 48**

Subject outlines, study aids, **Jurisp 154-156**

Subject summaries, study aids, **Jurisp 153, 154**

Summaries, subject summaries as study aids, **Jurisp 153, 154**

Summer clerkships, **Jurisp 210, 211**

Taking exam, generally, **Jurisp 169-191**

Thesauri, law libraries, **Jurisp 91, 92**

Thinking like a lawyer, **Jurisp 48, 49**

Time for self, **Jurisp 198, 199**

Torts
- first year course, **Jurisp 64**
- sample exam questions and answers, **Jurisp 310-355**

Treatises, law libraries, **Jurisp 87, 88**

Values, **Jurisp 200**

Visiting law school, preparation for entering law school, **Jurisp 10, 11**

Writing, legal writing as first year curriculum, **Jurisp 65, 66**

HUMAN RIGHTS

International Human Rights (this index)

Public International Law (this index)

HUSBAND AND WIFE

Federal Estate and Gift Taxation (this index) generally

ILLEGALITY

Landlord and Tenant (this index)

IMMIGRATION LAW AND PROCEDURE

Academic students, nonimmigrant visas, **Immigration 134**

Adjustment of status, nonimmigrant visas, **Immigration 149**

Administrative appeals, relief from deportation, **Immigration 201, 202**

Administrative Appeals Unit, administrative structure of immigration law, **Immigration 80**

IMMIGRATION LAW AND PROCEDURE—Cont'd

Administrative structure of immigration law, generally, **Immigration 71-85**

Appeals, **Immigration 80, 199-223**

Artists internatinoally recognized, nonimmigrant visas, **Immigration 145**

Asylum

- generally, **Immigration 239-260**
- criminal activity, denial of asylum as immigration consequences of, **Immigration 438, 439**
- right to grant or receive, **Immigration 270-274**

Athletes internatinoally recognized, nonimmigrant visas, **Immigration 145**

Birth, citizenship at, **Immigration 284-288**

Board of Immigration Appeals, administrative structure of immigration law, **Immigration 79**

Canadian business travelers and their families, nonimmigrant visas, **Immigration 146**

Capacity to use courts, **Immigration 384-388**

Certification, visas, **Immigration 117-124**

Change of status, student nonimmigrant visas, **Immigration 159, 160**

Citizenship

- generally, **Immigration 278-348**
- false claim to citizenship, criminal aspects of immigration, **Immigration 424, 425**
- fiancee or fiance of U.S. citizenship, nonimmigrant visas, **Immigration 141, 142**

Colonial immigration, **Immigration 1-3**

Commerce power, source of federal power to regulate immigration and naturalization, **Immigration 50**

Communists, grounds for exclusion, **Immigration 41, 42**

Compliance failure

- deportation proceedings, **Immigration 428-431**
- registration requirements, **Immigration 421, 422**

Concealing alien, **Immigration 415, 416**

Concepts of citizenship, **Immigration 278-284**

Congressional role in immigration process, generally, **Immigration 86-101**

IMMIGRATION LAW AND PROCEDURE—Cont'd

Conspiracy, criminal aspects of immigration, **Immigration 427, 428**
Constitutional provisions, source of federal power to regulate immigration and naturalization, **Immigration 51, 52**
Continued presence in United States, facilitating alien's unlawful entry or, **Immigration 411-420**
Crew members, nonimmigrant visas, **Immigration 132**
Crime related exclusion, **Immigration 41**
Criminal aspects of immigration, generally, **Immigration 405-439**
Delegated versus inherent power, source of federal power to regulate immigration and naturalization, **Immigration 52-55**
Denaturalization, **Immigration 325-335**
Denial of asylum, immigration consequences of criminal activity, **Immigration 438, 439**
Deportation
    generally, **Immigration 42, 43, 164-223**
    compliance failure, deportation proceedings, **Immigration 428-431**
    criminal activity, immigration consequences of, **Immigration 436-438**
    rights of alien during deportation hearing, **Immigration 193-195**
    suspension of deportation, congressional role in immigration process, **Immigration 101**
Diplomatic personnel, nonimmigrant visas, **Immigration 129, 130**
Discretion, relief from deportation, **Immigration 206-223**
Discrimination on basis of alienage, **Immigration 351-383**
Diversity immigrants, visas, **Immigration 114, 115**
Diversity visas, **Immigration 37**
Dual nationality, **Immigration 282-284**
Duration of status, student nonimmigrant visas, **Immigration 152, 153**
Early U.S. immigration policy, **Immigration 3-6**
Education rights of aliens, **Immigration 388-390**

IMMIGRATION LAW AND PROCEDURE—Cont'd

Employment
generally, **Immigration 34-37**
student nonimmigrant visas, **Immigration 154-157**
temporary workers, nonimmigrant visas, **Immigration 135-139**
unlawful employment of aliens, **Immigration 431, 432**
visas, employment-related, **Immigration 111-114**
Entry and reentry
exclusion, **Immigration 229, 230**
facilitating alien's unlawful entry or continued presence in United States, **Immigration 411-420**
right to enter, **Immigration 263, 264**
unlawful entry, **Immigration 406-410**
visas, **Immigration 125-127**
Estoppel, relief from deportation, **Immigration 221-223**
Ethical dimensions of immigration practice, **Immigration 440-459**
Exchange visitors, nonimmigrant visas, **Immigration 139-141**
Exclusion
generally, **Immigration 224-234**
criminal activity, **Immigration 226, 433-436**
grounds for, **Immigration 40-42**
judicial review, relief from deportation and exclusion, **Immigration 202-206**
Executive branch, functions of Federal Government in regulating immigration, **Immigration 69, 70**
Executive consultation with congress, congressional role in immigration process, **Immigration 98-100**
Executive Office of Immigration Review, administrative structure of immigration law, **Immigration 77-80**
Exit, freeom of, **Immigration 261-263**
Expatriation, **Immigration 336-348**
Extraordinary ability, nonimmigrant visas for aliens with, **Immigration 144**
Facilitating alien's unlawful entry or continued presence in United States, **Immigration 411-420**
False claim to citizenship, criminal aspects of immigration, **Immigration 424, 425**

IMMIGRATION LAW AND PROCEDURE—Cont'd
False statements, criminal aspects of immigration, **Immigration 422-428**
Family
  Canadian business travelers and their families, nonimmigrant visas, **Immigration 146**
  marriage fraud, **Immigration 42, 428**
  relatives of employees of international organizations, nonimmigrant visas, **Immigration 143, 144**
  sponsorship, **Immigration 33, 34, 110, 111**
  student's family, nonimmigrant visas, **Immigration 151**
  visas, **Immigration 110, 111, 143, 144, 146, 151**
Federal benefit program eligibility of aliens, **Immigration 390-394**
Fiancee or fiance of U.S. citizenship, nonimmigrant visas, **Immigration 141, 142**
Fraud
  criminal aspects of immigration, **Immigration 422-428**
  deportation, marriage fraud as grounds for, **Immigration 42**
  marriage fraud, **Immigration 42, 428**
Freedom of movement, **Immigration 261-277**
Good moral character not established, immigration consequences of criminal activity, **Immigration 438**
Harboring alien, **Immigration 415, 416**
Health and Human Services Department, administrative structure of immigration law, **Immigration 84**
Health related exclusion, **Immigration 40, 41, 225, 226**
Hearings
  deportation, **Immigration 175-199**
  exclusion, **Immigration 231, 232**
  rights of alien during deportation hearing, **Immigration 193-195**
History of U.S. immigration law and policy, **Immigration 1-48**
Hong Kong inhabitants
  Immigration Act of 1990, **Immigration 37, 38**
  visas, **Immigration 115**
Immigration Act of 1990, **Immigration 32-44**
Immigration and Nationality Act of 1952, **Immigration 15-21**

IMMIGRATION LAW AND PROCEDURE—Cont'd

Immigration and Naturalization Service, **Immigration 74-77, 96, 97**

Immigration Courts, administrative structure of immigration law, **Immigration 77-79**

Immigration Reform and Control Act of 1986 (IRCA), **Immigration 22-32**

Information media representatives, nonimmigrant visas, **Immigration 139**

Interdiction, exclusion, **Immigration 232-234**

International organization representatives, nonimmigrant visas, **Immigration 134, 135**

Intracompany transferees, nonimmigrant visas, **Immigration 142, 143**

In-transit visitors, nonimmigrant visas, **Immigration 131**

Issuance, visas, **Immigration 125-127**

Judicial review, relief from deportation, **Immigration 202-206**

Judiciary, functions of Federal Government in regulating immigration, **Immigration 62-68**

Jurisdiction, refugees and asylum, **Immigration 245, 246**

Jus soli and jus sanguinis principles, **Immigration 280-282**

Justice Department, administrative structure of immigration law, **Immigration 74-81**

Labor Department, administrative structure of immigration law, **Immigration 81-84**

Land ownership rights of aliens, **Immigration 396-399**

Legislature, functions of Federal Government in regulating immigration, **Immigration 62**

Loss of nationality, **Immigration 324-348**

Marriage fraud, **Immigration 42, 428**

Members of congress as ombudsmen, congressional role in immigration process, **Immigration 95, 96**

Migrant workers' rights, **Immigration 274-277**

Military service, rights of aliens, **Immigration 399, 400**

Misrepresentation, **Immigration 42, 422-428**

Moral and policy issues, grounds for deportation, **Immigration 45-48**

IMMIGRATION LAW AND PROCEDURE—Cont'd

Motion to reopen or reconsider, relief from deportation, **Immigration 199-201**

Movement, freedom of, **Immigration 261-277**

Nationality, loss of, **Immigration 324-348**

National security concerns, grounds for deportation, **Immigration 42, 43**

National sovereignty, source of federal power to regulate immigration and naturalization, **Immigration 50, 51**

Naturalization, generally, **Immigration 39, 40, 296-324**

Noncitizens' rights, **Immigration 277**

Nonimmigrant visas, generally, **Immigration 128-163**

Numerical limitations, visas, **Immigration 103-115**

Oversight of INS, congressional role in immigration process, **Immigration 96, 97**

Parole, exclusion, **Immigration 230, 231**

Perjury, criminal aspects of immigration, **Immigration 422-424**

Permanent resident procedures for alients inside U.S., visas, **Immigration 127**

Permissible and impermissible state regulations, source of federal power to regulate immigration and naturalization, **Immigration 58-61**

Permits, fraud and misuse of, **Immigration 425-427**

Petitions, visas, **Immigration 117-124**

Plenary congressional power, source of federal power to regulate immigration and naturalization, **Immigration 55-58**

Practical training, student nonimmigrant visas, **Immigration 157-159**

Preference visas, **Immigration 109-115**

Prehearing, procedures for deportation, **Immigration 175-188**

Private legislation, congressional role in immigration process, **Immigration 88-95**

Procedural process, exclusion, **Immigration 229-234**

Procedural requirements for nonimmigrant visas, **Immigration 146-148**

Procedures for deportation, generally, **Immigration 175-199**

Quota laws, generally, **Immigration 10-15**

IMMIGRATION LAW AND PROCEDURE—Cont'd

Reconsider, relief from deportation, **Immigration 199-201**
Refugees, generally, **Immigration 38, 235-239, 267-270**
Registration requirements, compliance failure, **Immigration 421, 422**
Relatives of employees of international organizations, nonimmigrant visas, **Immigration 143, 144**
Reopen, relief from deportation, **Immigration 199-201**
Reporting client's activities, ethical dimensions of immigration practice, **Immigration 443-445**
Restrictions, generally, **Immigration 6-10**
Return, right to, **Immigration 263**
Rights of aliens in United States, generally, **Immigration 349-404**
Scope of federal power, source of federal power to regulate immigration and naturalization, **Immigration 55-61**
Security and related grounds for exclusion, **Immigration 14, 227, 228**
Shielding alien, **Immigration 415, 416**
Show cause order, deportation hearing, **Immigration 188, 189**
Source of federal power to regulate immigration and naturalization, **Immigration 49-55**
Sovereignty, source of federal power to regulate immigration and naturalization, **Immigration 50, 51**
Special immigrants, visas, **Immigration 115-117**
State Department, administrative structure of immigration law, **Immigration 71-73**
Stateless persons, rights of, **Immigration 265-267**
Stay of deportation, **Immigration 218, 219**
Students
  academic students, nonimmigrant visas, **Immigration 134**
  nonimmigrant visas, **Immigration 150-163**
  vocational students, nonimmigrant visas, **Immigration 143**
Suspension of deportation, **Immigration 101, 210-214**
Taxation, rights of aliens, **Immigration 400-404**
Temporary visitors, nonimmigrant visas, **Immigration 130, 131**
Temporary workers, nonimmigrant visas, **Immigration 135-139**
Travel, right to, **Immigration 264, 265**

IMMIGRATION LAW AND PROCEDURE—Cont'd

Treaty traders and investors, nonimmigrant visas, **Immigration 132-134**

United States Information Agency, administrative structure of immigration law, **Immigration 85**

Unlawful employment of aliens, **Immigration 431, 432**

Unlawful entry, **Immigration 406-410**

Violation of student status, student nonimmigrant visas, **Immigration 161-163**

Visas
- generally, **Immigration 102-127**
- diversity visas, **Immigration 37**
- fraud, criminal aspects of immigration, **Immigration 425-427**
- nonimmigrant visas, generally, **Immigration 128-149**
- students, nonimmigrant visas, **Immigration 150-163**

Vocational students, nonimmigrant visas, **Immigration 143**

Voluntary departure, relief from deportation, **Immigration 208-210**

Voting rights, **Immigration 383, 384**

Withholding of deportation, **Immigration 217, 218**

IMPLIED EXCEPTION

Insurance Law (this index)

IMPORTS OR EXPORTS

International Business Transactions (this index)

INDIVIDUAL EMPLOYEE RIGHTS

Generally, **Indiv Employee Rts 1-4**

Accommodation duty, discrimination, **Indiv Employee Rts 174-177**

Alcohol abuse, general concepts and current issues, **Indiv Employee Rts 358-366**

Americans With Disabilities Act
- generally, **Indiv Employee Rts 128, 129**
- screening employees, **Indiv Employee Rts 345**

Arbitration outside collective bargaining, **Indiv Employee Rts 206-208**

INDIVIDUAL EMPLOYEE RIGHTS—Cont'd
At-will employment, termination of employment, **Indiv Employee Rts 221-247**
Bargaining agreements, collective rights, **Indiv Employee Rts 198-206**
Benefit programs, **Indiv Employee Rts 296-318**
Collective bargaining agreements, collective rights, **Indiv Employee Rts 198-206**
Collective rights, **Indiv Employee Rts 178-220**
Common law
- generally, **Indiv Employee Rts 7-9**
- collective rights, **Indiv Employee Rts 178-181**
- privacy and reputation, **Indiv Employee Rts 83-98**

Compensation
- injury and disease, compensation for, **Indiv Employee Rts 33-82**
- unemployment compensation, termination of employment, **Indiv Employee Rts 253-263**
- workers' compensation statutes, **Indiv Employee Rts 41-68**

Constitutional provisions, generally, **Indiv Employee Rts 9-11, 131-152**
Constructive discharges and quits, **Indiv Employee Rts 341, 342**
Contracts, generally, **Indiv Employee Rts 8, 9**
Criminal matters
- mail tampering, **Indiv Employee Rts 117, 118**
- Omnibus Crime Control and Safe Streets Act, **Indiv Employee Rts 114-117**

Current issues, **Indiv Employee Rts 330-373**
Defamation, **Indiv Employee Rts 84-90**
Defenses of employer
- discrimination, **Indiv Employee Rts 166-172**
- OSHA, **Indiv Employee Rts 26-28**

Definitions
- disability, **Indiv Employee Rts 68**
- protected class, **Indiv Employee Rts 156-158**

Disabled workers
- Americans With Disabilities Act, **Indiv Employee Rts 128, 129**
- compensation of, **Indiv Employee Rts 33-35**

INDIVIDUAL EMPLOYEE RIGHTS—Cont'd

Disabled workers—Cont'd
  social security disability insurance program, compensation for injury and disease, **Indiv Employee Rts 68-75**
Discrimination
  generally, **Indiv Employee Rts 153-177**
  collective rights, **Indiv Employee Rts 190-193**
Drug abuse, general concepts and current issues, **Indiv Employee Rts 358-366**
Drug-Free Workplace Act of 1988, **Indiv Employee Rts 125-128**
Employee Polygraph Protection Act, **Indiv Employee Rts 118-125**
Employee Retirement Income Security Act, **Indiv Employee Rts 296-318**
Enforcement, OSHA, **Indiv Employee Rts 21-23**
Exchanges of union-management information, collective rights, **Indiv Employee Rts 196-198**
Fair Credit Reporting Act, **Indiv Employee Rts 110-114**
Fair Labor Standards Act, wage and hour regulation, **Indiv Employee Rts 273-290**
Family and Medical Leave Act, **Indiv Employee Rts 319-322**
Federal constitution, **Indiv Employee Rts 132-149**
Federal contractor labor standards, wage and hour regulation, **Indiv Employee Rts 290-292**
Federal regulation
  collective rights, **Indiv Employee Rts 181-218**
  wage and hour regulation, **Indiv Employee Rts 273-295**
Fifth Amendment, **Indiv Employee Rts 145-147**
First Amendment, **Indiv Employee Rts 132-139**
Fourteenth Amendment, **Indiv Employee Rts 147-149**
Fourth Amendment, **Indiv Employee Rts 139-145**
Freedom of Information Act, **Indiv Employee Rts 98-101**
Garnishment restriction, wage and hour regulation, **Indiv Employee Rts 294, 295**
General concepts and current issues, **Indiv Employee Rts 330-373**
Genetic screening of employees, **Indiv Employee Rts 348**

INDIVIDUAL EMPLOYEE RIGHTS—Cont'd

Good cause for discharge from employment, **Indiv Employee Rts 248-253**
Honesty testing, screening employees, **Indiv Employee Rts 347**
Human immunodeficiency virus (HIV), general concepts and current issues, **Indiv Employee Rts 366-373**
Identification of responsible parties, **Indiv Employee Rts 331-341**
Invasion of privacy, **Indiv Employee Rts 90-98**
Labor unions, generally, **Indiv Employee Rts 178-220**
Mail tampering, **Indiv Employee Rts 117, 118**
National Labor Management Relations Act, collective rights, **Indiv Employee Rts 181-188**
National Labor Relations Act
  generally, **Indiv Employee Rts 181-188**
  unfair labor practices under NLRA, collective rights, **Indiv Employee Rts 188-195**
Ninth Amendment, **Indiv Employee Rts 147-149**
Occupational diseases, workers' compensation statutes, **Indiv Employee Rts 45, 46**
Occupational Safety and Health Act, **Indiv Employee Rts 16-32**
Old age and survivors insurance, **Indiv Employee Rts 322-329**
Omnibus Crime Control and Safe Streets Act, **Indiv Employee Rts 114-117**
OSHA, **Indiv Employee Rts 16-32**
Pensions, **Indiv Employee Rts 296-318**
Physical safety, **Indiv Employee Rts 16-82**
Portal-to-Portal Act, wage and hour regulation, **Indiv Employee Rts 293, 294**
Prevention of injury and disease, **Indiv Employee Rts 16-33**
Privacy Act of 1974, **Indiv Employee Rts 101-110**
Privacy and reputation, **Indiv Employee Rts 83-152**
Private sector regulation, collective rights, **Indiv Employee Rts 181-211**
Proving discrimination, **Indiv Employee Rts 158-166**
Public sector regulation, collective rights, **Indiv Employee Rts 211-220**
Railway Labor Act, **Indiv Employee Rts 208-210**

INDIVIDUAL EMPLOYEE RIGHTS—Cont'd

Record keeping, OSHA, **Indiv Employee Rts 19-21**
Reference checks, screening employees, **Indiv Employee Rts 351**
Rehabilitation
  compensation for injury and disease, **Indiv Employee Rts 40**
  vocational rehabilitation, **Indiv Employee Rts 75-82**
Reputation, **Indiv Employee Rts 83-152**
Safety, **Indiv Employee Rts 16-82**
Screening employees, **Indiv Employee Rts 342-353**
Smoking, general concepts and current issues, **Indiv Employee Rts 353-358**
Social Security
  generally, **Indiv Employee Rts 322-329**
  disability insurance program, compensation for injury and disease, **Indiv Employee Rts 68-75**
State constitutions, **Indiv Employee Rts 149-152**
State legislation affecting employee privacy, **Indiv Employee Rts 129-131**
State regulation
  collective rights, **Indiv Employee Rts 210, 211**
  wage and hour regulation, **Indiv Employee Rts 295**
Statutory regulation, generally, **Indiv Employee Rts 4-6**
Surveillance, collective rights, **Indiv Employee Rts 188-190**
Termination of employment
  generally, **Indiv Employee Rts 221-272**
  constructive discharges and quits, **Indiv Employee Rts 341, 342**
Third party representation denied, collective rights, **Indiv Employee Rts 193-195**
Torts, generally, **Indiv Employee Rts 7, 8**
Traumatic injuries, workers' compensation statutes, **Indiv Employee Rts 41-45**
Unemployment compensation, termination of employment, **Indiv Employee Rts 253-263**
Unfair labor practices under NLRA, collective rights, **Indiv Employee Rts 188-195**
Unions, generally, **Indiv Employee Rts 178-220**
Vocational rehabilitation, **Indiv Employee Rts 75-82**

INDIVIDUAL EMPLOYEE RIGHTS—Cont'd
Wage and hour regulation, **Indiv Employee Rts 273-295**
Worker Adjustment and Retraining Notification Act, termination of employment, **Indiv Employee Rts 264-272**
Workers' compensation statutes, **Indiv Employee Rts 41-68**

INDORSEMENTS
Negotiable Instruments and Check Collection (this index)

INITIATIVE AND REFERENDUM
State Constitutional Law (this index)

INJUNCTIONS
Generally, **Inj 1, 2**
Abstention, equity jurisdiction, **Inj 118-125**
Abuse of court process, equity jurisdiction, **Inj 49-56**
Adequate remedy at law, equity jurisdiction, **Inj 34-57, 77-81**
Aiders and abettors, personal jurisdiction, **Inj 12-15**
Appeal
  generally, **Inj 233-243**
  enforcement of injunction, **Inj 230, 231**
  interlocutory injunction, appeal of, **Inj 177-179**
Appointive statutes, jurisdiction, **Inj 9**
Assignee of business, personal jurisdiction, **Inj 19**
Automatic stay, appeal of interlocutory injunctions, **Inj 240, 241**
Balancing equities, discretion in issuance of injunction, **Inj 132-142**
Bonds, interlocutory injunctions, **Inj 172-176**
Change or modification
  equity jurisdiction, **Inj 108-113**
  interlocutory injunctions, **Inj 176, 177**
Civil contempt
  criminal contempt, civil contempt distinguished from, **Inj 228-232**
  enforcement, **Inj 223-232**
Civil rights violations, equity jurisdiction, **Inj 69, 70**
Clean hands, equity jurisdiction, **Inj 97-104**
Comity, extraterritorial effect, **Inj 207-213**

INJUNCTIONS—Cont'd
Comparison of jurisdiction over person with subject matter jurisdiction, **Inj 28-30**
Confidential relations, equity jurisdiction, **Inj 42, 43**
Constitutional procedures, enforcement of injunction, **Inj 229**
Contempt
    civil contempt, **Inj 223-232**
    criminal contempt, **Inj 223-232**
    enforcement of injunction, **Inj 216-232**
Contract cases exceptions, discretion in issuance of injunctions, **Inj 137-139**
Costs to petitioner, enforcement of injunction, **Inj 231**
Criminal contempt
    civil contempt distinguished from criminal contempt, **Inj 228-232**
    enforcement of injunction, **Inj 223-232**
Criminal matters
    enforcement, criminal contempt, **Inj 217-223**
    equity jurisdiction, **Inj 49-52, 57-64, 76, 77**
Criminal prosecution, equity jurisdiction, **Inj 49-52**
Damages
    adequate remedy at law, **Inj 43, 44**
    equity jurisdiction, **Inj 131**
Definitions or distinctions
    civil contempt distinguished from criminal contempt, enforcement of injunction, **Inj 228-232**
    equity jurisdiction, **Inj 32-34**
Discretion
    generally, **Inj 3, 4**
    appeal of injunctions, **Inj 238, 239**
    equity jurisdiction, **Inj 126-149**
    extraterritorial effect, **Inj 199, 200**
    interlocutory injunctions, **Inj 179-181**
    issuance of injunction, **Inj 126-149**
Dismissal of action, enforcement of injunction, **Inj 230**
Distinguishing civil from criminal contempt, enforcement, **Inj 228-232**
Enforcement
    generally, **Inj 216-232**

INJUNCTIONS—Cont'd
Enforcement—Cont'd
  criminal statute, equity jurisdiction, **Inj 60-64**
  equity jurisdiction, **Inj 60-64, 81-94**
Equity court
  extraterritorial effect, **Inj 213-215**
  jurisdiction, **Inj 5-9**
  subject matter jurisdiction, **Inj 24, 25**
Equity jurisdiction, generally, **Inj 2, 3, 32-125**
Evidence
  equity jurisdiction, **Inj 108**
  interlocutory injunctions, **Inj 158, 171, 172**
Exceptions
  adequate remedy at law, **Inj 57**
  balancing harm, **Inj 137-140**
  discretion in issuance of injunction, **Inj 137-140**
Extraterritorial effect, **Inj 197-213**
Federal courts versus state courts, equity jurisdiction, **Inj 119, 120**
Federal rule, personal jurisdiction, **Inj 17-19**
Findings of fact, appeal of injunctions, **Inj 235, 236**
Freedom of speech and press
  discretion in issuance of injunction, **Inj 146-148**
  equity jurisdiction, **Inj 74, 75**
Harm, interlocutory injunctions, **Inj 158**
In rem jurisdiction, **Inj 21-23**
Insolvency
  equity jurisdiction, **Inj 130**
  impractical remedy at law, **Inj 46-48**
Interest in property or subject matter
  equity jurisdiction, **Inj 39-42**
  personal jurisdiction, **Inj 19-21**
Interlocutory injunctions
  generally, **Inj 150-196**
  appeal of, **Inj 240-243**
Irreparable harm to petitioner, interlocutory injunctions, **Inj 158**
Jurisdiction, generally, **Inj 2, 3, 5-31**
Jury trial right, equity jurisdiction, **Inj 76**
Laches doctrine, equity jurisdiction, **Inj 107-113**

INJUNCTIONS—Cont'd

Libel, equity jurisdiction, **Inj 74-81**
Limitation of actions, enforcement of injunction, **Inj 230**
Limitations or restrictions
- enforcement of injunction, statute of limitations, **Inj 230**
- subject matter jurisdiction, **Inj 24-26**

Mandatory versus prohibitory interlocutory injunctions, **Inj 162-170**
Modification. Change or modification, supra
Money damages unmeasurable, equity jurisdiction, **Inj 131**
Mootness, appeal of interlocutory injunctions, **Inj 241-243**
Multiple actions at law, equity jurisdiction, **Inj 45, 46**
Multiplicity of suits, equity jurisdiction, **Inj 130, 131**
Nuisance, equity jurisdiction, **Inj 58-60, 114, 115**
Office, personal jurisdiction, **Inj 16, 17**
Out of state property or activity, extraterritorial effect, **Inj 213-215**
Pardon power of executive, distinction between civil and criminal contempt, **Inj 231**
Parties, generally, **Inj 10-12**
Permanent injunctions, interlocutory injunctions, **Inj 190-194**
Person, jurisdiction over, generally, **Inj 9-23, 28-30**
Personal feelings injury, equity jurisdiction, **Inj 71-73**
Personal jurisdiction, generally, **Inj 9-23, 28-30**
Personal property, equity jurisdiction, **Inj 40-42**
Petitions
- costs, enforcement of injunction, **Inj 231**
- discretion in issuance of injunctions, petition favored, **Inj 148, 149**
- enforcement of injunction, **Inj 230, 123**
- interlocutory injunctions, **Inj 158**
- voluntary dismissal of action, enforcement of injunction, **Inj 230**

Political questions, equity jurisdiction, **Inj 121-125**
Pollution, discretion in issuance of injunction, **Inj 144-146**
Preliminary injunctions, interlocutory injunctions, **Inj 189, 190**
Privacy rights violations, equity jurisdiction, **Inj 70, 71**
Privity, personal jurisdiction, **Inj 12**

INJUNCTIONS—Cont'd
Property and property rights
equity jurisdiction, **Inj 39-42, 64-69, 75, 76**
jurisdiction over successor in interest in, **Inj 19-21**
personal property, equity jurisdiction, **Inj 40-42**
real property, equity jurisdiction, **Inj 39, 40, 129, 130**
Prospective harm, discretion in issuance of injunction, **Inj 140-142**
Public interest, discretion in issuance of injunction, **Inj 142-149**
Quasi in rem jurisdiction, **Inj 21-23**
Real property, equity jurisdiction, **Inj 39, 40, 129, 130**
Res judicata
extraterritorial effect, **Inj 197-206**
interlocutory injunctions, **Inj 179**
Rulings of law, appeal of injunctions, **Inj 237, 238**
Standing, equity jurisdiction, **Inj 113-118**
Standing to raise issue of lack of jurisdiction, **Inj 31**
Statutes
discretion in issuance of injunctions, statutory exceptions, **Inj 139, 140**
interlocutory injunctions, **Inj 179-181**
Stay, appeal of interlocutory injunctions, **Inj 240, 241**
Subject matter jurisdiction, generally, **Inj 23-31**
Successors, personal jurisdiction, **Inj 16-21**
Supersedeas writ, appeal of interlocutory injunctions, **Inj 240, 241**
Taxpayer suits, equity jurisdiction, **Inj 116-118**
Temporary restraining orders, interlocutory injunctions, **Inj 181-189**
Torts, equity jurisdiction, **Inj 52-56**
Unique personal property, equity jurisdiction, **Inj 40-42**
United Mine Workers' situation, enforcement of injunction, **Inj 231, 232**
Vacation, interlocutory injunctions, **Inj 176, 177**
Value of subject matter, equity jurisdiction, **Inj 109-113**
Vesting, jurisdiction, **Inj 9**
Voluntary dismissal of action, enforcement of injunction, **Inj 230**

INSOLVENCY
Injunctions (this index)
Insurance Law (this index)
  Bankruptcy or insolvency

INSURABLE INTEREST
Insurance Law (this index)

INSURANCE LAW
Accident insurance, subrogation, **Insur 287**
Affirmative warranty, defenses of insurer, **Insur 203**
Agents' representations, defenses of insurer, **Insur 200**
All risk versus specified risk, definition of risks, **Insur 131-133**
Alternative claims by third party, insurer's duty to defend, **Insur 258, 259**
Ambiguous claims, insurer's duty to defend, **Insur 257, 258**
Annual statements, methods of statutory regulation, **Insur 382**
Appeal, insurer's duty to defend, **Insur 272, 273**
Appraisal
  filing claims, procedures for, **Insur 184**
  measure of recovery, appraisal clauses, **Insur 253-256**
Articles of commerce, measure of recovery, **Insur 237**
Art Law (this index)
Assignment, bad faith causes of action, **Insur 309-311**
Assignments
  defenses of insurer, **Insur 200**
  insurer's duty to defend, assignment of claims, **Insur 274**
  persons insured, **Insur 156-163**
Attorney's conflict of interest, insurer's duty to defend, **Insur 274-281**
Avoidance of policy, defenses of insurer, **Insur 193**
Bad faith causes of action, generally, **Insur 299-331**
Bankruptcy or insolvency
  bad faith causes of action, insolvency of insured, **Insur 315, 316**
  statutory regulation, methods of, **Insur 382**
Belief or opinion, defenses of insurer, **Insur 197-199**

INSURANCE LAW—Cont'd
Bid bonds, construction related bonds, **Insur 350-352**
Binders, written binders, **Insur 67, 68**
Bonds, generally, **Insur 339-367**
Cancellation of insurance policy, generally, **Insur 74-76**
Casualty insurance
  generally, **Insur 19-31**
  subrogation, **Insur 289**
Chose in action, persons insured, **Insur 156, 157**
Coinsurance, measure of recovery, **Insur 243-247**
Commercial general liability policies, generally, **Insur 43-51**
Common instances of estoppel, **Insur 233-236**
Communicating waiver, methods of, **Insur 225-227**
Concealment, defenses of insurer, **Insur 188-192**
Conflict of interest
  insurer's control of defense, **Insur 270, 271**
  insurer's duty to defend, conflict of interest in counsel, **Insur 274-281**
Consideration, limitations on waiver, **Insur 228, 229**
Construction related bonds, **Insur 350-359**
Contract versus tort, bad faith causes of action, **Insur 309**
Conventional subrogation, **Insur 297, 298**
Cooperation
  defenses of insurer, cooperation duty of insured, **Insur 219-222**
  filing claims procedures, cooperation of insured, **Insur 183**
Counter defenses to insurable interest doctrine, **Insur 104, 105**
Court-created duty, insurer's duty to defend, **Insur 273**
Court interpretation of warranties and conditions, defenses of insurer, **Insur 203-205**
Coverage, limitations on waiver as to, **Insur 230**
Damages, title insurance, **Insur 53, 54**
Declaratory judgment, self-protection methods for insurer, **Insur 266**
Defects, definition of risks, **Insur 126**
Defense
  bad faith causes of action, **Insur 322**

INSURANCE LAW—Cont'd
Defense—Cont'd
 control of defense, insurer's, **Insur 269-271**
 duty of insurer to defend, **Insur 257-281**
 insurer's defenses, generally, **Insur 188-224**
 reinsurance, **Insur 335-337**
 standing to raise defense of insurable interest, **Insur 103, 104**
 subrogation, **Insur 293-295**
Definition or distinction
 accident, definition of risks, **Insur 128-131**
 estoppel, **Insur 231, 232**
 insurable interest, distinction between property and life insurance, **Insur 81, 82**
 insurable interest in relation to property insurance, **Insur 82**
 insured, **Insur 138**
 misrepresentations, defenses of insurer, **Insur 192, 193**
 risks, **Insur 106-137**
 subrogation, **Insur 282, 283**
 waiver, **Insur 224, 225**
 warranties and conditions, defenses of insurer, **Insur 201-203**
Direct action statutes, procedures for filing claims, **Insur 186, 187**
Discharge of duty to defend by payment of proceeds, **Insur 262, 263**
Discrimination, regulation of insurance, **Insur 374**
Duties
 breach of duty of care, remedies for, **Insur 265**
 cooperation duty of insured, defenses of insurer, **Insur 219-222**
 insurer's duty to defend, **Insur 257-281**
 title insurance, duty to defend, **Insur 54**
Endowment life insurance, **Insur 10**
Entire policy, persons insured, **Insur 157**
Evidence, bad faith causes of action, **Insur 319-322**
Exceptions or exclusions
 friendly fire, implied exception for, **Insur 126-128**
 implied exception, infra
 intentional conduct, implied exception for, **Insur 119-126**
 liability insurance, exclusions, **Insur 44-51**
 title insurance exclusions, **Insur 52, 53**

INSURANCE LAW—Cont'd
Excess insurer, bad faith causes of action, **Insur 311-314**
Express waiver, **Insur 225**
Facts, limitations on waiver in regard to, **Insur 229, 230**
Failure to defend, remedies for, **Insur 263-265**
Fidelity bonds, **Insur 359-365**
Filing claims, procedures for, **Insur 178-187**
Fire and casualty insurance, generally, **Insur 19-31**
First-party insurance, bad faith causes of action, **Insur 317-329**
Friendly fire, implied exception for, **Insur 126-128**
Functional definition, **Insur 1-6**
Group insurance, life insurance, **Insur 13-29**
Health and disability insurance, generally, **Insur 35-43**
Health Care Law and Ethics (this index)
History, regulation of insurance, **Insur 368-372**
Hospitalization insurance, subrogation, **Insur 287-279**
Identification of insured, **Insur 139-156**
Implied exception
  friendly fire, implied exception for, **Insur 126-128**
  intentional conduct, implied exception for, **Insur 119-126**
  normal wear and tear or inherent defect, implied exception for, **Insur 126**
Implied waiver, **Insur 226, 227**
Incontestability clause
  defenses of insurer, **Insur 213-218**
  reinstatement of lapsed policy, **Insur 164, 165**
Indemnity insurance, reinsurance, **Insur 334, 335**
Industrial life insurance, **Insur 11, 12**
Inherent defect, implied exception for, **Insur 126**
Inland marine insurance, generally, **Insur 32-35**
Insurable interest
  generally, **Insur 77-105**
  reinsurance, **Insur 333, 334**
Intentional conduct, implied exception for, **Insur 119-126**
Interpretation by court of warranties and conditions, defenses of insurer, **Insur 203-205**
Interpretation of representation, defenses of insurer, **Insur 197**

INSURANCE LAW—Cont'd
Lapsed policy, reinstatement of, **Insur 163-165**
Legal interest versus factual expectancy, insurable interest in relation to property insurance, **Insur 82-92**
Legislature, regulation of insurance, **Insur 368-380**
Liability insurance
  generally, **Insur 43-51**
  reinsurance, **Insur 334, 335**
  subrogation, **Insur 285**
  third party interests in liability insurance, **Insur 173-176**
License and permit bonds, **Insur 367**
Licensing, methods of statutory regulation, **Insur 380, 381**
Life insurance
  generally, **Insur 7-29**
  assignments, **Insur 159-163**
  distinction between property and life insurance, insurable interest, **Insur 81, 82**
  insurable interest in relation to life insurance, **Insur 94-103**
  subrogation, **Insur 285, 286**
Life tenant/remainderman, special problems of, **Insur 171-173**
Limitations
  defenses of insurer, limitations on coverage, **Insur 208-213**
  waiver and estoppel, **Insur 227-232**
Marine insurance, generally, **Insur 31-35**
Materiality, defenses of insurer, **Insur 193-195**
McCarran-Ferguson Act, regulation of insurance, **Insur 377-380**
Measure of recovery, **Insur 237-256**
Medical insurance, subrogation, **Insur 287-279**
Miller Act requirements, construction related bonds, **Insur 355-359**
Misrepresentations, defenses of insurer, **Insur 192-201**
Mortgagor/mortgagee, special problems of, **Insur 168-171**
Multiple causes of action, insurer's duty to defend, **Insur 259**
Multiple coverage, insurer's duty to defend, **Insur 271, 272**
Mutual life insurance, **Insur 12**
No-action clauses, procedures for filing claims, **Insur 185, 186**
No-fault compensation, generally, **Insur 55-61**

INSURANCE LAW—Cont'd
Nonwaiver agreement, self-protection methods for insurer, **Insur 266-268**
Notice
  filing claims procedures, notice of loss, **Insur 178, 179**
  reservation of rights notice, self-protection methods for insurer, **Insur 269-271**
Obligation of insured to correct representations, defenses of insurer, **Insur 196**
Oral contracts, generally, **Insur 66, 67**
Original insured's rights against reinsurer, **Insur 337, 338**
Other insurance clauses, measure of recovery, **Insur 247-250**
Parol evidence rule
  limitations, **Insur 228**
  waiver and estoppel, **Insur 228, 232, 233**
Payment bonds, construction related bonds, **Insur 355-359**
Penalty statutes, methods of statutory regulation, **Insur 382, 383**
Performance bonds, construction related bonds, **Insur 352-355**
Persons insured, **Insur 138-177**
Policy limitations on waiver, **Insur 230, 231**
Pollution exclusion, liability insurance, **Insur 48-51**
Premiums
  generally, **Insur 68-71**
  return of premiums, defenses of insurer, **Insur 199**
Principal/surety relationship, bonds, **Insur 339-345**
Promissory warranty, defenses of insurer, **Insur 203**
Proof of loss, procedures for filing claims, **Insur 179-182**
Property insurance
  assignments, **Insur 158, 159**
  definitions and distinctions, insurable interest, **Insur 81, 82**
  insurable interest, **Insur 81-94**
  legal interest versus factual expectancy, insurable interest in relation to property insurance, **Insur 82-92**
  life insurance, distinction between property and, **Insur 81, 82**
  subrogation, **Insur 285**
Public interest, limitations on waiver, **Insur 227, 228**
Public official bonds, **Insur 365-367**
Rating legislation, regulation of insurance, **Insur 372-374**

INSURANCE LAW—Cont'd
Real estate, special problems of vendor/vendee, **Insur 165-168**
Real party in interest, subrogation, **Insur 295, 296**
Reasonable expectations rule, definition of risks, **Insur 133-137**
Reciprocal causes of action, bad faith causes of action, **Insur 329-331**
Regulation of insurance, **Insur 368-383**
Reinstatement of lapsed policy, **Insur 163-165**
Reinsurance, generally, **Insur 332-338**
Release, bad faith causes of action, **Insur 316, 317**
Reliance, defenses of insurer, **Insur 195, 196**
Remedies
  bad faith causes of action, **Insur 314, 315, 323-328**
  insurer's duty to defend, **Insur 263-266**
  subrogation, **Insur 290-293**
Renewal of policy, defenses of insurer, **Insur 200, 201**
Reservation of rights notice, self-protection methods for insurer, **Insur 269-271**
Reserve fund, generally, **Insur 71-73**
Return of premiums, defenses of insurer, **Insur 199**
Risk distribution, **Insur 2, 3**
Self-protection methods for insurer, **Insur 266-269**
Settlement, insurer's duty in regard to, **Insur 273**
Stacking of uninsured or underinsured motorist coverage, **Insur 64-66**
Standard form requirements, methods of statutory regulation, **Insur 381**
Standard of proof, bad faith causes of action, **Insur 319-322**
Standing to raise defense of insurable interest, **Insur 103, 104**
Statute of frauds, reinsurance, **Insur 334**
Statute of limitations, bad faith causes of action, **Insur 322, 323**
Statutes protective of insureds as defenses of insurer, warranties and conditions, **Insur 205-208**
Statutory regulation, methods of, **Insur 380-383**
Subrogation
  generally, **Insur 282-298**
  bad faith causes of action, **Insur 328, 329**

INSURANCE LAW—Cont'd

Subsequent damage, procedures for filing claims, **Insur 184**
Substantial membership, **Insur 3, 4**
Successors in interest, title insurance, **Insur 54**
Surgical insurance, subrogation, **Insur 287-279**
Surplus, generally, **Insur 73**
Surrender value, generally, **Insur 73**
Term life insurance, **Insur 8-10**
Third parties
  alternative claims by third party, insurer's duty to defend, **Insur 258, 259**
  bad faith causes of action, third party claims, **Insur 300-317**
  liability insurance, third party interests in, **Insur 173-176**
  subrogation, **Insur 293**
Time
  filing claims, procedures for, **Insur 182, 183**
  reinstatement of lapsed policy, **Insur 165**
  untimely withdrawal of insurer, remedies for, **Insur 265, 266**
Title insurance, generally, **Insur 51-54**
Torts
  bad faith causes of action, contract versus tort, **Insur 309**
  immunity, **Insur 176, 177**
Unauthorized insurers, regulation of insurance, **Insur 380**
Underwriter, insurer as, **Insur 5**
Unfair competition, regulation of insurance, **Insur 375, 376**
Uninsured and underinsured motorist coverage, generally, **Insur 62-66**
Unique property, measure of recovery, **Insur 238-243**
Unlawful contracts, definition of risks, **Insur 106-119**
Unnecessary allegations, insurer's duty to defend, **Insur 261, 262**
Untimely withdrawal of insurer, remedies for, **Insur 265, 266**
Untrue statement of facts in complaint, insurer's duty to defend, **Insur 260, 261**
Valued policies, measure of recovery, **Insur 250-253**
Waiver and estoppel
  generally, **Insur 223-236**
  common instances of estoppel, **Insur 233-236**
  communicating waiver, methods of, **Insur 225-227**

INSURANCE LAW—Cont'd
Waiver and estoppel—Cont'd
consideration, limitations on waiver, **Insur 228, 229**
counter defenses to insurable interest doctrine, **Insur 104, 105**
coverage, limitations on waiver as to, **Insur 230**
definitions
estoppel, **Insur 231, 232**
waiver, **Insur 224, 225**
express waiver, **Insur 225**
facts, limitations on waiver in regard to, **Insur 229, 230**
implied waiver, **Insur 226, 227**
limitations, **Insur 227-232**
nonwaiver agreement, self-protection methods for insurer, **Insur 266-268**
parol evidence rule, **Insur 228, 232, 233**
policy limitations on waiver, **Insur 230, 231**
public interest, limitations on waiver, **Insur 227, 228**
Warranties and conditions
defenses of insurer, **Insur 201-208**
limitations on coverage compared with warranties and conditions, **Insur 210-213**
Wear and tear, implied exception for normal, **Insur 126**
Whole-life insurance, **Insur 7, 8**
Workers' Compensation and Employee Protection Laws (this index)
Work product exclusion, liability insurance, **Insur 44-48**
Written binders, generally, **Insur 67, 68**

INTELLECTUAL PROPERTY
Generally, **Intell Prop 1 et seq.**

INTEREST IN PROPERTY OR SUBJECT MATTER
Estates in Land and Future Interests (this index)
Injunctions (this index)
Insurance Law (this index)
Professional Responsibility (this index)

INTEREST ON LAWYERS' TRUST ACCOUNT (IOLTA) FUNDS
Professional Responsibility (this index)

INTEREST ON MONEY
International Taxation (this index)

INTERLOCUTORY INJUNCTIONS
Injunctions (this index)

INTERNAL UNION AFFAIRS
Labor Law (this index)

INTERNATIONAL BUSINESS TRANSACTIONS
Act of State Doctrine in commercial transactions, **Intn'l Bus 391-414**
Arbitration, dispute settlement, **Intn'l Bus 312-359**
Back to back letters of credit, international trading of goods, **Intn'l Bus 179-183**
Banks, money and international business transactions, **Intn'l Bus 188-191**
Banks and banking, money and international business transactions, **Intn'l Bus 195-197**
Bills of lading, international trading of goods, **Intn'l Bus 121-123, 132-138**
Choice of law, international trading of goods, **Intn'l Bus 50-53**
CISG (contracts for international sale of goods), **Intn'l Bus 40-46**
CMEA (Council for Mutual Economic Assistance), international business transactions in nonmarket and transition economy nations, **Intn'l Bus 306, 307**
COMECON (Council for Mutual Economic Assistance), international business transactions in nonmarket and transition economy nations, **Intn'l Bus 306, 307**
Commercial terms, international trading of goods, **Intn'l Bus 93-113**
Consensus, negotiating international business transactions, **Intn'l Bus 21-23**
Copyright protection, technology transfers, **Intn'l Bus 232-234**

INTERNATIONAL BUSINESS TRANSACTIONS —Cont'd

Council for Mutual Economic Assistance, international business transactions in nonmarket and transition economy nations, **Intn'l Bus 306, 307**
Counterclaims, immunity of states in commercial transactions, **Intn'l Bus 388, 389**
Countertrade, international business transactions in nonmarket and transition economy nations, **Intn'l Bus 302-304**
Culture, negotiating international business transactions, **Intn'l Bus 29-31**
Currency issues, international business transactions in nonmarket and transition economy nations, **Intn'l Bus 298, 299**
Defenses, international trading of goods, **Intn'l Bus 171-179**
Definition of nonmarket and transition economy nations, **Intn'l Bus 285-289**
Delivery or misdelivery, international trading of goods, **Intn'l Bus 123-128**
Deposits, money and international business transactions, **Intn'l Bus 208-212**
Description or misdescription, international trading of goods, **Intn'l Bus 128-132**
Dispute settlement, litigation and arbitration, **Intn'l Bus 312-359**
Distributorship agreements, market economy nations, **Intn'l Bus 269-276**
Drafting CISG (contracts for international sale of goods), **Intn'l Bus 40-46**
Electronic bills of lading, international trading of goods, **Intn'l Bus 133-138**
Electronic letters of credit, international trading of goods, **Intn'l Bus 160-167**
Enforcement, dispute settlement, **Intn'l Bus 323-327, 342-347**
Eurodollars, money and international business transactions, **Intn'l Bus 208-212**
Exceptions
  Act of State Doctrine in commercial transactions, **Intn'l Bus 408-412**
  immunity of states in commercial transactions, **Intn'l Bus 378-388**

INTERNATIONAL BUSINESS TRANSACTIONS —Cont'd

Exchange and exchange controls, money and international business transactions, **Intn'l Bus 201-208**

Execution of judgment, immunity of states in commercial transactions, **Intn'l Bus 389, 390**

Financing, international trading of goods, **Intn'l Bus 139-183**

Foreign exchange and exchange controls, money and international business transactions, **Intn'l Bus 201-205**

Foreign Sovereign Immunities Act of 1976, **Intn'l Bus 371-373**

Forged bill of lading, international trading of goods, **Intn'l Bus 132, 133**

Formation of contract, international trading of goods, **Intn'l Bus 61-69**

Forum selection clause, dispute settlement, **Intn'l Bus 327-335**

Franchises, technology transfers, **Intn'l Bus 237-242**

Fraud defense, international trading of goods, **Intn'l Bus 171-179**

FTOs, international business transactions in nonmarket and transition economy nations, **Intn'l Bus 293-297**

Goods, international trading of, **Intn'l Bus 38-138**

Gray market goods, technology transfers, **Intn'l Bus 249-253**

ICSID (international arbitral rules), dispute settlement, **Intn'l Bus 354-359**

Immunity of states in commercial transactions, **Intn'l Bus 360-390**

Imports or exports

- export financing programs, money and international business transactions, **Intn'l Bus 193-195**
- international business transactions in nonmarket and transition economy nations, **Intn'l Bus 300-302, 304-306**

Intellectual property rights, technology transfers, **Intn'l Bus 218-256**

International Court of Justice, dispute settlement, **Intn'l Bus 313-315**

International Monetary System, **Intn'l Bus 184-188**

Introduction, **Intn'l Bus 1**

Jurisdiction, immunity of states in commercial transactions, **Intn'l Bus 375, 376**

INTERNATIONAL BUSINESS TRANSACTIONS —Cont'd

Language, negotiating international business transactions, **Intn'l Bus 31-36**

Letters of credit, international trading of goods, **Intn'l Bus 139, 140, 160-171, 179-183, 299, 300**

Litigation, dispute settlement, **Intn'l Bus 312-359**

Loans, money and international business transactions, **Intn'l Bus 208-212**

Market economy nations, international business transactions in, **Intn'l Bus 257-284**

Money and international business transactions, **Intn'l Bus 184-215**

National monetary systems, money and international business transactions, **Intn'l Bus 191-193**

Negotiation, generally, **Intn'l Bus 19-37**

Nonmarket and transition economy nations, international business transactions in, **Intn'l Bus 285-311**

Offshore banking, money and international business transactions, **Intn'l Bus 195-197**

Patents, technology transfers, **Intn'l Bus 218-256**

Payment against documents transaction, international trading of goods, **Intn'l Bus 114-121**

Piracy, technology transfers, **Intn'l Bus 245-249**

Planning for renegotiation, negotiating international business transactions, **Intn'l Bus 36, 37**

Pricing, money and international business transactions, **Intn'l Bus 212-215**

Recognition of foreign judgments, dispute settlement, **Intn'l Bus 323-327**

Regional and other development banks, money and international business transactions, **Intn'l Bus 188-191**

Renegotiation, negotiating international business transactions, **Intn'l Bus 36, 37**

Revolving letters of credit, international trading of goods, **Intn'l Bus 179-183**

INTERNATIONAL BUSINESS TRANSACTIONS —Cont'd

Risks
exchange risk, money and international business transactions, **Intn'l Bus 205-208**
loss, risk of, **Intn'l Bus 88-90**
Role playing, negotiating international business transactions, **Intn'l Bus 25, 26**
Sales agent agreements, market economy nations, **Intn'l Bus 269-276**
Sales international trading of goods, **Intn'l Bus 38-40, 139, 140**
Separation of powers, Act of State Doctrine in commercial transactions, **Intn'l Bus 403-408**
Service of process, immunity of states in commercial transactions, **Intn'l Bus 377, 378**
Sovereign immunity, **Intn'l Bus 360-390**
Standby letters of credit, international trading of goods, **Intn'l Bus 167-171**
STOs, international business transactions in nonmarket and transition economy nations, **Intn'l Bus 293-297**
Swedish Chamber of Commerce, dispute settlement, **Intn'l Bus 347-349**
Tax havens, money and international business transactions, **Intn'l Bus 195-197**
Teams, negotiating international business transactions, **Intn'l Bus 23-25**
Technology transfers, **Intn'l Bus 216-256, 263-269, 276-284, 307, 308**
Timing, negotiating international business transactions, **Intn'l Bus 26, 27**
Trademark protection, technology transfers, **Intn'l Bus 227-230**
Trade-related intellectual property rights, technology transfers, **Intn'l Bus 218-256**
Trans-border data flows, technology transfers, **Intn'l Bus 253, 254**
Transfer pricing, money and international business transactions, **Intn'l Bus 212-215**

INTERNATIONAL BUSINESS TRANSACTIONS —Cont'd

Transition economy nations, international business transactions in, **Intn'l Bus 285-311**
Treaties, dispute settlement, **Intn'l Bus 316, 317**
UNCITRAL (international arbitral rules), dispute settlement, **Intn'l Bus 354-359**
Uruguay Round TRIPs Agreement, technology transfers, **Intn'l Bus 218, 219**
Waiver
  Act of State Doctrine in commercial transactions, **Intn'l Bus 409, 410**
  sovereign immunity, **Intn'l Bus 378-381**

INTERNATIONAL ENVIRONMENTAL LAW

Generally, **Intn'l Environ 1-68**
Accidental pollution, vessel-based pollution, **Intn'l Environ 255-258**
Air pollution, generally, **Intn'l Environ 297-313**
Anadromous species, conservation of marine living resources, **Intn'l Environ 289, 289**
Antarctica, multilateral environmental problems, **Intn'l Environ 167-189**
Archeological importance of Antarctica, multilateral environmental problems, **Intn'l Environ 168, 169**
Assistance Convention (1986 IAEA Convention on Assistance in Cases of Nuclear Accident or Radiological Emergency), **Intn'l Environ 387, 388**
Bamako Convention, toxic and hazardous substances, **Intn'l Environ 224-226**
Basel Convention, toxic and hazardous substances, **Intn'l Environ 219-224**
Biodiversity, generally, **Intn'l Environ 84-123**
Bonn Convention, biodiversity, **Intn'l Environ 118-122**
Catadromous species, conservation of marine living resources, **Intn'l Environ 290**

INTERNATIONAL ENVIRONMENTAL LAW —Cont'd

CCAMLR (1980 Convention on Conservation of Antarctic Marine Living Resources), multilateral environmental problems, **Intn'l Environ 177-180**

Chemicals
- ozone depletion, **Intn'l Environ 155, 156**
- toxic and hazardous substances, **Intn'l Environ 215-226**

Civilian nuclear energy, **Intn'l Environ 359-361, 382-396**

CLC (1969 International Convention on Civil Liability for Oil Pollution), vessel-based pollution, **Intn'l Environ 259-261**

Compliance mechanisms, implementation, **Intn'l Environ 48-53**

Continental shelf, conservation of marine living resources, **Intn'l Environ 282**

Convention on Biological Diversity (CBD), **Intn'l Environ 90-106**

CRAMRA (1988 Antarctic Mineral Resources Convention), multilateral environmental problems, **Intn'l Environ 180**

Custom, sources and forms of international environmental law, **Intn'l Environ 26-31**

Customary law, use and testing of nuclear weapons, **Intn'l Environ 369-382**

Decreasing resources, global problems, **Intn'l Environ 70-72**

Desertification, generally, **Intn'l Environ 345-354**

Diplomatic avenues, implementation, **Intn'l Environ 54**

Driftnet fishing, conservation of marine living resources, **Intn'l Environ 295, 296**

Dumping, generally, **Intn'l Environ 263-271**

ECE Treaty (1992 ECE Convention on Protection and use of Transboundary Watercourses and Lakes), transboundary water pollution, **Intn'l Environ 333-336**

Economic importance of Antarctica, multilateral environmental problems, **Intn'l Environ 169, 170**

EEZ (Exclusive Economic Zone), conservation of marine living resources, **Intn'l Environ 280-282**

Funding, International Convention on Establishment of an International Fund for Compensation for Oil Pollution Damage, **Intn'l Environ 261, 262**

INTERNATIONAL ENVIRONMENTAL LAW —Cont'd

Future of IEL, **Intn'l Environ 397-411**

General principles of law, sources and forms of international environmental law, **Intn'l Environ 31-33**

Geo-physical character of Antarctica, multilateral environmental problems, **Intn'l Environ 167, 168**

Global climate change, generally, **Intn'l Environ 124-151**

Global organizations, implementation, **Intn'l Environ 41-44**

Global problems, generally, **Intn'l Environ 69-166**

Hazardous substances, generally, **Intn'l Environ 190-226**

Hazardous wastes, generally, **Intn'l Environ 218-226**

Highly migratory species (HMS), conservation of marine living resources, **Intn'l Environ 286**

High seas, International Convention Relating to Intervention on the High Seas in Cases of Oil Pollution Casualties, **Intn'l Environ 257, 258**

ICRW (International Convention for the Regulation of Whaling), conservation of marine living resources, **Intn'l Environ 292-295**

Implementation, generally, **Intn'l Environ 39-68**

Institutions, implementation, **Intn'l Environ 40-48**

Judicial matters
- implementation, judicial remedies, **Intn'l Environ 54-65**
- sources and forms of international environmental law, judicial decisions, **Intn'l Environ 33-36**

Jurisdiction
- implementation, **Intn'l Environ 56-60**
- marine living resources conservation, jurisdiction zones, **Intn'l Environ 279-283**
- nuclear weapons, use and testing of, **Intn'l Environ 373-375**

Land-based pollution, generally, **Intn'l Environ 227-240**

Legal response
- air pollution, **Intn'l Environ 301-313**
- Antarctica, multilateral environmental problems, **Intn'l Environ 172-189**
- biodiversity, **Intn'l Environ 90-123**
- desertification, **Intn'l Environ 350-354**
- dumping, **Intn'l Environ 266-271**

INTERNATIONAL ENVIRONMENTAL LAW —Cont'd

Legal response—Cont'd
- global climate change, **Intn'l Environ 131-151**
- land-based pollution, **Intn'l Environ 234-240**
- marine living resources, conservation of, **Intn'l Environ 278-296**
- nuclear damage, **Intn'l Environ 364-396**
- ozone depletion, **Intn'l Environ 158-166**
- population, **Intn'l Environ 78-83**
- toxic and hazardous substances, **Intn'l Environ 211-226**
- transboundary air pollution, **Intn'l Environ 301-313**
- transboundary water pollution, **Intn'l Environ 320-344**
- vessel-based pollution, **Intn'l Environ 248-262**
- water pollution, **Intn'l Environ 320-344**

Liability
- CLC (1969 International Convention on Civil Liability for Oil Pollution), vessel-based pollution, **Intn'l Environ 259-261**
- 1963 IAEA Convention on Civil Liability for Nuclear Damage, **Intn'l Environ 395, 396**
- nuclear damage, **Intn'l Environ 388-396**
- vessel-based pollution, **Intn'l Environ 258-262**

London Convention, Convention on the Prevention of Marine Pollution by Dumping of Wastes and Other Matter (1972 London Convention), **Intn'l Environ 267-270**

LRTAP (Convention on Long-Range Transboundary Air Pollution), **Intn'l Environ 304-309**

Mammals, conservation of marine living resources, **Intn'l Environ 287-289**

Marine living resources, generally, **Intn'l Environ 272-296**

MARPOL (1973/1978 International Convention for Prevention of Pollution from Ships), vessel-based pollution, **Intn'l Environ 249-251**

Migratory species of wild animals, biodiversity, **Intn'l Environ 118-122**

Mineral resources (1988 Antarctic Mineral Resources Convention), multilateral environmental problems, **Intn'l Environ 180**

INTERNATIONAL ENVIRONMENTAL LAW —Cont'd

Montreal Guidelines for Protection of Marine Environment Against Pollution from Land-based Sources, **Intn'l Environ 236, 237**

Montreal Protocol, ozone depletion, **Intn'l Environ 159, 160**

Multilateral environmental problems, generally, **Intn'l Environ 167-411**

1959 Antarctic Treaty, multilateral environmental problems, **Intn'l Environ 174-176**

1960 Paris Convention on Third Party Liability in Field of Nuclear Energy, **Intn'l Environ 393, 394**

1963 IAEA Convention on Civil Liability for Nuclear Damage, **Intn'l Environ 395, 396**

1991 Antarctic Environment Protocol, multilateral environmental problems, **Intn'l Environ 181-189**

1994 Convention on Nuclear Safety, **Intn'l Environ 384-386**

Nitrogen oxides, transboundary air pollution, **Intn'l Environ 307, 308**

Nongovernmental organizations (NGOs), implementation, **Intn'l Environ 46-48**

Notification Convention (1986 IAEA Convention on Early Notification of Nuclear Accident), **Intn'l Environ 386, 387**

Nuclear damage, generally, **Intn'l Environ 355-396**

Nuclear waste, **Intn'l Environ 361, 362**

Oil pollution

- funding, International Convention on Establishment of an International Fund for Compensation for Oil Pollution Damage, **Intn'l Environ 261, 262**
- high seas, International Convention Relating to Intervention on the High Seas in Cases of Oil Pollution Casualties, **Intn'l Environ 257, 258**
- OPRC (International Convention on Oil Pollution Preparedness, Response and Cooperation), vessel-based pollution, **Intn'l Environ 256**

Operational pollution, vessel-based pollution, **Intn'l Environ 248-255**

INTERNATIONAL ENVIRONMENTAL LAW —Cont'd

OPRC (International Convention on Oil Pollution Preparedness, Response and Cooperation), vessel-based pollution, **Intn'l Environ 256**

Organizations, implementation, **Intn'l Environ 40-48**

Ozone depletion, generally, **Intn'l Environ 152-166**

Pesticides, toxic and hazardous substances, **Intn'l Environ 212-215**

Population, global problems, **Intn'l Environ 69-83**

Ramsar Convention, biodiversity, **Intn'l Environ 115-118**

Remedial objectives
- air pollution, **Intn'l Environ 300, 301**
- biodiversity, **Intn'l Environ 89, 90**
- desertification, **Intn'l Environ 349, 350**
- dumping, **Intn'l Environ 263**
- global climate change, **Intn'l Environ 129-131**
- global problems, **Intn'l Environ 74-78**
- land-based pollution, **Intn'l Environ 232-234**
- marine living resources, conservation of, **Intn'l Environ 277, 278**
- nuclear damage, **Intn'l Environ 362-364**
- ozone depletion, **Intn'l Environ 157, 158**
- toxic and hazardous substances, **Intn'l Environ 203-211**
- transboundary air pollution, **Intn'l Environ 300, 301**
- transboundary water pollution, **Intn'l Environ 318-320**
- vessel-based pollution, **Intn'l Environ 246-248**
- water pollution, **Intn'l Environ 318-320**

Rhine River, transboundary water pollution, **Intn'l Environ 336-339**

Scientific importance of Antarctica, multilateral environmental problems, **Intn'l Environ 168, 169**

Seals
- conservation of marine living resources, **Intn'l Environ 288, 289**
- multilateral environmental problems, Seals Convention of 1972, **Intn'l Environ 176, 177**

Seals Convention of 1972, multilateral environmental problems, **Intn'l Environ 176, 177**

INTERNATIONAL ENVIRONMENTAL LAW —Cont'd

Sources and forms of international environmental law, **Intn'l Environ 15-38**

States
- implementation, **Intn'l Environ 60-65**
- nuclear damage, state responsibility, **Intn'l Environ 388-392**

Stockholm Conference on the Human Environment, **Intn'l Environ 3-8**

Straddling stocks, conservation of marine living resources, **Intn'l Environ 284-286**

Sulphur emissions, transboundary air pollution, **Intn'l Environ 305-307**

Toxic and hazardous substances, generally, **Intn'l Environ 190-226**

Transboundary air pollution, generally, **Intn'l Environ 297-313**

Transboundary water pollution, generally, **Intn'l Environ 314-344**

Treaties
- dumping, regional treaties, **Intn'l Environ 270, 271**
- international treaties related to biological diversity, **Intn'l Environ 107-122**
- land-based pollution, regional treaties, **Intn'l Environ 237-240**
- 1959 Antarctic Treaty, multilateral environmental problems, **Intn'l Environ 174-176**
- sources and forms of international environmental law, **Intn'l Environ 17-26**

UNCLOS (United Nations Convention on the Law of the Sea)
- generally, **Intn'l Environ 8-10**
- dumping, **Intn'l Environ 266, 267**
- land-based pollution, **Intn'l Environ 234-236**
- marine living resources, conservation of, **Intn'l Environ 278-290**
- vessel-based pollution, **Intn'l Environ 252-255**

UNEP Regional Sea Programme, conservation of marine living resources, **Intn'l Environ 290, 290**

INTERNATIONAL ENVIRONMENTAL LAW —Cont'd

UNEP (1987 UNEP London Guidelines for Exchange of Information on Chemicals in International Trade), toxic and hazardous substances, **Intn'l Environ 215-218**

UNESCO, 1972 UNESCO convention concerning protection of world cultural and natural heritage, **Intn'l Environ 113-115**

United Nations Conference on Environment and Development (UNCED), **Intn'l Environ 12-14**

United States/Canada
- transboundary air pollution, **Intn'l Environ 310, 311**
- transboundary water pollution, **Intn'l Environ 339-342**

United States/Mexico
- transboundary air pollution, **Intn'l Environ 312, 313**
- transboundary water pollution, **Intn'l Environ 342-344**

Vessel-based pollution, generally, **Intn'l Environ 241-262**

Volatile organic compounds, transboundary air pollution, **Intn'l Environ 308, 309**

Wastes
- dumping, Convention on the Prevention of Marine Pollution by Dumping of Wastes and Other Matter (1972 London Convention), **Intn'l Environ 267-270**
- hazardous wastes, generally, **Intn'l Environ 218-226**
- nuclear waste, **Intn'l Environ 361, 362**

Waterfowl habitat, biodiversity, **Intn'l Environ 115-118**

Water pollution, generally, **Intn'l Environ 314-344**

Weapons, use and testing of nuclear weapons, **Intn'l Environ 356-359, 365-382**

Wetlands, biodiversity, **Intn'l Environ 115-118**

Whaling, conservation of marine living resources, **Intn'l Environ 292-295**

World Commission on Environment and Development, **Intn'l Environ 10-12**

World Heritage Convention, biodiversity, **Intn'l Environ 113-115**

INTERNATIONAL HUMAN RIGHTS

Advisory jurisdiction, Inter-American Court of Human Rights, **Intn'l Human Rts 217-219**

INTERNATIONAL HUMAN RIGHTS—Cont'd

African System of Human and Peoples' Rights, **Intn'l Human Rts 228-247**
Apartheid, international convention on suppression and punishment of crime of, **Intn'l Human Rts 67, 68**
Bill of Human Rights, United Nations, **Intn'l Human Rts 28-57**
Bureau for Democracy, Human Rights, and Labor, United States and international human rights, **Intn'l Human Rts 308-310**
Charters
  Organization of American States (OAS), Inter-American Human Rights System, **Intn'l Human Rts 176-194**
  United Nations charter, **Intn'l Human Rts 21-28, 78-99**
Children, convention on rights of, **Intn'l Human Rts 76-78**
Contentious jurisdiction, Inter-American Court of Human Rights, **Intn'l Human Rts 207-211; Intn'l Human Rts 207-215**
Convention-based system, Inter-American Human Rights System, **Intn'l Human Rts 194-227**
Courts, International human rights laws in U.S. courts, **Intn'l Human Rts 310-317**
Customary international law, International human rights laws in U.S. courts, **Intn'l Human Rts 315-317**
Discrimination
  racial discrimination, international convention on elimination of all forms of, **Intn'l Human Rts 61-67**
  UN charter-based institutions, **Intn'l Human Rts 82-85**
  women, convention on elimination of all forms of discrimination against, **Intn'l Human Rts 68-72**
Economic aid cutoff, United States and international human rights, **Intn'l Human Rts 300-305**
Emerging caselaw, Inter-American Court of Human Rights, **Intn'l Human Rts 221-227**
Enforcement
  European Commission of Human Rights, enforcement mechanism of, **Intn'l Human Rts 110-112**
  European social charter, **Intn'l Human Rts 155-159**
European Court of Human Rights, **Intn'l Human Rts 133-147**
European social charter, **Intn'l Human Rts 151-159**
European system for protection of human rights, **Intn'l Human Rts 102-113**

INTERNATIONAL HUMAN RIGHTS—Cont'd
European Union, **Intn'l Human Rts 147-150**
Exhaustion of remedies, enforcement mechanism of convention, **Intn'l Human Rts 117-123**
Geneva Conventions and Protocols, **Intn'l Human Rts 249-272**
Genocide, covenant on prevention and punishment of crime of, **Intn'l Human Rts 58-61**
Gross violations of human rights, procedures for dealing with, **Intn'l Human Rts 87**
Helsinki Final Act, Organization for Security and Cooperation in Europe (OSCE), **Intn'l Human Rts 160-163**
Historical antecedents of law, **Intn'l Human Rts 1-20**
Humanitarian laws, generally, **Intn'l Human Rts 248-272**
Institutions, UN charter-based, **Intn'l Human Rts 78-99**
Inter-American Commission on Human Rights, **Intn'l Human Rts 199-207**
Inter-American Court of Human Rights, **Intn'l Human Rts 207-227**
Inter-American Human Rights System, **Intn'l Human Rts 174-227**
International Financial Institutions (IFIs), United States and international human rights, **Intn'l Human Rts 306, 307**
International human rights laws in U.S. courts, **Intn'l Human Rts 310-317**
Interpretation of rights guaranteed, European Court of Human Rights, **Intn'l Human Rts 141-147**
Interstate complaints, enforcement mechanism of convention, **Intn'l Human Rts 110-112**
Intervention, pre-World War II law, **Intn'l Human Rts 3-5**
Judgments, European Court of Human Rights, **Intn'l Human Rts 139-141**
Judicial and quasi-judicial proceedings, nongovernmental human rights organizations, **Intn'l Human Rts 324-326**
Jurisdiction
- European Court of Human Rights, **Intn'l Human Rts 133-137**
- Inter-American Court of Human Rights, **Intn'l Human Rts 207-211, 217-219**

INTERNATIONAL HUMAN RIGHTS—Cont'd

Labor standards, pre-World War II law, **Intn'l Human Rts 9, 10**
League of Nations, pre-World War II law, **Intn'l Human Rts 7-13**
Lobbyists, nongovernmental human rights organizations as, **Intn'l Human Rts 321-323**
Military aid cutoff, United States and international human rights, **Intn'l Human Rts 300-305**
Ministers, committee of, **Intn'l Human Rts 128-133**
Minorities, UN subcommission on prevention of discrimination and protection of, **Intn'l Human Rts 82-85**
Modus operandi, enforcement mechanism of convention, **Intn'l Human Rts 123, 134**
Nongovernmental human rights organizations, **Intn'l Human Rts 318-329**
Opinions, Inter-American Court of Human Rights, **Intn'l Human Rts 220, 221**
Optional protocol, United Nations, **Intn'l Human Rts 48-51**
Organization for Security and Cooperation in Europe (OSCE), **Intn'l Human Rts 159-173**
Organization of American States (OAS), Inter-American Human Rights System, **Intn'l Human Rts 176-194**
Postadmissibility proceedings, enforcement mechanism of convention, **Intn'l Human Rts 124-128**
Pre-World War II law, **Intn'l Human Rts 1-20**
Private petitions, enforcement mechanism of convention, **Intn'l Human Rts 112-115**
Quasi-judicial proceedings, nongovernmental human rights organizations, **Intn'l Human Rts 324-326**
Racial discrimination, international convention on elimination of all forms of, **Intn'l Human Rts 61-67**
San Francisco Conference, United Nations charter, **Intn'l Human Rts 22, 23**
Sex discrimination, convention on elimination of all forms of discrimination against women, **Intn'l Human Rts 68-72**
Six month rule, enforcement mechanism of convention, **Intn'l Human Rts 117-123**
Specialized agencies, **Intn'l Human Rts 99-101**

INTERNATIONAL HUMAN RIGHTS—Cont'd
State obligations and measures of implementation, African System of Human and Peoples' Rights, **Intn'l Human Rts 237-247**
Torture and other cruel, inhuman or degrading treatment, convention against, **Intn'l Human Rts 72-76**
Treaties
International human rights laws in U.S. courts, **Intn'l Human Rts 311-315**
pre-World War II law, **Intn'l Human Rts 5-7**
United Nations, **Intn'l Human Rts 58-78**
United Nations human rights system, **Intn'l Human Rts 21-101**
United States and international human rights, **Intn'l Human Rts 276-298**
Universal declaration of human rights, United Nations, **Intn'l Human Rts 29-38**
Women
discrimination against women, convention on elimination of all forms of, **Intn'l Human Rts 68-72**
status of women, UN commission on, **Intn'l Human Rts 85, 86**

INTERNATIONAL LAW
Public International Law (this index)

INTERNATIONAL MATTERS
Business transactions. **International Business Transactions** (this index)
Environmental law. **International Environmental Law** (this index)
Human rights. **International Human Rights** (this index)
Investment. **International Trade and Investment** (this index)
Public International Law (this index)
Taxation. **International Taxation** (this index)
Trade. **International Trade and Investment** (this index)

INTERNATIONAL TAXATION
Generally, **Intn'l Tax 1-26**

INTERNATIONAL TAXATION—Cont'd
Accounts payable, foreign currency, **Intn'l Tax 298-300**
Accounts receivable, foreign currency, **Intn'l Tax 298-300**
Accuracy-related penalty, intercompany pricing, **Intn'l Tax 240, 241**
Acquisition of foreign currency, **Intn'l Tax 294, 295, 297, 298**
Active trade or business exception, international tax-free transactions, **Intn'l Tax 314-317**
Adjustments
  intercompany pricing, **Intn'l Tax 238-240**
  stock basis, controlled foreign corporations, **Intn'l Tax 271, 272**
Advance pricing agreements, intercompany pricing, **Intn'l Tax 243-245**
Assignment rules, income tax treaty provisions, **Intn'l Tax 115-126**
Avoidance of double taxation, income tax treaty provisions, **Intn'l Tax 126, 127**
Bank deposits, nonbusiness income from U.S. sources, **Intn'l Tax 44, 45**
Basic U.S. jurisdictional tax principles, generally, **Intn'l Tax 11-26**
Bilateral income tax treaty network, **Intn'l Tax 105-107**
Borrowing foreign currency, **Intn'l Tax 295-297**
Boycott provisions, **Intn'l Tax 349-362**
Branch loss recapture rule, international tax-free transactions, **Intn'l Tax 323, 324**
Branch profits tax, taxing rules, **Intn'l Tax 48-54**
Bribery provisions, **Intn'l Tax 360-362**
Business activity in foreign countries, generally, **Intn'l Tax 138-144**
Capital
  contributions to capital and transfers to estates, trusts and partnerships, international tax-free transactions, **Intn'l Tax 324, 325**
  nonbusiness income from U.S. sources, capital gains, **Intn'l Tax 48-54**

INTERNATIONAL TAXATION—Cont'd

Central problem of international taxation, generally, **Intn'l Tax 2, 3**

Citizenship and residency, basic U.S. jurisdictional tax principles, **Intn'l Tax 18-23**

Classification rules, income tax treaty provisions, **Intn'l Tax 115-126**

Comparable profits method, intercompany pricing, **Intn'l Tax 227-231**

Computation
- credit, computing direct or indirect foreign tax credit, **Intn'l Tax 162-171**
- estate taxation for resident and nonresident aliens, **Intn'l Tax 372, 373, 376, 379**
- generation-skipping transfer tax, resident and nonresident aliens, **Intn'l Tax 379**
- gift tax, resident and nonresident aliens, **Intn'l Tax 376**

Contributions to capital and transfers to estates, trusts and partnerships, international tax-free transactions, **Intn'l Tax 324, 325**

Controlled foreign corporations, generally, **Intn'l Tax 249-284**

Conversion, foreign currency, **Intn'l Tax 303-307**

Corporations
- citizenship and residency, basic U.S. jurisdictional tax principles, **Intn'l Tax 21-23**
- inbound transactions, **Intn'l Tax 16, 17**
- shareholders, controlled foreign corporations, **Intn'l Tax 253-271**
- stock or securities exception, international tax-free transactions, **Intn'l Tax 317-319**

Credit
- controlled foreign corporations, foreign tax credit, **Intn'l Tax 272-274**
- estate taxation for resident and nonresident aliens, credits subtracted to determine tax due, **Intn'l Tax 373, 374**
- foreign tax credit, generally, **Intn'l Tax 145-195**
- generation-skipping transfer tax, credits subtracted to determine, **Intn'l Tax 379**
- resident and nonresident aliens, **Intn'l Tax 373, 374, 379**

Currency, foreign currency, **Intn'l Tax 285-308**

INTERNATIONAL TAXATION—Cont'd
Deductions
  estate taxation for resident and nonresident aliens, **Intn'l Tax 370-372**
  generation-skipping transfer tax, resident and nonresident aliens, **Intn'l Tax 378, 379**
  source rules, deduction allocation rules, **Intn'l Tax 92-104**
Definitions
  controlled foreign corporations, **Intn'l Tax 250-253**
  income tax, foreign tax credit, **Intn'l Tax 153-157**
  income tax treaty provisions, **Intn'l Tax 114, 115**
Development of model income tax treaties, **Intn'l Tax 109-111**
Discrimination
  hiring practices, international boycott provisions, **Intn'l Tax 355**
  income tax treaty provisions, nondiscrimination, **Intn'l Tax 130-132**
  refusals to do business, international boycott provisions, **Intn'l Tax 353-355**
  shipping and insurance arrangements, international boycott provisions, **Intn'l Tax 355, 356**
Disposition of foreign currency, **Intn'l Tax 294, 295, Tax 297, 298**
Dividends
  branch profits tax, taxing rules, **Intn'l Tax 53, 54**
  income source rules, **Intn'l Tax 77, 78**
  nonbusiness income from U.S. sources, **Intn'l Tax 45, 46**
Double taxation
  avoidance of double taxation, income tax treaty provisions, **Intn'l Tax 126, 127**
  economics of juridical double taxation, **Intn'l Tax 3-6**
  foreign tax credit, **Intn'l Tax 145-150**
Economics of international trade
  generally, **Intn'l Tax 1, 2**
  double taxation, economics of juridical double taxation, **Intn'l Tax 3-6**
  foreign sales corporations, economic processes, **Intn'l Tax 338-340**
Effectively connected income, taxing rules, **Intn'l Tax 32-37**

INTERNATIONAL TAXATION—Cont'd
Eligibility, foreign tax credit, **Intn'l Tax 152, 153**
Engaged in trade or business in United States, taxing rules, **Intn'l Tax 28-32**
Estates, trusts and partnerships, international tax-free transactions, **Intn'l Tax 324, 325**
Estate tax purposes, resident and nonresident aliens, **Intn'l Tax 363-381**
Exceptions, exemptions or exclusions
  active trade or business exception, international tax-free transactions, **Intn'l Tax 314-317**
  foreign income exclusion, business activity in foreign countries, **Intn'l Tax 141-143**
  generation-skipping transfer tax, resident and nonresident aliens, **Intn'l Tax 378, 379**
  gift tax exclusions, resident and nonresident aliens, **Intn'l Tax 375, 376**
  resident and nonresident aliens, **Intn'l Tax 375, 376, 378, 379**
  stock or securities exception, international tax-free transactions, **Intn'l Tax 317-319**
Exchange of information and administrative assistance, income tax treaty provisions, **Intn'l Tax 134-136**
Expatriates, basic U.S. jurisdictional tax principles, **Intn'l Tax 23-25**
Export related income, foreign sales corporations, **Intn'l Tax 336, 337**
FDAP income, nonbusiness income from U.S. sources, **Intn'l Tax 47, 48**
Filing requirements, taxing rules, **Intn'l Tax 63-65**
FIRPTA withholding, taxing rules, **Intn'l Tax 70-72**
Foreign currency, **Intn'l Tax 285-308**
Foreign income exclusion, business activity in foreign countries, **Intn'l Tax 141-143**
Foreign sales corporations, special incentives and disincentives, **Intn'l Tax 332-348**
Foreign tax credit, controlled foreign corporations, **Intn'l Tax 272-274**
Forward contracts, foreign currency, **Intn'l Tax 300, 301**

INTERNATIONAL TAXATION—Cont'd

Functional foreign currency, **Intn'l Tax 290-292**
Futures contracts, foreign currency, **Intn'l Tax 300, 301**
Generation-skipping tax purposes, resident and nonresident aliens, **Intn'l Tax 364-367, 377-379**
Gift tax purposes, resident and nonresident aliens, **Intn'l Tax 363-381**
Governments of foreign countries, taxing rules, **Intn'l Tax 61-63**
Gross estate, estate taxation for resident and nonresident aliens, **Intn'l Tax 367-370**
Growth of international trade, generally, **Intn'l Tax 1**
Hedging, foreign currency, **Intn'l Tax 301-303**
High withholding tax interest, foreign tax credit, **Intn'l Tax 180**
Hiring practices as discriminatory, international boycott provisions, **Intn'l Tax 355**
Housing cost amount, business activity in foreign countries, **Intn'l Tax 143, 144**
Inbound transactions, basic U.S. jurisdictional tax principles, **Intn'l Tax 13-18**
Income source rules, **Intn'l Tax 74-92**
Income tax
  intercompany pricing, income tax treaties, **Intn'l Tax 242, 243**
  shareholders, controlled foreign corporations, **Intn'l Tax 253-271**
  treaties, **Intn'l Tax 105-137, 242, 243**
Increase in earnings invested in U.S. property, controlled foreign corporations, **Intn'l Tax 268-271**
Information reporting, taxing rules, **Intn'l Tax 73**
Insurance arrangements as discriminatory, international boycott provisions, **Intn'l Tax 355, 356**
Intangible assets, international tax-free transactions, **Intn'l Tax 319-323**
Intercompany pricing, **Intn'l Tax 196-248**
Interest on money
  branch profits tax, taxing rules, **Intn'l Tax 52, 53**
  deduction allocation rules, source rules, **Intn'l Tax 97-101**

INTERNATIONAL TAXATION—Cont'd
Interest on money—Cont'd
high withholding tax interest, foreign tax credit, **Intn'l Tax 180**
income source rules, **Intn'l Tax 75-77**
nonbusiness income from U.S. sources, **Intn'l Tax 39-45**
Interpretation of U.S. income tax treaties, **Intn'l Tax 111, 112**
Investments in U.S. real property, taxing rules, **Intn'l Tax 54-60**
Jurisdictional tax principles, generally, **Intn'l Tax 11-26**
Lending foreign currency, **Intn'l Tax 295-297**
Licenses of intangible property, intercompany pricing, **Intn'l Tax 216-226**
Limitations
foreign tax credit, limitations on, **Intn'l Tax 171-194**
income tax treaty provisions, limitation on benefits, **Intn'l Tax 127-130**
Liquidating corporation, international tax-free transactions, **Intn'l Tax 319**
Loans, intercompany pricing, **Intn'l Tax 226, 227**
Management, foreign sales corporations, **Intn'l Tax 337, 338**
Mutual agreement procedure, income tax treaty provisions, **Intn'l Tax 132-134**
Nonbusiness income from U.S. sources, **Intn'l Tax 38-73**
Nondiscrimination, income tax treaty provisions, **Intn'l Tax 130-132**
Nonoutbound transactions, international tax-free transactions, **Intn'l Tax 325-331**
Option contracts, foreign currency, **Intn'l Tax 300, 301**
Original issue discount, nonbusiness income from U.S. sources, **Intn'l Tax 39, 40**
Outbound transactions
basic U.S. jurisdictional tax principles, **Intn'l Tax 11-13**
international tax-free transactions, **Intn'l Tax 313-325**
Partnerships
contributions to capital and transfers to estates, trusts and partnerships, international tax-free transactions, **Intn'l Tax 324, 325**
inbound transactions, **Intn'l Tax 17, 18**
withholdings, taxing rules, **Intn'l Tax 72, 73**

INTERNATIONAL TAXATION—Cont'd

Penalties for intercompany pricing, accuracy-related penalty, **Intn'l Tax 240, 241**

Personal property, income source rules, **Intn'l Tax 82-89**

Personal services, income source rules, **Intn'l Tax 78-81**

Portfolio interest, nonbusiness income from U.S. sources, **Intn'l Tax 40-44**

Preexisting trade or business, taxing rules, **Intn'l Tax 36, 37**

Prices and pricing, intercompany pricing, **Intn'l Tax 196-248**

Profits
- comparable profits method, intercompany pricing, **Intn'l Tax 227-231**
- split profits, intercompany pricing, **Intn'l Tax 231-235**

Qualification of foreign sales corporations, special incentives and disincentives, **Intn'l Tax 334-336**

Real property
- foreign investments in U.S. real property, taxing rules, **Intn'l Tax 54-60**
- income source rules, **Intn'l Tax 82**

Rebated taxes and subsidies, foreign tax credit, **Intn'l Tax 157, 158**

Receivables, accounts receivable, foreign currency, **Intn'l Tax 298-300**

Refusals to do business as discriminatory, international boycott provisions, **Intn'l Tax 353-355**

Relatives, reporting requirements for related taxpayers, **Intn'l Tax 245-248**

Rents and rentals
- income source rules, **Intn'l Tax 81, 82**
- intercompany pricing, rentals of tangible property, **Intn'l Tax 216**
- nonbusiness income from U.S. sources, **Intn'l Tax 46**

Reporting requirements for related taxpayers, intercompany pricing, **Intn'l Tax 245-248**

Research and experimental expenditures, source rules, **Intn'l Tax 101-104**

Residence
- estate tax purposes, resident and nonresident aliens, **Intn'l Tax 363-381**

INTERNATIONAL TAXATION—Cont'd

Residence—Cont'd
 source rule purposes, **Intn'l Tax 91, 92**
Residents, business activity in foreign countries, **Intn'l Tax 140-144**
Royalties, income source rules, **Intn'l Tax 81, 82**
Rules, generally, **Intn'l Tax 27-73**
Sailing permits, taxing rules, **Intn'l Tax 65**
Sales
 foreign sales corporations, special incentives and disincentives, **Intn'l Tax 332-348**
 intercompany pricing, **Intn'l Tax 204-214**
Services
 intercompany pricing, **Intn'l Tax 214-216**
 nonbusiness income from U.S. sources, **Intn'l Tax 46, 47**
 personal services, income source rules, **Intn'l Tax 78-81**
Shareholders, controlled foreign corporations, **Intn'l Tax 253-271**
Shipping arrangements as discriminatory, international boycott provisions, **Intn'l Tax 355, 356**
Small corporations, foreign sales corporations, **Intn'l Tax 346-348**
Soak-up taxes, foreign tax credit, **Intn'l Tax 158**
Social security benefits, nonbusiness income from U.S. sources, **Intn'l Tax 47**
Source rules, **Intn'l Tax 74-104**
Special incentives and disincentives, **Intn'l Tax 332-362**
Split profits, intercompany pricing, **Intn'l Tax 231-235**
Statutes, foreign tax credit, **Intn'l Tax 145-150**
Stock and stockholders
 controlled foreign corporations, shareholders, **Intn'l Tax 253-271**
 international tax-free transactions, stock or securities exception, **Intn'l Tax 317-319**
Subpart F income, controlled foreign corporations, **Intn'l Tax 254-268**
Tax-free transactions, generally, **Intn'l Tax 309-331**
Tax sparing, income tax treaty provisions, **Intn'l Tax 136, 137**
Transfer tax provisions, generally, **Intn'l Tax 363-381**

INTERNATIONAL TAXATION—Cont'd

Translation, foreign currency, **Intn'l Tax 303-307**

Transportation income, taxing rules, **Intn'l Tax 60, 61**

Treaties

basic U.S. jurisdictional tax principles, **Intn'l Tax 25, 26**

estate, gift, and generation-skipping transfer tax, **Intn'l Tax 379-381**

foreign tax credit, **Intn'l Tax 194, 195**

income tax treaties, **Intn'l Tax 105-137, 242, 243**

intercompany pricing, **Intn'l Tax 242, 243**

Trusts, contributions to capital and transfers to estates, trusts and partnerships, **Intn'l Tax 324, 325**

United States shareholders, controlled foreign corporations, **Intn'l Tax 250-253**

United States transfer tax provisions, generally, **Intn'l Tax 363-381**

Withholding

high withholding tax interest, foreign tax credit, **Intn'l Tax 180**

Withholding, taxing rules, **Intn'l Tax 65-73**

INTERNATIONAL TRADE AND INVESTMENT

Agriculture

European Union, common agricultural policy, **Intn'l Trade & Invest 304-306**

Uruguay Round Agreement on Agriculture, restrictions on imports, **Intn'l Trade & Invest 97-99**

Ancom trade rules and industrial development programs, regional economic integration, **Intn'l Trade & Invest 409-412**

Andean multinationsl, regional economic integration, **Intn'l Trade & Invest 414**

Assessing risk of nationalization, taking of foreign investment property by governments, **Intn'l Trade & Invest 215, 216**

Association of Southeast Asian Nations (ASEAN), **Intn'l Trade & Invest 396-401**

Attorneys, corporate counsel of multinational enterprise (MNE), **Intn'l Trade & Invest 49-53**

Bilateral investment treaties, variations on foreign investments, **Intn'l Trade & Invest 195-198**

INTERNATIONAL TRADE AND INVESTMENT —Cont'd

Boycott provisions of export laws, **Intn'l Trade & Invest 154-158**
Canada-U.S. free trade, NAFTA, **Intn'l Trade & Invest 346, 347**
Canadian Free Trade Agreement (CFTA), **Intn'l Trade & Invest 346-360**
Capital, free movement of, European Union, **Intn'l Trade & Invest 301-303**
Commission and lawmaking,, European Union, **Intn'l Trade & Invest 272-275**
Common agricultural policy, European Union, **Intn'l Trade & Invest 304-306**
Community transport policy, European Union, **Intn'l Trade & Invest 303, 304**
Competition
  European Union, competition rules, **Intn'l Trade & Invest 313-344**
  restriction on imports, **Intn'l Trade & Invest 119-121**
Computing value of taken investment, taking of foreign investment property by governments, **Intn'l Trade & Invest 231-223**
Controls on exports, generally, **Intn'l Trade & Invest 143-166**
Conventions, European Union, **Intn'l Trade & Invest 309**
Corporate counsel, multinational enterprise (MNE), **Intn'l Trade & Invest 49-53**
Council of Ministers,, European Union, **Intn'l Trade & Invest 271, 272**
Court of International Trade, restriction on imports, **Intn'l Trade & Invest 141, 142**
Customs, restrictions on imports, **Intn'l Trade & Invest 109-118**
Developed, market economy nations, restrictions on, **Intn'l Trade & Invest 187-195**
Developing nations, restrictions on foreign investments, **Intn'l Trade & Invest 171-177**
Dispute settlement
  CFTA, dispute settlement under, **Intn'l Trade & Invest 358-360**
  insuring against risks of foreign investment losses, **Intn'l Trade & Invest 254-257**

INTERNATIONAL TRADE AND INVESTMENT —Cont'd

Dispute settlement—Cont'd
NAFTA, dispute settlement under, **Intn'l Trade & Invest 384-386**
settlement of investment disputes, **Intn'l Trade & Invest 203-205**
WTO, dispute settlement under, restrictions on imports, **Intn'l Trade & Invest 79-90**
Dumping and antidumping duties, restriction on imports, **Intn'l Trade & Invest 121-128**
Duty free access to United States, **Intn'l Trade & Invest 118, 119**
East Asian integration, regional economic integration, **Intn'l Trade & Invest 414-416**
Economics
CFTA, **Intn'l Trade & Invest 347-350**
NAFTA, **Intn'l Trade & Invest 347, 350, 363-365**
Eligibility, insuring against risks of foreign investment losses, **Intn'l Trade & Invest 247, 248, 252-254**
Employment
international employment agreement, movement of people across national borders, **Intn'l Trade & Invest 436, 437**
Employment of local personnel, movement of people across national borders, **Intn'l Trade & Invest 424-426**
Enforcement of law, European Union, **Intn'l Trade & Invest 288-291**
Environment, side agreements on under NAFTA, **Intn'l Trade & Invest 386, 387**
Escape clause proceedings, restriction on imports, **Intn'l Trade & Invest 137-141**
Establishment right, European Union, **Intn'l Trade & Invest 298, 299**
European Court of Justice and Court of First Instance, European Union, **Intn'l Trade & Invest 280-284**
European parliament, European Union, **Intn'l Trade & Invest 275-279**
European Union
generally, **Intn'l Trade & Invest 265-312**

INTERNATIONAL TRADE AND INVESTMENT —Cont'd

European Union—Cont'd
 competition rules, **Intn'l Trade & Invest 313-344**
 extraterritorial antitrust laws, **Intn'l Trade & Invest 339-344**
 NAFTA, comparison with, **Intn'l Trade & Invest 387, 388**

Exemptions, European Union competition rules, **Intn'l Trade & Invest 313-323**

Expatriate compensation planning, movement of people across national borders, **Intn'l Trade & Invest 433-436**

Export Administration Act (EAA)
 controls on exports, **Intn'l Trade & Invest 146-148**
 sanctions for EAA violations, controls on exports, **Intn'l Trade & Invest 153**

Exports, controls on, generally, **Intn'l Trade & Invest 143-166**

Expropriation and nationalization in international law, taking of foreign investment property by governments, **Intn'l Trade & Invest 220-227**

Extraterritorial antitrust laws, European Union, **Intn'l Trade & Invest 339-344**

Foreign Corrupt Practices Act, **Intn'l Trade & Invest 158-161**

Foreign investments
 generally, **Intn'l Trade & Invest 34-40**
 variations on foreign investments, **Intn'l Trade & Invest 167-206**

Free movement of capital, European Union, **Intn'l Trade & Invest 301-303**

Free movement of goods or workers, European Union, **Intn'l Trade & Invest 291-298**

General Agreement on Tariffs and Trade (GATT)
 restrictions on imports, **Intn'l Trade & Invest 62-78**
 WTO, foreign investment under GATT and, **Intn'l Trade & Invest 201, 202**

Immigration laws of United States, movement of people across national borders, **Intn'l Trade & Invest 430-433**

Insuring against risks of foreign investment losses, generally, **Intn'l Trade & Invest 238-264**

International Trade Commission (ITC), import adjustments and, **Intn'l Trade & Invest 108, 109**

INTERNATIONAL TRADE AND INVESTMENT —Cont'd

Introduction, generally, **Intn'l Trade & Invest 1-17**
Joint ventures, Association of Southeast Asian Nations (ASEAN), **Intn'l Trade & Invest 401-404**
Labor
movement of people across national borders, **Intn'l Trade & Invest 418-424**
side agreements on under NAFTA, **Intn'l Trade & Invest 386, 387**
Libyan Law Nationalizing Bunker Hunt Interests, taking of foreign investment property by governments, **Intn'l Trade & Invest 217-220**
Licenses and licensing, controls on exports, **Intn'l Trade & Invest 148-153**
Limitations or restrictions
developed, market economy nations, **Intn'l Trade & Invest 187-195**
restrictions on foreign investments, **Intn'l Trade & Invest 171-177**
Local personnel, movement of people across national borders, **Intn'l Trade & Invest 424-426**
Movement of people across national borders, **Intn'l Trade & Invest 417-437**
Multilateral investment guarantee agency, insuring against risks of foreign investment losses, **Intn'l Trade & Invest 259-264**
Multinational enterprise (MNE), generally, **Intn'l Trade & Invest 40-55**
Multinational Trade Negotiations, GATT, restrictions on imports, **Intn'l Trade & Invest 67-70**
NAFTA (North American Free Trade Agreement)
generally, **Intn'l Trade & Invest 345-388**
comparison with European Union, **Intn'l Trade & Invest 387, 388**
Nationalization
taking of foreign investment property by governments, **Intn'l Trade & Invest 209-227**
United States laws affecting nationalization process, taking of

INTERNATIONAL TRADE AND INVESTMENT —Cont'd

Nationalization—Cont'd
foreign investment property by governments, **Intn'l Trade & Invest 234-237**
valuation of nationalized property, taking of foreign investment property by governments, **Intn'l Trade & Invest 227-230**
Negotiations, restrictions on imports, **Intn'l Trade & Invest 59-62**
Nonmarket and transition economy nations, restrictions on foreign investments, **Intn'l Trade & Invest 171-177**
Nontariff trade barriers, **Intn'l Trade & Invest 93, 94**
OPIC history and structure, insuring against risks of foreign investment losses, **Intn'l Trade & Invest 243-264**
Passports, movement of people across national borders, **Intn'l Trade & Invest 426, 427**
Patterns of world trade, **Intn'l Trade & Invest 21-28**
President of United States, controls on exports, **Intn'l Trade & Invest 145, 146**
Private insurers, insuring against risks of foreign investment losses, **Intn'l Trade & Invest 257-259**
Privatization, variations on foreign investments, **Intn'l Trade & Invest 183-186**
Public procurement, restrictions on imports, **Intn'l Trade & Invest 99-105**
Quotas, import quotas and licenses, **Intn'l Trade & Invest 91-93**
Regional economic integration, **Intn'l Trade & Invest 389-416**
Restrictions on imports, generally, **Intn'l Trade & Invest 56-142**
Review, controls on exports, **Intn'l Trade & Invest 151-153**
Sanctions for EAA violations, controls on exports, **Intn'l Trade & Invest 153**
Section 301 of Trade Act of 1974, controls on exports, **Intn'l Trade & Invest 161-166**
Services, freedom to provide, European Union, **Intn'l Trade & Invest 299-301**
Settlement
dispute settlements, supra

INTERNATIONAL TRADE AND INVESTMENT —Cont'd

Settlement—Cont'd
- United States Foreign Claims Settlement Commission, taking of foreign investment property by governments, **Intn'l Trade & Invest 230, 231**

Side agreements on labor and environment, NAFTA, **Intn'l Trade & Invest 386, 387**

Standards, restrictions on imports, **Intn'l Trade & Invest 105-108**

Subsidies and countervailing duties, restriction on imports, **Intn'l Trade & Invest 128-137**

Taking of foreign investment property by governments, generally, **Intn'l Trade & Invest 207-237**

Taxation, European Union, **Intn'l Trade & Invest 306, 307**

Trade Act of 1974, controls on exports, **Intn'l Trade & Invest 161-166**

Trade relations, European Union, **Intn'l Trade & Invest 307-309**

Transition economy nations, restrictions on foreign investments, **Intn'l Trade & Invest 171-183**

Treaties
- bilateral investment treaties, variations on foreign investments, **Intn'l Trade & Invest 195-198**
- labor law treaties, movement of people across national borders, **Intn'l Trade & Invest 418-420**

United States Foreign Claims Settlement Commission, taking of foreign investment property by governments, **Intn'l Trade & Invest 230, 231**

United States laws affecting nationalization process, taking of foreign investment property by governments, **Intn'l Trade & Invest 234-237**

United States trade laws, generally, **Intn'l Trade & Invest 28-34**

Uruguay Round Agreement on Agriculture, restrictions on imports, **Intn'l Trade & Invest 97-99**

Valuation of nationalized property, taking of foreign investment property by governments, **Intn'l Trade & Invest 227-230**

Variations on foreign investments, **Intn'l Trade & Invest 167-206**

INTERNATIONAL TRADE AND INVESTMENT —Cont'd

Visas, movement of people across national borders, **Intn'l Trade & Invest 427-430**

World trade and multinational enterprises, generally, **Intn'l Trade & Invest 18-55**

World Trade Organization (WTO)
- dispute settlement under WTO, **Intn'l Trade & Invest 79-90**
- GATT, foreign investment under GATT and WTO, **Intn'l Trade & Invest 201, 202**
- restrictions on imports, **Intn'l Trade & Invest 70-90**

INTERNATIONAL TRADE AND INVESTMENTS

Economics
- taxation. **International Taxation** (this index)

INTERPRETATION

Construction and Interpretation (this index)

INTERVIEWS AND INTERVIEWING

Legal Interviewing and Counseling (this index)

INVESTIGATIONS

Tax Procedure and Tax Fraud (this index)

INVESTMENTS

International Trade and Investment (this index)

IOLTA FUNDS (INTEREST ON LAWYERS' TRUST ACCOUNT FUNDS)

Professional Responsibility (this index)

JUDGES

State Constitutional Law (this index)

JUDICIAL MATTERS

Courts (this index)

JUDICIAL POWER
State Constitutional Law (this index)

JUDICIAL PROCESS
Generally, **Judicial Proc 1, 2**
Abstention, judicial lawmaking, **Judicial Proc 152-156**
Administrative interpretation, statutes and, **Judicial Proc 254-259**
Appellate review, **Judicial Proc 36-46**
Authority, precedent and, **Judicial Proc 101-104**
Avoidance, rule of, **Judicial Proc 299-301**
Bad law, **Judicial Proc 65-67**
Canons of construction, **Judicial Proc 237-242**
Changing common law, **Judicial Proc 161-183**
Common law
  generally, **Judicial Proc 7-11**
  adjudication, **Judicial Proc 48-183**
  statutes in derogation of, **Judicial Proc 242, 243**
Comparing statutes and constitutions, **Judicial Proc 276, 277**
Concurrence, craftsmanship, **Judicial Proc 22-24**
Constitutional law, **Judicial Proc 275-301**
Construction and interpretation
  generally, **Judicial Proc 237-242**
  administrative interpretation, statutes and, **Judicial Proc 254-259**
  constitutional interpretation, **Judicial Proc 275-301**
  legislative control of interpretation, **Judicial Proc 231, 232**
  private interpretation, effect of, **Judicial Proc 259-262**
  statutory interpretation, **Judicial Proc 184-274**
  strict construction of penal statutes, **Judicial Proc 243-249**
Craftsmanship, **Judicial Proc 12-47**
Definitions, **Judicial Proc 52, 53**
Desuetude, **Judicial Proc 270-273**
Dictum, precedents, **Judicial Proc 81-83**
Discretion, judicial lawmaking, **Judicial Proc 157-160**
Dissent, craftsmanship, **Judicial Proc 19-22**
Distinguishing precedent, **Judicial Proc 86-88**
Equally divided court, **Judicial Proc 29, 30**

JUDICIAL PROCESS—Cont'd
Equity of statute revisited, **Judicial Proc 273, 274**
First impression, case of, **Judicial Proc 90-97**
Fundamental values role, **Judicial Proc 233-237**
Goals, common law adjudication, **Judicial Proc 48-70**
Horizontal power, sources of judicial power, **Judicial Proc 4**
Intent, understanding the task, **Judicial Proc 201-206**
Interpretation. Construction and interpretation, supra
Lawmaking, generally, **Judicial Proc 107-160**
Legal reasoning, precedents, **Judicial Proc 104-106**
Legislative matters
  generally, **Judicial Proc 249-254**
  control of interpretation, **Judicial Proc 231, 232**
  understanding the statute, legislative history, **Judicial Proc 213-226**
Lenity, rule of, **Judicial Proc 296-299**
Limits on judicial lawmaking, **Judicial Proc 143-152**
Name-calling, **Judicial Proc 70**
Opinion, craftsmanship, **Judicial Proc 12-20, 24-28, 30-34**
Originalism, **Judicial Proc 279-291**
Overrulings, changing common law, **Judicial Proc 161-182**
Penal statutes, strict construction of, **Judicial Proc 243-249**
Plain meaning rule, understanding the task, **Judicial Proc 206-212**
Plurality opinions, craftsmanship, **Judicial Proc 24-27**
Postenactment evidence of legislative history, **Judicial Proc 249, 250**
Precedent, **Judicial Proc 71-106, 108-143, 296-301**
Private interpretation, effect of, **Judicial Proc 259-262**
Publication of opinions, **Judicial Proc 30-34**
Purpose, understanding the task, **Judicial Proc 201-206**
Reasoned opinion, **Judicial Proc 55-65**
Redoing precedent, **Judicial Proc 88-90**
Role of trial court, **Judicial Proc 46, 47**
Separate opinions, craftsmanship, **Judicial Proc 18, 19, 28**
Sources of judicial power, **Judicial Proc 4-11**
Stare decisis, **Judicial Proc 71-106, 262-269**

JUDICIAL PROCESS—Cont'd
State appellate courts, separate opinions in, **Judicial Proc 28**
Statutory interpretation, **Judicial Proc 184-274**
Strict construction of penal statutes, **Judicial Proc 243-249**
Style of opinion, **Judicial Proc 68, 69**
Subsequent developments, **Judicial Proc 249-274**
Summary disposition, stare decisis problem, **Judicial Proc 97-101**
Synthesis, **Judicial Proc 291-295**
Understanding, **Judicial Proc 212-249**
Understanding the task, **Judicial Proc 184-212**
Vertical power, **Judicial Proc 6, 7**

JUDICIAL REVIEW
Appeal and Error (this index)

JUDICIARY
Comparative Legal Traditions (this index)

JURISDICTION
Federal Jurisdiction (this index)
International Environmental Law (this index)
International Human Rights (this index)

JURISPRUDENCE
Generally, **Jurisp 1-6**
Adjustment of purposes, idealist theories of law as, **Jurisp 148-151**
African civilization, nonuniversality law, **Jurisp 57-75**
American realist theories of law, **Jurisp 255-272**
Anthropology, natural law as based on, **Jurisp 122-125**
Auxiliary in stage of economic determination, historical theories of law, **Jurisp 209-212**
Chinese civilization, nonuniversality law, **Jurisp 22-36**
Command theory of law of the utilitarians, later positivist theories of law, **Jurisp 179-185**

JURISPRUDENCE—Cont'd

Conative impulse, Scandinavian realist theories of law, **Jurisp 273-276**
Critical legal studies movement and offshoots, **Jurisp 296-346**
Criticisms
- American realist theories of law, **Jurisp 266-272**
- critical legal studies movement and offshoots, **Jurisp 314-320**
- divine and prophetic theories of law, **Jurisp 82, 83**
- early positivist theories of law, **Jurisp 178, 179**
- historical theories of law, **Jurisp 212-222**
- idealist theories of law, **Jurisp 154-169**
- later positivist theories of law, **Jurisp 189-204**
- modern theories of natural law, **Jurisp 128-137**
- natural law, early theories of, **Jurisp 95-113**
- phenomenological theories of law, **Jurisp 293-295**
- psychological theory of law, **Jurisp 253, 254**
- Scandinavian realist theories of law, **Jurisp 282, 283**
- sociological theories of law, **Jurisp 236-245**

Defining law, **Jurisp 350-352**
Deontology, natural law as, **Jurisp 119, 120**
Development in history of personal conditions from status to contract, historical theories of law, **Jurisp 207-209**
Divine and prophetic theories of law, **Jurisp 81-83**
Early positivist theories of law, **Jurisp 172-179**
Early theories of natural law, **Jurisp 84-113**
Empiricist epistemology, theories of law in, **Jurisp 171-352**
Ethical jurisprudence, natural law as, **Jurisp 125-127**
Feminist jurisprudence, critical legal studies movement and offshoots, **Jurisp 320-341**
Free law, sociological theories of law, **Jurisp 234-236**
Generalization of potential legal effect and considerations weighed by courts in decision of cases, American realist theories of law, **Jurisp 263, 264**
God, natural law as law of, **Jurisp 90-95**
Han Fei Tzu, early positivist theories of law, **Jurisp 177**
Harmonizing voluntary actions, idealist theories of law as, **Jurisp 138-143**
Historical theories of law, **Jurisp 205-222**
Idealist epistemology, theories of law in, **Jurisp 138-169**

JURISPRUDENCE—Cont'd
Idealist theories of law, **Jurisp 138-169**
Idea of freedom, idealist theories of law as, **Jurisp 143-148**
Ideological incipience in theories about law, **Jurisp 78, 80**
Independent imperatives, Scandinavian realist theories of law, **Jurisp 276-278**
Indian civilization, nonuniversality law, **Jurisp 36-49**
Inner morality of law, natural law as, **Jurisp 127, 128**
Inner order of human associations,, sociological theories of law, **Jurisp 227-229**
Irreconcilable epistemologies in theories about law, **Jurisp 76-79**
Japanese civilization, nonuniversality law, **Jurisp 49-57**
Jurisprudence of interests, sociological theories of law, **Jurisp 232-234**
Justice by nature, natural law as, **Jurisp 86-88**
Kautilya, early positivist theories of law, **Jurisp 172, 173**
Later positivist theories of law, **Jurisp 178, 179**
Legal polycentricity, **Jurisp 347-349**
Manifestation of spirit of people in history, historical theories of law, **Jurisp 205-207**
Metaphysical-rational epistemology, theories of law in, **Jurisp 81-137**
Modern theories of natural law, **Jurisp 113-137**
Morals, natural law as, **Jurisp 117, 118**
Natural law theories, **Jurisp 84-137**
Nonuniversality law, **Jurisp 7-75**
Normative theory of law, later positivist theories of law, **Jurisp 185-187**
Objective conditions of social solidarity,, sociological theories of law, **Jurisp 229-232**
Objectively given value, natural law as, **Jurisp 114-116**
Phenomenological theories of law, **Jurisp 284-295**
Philosophical framework of American realism, American realist theories of law, **Jurisp 256-258**
Positivist and existentialist approach, phenomenological theories of law, **Jurisp 292, 293**
Positivist theories of law, **Jurisp 171-204**

JURISPRUDENCE—Cont'd

Preparation for study of theories of law, **Jurisp 7-80**
Principle of legal evolution, idealist theories of law as, **Jurisp 151-154**
Prophecy of what courts will do, American realist theories of law, **Jurisp 260, 261**
Psychoanalytical point of view, American realist theories of law, **Jurisp 264-266**
Psychological theory of law, **Jurisp 246-254**
Race theory, critical legal studies movement and offshoots, **Jurisp 341-346**
Right reason, natural law as law of, **Jurisp 88-90**
Rules of conduct laid down by judges, American realist theories of law, **Jurisp 259, 260**
Rule theory of law, later positivist theories of law, **Jurisp 187-189**
Scandinavian realist theories of law, **Jurisp 273-283**
Scheme of interpretation for set of social facts that constituting counterpart of legal norms, Scandinavian realist theories of law, **Jurisp 280-282**
Shang Iang, early positivist theories of law, **Jurisp 174-176**
Shuen Tao, early positivist theories of law, **Jurisp 176**
Social welfare, Scandinavian realist theories of law, **Jurisp 279, 280**
Sociological theories of law, **Jurisp 223-245**
Sociology, natural law as related to, **Jurisp 120-122**
Value philosophy approach, phenomenological theories of law, **Jurisp 290-292**
Virtue, natural law as law of, **Jurisp 84-86**
Western civilization, nonuniversality law, **Jurisp 9-22**
What certain officials do about disputes, American realist theories of law, **Jurisp 261, 262**

JUSTICE DEPARTMENT

Tax Procedure and Tax Fraud (this index)

LABOR ARBITRATION LAW AND PRACTICE

Generally, **Labor Arb 1 et seq.**

GENERAL INDEX

References are to Titles and Pages

LABOR LAW

Ally Doctrine, **Labor 122-132**

Antitrust laws, labor and, **Labor 231-263**

Appeals

  consumers, appeals to, **Labor 143-149**

  secondary employees, appeals to, **Labor 132-143**

Appropriate bargaining units, selection of bargaining representative, **Labor 23-34**

Area standards picketing, organizational picketing, **Labor 81, 82**

Bargaining duty, generally, **Labor 181-230**

Boycotts

  appeals to secondary employees, **Labor 132-143**

  secondary boycotts, generally, **Labor 119-180**

Campaign propaganda, selection of bargaining representative, **Labor 52-60**

Certification as remedy for employer misconduct, selection of bargaining representative, **Labor 61-68**

Collective bargaining

  duty to bargain, generally, **Labor 181-230**

  enforcement of collective bargaining agreements, generally, **Labor 264-308**

  selection of bargaining representative, **Labor 17-68**

Concerted activity, generally, **Labor 84-118**

Constitutional protection, organizational picketing, **Labor 69-71**

Construction industry, recognitional picketing in, **Labor 83**

Damages for § 8(b)(4) violations, **Labor 178, 179**

Discharges, employer economic responses to concerted employee activity, **Labor 93-102**

Discipline

  Labor Management Reporting and Disclosure Act (LMRDA) regulation of internal union affairs, **Labor 353-361**

  NLRA regulation of internal union affairs, **Labor 336-344**

Distribution of literature, selection of bargaining representative, **Labor 43-52**

Domination and assistance, employer economic responses to concerted employee activity, **Labor 104-106**

Duty to bargain, generally, **Labor 181-230**

Early regulation by law and statutory overview, **Labor 1-7**

LABOR LAW—Cont'd

Elections
  bargaining representative, **Labor 17-68**
  officers, Labor Management Reporting and Disclosure Act (LMRDA) regulation of internal union affairs, **Labor 361-366**
Employer economic responses to concerted employee activity, **Labor 84-118**
Enforcement of collective bargaining agreements, generally, **Labor 264-308**
Exceptions, federal preemption of state legislation, **Labor 324-328**
Exclusivity, selection of bargaining representative, **Labor 17-23**
Exhaustion of internal union remedies, Labor Management Reporting and Disclosure Act (LMRDA) regulation of internal union affairs, **Labor 358**
Featherbedding, **Labor 179, 180**
Federal preemption of state legislation, **Labor 309-328**
Fiduciary duties of union officers, Labor Management Reporting and Disclosure Act (LMRDA) regulation of internal union affairs, **Labor 373-379**
Free speech and assembly, Labor Management Reporting and Disclosure Act (LMRDA) regulation of internal union affairs, **Labor 345-353**
Good faith bargaining, **Labor 181-192**
Grievance arbitration, enforcement of collective bargaining agreements, **Labor 264-281**
Hot cargo agreements, **Labor 149-156**
Inducements, employer economic responses to concerted employee activity, **Labor 102-104**
Internal union affairs
  Labor Management Reporting and Disclosure Act (LMRDA) regulation of internal union affairs, **Labor 345-379**
  NLRA regulation of, **Labor 329-344**
International Trade and Investment (this index)
  employers and employees
    Labor
Judicial control of union activity prior to Wagner Act, **Labor 1-4**

LABOR LAW—Cont'd

Judicial review of board representation procedures, selection of bargaining representative, **Labor 34-37**

Jurisdictional disputes between unions, **Labor 167-178**

Labor Management Reporting and Disclosure Act (LMRDA) regulation of internal union affairs, **Labor 345-379**

Landrum-Griffin Act, generally, **Labor 7**

Last word on employer intent, employer economic responses to concerted employee activity, **Labor 111-118**

Lockouts, employer economic responses to concerted employee activity, **Labor 111-118**

Management restructuring, employer economic responses to concerted employee activity, **Labor 106-110**

Meaning of concerted activity, **Labor 84-89**

Members and membership policy, NLRA regulation of internal union affairs, **Labor 333-344**

Multiemployer and multiunion bargaining, **Labor 201-206**

National Labor Relations Act (NLRA)
- federal preemption of state legislation, **Labor 309-319**
- internal union affairs, regulation of, **Labor 329-344**

National Labor Relations Board (NLRB) structure and procedure, **Labor 8-16**

No-strike clause, enforcement of, **Labor 281-289**

Officers
- election of union officers, Labor Management Reporting and Disclosure Act (LMRDA) regulation of internal union affairs, **Labor 361-366**
- fiduciary duties of union officers, Labor Management Reporting and Disclosure Act (LMRDA) regulation of internal union affairs, **Labor 373-379**

Organizational picketing, **Labor 69-83**

Picketing
- area standards picketing, organizational picketing, **Labor 81, 82**
- constitutional protection, organizational picketing, **Labor 69-71**
- organizational picketing, **Labor 69-83**
- publicity picketing under Section 8(b)(7)(C), organizational picketing, **Labor 79, 80**

LABOR LAW—Cont'd
Picketing—Cont'd
recognitional picketing in construction industry, organizational picketing, **Labor 83**
Preemption, federal preemption of state legislation, **Labor 309-328**
Protected status, loss of, **Labor 89-93**
Protection of property, selection of bargaining representative, **Labor 37-43**
Publicity picketing under Section 8(b)(7)(C), organizational picketing, **Labor 79, 80**
Recognitional picketing in construction industry, organizational picketing, **Labor 83**
Refusals
bargain, remedies for refusal to bargain, **Labor 219-225**
hire, refusal to hire, employer economic responses to concerted employee activity, **Labor 93-102**
Remedies
exhaustion of internal union remedies, Labor Management Reporting and Disclosure Act (LMRDA) regulation of internal union affairs, **Labor 358**
refusal to bargain, remedies for, **Labor 219-225**
Representation
bargaining and contract enforcement, representation duty, **Labor 300-308**
National Labor Relations Board structure and procedure, representation cases, **Labor 13-16**
Restructuring management, employer economic responses to concerted employee activity, **Labor 106-110**
Secondary boycotts, generally, **Labor 119-180**
Security devices, NLRA regulation of internal union affairs, **Labor 329-333**
Solicitation, selection of bargaining representative, **Labor 43-52**
Strikes, enforcement of no-strike clause, **Labor 281-289**
Subjects of bargaining, **Labor 193-201**
Successor employers, contractual and bargaining obligations of, **Labor 289-300**
Taft-Hartley Act, generally, **Labor 6**
Terminating duty to bargain, **Labor 225-230**

LABOR LAW—Cont'd

Term of existing agreement, bargaining during, **Labor 207-219**
Trusteeships, Labor Management Reporting and Disclosure Act (LMRDA) regulation of internal union affairs, **Labor 367-373**
Unfair labor practice cases, National Labor Relations Board structure and procedure, **Labor 10-13**
Wagner Act, generally, **Labor 1-5**
Work preservation, **Labor 156-166**

LANDLORD AND TENANT

Abandonment, termination of lease, **Sales & Leases Goods 46-53**
Appraisal leases, rent reserved in lease, **Sales & Leases Goods 260, 261**
Assignment, **Sales & Leases Goods 208-211, 226, 227, 271, 287, 288**
Change. Modification or change, infra
Common areas, repairs and improvements, **Sales & Leases Goods 90-95**
Concurrent leases, **Sales & Leases Goods 223, 224**
Construction and operation of renewal and extension provisions, **Sales & Leases Goods 248-250**
Consumer price index leases, rent reserved in lease, **Sales & Leases Goods 260**
Covenants running with the land, **Sales & Leases Goods 226-244**
Criminal acts of third parties, interference with tenant's possession and use of premises, **Sales & Leases Goods 79-81**
Dangerous conditions, injury to persons and property outside leased property, **Sales & Leases Goods 176-178**
Defenses, **Sales & Leases Goods 151-159**
Definition of rent, **Sales & Leases Goods 256, 257**
Destruction of premises, termination of lease, **Sales & Leases Goods 44-46**
Distress for rent, **Sales & Leases Goods 282-289**
Duration of lease
  generally, **Sales & Leases Goods 12, 13, 15**
  tenancy at sufferance, **Sales & Leases Goods 19**
  tenancy at will, **Sales & Leases Goods 18**
Eminent domain proceedings, **Sales & Leases Goods 81-84**

LANDLORD AND TENANT—Cont'd
English rule, possession and use of demised premises, **Sales & Leases Goods 67-69**
Estoppel. Waiver or estoppel, infra
Eviction, retaliatory eviction, **Sales & Leases Goods 145-150**
Expiration of landlord's estate, termination of lease, **Sales & Leases Goods 54-60**
Express covenants, **Sales & Leases Goods 87-169**
Extensions and renewals
construction and operation of renewal and extension provisions, **Sales & Leases Goods 248-250**
distinction between extensions and renewals, **Sales & Leases Goods 246-248**
Fitness for use, possession and use of demised premises, **Sales & Leases Goods 69-76**
Fixtures, changes in condition of demised premises, **Sales & Leases Goods 198-205**
Government regulations, repairs and improvements, **Sales & Leases Goods 98-101**
Habitability, implied warranty of, **Sales & Leases Goods 110-145**
Historical background, **Sales & Leases Goods 1-10**
Holdover problem, termination of lease, **Sales & Leases Goods 60-65**
Illegality
possession and use of demised premises, illegal use, **Sales & Leases Goods 76**
termination of lease, illegality and frustration of purpose, **Sales & Leases Goods 33-44**
Implied warranty of habitability, **Sales & Leases Goods 110-145**
Improvements, generally, **Sales & Leases Goods 86-205**
Injury to persons and property outside leased property, **Sales & Leases Goods 173-182**
Insurance, generally, **Sales & Leases Goods 291-293**
Interference with tenant's possession and use of premises, **Sales & Leases Goods 77-81**
Knowledge of tenant, negligent repairs, **Sales & Leases Goods 171, 172**
Landlord's liens, **Sales & Leases Goods 278-282**

LANDLORD AND TENANT—Cont'd

Latent defects, possession and use of demised premises, **Sales & Leases Goods 72, 73**

Liens

- landlord's liens, **Sales & Leases Goods 278-282**
- statutory liens, **Sales & Leases Goods 280-282**

Massachusetts rule, negligent repairs, **Sales & Leases Goods 170, 171**

Modification or change

- agreements to modify rent, **Sales & Leases Goods 263, 264**
- condition of demised premises, changes in, **Sales & Leases Goods 182-205**
- distress for rent, **Sales & Leases Goods 288, 289**

Mortgage of reversion, **Sales & Leases Goods 224, 225**

Negligent repairs, **Sales & Leases Goods 169-173**

Options to purchase, **Sales & Leases Goods 245, 246, 250-255**

Payment of rent, generally, **Sales & Leases Goods 264-270**

Percentage leases, rent reserved in lease, **Sales & Leases Goods 261, 262**

Periodic tenancy, **Sales & Leases Goods 13-17**

Possession and use of demised premises, **Sales & Leases Goods 66-85**

Remedies of landlord for nonpayment of rent, **Sales & Leases Goods 272, 273**

Renewals. Extensions and renewals, supra

Rent and security, generally, **Sales & Leases Goods 256-290**

Repairs, generally, **Sales & Leases Goods 86-205**

Restraints on alienation, **Sales & Leases Goods 222, 223**

Retaliatory eviction, **Sales & Leases Goods 145-150**

Reversion

- lease in, **Sales & Leases Goods 223**
- mortgage of reversion, **Sales & Leases Goods 224, 225**

Running with the land, **Sales & Leases Goods 226-244**

Security deposits, **Sales & Leases Goods 274-277**

Self-help, termination of lease, **Sales & Leases Goods 55-58**

Setup leases, rent reserved in lease, **Sales & Leases Goods 259, 260**

LANDLORD AND TENANT—Cont'd

Special limitations, termination of lease, **Sales & Leases Goods 21, 22**
Statutes
- distress for rent, statutory modification, **Sales & Leases Goods 288, 289**
- liens, statutory liens, **Sales & Leases Goods 280-282**
- repairs, statutory duty to repair, **Sales & Leases Goods 101-110, 180, 181**
- several tenancies, statutory modification of, **Sales & Leases Goods 20**

Sublease, covenants running with the land, **Sales & Leases Goods 227, 228**
Summary process statutes, termination of lease, **Sales & Leases Goods 58-60**
Surrender, termination of lease, **Sales & Leases Goods 46-53**
Taxes, generally, **Sales & Leases Goods 294-299**
Tenancy at sufferance, **Sales & Leases Goods 19, 20**
Tenancy at will, **Sales & Leases Goods 17-19**
Term for years, **Sales & Leases Goods 12, 13**
Termination of lease
- generally, **Sales & Leases Goods 15-17, 21-65**
- tenancy at sufferance, **Sales & Leases Goods 19, 20**
- tenancy at will, **Sales & Leases Goods 18, 19**

Third parties
- changes in condition of demised premises, **Sales & Leases Goods 183, 184**
- distress for rent, **Sales & Leases Goods 286, 287**
- interference with tenant's possession and use of premises, **Sales & Leases Goods 77-81**

Transfers, generally, **Sales & Leases Goods 206-244**
Waiver or estoppel
- distress for rent, waiver, **Sales & Leases Goods 288**
- title, estoppel to deny landlord's title, **Sales & Leases Goods 289, 290**

Warranties, implied warranty of habitability, **Sales & Leases Goods 110-145**
Waste, changes in condition of demised premises, **Sales & Leases Goods 188-198**

LANDLORD AND TENANT—Cont'd

Wear and tear, changes in condition of demised premises, **Sales & Leases Goods 184-187**

LAND USE

Aesthetics and preservation of historical and cultural resources, **Land Use 254-265**
Age discrimination, zoning and discrimination, **Land Use 242-245**
Agriculture, natural resources, **Land Use 267, 268**
Airspace utilization, **Land Use 313-316**
Amendments, zoning, **Land Use 178-180**
Antitrust issues in land development decisions, **Land Use 139, 140**
Apartments, exclusionary zoning, **Land Use 224-226**
Architectural considerations, aesthetics and preservation of historical and cultural resources, **Land Use 258, 259**
Beaches, natural resources, **Land Use 269-272**
Billboards, aesthetics and preservation of historical and cultural resources, **Land Use 254-257**
Buffer zones, **Land Use 194, 195**
Cluster zones, **Land Use 190-194**
Coastlines, natural resources, **Land Use 269-272**
Commerce, exclusionary zoning, **Land Use 221-223**
Commercial areas, nuisances in, **Land Use 26, 27**
Common law controls on use of land, generally, **Land Use 11-31**
Compensation
    eminent domain, **Land Use 156-158**
    unconstitutional land use regulation, **Land Use 84-88**
Conditional rezoning, **Land Use 180-183**
Conditional use permits, zoning, **Land Use 186-188**
Condominiums, exclusionary zoning, **Land Use 224-226**
Consequential damages, eminent domain, **Land Use 158, 159**
Constitutional law, compensation or damages for unconstitutional land use regulation, **Land Use 84-88**
Construction of restrictive covenants, **Land Use 44, 45**
Consumption of energy, **Land Use 318-320**

LAND USE—Cont'd

Contract or conditional rezoning, **Land Use 180-183**
Control of land use, generally, **Land Use 1-10**
Covenants, easements compared to, **Land Use 33-35**
Damages
  consequential damages, eminent domain, **Land Use 158, 159**
  unconstitutional land use regulation, **Land Use 84-88**
Defeasible fees, private law devices, **Land Use 32, 33**
Development of land
  aesthetics and preservation of historical and cultural resources, **Land Use 262-265**
  regulation of, **Land Use 80-140**
Discrimination, zoning and, **Land Use 210-253**
Easements, private law devices, **Land Use 33-38**
Eminent domain and police power, generally, **Land Use 141-171**
Endangered species, environmental controls, **Land Use 283-289**
Energy and space, **Land Use 311-324**
Enforcement
  private law devices, **Land Use 47, 48**
  standing to enforce restrictions, **Land Use 46, 47**
Environmental concerns
  controls, generally, **Land Use 117-120, 275-295**
  energy and space, environmentalists, **Land Use 320-322**
  flood plains, wetlands and open lands, regulation of, **Land Use 95-104**
  nuisance doctrine and environmental regulation, **Land Use 30**
Equitable balance, energy and space, **Land Use 322-324**
Equitable servitudes and restrictive covenants, generally, **Land Use 38, 39**
Exceptions or exemptions
  nuisance exception, regulation of land development, **Land Use 88-90**
  special exceptions, zoning, **Land Use 186-188**
Exclusionary zoning, **Land Use 210-245**
Fair market value rule, eminent domain, **Land Use 149-151**
Federal pollution legislation, environmental controls, **Land Use 280, 281**
Federal taxing and spending, **Land Use 309, 310**

LAND USE—Cont'd

Fees, private law devices, **Land Use 32, 33**
Floating zones, **Land Use 188-190**
Flood plains, regulation of, **Land Use 95-105**
Forests, natural resources, **Land Use 268, 269**
Group homes, exclusionary zoning, **Land Use 229-233**
Hazardous waste, environmental controls, **Land Use 281-283**
Housing
  low-cost housing, inclusionary zoning, **Land Use 245-251**
  racial exclusion, housing discrimination, **Land Use 236-240**
Implied easements, private law devices, **Land Use 37, 38**
Inclusionary zoning, **Land Use 245-253**
Industrial areas, nuisances in, **Land Use 26, 27**
Industry, exclusionary zoning, **Land Use 221-223**
In gross, easements appurtenant and, **Land Use 35-37**
Initiative and referendum, zoning, **Land Use 202-205**
Inquiry notice of restrictions, **Land Use 41-43**
Institutional uses, exclusionary zoning, **Land Use 229-233**
Interest in land, restrictions on as constituting, **Land Use 43, 44**
Intergovernmental zoning conflicts, **Land Use 205-209**
Inverse condemnation, **Land Use 160-162**
Judicial review
  environmental controls, **Land Use 279, 280**
  zoning, **Land Use 195-198**
Junkyards, aesthetics and preservation of historical and cultural resources, **Land Use 259, 260**
Just compensation, eminent domain, **Land Use 149-151**
Landmark preservation, aesthetics and preservation of historical and cultural resources, **Land Use 261, 262**
Large lot zoning requirements, **Land Use 215-219**
Low-cost housing, inclusionary zoning, **Land Use 245-251**
Maps, planning process, **Land Use 56-58**
Master plan, **Land Use 52-79**
Minimum building size, exclusionary zoning, **Land Use 219-221**
Mobile homes, exclusionary zoning, **Land Use 226-229**
Modification, private law devices, **Land Use 50, 51**
National Environmental Policy Act, **Land Use 276-279**

LAND USE—Cont'd
Natural resources, **Land Use 266-274**
New towns, planning process, **Land Use 69-74**
Nonconforming uses, zoning, **Land Use 199-202**
Notices, inquiry notice of restrictions, **Land Use 41-43**
Nuisance, common law controls on use of land, **Land Use 16-31**
Nuisance exception, regulation of land development, **Land Use 88-90**
Official maps, planning process, **Land Use 56-58**
Open lands, regulation of, **Land Use 95-105**
Open space preservation, **Land Use 105**
Parol representations regarding covenants, **Land Use 45, 46**
Permissive waste, common law controls on use of land, **Land Use 15**
Planned unit developments and cluster zones, **Land Use 190-194**
Plans and planning
  generally, **Land Use 52-79**
  energy, consumption of, **Land Use 318-320**
  zoning, planned unit developments and cluster zones, **Land Use 190-194**
Police power, generally, **Land Use 80-84**
Pollution, environmental controls, **Land Use 280, 281**
Prescriptive easements, private law devices, **Land Use 37, 38**
Private law devices, **Land Use 32-51**
Private schools, exclusionary zoning, **Land Use 233-236**
Property rights and police power, generally, **Land Use 80-84**
Public facilities, common law controls on use of land, **Land Use 27, 28**
Publicly owned land, planning process, **Land Use 68, 69**
Racial exclusion, housing discrimination, **Land Use 236-240**
Real covenants running with the land, **Land Use 39, 40**
Recapture of unearned increment, taxation and control of land use, **Land Use 308, 309**
Regional taxation, **Land Use 300-303**
Religious institutions, exclusionary zoning, **Land Use 233-236**
Removal of earth, restrictions on, **Land Use 266, 267**
Restrictive covenants, generally, **Land Use 38, 39**

LAND USE—Cont'd
Rivers, natural resources, **Land Use 272, 273**
Rural areas, nuisances in, **Land Use 19-22**
Schools, exclusionary zoning, **Land Use 233-236**
Sign regulations, aesthetics and preservation of historical and cultural resources, **Land Use 254-257**
Single-family classification, exclusionary zoning, **Land Use 211-215**
Special exceptions, zoning, **Land Use 186-188**
Special use permits, zoning, **Land Use 186-188**
Spot zoning, **Land Use 176-178**
Standing to enforce restrictions, **Land Use 46, 47**
State legislation, environmental controls, **Land Use 290**
Streams, natural resources, **Land Use 272, 273**
Subdivisions
  regulation of land development, **Land Use 120-139**
  taxation and control of land use, subdivision restrictions, **Land Use 298-300**
Taxation and control of land use, **Land Use 296-310**
Termination of restrictive covenants, **Land Use 48-50**
Towns, planning process for new towns, **Land Use 69-74**
Transfer of development rights, aesthetics and preservation of historical and cultural resources, **Land Use 262-265**
Transition zones, **Land Use 194, 195**
Trespass or nuisance, **Land Use 30, 31**
Underground space, utilization of, **Land Use 316, 317**
Unearned increment, taxation and control of land use, **Land Use 308, 309**
Urban growth
  regulation of, **Land Use 106-117**
  taxation and control of land use, **Land Use 303-306**
Variances, **Land Use 183-186**
Voluntary waste, common law controls on use of land, **Land Use 13-15**
Waiver, private law devices, **Land Use 50, 51**
Waste, common law controls on use of land, **Land Use 11-15**
Wetlands, regulation of, **Land Use 95-105**

LAND USE—Cont'd
Zoning
generally, **Land Use 172-209**
discrimination, zoning and, **Land Use 210-253**
nuisances in zoned areas, **Land Use 28, 29**
taxation and control of land use, **Land Use 298-300**

LANHAM ACT
Generally, **Unfair Trade 105 et seq.**

LAW, THE STUDY AND PRACTICE OF
Argument, **Law Study & Prac 75, 221-249**
Authority, **Law Study & Prac 40**
Briefs, **Law Study & Prac 12, 13, 77-94**
Burden of proof, **Law Study & Prac 177**
Canned briefs, **Law Study & Prac 100**
Career choices, generally, **Law Study & Prac 319-342**
Cases, **Law Study & Prac 7-39, 63-94, 172-202**
Classes, **Law Study & Prac 98, 158-169, 300-306, 336-338**
Clerking, **Law Study & Prac 306-311**
Clerkships, **Law Study & Prac 328, 329**
Clinical courses, **Law Study & Prac 305**
Compromise and settlement. **Legal Negotiation** (this index)
Controlling authority, **Law Study & Prac 40**
Course selection, **Law Study & Prac 300-306, 336-338**
Depositions, generally, **Law Study & Prac 189-193**
Dicta, **Law Study & Prac 88-90**
Directed verdict, **Law Study & Prac 180**
Discovery, generally, **Law Study & Prac 189-193**
Drafting. **Legal Drafting** (this index)
Economics. **Law and Economics** (this index)
Ethics, **Law Study & Prac 52, 53, 206, 228-230**
Evidence, **Law Study & Prac 206-208, 211, 212**
Examinations
How to Study Law and Take Law Exams (this index)
Exams, **Law Study & Prac 112-149**
Fees, **Law Study & Prac 173, 174**

LAW, THE STUDY AND PRACTICE OF—Cont'd
Flunking out, **Law Study & Prac 152-154**
Hard/soft metaphor, **Law Study & Prac 167, 168**
High school teaching programs, **Law Study & Prac 314-318**
Holding, **Law Study & Prac 88-90**
Hypotheticals, use of, **Law Study & Prac 30-33**
Impeachment, **Law Study & Prac 189-191**
Interviews and interviewing. **Legal Interviewing and Counseling** (this index)
Intuition, **Law Study & Prac 33**
Journals, **Law Study & Prac 107-110, 335, 336**
Judgment n.o.v., **Law Study & Prac 180**
Juries, **Law Study & Prac 175-179, 198, 199**
Law review, **Law Study & Prac 297-300**
Learning, **Law Study & Prac 9, 10, 18-22, 97, 60-62, 97-104, 110, 111, 248, 249**
Legal argument, generally, **Law Study & Prac 221-249**
Legal education, **Law Study & Prac 91-93, 294-296, 306-309**
Legal movies, **Law Study & Prac 313**
Legal novels and plays, **Law Study & Prac 312, 313, 340**
Legal research, generally, **Law Study & Prac 250-266**
Legal response. **International Environmental Law** (this index)
Legal scholars. **Comparative Legal Traditions** (this index)
Legal traditions. **Comparative Legal Traditions** (this index)
Legal writing, generally, **Law Study & Prac 267-294**
Legal Writing (this index)
Legislative Law and Process (this index)
Moot court, **Law Study & Prac 221-249**
Motions, **Law Study & Prac 194-197**
Natural law, **Law Study & Prac 46-50**
Negotiation. **Legal Negotiation** (this index)
Operative facts, **Law Study & Prac 83, 84**
Opinion evidence, **Law Study & Prac 206-209**
Outlines, **Law Study & Prac 98-101**
Pain and suffering, **Law Study & Prac 176, 178**
Ping pong and the law, **Law Study & Prac 18-22**

LAW, THE STUDY AND PRACTICE OF—Cont'd
Planning, **Law Study & Prac 174-184, 252-254**
Pleadings, illustrated, **Law Study & Prac 172-201**
Precedent, **Law Study & Prac 7-39, 41-50**
Pretrial Litigation (this index)
Pretrial process, generally, **Law Study & Prac 172-197**
Problem solving, **Law Study & Prac 253, 254**
Pro bono activities, **Law Study & Prac 313-318**
Procedural law/substantive law, **Law Study & Prac 195**
Psychological aspects, generally, **Law Study & Prac 150-170**
Relativity, **Law Study & Prac 46-50**
Research. **Legal Research** (this index)
Restatement movement, **Law Study & Prac 45, 46**
Retroactivity, **Law Study & Prac 73, 74**
Scholars. **Comparative Legal Traditions** (this index)
Second case in the world, **Law Study & Prac 7-18**
Slippery slopes, **Law Study & Prac 233-235**
Socratic method, **Law Study & Prac 160-167**
Statutes, **Law Study & Prac 34-39, 256**
Study, how much time, **Law Study & Prac 107**
Study groups, **Law Study & Prac 101-104**
Substantive law/procedural law, **Law Study & Prac 195**
Teaching yourself, **Law Study & Prac 60-62, 248, 249**
Time. **Legal Negotiation** (this index)
Traditions. **Comparative Legal Traditions** (this index)
Trials, overview, **Law Study & Prac 198-202**
Uniform state laws, **Law Study & Prac 45, 46**
Values, **Law Study & Prac 46-50, 52, 53, 206, 228-230**
Writing. **Legal Writing** (this index)

LAW AND ECONOMICS
Agency regulation, economics of government regulation, **Law & Eco 224-234**
Allocations, **Law & Eco 28, 29, 91, 92, 240-242**
Antitrust Law and Economics (this index)
Arrow's theorem and possible solutions, public choice, **Law & Eco 274-281**

LAW AND ECONOMICS—Cont'd

Assignment of rights, **Law & Eco 60-62, 145-149**
Assumption of risk, **Law & Eco 159, 160, 174**
Bargaining problems, Coase theorem and related property issues, **Law & Eco 64-67**
Capacity, formation of contract, **Law & Eco 94-97**
Choices and preferences, terms and controversies in law and economics, **Law & Eco 38-41**
Collateral source rule, **Law & Eco 176**
Comparative negligence, **Law & Eco 154-159, 174, 175**
Comparison of perfect competition and monopoly, limits on, **Law & Eco 207-210**
Consideration requirement, formation of contract, **Law & Eco 101-109**
Contestable markets, economics of government regulation, **Law & Eco 235, 236**
Contract law applications, **Law & Eco 82-141**
Contributory negligence, **Law & Eco 151-154, 174, 175**
Conventional doctrine, economics of tort law, **Law & Eco 151, 152**
Cost curves, economics of antitrust, **Law & Eco 195-199**
Costs, **Law & Eco 143-145, 193-199, 242-256**
Cross-elasticity, market definition and, **Law & Eco 213-215**
Cross-subsidization, economics of government regulation, **Law & Eco 232-234**
Damages, generally, **Law & Eco 175-182**
Defenses, **Law & Eco 172-175**
Definitions, **Law & Eco 210-218**
Demand, supply and, **Law & Eco 184-189, 216-218**
Distributive consequences, economics of tort law, **Law & Eco 150, 151**
Duplicating friction-free exchanges, Coase theorem and related property issues, **Law & Eco 70-76**
Duress, formation of contract, **Law & Eco 97-99**
Efficiency, **Law & Eco 27-35, 152-154, 161-165**
Elasticity, generally, **Law & Eco 15-19**
Equilibrium, **Law & Eco 10-13, 189-192, 199-201**

LAW AND ECONOMICS—Cont'd

Excessive competition, economics of government regulation, **Law & Eco 236-239**

Exculpatory provisions, contract law and distributive goals, **Law & Eco 112-118**

Excuses for nonperformance, contract remedies, **Law & Eco 138-141**

Exogenous and endogenous effect, terms and controversies in law and economics, **Law & Eco 52, 53**

Externalities, reactions to transaction costs and externalities, **Law & Eco 242-256**

Extremes, economics of antitrust, **Law & Eco 183-218**

Formation of contract, **Law & Eco 91-109**

Future losses, damages for, **Law & Eco 176-180**

Geographic markets, economics of antitrust, **Law & Eco 215, 216**

Government regulation, economics of generally, **Law & Eco 219-256**

Hand formula, economics of tort law, **Law & Eco 149, 150**

Inherently scarce resources allocated, economics of government regulation, **Law & Eco 240-242**

Legislation, economic theory of, **Law & Eco 281-289**

Lerner Index, economics of antitrust, **Law & Eco 211, 212**

Liability, **Law & Eco 145-149, 160-165, 172-175**

Limits on comparison of perfect competition and monopoly, economics of antitrust, **Law & Eco 207-210**

Logrolling, Arrow's theorem and possible solutions, **Law & Eco 279, 280**

Marginal analysis generally, **Law & Eco 25, 26**

Marginal costs equals marginal revenue rule, economics of antitrust, **Law & Eco 193-195**

Markets and marketing, **Law & Eco 10-13, 20-25, 189-192, 210-218, 235, 236**

Models, refining negligence model, **Law & Eco 151-154**

Monopoly, generally, **Law & Eco 202-204**

Natural monopoly rationale, economics of government regulation, **Law & Eco 220-236**

Negative externalities and property rights, terms and controversies in law and economics, **Law & Eco 42-45**

LAW AND ECONOMICS—Cont'd

Negligence, **Law & Eco 149-159, 174, 175**

Offer and acceptance, formation of contract, **Law & Eco 99-101**

Pareto optimality and superiority, terms and controversies in law and economics, **Law & Eco 30-33**

Perfect competition, generally, **Law & Eco 204-207**

Positive externalities and property rights, terms and controversies in law and economics, **Law & Eco 45-49**

Private risk allocation, contract law applications, **Law & Eco 91, 92**

Producer and consumer surplus, economics of antitrust, **Law & Eco 189-192**

Public choice, generally, **Law & Eco 257-289**

Punitive damages, **Law & Eco 181, 182**

Rational maximizer of self-interest, terms and controversies in law and economics, **Law & Eco 36-38**

Rawls' Theory of Justice, public choice, **Law & Eco 266-268**

Reactions to transaction costs and externalities, economics of government regulation, **Law & Eco 242-256**

Reconciling contributory negligence and efficiency, economics of tort law, **Law & Eco 152-154**

Refining negligence model or standard, economics of tort law, **Law & Eco 151-159**

Remedies, contract remedies, **Law & Eco 126-138**

Rescue duty, economics of tort law, **Law & Eco 171, 172**

Risk-aversion and loss spreading, economics of tort law, **Law & Eco 165-171**

Scarcity, allocation of inherently scarce resources, economics of government regulation, **Law & Eco 240-242**

Single-peaked preferences, Arrow's theorem and possible solutions, **Law & Eco 280, 281**

Specific performance, contract remedies, **Law & Eco 130-133**

Standards, negligence standard, **Law & Eco 149-159**

Strict liability, **Law & Eco 160-165, 172-175**

Subsidization, economics of government regulation, **Law & Eco 232-234**

Superiority, pareto optimality and, **Law & Eco 30-33**

Supply and demand, **Law & Eco 184-189, 216-218**

LAW AND ECONOMICS—Cont'd
Surplus, economics of antitrust, **Law & Eco 189-192**
Terms and controversies in law and economics, **Law & Eco 27-55**
Tort law, economics of generally, **Law & Eco 142-182**
Transaction costs, **Law & Eco 62-64, 70-76, 242-256**
Unforeseen misuse as defense to strict liability, economics of tort law, **Law & Eco 173, 174**
Unreasonable assumption of risk as defense to strict liability, economics of tort law, **Law & Eco 174**
Utilitarianism, public choice, **Law & Eco 263-266**
Voting preferences, **Law & Eco 270-281**
Wealth effect, Coase theorem and related property issues, **Law & Eco 67-70**

LAW EXAMS
How to Study Law and Take Law Exams (this index)

LAW OF THE SEA
Admiralty (this index)

LEASES
Landlord and Tenant (this index)
Sales and Leases of Goods (this index)

LEGAL DRAFTING
Abetting unauthorized practice of law, ethics of drafting, **Legal Draft 351, 352**
Accuracy, **Legal Draft 3-5**
Advertising specialization or concentration, ethics of drafting, **Legal Draft 324**
Agency interpretation, rule favoring, **Legal Draft 261**
Ambiguities, **Legal Draft 29, 30, 105-152, 284**
Appropriations, parts of statute, **Legal Draft 313**
Assignment, parts of contract, **Legal Draft 292**
Attorney-client privilege, ethics of drafting, **Legal Draft 336-338**
Borrowed language rule, **Legal Draft 260**

LEGAL DRAFTING—Cont'd

Brevity, **Legal Draft 5-7**
Caption, parts of contract, **Legal Draft 287**
Characteristics, **Legal Draft 3-8, 45, 46**
Checklists, **Legal Draft 59, 60, 67-81**
Choice of law, parts of contract, **Legal Draft 290, 291**
Choosing right concept, **Legal Draft 82-96**
Clarity, **Legal Draft 5, 183-196**
Classification, organization, **Legal Draft 100, 101**
Combining full and partial definitions, **Legal Draft 219, 220**
Common law rules, interpretation rules, **Legal Draft 246-266**
Communication, ethics of drafting, **Legal Draft 332, 333**
Competence, ethics of drafting, **Legal Draft 325, 326**
Computers, drafting with, **Legal Draft 314-322**
Conciseness, **Legal Draft 157-183**
Confidentiality, ethics of drafting, **Legal Draft 335-338**
Conflict of interest, ethics of drafting, **Legal Draft 338-347**
Consequences, **Legal Draft 105-107, 227-244**
Consistency, **Legal Draft 153-156**
Context of document, determination of, **Legal Draft 46-50**
Contextual ambiguity, **Legal Draft 107-111**
Contract drafting, **Legal Draft 280-294**
Costs of bad drafting, **Legal Draft 18, 19**
Criminal matters, **Legal Draft 252, 253, 329-332**
Date, parts of statute, **Legal Draft 311-313**
Definitions, **Legal Draft 30, 82, 105, 204-226, 289, 310**
Delegation, parts of contract, **Legal Draft 292**
Developing organization, planning and preparation, **Legal Draft 28, 29**
Diligence, ethics of drafting, **Legal Draft 325, 326**
Doubly ensuring intended consequences, **Legal Draft 243, 244**
Effective date, parts of statute, **Legal Draft 311, 312**
Ejusdem generis rule, **Legal Draft 256-258**
Enacting clause, parts of statute, **Legal Draft 308**
Enforcement mechanisms, parts of statute, **Legal Draft 310, 311**
Ethics, **Legal Draft 17, 323-352**

LEGAL DRAFTING—Cont'd

Expressio unius est exclusio alterius, **Legal Draft 255, 256**
Factual concepts, choosing right concept, **Legal Draft 85-89**
Factual context of document, determination of, **Legal Draft 48-50**
Fees, ethics of drafting, **Legal Draft 333-335**
Findings, parts of statute, **Legal Draft 309**
Flow charts, drafting with computers, **Legal Draft 321**
Force majeure, parts of contract, **Legal Draft 293**
Form, drafting within the law, **Legal Draft 51-53**
Former clients, solicitation of, **Legal Draft 324, 325**
Four corner rules, interpretation rules, **Legal Draft 248, 249**
Fraudulent transactions, ethics of drafting, **Legal Draft 329-332**
Free drafting services, provision of, **Legal Draft 352**
Full definitions, **Legal Draft 215-217, 219, 220**
Gaps, contract drafting, **Legal Draft 284**
Grammar checks, drafting with computers, **Legal Draft 320**
Handwritten words prevail over printed words, **Legal Draft 265, 266**
Heading, parts of contract, **Legal Draft 287**
Housekeeping provisions, **Legal Draft 290-294, 311-313**
Identification, **Legal Draft 24, 25, 27, 28, 43, 44**
Implied terms, drafting within the law, **Legal Draft 58, 59**
Incorporation by reference, **Legal Draft 212-214**
Informative writing, **Legal Draft 8**
In pari materia, rule of construing statutes, **Legal Draft 262-264**
Intellectual exercise, drafting as, **Legal Draft 10-15**
Intent, **Legal Draft 248-252, 281-283**
Interpretation rules, **Legal Draft 31, 245-266**
Introductory paragraph, parts of contract, **Legal Draft 287**
Knowledge of audience, **Legal Draft 43-46**
Last modification rule, **Legal Draft 266**
Layout of document, **Legal Draft 267-279**
Legal concepts, choosing right concept, **Legal Draft 83-85**
Legal context of document, determination of, **Legal Draft 47, 48**
Legislative drafting, **Legal Draft 295-313**
Les posterior derogat priori rule, **Legal Draft 264**

LEGAL DRAFTING—Cont'd
Liberal construction rule, **Legal Draft 255**
Liquidated damages, parts of contract, **Legal Draft 293**
Literary exercise, drafting as, **Legal Draft 15-17**
Litigation-related writing, **Legal Draft 8, 9**
Location, **Legal Draft 223, 224**
Macro collections, drafting with computers, **Legal Draft 321**
Mailings, ethics of drafting, **Legal Draft 324**
Mass mailings, ethics of drafting, **Legal Draft 324**
Meaning, drafting within the law, **Legal Draft 53-55**
Merger clause, parts of contract, **Legal Draft 292**
Mischief rule, interpretation rules, **Legal Draft 249-251**
Modification, parts of contract, **Legal Draft 291**
Noscitur a sociis rule, **Legal Draft 258, 259**
Notarization, parts of contract, **Legal Draft 294**
Notices, parts of contract, **Legal Draft 292**
Objectives, **Legal Draft 22, 23, 36-43, 327-329**
Organization, **Legal Draft 97-104**
Partial definitions, **Legal Draft 217-219, 219, 220**
Parts of contract, **Legal Draft 286-294**
Penalties, parts of statute, **Legal Draft 311**
Permission and authorization, drafting within the law, **Legal Draft 57, 58**
Persuasive writing, **Legal Draft 8**
Plain meaning, interpretation rules, **Legal Draft 248, 249**
Planning, **Legal Draft 21-29**
Postexecution monitoring, **Legal Draft 35**
Preemption, parts of statute, **Legal Draft 313**
Preparation, **Legal Draft 21-29**
Preventive lawyering, drafting as form of, **Legal Draft 9, 10**
Private law documents, legislative compared to, **Legal Draft 296-304**
Readability indexes, **Legal Draft 197, 198**
Recitals, parts of contract, **Legal Draft 287-289**
Recurring problems, contract drafting, **Legal Draft 280-285**
Reddendo singula singulis rule, **Legal Draft 259, 260**

LEGAL DRAFTING—Cont'd

Remedies, parts of statute, **Legal Draft 311**
Repeals, parts of statute, **Legal Draft 312, 313**
Representation, ethics of drafting, **Legal Draft 326-332**
Research, generally, see **Legal Research** (this index)
Research, planning and preparation, **Legal Draft 25**
Review, **Legal Draft 32-34**
Revision, **Legal Draft 32-34**
Savings clause, parts of statute, **Legal Draft 312**
Semantic ambiguity, **Legal Draft 111-133**
Sequence, organization, **Legal Draft 101-104**
Severability, **Legal Draft 290, 313**
Sexist language, **Legal Draft 198-203**
Short title section, parts of statute, **Legal Draft 309**
Signature blocks, parts of contract, **Legal Draft 294**
Simplicity, **Legal Draft 7, 183-196**
Software programs, drafting with computers, **Legal Draft 318-321**
Solicitation, ethics of drafting, **Legal Draft 323-325**
Statutes, **Legal Draft 60-63, 245, 246, 307-313**
Strict construction rule, interpretation rules, **Legal Draft 252-255**
Style and usage, **Legal Draft 30, 153-203, 320**
Substance, **Legal Draft 55-59, 64-81**
Substantive matters, **Legal Draft 32-34, 210-212, 289, 290, 310**
Survivability, parts of contract, **Legal Draft 292**
Syntactic ambiguity, **Legal Draft 133-152**
Termination date, parts of statute, **Legal Draft 313**
Terms creating legal consequences, **Legal Draft 30, 31, 227-244**
Testing definitions, **Legal Draft 225, 226**
Testing for substantive gaps, **Legal Draft 77-81**
Third parties, ethics of drafting, **Legal Draft 347-349**
Title, parts of statute, **Legal Draft 308**
Tone, **Legal Draft 7, 8**
Typed words prevail over printed words, **Legal Draft 265, 266**
Typography and layout of document, **Legal Draft 267-279**
Unanticipated events, contract drafting, **Legal Draft 284, 285**

LEGAL DRAFTING—Cont'd

Uniformity, terms creating legal consequences, **Legal Draft 229-231**
Vest pocket definitions, **Legal Draft 214, 215**
Waiver, parts of contract, **Legal Draft 291, 292**
Writing, generally, see **Legal Writing** (this index)

LEGAL INTERVIEWING AND COUNSELING

Active listening, **Legal Interview 178-184, 337-348**
Affection, **Legal Interview 112, 113**
Analyzing moral influence, **Legal Interview 265-271**
Appendix A, counseling profession, **Legal Interview 317-320**
Appendix B, exercises, **Legal Interview 321-357**
Argument for collaboration, sharing authority and collaborative decisionmaking, **Legal Interview 228-230**
Arrangement of people, **Legal Interview 224-226**
Association of ideas, interventions and skills, **Legal Interview 191, 192**
Authority or authorization, **Legal Interview 51-56, 228-248, 362-371**
Basic theories of counseling, **Legal Interview 131-139**
Bibliography, **Legal Interview 16, 377-395**
Body language, skills, **Legal Interview 187, 188**
Chapter references, **Legal Interview 372-376**
Choices, **Legal Interview 176-178, 355-357**
Collaborative matters, **Legal Interview 228-248, 355-357**
Companionship, **Legal Interview 133, 134, 139-163**
Competition, generally, **Legal Interview 86, 87**
Concealed meaning, interventions and skills, **Legal Interview 192**
Conduct, **Legal Interview 261-265**
Consequences and procedure, interventions, **Legal Interview 200**
Consistency or inconsistency, interventions and skills, **Legal Interview 191**
Content and process, generally, **Legal Interview 74-82**
Continuing threats to working relationship, **Legal Interview 93-104**

LEGAL INTERVIEWING AND COUNSELING —Cont'd
Counseling bibliography, **Legal Interview 377-395**
Counseling profession, Appendix A, **Legal Interview 317-320**
Counseling theories, exercises, **Legal Interview 331, 332**
Counselor, lawyer as, **Legal Interview 6-8**
Countertransference, **Legal Interview 56-61**
Creative problem-solving, **Legal Interview 291-296**
Criminal conduct, client conduct that is illegal but seems moral, **Legal Interview 263**
Culture, interventions, **Legal Interview 207**
Decision, movement from choice to, **Legal Interview 176-178**
Deference, generally, **Legal Interview 76-78**
Demeanor, **Legal Interview 79**
Dependence, **Legal Interview 87-92, 217-227**
Dilemma, interventions, **Legal Interview 203, 204**
Directive styles, basic theories of counseling, **Legal Interview 135, 136**
Discovery, understanding ourselves, **Legal Interview 272, 273**
Discrepancy, interventions, **Legal Interview 198, 199**
Disguise, lawyer persona and feelings it disguises, **Legal Interview 38-61**
Ecology, **Legal Interview 217-221**
Epilogue on learning, **Legal Interview 297 et seq.**
Establishment of working relationship, **Legal Interview 62-104**
Exercises, Appendix B, **Legal Interview 321-357**
Expectations of client, **Legal Interview 72-74**
Experimentation, interventions, **Legal Interview 202, 203**
Facts, generally, **Legal Interview 8-10, 105-130**
Feedback, interventions and skills, **Legal Interview 192-197**
Feelings, generally, **Legal Interview 8-10, 46-51**
Foundation for companionship model, **Legal Interview 139-163**
Gaps and inconsistencies, interventions and skills, **Legal Interview 191**
Gathering facts, **Legal Interview 107-125**
Gestalt, foundation for companionship model, **Legal Interview 140-143**

LEGAL INTERVIEWING AND COUNSELING —Cont'd

Getting the facts, generally, **Legal Interview 105-130**
Hard choices, exercises, **Legal Interview 355-357**
Help and helping, **Legal Interview 111, 112, 131-163**
Heroic, need to be, **Legal Interview 51-56**
Honesty or dishonesty, **Legal Interview 120-122**
Identity, understanding ourselves, **Legal Interview 273-285**
Illegality, client conduct that is illegal but seems moral, **Legal Interview 263**
Imagination, **Legal Interview 230-235, 322**
Inconsistencies and gaps, interventions and skills, **Legal Interview 191**
Influence, **Legal Interview 259-271, 358-362**
Initial threats to working relationship, **Legal Interview 83-92**
Interpreties theories, basic theories of counseling, **Legal Interview 136-139**
Interventions, generally, **Legal Interview 198-209**
Interviewing, generally, **Legal Interview 105-130**
Introduction, **Legal Interview 1-16**
Johari Window, foundation for companionship model, **Legal Interview 148-158**
Judgment, moral feeling and moral judgment, **Legal Interview 251-258**
Kinsey Model, **Legal Interview 110, 111**
Law office, **Legal Interview 105-107, 249, 250**
Lawyer as interviewer and counselor, generally, **Legal Interview 6-8, 10-16**
Learning about people, **Legal Interview 297-302**
Lies, **Legal Interview 120-122**
Listening, active listening, **Legal Interview 178-184, 337-348**
Litigation facts, **Legal Interview 105-107**
Logic, interventions, **Legal Interview 208**
Mask, learning the mask, **Legal Interview 38**
Meaning, **Legal Interview 114-116, 192**
Mechanics, **Legal Interview 125-130**
Models, **Legal Interview 110, 111, 131-163**

LEGAL INTERVIEWING AND COUNSELING —Cont'd

Morals, generally, **Legal Interview 122-125**
Movement from choice to decision, interventions and skills, **Legal Interview 176-178**
Nondirective styles, basic theories of counseling, **Legal Interview 134, 135**
Nonverbal communication, skills, **Legal Interview 187, 188**
Open and closing sentences, interventions and skills, **Legal Interview 189**
Openness, generally, **Legal Interview 79-82**
Payoff, generally, **Legal Interview 113, 114**
Persona, **Legal Interview 38-61**
Personal climate, generally, **Legal Interview 62-72**
Perspective, interventions, **Legal Interview 204, 205**
Phases in legal counseling, interventions and skills, **Legal Interview 164-176**
Place, generally, **Legal Interview 210-227**
Power, problem of, **Legal Interview 51-56**
Presence, **Legal Interview 116**
Problems, **Legal Interview 258-265, 276-285, 291-296**
Procedure and consequences, interventions, **Legal Interview 200**
Process, generally, **Legal Interview 74-82**
Professional authority, exercises, **Legal Interview 362-371**
Projection, **Legal Interview 93-104**
Psychoanalytic theory, foundation for companionship model, **Legal Interview 143-148**
Psychological theory, interventions, **Legal Interview 199**
Public interest, client conduct seems legal but not to serve, **Legal Interview 263-265**
Purpose, **Legal Interview 221-224**
Questions, skills, **Legal Interview 184-187**
Recurrent references, interventions and skills, **Legal Interview 190, 191**
References, **Legal Interview 190, 191, 372-376**
Reflective writing, **Legal Interview 302-316**
Relationship, interventions, **Legal Interview 200-202**

LEGAL INTERVIEWING AND COUNSELING —Cont'd

Resource, imagining client as, **Legal Interview 230-235**
Responding to role-identity problem, understanding ourselves, **Legal Interview 276-285**
Role, understanding ourselves, **Legal Interview 273-285**
Self-determination and moral concerns of client, exercises, **Legal Interview 334-337**
Self-understanding, **Legal Interview 272-296**
Sense of place, exercises, **Legal Interview 357, 358**
Sharing authority and collaborative decisionmaking, **Legal Interview 228-248**
Shifts in conversation, interventions and skills, **Legal Interview 189, 190**
Skills, generally, **Legal Interview 178-188**
Solution-seeking, interventions, **Legal Interview 208, 209**
Solving problems and telling stories, **Legal Interview 17-37**
Space, **Legal Interview 210-227**
Speech, talking like a lawyer, **Legal Interview 38-41**
Structure, interventions, **Legal Interview 205, 206**
Talking like a lawyer, **Legal Interview 38-41**
Technical devices, **Legal Interview 116-120**
Telling stories and solving problems, **Legal Interview 17-37**
Territoriality, **Legal Interview 226, 227**
Themes, interventions and skills, **Legal Interview 190, 191**
Theories, **Legal Interview 131-163, 331, 332**
Things to look for and do in legal counseling, **Legal Interview 189 et seq.**
Thinking like a lawyer, **Legal Interview 41-46**
Threats, **Legal Interview 83-104, 329-331**
Time, **Legal Interview 215-217**
Transactional analysis, foundation for companionship model, **Legal Interview 158-163**
Transference, generally, **Legal Interview 93-104**
Trust, **Legal Interview 114**
Understanding ourselves, **Legal Interview 272-296**

LEGAL INTERVIEWING AND COUNSELING —Cont'd

Using the Johari Window, foundation for companionship model, **Legal Interview 155-158**

Writing, reflective writing, **Legal Interview 302-316**

LEGAL NEGOTIATION

Generally, **Legal Nego 1-31**

Agenda, environmental considerations and grounds for negotiating, **Legal Nego 144**

Agreement, generally, **Legal Nego 220-230**

Attorneys
- case evaluation skills, **Legal Nego 32-34**
- effectiveness of counsel, **Legal Nego 48, 49**

Bargaining, **Legal Nego 128-214**

Best alternative to negotiated agreement, **Legal Nego 57-69**

Body language, nonverbal behavior in negotiating sessions, **Legal Nego 179, 180**

Breaks, negotiation of, **Legal Nego 209-211**

Civil disputes, **Legal Nego 23-25**

Clarification of law, legal disputes not to be negotiated, **Legal Nego 79**

Closure, **Legal Nego 215-220**

Combinations of styles and strategies of negotiating, **Legal Nego 110-112**

Communication and information exchange, **Legal Nego 166-180**

Competent representation, obligation of, **Legal Nego 8-12**

Competition, **Legal Nego 95-103, 211-214**

Compromise and settlement
- generally, **Legal Nego 70-76**
- defects in compromise and settlement agreements, **Legal Nego 238-242**
- interpretation of settlement, **Legal Nego 231-233**
- offers, **Legal Nego 70-75**
- unwillingness to compromise, legal disputes not to be negotiated, **Legal Nego 81**

Conceptualization of case, **Legal Nego 153-166**

Consent, **Legal Nego 15-19**

LEGAL NEGOTIATION—Cont'd

Contractual transactions, **Legal Nego 21-23**
Cooperative style of negotiating, **Legal Nego 88-95**
Criminal cases, **Legal Nego 27-29**
Damage, elements and measures of, **Legal Nego 35-38**
Damages, range of, **Legal Nego 51, 52**
Defects in compromise and settlement agreements, **Legal Nego 238-242**
Development of law, legal disputes not to be negotiated, **Legal Nego 79**
Divorce cases, **Legal Nego 29, 30**
Domestic relations problems, **Legal Nego 29, 30**
Effectiveness of counsel, **Legal Nego 48, 49**
Entrapment, **Legal Nego 208, 209**
Environmental considerations and grounds for negotiating, **Legal Nego 128-145**
Escalation of conflict, **Legal Nego 208, 209**
Ethics, professional ethical rules, **Legal Nego 8, 9**
Evaluation of cases, **Legal Nego 32-81**
Face saving, **Legal Nego 198-200**
Fairness in negotiation results, **Legal Nego 233-238**
Final breakdown, **Legal Nego 230, 231**
Final disbursements, **Legal Nego 242, 243**
Format, environmental considerations and grounds for negotiating, **Legal Nego 142, 143**
Frivolous suits, **Legal Nego 78, 79**
Goals, **Legal Nego 57-69**
Impossibly difficult cases, legal disputes not to be negotiated, **Legal Nego 80**
Ineffective competitive negotiators, dealing with, **Legal Nego 211-214**
Information exchanges, **Legal Nego 128-214**
Informed consent, **Legal Nego 15-19**
Insurance coverage, **Legal Nego 49**
International legal negotiations, **Legal Nego 30, 31**
Interpretation of settlement, **Legal Nego 231-233**
Intimidation, **Legal Nego 193-198**

LEGAL NEGOTIATION—Cont'd

Intolerably offensive opponents, legal disputes not to be negotiated, **Legal Nego 80**

Inventing options, **Legal Nego 153-166**

Irritating competitive negotiators, dealing with, **Legal Nego 211-214**

Labor-management negotiations, **Legal Nego 25-27**

Leverage, **Legal Nego 49**

Location, environmental considerations and grounds for negotiating, **Legal Nego 129-132**

Malpractice, legal malpractice, **Legal Nego 11, 12**

Minimum dispositions, **Legal Nego 57-69**

Narrowing difference and closure, **Legal Nego 215-220**

Nonverbal behavior in negotiating sessions, **Legal Nego 179, 180**

Nuisance suits, **Legal Nego 78, 79**

Obnoxious opponents, legal disputes not to be negotiated, **Legal Nego 80**

Offer of compromise or settlement, **Legal Nego 70-76, 145-153, 180-183**

Opening negotiation and making opening offers, **Legal Nego 145-153**

Options, inventing options, **Legal Nego 153-166**

Persuasion, **Legal Nego 128-214**

Physical setting, environmental considerations and grounds for negotiating, **Legal Nego 132-136**

Presenting favorable conceptualization of case, **Legal Nego 153-166**

Professional economic analysis, **Legal Nego 56**

Professional ethical rules, **Legal Nego 8, 9**

Promises, **Legal Nego 201-208**

Pure nuisance suits, **Legal Nego 78, 79**

Restarting stalled negotiations, **Legal Nego 209-211**

Satisfaction of demand for trial, legal disputes not to be negotiated, **Legal Nego 79, 80**

Single negotiating text, environmental considerations and grounds for negotiating, **Legal Nego 144, 145**

Stages of legal negotiations, **Legal Nego 112-127**

LEGAL NEGOTIATION—Cont'd
Stalled negotiations, **Legal Nego 209-211**
Statute of limitations, effect of negotiations on, **Legal Nego 77**
Strategies of negotiating, **Legal Nego 103-110**
Styles of negotiating, **Legal Nego 82-103, 110-112**
Surveillance, environmental considerations and grounds for negotiating, **Legal Nego 139-142**
Tactics, **Legal Nego 128-214**
Target points, **Legal Nego 57-69**
Taxation, **Legal Nego 46-48**
Threats, **Legal Nego 201-208**
Time
  environmental considerations and grounds for negotiating, time considerations, **Legal Nego 137-139**
  payments, timing of, **Legal Nego 38-45**
  pressure and deadlines, **Legal Nego 216-218**
Transference factors, **Legal Nego 200, 201**
Truth in legal negotiation, **Legal Nego 183-193**
Unwillingness to compromise, legal disputes not to be negotiated, **Legal Nego 81**

LEGAL RESEARCH
Generally, **Legal Research 1-15**
Adjudications, international law, **Legal Research 307-313**
Administrative law, **Legal Research 192-220**
American Law Reports Annotations, **Legal Research 81-89**
Annotations, **Legal Research 81-89**
Arbitrations, international law, **Legal Research 312, 313**
Bibliographic guides, research in English language, **Legal Research 334, 335**
Briefs, specialized and practice materials, **Legal Research 254, 255**
Case law
  English and commonwealth law, **Legal Research 316-321**
  international law, **Legal Research 284, 285**
CD-ROM materials, **Legal Research 117, 118**
Civil law system, **Legal Research 330-341**

LEGAL RESEARCH—Cont'd
Constitutions, **Legal Research 121-159**
Court reports, **Legal Research 16-48**
Court rules, specialized and practice materials, **Legal Research 250-252**
Dictionaries, English and commonwealth law, **Legal Research 328, 329**
Digests
  generally, **Legal Research 49-70**
  international law, **Legal Research 286, 287**
Directories, reference resources, **Legal Research 263-267**
Drafting, generally, see **Legal Drafting** (this index)
Electronic resources
  generally, **Legal Research 98-120**
  CD-ROM materials, **Legal Research 117, 118**
  Internet, **Legal Research 119**
  online full-text databases, **Legal Research 235, 236**
  specialized and practice materials, **Legal Research 249, 250**
  state court reports, **Legal Research 47, 48**
  Supreme Court of the United States, **Legal Research 35**
Encyclopedias
  generally, **Legal Research 89-96**
  English and commonwealth law, **Legal Research 326, 327**
  research in English language, **Legal Research 333, 334**
English and commonwealth law, **Legal Research 315-329**
English language, research in, **Legal Research 332-337**
Ethics, specialized and practice materials, **Legal Research 252, 253**
Executive agreements, international law, **Legal Research 271-284**
Federal legislative history sources, **Legal Research 162-189**
Federal statutes, **Legal Research 125-141**
Formbooks, specialized and practice materials, **Legal Research 255, 256**
Handbooks, reference resources, **Legal Research 257-260**
History, **Legal Research 160-191**
International law, **Legal Research 269-314**
International organizations, **Legal Research 300-307**

LEGAL RESEARCH—Cont'd
Internet resources, **Legal Research 119**
Legislative history, **Legal Research 160-191**
Local charters and ordinances, **Legal Research 157, 158**
Looseleaf services
  specialized and practice materials, **Legal Research 239-248**
  Supreme Court of the United States, **Legal Research 32-34**
Lower federal courts, court reports, **Legal Research 35-41**
National reporter system, state courts, **Legal Research 44-47**
News sources, reference resources, **Legal Research 262, 263**
Official reports, state courts, **Legal Research 41-44**
Online full-text databases, **Legal Research 235, 236**
Organizations, international organizations, **Legal Research 300-307**
Periodicals
  generally, **Legal Research 228-237**
  English and commonwealth law, **Legal Research 327, 328**
Practice materials, **Legal Research 238-256**
Records, specialized and practice materials, **Legal Research 254, 255**
Reference resources, **Legal Research 257-268**
Regulations, English and commonwealth law, **Legal Research 324-326**
Restatements of the law
  generally, **Legal Research 225-228**
  international law, **Legal Research 286, 287**
Secondary materials
  generally, **Legal Research 221-237**
  English and commonwealth law, secondary sources, **Legal Research 326-329**
Shepards
  citations, **Legal Research 70-79**
  statutes, Shepardizing statutes, **Legal Research 149-154**
Specialized and practice materials, **Legal Research 238-256**
State courts, court reports, **Legal Research 41-48**
State legislative history, **Legal Research 189, 190**
State statutes, **Legal Research 143-149**
Statistics, reference resources, **Legal Research 260-262**

LEGAL RESEARCH—Cont'd
Statutes
generally, **Legal Research 121-159**
English and commonwealth law, **Legal Research 321-324**
international law, **Legal Research 284, 285**
Summaries of foreign law, research in English language, **Legal Research 335-337**
Supreme Court of the United States, **Legal Research 23-35**
Supreme Court Reporter and Lawyers' Edition, **Legal Research 28-32**
Texts
generally, **Legal Research 222-225**
online full-text databases, **Legal Research 235, 236**
Translations of foreign law, research in English language, **Legal Research 335-337**
Treaties
generally, **Legal Research 222-225**
international law, **Legal Research 271-284, 294-300**
Treatises
English and commonwealth law, **Legal Research 327, 328**
language, research in English language, **Legal Research 333, 334**
Uniform laws and model acts, **Legal Research 154-157**
United States Constitution, **Legal Research 142, 143**
United States Reports, **Legal Research 24-27**
Writing, generally, see **Legal Writing** (this index)
Yearbooks, international law, **Legal Research 313, 314**

LEGAL SCHOLARS
Comparative Legal Traditions (this index)

LEGAL TRADITIONS
Comparative Legal Traditions (this index)

LEGAL WRITING
Generally, **Legal Writing 1-25**
Adding comments to documents, advanced word processing, **Legal Writing 319, 320**

LEGAL WRITING—Cont'd

Advanced word processing, **Legal Writing 310-330**
Ambiguous sentences, principles for avoiding, **Legal Writing 75-78**
Analogies, case law analysis, **Legal Writing 213-220**
Analysis, common units of legal writing, **Legal Writing 12-14**
Apostrophe, use of, **Legal Writing 157-160**
Appellate brief, **Legal Writing 284-296**
Archaic legalisms, omission of, **Legal Writing 101, 102**
Automatic cross-referencing, advanced word processing, **Legal Writing 324-326**
Basic word processing functions, **Legal Writing 18-25**
Brackets, use of, **Legal Writing 161**
Briefs, appellate brief, **Legal Writing 284-296**
Case law
  analogies, case law analysis, **Legal Writing 213-220**
  construction or interpretation, statutory analysis, **Legal Writing 229-239**
  distinctions, case law analysis, **Legal Writing 213-220**
  office memorandum, statutory analysis without case law, **Legal Writing 207-212**
  synthesis of rule, case law analysis, **Legal Writing 220-229**
Case statements, common units of legal writing, **Legal Writing 10-12**
Citations, punctuation of, **Legal Writing 161, 162**
Client letter, **Legal Writing 297-309**
Colon, use of, **Legal Writing 152, 153**
Comma, use of, **Legal Writing 142-150**
Comparing documents, advanced word processing, **Legal Writing 317-319**
Confusing sentences, principles for avoiding, **Legal Writing 75-78**
Construction or interpretation, statutory analysis, case law interpretation, **Legal Writing 229-239**
Controlling tone, art of persuasive writing, **Legal Writing 243-248**
Court, documents prepared for, **Legal Writing 262-296**

LEGAL WRITING—Cont'd

Cross-referencing, advanced word processing, **Legal Writing 324-326**
Dash, use of, **Legal Writing 155, 156**
Distinctions, case law analysis, **Legal Writing 213-220**
Ellipsis points, use of, **Legal Writing 175-177**
Enhancement of readability, techniques for, **Legal Writing 62-68**
Equivocations, avoidance of, **Legal Writing 105, 106**
Evaluations, common units of legal writing, **Legal Writing 12-14**
Fact statements, common units of legal writing, **Legal Writing 8**
Footnoting, advanced word processing, **Legal Writing 321-323**
Form and content
  law office memorandum, **Legal Writing 183-203**
  letter to client, **Legal Writing 303-309**
Gender-linked pronouns, use of, **Legal Writing 171, 172**
Glossary of words commonly misused, **Legal Writing 111-139**
Grammar
  generally, **Legal Writing 162-172**
  basic word processing functions, grammar programs, **Legal Writing 23-25**
Hyphen, use of, **Legal Writing 154, 155**
Inductive/deductive distinction, **Legal Writing 15, 16**
Italics, use of, **Legal Writing 173-175**
Language in legal setting, principles for making word choices, **Legal Writing 100-108**
Large-scale organization, **Legal Writing 26-42**
Law blocks creation, advanced word processing, **Legal Writing 321**
Law office memorandum, **Legal Writing 178-239**
Legal setting, language in, **Legal Writing 99-139**
Letter to client, **Legal Writing 297-309**
Mechanics, **Legal Writing 173-177**
Memorandum
  law office memorandum, **Legal Writing 178-239**
  trial court memoranda, documents prepared for court, **Legal Writing 262-284**
Nonsubstantive place-fillers, transitions to avoid, **Legal Writing 93, 94**

LEGAL WRITING—Cont'd
Numerals, use of, **Legal Writing 177**
Offices, law office memorandum, **Legal Writing 178-239**
Order of preparation of memorandum sections, law office memorandum, **Legal Writing 203, 204**
Outlining, advanced word processing, **Legal Writing 312-315**
Paragraphs
  organization of, **Legal Writing 43-50**
  transitional, **Legal Writing 87-89**
Parentheses, use of, **Legal Writing 153, 154**
Personal pronouns, use of, **Legal Writing 167, 168**
Persuasive writing, art of, **Legal Writing 240-261**
Pleading design, advanced word processing, **Legal Writing 326-328**
Pronouns
  generally, **Legal Writing 167-171**
  gender-linked pronouns, use of, **Legal Writing 171, 172**
Punctuation, **Legal Writing 142-162**
Questions, common units of legal writing, **Legal Writing 7, 8**
Quotation marks, use of, **Legal Writing 157**
Readability, techniques to enhance, **Legal Writing 62-68**
Redundancy in legal writing, **Legal Writing 108-110**
Reflexive pronouns, use of, **Legal Writing 168, 169**
Research, generally, see **Legal Research** (this index)
Revision of sentences, **Legal Writing 78-85**
Rhetorical devices, art of persuasive writing, **Legal Writing 249-261**
Rules, common units of legal writing, **Legal Writing 8, 10, 14, 15**
Semicolon, use of, **Legal Writing 150-152**
Sentences
  ambiguous sentences, principles for avoiding, **Legal Writing 75-78**
  confusing sentences, principles for avoiding, **Legal Writing 75-78**
  design and construction, **Legal Writing 50-61**
  patterns, **Legal Writing 68-74**
  revision of sentences, **Legal Writing 78-85**

LEGAL WRITING—Cont'd

Sentences—Cont'd
- substantive transitions between sentences, **Legal Writing 91, 92**
- transitional, **Legal Writing 89-92**

Slash or virgule, use of, **Legal Writing 156, 157**
Small-scale organization, **Legal Writing 43-85**
Statutory analysis
- case law interpretation, **Legal Writing 229-239**
- office memorandum, statutory analysis without case law, **Legal Writing 207-212**

Style checker programs, basic word processing functions, **Legal Writing 23-25**
Subject-verb agreement, **Legal Writing 162-166**
Subjunctive mood, use of, **Legal Writing 172, 173**
Substantive transitions between sentences, **Legal Writing 91, 92**
Synthesis of rule, case law analysis, **Legal Writing 220-229**
Table of authorities, advanced word processing, **Legal Writing 315-317**
Transitions and transitional words, **Legal Writing 86-98**
Trial court memoranda, documents prepared for court, **Legal Writing 262-284**
Typographical conventions, **Legal Writing 177**
Variety in transitional words, **Legal Writing 94-98**
Virgule, use of, **Legal Writing 156, 157**
Westlaw, integrating word processing with, **Legal Writing 328-331**
Westmate, integrating word processing with, **Legal Writing 328-331**
Who, which, or that, which to use, **Legal Writing 169-171**
Who or whom, use of, **Legal Writing 166, 167**
Word processing
- advanced word processing, **Legal Writing 310-330**
- basic word processing functions, **Legal Writing 18-25**

LEGISLATIVE LAW AND PRACTICE

State Constitutional Law (this index)

GENERAL INDEX

References are to Titles and Pages

LEGISLATIVE LAW AND PROCESS

Generally, **Legis Law & Proc 1-12**
Acquiescence, **Legis Law & Proc 7, 8**
Advocacy, **Legis Law & Proc 91-133**
Agency bill making, **Legis Law & Proc 143, 144**
Allocator of resources, legislature as, **Legis Law & Proc 222-225**
Amendment sections, bill drafting, **Legis Law & Proc 169-171**
Apportionment, struggle for legislative power, **Legis Law & Proc 250-253**
Appropriations, **Legis Law & Proc 123-133, 223, 224**
Attainder bills, constitutional rules aimed at legislatures, **Legis Law & Proc 283, 284**
Authors chosen, legislative advocacy, **Legis Law & Proc 99-103**
Bicameral-unicameral, universal institution, **Legis Law & Proc 22, 23**
Bill of rights, legal limitations on legislative power, **Legis Law & Proc 235, 236**
Borrowed bills, sources of ideas and bills, **Legis Law & Proc 135, 136**
Budget resolutions, appropriations advocacy, **Legis Law & Proc 132**
Candidates, sources of ideas and bills, **Legis Law & Proc 137**
Canons of statutory construction, **Legis Law & Proc 306-311**
Character of legislative law, **Legis Law & Proc 207-213**
Charters, search for sanctions, **Legis Law & Proc 151, 152**
Chief executives, sources of ideas and bills, **Legis Law & Proc 137**
Codification and recodification, packaging bills, **Legis Law & Proc 195, 196**
Committees, generally, **Legis Law & Proc 25-27**
Common drafting errors, **Legis Law & Proc 181-188**
Compromise to acquiescence, legislative advocacy, **Legis Law & Proc 113, 114**
Congressional delegation, sources of legislative power, **Legis Law & Proc 205, 206**
Consensus, legislative advocacy, **Legis Law & Proc 103-109**
Constitutional law, **Legis Law & Proc 236-239, 262-292**

LEGISLATIVE LAW AND PROCESS—Cont'd

Courts, lawmaking roles of, **Legis Law & Proc 319-327**
Criminal penalties, search for sanctions, **Legis Law & Proc 146-148**
Crises, appropriations advocacy, **Legis Law & Proc 131, 132**
Cross references, common drafting errors, **Legis Law & Proc 187, 188**
Crusher bills, packaging bills, **Legis Law & Proc 196-199**
Definitions, **Legis Law & Proc 177-181, 293, 294**
Delayed impact debate, legislative advocacy, **Legis Law & Proc 114, 115**
Delegation of power, constitutional rules aimed at legislatures, **Legis Law & Proc 284-290**
Direct democracy, structural limitations on legislative power, **Legis Law & Proc 246-249**
Double subject, constitutional rules aimed at legislatures, **Legis Law & Proc 290, 291**
Drafting bills, generally, **Legis Law & Proc 159-204**
Due process, **Legis Law & Proc 54-63, 272-275**
Education, **Legis Law & Proc 91-94, 152-155**
Effective date and time, bill drafting, **Legis Law & Proc 167, 168**
Elections and campaigns, struggle for legislative power, **Legis Law & Proc 253-261**
Enacting clause, bill drafting, **Legis Law & Proc 167**
Enrolled bill rule, judicial supervision of legislative process, **Legis Law & Proc 84, 85**
Equal protection, major foundations for constitutional challenge, **Legis Law & Proc 270-272**
Ethics, questions of, **Legis Law & Proc 42-53**
Exception, statutory interpretation, **Legis Law & Proc 295, 296**
Executive role, **Legis Law & Proc 77-83, 126, 127**
Ex post facto criminal laws, constitutional rules aimed at legislatures, **Legis Law & Proc 283**
Extended institution, **Legis Law & Proc 23**
Federal courts versus state courts, structural limitations on legislative power, **Legis Law & Proc 243-245**
Federal supremacy, structural limitations on legislative power, **Legis Law & Proc 241, 2424**

LEGISLATIVE LAW AND PROCESS—Cont'd

Fines and penalties, search for sanctions, **Legis Law & Proc 146-149**
Fiscal crises, appropriations advocacy, **Legis Law & Proc 131, 132**
Form of legislative law, **Legis Law & Proc 213-217**
Franchises, search for sanctions, **Legis Law & Proc 151, 152**
Gerrymandering, struggle for legislative power, **Legis Law & Proc 252, 253**
Golden rule exception, statutory interpretation, **Legis Law & Proc 295, 296**
Governmental process, bill creation as, **Legis Law & Proc 141-144**
Grammar, common drafting errors, **Legis Law & Proc 188**
Half-step bills, packaging bills, **Legis Law & Proc 202, 203**
Headnotes, bill drafting, **Legis Law & Proc 176, 177**
History, **Legis Law & Proc 311-318**
Horizontal editing, common drafting errors, **Legis Law & Proc 181, 182**
How to Study Law and Take Law Exams (this index)
Ideas for legislation, **Legis Law & Proc 134-158**
Impact of constitutions, **Legis Law & Proc 262-292**
Impact statements, search for sanctions, **Legis Law & Proc 155**
Implied amendment, bill drafting, **Legis Law & Proc 169-171**
Incorporation by reference, constitutional rules aimed at legislatures, **Legis Law & Proc 287-289**
Inertia, **Legis Law & Proc 8-10**
Initiative and referendum, **Legis Law & Proc 246-249, 289, 290**
Intent, **Legis Law & Proc 191, 192, 293-298**
Investigator, legislature as, **Legis Law & Proc 225-228**
Jargon, common drafting errors, **Legis Law & Proc 185, 186**
Journal entry rule, judicial supervision of legislative process, **Legis Law & Proc 85-89**
Judicial Process (this index)
Judicial review of constitutionality, **Legis Law & Proc 262-267**
Judicial supervision of legislative process, **Legis Law & Proc 84-90**

LEGISLATIVE LAW AND PROCESS—Cont'd

Latin, canons of statutory construction, **Legis Law & Proc 309, 310**

Leadership, generally, **Legis Law & Proc 29, 30**

Legal limitations on legislative power, **Legis Law & Proc 235-240**

Legislative institutions, generally, **Legis Law & Proc 13-53**

Licenses and permits, search for sanctions, **Legis Law & Proc 151, 152**

Limitations on legislative power, **Legis Law & Proc 229-249**

Line-item versus program budgeting, appropriations advocacy, **Legis Law & Proc 128-131**

Lists and modifiers, common drafting errors, **Legis Law & Proc 186, 187**

Lobbyists, generally, **Legis Law & Proc 24, 25**

Local government, legislature as operator of government, **Legis Law & Proc 219**

Local units, sources of legislative power, **Legis Law & Proc 207**

Major foundations for constitutional challenge, **Legis Law & Proc 269-277**

Making a bill, generally, **Legis Law & Proc 134-204**

Mandates, processing bills, **Legis Law & Proc 63-67**

Mandatory provisions, bill drafting, **Legis Law & Proc 166-171**

Members, **Legis Law & Proc 35-41**

Misplaced duty, common drafting errors, **Legis Law & Proc 184, 185**

Model bills, sources of ideas and bills, **Legis Law & Proc 135, 136**

Nonretroactivity, **Legis Law & Proc 172-174, 281-284**

Norms, generally, **Legis Law & Proc 30-33**

Omnibus bills, packaging bills, **Legis Law & Proc 200, 201**

One person, one vote, struggle for legislative power, **Legis Law & Proc 251, 252**

Operator of government, legislature as, **Legis Law & Proc 218-228**

Organized interests, sources of ideas and bills, **Legis Law & Proc 136, 137**

LEGISLATIVE LAW AND PROCESS—Cont'd

Oversight, legislature as operator of government, **Legis Law & Proc 219-221**
Packaging bills, **Legis Law & Proc 192-204**
Parallelism, common drafting errors, **Legis Law & Proc 186**
Past and future, legal limitations on legislative power, **Legis Law & Proc 240**
Perspectives on legislative power, **Legis Law & Proc 205-262**
Persuasion, legislative advocacy, **Legis Law & Proc 91-94, 97-99**
Petitions, obligation to petitions, **Legis Law & Proc 4-6**
Plain meaning approach, statutory interpretation, **Legis Law & Proc 295, 296**
Policy making, **Legis Law & Proc 205-262**
Political candidates, sources of ideas and bills, **Legis Law & Proc 137**
Political reality as limitation, **Legis Law & Proc 229, 230**
Preferred freedoms, major foundations for constitutional challenge, **Legis Law & Proc 270**
Private rights, search for sanctions, **Legis Law & Proc 155**
Processing bills, **Legis Law & Proc 54-90**
Publicity, search for sanctions, **Legis Law & Proc 152-155**
Public policy, legislature as allocator of resources, **Legis Law & Proc 222, 223**
Purpose clauses, bill drafting, **Legis Law & Proc 175, 176**
Reordering priorities, appropriations advocacy, **Legis Law & Proc 127, 128**
Repeal sections, bill drafting, **Legis Law & Proc 169-171**
Republican system, sources of legislative power, **Legis Law & Proc 205**
Residual power of states, sources of legislative power, **Legis Law & Proc 206, 207**
Retroactivity or nonretroactivity, **Legis Law & Proc 172-174, 281-284**
Riders, appropriations advocacy, **Legis Law & Proc 132, 133**
Rigidity of statute law, character of legislative law, **Legis Law & Proc 210-212**
Running government, **Legis Law & Proc 218-228**

LEGISLATIVE LAW AND PROCESS—Cont'd
Sanctions, **Legis Law & Proc 144-158, 230, 231**
Savings clauses, bill drafting, **Legis Law & Proc 172-174**
Seniority, generally, **Legis Law & Proc 33-35**
Separateness of courts and legislatures, **Legis Law & Proc 319-324**
Separation of powers, **Legis Law & Proc 242, 243, 320**
Severability, **Legis Law & Proc 174, 175, 265, 266**
Short titles, bill drafting, **Legis Law & Proc 176**
Significance of committee hearings, legislative advocacy, **Legis Law & Proc 94-96**
Societal pressure, legislative advocacy, **Legis Law & Proc 96, 97**
Softening issues tactic, legislative advocacy, **Legis Law & Proc 109-114**
Sources of ideas and bills, **Legis Law & Proc 134-140**
Sources of legislative power, **Legis Law & Proc 205-207**
Special legislation, constitutional rules aimed at legislatures, **Legis Law & Proc 278-280**
State boundary, legal limitations on legislative power, **Legis Law & Proc 239, 240**
Statutory interpretation, **Legis Law & Proc 293-327**
Structural limitations on legislative power, **Legis Law & Proc 241-245**
Struggle for legislative power, **Legis Law & Proc 250-261**
Subcommittees, **Legis Law & Proc 27-29, 124-126**
Tactical drafting, **Legis Law & Proc 189-192**
Taxation, legislature as allocator of resources, **Legis Law & Proc 224, 225**
Techniques for bill drafting, **Legis Law & Proc 159-166**
Title, **Legis Law & Proc 166, 167, 291, 292**
Trailer bills, packaging bills, **Legis Law & Proc 203, 204**
Typical hurdles in one house, **Legis Law & Proc 67-77**
Uniform Statutory Construction Act, **Legis Law & Proc 171, 172**
Universal institution, **Legis Law & Proc 22-35**
Vagueness, tactical drafting, **Legis Law & Proc 191, 192**
Veto, legislature as operator of government, **Legis Law & Proc 221, 222**

LEGISLATIVE LAW AND PROCESS—Cont'd
Words, legislation is, **Legis Law & Proc 10-12**

LIABILITIES
Federal Income Taxation of Partners and Partnerships (this index)
Hazardous Wastes and Toxic Substances, Law of (this index)
International Environmental Law (this index)
Medical Liability (this index)
Partnership. **Federal Income Taxation of Partners and Partnerships** (this index)

LIABILITY INSURANCE
Insurance Law (this index)

LIENS
Real Estate Finance (this index)

LIFE INSURANCE
Insurance Law (this index)

LIMITATIONS AND RESTRICTIONS
Injunctions (this index)
Insurance Law (this index)
International Taxation (this index)
International Trade and Investment (this index)
Medical Liability (this index)
State Constitutional Law (this index)

LIMITED LIABILITY COMPANY
Partnership and LLC (this index)

LIQUIDATION
Federal Income Taxation of Partners and Partnerships (this index)

LISTENING

Trial and Practice Skills (this index)

LITIGATION

Section 1983 Litigation (this index)

LOCAL GOVERNMENT LAW

Abandonment, disposition and loss of municipal property, **Loc Govt 305, 306**
Abutters, acquisition of property under eminent domain, **Loc Govt 280, 281**
Acquisition of property by contract, **Loc Govt 247-271**
Additional considerations relevant to expenditures of municipal corporations, **Loc Govt 394-397**
Administrative functions restricted, problems of organization and operation, **Loc Govt 130-136**
Adverse possession, **Loc Govt 272-279, 312, 313**
Agency, acquisition of property by contract, **Loc Govt 267, 268**
Alterations, formation of local government, **Loc Govt 59-67, 74-96**
Annexation, boundary changes, **Loc Govt 75-80**
Apportionment, just compensation for acquisition of property under eminent domain, **Loc Govt 291-297**
Appraisal, just compensation for acquisition of property under eminent domain, **Loc Govt 291-293**
Arbitration, problems of organization and operation, **Loc Govt 123**
Avoidance, debt limitations, **Loc Govt 384-386**
Bankruptcy, borrowing, **Loc Govt 381, 382**
Bidding requirements, acquisition of property by contract, **Loc Govt 258-266**
Bonds, **Loc Govt 374-383, 387, 388**
Borrowing, generally, **Loc Govt 374-393**
Boundary changes, formation of local government, **Loc Govt 74-96**
Certificates of participation, debt limitations, **Loc Govt 386, 387**
Challenged employment practices, problems of organization and operation, **Loc Govt 108-120**

LOCAL GOVERNMENT LAW—Cont'd

Change of use of property held in fee, limitations on municipal use of acquired property, **Loc Govt 304**

Citizen litigation with local governments, **Loc Govt 398-430**

Civil service, problems of organization and operation, **Loc Govt 125**

Claim notice, citizen tort claims against local government, **Loc Govt 401**

Classification, taxation, **Loc Govt 320, 321**

Collective bargaining, problems of organization and operation, **Loc Govt 121, 122, 125**

Commerce, taxation, **Loc Govt 323-327**

Comparable worth, problems of organization and operation, **Loc Govt 128, 129**

Compulsory transfer, disposition and loss of municipal property by eminent domain, **Loc Govt 313, 314**

Conflict of interest, **Loc Govt 100-106, 252-254**

Consequential and severance damages, acquisition of property under eminent domain, **Loc Govt 297-300**

Constitutionality, **Loc Govt 20, 83-89, 301, 302, 347-351, 394, 395**

Contiguity, boundary changes, **Loc Govt 84**

Contracts, **Loc Govt 247-271, 268, 269, 283**

Contribution, citizen tort claims against local government, **Loc Govt 409-412**

Corporation, local income taxes, **Loc Govt 337, 338**

Damages, **Loc Govt 297-300, 409-412**

Debt limitations, borrowing, **Loc Govt 383-389**

Dedication, acquisition of property, **Loc Govt 272-279**

De facto taking, acquisition of property under eminent domain, **Loc Govt 289-291**

Defect notice, citizen tort claims against local government, **Loc Govt 401**

Defensive incorporation, boundary changes, **Loc Govt 84-86**

Delegation of implementation authority, problems of organization and operation, **Loc Govt 136-142**

Dillon's Rule, sources of local governing powers, **Loc Govt 18**

LOCAL GOVERNMENT LAW—Cont'd

Directory considerations common to statutory incorporation or alteration procedures, **Loc Govt 67**

Disease testing, problems of organization and operation, **Loc Govt 126-128**

Disposition and loss of municipal property, **Loc Govt 305-314**

Dissolution, division and detachment, boundary changes, **Loc Govt 81-83**

Drug testing, problems of organization and operation, **Loc Govt 126-128**

Due process, **Loc Govt 118-120, 321, 322**

Easements, **Loc Govt 276, 277, 281, 282**

Elections, problems of organization and operation, **Loc Govt 142-154**

Eminent domain, **Loc Govt 279-300, 313, 314**

Employees, problems of organization and operation, **Loc Govt 97-99**

Equal protection, **Loc Govt 109, 110, 322, 323**

Estoppel to claim title, disposition and loss of municipal property, **Loc Govt 312, 313**

Excess condemnation, acquisition of property under eminent domain, **Loc Govt 286-288**

Execution, citizen tort claims against local government, **Loc Govt 409-412**

Executive functions restricted, problems of organization and operation, **Loc Govt 130-136**

Fair market value, just compensation for acquisition of property under eminent domain, **Loc Govt 291-297**

Federal Taxation, **Loc Govt 391-393, 430**

Fee simple absolute, acquisition, **Loc Govt 274-276**

First Amendment, **Loc Govt 116-118, 379-381**

Fiscal crises, borrowing, **Loc Govt 379-381**

Flexibility of municipality, acquisition of property upon, **Loc Govt 277-279**

Forfeiture, disposition and loss of municipal property, **Loc Govt 313**

Formation of local government, **Loc Govt 67-74**

LOCAL GOVERNMENT LAW—Cont'd

Fourteenth Amendment, problems of organization and operation, **Loc Govt 142-154**

Franchises, disposition and loss of municipal property, **Loc Govt 307-309**

Gifts, **Loc Govt 272-279, 310, 311**

Highest and best use factors, just compensation for acquisition of property under eminent domain, **Loc Govt 293, 294**

Holding city to present use, limitations on municipal use of acquired property, **Loc Govt 302-304**

Immunity of municipality, citizen tort claims against local government, **Loc Govt 402-409**

Implied powers, sources of local governing powers, **Loc Govt 26, 27**

Income taxes, **Loc Govt 333-338**

Inconsistent private uses, limitations on municipal use of acquired property, **Loc Govt 300, 301**

Indemnity, citizen tort claims against local government, **Loc Govt 409-412**

Injury notice, citizen tort claims against local government, **Loc Govt 401**

Interest rate on bonds, borrowing, **Loc Govt 376-379**

Intergovernmental transfers, sources of revenue, **Loc Govt 371-373**

Inverse condemnation, acquisition of property under eminent domain, **Loc Govt 289-291**

Judicial functions restricted, problems of organization and operation, **Loc Govt 130-136**

Just compensation, acquisition of property under eminent domain, **Loc Govt 291-297**

Land use, **Loc Govt 155-314**

Leases and leaseholds, **Loc Govt 293, 306, 307, 386**

Legislative functions restricted, problems of organization and operation, **Loc Govt 130-136**

Licensing, taxation, **Loc Govt 329-333**

Limitations and restrictions, **Loc Govt 29-44, 130-136, 266, 267, 282, 283, 300-304, 383-391, 394-397**

LOCAL GOVERNMENT LAW—Cont'd

Mandatory considerations common to statutory incorporation or alteration procedures, **Loc Govt 67**
Market value, just compensation for acquisition of property under eminent domain, **Loc Govt 291-297**
Mortgage, disposition and loss of municipal property, **Loc Govt 310, 311**
Municipal corporations, generally, **Loc Govt 21, 22**
Necessity use requirements, acquisition of property under eminent domain, **Loc Govt 284**
Nondelegation doctrine, sources of local governing powers, **Loc Govt 23-26**
Nonhome rule municipalities, sources of local governing powers, **Loc Govt 21, 22**
Notes, borrowing, **Loc Govt 374**
Notice requirements, citizen tort claims against local government, **Loc Govt 400-402**
Nuisances, limitations on municipal use of acquired property, **Loc Govt 300**
Officers, **Loc Govt 99, 100, 397**
Personal property taxes, **Loc Govt 338, 339**
Pledge, disposition and loss of municipal property, **Loc Govt 310, 311**
Plenary power, limitations on state power over municipal corporations, **Loc Govt 29, 30**
Police power, land use, **Loc Govt 155-189**
Political realities, boundary changes, **Loc Govt 83-89**
Power, generally, **Loc Govt 1-58**
Prescription, acquisition of property, **Loc Govt 272-279**
Privatization, problems of organization and operation, **Loc Govt 129, 130**
Property taxes, **Loc Govt 338-351**
Public employees unions, problems of organization and operation, **Loc Govt 120-130**
Public use or purpose, acquisition of property under eminent domain, **Loc Govt 283-286**
Quick condemnation, acquisition of property under eminent domain, **Loc Govt 288, 289**

LOCAL GOVERNMENT LAW—Cont'd
Real property taxes, **Loc Govt 339-342**
Residency requirements, problems of organization and operation, **Loc Govt 106-108**
Resolution of competing power considerations, **Loc Govt 44-58**
Restitution and relief, acquisition of property by contract, **Loc Govt 269-271**
Restrictive covenants, acquisition of property under eminent domain, **Loc Govt 282, 283**
Retroactivity of invalidation of local income taxes, **Loc Govt 336, 337**
Revenue bonds, debt limitations, **Loc Govt 387, 388**
Revenues, generally, **Loc Govt 315-397**
Sale, disposition and loss of municipal property, **Loc Govt 311, 312**
Sales and use taxes, **Loc Govt 351-355**
Scenic and development easements, acquisition of property under eminent domain, **Loc Govt 281, 282**
§ 1983, claims against local government under, **Loc Govt 412-422**
Severance damages, acquisition of property under eminent domain, **Loc Govt 297-300**
Sources of local governing powers, **Loc Govt 14-28**
Sovereignty, sources of local governing powers, **Loc Govt 14-18**
Special tax assessments, **Loc Govt 356-369**
Standing, citizen litigation with local governments, **Loc Govt 422-424**
Statutes, **Loc Govt 21, 63-67, 400**
Statutes of limitations, citizen tort claims against local government, **Loc Govt 400**
Streets, **Loc Govt 280, 281, 309, 310**
Strikes, problems of organization and operation, **Loc Govt 124, 125**
Substitution, just compensation for acquisition of property under eminent domain, **Loc Govt 291-297**
Taxation, generally, **Loc Govt 319-369**
Taxpayers' suits, citizen litigation with local governments, **Loc Govt 426-428, 430**

LOCAL GOVERNMENT LAW—Cont'd

TDRs, just compensation for acquisition of property under eminent domain, **Loc Govt 295-297**

Tort claims against local government by citizens, **Loc Govt 399-412**

Transfer development rights, just compensation for acquisition of property under eminent domain, **Loc Govt 295-297**

Ultra vires, citizen tort claims against local government, **Loc Govt 399, 400**

Uniformity, taxation, **Loc Govt 328, 329**

Unlawful expenditures, liability of municipal officer for, **Loc Govt 397**

Utility revenues and user fees, **Loc Govt 370, 371**

Vacation of streets, disposition and loss of municipal property, **Loc Govt 309, 310**

LOCAL TAXATION

State and Local Taxation and Finance (this index)

LOOSELEAF SERVICES

Legal Research (this index)

LOSSES

Federal Income Taxation of Partners and Partnerships (this index)

MANDATORY MATTERS

Professional Responsibility (this index)

MARITAL DEDUCTIONS

Federal Estate and Gift Taxation (this index) generally

MARITIME LAW

Admiralty (this index)

MARKETS AND MARKETING

Common market. **European Union** (this index)

MARKETS AND MARKETING—Cont'd
European Union (this index)

MASS COMMUNICATIONS
Generally, **Mass Comm 1 et seq.**

MEDICAL LIABILITY
Generally, **Med Liab 1-23**
Affirmative defenses, **Med Liab 137-166**
After-discovered dangers, duty to disclose, **Med Liab 110-113**
Arbitration
  changing litigation system, **Med Liab 251-253**
  limitations on liability, **Med Liab 160, 161**
Assault and battery
  informed decision making, battery versus negligence, **Med Liab 86-88**
  intentional torts, **Med Liab 65-69**
Assumption of risk, affirmative defenses, **Med Liab 154-156**
Avoidable consequences, affirmative defenses, **Med Liab 153**
Best judgment rule, negligence based claims, **Med Liab 34-36**
Birth, damages for wrongful birth, **Med Liab 128-130**
Caps
  attorneys' fees, caps on, **Med Liab 255-257**
  malpractice awards, caps on, **Med Liab 253-255**
Causation, establishment of, **Med Liab 115-127**
Changing litigation system, **Med Liab 251-253**
Charitable immunity, **Med Liab 162, 163**
Civil rights violation, intentional torts, **Med Liab 83-85**
Comparative negligence, affirmative defenses, **Med Liab 151, 152**
Competency of experts, proving professional standard, **Med Liab 38-41**
Confidential information disclosure, intentional torts, **Med Liab 75-78**
Consent
  duty, consensual relationships, **Med Liab 6-10**
  informed decision making, **Med Liab 89-99**
Contract, generally, **Med Liab 217-231**
Contributory negligence, affirmative defenses, **Med Liab 149-151**

MEDICAL LIABILITY—Cont'd
Corporate responsibility, vicarious liability, **Med Liab 204-212**
Countersuits, **Med Liab 257-259**
Damages
  generally, **Med Liab 127-136**
  punitive damages, **Med Liab 133, 134**
Defamation, intentional torts, **Med Liab 70, 71**
Defenses, **Med Liab 137-166**
Dignitary torts, damages, **Med Liab 130, 131**
Disclosure
  informed decision making, disclosure duty, **Med Liab 102-110**
  intentional torts, disclosure of confidential information, **Med Liab 75-78**
Duty, generally, **Med Liab 1-23**
Economic interests, informed decision making, **Med Liab 108, 109**
Emergency circumstances, **Med Liab 4-6**
Emotional distress and outrage, intentional torts, **Med Liab 78-83**
Employees and independent contractors, hospital liability, **Med Liab 193-195**
Establishment of professional relationship, **Med Liab 1-23**
Evidence of professional standard, negligence based claims, **Med Liab 36-62**
Exceptions
  disclosure duty, informed decision making, **Med Liab 105-108**
  experts, proving professional standard, **Med Liab 41-62**
Exculpatory clauses, limitations on liability, **Med Liab 159, 160**
Exemplary damages, **Med Liab 133, 134**
Experimental procedures, duty to disclose, **Med Liab 109**
Expert testimony, proving professional standard, **Med Liab 38-41**
False imprisonment, intentional torts, **Med Liab 71-73**
Good Samaritan laws, **Med Liab 146-149**
Governmental immunity, **Med Liab 164, 165**
Health maintenance organizations, vicarious liability, **Med Liab 186-190**
HIV status of physician, duty to disclose, **Med Liab 109, 110**

MEDICAL LIABILITY—Cont'd
Hospital liability, **Med Liab 191-216**
Implied consent, informed decision making, **Med Liab 95-98**
Independent contractors, hospital liability, **Med Liab 193-195**
Informed decision making, **Med Liab 86-114**
Intentional torts, **Med Liab 63-85**
Invasion of privacy, intentional torts, **Med Liab 73, 74**
Last clear chance, affirmative defenses, **Med Liab 153**
Limitations
 generally, **Med Liab 137-166**
 duty, limits of, **Med Liab 15-23**
Limitations on liability, **Med Liab 156-161**
Locality rules, negligence based claims, **Med Liab 27-34**
Misrepresentation, intentional torts, **Med Liab 74, 75**
Negligence theory, generally, **Med Liab 1**
Partnerships, vicarious liability, **Med Liab 182, 183**
Patient dumping, vicarious liability, **Med Liab 212-216**
Prior tortfeasors, affirmative defenses, **Med Liab 154**
Privacy invasion, intentional torts, **Med Liab 73, 74**
Privileges and immunities, **Med Liab 161-166**
Product liability, **Med Liab 227-229**
Professional corporation, vicarious liability, **Med Liab 183-186**
Proving professional standard, negligence based claims, **Med Liab 36-62**
Punitive damages, **Med Liab 133, 134**
Reform
 damage awards and malpractice reform, **Med Liab 134-136**
 litigation system, **Med Liab 232-259**
Refusal
 informed decision making, refusal of treatment, **Med Liab 99-101**
 limits of duty, refusal to provide treatment, **Med Liab 21-23**
Releases, limitations on liability, **Med Liab 156-159**
Res ipsa loquitur, proving professional standard, **Med Liab 54-62**
Respectable minority rule, negligence based claims, **Med Liab 26, 27**
Respondeat superior, hospital liability, **Med Liab 191-193**

MEDICAL LIABILITY—Cont'd
School and locality rules, negligence based claims, **Med Liab 27-34**
Standard of care, negligence based claims, **Med Liab 24-36**
Standards, proving professional standard, **Med Liab 36-62**
Statutes
  immunity, statutory immunity, **Med Liab 165, 166**
  limitation of actions, **Med Liab 137-146**
  rate freeze on malpractice premiums, **Med Liab 257**
Statutes of limitations, **Med Liab 137-146**
Strict liability, **Med Liab 230, 231**
Subsequent tortfeasors, affirmative defenses, **Med Liab 154**
Substituted consent, informed decision making, **Med Liab 95-98**
Vicarious liability
  generally, **Med Liab 167-190**
  hospital liability, **Med Liab 195-204**
Voluntary termination, limits of duty, **Med Liab 16-21**
Warranty, generally, **Med Liab 217-231**
Wrongful life and wrongful birth, damages, **Med Liab 128-130**

MEDICARE
Health Care Law and Ethics (this index)

MEMORANDUM
Legal Writing (this index)

MENTAL HEALTH AND DISABILITY LAW
ABA model rules and code of professional conduct, **Mental Health & Disab 138-140**
Abolition of insanity defense, **Mental Health & Disab 271, 272**
Access to records, **Mental Health & Disab 127, 128**
Adjustment disorder, **Mental Health & Disab 40, 41**
Ad litem guardian, **Mental Health & Disab 229**
Administrative regulation and remediation, mental health professionals, **Mental Health & Disab 14-19**
Affirmative action programs, protection of mentally disabled from employment discrimination, **Mental Health & Disab 319, 320**

MENTAL HEALTH AND DISABILITY LAW —Cont'd

Alcoholics, protection of mentally disabled from employment discrimination, **Mental Health & Disab 316, 317**
Allocation among mental health professionals, **Mental Health & Disab 19, 20**
American Law Institute Test, **Mental Health & Disab 261-263**
Americans With Disabilities Act, protection of mentally disabled from employment discrimination, **Mental Health & Disab 307-310**
Anxiety disorders, **Mental Health & Disab 37**
Appointment of guardian, **Mental Health & Disab 217-219**
Attorneys, **Mental Health & Disab 130-144, 237, 238**
Automatism defense, **Mental Health & Disab 264, 265**
Bail, competency to stand trial, **Mental Health & Disab 250**
Behavior modification programs, right to refuse, **Mental Health & Disab 199, 200**
Capital punishment, **Mental Health & Disab 273-275, 296-305**
Civil commitment, generally, **Mental Health & Disab 142-183**
Civil rights laws, **Mental Health & Disab 88-90**
Classifications and definitions of mental disorders, **Mental Health & Disab 31-41**
Clinical psychiatric evidence, **Mental Health & Disab 46-64**
Community services, right to treatment, **Mental Health & Disab 209-211**
Competency to stand trial, **Mental Health & Disab 234-254**
Compulsive gamblers, protection of mentally disabled from employment discrimination, **Mental Health & Disab 317**
Confidentiality, **Mental Health & Disab 18, 112-129**
Confrontation clause, **Mental Health & Disab 126, 127, 173-177**
Constitutional law, **Mental Health & Disab 131, 132, 248-251, 290-294, 296-305, 310-312**
Controlled studies, **Mental Health & Disab 13, 14, 19**
Criminal defenses, generally, **Mental Health & Disab 255-272**
Dangerous propensities of patients, **Mental Health & Disab 119, 120**
Defamation actions, **Mental Health & Disab 115, 116**

MENTAL HEALTH AND DISABILITY LAW —Cont'd

Defenses, generally, **Mental Health & Disab 255-272**
Diagnosis and treatment, generally, **Mental Health & Disab 12-14**
Diminished capacity doctrine, **Mental Health & Disab 265-267**
Discipline, **Mental Health & Disab 17, 18, 340, 341**
Disclosures, **Mental Health & Disab 119, 120**
Dissociative disorders, **Mental Health & Disab 37, 38**
Drug and alcohol treatment records, confidentiality of, **Mental Health & Disab 128, 129**
DSM-IV, definition of mental disorder, **Mental Health & Disab 42**
Duress as defense, **Mental Health & Disab 269**
Durham Rule, **Mental Health & Disab 261**
Education of mentally handicapped, **Mental Health & Disab 331-341**
Electroconvulsive therapy, right to refuse, **Mental Health & Disab 197, 198**
Emergency detention and screening, **Mental Health & Disab 164-166**
Employment discrimination, protection of mentally disabled from, **Mental Health & Disab 306-320**
Ethical issues, **Mental Health & Disab 302-304**
Experts, **Mental Health & Disab 46-64, 137, 138**
Factitious disorders, **Mental Health & Disab 39, 40**
Fair Housing Amendment Act, **Mental Health & Disab 323, 324, 329, 330**
Guardianship, generally, **Mental Health & Disab 214-233**
Guilty but mentally ill as defense, **Mental Health & Disab 269, 270**
Health maintenance organizations, mental health professionals, **Mental Health & Disab 21**
Housing, generally, **Mental Health & Disab 321-327**
Informed consent, **Mental Health & Disab 91-111, 186-188, 301, 302**
Insanity defense tests, **Mental Health & Disab 257-263**

MENTAL HEALTH AND DISABILITY LAW —Cont'd

Involuntary admission, generally, **Mental Health & Disab 166-169**
Irresistible impulse test, **Mental Health & Disab 259-261**
Judicial remedies, protection of mentally disabled from employment discrimination, **Mental Health & Disab 318, 319**
Justification, **Mental Health & Disab 146-153, 256, 257**
Limited choices, mental health professionals, **Mental Health & Disab 8**
Malpractice, **Mental Health & Disab 65, 66**
Managed care, mental health professionals, **Mental Health & Disab 21**
Mentally retarded persons, **Mental Health & Disab 211, 279, 280, 304, 305**
M'Naghten Rule, **Mental Health & Disab 258, 259**
Mood disorders, **Mental Health & Disab 36, 37**
Myth, mental illness as, **Mental Health & Disab 42-45**
Negligence, **Mental Health & Disab 65-72, 77-88**
Nonnegligence theories, **Mental Health & Disab 88-90**
Nontherapist, counseling by, **Mental Health & Disab 73, 74**
Notice of public trial, civil commitment, **Mental Health & Disab 173, 174**
Organic mental syndromes and disorders, **Mental Health & Disab 32, 33**
Parens patriae, civil commitment, **Mental Health & Disab 159-161**
Patient access to records, **Mental Health & Disab 127, 128**
Personality disorder, **Mental Health & Disab 41**
Professionals, **Mental Health & Disab 1-21**
Provocation defense, **Mental Health & Disab 268, 269**
Psychiatric nurse, **Mental Health & Disab 6, 7**
Psychiatric social worker, **Mental Health & Disab 6**
Psychiatrists, **Mental Health & Disab 2-4**
Psychoactive substance use disorders, **Mental Health & Disab 33**
Psychoanalysts, **Mental Health & Disab 5, 6**
Psychologists, **Mental Health & Disab 4, 5**

MENTAL HEALTH AND DISABILITY LAW —Cont'd

Psychosurgery, right to refuse, **Mental Health & Disab 198, 199**
Psychotropic medication, **Mental Health & Disab 188-197, 289, 290**
Public trial, civil commitment, **Mental Health & Disab 173-177**
Reasonable accommodation in private sector, protection of mentally disabled from employment discrimination, **Mental Health & Disab 317, 318**
Records, **Mental Health & Disab 127-129**
Refusal to consent to psychiatric treatment, right to, **Mental Health & Disab 184-200, 289-295**
Rehabilitation Act of 1973, protection of mentally disabled from employment discrimination, **Mental Health & Disab 306, 307**
Reimbursement for treatment, **Mental Health & Disab 209**
Release procedures, civil commitment, **Mental Health & Disab 177, 178**
Reporting requirements, **Mental Health & Disab 118, 119**
Research, informed consent, **Mental Health & Disab 106-111**
Right to treatment, generally, **Mental Health & Disab 201-213**
Schizophrenia, **Mental Health & Disab 33-35**
Self-defense, **Mental Health & Disab 267, 278**
Self-incrimination, **Mental Health & Disab 248-250, 283, 284**
Sentence and punishment, **Mental Health & Disab 273-288**
Sex and sexual offenses, **Mental Health & Disab 18, 19, 38, 79-81, 284-288**
Sleep disorders, **Mental Health & Disab 38, 39**
Social security disability benefits, **Mental Health & Disab 342-347**
Somatoform disorders, **Mental Health & Disab 37**
Sovereign immunity, tort theories, **Mental Health & Disab 75-77**
Speedy trial, competency to stand trial, **Mental Health & Disab 250, 251**
Statutory reporting requirements, **Mental Health & Disab 118, 119**
Student records, education of mentally handicapped, **Mental Health & Disab 338-340**
Suicide, **Mental Health & Disab 77-79**

MENTAL HEALTH AND DISABILITY LAW —Cont'd

Termination of social security disability benefits, **Mental Health & Disab 346, 347**
Voluntary admission, generally, **Mental Health & Disab 178-183**
Waiver of counsel, competency to stand trial, **Mental Health & Disab 237, 238**
Warning duty, **Mental Health & Disab 86-88**
Witnesses, confrontation clause, **Mental Health & Disab 126, 127**
Wrongful disclosure, **Mental Health & Disab 115-118**
Zoning, generally, **Mental Health & Disab 327-330**

MEXICO

United States/Mexico. **International Environmental Law** (this index)

MILITARY LAW

Absence offenses, **Mil 190-193**
Administrative claim remedies, tort claims of servicemembers, **Mil 337-340**
Administrative corrective measures, **Mil 105-107**
Administrative review, discharge and administrative separation, **Mil 313-317**
Air warfare, **Mil 258-263**
Alcohol related offenses, **Mil 188, 189**
Apprehension through trial, criminal process from, **Mil 142-169**
Article 15, **Mil 107-116**
Article 139, **Mil 116**
Assembly, First Amendment rights, **Mil 92-94**
Association, First Amendment rights, **Mil 94**
Biological weapons, **Mil 267, 268**
Board of Correction of Military Records, discharge and administrative spearation, **Mil 314, 315**
Chemical weapons, **Mil 267, 268**
Civilian review of courts-martial, **Mil 179-182**
Combat-related offenses, **Mil 199-201**

MILITARY LAW—Cont'd

Commissioned officers, dismissal of, **Mil 310-313**
Compensation for injury and death of servicemenbers and veterans, **Mil 318-352**
Conscientious objection, discharges of enlisted personnel, **Mil 305, 306**
Conscription, **Mil 62-72**
Constitutional law, generally, **Mil 73-102**
Conventional weapons, **Mil 265-267**
Court of Criminal Appeals, review of courts-martial, **Mil 174-176**
Courts-martial, **Mil 117-142, 169-182**
Criminal justice system of military, generally, **Mil 103-228**
Customary law of armed conflict, **Mil 255-258**
Damages, tort claims of servicemembers, **Mil 336, 337**
Death, compensation for injury and death of servicemenbers and veterans, **Mil 318-352**
Defenses to criminal liability, criminal justice system of military, **Mil 207-210**
Definitions, **Mil 231-233**
Discharge and administrative separation, **Mil 281-317**
Discharge review boards, **Mil 313, 314**
Drug related offenses, **Mil 188, 189**
Due process rights of servicemenbers, **Mil 74-77**
Duties and orders offenses, **Mil 193-197**
Eligibility criteria for veterans' benefits, compensation for injury and death, **Mil 344**
Enlisted personnel, **Mil 41-57, 283-310**
Entry into military, **Mil 41-72**
Equal protection, **Mil 78-81**
Exhaustion of administrative remedies, discharge and administrative separation, **Mil 315, 316**
Federal Tort Claims Act, tort claims of servicemembers, **Mil 319-337**
Feres Doctrine, tort claims of servicemembers, **Mil 322-325**
First Amendment rights, **Mil 81-94**
Foreign Claims Act, tort claims of servicemembers, **Mil 339, 340**

MILITARY LAW—Cont'd

Formal investigation, criminal justice system of military, **Mil 146, 147**
General courts-martial, **Mil 124, 125**
Geneva Conventions, **Mil 242-254**
Genocide Convention of 1948, **Mil 250, 251**
Government contractors' immunity, tort claims of servicemembers, **Mil 335, 336**
Hague Conventions of 1907, **Mil 242**
Homicidal offenses, **Mil 185-186**
Homosexuality, **Mil 47-49, 307-310**
Hospital programs, veterans' benefits, **Mil 350, 351**
Injunctions, judicial review of discharge and administrative separation, **Mil 316, 317**
Injuries, compensation for injury and death of servicemenbers and veterans, **Mil 318-352**
Insurance, veterans' benefits, **Mil 351, 352**
International armed conflict, **Mil 231-236**
International covenant on civil and political rights, **Mil 254, 255**
Judge advocate general, review of courts-martial, **Mil 173, 174**
Judicial review, **Mil 52, 53, 315-317**
Jurisdiction, **Mil 125-142, 315**
Law of armed conflict, generally, **Mil 229-280**
Malpractice, tort claims of servicemembers, **Mil 334, 335**
Military Claims Act, tort claims of servicemembers, **Mil 337, 338**
Military Personnel and Civilian Employees Claims Act, tort claims of servicemembers, **Mil 340, 341**
Modern warfare, application of law of armed conflict to particular issues of, **Mil 258**
National Guard Tort Claims Act, tort claims of servicemembers, **Mil 339**
National Security Constitution, **Mil 1-40**
Naval warfare, law of armed conflict, **Mil 263-265**
New trial petition, review of courts-martial, **Mil 177, 178**
Nuclear weapons, **Mil 268, 269**
Nursing homes, veterans' benefits, **Mil 350, 351**
Officer appointments, **Mil 57-60**

MILITARY LAW—Cont'd
Petitions and communications with congress, First Amendment rights, **Mil 93, 94**
Pleas, criminal justice system of military, **Mil 156-159**
Political participation, First Amendment rights, **Mil 87, 88**
Preliminary injunctions, judicial review, **Mil 316, 317**
Preparation for trial, criminal justice system of military, **Mil 148-151**
Pretrial plea bargaining, criminal justice system of military, **Mil 156-159**
Protection of national security, **Mil 31-40**
Protocols I and II to Geneva Conventions of 1948, **Mil 251-254**
Publications, First Amendment rights, **Mil 88-92**
Public employment preference rights of veterans, constitutional and statutory rights of servicemenbers, **Mil 101, 102**
Punishment, criminal justice system of military, **Mil 210, 211**
Redressing acts in violation of law of armed conflict, **Mil 270-280**
Reemployment rights of servicemen, constitutional and statutory rights of servicemenbers, **Mil 99-101**
Rehabilitation programs, veterans' benefits, **Mil 350, 351**
Religion, First Amendment rights, **Mil 82, 83**
Reservists, activation of, **Mil 60-62**
Residency and tax situs, constitutional and statutory rights of servicemenbers, **Mil 95, 96**
Restrictions on freedom, criminal justice system of military, **Mil 142-144**
Review of courts-martial, criminal justice system of military, **Mil 169-182**
Right to counsel, constitutional safeguards, **Mil 223-228**
Search and seizure, criminal justice system of military, **Mil 213-221**
Self-incrimination, criminal justice system of military, **Mil 221-223**
Sentencing procedures, criminal justice system of military, **Mil 164-166**
Sex offenses, **Mil 186, 187**
Soldiers' and Sailors' Civil Relief Act, constitutional and statutory rights of servicemenbers, **Mil 96-99**

MILITARY LAW—Cont'd
Special courts-martial, **Mil 121-124**
Speech, First Amendment rights, **Mil 84-88**
Speedy trial, criminal justice system of military, **Mil 152-156**
Staff judge advocate, review of courts-martial, **Mil 172, 173**
Stratagems, treachery or perfidy, law of armed conflict, **Mil 269, 270**
Summary courts-martial, **Mil 118-121**
Superior-subordinate relationship offenses, **Mil 197-199**
Symbolic expression, First Amendment rights, **Mil 88**
Tax situs, constitutional and statutory rights of servicemenbers, **Mil 95, 96**
Text and doctrine of National Security Constitution, **Mil 2-27**
Theft offenses, **Mil 187, 188**
Tort claims of servicemembers, compensation for injury and death of servicemenbers and veterans, **Mil 319-341**
Treaties relating to armed conflict, **Mil 240-255**
Trial, generally, **Mil 159-169**
United States Court of Appeals for Armed Forces, review of courts-martial, **Mil 176, 177**
Veterans, **Mil 101, 102, 342-352**
Voting right, constitutional and statutory rights of servicemenbers, **Mil 95**
Weapons systems, **Mil 265-269**

MINES AND MINERALS
Energy and Natural Resources Law (this index)
Hard rock mining and minerals. **Energy and Natural Resources Law** (this index)
Water Law (this index)

MIRANDA RULES
Generally, **Crim Proc-Const Lim 198-227, 306-310**

MODERN PUBLIC LAND LAW
Access to federal land, **Pub Land 35-40**
Acquisition of public domain, generally, **Pub Land 13, 14, 28-30**

MODERN PUBLIC LAND LAW—Cont'd

Alaska, **Pub Land 7, 23, 31-33, 245, 246, 256-258**
Alaska National Interest Lands Conservation Act, **Pub Land 34, 39, 80, 88, 250, 256-258, 311**
Antiquities Act of 1906, **Pub Land 25, 33, 34, 80, 291**
Archaeological Resources protection Act of 1979, **Pub Land 292, 293; Pub Land 293**
Areas of critical environmental concern, **Pub Land 223**
Assimilative Crimes Act, **Pub Land 43**
Bald and Golden Eagle Protection Act, **Pub Land 230**
Bureau of Land Management, **Pub Land 2, 32, 46, 62, 117, 118, 148-150, 201-204, 215, 221-231, 252**
Bureau of Reclamation, **Pub Land 274, 275**
California desert conservation area, **Pub Land 222, 223, 323**
Classification, **Pub Land 79, 82**
Classification and Multiple Use Act of 1964, **Pub Land 32, 79, 82**
Clean Air Act, **Pub Land 297, 298**
Clean Water Act, **Pub Land 58, 125, 127, 162, 190, 191, 195, 202**
Coal leasing, generally, **Pub Land 153-155 et seq.**
Colorado River Storage Project Act, **Pub Land 298**
Columbia River Gorge National Scenic Area Act, **Pub Land 125**
Commerce clause, **Pub Land 49, 115, 116, 232-234**
Concessions Policy Act, **Pub Land 266**
Condemnation, **Pub Land 28, 29**
Conservation, age of, **Pub Land 12, 24, 30, 31**
Corps of Engineers, **Pub Land 303**
Desert Lands Act, **Pub Land 19, 37, 113, 114**
Disposition, **Pub Land 12, 15-24**
Enclave clause, **Pub Land 41-44**
Endangered Species Act, generally, **Pub Land 231, 235**
Equal footing doctrine, **Pub Land 16, 17**
Equal protection clause, **Pub Land 233, 265**
Exchanges of land, **Pub Land 87-89**
External threats, **Pub Land 249, 250, 294-299**
Federal Coal Leasing Act Amendments of 1976, **Pub Land 153-155 et seq.**

MODERN PUBLIC LAND LAW—Cont'd
Federal implied reserved water rights, **Pub Land 53, 114-120**
Federal Land Exchange Facilitation Act, **Pub Land 88**
Federal Land Policy and Management Act, generally, **Pub Land 2, 3, 32, 37, 39, 40, 52, 53, 60, 61, 67, 82-89**
Federal Onshore Oil and Gas Leasing Reform Act, **Pub Land 164-168**
Federal Power Act, **Pub Land 18, 123**
Federal Property and Administrative Services Act, **Pub Land 89**
Federal Timber Contract Payment Modification Act of 1984, **Pub Land 182**
Federal Tort Claims Act, **Pub Land 283-288**
First Amendment, **Pub Land 276**
Fish and Wildlife Coordination Act, **Pub Land 231**
Fish and Wildlife Service, **Pub Land 33, 240-243, 246-249, 251, 311**
Fisheries Conservation and Management Act, **Pub Land 231**
Forest and Rangeland Renewable Resources Planning Act, **Pub Land 195, 196**
Forest Reserve Amendment to General Revision Act, **Pub Land 25, 29**
Forest Service Organic Act, **Pub Land 25, 31, 52, 145-147, 175, 183, 206, 272-274**
General mining law, **Pub Land 8, 9, 21, 26, 128-145, 301, 321**
Geothermal leasing, **Pub Land 169, 298**
Geothermal Steam Act, **Pub Land 169, 298**
Grazing in wilderness areas, rangeland resource, **Pub Land 308**
Hells Canyon National Recreation Area Act, **Pub Land 271, 272**
Historic Sites Act of 1935, **Pub Land 293, 294**
Homesteading, **Pub Land 2, 19, 20, 170**
Interior Department, generally, **Pub Land 1, 2**
Judicial review, generally, **Pub Land 73, 74**
Jurisdiction clause, **Pub Land 41-44**
Lacey Act, **Pub Land 230**
Land and Water Conservation Fund, **Pub Land 33, Pub Land 54,; Pub Land 33, 54, 261-263**
Land use planning, **Pub Land 176, 177, 195-201, 222, 223, 225, 226, 268, 269, 303, 304**

MODERN PUBLIC LAND LAW—Cont'd

Legislative veto, **Pub Land 85**
Livestock grazing, **Pub Land 10, 46, 62, 212-221, 224-231, 308**
Marine Mammal Protection Act, **Pub Land 231**
McCarren Amendment, **Pub Land 120**
Migratory Bird Treaty Act, **Pub Land 230, 249**
Mineral Leasing Act of 1920, **Pub Land 9, 18, 27, 50, 51, 82, 151**
Mineral resource, generally, **Pub Land 8, 9**
Modern public land law defined, **Pub Land 3-6**
Multiple-Use, Sustained-Yield Act of 1960, **Pub Land 31, 183-187, 252, 272**
National Environmental Policy Act, generally, **Pub Land 39**
National Forest Management Act of 1976, **Pub Land 31, 70, 176-182, 195-201**
National Forest Service, generally, **Pub Land 2**
National Forest Ski Area Act of 1986, **Pub Land 273**
National Forest System, generally, **Pub Land 2**
National Historic Preservation Act of 1966, **Pub Land 294**
National Park Service, **Pub Land 1, 2, 93, 94, 265, 295-297**
National Park System, generally, **Pub Land 1, 2**
National recreation areas, **Pub Land 269-272**
National Trails System Act, generally, **Pub Land 269-272**
National Wild and Scenic Rivers Act of 1968, **Pub Land 162, 299-305**
National wilderness preservation system, **Pub Land 34, 118, 162, 280, 281, 290, 305-323**
National Wildlife Refuge System, **Pub Land 2, 26, 32, 33, 162, 246-249, 281**
Off-road vehicle use, **Pub Land 222, 223, 277-282**
Oil and gas leasing, **Pub Land 163-169**
Oregon and California Act, Bureau of Land Management, **Pub Land 201, 203, 204**
Pacific Northwest Electric Power Planning and Conservation Act, **Pub Land 124, 125**
Payments in Lieu of Taxes Act, **Pub Land 55**
Pickett Act, **Pub Land 27**
Pollution, **Pub Land 127, 191, 202, 223, 297, 298, 302**

MODERN PUBLIC LAND LAW—Cont'd
Preemption, **Pub Land 49-55**
Preservation, age of, **Pub Land 12**
Preservation resource, **Pub Land 11, 162, 289-305**
Private holdings, land acquisition of, **Pub Land 302**
Privileges and immunities clause, access to wildlife, **Pub Land 233**
Project Bold, **Pub Land 89**
Property clause, **Pub Land 44-46, 48, 19, 115, 116, 234, 294**
Public Rangeland Improvement Act, **Pub Land 214, 218, 219, 226**
Public trust, **Pub Land 91-94, 295-297**
R. S. 2477, **Pub Land 38**
Rangeland resource, **Pub Land 10, 46, 62, 212-221, 224-231, 308**
Reclamation Act, **Pub Land 18, 22, 121, 122**
Recreational purposes, acquisition of land for, **Pub Land 260-264**
Recreation and Public Purposes Act of 1926, **Pub Land 89, 90**
Recreation resource, **Pub Land 10, 11, 259, 264-282**
Refuge Recreation Act of 1962, **Pub Land 247, 248, 260, 261**
Reservations, **Pub Land 78, 289**
Sagerbrush Rebellion, **Pub Land 24, 44, 90, 205**
Sales of land, **Pub Land 89-91**
Sikes Act, **Pub Land 231**
Stock-Raising Homestead Act of 1916, **Pub Land 19, 20, 27, 170-172**
Submerged Lands Act of 1953, **Pub Land 16, 18**
Supremacy Clause, preemption, **Pub Land 49-55**
Surface Mining Control and Reclamation Act of 1977, **Pub Land 161, 162, 172-174**
Takings clause, **Pub Land 55-63, 150, 151, 160, 173, 174, 270, 271, 274, 275**
Taylor Grazing Act, **Pub Land 2, 18, 30, 79, 207-212**
Timber resource, **Pub Land 9, 10, 25, 31, 52, 70, 145-147, 175-183, 187-190, 194-204, 206, 272-274, 309, 310**
Tongass Timber Reform Act, **Pub Land 257**
Unlawful Inclosures Act, **Pub Land 36, 47, 206**
Water resource, **Pub Land 8, 110-120, 125-127, 173, 175, 260**

MODERN PUBLIC LAND LAW—Cont'd
Watershed, **Pub Land 125-127, 173, 175, 260**
Weeks Act, **Pub Land 173, 175, 260**
Wild, Free-roaming Horses and Burros Act, **Pub Land 46, 62, 227-231**
Wild and scenic rivers, **Pub Land 162, 299-305**
Wilderness Act of 1964, **Pub Land 34, 118, 162, 280, 281, 290, 305-323**
Wildlife refuge, **Pub Land 2, 26, 32, 33, 162, 246-249, 281**
Wildlife resource, **Pub Land 231, 235**
Wildlife resource, generally, **Pub Land 1, 2**
Wise use movement, **Pub Land 24**
Withdrawals, **Pub Land 25, 78-82, 289**
Yellowstone National Park, **Pub Land 7, 25, 79, 169, 251, 289, 298**

MODIFICATION
Change or Modification (this index)

MONOPOLIES AND RESTRAINTS OF TRADE
Health Care Law and Ethics (this index)

MUSEUM ORGANIZATION
Art Law (this index)

MUSEUM POLICIES
Art Law (this index)

NATIONAL FORESTS
Energy and Natural Resources Law (this index)

NATIONALIZATION
International Trade and Investment (this index)

NATIONAL LABOR RELATIONS ACT
Individual Employee Rights (this index)
Labor Law (this index)

NATURAL RESOURCES

Energy and Natural Resources Law (this index)

NEGOTIABLE INSTRUMENTS AND CHECK COLLECTION

Generally, **Neg Inst 1-16**
Absolute liability, additional warranty of, **Neg Inst 264, 265**
Accommodation parties, ordinary or personal defenses, **Neg Inst 304-318**
Accord and satisfaction, underlying obligations, **Neg Inst 122, 123**
Alteration
  material alteration, transfer warranties, **Neg Inst 261**
  real defenses, **Neg Inst 299**
  risk allocation, alteration of check, **Neg Inst 492, 493**
Availability of funds, checks, **Neg Inst 438-449**
Banks and banking
  duties of collecting bank, checks, **Neg Inst 414-422**
  electronic banking, **Neg Inst 285-287**
  final payment by payor bank, checks, **Neg Inst 422-438**
  form and function of checks, **Neg Inst 395-397**
  funds availability, checks, **Neg Inst 438-449**
  multiple banks, presentment of check for payment, **Neg Inst 406-422**
  payor bank, presentment of check for payment, **Neg Inst 398-406**
Cancellation, discharge of liability, **Neg Inst 166**
Capacity or incapacity
  real defenses, **Neg Inst 295**
  signer, contract liability on instruments, **Neg Inst 90-105**
  wrongful honor in absence of fraud or forgery, **Neg Inst 484, 485**
Cash, unauthorized use of, **Neg Inst 523, 524**
Cashier's checks, liability of special instruments, **Neg Inst 105-109**
Certificates of deposit, **Neg Inst 23, 24, 31**
Certified checks, liability of special instruments, **Neg Inst 105-109**

NEGOTIABLE INSTRUMENTS AND CHECK COLLECTION—Cont'd
Check collection, generally, **Neg Inst 387-466**
Claims, generally, **Neg Inst 327-329**
Competency or incompetency. Capacity or incapacity, supra
Contracts
  defenses, contract law, **Neg Inst 319-323**
  liability on instruments, **Neg Inst 81-123**
Conversion, **Neg Inst 521-523**
Credit cards, unauthorized use of, **Neg Inst 524, 525**
Damages, incidental damages, **Neg Inst 284, 285**
Date of instrument, **Neg Inst 78, 79**
Death of customer, wrongful honor in absence of fraud or forgery, **Neg Inst 484, 485**
Declaration, negotiability or not by, **Neg Inst 74, 75**
Defenses
  generally, **Neg Inst 289-329**
  contract law, **Neg Inst 319-323**
  discharge of liability, **Neg Inst 167**
  ordinary or personal defenses, **Neg Inst 301-323**
  payor banks, **Neg Inst 501-521**
  transfer warranties, **Neg Inst 262**
Defining conditions and mechanics of satisfying them, **Neg Inst 133-153**
Deposits
  certificates of deposit, **Neg Inst 23, 24, 31**
  dishonored checks, **Neg Inst 458-460**
  payor bank, relationship between customer and, **Neg Inst 468, 469**
  presentment of check for payment, **Neg Inst 409-413**
Destroyed checks, **Neg Inst 485-487**
Discharge of liability
  generally, **Neg Inst 157-167**
  ordinary or personal defenses, **Neg Inst 303, 304**
Dishonor
  checks, **Neg Inst 449-466**
  defining conditions and mechanics of satisfying them, **Neg Inst 133-143**
  wrongful dishonor, generally, **Neg Inst 470-474**

NEGOTIABLE INSTRUMENTS AND CHECK COLLECTION—Cont'd
Drafts, **Neg Inst 24, 25, 31-36, 105, 135-137**
Duress, real defenses, **Neg Inst 294, 295**
Duties of collecting bank, checks, **Neg Inst 414-422**
Early law of commercial paper, **Neg Inst 5, 6**
Electronic banking, **Neg Inst 285-287**
Electronic fund transfers, unauthorized use of, **Neg Inst 525-527**
Enforcement
  entitlement to enforce, transfer warranties, **Neg Inst 259, 260**
  instruments as property, **Neg Inst 176-203**
Entitlement to enforce, transfer warranties, **Neg Inst 259, 260**
Evidence of dishonor, defining conditions and mechanics of satisfying them, **Neg Inst 143**
Excuse of conditions or delay, **Neg Inst 153-155**
Expedited Funds Availability Act, checks, **Neg Inst 441-449**
Expeditious return, dishonored checks, **Neg Inst 449-466**
Final or finality
  payor bank, final payment by, **Neg Inst 422-438**
  presentment warranties, **Neg Inst 267-270**
Fixed amount, requisites of negotiability, **Neg Inst 57-59**
Form and function of checks, **Neg Inst 387-397**
Fraud and forgery
  real defenses, **Neg Inst 296-299**
  risk allocation, **Neg Inst 491-529**
  wrongful honor in absence of, **Neg Inst 474-484**
Fraudulent alteration, discharge of liability, **Neg Inst 165**
Holder in due course, **Neg Inst 167, 266, 331-386**
Illegality, real defenses, **Neg Inst 295, 296**
Incidental damages, **Neg Inst 284, 285**
Incomplete instruments, **Neg Inst 76-78**
Indorsements
  failure to satisfy conditions, **Neg Inst 126-129**
  forged, risk allocation, **Neg Inst 495, 496**
  instruments as property, **Neg Inst 210-251**
  ordinary or personal defenses, **Neg Inst 304-318**
  retroactive indorsements, instruments as property, **Neg Inst 240-251**

NEGOTIABLE INSTRUMENTS AND CHECK COLLECTION—Cont'd
Infancy, real defenses, **Neg Inst 294**
Insolvency proceedings, **Neg Inst 263, 298**
International law, **Neg Inst 16**
Joint obligors, liability of, **Neg Inst 112, 113**
Lack of words of negotiability, **Neg Inst 76**
Limitations or restrictions, **Neg Inst 249-251, 376-386**
Lost checks, **Neg Inst 485-487**
Material alteration, transfer warranties, **Neg Inst 261**
Money, requisites of negotiability, **Neg Inst 57**
Money orders, liability of special instruments, **Neg Inst 109-111**
Multiple banks, presentment of check for payment, **Neg Inst 406-422**
Nature of instruments, generally, **Neg Inst 17-21**
Negotiation, instruments as property, **Neg Inst 207-240**
Notes, defining conditions and mechanics of satisfying them, **Neg Inst 134**
Notice
  defining conditions and mechanics of satisfying them, **Neg Inst 149-153**
  dishonored checks, **Neg Inst 149-153, 449-466**
  real defenses, notice of discharge, **Neg Inst 299, 300**
On demand, requisites of negotiability, **Neg Inst 60-64**
Order
  requisites of negotiability, **Neg Inst 44-48**
  requisites of negotiability, order or bearer, **Neg Inst 64-72**
  wrongful honor in absence of fraud or forgery, order closing account, **Neg Inst 482, 483**
Ordinary or personal defenses, **Neg Inst 301-323**
Payor bank
  defenses, **Neg Inst 501-521**
  dishonored checks, **Neg Inst 449-455**
  final payment by payor bank, checks, **Neg Inst 422-438**
  presentment of check for payment, **Neg Inst 398-406**
  relationship between customer and, **Neg Inst 467-489**
  wrongful honor, remedies for, **Neg Inst 487-489**

NEGOTIABLE INSTRUMENTS AND CHECK COLLECTION—Cont'd

Per se negligence defenses, payor bank defenses, **Neg Inst 512-521**
Place of payment, **Neg Inst 80**
Post-dated checks, wrongful honor in absence of fraud or forgery, **Neg Inst 483**
Presentment
    generally, **Neg Inst 398-422**
    defining conditions and mechanics of satisfying them, **Neg Inst 144-149**
    warranties, **Neg Inst 267-282**
Promise, requisites of negotiability, **Neg Inst 44-48**
Promissory notes, **Neg Inst 22, 23, 27-31**
Property, instruments as, **Neg Inst 169-251**
Real defenses, **Neg Inst 293-301**
Recoupment, **Neg Inst 324-327**
Regulation CC, **Neg Inst 397, 441-449, 463-466**
Remedying breach of warranty, **Neg Inst 282-285**
Requisites of negotiability, **Neg Inst 39-80**
Restitution, **Neg Inst 253-288, 488, 489**
Retroactive indorsements, instruments as property, **Neg Inst 240-251**
Risk allocation, generally, **Neg Inst 491-529**
Satisfaction, **Neg Inst 126-153**
Secondary liability, conditions of, **Neg Inst 125-155**
Signatures, **Neg Inst 43, 44, 81-105, 261**
Stale checks, wrongful honor in absence of fraud or forgery, **Neg Inst 484**
Statutes of limitations, instruments as property, **Neg Inst 202, 203**
Stolen checks, **Neg Inst 485-487**
Subrogation defense, payor banks, **Neg Inst 502, 503**
Supplemental role of federal law, **Neg Inst 15**
Suretyship defenses, ordinary or personal defenses, **Neg Inst 304-318**
Teller's checks, liability of special instruments, **Neg Inst 105-109**
Tender of payment, discharge of liability, **Neg Inst 164**

NEGOTIABLE INSTRUMENTS AND CHECK COLLECTION—Cont'd
Transfer warranties, **Neg Inst 256-266**
Travelers' checks, liability of special instruments, **Neg Inst 111, 112**
Trust indorsements, instruments as property, **Neg Inst 249**
Unauthorized use of other payment instruments, **Neg Inst 523-529**
Unconditional, requisites of negotiability, **Neg Inst 48-57**
Underlying obligations, **Neg Inst 113-123**
Uniform Commercial Code, generally, **Neg Inst 7-14**
Uniform Negotiable Instruments Law, **Neg Inst 7**
Warranties, **Neg Inst 253-288, 487, 488**
Writing, requisites of negotiability, **Neg Inst 42, 43**
Wrongful dishonor, generally, **Neg Inst 470-474**

NEGOTIATION
Government Contracts (this index)
Legal Negotiation (this index)
Public International Law (this index)
Trial and Practice Skills (this index)
Uniform Commercial Code (this index)

NLRA (NATIONAL LABOR RELATIONS ACT)
Labor Law (this index)

NOTICE
Insurance Law (this index)
Negotiable Instruments and Check Collection (this index)

OBSCENITY
Art Law (this index)

OCEAN MANAGEMENT
Generally, **Coastal and Ocean 1 et seq.**

OFFICERS

Labor Law (this index)

OIL AND GAS LAW

Generally, **Oil & Gas 1-57**
Ad coleum doctrine, **Oil & Gas 8, 9**
Administrative clauses, oil and gas lease savings clauses, **Oil & Gas 259-268**
Adverse possession, creation and transfer of oil and gas interests by, **Oil & Gas 76-83**
Assumpsit, protection of oil and gas rights, **Oil & Gas 53, 54**
Balancing agreements, gas contracts, **Oil & Gas 385-387**
Carried interest, **Oil & Gas 47, 48**
Cessation of production clauses, oil and gas lease savings clauses, **Oil & Gas 256-258**
Common implied covenants, implied covenants in oil and gas leases, **Oil & Gas 302-336**
Conservation laws, limits to rule of capture, **Oil & Gas 15-28**
Constructive production, oil and gas lease savings clauses providing for, **Oil & Gas 227-258**
Contracts, generally, **Oil & Gas 367-388**
Conveyance of oil and gas rights, generally, **Oil & Gas 59-75**
Correlative rights doctrine, limits to rule of capture, **Oil & Gas 13, 14**
Creation and transfer of oil and gas interests, generally, **Oil & Gas 59-83**
Damage to lease value, **Oil & Gas 49-52**
Deductions, **Oil & Gas 273-276, 350-352**
Definitions and distinctions, **Oil & Gas 114-131**
Delay rentals, **Oil & Gas 195-225, 356, 357**
Delivery conditions, gas contracts, **Oil & Gas 385**
Depletion, taxation, **Oil & Gas 352-355**
Description, conveyance of oil and gas leases, **Oil & Gas 64-68**
Development
- generally, **Energy 439-449**
- taxation of oil and gas development, **Oil & Gas 361-366**

OIL AND GAS LAW—Cont'd

Diligent and proper operation, implied covenants in oil and gas leases, **Oil & Gas 334-336**

Division of orders, oil and gas contracts, **Oil & Gas 387, 388**

Drainage, **Oil & Gas 12, 13, 318-327**

Drilling, generally, **Oil & Gas 3-5**

Ejectment and conversion, protection of oil and gas rights, **Oil & Gas 55-57**

Equipment costs, taxation of oil and gas development, **Oil & Gas 366**

Escaped hydrocarbons, limits to rule of capture, **Oil & Gas 10, 11**

Essential clauses in modern oil and gas leases, **Oil & Gas 163-225**

Execution, conveyance of oil and gas leases, **Oil & Gas 69-75**

Farmout agreements, oil and gas contracts, **Oil & Gas 369-371**

Fee interest, **Oil & Gas 36, 37**

Force majeure clauses, oil and gas lease savings clauses, **Oil & Gas 247-250**

Fractional interest problems, **Oil & Gas 131-144**

Future, implied covenants in oil and gas leases, **Oil & Gas 336, 337**

Granting clause, essential clauses in modern oil and gas leases, **Oil & Gas 167-184**

Habendum clause, oil and gas leases, **Oil & Gas 184-195**

Implied covenants, **Oil & Gas 296-337, 342-345**

Intangible drilling costs, **Oil & Gas 350-352, 365**

International Environmental Law (this index)

Interpretive problems in oil and gas conveyancing, generally, **Oil & Gas 111-162**

Joint ownership of oil and gas rights, generally, **Oil & Gas 84-110**

Leases, generally, **Energy 279-283; Oil & Gas 163-348**

Limits to rule of capture, **Oil & Gas 10-28**

Markets and market value, generally, **Oil & Gas 276-278**

Mineral interest, **Oil & Gas 37-40**

Mother Hubbard problem, land covered by lease, **Oil & Gas 170-172**

OIL AND GAS LAW—Cont'd

Net profits interest, **Oil & Gas 46, 47**
Operating agreements, oil and gas contracts, **Oil & Gas 371-375**
Ownership of oil and gas rights, generally, **Oil & Gas 8-35**
Parties designated, conveyance of oil and gas leases, **Oil & Gas 68, 69**
Partnerships, taxation of oil and gas development, **Oil & Gas 362, 363**
Price of gas contracts, **Oil & Gas 379-381**
Production payment, **Oil & Gas 45, 46**
Protection of oil and gas rights, generally, **Oil & Gas 49-57**
Quitclaim deed, conveyance of oil and gas rights, **Oil & Gas 61, 62**
Reasonable prudent operator standard, implied covenants in oil and gas leases, **Oil & Gas 299-302**
Royalties, generally, **Oil & Gas 144, 145, 150-159**
Rule of capture, generally, **Oil & Gas 9, 10**
Sale/sublease distinction, taxation of transfer of mineral rights, **Oil & Gas 357-359**
Shut-in royalty clauses, oil and gas lease savings clauses, **Oil & Gas 250-256**
Slander of title, **Oil & Gas 52, 53**
Support agreements, oil and gas contracts, **Oil & Gas 368, 369**
Surface interest, **Oil & Gas 41, 42**
Surveys, conveyance of oil and gas leases, **Oil & Gas 66-68**
Take-or-pay and other royalty disputes, **Oil & Gas 288-293**
Take provisions, gas contracts, **Oil & Gas 382, 383**
Taxation, generally, **Oil & Gas 349-366**
Term of gas contracts, **Oil & Gas 378, 379**
Timber, federal timber law, **Energy 336-338**
Top leasing, **Oil & Gas 159-162**
Uses permitted by grant, oil and gas leases, **Oil & Gas 172-184**
Value or valuation, damage to lease value, **Oil & Gas 49-52**
Warranty deed, conveyance of oil and gas rights, **Oil & Gas 60, 61**

OLDER PERSONS
Elder Law (this index)

OPTIONAL ADJUSTMENTS
Federal Income Taxation of Partners and Partnerships (this index)

ORDER
Negotiable Instruments and Check Collection (this index)

ORGANS
Health Care Law and Ethics (this index)

OUTBOUND TRANSACTIONS
International Taxation (this index)

OUTLINES AND OUTLINING
How to Study Law and Take Law Exams (this index)

OVERBREADTH AND VAGUENESS
First Amendment (this index)

OVERPAYMENTS
Tax Procedure and Tax Fraud (this index)

PARAGRAPHS
Legal Writing (this index)

PARLIAMENTARY GOVERNMENT
Comparative Legal Traditions (this index)

PAROL EVIDENCE RULE
Insurance Law (this index)

PARTNERSHIP
Agency-Partnership (this index)

PARTNERSHIP—Cont'd
Federal Income Taxation of Partners and Partnerships (this index)
International Taxation (this index)
Limited liability company. **Partnership and LLC** (this index)

PARTNERSHIP AND LLC
Accounting, **Partn & LLC 174, 175**
Agency relationship, **Partn & LLC 4-6, 11, 19 et seq., 39, 48-56, 114, 139-141**
Agent, **Partn & LLC 10, 17, 21, 22, 36-39, 45-54, 67, 114, 126-129**
Aggregate theory of partnership, **Partn & LLC 150, 151**
Ambiguous principal, **Partn & LLC 14, 15**
Apparent authority, **Partn & LLC 105-111, 140, 141**
Authority, **Partn & LLC 99, 100, 103-111, 139-141**
Borrowed servants, **Partn & LLC 14**
Charging order, **Partn & LLC 179, 180**
Co-agency, **Partn & LLC 20**
Contribution, **Partn & LLC 57, 58, 90**
Co-principal doctrine, **Partn & LLC 94**
Covenants not to compete, **Partn & LLC 54**
Custom, **Partn & LLC 103, 106**
Death of party to an agency relationship, **Partn & LLC 140**
Deep pocket theory, **Partn & LLC 66**
Derivative suits by limited partners, **Partn & LLC 211**
Disclosure, fiduciary duties, **Partn & LLC 48, 49**
Dissociation of partner, **Partn & LLC 186**
Dissolution of partnership, **Partn & LLC 58, 184, 185, 194, 200**
Dual priorities rule, **Partn & LLC 178**
Enterprise liability, **Partn & LLC 77**
Entity theory of partnership, **Partn & LLC 151**
Equal dignity rule, **Partn & LLC 102**
Estoppel, **Partn & LLC 87, 88, 111-113**
Exculpatory clause, effect of, **Partn & LLC 86, 87**
Express authority, **Partn & LLC 99, 100**

PARTNERSHIP AND LLC—Cont'd

Fellow servant rule, **Partn & LLC 40**
Fiduciary, definition of, **Partn & LLC 8, 48**
Fiduciary duties, **Partn & LLC 48-54**
Fraud, **Partn & LLC 82-87**
Frolic or detour, **Partn & LLC 73**
General agent, **Partn & LLC 21, 114**
Going and coming rule, **Partn & LLC 75**
Good will, **Partn & LLC 184, 197**
Implied authority, **Partn & LLC 103, 104**
Imputed contributory negligence, **Partn & LLC 82, 90**
Imputed knowledge, **Partn & LLC 136-138**
Incidental authority, **Partn & LLC 103**
Indemnity, **Partn & LLC 36, 37, 46, 47, 90**
Independent contractor, **Partn & LLC 17, 68-72**
Inherent agency power, **Partn & LLC 115, 116**
Jingle rule, **Partn & LLC 178**
Joint enterprise, **Partn & LLC 89, 90**
Joint venture, **Partn & LLC 91**
Lien of agent, **Partn & LLC 39**
Limited liability limited partnership, **Partn & LLC 32**
Limited liabliity company, **Partn & LLC 33, 34, 61, 62, 220-223**
Limited liabliity partnership, **Partn & LLC 30, 31**
Limited partner, **Partn & LLC 208-212**
Limited partnership, **Partn & LLC 32, 207-215**
Liquidation rights of partners, **Partn & LLC 188, 189**
LLC, **Partn & LLC 33, 217-223**
LLLP, **Partn & LLC 32, 215, 216**
LLP, **Partn & LLC 30**
Loaned employees, **Partn & LLC 14**
Loyalty, fiduciary duties, **Partn & LLC 50-54**
Master and servant, **Partn & LLC 11, 12, 63-66, 88**
Misrepresentation, **Partn & LLC 82-87**
Nondelegable duty doctrine, **Partn & LLC 71, 72**
Nonservant agent, **Partn & LLC 17**
Notice, **Partn & LLC 134**

PARTNERSHIP AND LLC—Cont'd
Partially disclosed principal, **Partn & LLC 22**
Partner, generally, **Partn & LLC 57-60**
Partnership, generally, **Partn & LLC 29**
Power coupled with an interest, **Partn & LLC 140**
Power given as security, **Partn & LLC 139**
Power of attorney, **Partn & LLC 100-102**
Principal, **Partn & LLC 9, 10, 36-38, 40, 43**
Punitive damages against employer, **Partn & LLC 80, 81**
Qui facit per alium facit per se, **Partn & LLC 10**
Ratification, **Partn & LLC 130-133**
Re-entry after frolic, **Partn & LLC 74**
Respondeat superior, **Partn & LLC 11, 63**
RULPA, **Partn & LLC 32, 206**
RUPA, **Partn & LLC 29, 145**
Scope of employment, **Partn & LLC 73-80**
Servant, **Partn & LLC 12**
Sole actor rule, **Partn & LLC 137, 138**
Special agent, **Partn & LLC 21**
Subagent, **Partn & LLC 19, 39**
Taxation, **Partn & LLC 28, 33, 218, 219**
Termination of authority, **Partn & LLC 139-141**
Trade secrets, **Partn & LLC 53**
ULLCA, **Partn & LLC 33, 61, 62, 217-223**
ULPA, **Partn & LLC 32, 206**
Undisclosed principal, **Partn & LLC 22, 118, 120, 121, 123, 124**
Unincorporated associations, **Partn & LLC 93, 94**
UPA, **Partn & LLC 29, 144**
Vicarious tort liability, **Partn & LLC 87, 88, 96**
Warranty of authority of agent, **Partn & LLC 128**
Winding up of partnership, **Partn & LLC 198-202**
Worker's compensation laws, **Partn & LLC 41, 42, 129**

PATENTS
Generally, **Intell Prop 1 et seq.**

PAYOR BANK
Negotiable Instruments and Check Collection (this index)

PENALTIES AND INTEREST
Tax Procedure and Tax Fraud (this index)

PERFORMANCE
Uniform Commercial Code (this index)

PERIODICALS
Legal Research (this index)

PERSONAL PROPERTY
Abandoned chattel, finders, **Pers Prop 165-168**
Abandoned personal property, **Pers Prop 45-84**
Acceptance, gifts, **Pers Prop 323, 324**
Accession and confusion, **Pers Prop 369-379**
Adverse possession of personal property, **Pers Prop 349-368**
Armory rule, prior possession, **Pers Prop 128, 129, 132-145**
Bailments, **Pers Prop 196-250**
Bank accounts, **Pers Prop 325-348**
Bee hive cases, **Pers Prop 31-33**
Bulky chattel, finders, **Pers Prop 169**
Burden of proof, bailments, **Pers Prop 224-227, 234-244**
Buried treasure, finders, **Pers Prop 172-181**
Causa mortis gifts, **Pers Prop 318-322**
Commercial bailments, **Pers Prop 231-250**
Common carriers, commercial bailments, **Pers Prop 233, 234**
Common law estates, **Pers Prop 380-386**
Conditional gifts, **Pers Prop 308-313**
Conversion, accession and confusion, **Pers Prop 372, 373**
Corporate stock as gift, **Pers Prop 301-305**
Custom, wild animals and first possession, **Pers Prop 14-17**
Damages
    accession and confusion, **Pers Prop 372, 373**
    bailments, **Pers Prop 227-229**

PERSONAL PROPERTY—Cont'd
Damages—Cont'd
prior possession, **Pers Prop 130, 131, 154-156**
Deed of gifts, **Pers Prop 290-292**
Defense of jus tertii, prior possession, **Pers Prop 134-137**
Delivery or misdelivery
bailments, misdelivery, **Pers Prop 229, 230, 244, 245**
commercial bailments, misdelivery, **Pers Prop 244, 245**
donative intent, **Pers Prop 314-317**
gifts, **Pers Prop 287-305**
Distinctions, sales distinguished from bailments, **Pers Prop 216, 217**
Donative intent, gift, **Pers Prop 305-317**
Election, first possessors and forms of action, **Pers Prop 117, 118**
Engagement presents, **Pers Prop 308-313**
Entrusting chattel, good faith purchasers, **Pers Prop 270-275**
Escheat, finders, **Pers Prop 188**
Estray statutes, **Pers Prop 25, 26**
Extinguishment of title, good faith purchasers, **Pers Prop 264, 265**
Fee tails, common law estates, **Pers Prop 382, 383**
Finders
generally, **Pers Prop 158-195**
bailments, **Pers Prop 200-208**
Forms of action, **Pers Prop 85-118**
Fungible goods, bailments, **Pers Prop 220, 221**
Future interests, common law estates, **Pers Prop 384, 385**
Gifts, **Pers Prop 286-324**
Good faith purchasers, **Pers Prop 251-285**
Identify of fraudulent purchaser, good faith purchasers, **Pers Prop 276-279**
Insurable interest, good faith purchasers, **Pers Prop 261-263**
Intangible personal property, finders, **Pers Prop 188-195**
Inter vivos right to withdraw, joint bank accounts, **Pers Prop 334-338**
Joint bank accounts, **Pers Prop 325-348**
Joint tenancy, common law estates, **Pers Prop 386**

PERSONAL PROPERTY—Cont'd
Judicial opinions, abandoned personal property, **Pers Prop 51-57**
Jus tertii defense, prior possession, **Pers Prop 134-137**
Justification, prior possession, **Pers Prop 129, 130**
Landowners as first possessors, **Pers Prop 26-31**
Licenses, bailments, **Pers Prop 209-217**
Liens, good faith purchasers, **Pers Prop 279-285**
Limitations on warehouser liability, commercial bailments, **Pers Prop 245-249**
Limited entry cases, finders, **Pers Prop 169-172**
Lost chattel, finders, **Pers Prop 165-168**
Mislaid chattel, finders, **Pers Prop 165-168**
Negligent entrustment, bailments, **Pers Prop 215**
Parking lots, bailments, **Pers Prop 210-213**
Personal injuries, bailments, **Pers Prop 214, 215**
Photographs, bailments, **Pers Prop 213, 214**
Present estates, common law estates, **Pers Prop 381-384**
Prior possession, **Pers Prop 119-157**
Private place, finders, **Pers Prop 164, 165**
Public place, finders, **Pers Prop 164, 165**
Rationi soli in United States, **Pers Prop 38-44**
Real property, accession and confusion, **Pers Prop 377-379**
Remainders, common law estates, **Pers Prop 381-384**
Replevin, prior possession, **Pers Prop 120-128, 132-145**
Resale, good faith purchasers, **Pers Prop 275, 276**
Return of chattel, bailments, **Pers Prop 217-221, 230, 231**
Rewards, finders, **Pers Prop 185-188**
Right to sue, bailments, **Pers Prop 205-208**
Rule against perpetuities, common law estates, **Pers Prop 385**
Rule in Shelley's Case, common law estates, **Pers Prop 382**
Rule in Wild's Case, common law estates, **Pers Prop 383**
Safe deposit boxes, bailments, **Pers Prop 209, 210**
Sales, bailments, **Pers Prop 209-217**
Salvage
  finders, **Pers Prop 174-181**
  prior possession, **Pers Prop 156**

PERSONAL PROPERTY—Cont'd

Small chattel, finders, **Pers Prop 169**
Soil, finders of chattel embedded in or on top of, **Pers Prop 168, 169**
Standard of care, bailments, **Pers Prop 221-223, 232-234**
Statutes of limitations, adverse possession of personal property, **Pers Prop 350-368**
Statutory treatment of joint bank accounts, **Pers Prop 328-332**
Stock as gift, **Pers Prop 301-305**
Stolen chattel, good faith purchasers, **Pers Prop 261-263**
Successive finders, prior possession, **Pers Prop 146-156**
Sunken treasure, finders, **Pers Prop 174-181**
Survivors and survivorship, joint bank accounts, **Pers Prop 338-348**
Tenancy by the entireties, common law estates, **Pers Prop 385, 386**
Tenancy in common, common law estates, **Pers Prop 386**
Theft from warehouse, commercial bailments, **Pers Prop 242-244**
Third parties
    abandoned personal property, third party rights, **Pers Prop 57-59**
    gifts through, **Pers Prop 299-301**
Title, good faith purchasers, **Pers Prop 255-260, 264, 265**
Totten Trust, joint bank accounts, **Pers Prop 345-348**
Transfer, good faith purchasers, **Pers Prop 267**
Treasure trove, finders, **Pers Prop 172-181**
Trover, prior possession, **Pers Prop 120-128**
Unclaimed personal property, finders, **Pers Prop 188-195**
Uniform Commercial Code
    adverse possession of personal property, **Pers Prop 354**
    good faith purchasers, **Pers Prop 265-276**
Value, good faith purchasers, **Pers Prop 268, 269**
Void and voidable title, good faith purchasers, **Pers Prop 255-260**
Warehouses and warehousemen, commercial bailments, **Pers Prop 232, 233, 242-249**
Wild animals and first possession, **Pers Prop 1-44**
Withdrawal rights, joint bank accounts, **Pers Prop 334-338**

PERSONAL PROPERTY—Cont'd
Worthier Title Doctrine, common law estates, **Pers Prop 383, 384**
Wreck of the sea, finders, **Pers Prop 174-181**

PESTICIDES
Hazardous Wastes and Toxic Substances, Law of (this index)

PETITIONS
Injunctions (this index)

PICKETING
Labor Law (this index)

PLANNING
Trial and Practice Skills (this index)

PLANS OR PLANNING
Estate Planning (this index)
Land Use (this index)

PORNOGRAPHY
Art Law (this index)
First Amendment (this index)

PREMIUMS
Insurance Law (this index)

PREPARATION
How to Study Law and Take Law Exams (this index)

PRESENTMENT
Negotiable Instruments and Check Collection (this index)

PRESS
Freedom of speech and press
    Injunctions (this index)

GENERAL INDEX

References are to Titles and Pages

PRETRIAL LITIGATION

Active listening, interviewing techniques, **Pretr Lit 25-27**
Admission requests, **Pretr Lit 229-236**
Amendment of pleadings, **Pretr Lit 95-97**
Answer, responses to complaint, **Pretr Lit 113-119**
Argument, motion argument, **Pretr Lit 282-290**
Attorney-client relationship, establishment of, **Pretr Lit 8-30**
Certification, disclosure and discovery, **Pretr Lit 154-157**
Complaint, **Pretr Lit 64-128**
Compulsory motions, judicial intervention into discovery and disclosure process, **Pretr Lit 246-249**
Concluding remarks, **Pretr Lit 18-20**
Conferences, pretrial, **Pretr Lit 313-320**
Consolidation of defenses, responses to complaint, **Pretr Lit 100-102**
Counterclaims, responses to complaint, **Pretr Lit 120-124**
Cross-claims, responses to complaint, **Pretr Lit 124-126**
Defenses, **Pretr Lit 98-102, 212-218**
Defining client's problem, **Pretr Lit 13, 14**
Depositions, **Pretr Lit 180-218**
Disclosure and scope of civil discovery, generally, **Pretr Lit 129-157**
Discovery and disclosure, generally, **Pretr Lit 129-157**
Dismissal motion, responses to complaint, **Pretr Lit 104-109**
Drafting interrogatories, **Pretr Lit 162-172**
Establishment of attorney-client relationship, **Pretr Lit 8-30**
Ethics of negotiation, **Pretr Lit 356-359**
Evaluating case for settlement, **Pretr Lit 334-339**
Examination, requests for, **Pretr Lit 225-228**
Expert witnesses, **Pretr Lit 133, 134, 147-150, 203-205**
Factual investigation, **Pretr Lit 46-63**
Federal Rules of Civil Procedure, depositions under, **Pretr Lit 180-188**
Follow-up questioning by attorney, **Pretr Lit 16-18**
Forum change, pretrial motion for, **Pretr Lit 265-268**
Initial attorney-client interview, structure of, **Pretr Lit 10**

PRETRIAL LITIGATION—Cont'd
Initial disclosures, **Pretr Lit 130-133**
Interrogatories, **Pretr Lit 158-179**
Intervention, judicial intervention into discovery and disclosure process, **Pretr Lit 237-257**
Interviewing client, **Pretr Lit 8-30**
Investigation and planning, **Pretr Lit 31-63**
Judicial intervention into discovery and disclosure process, **Pretr Lit 237-257**
Judicial involvement in pretrial process, **Pretr Lit 329-332**
Law governing pretrial litigation, generally, **Pretr Lit 3-6**
Legal research, **Pretr Lit 39-46**
Memorializing the settlement, **Pretr Lit 360-364**
Modern pleading and practice, **Pretr Lit 81-89**
Motions, generally, **Pretr Lit 258-290**
Negotiation and settlement, **Pretr Lit 333-364**
Orders, pretrial, **Pretr Lit 320-329**
Planning, **Pretr Lit 31-63, 150-154**
Preparation, **Pretr Lit 34-39, 192-194, 205-212**
Prerequisites to suit, complaint as, **Pretr Lit 64-72**
Privilege, general scope of discovery under Rule 26(b), **Pretr Lit 141-143**
Production of documents, requests for, **Pretr Lit 219-225**
Protective orders motions, judicial intervention into discovery and disclosure process, **Pretr Lit 241-246**
Relevance, general scope of discovery under Rule 26(b), **Pretr Lit 135-141**
Relief, **Pretr Lit 15, 16, 74-81**
Responses, **Pretr Lit 98-128, 172-179**
Retaining attorney, **Pretr Lit 27-30**
Role of layer in pretrial litigation, **Pretr Lit 6, 7**
Rule 11 pleading requirements, **Pretr Lit 89-94**
Rule 12 motions, responses to complaint, **Pretr Lit 103-112**
Rule 33 interrogatory, **Pretr Lit 158-162**
Sanction motions, judicial intervention into discovery and disclosure process, **Pretr Lit 249-257**
Settlement and negotiation, **Pretr Lit 333-364**

PRETRIAL LITIGATION—Cont'd
Statements of witnesses, investigative techniques, **Pretr Lit 60-63**
Strategy of pretrial motion, **Pretr Lit 271-275**
Structure, **Pretr Lit 10, 47-56**
Summary judgment, **Pretr Lit 291-312**
Supplementation, disclosure and discovery, **Pretr Lit 154-157**
Techniques, **Pretr Lit 20-27, 197-203**
Third parties, **Pretr Lit 126-128, 353-356**
Timing of action, motion affecting, **Pretr Lit 268, 269**
Waiver of defenses, responses to complaint, **Pretr Lit 100-102**
Witnesses, **Pretr Lit 59-63, 133, 134, 147-150, 203-205, 205-212**
Work-product doctrine, disclosure and discovery, **Pretr Lit 143-147**
Written motion papers, **Pretr Lit 275-282**

PRIORITIES
Secured Transactions (this index)
Uniform Commercial Code (this index)

PRIOR RESTRAINT
First Amendment (this index)

PRISONS AND PRISONERS
Sentencing, Corrections, and Prisoners' Rights, Law of (this index)

PROBATE
Uniform Probate Code (this index)

PROCUREMENTS
Government Contracts (this index)

PRODUCTS LIABILITY
Generally, **Prod Liab 1 et seq.**

PROFESSIONAL RESPONSIBILITY

Acceptance of questionable cases, adversary system, **Prof Resp 320-325**
Accounting, fiduciary responsibilities, **Prof Resp 255**
Adjudicative responsibilities, lawyer as judge, **Prof Resp 468-471**
Administrative responsibilities, lawyer as judge, **Prof Resp 471, 472**
Administrative tribunals, unauthorized practice of law, **Prof Resp 127-130**
Admission to bar, maintenance of professional standards, **Prof Resp 50-53, 62-64**
Adversary system, generally, **Prof Resp 304-361**
Advertising, **Prof Resp 178-187, 283, 384**
Advisor, lawyer as, **Prof Resp 395-399**
Age requirements, maintenance of professional standards, **Prof Resp 47-50**
Alternative dispute resolution, **Prof Resp 419-456**
Antitrust restraints, unauthorized practice of law, **Prof Resp 141-144**
Appearance of impropriety, lawyer as judge, **Prof Resp 467, 467**
Apprenticeships, maintenance of professional standards, **Prof Resp 42-45**
Arbitral tribunals, unauthorized practice of law, **Prof Resp 127-130**
Assistants, unauthorized practice of law, **Prof Resp 121, 122**
Attorney-client relationship, generally, **Prof Resp 195-303**
Attorneys' fees, generally, **Prof Resp 262-292**
Attorneys' liens, **Prof Resp 287-289**
Availability, duty to make legal services available, **Prof Resp 145-155**
Character requirements, maintenance of professional standards, **Prof Resp 50-60**
Citizenship requirements, maintenance of professional standards, **Prof Resp 47-50**
Clinics, duty to make legal services available, **Prof Resp 170-172**
Code of Professional Responsibility, duty to ensure competence, **Prof Resp 74-78**

PROFESSIONAL RESPONSIBILITY—Cont'd
Collection, attorneys' fees, **Prof Resp 284-287**
Commercial speech, advertising, **Prof Resp 180-182**
Commingling, fiduciary responsibilities, **Prof Resp 255-258**
Committees on professional ethics, role of organized bar, **Prof Resp 37, 38**
Competency, **Prof Resp 42-47, 72-110**
Conduct at trial, specific obligations of advocate, **Prof Resp 343-361**
Confidentiality, **Prof Resp 195-221, 224**
Conflict of interest, **Prof Resp 222-253, 383,384**
Constitutional defenses to moral character inquiries, maintenance of professional standards, **Prof Resp 54, 55**
Contingent fees, **Prof Resp 271-277**
Continuing legal education, duty to ensure competence, **Prof Resp 100-102**
Corporations
- attorney-client relationship, corporate communications, **Prof Resp 200, 201**
- employee, lawyer as, **Prof Resp 406-415**
- unauthorized practice of law, **Prof Resp 134-137**

Delay, specific obligations of advocate, **Prof Resp 325, 326**
Development of organized bar, **Prof Resp 27-32**
Discipline and disciplinary proceedings
- competence, duty to ensure, **Prof Resp 78-81, 98-100**
- maintenance of professional standards, **Prof Resp 55-60, 64-71**
- prosecuting attorneys, **Prof Resp 392-394**

Discretion of prosecuting attorneys to charge with crime, **Prof Resp 379-381**
Education
- continuing legal education, duty to ensure competence, **Prof Resp 100-102**
- maintenance of professional standards, **Prof Resp 42-45**
- recertification examinations, duty to ensure competence, **Prof Resp 103**

Enforcement, unauthorized practice of law, **Prof Resp 139-144**
Ethical concerns of private lawyer serving as neutral, alternative dispute resolution, **Prof Resp 422-451**

PROFESSIONAL RESPONSIBILITY—Cont'd

Examinations
maintenance of professional standards, **Prof Resp 45-47**
recertification examinations, duty to ensure competence, **Prof Resp 103**
Exceptions to confidentiality, attorney-client relationship, **Prof Resp 202-221**
Extra-judicial activities, lawyer as judge, **Prof Resp 473-477**
Fair trial/free press conflict, **Prof Resp 362-376**
Fiduciary responsibilities, **Prof Resp 254-261**
First Amendment, advertising, **Prof Resp 180-182**
Government employee, lawyer as, **Prof Resp 415-418**
Group prepaid legal services, duty to make legal services available, **Prof Resp 165-170**
Impropriety, lawyer as judge, **Prof Resp 467, 467**
Ineffective assistance of counsel, duty to ensure competence, **Prof Resp 90-92**
Interest on Lawyers' Trust Account (IOLTA) Funds
commingling, fiduciary responsibilities, **Prof Resp 257, 258**
Legal Aid and Public Defender services, **Prof Resp 161, 162**
Interference with client-attorney relationship, prosecuting attorneys, **Prof Resp 391, 392**
IOLTA. Interest on Lawyers' Trust Account (IOLTA) Funds, supra
Jail-house lawyers, duty to make legal services available, **Prof Resp 176**
Judge, lawyer as, **Prof Resp 457-477**
Judicare, duty to make legal services available, **Prof Resp 163-165**
Judicial control of unauthorized practice of law, **Prof Resp 122, 123**
Law students, duty to make legal services available, **Prof Resp 174-176**
Legal Aid services, **Prof Resp 157-163**
Legal clerks, unauthorized practice of law, **Prof Resp 121, 122**
Legal profession, generally, **Prof Resp 1-11**
Legal services corporation, Legal Aid and Public Defender services, **Prof Resp 159-161**

PROFESSIONAL RESPONSIBILITY—Cont'd

Legislature, lawyer and, **Prof Resp 484-494**
Liens, attorneys' liens, **Prof Resp 287-289**
Lobbyist, lawyer and, **Prof Resp 493, 494**
Loyalty, conflict of interest, **Prof Resp 223**
Lying client or witness, specific obligations of advocate, **Prof Resp 326-342**
Maintenance of professional standards, **Prof Resp 39-71**
Malpractice liability, duty to ensure competence, **Prof Resp 81-90**
Mandatory matters
  State Bar Associations, mandatory membership, **Prof Resp 32-37**
  withdrawal from employment as mandatory, **Prof Resp 296-298**
Media, fair trial/free press conflict, **Prof Resp 362-376**
Misappropriation, fiduciary responsibilities, **Prof Resp 258, 259**
Model Rules of Professional Conduct, duty to ensure competence, **Prof Resp 74-78**
Moral character inquiries, constitutional defenses to, **Prof Resp 54, 55**
Negotiator, lawyer as, **Prof Resp 399-404**
Office of Economic Opportunity (OEO), Legal Aid and Public Defender services, **Prof Resp 159**
Organized bar, role of, **Prof Resp 27-38**
Personal responsibilities, professional versus, **Prof Resp 495-504**
Plea bargaining, prosecuting attorneys, **Prof Resp 381, 382**
Police supervision, prosecuting attorneys, **Prof Resp 390, 391**
Preparation for trial, adversary system, **Prof Resp 314-320**
Press, fair trial/free press conflict, **Prof Resp 362-376**
Procedural standards, maintenance of professional standards, **Prof Resp 61-71**
Professional examinations, maintenance of professional standards, **Prof Resp 45-47**
Prosecuting attorneys, generally, **Prof Resp 377-394**
Public Defender services, **Prof Resp 157-163**
Public image of lawyers, **Prof Resp 12-18**

PROFESSIONAL RESPONSIBILITY—Cont'd

Public interest
duty to make legal services available, public interest law, **Prof Resp 172, 173**
unauthorized practice of law, public interest test, **Prof Resp 120, 121**
Public leader and law reformer, lawyer as, **Prof Resp 478-483**
Qualification or disqualification
judge, lawyer as, **Prof Resp 459-467**
maintenance of professional standards, **Prof Resp 42-47**
Quasi-judicial activities, lawyer as judge, **Prof Resp 472, 473**
Questionable cases, acceptance of, **Prof Resp 320-325**
Recertification examinations, duty to ensure competence, **Prof Resp 103**
Recordkeeping, fiduciary responsibilities, **Prof Resp 255**
Referrals, duty to make legal services available, **Prof Resp 173**
Residence requirements, maintenance of professional standards, **Prof Resp 47-50**
Rule 11 sanctions, duty to ensure competence, **Prof Resp 98-100**
Security funds of client, fiduciary responsibilities, **Prof Resp 259, 260**
Self-representation, unauthorized practice of law, **Prof Resp 134-137**
Sherman Act, advertising, **Prof Resp 179, 180**
Solicitation, **Prof Resp 187-193**
Specialization, duty to ensure competence, **Prof Resp 101-110**
Staff counsel to legislature, lawyer and, **Prof Resp 492**
Standards of professional responsibility, **Prof Resp 19-26**
State Bar Associations, mandatory membership, **Prof Resp 32-37**
Substantial interest requirement, advertising, **Prof Resp 182-187**
Supervision of police, prosecuting attorneys, **Prof Resp 390, 391**
Television in courtroom, **Prof Resp 373-376**
Termination of employment, **Prof Resp 289-303**
Unauthorized practice of law, **Prof Resp 111-144**
Waivers, unauthorized practice of law, **Prof Resp 121**
Withdrawal from employment, **Prof Resp 294-303**
Written fee agreement, **Prof Resp 277, 278**

PROFITS
International Taxation (this index)

PRONOUNS
Legal Writing (this index)

PROPERTY
Energy and Natural Resources Law (this index)
How to Study Law and Take Law Exams (this index)
Injunctions (this index)
Insurance Law (this index)
Personal Property (this index)
Real Property (this index)

PROPORTIONATE OR DISPROPORTIONATE
Federal Income Taxation of Partners and Partnerships (this index)

PROPOSALS
Tax Procedure and Tax Fraud (this index)

PUBLIC INTEREST
Professional Responsibility (this index)

PUBLIC INTERNATIONAL LAW
Generally, **Pub Intn'l Law 1-18**
Act of State, sovereign immunity, **Pub Intn'l Law 233-242**
Advisory jurisdiction, International Court of Justice, **Pub Intn'l Law 85, 86**
African System, regional human rights law and institutions, **Pub Intn'l Law 140, 141**
Alien Tort Statute, customary international law in U.S. law, **Pub Intn'l Law 212-214**
Antitrust, Act of state in, **Pub Intn'l Law 241, 242**
Arbitration
  international legal research sources, arbitral decisions, **Pub Intn'l Law 252-254**

PUBLIC INTERNATIONAL LAW—Cont'd
Arbitration—Cont'd
quasi-judicial methods of dispute settlement, **Pub Intn'l Law 68-73**
Benelux Court of Justice, **Pub Intn'l Law 89**
Binding character of United Nations resolutions, **Pub Intn'l Law 42, 43**
Casebooks, international legal research sources, **Pub Intn'l Law 247, 248**
Comity, jurisdictional principles in United States law, **Pub Intn'l Law 177-182**
Compromis, quasi-judicial methods of dispute settlement, **Pub Intn'l Law 71**
Conciliation, dispute settlement, **Pub Intn'l Law 66-68**
Conduct and effects test, jurisdictional principles in United States law, **Pub Intn'l Law 175-177**
Connally reservation, contentious jurisdiction of International Court of Justice, **Pub Intn'l Law 79-81**
Consent
arbitration, quasi-judicial methods of dispute settlement, **Pub Intn'l Law 70**
treaties, international law of, **Pub Intn'l Law 95, 96**
Construction or interpretation, international law of treaties, **Pub Intn'l Law 105-107**
Contentious jurisdiction, International Court of Justice, **Pub Intn'l Law 76-84**
Conventional international law, **Pub Intn'l Law 24-26**
Court of Justice of European Communities, **Pub Intn'l Law 86-88**
Courts, international, **Pub Intn'l Law 74-90**
Customary international law, **Pub Intn'l Law 22-24, 208-214**
Defense treaties, regional, **Pub Intn'l Law 62, 63**
Definitions, **Pub Intn'l Law 1-3, 45, 46, 92-99, 142**
Digests, international legal research sources, **Pub Intn'l Law 254-256**
Diplomatic and related immunities, **Pub Intn'l Law 215-221**
Dispute settlement, **Pub Intn'l Law 64-90**

PUBLIC INTERNATIONAL LAW—Cont'd
Encyclopedias, international legal research sources, **Pub Intn'l Law 245, 246**
Enforcement, relevance and function of international law, **Pub Intn'l Law 10-13**
European communities, supranational organizations and, **Pub Intn'l Law 51 et seq.**
European Court of Human Rights, **Pub Intn'l Law 88, 89**
European System, regional human rights law and institutions, **Pub Intn'l Law 128-132**
Federal supremacy, foreign relation laws in United States, **Pub Intn'l Law 186-189**
Force, United Nations and use of, **Pub Intn'l Law 57-59**
Foreign Sovereign Immunities Act (FSIA), **Pub Intn'l Law 225-233**
Geneva Conventions, international humanitarian law, **Pub Intn'l Law 142-146**
Humanitarian law, international, **Pub Intn'l Law 142-147**
Human rights
  European Court of Human Rights, **Pub Intn'l Law 88, 89**
  Inter-American Court of Human Rights, **Pub Intn'l Law 89, 90**
  international law of human rights, **Pub Intn'l Law 116-147**
  regional human rights law and institutions, **Pub Intn'l Law 128-141**
ICJ statute, sources of international law, **Pub Intn'l Law 20-27**
Immunities, **Pub Intn'l Law 215-242**
Individuals' rights, **Pub Intn'l Law 115-158**
Injuries to aliens, generally, **Pub Intn'l Law 147-158**
Inter-American Court of Human Rights, **Pub Intn'l Law 89, 90**
Inter-American System, regional human rights law and institutions, **Pub Intn'l Law 132-139**
International Court of Justice, **Pub Intn'l Law 75-86**
International humanitarian law, **Pub Intn'l Law 142-147**
Interpretation, international law of treaties, **Pub Intn'l Law 105-107**
Invalidity of treaties, **Pub Intn'l Law 107-114**

PUBLIC INTERNATIONAL LAW—Cont'd

Iranian Hostages Case, diplomatic and related immunities, **Pub Intn'l Law 219**

Judicial decisions, international legal research sources, **Pub Intn'l Law 252-254**

Jurisdiction, **Pub Intn'l Law 76-86, 159-185**

Legal research sources, **Pub Intn'l Law 243-257**

Lotus Case, jurisdiction, **Pub Intn'l Law 161-163**

Mediation, dispute settlement, **Pub Intn'l Law 66-68**

Nationality, international jurisdictional principles, **Pub Intn'l Law 163-167**

National security considerations, contentious jurisdiction of International Court of Justice, **Pub Intn'l Law 82, 83**

Negotiation
- dispute settlement, **Pub Intn'l Law 65-68**
- treaties, international law of, **Pub Intn'l Law 94, 95**

Nicaragua amendment, contentious jurisdiction of International Court of Justice, **Pub Intn'l Law 81, 82**

Nonjudicial methods, dispute settlement, **Pub Intn'l Law 65-68**

Observance, international law of treaties, **Pub Intn'l Law 104-107**

Pacta sunt servanda, international law of treaties, **Pub Intn'l Law 104**

Passive personality principle, international jurisdictional principles, **Pub Intn'l Law 174**

Peacekeeping, United Nations and, **Pub Intn'l Law 56-61**

Periodical literature, international legal research sources, **Pub Intn'l Law 248-250**

Phenomenological rule, immunities, **Pub Intn'l Law 238, 239**

Political question doctrine, separation of powers in foreign affairs, **Pub Intn'l Law 193-195**

Quasi-judicial methods, dispute settlement, **Pub Intn'l Law 68-73**

Ratification, international law of treaties, **Pub Intn'l Law 96-98**

Reciprocity
- International Court of Justice, contentious jurisdiction of, **Pub Intn'l Law 77-79**

PUBLIC INTERNATIONAL LAW—Cont'd
Reciprocity—Cont'd
United States law, jurisdictional principles in, **Pub Intn'l Law 181, 182**
Regional human rights law and institutions, **Pub Intn'l Law 128-141**
Regional organizations, **Pub Intn'l Law 47-51, 61, 62**
Repertories of practice, international legal research sources, **Pub Intn'l Law 254-256**
Research sources, **Pub Intn'l Law 243-257**
Reservations, international law of treaties, **Pub Intn'l Law 98-103**
Restatements, international legal research sources, **Pub Intn'l Law 245, 246**
Secondary sources of international law, **Pub Intn'l Law 28-35**
Separation of powers in foreign affairs, **Pub Intn'l Law 189-208**
Settlement of disputes, **Pub Intn'l Law 64-90**
Signature, international law of treaties, **Pub Intn'l Law 96-98**
Sources of international law, generally, **Pub Intn'l Law 19-35**
Sovereign compulsion, jurisdictional principles in United States law, **Pub Intn'l Law 182-185**
Sovereign immunity, **Pub Intn'l Law 222-233**
Specialized agencies of United Nations, **Pub Intn'l Law 45-47**
State and international organization practice, international legal research sources, **Pub Intn'l Law 254-257**
State immunities, **Pub Intn'l Law 221, 222, 233-2442**
Supranational organizations, **Pub Intn'l Law 51-57**
Supremacy, foreign relation laws in United States, **Pub Intn'l Law 186-189**
Suspension of treaties, **Pub Intn'l Law 107-114**
Termination of treaties, **Pub Intn'l Law 107-114**
Territorial principle, international jurisdictional principles, **Pub Intn'l Law 167-172**
Treaties
generally, **Pub Intn'l Law 91-114**
diplomatic and related immunities, **Pub Intn'l Law 216-219**
immunity, exception, **Pub Intn'l Law 240, 241**
legal research sources, **Pub Intn'l Law 250-252**

PUBLIC INTERNATIONAL LAW—Cont'd
Treaties—Cont'd
regional defense treaties, **Pub Intn'l Law 62, 63**
Treatises, international legal research sources, **Pub Intn'l Law 243-245**
United Nations
generally, **Pub Intn'l Law 38-47**
force, use of, **Pub Intn'l Law 57-59**
individuals, rights of, **Pub Intn'l Law 118-127**
legal research sources, UN practice, **Pub Intn'l Law 256, 257**
peacekeeping, United Nations and, **Pub Intn'l Law 56-61**
United States law, jurisdictional principles in, **Pub Intn'l Law 174-185**
Universality principle, international jurisdictional principles, **Pub Intn'l Law 172, 173**
Voting procedures, United Nations, **Pub Intn'l Law 41, 42**
War powers, separation of powers in foreign affairs, **Pub Intn'l Law 206-208**
Yearbooks of International Law Commission, international legal research sources, **Pub Intn'l Law 246, 247**

PUBLIC LAND
Modern Public Land Law (this index)

PUBLIC OFFICERS AND EMPLOYEES
State Constitutional Law (this index)

PUBLIC SECTOR
Labor Arbitration Law and Practice (this index)

QUALIFICATION OR DISQUALIFICATION
Professional Responsibility (this index)

QUALIFICATIONS
State Constitutional Law (this index)

RCRA (RESOURCE CONSERVATION AND RECOVERY ACT)

Hazardous Wastes and Toxic Substances, Law of (this index)

READING QUESTIONS

Trial and Practice Skills (this index)

READINGS

How to Study Law and Take Law Exams (this index)

REAL ESTATE FINANCE

Generally, **Real Est Fin 1-230**

Acceleration, after default and before foreclosure, **Real Est Fin 154-159**

Adjustable rate mortgage (ARM), interest on money, **Real Est Fin 82-84**

After-acquired property, extent of mortgage coverage, **Real Est Fin 98, 99**

Alternatives to foreclosure, **Real Est Fin 172-174**

Applications, obtaining real estate financing, **Real Est Fin 24**

Assignments, **Real Est Fin 126-150, 165, 166**

Balloon loans, discharge of obligation and mortgage, **Real Est Fin 91, 92**

Bankruptcy, foreclosure, **Real Est Fin 196-198**

Banks and banking, **Real Est Fin 18-22**

Building and construction

- after default and before foreclosure, **Real Est Fin 153**
- mortgage market, construction financing, **Real Est Fin 12-16**

Buy-down mortgage, interest on money, **Real Est Fin 85, 86**

Commercial banks, **Real Est Fin 18, 19**

Commercial property, mortgage market, **Real Est Fin 16, 17**

Commitment, obtaining real estate financing, **Real Est Fin 24**

Community housing authorities, **Real Est Fin 24**

Comprehensive Environmental Response, Compensation, and Liability Act (CERCLA) of 1980, federal government involvement in financing process, **Real Est Fin 45, 46**

REAL ESTATE FINANCE—Cont'd

Condemnation awards, extent of mortgage coverage, **Real Est Fin 101**
Condominiums, financing of, **Real Est Fin 218-223**
Conflicting assignments, **Real Est Fin 138-140**
Constitutional issues, foreclosure by power of sale, **Real Est Fin 209-211**
Contract, obtaining real estate financing, **Real Est Fin 25, 26**
Conventional subrogation, **Real Est Fin 148, 149**
Conveyance of mortgaged property, transfer of mortgagor's interest, generally, **Real Est Fin 106-117**
Cooperatives, financing of, **Real Est Fin 216-218**
Credit unions, **Real Est Fin 23**
Damages, waste of mortgaged property, **Real Est Fin 104**
Death of mortgagor or mortgagee, transfer at, **Real Est Fin 145, 151**
Deed of trust, **Real Est Fin 49**
Default, generally, **Real Est Fin 152-174**
Defenses available against assignment of mortgage loan, **Real Est Fin 129-133**
Definitions, **Real Est Fin 1, 2, 152**
Description, mortgage market, **Real Est Fin 12, 13**
Discharge of obligation and mortgage, **Real Est Fin 89-96**
Due-on-sale clause, **Real Est Fin 86, 87, 118-125**
Easements, extent of mortgage coverage, **Real Est Fin 99, 100**
Equitable mortgages, **Real Est Fin 50-54**
Equity of redemption, **Real Est Fin 169-172, 214, 215**
Escrow accounts, discharge of obligation and mortgage, **Real Est Fin 92, 93**
Exemptions, usury, **Real Est Fin 87**
Extension of obligation, **Real Est Fin 89**
Extent of mortgage coverage, **Real Est Fin 98-103**
Federal action, reform measures, **Real Est Fin 225-227**
Federal government involvement in financing process, **Real Est Fin 33-46**
Federal preemption, usury, **Real Est Fin 88, 89**
Fixtures, **Real Est Fin 100, 101, 184, 185**

REAL ESTATE FINANCE—Cont'd

Foreclosure, generally, **Real Est Fin 6, 7, 195-215**
Fractional assignments, **Real Est Fin 140-145**
Further encumbrance of mortgaged property, **Real Est Fin 125**
Future advances, underlying obligations, **Real Est Fin 71-79**
Gar-St. Germain Depository Institutions Act of 1982, **Real Est Fin 121-123**
Guaranty programs, federal government involvement in financing process, **Real Est Fin 34-36**
Home Mortgage Disclosure Act of 1975, federal government involvement in financing process, **Real Est Fin 44, 45**
Housing subsidies, federal government involvement in financing process, **Real Est Fin 34**
Injunctions, waste of mortgaged property, **Real Est Fin 104, 105**
Installment land contract, **Real Est Fin 54-61**
Insurance and insurance proceeds, **Real Est Fin 20, 34-36, 101-103, 153**
Interest on money, generally, **Real Est Fin 80-89**
Interstate Land Sales Full Disclosure Act of 1968, federal government involvement in financing process, **Real Est Fin 40, 41**
Investment trusts, **Real Est Fin 21**
Judicial review, foreclosure by power of sale, **Real Est Fin 209**
Judicial sales, **Real Est Fin 199-209**
Late charges, discharge of obligation and mortgage, **Real Est Fin 93**
Lease, real estate financing devices, **Real Est Fin 61-68**
Liens
- mechanics' liens, priorities, **Real Est Fin 185-189**
- mortgages, generally, **Real Est Fin 1-10**
- tax liens, priorities, **Real Est Fin 190**

Life insurance companies, **Real Est Fin 20**
Lis pendens, priorities, **Real Est Fin 190, 191**
Loan contract, obtaining real estate financing, **Real Est Fin 25, 26**
Market, mortgage market, **Real Est Fin 12-46**
Marshalling, priorities, **Real Est Fin 191-194**
Mechanics' liens, priorities, **Real Est Fin 185-189**
Military service, foreclosure, **Real Est Fin 198, 199**

REAL ESTATE FINANCE—Cont'd

Modification of obligation, **Real Est Fin 89**

Mortgages, generally, **Real Est Fin 1-10, 47-49**

Mutual savings banks, **Real Est Fin 20**

National Flood Insurance program, federal government involvement in financing process, **Real Est Fin 41-43**

Nationwide foreclosure system, reform measures, **Real Est Fin 225, 226**

Obligation/security distinction, mortgages, **Real Est Fin 2**

One action rule, alternatives to foreclosure, **Real Est Fin 173, 174**

Operation of law, assignment by, **Real Est Fin 145-150**

Penalties, usury, **Real Est Fin 88**

Pension funds, **Real Est Fin 20**

Performance bonds, mortgage market, **Real Est Fin 12, 13**

Possession and rents, after default and before foreclosure, **Real Est Fin 159-168**

Power of sale, foreclosure by, **Real Est Fin 206-211**

Preemption, **Real Est Fin 88, 89, 226**

Prepayment, discharge of obligation and mortgage, **Real Est Fin 93-95**

Price level adjusted mortgage, interest on money, **Real Est Fin 84**

Principal and interest, after default and before foreclosure, **Real Est Fin 152**

Priorities, **Real Est Fin 175-194**

Purchase money mortgages, **Real Est Fin 47, 48, 177-179**

Real Estate Settlement Procedures Act of 1974, federal government involvement in financing process, **Real Est Fin 43, 44**

Receivers and receivership, after default and before foreclosure, **Real Est Fin 166-168**

Recording statutes, priorities, **Real Est Fin 175, 176**

Redemption, **Real Est Fin 4, 5, 8, 169-172, 212-215**

Reform, **Real Est Fin 224-230**

Release of mortgage, discharge of obligation and mortgage, **Real Est Fin 95**

Renewal of obligation, **Real Est Fin 89**

Rents, after default and before foreclosure, **Real Est Fin 159-168**

Rents and profits, extent of mortgage coverage, **Real Est Fin 103**

REAL ESTATE FINANCE—Cont'd

Residential property, mortgage market, **Real Est Fin 16, 17**
Restatement of property, mortgages, **Real Est Fin 230**
Revenue/equity mortgage, interest on money, **Real Est Fin 86**
Right to possession and rents, after default and before foreclosure, **Real Est Fin 159-168**
Sale and leaseback, real estate financing devices, **Real Est Fin 66-68**
Savings and loan associations, **Real Est Fin 19**
Secondary financing, **Real Est Fin 28-33**
Secondary mortgage market support institutions, federal government involvement in financing process, **Real Est Fin 36-38**
Securities, **Real Est Fin 27, 28, 150**
Service corporations, **Real Est Fin 23**
Shared appreciation mortgage (SAMs), interest on money, **Real Est Fin 84, 85**
State development agencies, **Real Est Fin 23, 24**
Statute of frauds, mortgages, **Real Est Fin 2, 3**
Statute of limitations, **Real Est Fin 95, 96, 196**
Statutory redemption, **Real Est Fin 212-215**
Strict foreclosure, **Real Est Fin 211, 212**
Subordination agreements, priorities, **Real Est Fin 179-184**
Subrogation, assignment by operation of law, **Real Est Fin 145-150**
Syndications, **Real Est Fin 23**
Taxation, **Real Est Fin 48, 49, 152, 190**
Title, mortgages, **Real Est Fin 9**
Transfer of interest, generally, **Real Est Fin 106-150**
Truth in Lending Act of 1968, federal government involvement in financing process, **Real Est Fin 38, 39**
Underlying obligations, **Real Est Fin 69-96**
Uniform Land Security Interest Act, **Real Est Fin 227-230**
Usury, interest on money, **Real Est Fin 87-89**
Waiver, **Real Est Fin 153, 154, 211, 214**
Waste, **Real Est Fin 103-105, 153**

GENERAL INDEX

References are to Titles and Pages

REAL PROPERTY

Abandonment, termination for, **Real Prop 121-127, 206-209, 239, 240**

Adverse possession, **Real Prop 1-27**

Adverse use, termination of easements, **Real Prop 209, 210**

Airspace, **Real Prop 376-378**

Appurtenant or in gross, easements, **Real Prop 173, 174**

Assignment, transfer of tenancy, **Real Prop 161, 162, 164-167, 215**

Boundaries, **Real Prop 392-394**

Color of title, adverse possession, **Real Prop 16, 17**

Common law estates, **Real Prop 28-84**

Community property, **Real Prop 97-101**

Concurrent ownership, **Real Prop 85-105**

Condominiums, **Real Prop 101-105**

Constructive notice, **Real Prop 325-331**

Contingent remainders, **Real Prop 43, 44, 53-56, 67, 68**

Continuous, adverse possession, **Real Prop 17-19**

Contract of sale, generally, **Real Prop 256-276**

Conveyancing, generally, **Real Prop 245-374**

Covenants running with the land, **Real Prop 211-243**

Creation of easements and licenses, **Real Prop 176-192**

Deed, transfer of title by, **Real Prop 277-312**

Delivery of deeds, transfer of title, **Real Prop 285-298**

Destruction, **Real Prop 53-56, 112, 113**

Disclosure duty, transfer of title by deed, **Real Prop 310-312**

Discrimination, contract of sale, **Real Prop 258**

Disrepair, conditions of, **Real Prop 135-160**

Dower, common law estates, **Real Prop 81-83**

Duration, adverse possession, **Real Prop 4-8**

Easements, **Real Prop 169-210, 212-214**

Ejectment, adverse possession, **Real Prop 2, 3**

Eminent domain, **Real Prop 117, 118, 378, 443, 444**

Enforcement of neighborhood restrictions, **Real Prop 231-239**

Environmental protection, **Real Prop 441-443**

Equitable conversion, contract of sale, **Real Prop 268-273**

REAL PROPERTY—Cont'd

Equitable interests in land, **Real Prop 56-66**
Equitable servitudes, privity, **Real Prop 226-231**
Estate for years (tenancy for a term), **Real Prop 29, 34**
Estate from period to period, **Real Prop 34, 35**
Estates in Land and Future Interests (this index)
Estoppel, termination of neighborhood restrictions, **Real Prop 241**
Eviction, possessory interest of tenant, **Real Prop 129**
Exclusionary zoning, judicial review, **Real Prop 469-473**
Exclusive, adverse possession, **Real Prop 19**
Execution of deeds, transfer of title, **Real Prop 278-285**
Executory interests, **Real Prop 58-60, 63, 64, 68**
Expenditures, concurrent ownership, **Real Prop 95-97**
Express words, creation of easements and licenses, **Real Prop 176-178**
Fee simple estates, **Real Prop 28, 31**
Fee tail estates, **Real Prop 29, 31-33**
Finance. **Real Estate Finance** (this index)
Fixtures, **Real Prop 395-398**
Future interests, common law estates, **Real Prop 37-46**
Gifts to heirs, **Real Prop 71-75**
Grant deed, transfer of title, **Real Prop 278**
Growth management, **Real Prop 438, 439**
Heirs, generally, **Real Prop 71-76**
Holdover tenants, **Real Prop 118-121, 129-131**
Horizontal privity, **Real Prop 222-224**
Hostile, adverse possession, **Real Prop 19-23**
Implication, creation of easements and licenses, **Real Prop 178-185**
Independent Covenants Doctrine, termination of tenancies, **Real Prop 113, 114**
Indestructibility of uses, equitable interests in land, **Real Prop 60, 61**
Inquiry notice, **Real Prop 331-340**
Installment land contracts, contract of sale, **Real Prop 273, 274**
Insurance, title insurance, **Real Prop 354-361**

REAL PROPERTY—Cont'd
Interests in land, generally, **Real Prop 1-243**
International Taxation (this index)
Judicial review, regulation of land use, **Real Prop 457-473**
Laches, termination of neighborhood restrictions, **Real Prop 241**
Landlord and tenant, **Real Prop 106-168**
Landmarks and historic districts, **Real Prop 440, 441**
Land Use (this index)
Life estates, **Real Prop 29, 33, 34**
Limitations of recording system, **Real Prop 350-353**
Mapping, **Real Prop 422-424**
Marital estates, common law estates, **Real Prop 80-84**
Marketable title, contract of sale, **Real Prop 258-268**
Merger, terminations by, **Real Prop 205, 206, 239, 240**
Modern Public Land Law (this index)
Mortgages, **Real Prop 362-374**
Necessity, creation of easements and licenses, **Real Prop 185, 186**
No shifting interests, rules regulating common law estates, **Real Prop 52, 53**
No springing interests, rules regulating common law estates, **Real Prop 49-52**
Notorious, adverse possession, **Real Prop 11**
Nuisance, **Real Prop 378, 407-411**
Ownership, adverse possession, **Real Prop 1-5**
Partition, concurrent ownership, **Real Prop 93**
Payment of taxes, adverse possession, **Real Prop 9, 10**
Performance or nonperformance, contract of sale, **Real Prop 273-276**
Periodic estate (tenancy from period to period), **Real Prop 29**
Periodic tenancy, landlord and tenant, **Real Prop 108, 109**
Possessory interest, **Real Prop 127-132, 169-171**
Prescription, **Real Prop 187-192, 240, 241**
Priorities, recording system, **Real Prop 313-353**
Privity, **Real Prop 222-225**
Profits, easements, **Real Prop 171, 172**

REAL PROPERTY—Cont'd

Qualities of possession required, adverse possession, **Real Prop 10-23**
Quality of estates, **Real Prop 35-37**
Quiet enjoyment, **Real Prop 114-116, 301, 302**
Quitclaim deed, transfer of title, **Real Prop 277, 278**
Real estate brokers, **Real Prop 246-255**
Recording system, **Real Prop 313-353**
Regulation of land use, **Real Prop 412-473**
Remainders, **Real Prop 41-46, 53-56, 63, 64, 67-69**
Rent, **Real Prop 132-135, 149-152**
Rents and profits, concurrent ownership, **Real Prop 93-97**
Restraints on alienation, **Real Prop 76-78**
Reversion, **Real Prop 37-39, 45, 46, 69**
Reverter, common law estates, **Real Prop 39, 40**
Rule against perpetuities, **Real Prop 66-71**
Rule in Shelley's Case, **Real Prop 71-75**
Running with the land, **Real Prop 211-243**
Seisin, **Real Prop 30, 31, 49, 81, 82, 300**
Severance, concurrent ownership, **Real Prop 91-93**
Spurious, easements, **Real Prop 174, 175**
Statute of frauds, contract of sale, **Real Prop 256-258**
Statute of limitations, adverse possession, **Real Prop 23-26**
Statute of uses, equitable interests in land, **Real Prop 61-64**
Statutory deed, transfer of title by deed, **Real Prop 299**
Stream water, **Real Prop 380-384**
Subdivision regulation, **Real Prop 433-438**
Subleases, transfer of tenancy, **Real Prop 161, 162, 167, 168**
Support of land, **Real Prop 387-391**
Surface water, **Real Prop 384, 385**
Surrender, termination of tenancies, **Real Prop 116, 117**
Survivorship, concurrent ownership, **Real Prop 89-91**
Tenancy at sufferance, **Real Prop 29, 30**
Tenancy at will, **Real Prop 29, 30, 109, 110**
Tenancy for term, landlord and tenant, **Real Prop 107, 108**
Termination, **Real Prop 39, 40, 69, 110-127, 144-149, 203-210, 239-243**

REAL PROPERTY—Cont'd
Title insurance, **Real Prop 354-361**
Torts, conditions of disrepair, **Real Prop 152-160**
Transfers, **Real Prop 46-49, 161-168, 192-194, 277-312, 372-374**
Trespass, **Real Prop 377, 399-406**
Unclean hands, termination of neighborhood restrictions, **Real Prop 241**
Underground water, **Real Prop 385, 386**
Use of land. **Land Use** (this index)
Validity or invalidity, termination of easements, **Real Prop 210**
Variations by tenant, scope of easements, **Real Prop 197-203**
Vertical privity, **Real Prop 224, 225**
Vested remainders, **Real Prop 44, 45, 68, 69**
Warranty deed, transfer of title, **Real Prop 278, 298, 299**
Waste, common law estates, **Real Prop 78-80**
Water, **Real Prop 379-386**
Worthier Title Doctrine, **Real Prop 75, 76**
Zoning, **Real Prop 412-433**

RECIPROCITY
Public International Law (this index)

REFORM
Medical Liability (this index)

REFUSAL
Medical Liability (this index)

REFUSALS
Labor Law (this index)

REGULATED INDUSTRIES
Generally, **Reg Indus 1-18**
Affected with public interest, legal basis of regulation, **Reg Indus 73-78**
Allocation problems, rates to customers, **Reg Indus 182-209**
Alternatives, **Reg Indus 273-290**

REGULATED INDUSTRIES—Cont'd
Antitrust, **Reg Indus 14-18, 291-323, 329-331**
Appeals, antitrusts, **Reg Indus 317-323**
Competition, **Reg Indus 227-232, 341-351**
Constitutional law, **Reg Indus 95-102, 244, 245**
Cost-based rate differentials, discrimination, **Reg Indus 172-175**
Cross-subsidization, minimum rate regulation, **Reg Indus 240, 241**
Customers, generally, **Reg Indus 159-209**
Deregulation, **Reg Indus 336-341**
Destructive competition, minimum rate regulation, **Reg Indus 227-232**
Discrimination, rates to customers, **Reg Indus 159-181**
Due process, legal basis of regulation, **Reg Indus 78-87**
Elasticity of demand, discrimination, **Reg Indus 175-177**
Entry, restrictions on, **Reg Indus 244-267**
Environmental regulation, integrating economic regulation and, **Reg Indus 351-359**
Equal access, **Reg Indus 341-351**
Expenses, **Reg Indus 91**
Failure, generally, **Reg Indus 332-370**
Fair rate of return, maximum price regulation, **Reg Indus 128-138**
Government ownership, alternatives to cost of service rate regulation, **Reg Indus 288-290**
Healthcare, managed competition, **Reg Indus 365-368**
Immunity, antitrusts, **Reg Indus 304-314**
Improvement of efficiency and product quality, regulation of level of, **Reg Indus 221-226**
Incentive regulation, **Reg Indus 359-365**
Internal cross-subsidization, minimum rate regulation, **Reg Indus 240, 241**
Investment and rate of return, **Reg Indus 90**
Jurisdiction, **Reg Indus 324-331**
Just and reasonable rates, **Reg Indus 209**
Legal basis of regulation, **Reg Indus 70-87**
Marginal cost rates, allocation problems, **Reg Indus 184-198**
Market failure, **Reg Indus 42-69**

REGULATED INDUSTRIES—Cont'd
Maximum price regulation, **Reg Indus 93-158**
Minimum rate regulation, generally, **Reg Indus 227-243, 266, 267**
Monopoly, restrictions on entry, **Reg Indus 247-254**
Multi-part rates, allocation problems, **Reg Indus 199-203**
Operating expenses, maximum price regulation, **Reg Indus 138-155**
Operating ratios, alternatives to cost of service rate regulation, **Reg Indus 277-279**
Peakload rates, allocation problems, **Reg Indus 203-209**
Predatory pricing, minimum rate regulation, **Reg Indus 235, 236**
Price freeze, alternatives to cost of service rate regulation, **Reg Indus 283-287**
Primary jurisdiction, **Reg Indus 324-331**
Quality, **Reg Indus 218-226, 233-235, 245-247**
Rate regulation, generally, **Reg Indus 88-92, 227-243, 277-290**
Rationing resources, **Reg Indus 254, 255, 268-276**
Reasons for regulating, **Reg Indus 19-69**
Reform, generally, **Reg Indus 332-370**
Restrictions on entry, **Reg Indus 244-267**
Revenue requirements, rate regulation, **Reg Indus 88-90**
Safety, minimum rate regulation, **Reg Indus 233-235**
Seasonal rates, allocation problems, **Reg Indus 203-209**
Service, regulation of level of, **Reg Indus 210-218**
Standard cost rates, alternatives to cost of service rate regulation, **Reg Indus 280-283**
Transition costs, **Reg Indus 368-370**
Unbundling, **Reg Indus 341-351**

REHABILITATION
Individual Employee Rights (this index)

REJECTION
Uniform Commercial Code (this index)

RELATIVES

Family Law (this index)

RELIGION, FREEDOM OF

First Amendment (this index)

RELIGION, THE STATE AND

Generally, **Relig 1 et seq.**
Aid or assistance, **Relig 195-238**
Autonomy, institutional, **Relig 116-124**
Colleges, assistance by government to religious institutions and activities, **Relig 214-217**
Compelled accommodation test, **Relig 80-115**
Constitutional interpretation, generally, **Relig 10-13**
De facto protestant establishment and enactment of Fourteenth Amendment, **Relig 56-62**
Definition of religion, **Relig 262-276**
Delegation of governmental power to religious groups, **Relig 192-194**
Differing Colonial patterns, **Relig 41-44**
Discrimination against religious conduct, **Relig 75-78**
Equal treatment, **Relig 17-19**
Establishment clause, **Relig 28-34, 131-147**
European background, **Relig 36-41**
Expanded definitions of religion, **Relig 263-271**
Expression, freedom of, **Relig 72-75**
First Amendment, generally, **Relig 5**
Founding generation, **Relig 44-56**
Fourteenth Amendment, de facto protestant establishment and enactment of, **Relig 56-62**
Free exercise of religion, **Relig 25-28, 69-147, 236-238**
Free speech, implications of, **Relig 236-238**
Government institutions and activities, religion in, generally, **Relig 148-194**
Government neutrality-private choice line of decisions, assistance by government to religious institutions and activities, **Relig 222-231**

RELIGION, THE STATE AND—Cont'd

History, generally, **Relig 35-68**
Incorporation of First Amendment, **Relig 6-8**
Internal autonomy decisions, **Relig 116-122**
Interpretation of religion clauses, **Relig 9-25**
Legislative accommodations of religion, **Relig 131-147**
Lemon test, establishment clause standards, **Relig 28-31**
Modern case law, assistance by government to religious institutions and activities, **Relig 205-231**
Neutrality as equal treatment, establishment clause standards, **Relig 34**
Nineteenth Century, de facto protestant establishment and enactment of Fourteenth Amendment, **Relig 56-62**
No endorsement, establishment clause standards, **Relig 32, 33**
Noncoercion and religious choice, **Relig 19-25, 33**
Philosophy, religion and politics in pluralistic liberal democracy, **Relig 252-261**
Political decision-making, religious influences on, **Relig 239-261**
Potential religion clause values, **Relig 13-25**
Protestant-Catholic school conflicts in the mid-1800s, assistance by government to religious institutions and activities, **Relig 203, 204**
Public schools, religious elements in, **Relig 150-182**
Religious Freedom Restoration Act, **Relig 124-129**
Religious pluralism, **Relig 62-68**
Religious test clause, **Relig 4, 5**
Resolving definition of religion problem, **Relig 271-275**
Restrictions on religious dissent, European background, **Relig 36-41**
Separation of church and state, **Relig 15-17**
Social services, assistance by government to religious institutions and activities, **Relig 217-222**
State constitutional prohibitions on religious aid, **Relig 234-236**
Traditional definitions of religion, **Relig 262, 263**
Virginia religious assessment controversy, assistance by government to religious institutions and activities, **Relig 200-203**
Wars of religion, European background, **Relig 36-41**

REMEDIES
Insurance Law (this index)
Labor Law (this index)
Objectives. **International Environmental Law** (this index)

REMOVAL
Federal Jurisdiction (this index)
State Constitutional Law (this index)

RENEWALS
Landlord and Tenant (this index)

RENTS AND RENTALS
International Taxation (this index)

REPRESENTATION
Attorneys (this index)
Labor Arbitration Law and Practice (this index)
Labor Law (this index)

RESEARCH
How to Study Law and Take Law Exams (this index)
Legal Research (this index)

RESIDENCE
International Taxation (this index)

RES JUDICATA
Injunctions (this index)

RESOURCE CONSERVATION AND RECOVERY ACT (RCRA)
Hazardous Wastes and Toxic Substances, Law of (this index)

RESPONSIBILITY
Professional Responsibility (this index)

RESTATEMENTS OF THE LAW
Legal Research (this index)

RETROACTIVITY
Tax Procedure and Tax Fraud (this index)

RETURNS
Tax Procedure and Tax Fraud (this index)

REVERSION
Landlord and Tenant (this index)

REVIEW
Health Care Law and Ethics (this index)

RISKS
International Business Transactions (this index)

SAFE HARBOR
Federal Income Taxation of Partners and Partnerships (this index)

SALES AND LEASES OF GOODS
Generally, **Sales & Leases Goods 1-29**
Acceptance, rights on improper tender, **Sales & Leases Goods 312-326**
Adequate assurance of performance, **Sales & Leases Goods 285-291**
Anticipatory repudiation, generally, **Sales & Leases Goods 276-285**
Approval of sale, **Sales & Leases Goods 163, 164, 212**
Assignment, title and rights of third parties, **Sales & Leases Goods 190-193**
Bailee, risk of loss, **Sales & Leases Goods 203-205**
Bills of lading, generally, **Sales & Leases Goods 110-114**
Carrier, risk of loss, **Sales & Leases Goods 199-203**
C.& F., performance, **Sales & Leases Goods 131**

SALES AND LEASES OF GOODS—Cont'd
C.I.F., performance, **Sales & Leases Goods 130, 131**
Consequential damages, monetary remedies, **Sales & Leases Goods 404-416**
Consignments, title and rights of third parties, **Sales & Leases Goods 164, 165**
Consumer lease defined, **Sales & Leases Goods 26-29**
Continuation of performance after breach, **Sales & Leases Goods 368-372**
Contract for sale defined, **Sales & Leases Goods 8-13**
Course of dealing, terms of contract, **Sales & Leases Goods 89, 90**
Course of performance, terms of contract, **Sales & Leases Goods 87-89**
Creditors' rights, **Sales & Leases Goods 187-190**
Crops, title and rights of third parties, **Sales & Leases Goods 157-159**
Damages, remedies, **Sales & Leases Goods 365-368, 400-416**
Definitions, **Sales & Leases Goods 1-29**
Delivery, nonmonetary remedies, **Sales & Leases Goods 372-385**
Destination contracts, **Sales & Leases Goods 128, 159, 160**
Documents of title, generally, **Sales & Leases Goods 109-116**
Energy and Natural Resources Law (this index)
Entrustment, third parties, **Sales & Leases Goods 166-176**
Estoppel, statute of frauds, **Sales & Leases Goods 62-64**
Examination of goods, **Sales & Leases Goods 244-246**
Exceptions, statute of frauds, **Sales & Leases Goods 56-62**
Exclusion of warranties, **Sales & Leases Goods 246-255**
Excuse for nonperformance, **Sales & Leases Goods 326-341**
Existing goods, **Sales & Leases Goods 22**
Express terms of contract, **Sales & Leases Goods 84-87**
Express warranties, **Sales & Leases Goods 215-224, 247-249**
F.A.S., performance, **Sales & Leases Goods 129, 130**
Federal Income Taxation of Partners and Partnerships (this index)
Finance lease defined, **Sales & Leases Goods 26-29**
Fitness, implied warranty of, **Sales & Leases Goods 242-244**

SALES AND LEASES OF GOODS—Cont'd

F.O.B., performance, **Sales & Leases Goods 129**
Formation of contract, generally, **Sales & Leases Goods 30-46**
Fungible goods, **Sales & Leases Goods 22, 23, 156, 157**
Future goods, **Sales & Leases Goods 22, 156**
Good faith, modification, **Sales & Leases Goods 77, 78**
Goods defined, **Sales & Leases Goods 13-19**
Identified goods, **Sales & Leases Goods 21, 22**
Implied warranties, generally, **Sales & Leases Goods 232-246**
Improper tender, rights on, **Sales & Leases Goods 306-326**
Incidental damages, remedies, **Sales & Leases Goods 365-368, 404-416**
Infringement, warranty against, **Sales & Leases Goods 231, 232**
Insolvency of seller or lessor, remedies, **Sales & Leases Goods 423-425**
Installment contracts, **Sales & Leases Goods 292-300**
Interference, **Sales & Leases Goods 225-231, 249, 250**
International Taxation (this index)
Lease agreement defined, **Sales & Leases Goods 8-13**
Lease contract defined, **Sales & Leases Goods 8-13**
Lease defined, **Sales & Leases Goods 8-13**
Leases of goods and services defined, **Sales & Leases Goods 13-19**
Letters of credit, generally, **Sales & Leases Goods 116-118**
Liquidated damages, **Sales & Leases Goods 365-368, 416**
Magnuson-Moss, warranty obligations, **Sales & Leases Goods 260-263**
Market price or rent, monetary remedies, **Sales & Leases Goods 395-399**
Market value standard, remedies, **Sales & Leases Goods 355-358**
Merchantability, warranty of, **Sales & Leases Goods 234-238**
Merchant defined, **Sales & Leases Goods 23-26**
Mixed sales defined, **Sales & Leases Goods 13-19**
Modification, **Sales & Leases Goods 74-82, 246-255**
Monetary remedies, **Sales & Leases Goods 348-372, 386-425**
Negligent tort, warranty obligations, **Sales & Leases Goods 267-269**

SALES AND LEASES OF GOODS—Cont'd

Negotiable documents of title, **Sales & Leases Goods 194**
Nonconforming goods, acceptance, **Sales & Leases Goods 44, 45**
Nonmonetary remedies, **Sales & Leases Goods 418-428**
Nonshipment contracts, performance, **Sales & Leases Goods 123-125**
Offer and acceptance, generally, **Sales & Leases Goods 31-46**
Open price, terms of contract, **Sales & Leases Goods 93-100**
Parol evidence, generally, **Sales & Leases Goods 64-73**
Passage of title, **Sales & Leases Goods 150-165**
Perfect tender rule, **Sales & Leases Goods 291, 292**
Performance, generally, **Sales & Leases Goods 119-148**
Possession and rights of creditors, **Sales & Leases Goods 187-190**
Price, obligation to pay, **Sales & Leases Goods 136-148**
Price defined, **Sales & Leases Goods 19-21**
Price standard, remedies, **Sales & Leases Goods 363-365**
Privity in regard to warranty, **Sales & Leases Goods 255-260**
Profit standard, remedies, **Sales & Leases Goods 359-363**
Public misrepresentation, warranty obligations, **Sales & Leases Goods 264-267**
Reclamation, nonmonetary remedies, **Sales & Leases Goods 379-385**
Rejection, **Sales & Leases Goods 162, 306-312**
Re-lease as remedy, **Sales & Leases Goods 349-355**
Remedies, generally, **Sales & Leases Goods 342-425**
Rent, **Sales & Leases Goods 19-21, 136-148, 363-365, 390, 391**
Replevin, nonmonetary remedies, **Sales & Leases Goods 422, 423**
Repossession, nonmonetary remedies, **Sales & Leases Goods 379-385**
Repudiation, generally, **Sales & Leases Goods 274-341**
Resale as remedy, **Sales & Leases Goods 349-355**
Restatement of Torts (Second), warranty obligations, **Sales & Leases Goods 269-273**
Return, **Sales & Leases Goods 163, 164, 212**
Revocation, **Sales & Leases Goods 162, 320-325**

SALES AND LEASES OF GOODS—Cont'd
Risk of loss, generally, **Sales & Leases Goods 195-212**
Sale defined, **Sales & Leases Goods 8-13**
Security interest, **Sales & Leases Goods 161, 162, 416, 417**
Shipment contracts, **Sales & Leases Goods 125-128, 160, 161**
Specific performance, nonmonetary remedies, **Sales & Leases Goods 418-421**
Statute of frauds, **Sales & Leases Goods 48-64, 79, 80**
Stopping delivery, nonmonetary remedies, **Sales & Leases Goods 376-379**
Sufficiency of writing, statute of frauds, **Sales & Leases Goods 52-55**
Tender obligations, performance, **Sales & Leases Goods 121-126**
Terms of contract, generally, **Sales & Leases Goods 83-108**
Third parties, **Sales & Leases Goods 149-194**
Time for tender, performance, **Sales & Leases Goods 131-136**
Title and rights of third parties, generally, **Sales & Leases Goods 149-194**
Unborn young of animals, title and rights of third parties, **Sales & Leases Goods 157-159**
Unconscionable terms of contract, **Sales & Leases Goods 101-108**
Unilateral contracts, acceptance in, **Sales & Leases Goods 45, 46**
Usage of trade, terms of contract, **Sales & Leases Goods 90, 91**
Voidable interests, third parties, **Sales & Leases Goods 176-187**
Waiver, modification and, **Sales & Leases Goods 80-82**
Warehouse receipts, generally, **Sales & Leases Goods 114-116**
Warranty obligations, generally, **Sales & Leases Goods 213-273**
Withholding delivery, nonmonetary remedies, **Sales & Leases Goods 374-376**

SALVAGE
Personal Property (this index)

SAMPLES
How to Study Law and Take Law Exams (this index)

SCHOLARS

Comparative Legal Traditions (this index)

SCHOOLS, STUDENTS AND TEACHERS, THE LAW OF

Abuse of child, student discipline, **Schools 185-190**
Academic discipline, student discipline, **Schools 192-194**
Acquired Immunodeficiency Syndrome (AIDS), education of disabled children, **Schools 251-253**
Act of God, civil liability, **Schools 289**
Admission, attendance in public schools, **Schools 7-14**
Affirmative action, employment discrimination, **Schools 420-423**
Age discrimination, teachers, **Schools 438-440**
AIDS (Acquired Immunodeficiency Syndrome), education of disabled children, **Schools 251-253**
Alcohol, freedom of speech and expression, **Schools 113, 114**
Amish exception, private schools, **Schools 31-33**
Assault and battery, civil liability, **Schools 268-270**
Assumption of risk, civil liability, **Schools 287-289**
Attendance in public schools, **Schools 6-38**
Attorneys' fees, education of disabled children, **Schools 253, 254**
Automobile search, **Schools 170-172**
Bible reading, religious activities in public schools, **Schools 128, 129**
Buckley Amendment, student records, **Schools 302-307**
Busing, racial segregation, **Schools 205, 206**
Canine searches, **Schools 165-167**
Censorship of books, **Schools 50-58**
Certification of teachers, terms and conditions of employment, **Schools 336-341**
Child abuse, student discipline, **Schools 185-190**
Civil liability, generally, **Schools 266-300**
Comparative negligence, civil liability, **Schools 286, 287**
Competency, student testing, **Schools 324, 325**
Compulsory attendance, **Schools 15-21**
Consent, search and seizure, **Schools 165**

SCHOOLS, STUDENTS AND TEACHERS, THE LAW OF—Cont'd

Constitutional torts, **Schools 297-300**
Contributory negligence, civil liability, **Schools 284, 285**
Conviction of crime, teacher dismissal for, **Schools 403-406**
Corporal punishment, student discipline, **Schools 180-185**
De facto segregation, **Schools 206-211**
Defamation, student records, **Schools 307-319**
Defenses for negligence, civil liability, **Schools 283-294**
De jure segregation, **Schools 206-211**
Desks, search and seizure, **Schools 169, 170**
Diagnostic and therapeutic services for parochial school students, public tax funds for religious schools, **Schools 144, 145**
Diploma, instructional programs, **Schools 61, 62**
Disabled children, education of, **Schools 222-254**
Disabled persons, discrimination against disabled teachers, **Schools 440-443**
Discipline, **Schools 177-194, 249-251**
Dismissal of teachers, **Schools 374-410**
Disparate treatment and disparate impact, employment discrimination, **Schools 416-418**
Drugs, freedom of speech and expression, **Schools 113, 114**
Drug testing, **Schools 173-175**
Due process, **Schools 65-95, 325-328, 375-385**
Educational malpractice, **Schools 294-297**
Eleventh Amendment, education of disabled children, **Schools 231**
Employment discrimination, **Schools 411-445**
Equal Access Act of 1984, religious activities in public schools, **Schools 132-138**
Equal Pay Act, sex discrimination, **Schools 428-430**
Equal protection, **Schools 217, 218, 256-261, 325-328, 412, 413**
Exemptions or exceptions, **Schools 29-33**
False imprisonment, civil liability, **Schools 271, 272**
Family and Medical Leave Act of 1993, teachers, **Schools 444, 445**
Field trip searches, **Schools 172, 173**

SCHOOLS, STUDENTS AND TEACHERS, THE LAW OF—Cont'd

Finances and funds, public tax funds for religious schools, **Schools 138-148**
Flags, freedom of speech and expression, **Schools 104**
Fourth Amendment, search and seizure, **Schools 158-165**
Freedom of speech and expression, **Schools 96-115, 353, 354**
Free exercise and establishment, **Schools 119, 120**
Functional literacy, student testing, **Schools 332-335**
Good and just cause, teacher dismissal, **Schools 408-410**
Graduation ceremonies prayer, religious activities in public schools, **Schools 129-131**
Hair codes, freedom of speech and expression, **Schools 106-108**
Home schooling, **Schools 21-28**
Homework, instructional programs, **Schools 62, 63**
Homosexuality, teacher dismissal for, **Schools 400-402**
How to Study Law and Take Law Exams (this index)
Illegal aliens, attendance in public schools, **Schools 13, 14**
Immediate temporary suspension, due process rights of students, **Schools 73, 74**
Immigration Law and Procedure (this index)
Immorality, **Schools 112, 395-403**
Immunity, civil liability, **Schools 289-292**
Individualized Education Program, **Schools 241, 242**
Individuals With Disability Act (IDEA), **Schools 227-229, 231-246**
In loco parentis, student discipline, **Schools 178, 179**
Instructional materials and equipment in parochial school, public tax funds for religious schools, **Schools 145, 146**
Instructional programs, **Schools 39-64**
Insubordination, teacher dismissal for, **Schools 392-395**
Intentional interference, civil liability, **Schools 267-272**
Interdistrict racial segregation, **Schools 216, 217**
Judicial review, student testing, **Schools 322, 323**
Last clear chance, civil liability, **Schools 292, 293**
Lemon test, religion in public schools and statute funding of religious schools, **Schools 121-125**

SCHOOLS, STUDENTS AND TEACHERS, THE LAW OF—Cont'd
Library books, censorship of, **Schools 55-58**
Local board prerogatives, terms and conditions of teacher employment, **Schools 341-345**
Lockers, search and seizure, **Schools 169, 170**
Malpractice, educational malpractice, **Schools 294-297**
Marriage, **Schools 36, 112**
Membership in student societies, freedom of speech and expression, **Schools 108-110**
Metal detector searches, **Schools 175, 176**
Negligence, civil liability, **Schools 273-294**
One-race schools, racial segregation, **Schools 204, 205**
Out-of-school activities, student discipline for, **Schools 190-192**
Parens patriae, compulsory attendance, **Schools 16, 17**
Parochial schools, **Schools 142-148**
Personal appearance, **Schools 104-108, 362-364**
Picketing, constitutional rights of teachers, **Schools 354-361**
Police involvement, search and seizure, **Schools 164, 165**
Prayer, religious activities in public schools, **Schools 128-132**
Pregnancy, **Schools 1101-112**
Privacy rights, **Schools 302-307, 319-321, 364-367**
Private schools, **Schools 28-36, 246, 247**
Professional Responsibility (this index)
Promotion, instructional programs, **Schools 59, 60**
Protests, freedom of speech and expression, **Schools 103, 104**
Publications by students, **Schools 149-156**
Public lewdness, teacher dismissal for, **Schools 403**
Public tax funds for religious schools, **Schools 138-148**
Public transportation of parochial school students, public tax funds for religious schools, **Schools 142, 143**
Race and racial discrimination, **Schools 195-221, 211-423**
Reasonable suspicion, search and seizure, **Schools 160, 161**
Records of students, **Schools 301-321**
Reimbursement of parochial schools for teacher-made tests, public tax funds for religious schools, **Schools 143, 144**

SCHOOLS, STUDENTS AND TEACHERS, THE LAW OF—Cont'd

Release time, religious activities in public schools, **Schools 126-128**

Religion and religious matters, generally, **Schools 116-148**

Save harmless laws, civil liability, **Schools 293, 294**

Search and seizure, **Schools 157-176**

Sectarian schools, private school for disabled children, **Schools 248**

Separate-but-equal, racial segregation, **Schools 195-199**

Sex discrimination, **Schools 255-265, 424-435**

Sex education, instructional programs, **Schools 63, 64**

Sexual orientation, teachers, **Schools 435**

Silent meditation, religious activities in public schools, **Schools 129**

Sit-ins, freedom of speech and expression, **Schools 103, 104**

Standardized testing and scoring in parochial schools, public tax funds for religious schools, **Schools 143**

State equal protection, racial segregation, **Schools 217, 218**

State funding of religious schools, **Schools 138-148**

Strict liability, civil liability, **Schools 272, 273**

Strip searches, **Schools 167-169**

Suspension, due process rights of students, **Schools 73, 74**

Taxation, public tax funds for religious schools, **Schools 138-148**

Tax credits and deductions for students in parochial schools, public tax funds for religious schools, **Schools 146-148**

Temporary suspension, due process rights of students, **Schools 73, 74**

Tenure, **Schools 348-350, 386-392**

Tests and testing, **Schools 143, 144, 173-175, 322-335**

Textbooks, **Schools 50-54, 141**

Title VI, employment discrimination, **Schools 413, 414**

Title VII, **Schools 414-416, 424-426**

Title IX, **Schools 261-265, 430-432**

Tobacco, freedom of speech and expression, **Schools 113, 114**

Transportation of parochial school students, public tax funds for religious schools, **Schools 142, 143**

SCHOOLS, STUDENTS AND TEACHERS, THE LAW OF—Cont'd
Transsexuality, teacher dismissal for, **Schools 402, 403**
Truancy, compulsory attendance, **Schools 17-19**
Unitary system, racial segregation, **Schools 211-216**
Vaccination, attendance in public schools, **Schools 36-38**
Weapons, freedom of speech and expression, **Schools 114, 115**

SEALS
International Environmental Law (this index)

SECONDARY MATERIALS
Legal Research (this index)

SECTION 1983 LITIGATION
Abrogation, sovereign immunity of state, **Sect 1983 Lit 112-115**
Abstention and related doctrines, **Sect 1983 Lit 22, 23, 255-286**
Accountability, municipal liability, **Sect 1983 Lit 87-92**
Administrative proceedings of state, preclusion and § 1983, **Sect 1983 Lit 245**
Ancillary awards of monetary relief, sovereign immunity of state, **Sect 1983 Lit 110-112**
Anticipatory relief, abstention and related doctrines, **Sect 1983 Lit 266-271**
Anti-Injunction Act, abstention and related doctrines, **Sect 1983 Lit 260, 261**
Arbitration, preclusion and § 1983, **Sect 1983 Lit 253, 254**
Arms of state, sovereign immunity of state, **Sect 1983 Lit 118-120**
Associational and third party standing, jurisdiction and procedure, **Sect 1983 Lit 343, 344**
Attorneys' fees, generally, **Sect 1983 Lit 191-212**
Authorized versus unauthorized official behavior, Parratt and scope of due process, **Sect 1983 Lit 42-44**
Bivens and federal officer liability, **Sect 1983 Lit 301-316**
Burden of pleading and proof, jurisdiction and procedure, **Sect 1983 Lit 331-333**

SECTION 1983 LITIGATION—Cont'd

Burford abstention, state administrative decisionmaking, **Sect 1983 Lit 284-286**
Causation, **Sect 1983 Lit 100, 101, 340, 341**
Choice of law and § 1983, **Sect 1983 Lit 213-228**
Class action litigation, jurisdiction and procedure, **Sect 1983 Lit 348, 349**
Coercive enforcement remedies, injunctions and declaratory relief, **Sect 1983 Lit 179-186**
Color of law, **Sect 1983 Lit 17-20, 26-32**
Compliance, relief from continuing injunctive relief, **Sect 1983 Lit 186, 187**
Congressional displacement, exceptions to statutory enforcement of federal laws under § 1983, **Sect 1983 Lit 78-80**
Consequences of exhausting state remedies, qualifications on no-exhaustion rule, **Sect 1983 Lit 25, 26**
Constitutional coverage of § 1983, generally, **Sect 1983 Lit 32-34**
Contempt, coercive enforcement of remedies, **Sect 1983 Lit 183-186**
Continuing injunctive relief, relief from, **Sect 1983 Lit 186-190**
Contraction, Bivens and federal officer liability, **Sect 1983 Lit 309-313**
Convicted criminals, **Sect 1983 Lit 23, 24, 252, 253**
Cruel and unusual punishments, official violence, **Sect 1983 Lit 59, 60**
Custodial settings, private violence and affirmative governmental duties, **Sect 1983 Lit 63-66**
Custom or policy, municipal liability, **Sect 1983 Lit 92-98**
Damages, generally, **Sect 1983 Lit 150-161**
Declaratory judgments, generally, **Sect 1983 Lit 176-179**
Default, § 1983 and habeas corpus, **Sect 1983 Lit 290-292**
DeShaney, limits of, **Sect 1983 Lit 69-73**
Discretion, supplemental jurisdiction over pendent claims and parties, **Sect 1983 Lit 324, 325**
Discriminatory procedures, State courts, **Sect 1983 Lit 235, 236**
Displacement of § 1983 by state remedies, State courts, **Sect 1983 Lit 239, 240**
Due process, **Sect 1983 Lit 35-55, 60-62**

SECTION 1983 LITIGATION—Cont'd

Early interpretations, **Sect 1983 Lit 5-9**
Enforcement, **Sect 1983 Lit 32, 33, 74-85**
Equitable relief, **Sect 1983 Lit 163-167, 181-183**
Exceptions to statutory enforcement of federal laws under § 1983, **Sect 1983 Lit 77-82**
Excessive force, generally, **Sect 1983 Lit 56-73**
Exhaustion of remedies, **Sect 1983 Lit 12-26**
Expansion, Bivens and federal officer liability, **Sect 1983 Lit 306-309**
Ex parte Young, abstention and related doctrines, **Sect 1983 Lit 266-271**
Facial versus as applied challenges, jurisdiction and procedure, **Sect 1983 Lit 349-351**
Fault in hiring, municipal liability, **Sect 1983 Lit 101, 102**
Federalism, **Sect 1983 Lit 172, 173, 261-274**
Federal litigation, choice of law and § 1983 generally, **Sect 1983 Lit 215, 216**
Federal Tort Claims and Westfall Act, Bivens and federal officer liability, **Sect 1983 Lit 316-319**
Freedom from trial, good faith immunities, **Sect 1983 Lit 130-133**
Good faith, personal immunities, **Sect 1983 Lit 126-149**
Guilty pleas, preclusion and § 1983, **Sect 1983 Lit 253, 254**
Habeas corpus, **Sect 1983 Lit 287-300**
Hard bargains, relief from continuing injunctive relief, **Sect 1983 Lit 187-189**
Hiring fault, municipal liability, **Sect 1983 Lit 101, 102**
Historical background, **Sect 1983 Lit 1-5**
Hybrid officials, personal immunities, **Sect 1983 Lit 145, 146**
Individual supervisory liability, municipal liability, **Sect 1983 Lit 102**
Individual versus official capacity suits, **Sect 1983 Lit 120, 333-335**
Injunctions, generally, **Sect 1983 Lit 162-190**
Intentional deprivations, state of mind and due process, **Sect 1983 Lit 40-42**
Interlocutory appealability, good faith immunities, **Sect 1983 Lit 135, 136**

SECTION 1983 LITIGATION—Cont'd

Irreparable harm, injunctions and declaratory relief, **Sect 1983 Lit 165, 166**
Judicial actors, personal immunities, **Sect 1983 Lit 136-140**
Judicial Elaboration of Fees Act, attorneys' fees, **Sect 1983 Lit 195-205**
Jurisdiction, **Sect 1983 Lit 320-351**
Justiciability, **Sect 1983 Lit 169-171, 335-349**
Law enforcement practices as unconstitutional, injunctions and declaratory relief, **Sect 1983 Lit 168-173**
Legislative actors, personal immunities, **Sect 1983 Lit 140-142**
Limitations, **Sect 1983 Lit 69-73, 123-125**
Litigation costs ofther than attorneys' fees, **Sect 1983 Lit 208, 209**
Local governments and officials, personal immunities, **Sect 1983 Lit 148, 149**
Monell consequences, municipal liability, **Sect 1983 Lit 90-92**
Monroe and modern § 1983 action, **Sect 1983 Lit 10-34**
Monroe versus Parratt, **Sect 1983 Lit 51-53**
Mootness, jurisdiction and procedure, **Sect 1983 Lit 347-349**
Municipal liability, **Sect 1983 Lit 86-102**
Negligent deprivations, state of mind and due process, **Sect 1983 Lit 40-42**
Notice of claim requirements under state law, permutations on no-exhaustion rule, **Sect 1983 Lit 21, 22**
Official violence, **Sect 1983 Lit 57-62**
Our Federalism, abstention and related doctrines, **Sect 1983 Lit 261-274**
Parolee violence, private violence and affirmative governmental duties, **Sect 1983 Lit 68**
Parratt and scope of due process, constitutionally compelled remedies, **Sect 1983 Lit 53-55**
Pendent claims under state law, sovereign immunity of state, **Sect 1983 Lit 123-125**
Pennhurst limitation, sovereign immunity of state, **Sect 1983 Lit 123-125**
Permutations, **Sect 1983 Lit 20-32**
Personal immunities, **Sect 1983 Lit 126-149**

SECTION 1983 LITIGATION—Cont'd

Pleading, **Sect 1983 Lit 237, 238, 329-333**
Pratt and scope of due process, **Sect 1983 Lit 35-55**
Preclusion and § 1983, **Sect 1983 Lit 241-254**
Preemption, enforcement of federal laws under § 1983, **Sect 1983 Lit 82-85**
Prison Litigation Reform Act, relief from continuing injunctive relief, **Sect 1983 Lit 189, 190**
Prisons and prisoners, **Sect 1983 Lit 63-65, 189, 190**
Private violence and affirmative governmental duties, **Sect 1983 Lit 63-73**
Prosecutorial and quasi-judicial immunities, **Sect 1983 Lit 142-144**
Prospective or retrospective relief, sovereign immunity of state, **Sect 1983 Lit 106-110**
Protected liberty and property, Parratt and scope of due process, **Sect 1983 Lit 44-47**
Public employees, private violence and affirmative governmental duties, **Sect 1983 Lit 68, 69**
Pullman, unclear questions of state law, **Sect 1983 Lit 275-286**
Qualifications on no-exhaustion rule, **Sect 1983 Lit 22-26**
Reasonableness assessed, good faith immunities, **Sect 1983 Lit 133-135**
Redressability, jurisdiction and procedure, **Sect 1983 Lit 341-343**
Release-dismissal agreement, preclusion and § 1983, **Sect 1983 Lit 253, 254**
Relitigation and limits, § 1983 and habeas corpus, **Sect 1983 Lit 289, 290**
Remedial details and federal common law, Bivens and federal officer liability, **Sect 1983 Lit 313-316**
Remedial discretion, injunctions and declaratory relief, **Sect 1983 Lit 173-176**
Removal, jurisdiction and procedure, **Sect 1983 Lit 327-329**
Respondeat superior liability, municipal liability, **Sect 1983 Lit 89, 90**
Retrospective versus prospective relief, sovereign immunity of state, **Sect 1983 Lit 106-110**
Ripeness, jurisdiction and procedure, **Sect 1983 Lit 344-346**

SECTION 1983 LITIGATION—Cont'd

Rooker-Feldman and related doctrines, preclusion and § 1983, **Sect 1983 Lit 249-252**

Searches and seizures, official violence, **Sect 1983 Lit 57-59**

Seminole Tribe, sovereign immunity of state, **Sect 1983 Lit 115-118**

Settlement, attorneys' fees and, **Sect 1983 Lit 209-212**

Sovereign immunity of state, **Sect 1983 Lit 103-125**

Standing to sue, jurisdiction and procedure, **Sect 1983 Lit 337-344**

State administrative remedies, permutations on no-exhaustion rule, **Sect 1983 Lit 20, 21**

State courts, generally, **Sect 1983 Lit 229-240**

State of mind, **Sect 1983 Lit 33, 34, 40-42**

Statutes, **Sect 1983 Lit 75-82, 192-195, 224-228**

Statutes of limitations, choice of law and § 1983, **Sect 1983 Lit 224-228**

Structural injunctions, **Sect 1983 Lit 167-176**

Subject matter jurisdiction, **Sect 1983 Lit 320-322**

Substantive due process, **Sect 1983 Lit 47-51, 60-62**

Supplemental jurisdiction over pendent claims and parties, **Sect 1983 Lit 322-325**

Supremacy clause claims, enforcement of federal laws under § 1983, **Sect 1983 Lit 82-85**

Taking of property, qualifications on no-exhaustion rule, **Sect 1983 Lit 24, 25**

Tax and Rate Injunction Acts, abstention and related doctrines, **Sect 1983 Lit 256-260**

Taxpayer standing, jurisdiction and procedure, **Sect 1983 Lit 339, 340**

Third party standing, jurisdiction and procedure, **Sect 1983 Lit 343, 344**

Timing and successive petitions, § 1983 and habeas corpus, **Sect 1983 Lit 292**

Tolling of statutes of limitations, choice of law and § 1983, **Sect 1983 Lit 226, 227**

Training failure as basis for municipal liability, **Sect 1983 Lit 98-102**

SECTION 1983 LITIGATION—Cont'd
Unclear questions of state law, Pullman, **Sect 1983 Lit 275-286**
Venue, jurisdiction and procedure, **Sect 1983 Lit 325-327**
Waiver, sovereign immunity of state, **Sect 1983 Lit 112-115**
Workplace safety, private violence and affirmative governmental duties, **Sect 1983 Lit 68, 69**
Younger, abstention and related doctrines, **Sect 1983 Lit 266-274**

SECURED TRANSACTIONS
Acceleration of payment, permitted and restricted, **Secur Trans 78, 79**
Accessions, **Secur Trans 32, 290, 291, 349, 350**
Account debtor, **Secur Trans 27, 28, 104-113, 341, 342**
Accounts, **Secur Trans 16, 17, 21, 22, 34, 52, 53, 96-98, 119, 120, 130, 209-211, 269-273**
After-acquired property, **Secur Trans 72-76, 319-323, 325**
Agreements, **Secur Trans 15, 16, 39, 54-81, 83, 183, 184, 204**
Amendment to financing statement, filing, **Secur Trans 186, 187**
Assignment of security interest, **Secur Trans 27, 28, 102-113, 120, 121, 137, 138, 191, 192, 341, 342**
Attachment of security interest, **Secur Trans 36, 37, 54-58, 83-89, 116-122**
Bank, security interest of, **Secur Trans 56, 57, 121, 277**
Bankruptcy or insolvency, **Secur Trans 121, 122, 230-233, 295-312, 319-332**
Bulk transfer, **Secur Trans 17, 18**
Certificate of title, **Secur Trans 131-133, 222-228**
Chattel mortgage, **Secur Trans 46, 47**
Chattel paper, **Secur Trans 16, 17, 21, 22, 33, 125, 129, 209, 212, 252-256**
Collateral, generally, **Secur Trans 28-36**
Conditional sale, **Secur Trans 47, 48**
Conflict of laws, **Secur Trans 115, 116, 120-129, 133-139, 142, 143, 204-213, 222-228**
Consignments, generally, **Secur Trans 53, 68-70**
Consumer goods, **Secur Trans 8, 9, 71, 75, 76, 106-110, 116-119, 148-150, 195, 196, 247-249, 351-355, 357, 358**

SECURED TRANSACTIONS—Cont'd
Continuation statement, filing, **Secur Trans 189, 190**
Contract rights, **Secur Trans 16, 17, 21, 22, 34, 52, 53, 96-98, 119, 120, 130, 209-211, 269-273**
Crops, **Secur Trans 60, 75, 76, 148-150, 178-182, 268, 269**
Debt, statement of, **Secur Trans 80, 96-98, 163**
Debtor, **Secur Trans 25-27, 95, 96**
Default, generally, **Secur Trans 335-337, 371-374**
Definition of secured transaction, **Secur Trans 12-17**
Deposit account, **Secur Trans 24, 25, 270. 327-331**
Documents, **Secur Trans 32, 122-125, 127, 129, 208, 209, 256, 257**
Equipment, **Secur Trans 29, 121, 148-150, 249, 250**
Equipment trust, generally, **Secur Trans 53**
Excluded transactions, generally, **Secur Trans 18-25**
Factors liens, **Secur Trans 52**
Farm equipment, **Secur Trans 121, 148-150, 249, 250**
Farm products, **Secur Trans 29, 30, 60, 75, 76, 148-150, 178-182, 233, 244-247, 268, 269**
Federal law, **Secur Trans 18, 19, 130, 131, 246, 247**
Field warehousing, **Secur Trans 39-42**
Filing, **Secur Trans 129-131, 145-161, 173, 174, 184-193, 196-203, 234-236, 262-264**
Financing statement, **Secur Trans 162-172, 174-184, 186, 187**
Fixtures, **Secur Trans 31, 32, 117-119, 150-154, 178-182, 282-290, 349-351**
Future advances, **Secur Trans 76-78, 250-2552, 259-261, 280, 281**
General intangibles, **Secur Trans 34, 130, 209-211**
Goods, **Secur Trans 29-32, 115, 116, 120-129, 133-139, 142, 143, 204-213, 222-228**
Government or agency, transfer by excluded, **Secur Trans 20, 21**
Insolvency or bankruptcy, **Secur Trans 121, 122, 230-233, 295-312, 319-332**
Instruments, **Secur Trans 32, 33, 42-45, 122-127, 207-209, 215, 252-257**
Insurance policy, transfer of rights excluded, **Secur Trans 22, 23**

SECURED TRANSACTIONS—Cont'd
Inventory, **Secur Trans 30, 31, 264-268**
Investment securities, **Secur Trans 32, 33, 42-45, 57, 58, 122-127, 209, 209, 215, 260**
Judgment, assignment excluded, **Secur Trans 23**
Lease, **Secur Trans 53, 66-68, 196, 197**
Liens, generally, **Secur Trans 19, 20, 232, 233**
Minerals, gas or oil, **Secur Trans 36, 60, 61, 150-154, 178, 180, 211, 214, 244**
Mobile goods, **Secur Trans 36, 212**
Money, **Secur Trans 36, 126**
Motor vehicles, certificate of title, **Secur Trans 131-133, 222-228**
Multistate transactions, **Secur Trans 115, 116, 120-129, 133-139, 142, 143, 204-213, 222-228**
Place of filing, **Secur Trans 130, 131, 145-161**
Pledge, **Secur Trans 37-45, 55, 56, 92-94, 125-129, 335**
Priorities
  generally, **Secur Trans 229-231**
  between secured parties, **Secur Trans 257-273, 291-294**
  buyers of collateral, **Secur Trans 236-257**
Proceeds, **Secur Trans 35, 63, 64, 81, 133-137, 182, 183, 269-273, 325, 327-331**
Products of collateral, **Secur Trans 182, 183, 291, 292, 325**
Purchase money security interest, **Secur Trans 49-51, 116-119, 121, 234-236, 262-271**
Real estate, **Secur Trans 23, 24, 31, 32, 60, 61, 117-119, 150-154, 178-182, 282-290, 349-351**
Release, filing statement of, **Secur Trans 192, 193**
Sale, **Secur Trans 16, 17, 57, 65, 66, 98-101, 121, 236-257, 275, 276, 331, 332, 337, 338, 349-356, 358, 359-370**
Sale or disposition upon default, **Secur Trans 337, 338, 349-356, 358, 359-370**
Secured party, **Secur Trans 26, 27, 100, 101, 229-231, 236-257, 257-273, 291-294, 335-338, 341-343**
Securities, **Secur Trans 32, 33, 42-45, 57, 58, 122-127, 209, 209, 215, 260**
Security agreement, **Secur Trans 39, 54-81, 183, 184**
Security interest, **Secur Trans 13, 36, 37, 54-58, 83-89, 116-122**

SECURED TRANSACTIONS—Cont'd
Setoff, **Secur Trans 23, 104-110**
Signature, **Secur Trans 58, 59, 166-170**
Subordination permitted, **Secur Trans 82**
Termination statement, **Secur Trans 193-196**
Timber, **Secur Trans 35, 60, 150, 151, 179**
Title, **Secur Trans 64, 65, 89, 90**
Tort claim, transfer excluded, **Secur Trans 24**
Transmitting utility, **Secur Trans 154, 179**
Trust receipts, **Secur Trans 51, 52**
Uniform Commercial Code, generally, **Secur Trans 1-17**
Unpaid seller, **Secur Trans 275, 276, 331, 332**
Value, necessity of, **Secur Trans 84-87**
Wage claim, transfer excluded, **Secur Trans 20**
Warranties, **Secur Trans 98-101**

SECURITIES REGULATION
Generally, **Securities Reg 1 et seq.**

SENIOR CITIZENS
Elder Law (this index)

SENTENCES
Legal Writing (this index)

SENTENCING, CORRECTIONS, AND PRISONERS' RIGHTS, LAW OF
Access to courts, prisoner's rights as to, **Sentencing 175-189**
Affirmative defenses, mechanics of litigating prisoners' § 1983 suits, **Sentencing 331-340**
Association, freedom of as right of prisoners, **Sentencing 164-168**
Attorneys' fees, prisoner's § 1983 suit remedies, **Sentencing 352-357**
Bivens actions, mechanics of litigating prisoners' § 1983 suits, **Sentencing 324, 325**
Breaches of plea agreements, **Sentencing 24-28**

SENTENCING, CORRECTIONS, AND PRISONERS' RIGHTS, LAW OF—Cont'd

Cause of action, mechanics of litigating prisoners' § 1983 suits, **Sentencing 318-324**
Classification, transfers, and withholding of privileges, **Sentencing 202-227**
Community based sanctions, **Sentencing 68-89**
Community service, community-based sentencing options, **Sentencing 85-89**
Complaints, mechanics of litigating prisoners' § 1983 suits, **Sentencing 317-330**
Conditions of confinement, **Sentencing 265-272**
Constraints of government during and after plea process, **Sentencing 28-38**
Contempt proceedings, enforcement of court orders through, **Sentencing 369, 370**
Corrections law and prisoner's rights, generally, **Sentencing 139-148**
Cruel and unusual punishment, generally, **Sentencing 128-137, 255-280**
Damages, § 1983 suits remedies, **Sentencing 341-344**
Day-reporting centers, community-based sentencing options, **Sentencing 74**
Death penalty, **Sentencing 111-127**
Defenses, mechanics of litigating prisoners' § 1983 suits, **Sentencing 331-340**
Disciplinary proceedings, generally, **Sentencing 139-148**
Due process, **Sentencing 190-198, 202-221, 246-254**
Economic sanctions, community-based sentencing options, **Sentencing 76-84**
Eighth Amendment, generally, **Sentencing 128-137, 255-280**
Enforcement of court orders, remedies, **Sentencing 369, 370**
Equal protection, prisoner's rights, **Sentencing 221-227**
Equitable relief, prisoners' § 1983 suit remedies, **Sentencing 345-351**
Exhaustion of remedies, mechanics of litigating prisoners' § 1983 suits, **Sentencing 339, 340**
Factors considered at sentencing, **Sentencing 55-67**

SENTENCING, CORRECTIONS, AND PRISONERS' RIGHTS, LAW OF—Cont'd

First Amendment, prisoners' rights, **Sentencing 149-174**

Force, use of as cruel and unusual punishment, **Sentencing 272-280**

Fourth Amendment searches and seizures, prisoner's rights, **Sentencing 228-245**

Guilty pleas, **Sentencing 12-38**

Home confinement, community-based sentencing options, **Sentencing 74-76**

Immunity, mechanics of litigating prisoners' § 1983 suits, **Sentencing 331-338**

Intelligent guilty pleas, **Sentencing 14-23**

Jurisdiction, mechanics of litigating prisoners' § 1983 suits, **Sentencing 325, 326**

Limitation of actions, mechanics of litigating prisoners' § 1983 suits, **Sentencing 338**

Litigation of prisoners' rights, **Sentencing 317-371**

Medical care, **Sentencing 256-265**

Miranda warnings, **Sentencing 198-201**

Modification of court orders, remedies, **Sentencing 357-368**

Mootness, mechanics of litigating prisoners' § 1983 suits, **Sentencing 338, 339**

Official immunity, mechanics of litigating prisoners' § 1983 suits, **Sentencing 332-338**

Options for community-based sentencing, **Sentencing 70-84**

Parole and probation, generally, **Sentencing 281-304**

Personal injuries, due process claims for, **Sentencing 246-254**

Plea bargaining, **Sentencing 12-38**

Prisoners' rights. Corrections law and prisoner's rights, supra

Privacy, prisoner's rights, **Sentencing 235-245**

Probation and parole, generally, **Sentencing 281-304**

Procedural due process, corrections law and prisoner's rights, **Sentencing 190-198**

Property deprivations, due process claims for, **Sentencing 246-254**

Protection of inmates, use of force and as cruel and unusual punishment, **Sentencing 272-280**

SENTENCING, CORRECTIONS, AND PRISONERS' RIGHTS, LAW OF—Cont'd
Psychiatric care, **Sentencing 256-265**
Purposes of criminal sentences, **Sentencing 2**
Reform of sentencing proposals, **Sentencing 8-11**
Release, prisoner's rights upon, **Sentencing 305-316**
Release on parole, prisoner's rights, **Sentencing 295-304**
Religion, freedom of as prisoner's right, **Sentencing 169-174**
Remedies, litigation of prisoners' rights, **Sentencing 341-371**
Restoration of rights of released prisoners, **Sentencing 313-316**
Restricted opportunities and rights of released prisoners, **Sentencing 305-313**
Revocation of probation and parole, prisoner's rights as to, **Sentencing 283-295**
Searches and seizures, prisoner's rights, **Sentencing 228-245**
§ 1983 suits, **Sentencing 317-357**
Self-incrimination privilege in correctional context, prisoner's rights, **Sentencing 198-201**
Sentencing, generally, **Sentencing 1-137**
Sovereign immunity, mechanics of litigating prisoners' § 1983 suits, **Sentencing 331, 332**
Speech, freedom of as prisoner's right, **Sentencing 149-164**
Statute of limitations, mechanics of litigating prisoners' § 1983 suits, **Sentencing 338**
Statutes, **Sentencing 90-110, 338**
Sufficiency of complaint, mechanics of litigating prisoners' § 1983 suits, **Sentencing 326-330**
Transfers, classification, and withholding of privileges, **Sentencing 202-227**
Voluntary guilty pleas, **Sentencing 14-23**
Withholding of privileges, **Sentencing 202-227**

SERVICES
Corporations (this index)
Federal Income Taxation of Partners and Partnerships (this index)
International Taxation (this index)

SETTLEMENT

Compromise and Settlement (this index)

SEX DISCRIMINATION

Abortion, **Sex Discrim 13-25, 26-34, 223**
Affirmative action, **Sex Discrim 5, 62, 82, 83, 120-122, 182-190, 281-286, 288, 290, 293**
Age Discrimination in Employment Act, **Sex Discrim 197**
AIDS, **Sex Discrim 9, 39, 357**
Alimony, **Sex Discrim 159**
Bennett Amendment, Title VII, **Sex Discrim 196, 226-259, 263, 264**
Bill of Rights, **Sex Discrim 55-59, 63-69, 77-91, 110-112, 129-133, 183**
Bona fide occupational qualification, Title VII, **Sex Discrim 226, 265-274**
Caesarean sections, **Sex Discrim 36**
Child custody, **Sex Discrim 80, 117, 156, 163-166**
Child support, **Sex Discrim 117, 139, 156, 166-168**
Civic responsibilities, **Sex Discrim 1, 62, 120-122, 127-129**
Civil law distinct from criminal law, **Sex Discrim 8**
Civil remedies, **Sex Discrim 130-135, 195**
Civil war statutes, **Sex Discrim 196, 279**
Classification, statutory, **Sex Discrim 4 et seq.**
Community property, marital partners, **Sex Discrim 154, 155**
Comparable work, Equal Pay Act, **Sex Discrim 196, 199-216, 226-259, 263, 264, 274-279**
Comparable worth, **Sex Discrim 196, 225-244, 256, 258-260, 263, 264**
Compensatory legislation, **Sex Discrim 82, 83**
Contraception, **Sex Discrim 9-12, 19, 34, 35, 38-46**
Criminal law, **Sex Discrim 8, 11, 13-34, 51, 96-366, 368, 372-376**
Criminal procedure, **Sex Discrim 1, 62, 127-129, 353, 357, 360, 366-376**
Divorce and dissolution, **Sex Discrim 2, 54, 72, 80, 108, 117, 139, 154-168**
Domestic partners, **Sex Discrim 1, 2, 9, 54, 71 et seq.**

SEX DISCRIMINATION—Cont'd
Domicile, wives' disabilities, **Sex Discrim 1, 71, 70-82, 125-127, 150**
Due process clause, **Sex Discrim 1, 55-61, 63-69, 77-91, 110-112, 183**
Education, **Sex Discrim 51, 54, 73, 79, 96, 131, 137, 144-148, 231, 232, 237, 255, 293-304**
Employees Retirement Income Security Act, **Sex Discrim 160, 161, 176, 307**
Employment, generally, **Sex Discrim 9**
Equal Credit Opportunity Act, **Sex Discrim 305-307**
Equal Employment Opportunity Commission, **Sex Discrim 274**
Equal Pay Act, **Sex Discrim 196, 199-216, 226-259, 263, 264, 274-279**
Equal protection clause, **Sex Discrim 55-58, 66-69, 71-87, 94, 96-101, 109, 120, 144-148, 181, 188**
Equal Rights Amendment, Federal, **Sex Discrim 78, 95, 377-380**
Equal Rights Amendment, State, **Sex Discrim 4, 62, 78, 95, 107-109, 120-122, 146-148, 160, 309, 377**
Executive orders, **Sex Discrim 197**
Fair Labor Standards Act, **Sex Discrim 200**
First Amendment rights, **Sex Discrim 129, 133-137**
Fourteenth Amendment, **Sex Discrim 55-59, 63-69, 77-91, 110-112, 183**
Fundamental rights, generally, **Sex Discrim 1**
Gender, **Sex Discrim 4 et seq.**
Gender neutral statutes, **Sex Discrim 4, 69, 76, 85, 90, 92-106, 129-131, 145, 179-181, 185, 186, 188, 238-243, 339-343**
Gender standard of review, **Sex Discrim 4, 69, 76, 90, 92-106, 145, 181, 185, 186, 188**
Harassment, **Sex Discrim 194-196, 238-243**
Health care, **Sex Discrim 9, 34, 35, 37-51, 325, 375**
Housing, **Sex Discrim 197**
Immunity, **Sex Discrim 104, 112, 150, 151, 347-350**
Incest, **Sex Discrim 20, 51, 317, 318**
Incorporation, **Sex Discrim 63-65**
Indian Child Welfare Act, **Sex Discrim 166**

SEX DISCRIMINATION—Cont'd
Indians, tribal, **Sex Discrim 123-125**
Insurance, **Sex Discrim 307, 308**
Intent, invidious, **Sex Discrim 183, 200, 216, 227, 228, 234, 237**
Jury, women's exclusion, **Sex Discrim 1, 62, 87, 127-129**
Labor unions, **Sex Discrim 196, 218**
Language, **Sex Discrim 1, 4, 55, 57, 60, 87, 99, 103, 109, 114-119, 362, 377, 378**
Law, **Sex Discrim 3-5, 57, 109**
Majority, age of, **Sex Discrim 73, 86, 88**
Marital partners, **Sex Discrim 1, 2, 9, 54, 71, 72, 77, 80-82, 108, 117, 125-127, 139, 150-168, 313-321, 338; Sex Discrim 372**
Medical malpractice, **Sex Discrim 39, 49**
Men, generally, **Sex Discrim 2, 5, 9**
Military service, **Sex Discrim 49, 80, 83, 96, 97, 101-106, 120**
Minority women, **Sex Discrim 9, 104, 123-125, 166, 180, 193, 230, 352, 375**
Names, **Sex Discrim 54, 125-127**
National Labor Relations Act, **Sex Discrim 196**
Necessaries and support obligation, marital partners, **Sex Discrim 152, 153**
Nonmarital partners, **Sex Discrim 80, 117, 137-148, 156, 163-174, 180**
Pay equity, **Sex Discrim 196, 225, 227-244, 256, 258-260**
Pensions, **Sex Discrim 160-163, 264, 265**
Police power, state, **Sex Discrim 54, 55, 63-65, 110**
Pornography, **Sex Discrim 129-131, 339-343**
Precedent, **Sex Discrim 18, 343**
Pregnancy, **Sex Discrim 9-51, 83-86, 137, 138, 215, 223, 230, 253, 325, 375**
Prisons and jails, **Sex Discrim 351, 372-376**
Privacy, right of, **Sex Discrim 4, 10, 36, 69, 137-143, 355, 372**
Privileges and immunities clause, **Sex Discrim 55, 57**
Product liability, **Sex Discrim 38-49**
Prostitution, **Sex Discrim 100-356**
Public accommodations, **Sex Discrim 133-136, 308-310**
Rape, **Sex Discrim 20, 97-99, 328, 330, 332-338, 345, 368**

SEX DISCRIMINATION—Cont'd
Rational basis test, **Sex Discrim 66, 67, 72-87, 144, 181**
Regulations, **Sex Discrim 293**
Service clubs, public accommodations, **Sex Discrim 133-136, 308-310**
Sexual stereotyping, **Sex Discrim 1, 4, 55, 57, 60, 87, 99, 103, 109, 114-119, 362, 377, 378**
Single sex partners, **Sex Discrim 140-143, 164**
Social Security Act, **Sex Discrim 81, 175-180**
Sports, **Sex Discrim 144-148**
Standards of review, generally, **Sex Discrim 65, 93**
Sterilization, **Sex Discrim 11, 34, 35, 44**
Strict scrutiny, **Sex Discrim 67-69, 74, 81, 86, 109, 188**
Surrogacy, **Sex Discrim 8, 167-169**
Title IX, **Sex Discrim 196, 215, 217-279, 283, 284, 293-304**
Torts, **Sex Discrim 150-152, 154**

SHEPARDS
Legal Research (this index)

SKILLS
Trial and Practice Skills (this index)

SOCIAL SECURITY
Individual Employee Rights (this index)

SOCRATIC METHOD
How to Study Law and Take Law Exams (this index)

SOURCES OF LAW
Comparative Legal Traditions (this index)

SPEECH
Freedom of speech and press
  Injunctions (this index)

SPORTS LAW

Acceptance, formation of contracts, **Sports 2**
Administration, amateur sports, **Sports 201, 202**
Agents, **Sports 15-25, 218-220**
Amateur sports, generally, **Sports 201-205**
Amateur Sports Act of 1978, international sports, **Sports 249-251**
Americans with Disabilities Act, handicapped athlete, **Sports 232-234**
Anticipating reasonably foreseeable dangers, referee liability, **Sports 137, 138**
Antimarriage rules, eligibility, **Sports 217, 218**
Antitrust, generally, **Sports 52-70**
Arbitration and mediation, **Sports 47-51**
Assignment, **Sports 10, 28**
Assumption of risk, defenses, **Sports 156-167**
Baseball, **Sports 56, 57, 105-108, 163-166**
Battery, criminal liability, **Sports 198**
Boycotts, international sports, **Sports 252, 253**
Cable TV, antitrust, **Sports 67, 68**
Canadian Approach, criminal liability, **Sports 199, 200**
Car racing, **Sports 109-111, 161-163, 176, 177**
Charitable immunity, defenses, **Sports 184, 185**
Children, **Sports 92, 111-113, 166, 167, 177, 178**
Coach liability, generally, **Sports 122-133**
Collateral agreements, **Sports 8, 9**
Colleges and universities, **Sports 189, 235-246**
College scholarships, generally, **Sports 235-246**
Comparative negligence, defenses, **Sports 169, 170**
Competent coaches, school liability for failure to hire, **Sports 118**
Concerted activities, labor law, **Sports 45-47**
Conflicts of interest, agents, **Sports 18, 19**
Construction, facility liability, **Sports 93, 94**
Contact and noncontact sports, **Sports 100, 101, 278, 279**
Contracts, generally, **Sports 1-14**
Contributory negligence, defenses, **Sports 167-169**
Control of game, referee liability for failure to, **Sports 138, 139**

SPORTS LAW—Cont'd

Criminal liability, generally, **Sports 193-200**
Death penalty, NCAA, **Sports 259, 260**
Defamation, generally, **Sports 140-155**
Defenses, **Sports 11-13, 151-185**
Deferrals, financial considerations, **Sports 29-32**
Design, facility liability, **Sports 93, 94**
Discipline and penalties, generally, **Sports 257-264**
Discretionary acts, defense of sovereign immunity, **Sports 181-183**
Discrimination, sex discrimination, **Sports 275-288**
Drug testing, generally, **Sports 265-274**
Due process, drug testing, **Sports 273, 274**
Duties of agents, **Sports 16-18**
Education, **Sports 115-121, 189, 235-246, 260, 261**
Eligibility, generally, **Sports 206-225**
Employers and employees, **Sports 189-191, 246**
Enforcement of rules, referee liability for duty as to, **Sports 135, 136**
Equal protection, **Sports 273, 274, 284-287**
Equipment, school liability for failure to maintain, **Sports 120, 121**
ERAs of state, sex discrimination, **Sports 287, 288**
Estate planning, **Sports 36-38**
Exemptions, antitrust, **Sports 56-61**
Expressed assumption of risk, defenses, **Sports 160**
Facilities, **Sports 90-94, 113, 114, 120, 121**
Facility liability, **Sports 90-94**
Financial considerations, generally, **Sports 26-38**
Financial planning, generally, **Sports 33-38**
Foot races, waivers as defense, **Sports 175, 176**
Formation of contracts, **Sports 1-3**
Franchise movement, antitrust, **Sports 62-64**
Golf, **Sports 108, 109, 163-166**
Grievance, arbitration and mediation, **Sports 50**
Grove City and Civil Rights Restoration Act of 1987, sex discrimination, **Sports 281-284**

SPORTS LAW—Cont'd

Handicapped athlete, generally, **Sports 226-234**
High school sports, discipline and penalties, **Sports 260, 261**
Hockey, spectator injuries, **Sports 109-111**
Immunities, privileges and, **Sports 178-185, 207-210**
Implied assumption of risk, defenses, **Sports 160, 161**
Incorporation, financial considerations, **Sports 33**
Inherently violent sports, criminal liability, **Sports 196-198**
Instruction failure, school liability for, **Sports 118**
International sports, generally, **Sports 247-256**
Interpertation, formation of contracts, **Sports 2, 3**
Invasion of privacy, defamation, **Sports 149-151**
Investments, tax-sheltered investments, **Sports 32, 33**
Invitees, facility liability, **Sports 90-92**
Jockeys, assumption of risk defense, **Sports 161-163**
Labor law, generally, **Sports 39-51**
League versus league, antitrust, **Sports 64, 65**
Lockouts, **Sports 46, 47**
Maintenance and repair, facility liability, **Sports 93, 94**
Malpractice, generally, **Sports 75-86**
Mediation and arbitration, **Sports 47-51**
Medical malpractice, generally, **Sports 75-86**
Minors, **Sports 92, 111-113, 166, 167, 177, 178**
Mutuality as defense, contracts, **Sports 13**
National Labor Relations Act, **Sports 39-41**
NCAA, **Sports 22, 23, 204, 205, 258-260**
Negligence, generally, **Sports 71-75**
Negotiating contract, **Sports 13, 14**
NFL antitrust exemptions, **Sports 58**
No-agent rule, eligibility, **Sports 218-220**
No-cut, specialty clauses in contracts, **Sports 7, 8**
Noncontact sports, **Sports 100, 101, 278, 279**
Nonparticipants, workers' compensation, **Sports 191, 192**
Nonstatutory labor antitrust exemption, **Sports 58-61**
No pass, no play statutes, eligibility, **Sports 222-225**
No transfer rules, eligibility, **Sports 216, 217**

SPORTS LAW—Cont'd

Offer, formation of contracts, **Sports 1, 2**
Olympics, international sports, **Sports 247-249**
Option, specialty clauses in contracts, **Sports 6, 7**
Participant injuries, **Sports 95-103**
Penalties, generally, **Sports 257-264**
Pension plans, deferrals by, **Sports 29-31**
Per se defamation, **Sports 141-143**
Player restraints, antitrust, **Sports 61, 62**
Policy considerations, sovereign immunity defense, **Sports 183, 184**
Preparation of participants, coach liability for, **Sports 128-132**
Preservation of capital, financial planning, **Sports 34, 35**
Privacy, **Sports 149-151, 270-272**
Privileges and immunities, **Sports 178-185, 207-210**
Products liability, torts, **Sports 86, 87**
Professional sports, **Sports 94, 99, 100, 186-188, 261-267**
Proposition 48, eligibility, **Sports 220-222**
Protection against risk, financial planning, **Sports 35, 36**
Protection of participants, referee liability for duty as to, **Sports 136**
Public figures, defamation, **Sports 143-147**
Qualifications, coach liability, **Sports 125-138**
Racing cars, **Sports 109-111, 161-163, 176, 177**
Reasonableness of search, drug testing, **Sports 272, 273**
Red shirting rules, eligibility, **Sports 215, 216**
Referee liability, generally, **Sports 134-139**
Registration of agents, **Sports 19-23**
Rehabilitation Act, Section 504 of, **Sports 230-232**
Remedies, contracts, **Sports 10, 11**
Reserve, specialty clauses in contracts, **Sports 7**
Rule-making, amateur sports, **Sports 203**
Rule of repose, defamation, **Sports 148, 149**
Safety rules violation, participant injuries, **Sports 97, 98**
Salary, arbitration and mediation, **Sports 50, 51**
School liability, generally, **Sports 115-121**

SPORTS LAW—Cont'd

Schools, **Sports 115-121, 189, 235-246, 260, 261**
Scope of eligibility rules, **Sports 206, 207**
Section 504 of Rehabilitation Act, **Sports 230-232**
Separate but equal, sex discrimination, **Sports 277, 278**
Sex discrimination, generally, **Sports 275-288**
Skiing, assumption of risk defense, **Sports 163-166**
Sovereign immunity defense, **Sports 178-184**
Specialty clauses in contracts, **Sports 6-8**
Spectator injuries, **Sports 104-114**
Sportwriters, defamation, **Sports 140, 141**
Standard player's contract, **Sports 3-6**
State actors, eligibility, **Sports 210-212**
State legislation, registration of agents, **Sports 19, 20**
Status, **Sports 90, 202, 203**
Strict liability, torts, **Sports 88, 89**
Strikes, **Sports 46**
Substantially nonvested property, deferrals by, **Sports 31, 32**
Supervision, **Sports 119, 120, 132, 133**
Taxation, generally, **Sports 26-28**
Tax-sheltered investments, **Sports 32, 33**
Terminations, contracts, **Sports 9**
Third persons, participant injuries, **Sports 102, 103**
Title IX, sex discrimination, **Sports 279-284**
Torts, generally, **Sports 71-94**
TV packaging, antitrust, **Sports 66-68**
Unclean hands as defense, contracts, **Sports 12**
Unconscionability as defense, contracts, **Sports 12, 13**
Unions, generally, **Sports 39-51**
Universities, **Sports 189, 235-246**
Unreasonably hazardous conditions, facility liability, **Sports 92, 93**
Unsportmanlike conduct, participant injuries, **Sports 98, 99**
Vicarious liability, school liability, **Sports 117, 118**
Violation of safety rules, participant injuries, **Sports 97, 98**
Violence in sports, criminal liability, **Sports 193-195**

SPORTS LAW—Cont'd
Waivers, defenses, **Sports 172-178**
Warnings, **Sports 118, 136, 137, 170-172**
Warranty liability, torts, **Sports 89, 90**
Workers' compensation, generally, **Sports 186-192**
Wrestling, spectator injuries, **Sports 109-111**

STAFFING
Health Care Law and Ethics (this index)

STANDARDS
Tax Procedure and Tax Fraud (this index)

STATE AND LOCAL TAXATION AND FINANCE
Generally, **State & Loc Tax & Fin 1-4**
Accounting requirements, expenditure patterns, **State & Loc Tax & Fin 115-117**
Appropriations process, expenditure patterns, **State & Loc Tax & Fin 109-115**
Arbitrage bonds, **State & Loc Tax & Fin 184-186**
Auditing, expenditure patterns, **State & Loc Tax & Fin 115-117**
Bankruptcy, Federal Bankruptcy Code, **State & Loc Tax & Fin 101, 102, 210-218**
Bonds, **State & Loc Tax & Fin 143-186**
Budgetary requirements, expenditure patterns, **State & Loc Tax & Fin 108-121**
Capital expenditures, **State & Loc Tax & Fin 135-240**
Ceilings on debt, **State & Loc Tax & Fin 229-240**
Coal severance taxes, **State & Loc Tax & Fin 71, 72**
Collective bargaining and employee salaries, expenditure patterns, **State & Loc Tax & Fin 121-124**
Commerce clause, **State & Loc Tax & Fin 13-27**
Constitutional law, generally, **State & Loc Tax & Fin 5-29**
Consumer loan bonds, **State & Loc Tax & Fin 182**
Crises, state and local government responses to fiscal crises, **State & Loc Tax & Fin 132-134**
Debt financing, **State & Loc Tax & Fin 135-240**

STATE AND LOCAL TAXATION AND FINANCE —Cont'd

Definitions, **State & Loc Tax & Fin 138-143**
Due process clause, **State & Loc Tax & Fin 10-13**
Enabling legislation, compliance with state, **State & Loc Tax & Fin 218-229**
Entertainment taxes, **State & Loc Tax & Fin 67-69**
Equal protection clause, **State & Loc Tax & Fin 9, 10**
Estate and gift taxes, **State & Loc Tax & Fin 73-75**
Exemptions, tax exempt status of bonds, **State & Loc Tax & Fin 177-186**
Expenditure patterns, **State & Loc Tax & Fin 108-134**
Federal Bankruptcy Code, **State & Loc Tax & Fin 101, 102, 210-218**
Federal securities laws, **State & Loc Tax & Fin 201-207**
Fines, **State & Loc Tax & Fin 102, 103**
Full faith and credit obligation, **State & Loc Tax & Fin 186-190**
General obligation bonds, **State & Loc Tax & Fin 143-154**
Gross receipts taxes, **State & Loc Tax & Fin 66, 67**
Impact taxes, **State & Loc Tax & Fin 95-98**
Industrial development bonds (IBDs), **State & Loc Tax & Fin 170-172, 177-182**
Intergovernmental aid, **State & Loc Tax & Fin 103-107, 117-120**
Internal Revenue Code, **State & Loc Tax & Fin 100, 101, 207-210**
License fees, **State & Loc Tax & Fin 75-81**
Limits, expenditure patterns, **State & Loc Tax & Fin 124-126**
Long-term bonds, **State & Loc Tax & Fin 143-173**
Louisiana's first use tax, **State & Loc Tax & Fin 73**
Moral obligation bonds, **State & Loc Tax & Fin 165-169**
Mortgage subsidy bonds, **State & Loc Tax & Fin 182-184**
Multifamily housing bonds, **State & Loc Tax & Fin 182-184**
New York City stock transfer tax, **State & Loc Tax & Fin 69, 70**
Notes, short-term notes, **State & Loc Tax & Fin 172-177**
Oil and gas severance taxes, **State & Loc Tax & Fin 72, 73**
Personal property taxes, **State & Loc Tax & Fin 38-40**
Privileges and immunities clause, **State & Loc Tax & Fin 28, 29**

STATE AND LOCAL TAXATION AND FINANCE —Cont'd

Real estate special assessments and special benefit principle, **State & Loc Tax & Fin 81-90**

Real estate taxes, **State & Loc Tax & Fin 29-38**

Revenue bonds, **State & Loc Tax & Fin 154-165**

Sales and use taxes, **State & Loc Tax & Fin 43-67**

School finance requirements, expenditure patterns, **State & Loc Tax & Fin 126-131**

Securities, federal securities laws, **State & Loc Tax & Fin 201-207**

Severance taxes, **State & Loc Tax & Fin 70-73**

Short-term notes, **State & Loc Tax & Fin 172-177**

Special assessments, **State & Loc Tax & Fin 81-109**

Special benefit principle, real estate special assessments, **State & Loc Tax & Fin 81-90**

Special districts, revenue sources for, **State & Loc Tax & Fin 98-100**

Stock and stockholders, New York City stock transfer tax, **State & Loc Tax & Fin 69, 70**

Supremacy clause, **State & Loc Tax & Fin 27, 28**

User charges, special assessments and, **State & Loc Tax & Fin 81-109**

STATE CONSTITUTIONAL LAW

Generally, **State Const 1, 2**

Absurd results, literal meaning, **State Const 10-14**

Acreage restrictions, homestead exemptions, **State Const 247, 248**

Adequate and independent state ground, state declaration of rights, **State Const 37-42**

Ad valorem tax base, **State Const 223, 224**

Advisory opinions, judicial branch, **State Const 156, 157**

Alienation, homestead exemptions, **State Const 249**

Allocation of power between state and its subdivisions, **State Const 6**

Amendments to state constitutions, **State Const 264-275**

STATE CONSTITUTIONAL LAW—Cont'd

Appointment, governor's appointment power, **State Const 62-69**
Ballot summary, extrinsic evidence of meaning, **State Const 25-27**
Bonds, **State Const 212-214, 219-222, 225-227**
Charitable exemptions, taxation, **State Const 242-244**
Choice of rule of interpretation, **State Const 28, 29**
Clemency, governor, **State Const 69-73**
Compensation, legislators, **State Const 102-105**
Constitutional Convention, amendments to state constitutions, **State Const 272, 273**
Construction rules, **State Const 8-32**
Debt, revenue and taxation, **State Const 215, 216, 218, 219, 223-225**
Declaration of rights, **State Const 33-50**
Delegation
  judicial power, separation of powers, **State Const 189-191**
  legislative power, separation of powers, **State Const 188, 189**
Devise of homestead exemptions, **State Const 249, 250**
Discipline of judges, judicial branch, **State Const 165-169**
Education provisions, **State Const 252-254**
Elections
  amendments to state constitutions, **State Const 274, 275**
  governor, **State Const 52-57**
  legislators, **State Const 97-102**
  recall elections of public officials, **State Const 255, 256**
Estate taxes, **State Const 234, 235**
Evidence, intrinsic evidence of meaning, **State Const 14-19**
Executive branch, generally, **State Const 51-86**
Exemptions
  charitable exemptions, taxation, **State Const 242-244**
  homestead exemptions, **State Const 246-250**
  public property, tax exemption, **State Const 239-242**
  tax exemptions, **State Const 239-245**
Expressio unius est exclusio alterius, **State Const 14-17**
Expulsion, legislators, **State Const 97-102**
Extrinsic evidence of meaning, **State Const 19-27**

STATE CONSTITUTIONAL LAW—Cont'd
Federal Constitutional limitations, revenue and taxation, **State Const 211, 212**
Federal versus state constitutional power, **State Const 6, 7**
Future, state declaration of rights, **State Const 48-50**
General laws, legislative branch, **State Const 109-122**
General nonproperty tax provisions, **State Const 230, 231**
General obligation bonds, revenue and taxation, **State Const 219, 220**
Governor, generally, **State Const 51-86**
Historical role, state declaration of rights, **State Const 34, 35**
Home rule provisions, **State Const 203-208**
Homestead exemptions, **State Const 246-250**
Identical or similar constitutional provisions, state declaration of rights, **State Const 46-48**
Impeachment of state officials, **State Const 254, 255**
Income taxes, constitutional provisions pertaining to, **State Const 232-234**
Inconsistencies within constitutions, **State Const 17-19**
Initiative and referendum
- generally, **State Const 256-259**
- amendments to state constitutions by initiative petition, **State Const 269-272**
- revenue and taxation, **State Const 217, 218, 225**

Intent, literal meaning, **State Const 10-14**
Intrinsic evidence of meaning, **State Const 14-19**
Judges
- discipline of judges, **State Const 165-169**
- removal of judges, **State Const 165-169**
- retention of judges, **State Const 164, 165**
- selection of judges, **State Const 164, 165**

Judicial branch, generally, **State Const 123-169**
Judicial deference to and usurpation of legislative power, separation of powers, **State Const 172-176**
Judicial power
- executive usurpation of judicial power, separation of powers, **State Const 184-186**
- judicial power, separation of powers, **State Const 189-191**

STATE CONSTITUTIONAL LAW—Cont'd
Judicial power—Cont'd
legislative usurpation of judicial power, separation of powers, **State Const 186-188**
Jurisdiction, judicial branch, **State Const 142-151**
Just value, meaning of, **State Const 236, 237**
Lawyer governance and regulation of practice of law, judicial branch, **State Const 157-161**
Legislative branch, generally, **State Const 87-122**
Legislature and legislators
amendments to state constitutions, **State Const 265-268**
delegation of legislative power, **State Const 188, 189**
executive usurpation of legislative power, **State Const 182-184**
governor, **State Const 57-61**
interpretation of constitutions, extrinsic evidence of meaning, **State Const 22-25**
separation of powers, **State Const 172-189**
super majority requirements, revenue and taxation, **State Const 216, 217**
usurpation of power, **State Const 172-179, 186-188**
Lieutenant governor, **State Const 76-79**
Limitations and restrictions
alienation, homestead exemptions, **State Const 249**
bond restrictions, local government, **State Const 225-227**
constitutional restrictions on debt of local government, revenue and taxation, **State Const 223**
devise of homestead exemptions, **State Const 249, 250**
exercise of state power limited, generally, **State Const 2, 3**
homestead exemptions, **State Const 247-250**
imposition of tax, restrictions on, **State Const 227-245**
local govenment, **State Const 194-198, 202, 203, 225-227**
long term indebtedness, restrictions on, **State Const 212-227**
revenue and taxation, **State Const 211-215, 223-225**
special and local legislation, **State Const 109-122**
taxation, **State Const 211-215, 223-225, 227-245**
Literal meaning, intent, and absurd results, **State Const 10-14**
Local government, generally, **State Const 192-210**
Mandatory provisions, effect of, **State Const 29, 30**

STATE CONSTITUTIONAL LAW—Cont'd
Military power, governor, **State Const 74-76**
Origination clauses, legislative branch, **State Const 94-97**
Plain statement rule, state declaration of rights, **State Const 42-45**
Privileges, legislators, **State Const 97-102**
Public officers and employees
  executive officers and departments, **State Const 79-86**
  impeachment of state officials, **State Const 254, 255**
  recall elections of public officials, **State Const 255, 256**
  removal of state officials, **State Const 254, 255**
Public property, tax exemption, **State Const 239-242**
Qualifications
  governor, **State Const 52-57**
  judicial branch, **State Const 161-164**
  legislators, **State Const 97-102**
Reaffirmation of existing power, **State Const 4, 5**
Reapportinment, **State Const 259-261**
Recall elections of public officials, **State Const 255, 256**
Regulating exercise of state power, generally, **State Const 3, 4**
Removal
  governor's removal power, **State Const 62-69**
  judges, judicial branch, **State Const 165-169**
  state officials, **State Const 254, 255**
Repayment of debt, revenue and taxation, **State Const 224, 225**
Retention of judges, judicial branch, **State Const 164, 165**
Revenue, generally, **State Const 211-245**
Revision Commissions, amendments to state constitutions, **State Const 268, 269**
Rulemaking, judicial branch, **State Const 151-156**
Rules of construction, **State Const 8-32**
School districts, **State Const 208-210**
School lands and school fund, administration of, **State Const 262, 263**
Selection of judges, judicial branch, **State Const 164, 165**
Separation of powers, **State Const 170-191**
Sessions, legislative branch, **State Const 88-94**
Single subject requirement, legislative branch, **State Const 105-108**

STATE CONSTITUTIONAL LAW—Cont'd
Sovereign immunity, **State Const 261, 262**
Special and local legislation, limitations on, **State Const 109-122**
Statutes
generally, **State Const 251, 252**
judicial usurpation of legislative power, separation of powers, **State Const 176-179**
use of rules of, **State Const 31, 32**
Succession to office of governor, lieutenant governor, **State Const 76-79**
Taxation, generally, **State Const 211-245**
Term of office, governor, **State Const 52-57**
Title requirement, legislative branch, **State Const 108, 109**
Uniformity clauses, revenue and taxation, **State Const 227-230**
Use valuation, **State Const 237-239**
Usurpation of power, **State Const 172-188**
Value or valuation
just value, meaning of, **State Const 236, 237**
taxation according to valuation, requirement of, **State Const 235, 236**
use valuation, **State Const 237-239**
Waiver of sovereign immunity, **State Const 261, 262**

STATES
Constitutional law. **State Constitutional Law** (this index)
Courts. **Federal Jurisdiction** (this index)
Hazardous Wastes and Toxic Substances, Law of (this index)
International Environmental Law (this index)
Regulation
State and Local Taxation and Finance (this index)

STATUTE OF FRAUDS
Generally, **Contracts 138 et seq.**

STATUTE OF LIMITATIONS
Tax Procedure and Tax Fraud (this index)

STATUTES
Analysis. **Legal Writing** (this index)
Injunctions (this index)
Landlord and Tenant (this index)
Legal Research (this index)
Legal Writing (this index)
Medical Liability (this index)
State Constitutional Law (this index)

STOCK AND STOCKHOLDERS
International Taxation (this index)

STRUCTURE
Staffing. **Health Care Law and Ethics** (this index)

STUDIES AND STUDYING
Law, The Study and Practice of (this index)

SUBDIVISIONS
Land Use (this index)

SUBROGATION
Insurance Law (this index)

TAXATION
Federal Taxes (this index)
Fraud. **Tax Procedure and Tax Fraud** (this index)
International Taxation (this index)

TAX PROCEDURE AND TAX FRAUD
Generally, **First Amd 1-7**
ABA opinion, hazards and standards of tax practice, **First Amd 349-351**
Abuse of discretion, retroactive revocation of rulings, **First Amd 38-40**
Accuracy penalties, **First Amd 183-192**
Administrative appeals, audits, **First Amd 62-66**

TAX PROCEDURE AND TAX FRAUD—Cont'd
Administrative collection procedures, **First Amd 217-227**
Aiding and assisting, criminal provisions of IRC, **First Amd 307, 308**
Amount of tax involved, criminal investigations, **First Amd 263**
Appeals, audits, **First Amd 62-66**
Art Law (this index)
Assessment, collection process, **First Amd 210, 211**
Attempted evasion, criminal provisions of IRC, **First Amd 298-302**
Attorney-client privilege, IRS investigatory powers and techniques, **First Amd 295, 296**
Attorneys' fees, additional civil tax litigation considerations, **First Amd 139-147**
Audits, **First Amd 55-71**
Avoidance, evasion versus, **First Amd 3, 4**
Bank deposits method of proof of unreported income, federal tax crimes, **First Amd 323**
Burden of proof, additional civil tax litigation considerations, **First Amd 127-132**
Cash expenditures method of proof of unreported income, federal tax crimes, **First Amd 323, 324**
Choice of forum in civil tax litigation, **First Amd 95-126**
Churches, IRS summons power, **First Amd 287**
Circular 230, hazards and standards of tax practice, **First Amd 351-357, 361-365**
Circumstantial evidence, willfulness in tax crimes, **First Amd 328, 329**
Civil fraud penalty, **First Amd 156-165**
Civil penalties and interest, generally, **First Amd 149-176**
Closing agreements, audits, **First Amd 66-71**
Collateral agreements, audits, **First Amd 70**
Collateral estoppel, additional civil tax litigation considerations, **First Amd 132-139**
Collection process, generally, **First Amd 209-232**
Comparison of IRS summons and grand jury summons, **First Amd 290, 291**

TAX PROCEDURE AND TAX FRAUD—Cont'd

Compliance, IRS summons power, **First Amd 274-276**
Conferences, criminal investigations, **First Amd 263-267**
Confidentiality versus disclosure, generally, **First Amd 42-53**
Conspiracy, federal tax crimes, **First Amd 310-313**
Corporations (this index)
Criminal matters
  federal tax crimes, generally, **First Amd 298-324**
  investigations, generally, **First Amd 253-269**
  willfulness in tax crimes, **First Amd 325-342**
Defenses, willfulness in tax crimes, **First Amd 329-341**
Deficiencies
  interest on, **First Amd 176-178**
  statutes of limitations, deficiency assessment, **First Amd 72-82**
Definition, willfulness in tax crimes, **First Amd 326-328**
Delay, tax court proceedings instituted for, **First Amd 175, 176**
Delinquency penalties, **First Amd 150-152, 199-202**
Demand, collection process, **First Amd 210, 211**
Determination letters, informal IRS rulings, **First Amd 33**
Disciplinary action, hazards and standards of tax practice, **First Amd 363-365**
Disclosure
  confidentiality versus disclosure, generally, **First Amd 42-53**
  grand jury investigations, **First Amd 291, 292**
  voluntary disclosure, criminal investigations, **First Amd 262, 263**
Discretion, discriminatory treatment as abuse of discretion, **First Amd 38-40**
Discriminatory treatment as abuse of discretion, retroactive revocation of rulings, **First Amd 38-40**
Duration of federal tax lien, collection process, **First Amd 214**
Education of defendant, willfulness in tax crimes, **First Amd 341, 342**
Enforcement proceedings, IRS summons power, **First Amd 280-283**

TAX PROCEDURE AND TAX FRAUD—Cont'd
Evasion
attempted evasion, criminal provisions of IRC, **First Amd 298-302**
avoidance, evasion versus, **First Amd 3, 4**
Evidence
burden of proof, additional civil tax litigation considerations, **First Amd 127-132**
circumstantial evidence, willfulness in tax crimes, **First Amd 328, 329**
unreported income, federal tax crimes, **First Amd 320-324**
willfulness, **First Amd 263, 328, 329**
Exhaustion of administrative remedies, additional civil tax litigation considerations, **First Amd 145-147**
Expedited plea procedures, criminal investigations, **First Amd 267, 268**
Experience of defendant, willfulness in tax crimes, **First Amd 341, 342**
Extension by agreement for time limits on assessing deficiencies, statutes of limitations, **First Amd 79-81**
False document submitted, criminal provisions of IRC, **First Amd 309**
False statements
criminal provisions of IRC, **First Amd 305-307**
federal tax crimes, **First Amd 313**
Federal Estate and Gift Taxation (this index)
Federal Income Taxation of Partners and Partnerships (this index)
Federal Income Taxation (this index)
Federal tax crimes, generally, **First Amd 298-324**
Federal Taxes (this index)
Federal tax lien, collection process, **First Amd 211-217**
Fiduciaries, third-party liability, **First Amd 240, 241**
Fifth Amendment, IRS investigatory powers and techniques, **First Amd 293-295**
Freedom of Information Act, confidentiality versus disclosure, **First Amd 42-45**
Frivolous returns, penalties for, **First Amd 175**

TAX PROCEDURE AND TAX FRAUD—Cont'd

Generation-skipping transfer tax. **Federal Estate and Gift Taxation** (this index) generally
Gift taxes. **Federal Estate and Gift Taxation** (this index)
Grand jury investigations, generally, **First Amd 287-292**
Hazards of tax practice, generally, **First Amd 343-365**
Health of taxpayer
  criminal investigations, **First Amd 263**
  willfulness in tax crimes, **First Amd 341, 342**
Impact of IMPACT, hazards and standards of tax practice, **First Amd 358-361**
Impeding administration, criminal provisions of IRC, **First Amd 309, 310**
Income tax. **Corporations** (this index)
Increased fines, federal tax crimes, **First Amd 317-319**
Informal IRS rulings, **First Amd 24-36**
Information reporting penalties, **First Amd 181-183**
Innocent spouse rules, third-party liability, **First Amd 233-237**
Interest, generally, **First Amd 149-176**
International Taxation (this index)
Investigations
  criminal investigations, **First Amd 253-269**
  grand jury investigations, **First Amd 287-292**
  IRS investigatory powers and techniques, **First Amd 271-298**
IRS
  generally, **First Amd 5, 6**
  comparison of IRS summons and grand jury summons, **First Amd 290, 291**
  federal tax crimes, **First Amd 298-310**
  hazards and standards of tax practice, **First Amd 361-365**
  informal IRS rulings, **First Amd 24-36**
  investigatory powers and techniques, **First Amd 271-298**
Jeopardy and termination assessments, collection process, **First Amd 227-232**
John Doe summons, IRS summons power, **First Amd 286, 287**
Joint ABA/AICPA proposed standards, **First Amd 357, 358**
Judicial collection procedures, **First Amd 217-227**

TAX PROCEDURE AND TAX FRAUD—Cont'd

Judicial review of regulations, Treasury Department, **First Amd 14-17**

Jurisdictional requirements, choice of forum in civil tax litigation, **First Amd 100-104**

Justice Department
- generally, **First Amd 7**
- criminal investigations, **First Amd 263-267**

Legislative regulations, Treasury Department, **First Amd 13, 14**

Lesser included offenses, federal tax crimes, **First Amd 316, 317**

Letter rulings, informal IRS rulings, **First Amd 26-33**

Levy, judicial and administrative collection procedures, **First Amd 219-226**

Liens, collection process, **First Amd 211-217**

Mail fraud, federal tax crimes, **First Amd 314-316**

Major count policy, criminal investigations, **First Amd 268**

Mistake of law, willfulness in tax crimes, **First Amd 329-332**

Mitigation of statutory time limits, **First Amd 86-94**

Naked assessments, additional civil tax litigation considerations, **First Amd 130-132**

Negligence penalties, **First Amd 153-156**

Net worth method of proof of unreported income, federal tax crimes, **First Amd 322, 323**

Nolo contendere pleas, criminal investigations, **First Amd 269**

Notice, collection process, **First Amd 210, 211, 214, 215**

Objections, IRS summons power, **First Amd 276-280**

Obstructing administration, criminal provisions of IRC, **First Amd 309, 310**

Overpayments
- interest on, **First Amd 176-178**
- statutes of limitations, **First Amd 82-85**

Penalties and interest
- generally, **First Amd 149-176**
- federal tax crimes, **First Amd 317-319**

Perjury, federal tax crimes, **First Amd 313, 314**

Plea agreements, criminal investigations, **First Amd 267-269**

Powers of attorney, hazards and standards of tax practice, **First Amd 362, 363**

TAX PROCEDURE AND TAX FRAUD—Cont'd

Pre-IMPACT penalties, **First Amd 149-176**
Preparer penalties, **First Amd 173-175, 192-198**
Privacy Act, confidentiality versus disclosure, **First Amd 42-45**
Privileges and protections, IRS investigatory powers and techniques, **First Amd 293-297**
Procedural regulations, IRS and Treasury Department rulemaking, **First Amd 23, 24**
Promoter penalties, **First Amd 192-198**
Proposals
amendments of 1986, hazards and standards of tax practice, **First Amd 351-357**
Joint ABA/AICPA proposed standards, **First Amd 357, 358**
Protections and privileges, IRS investigatory powers and techniques, **First Amd 293-297**
Protester penalties, **First Amd 192-198**
Reasonable basis standard of tax practice, **First Amd 345-349**
Refunds, statutes of limitations, **First Amd 82-85**
Release of federal tax lien, collection process, **First Amd 215-217**
Res judicata, additional civil tax litigation considerations, **First Amd 132-139**
Resolution of audit, **First Amd 60-62**
Retroactivity
revocation of rulings, **First Amd 36-40**
Treasury Department regulations, **First Amd 17-23**
Returns
audits, selecting returns for, **First Amd 55, 56**
confidentiality versus disclosure, **First Amd 45-50**
frivolous returns, penalties for, **First Amd 175**
penalties, **First Amd 149-176, 178-208**
pre-IMPACT penalties, **First Amd 149-176**
Revenue rulings, informal IRS rulings, **First Amd 25, 26**
RICO, federal tax crimes, **First Amd 314-316**
Sale of seized property, judicial and administrative collection procedures, **First Amd 226, 227**
Search warrants, IRS investigatory powers and techniques, **First Amd 292, 293**

TAX PROCEDURE AND TAX FRAUD—Cont'd

Sentence and punishment
  federal tax crimes, **First Amd 317-319**
  penalties and interest, supra
Sentencing guidelines, federal tax crimes, **First Amd 317-319**
Service of summons, IRS investigatory powers and techniques, **First Amd 272, 273**
Settlements, audits, **First Amd 66-71**
Stacking criminal charges, federal tax crimes, **First Amd 316, 317**
Standards
  confidentiality versus disclosure, standard of review, **First Amd 50, 51**
  tax practice standards, generally, **First Amd 343-365**
State and Local Taxation and Finance (this index)
Statute of limitations
  generally, **First Amd 72-94**
  criminal provisions of IRC, **First Amd 310**
Steps involved in criminal investigations, **First Amd 257-261**
Strategic considerations, choice of forum in civil tax litigation, **First Amd 121-126**
Subpoena power, grand jury investigations, **First Amd 289, 290**
Substantial understatement penalty, **First Amd 165-171**
Summons, IRS investigatory powers and techniques, **First Amd 271-287**
Taxpayer protections, audits, **First Amd 58-60**
Technical advice, informal IRS rulings, **First Amd 33, 34**
Termination assessments, collection process, **First Amd 227-232**
Third parties
  IRS summons power, third party recordkeeper, **First Amd 283-286**
  liability, generally, **First Amd 233-252**
Transferees, third-party liability, **First Amd 237-240**
Treasury Department and the IRS, generally, **First Amd 5, 6**
Trust fund taxes, third-party liability, **First Amd 241-252**
Uncertainty in tax law, willfulness in tax crimes, **First Amd 332-341**

TAX PROCEDURE AND TAX FRAUD—Cont'd
United States Claims Court, choice of forum in civil tax litigation, **First Amd 118-121**
United States District Court, choice of forum in civil tax litigation, **First Amd 113-118**
United States Tax Court
- additional civil tax litigation considerations, **First Amd 128**
- choice of forum in civil tax litigation, **First Amd 97-113**
- delay, tax court proceedings instituted for, **First Amd 175, 176**

Unreported income, federal tax crimes, **First Amd 320-324**
Valuation penalties, **First Amd 171, 172**
Voluntary disclosure, criminal investigations, **First Amd 262, 263**
Waiver or estoppel, additional civil tax litigation considerations, **First Amd 132-139**
Willfulness
- generally, **First Amd 325-342**
- criminal provisions of IRC, willful failure to file or pay, **First Amd 303-305**

Wire fraud, federal tax crimes, **First Amd 314-316**
Work product doctrine, IRS investigatory powers and techniques, **First Amd 296, 297**
Written determinations, confidentiality versus disclosure, **First Amd 51-53**

TELECOMMUNICATIONS
Generally, **Mass Comm 1 et seq.**

TENANTS
Landlord and Tenant (this index)

TERMINATION
Employment. **Individual Employee Rights** (this index)
Labor Arbitration Law and Practice (this index)
Lease. **Landlord and Tenant** (this index)

TEXTS
Legal Research (this index)

THIRD PARTIES
Insurance Law (this index)
Landlord and Tenant (this index)
Personal Property (this index)
Tax Procedure and Tax Fraud (this index)
Uniform Commercial Code (this index)

TIERED PARTNERSHIPS
Federal Income Taxation of Partners and Partnerships (this index)

TIME
Federal Income Taxation of Partners and Partnerships (this index)
Insurance Law (this index)
Legal Negotiation (this index)

TORTS
Absolute liability, generally, **Torts 31**
Accord and satisfaction, generally, **Torts 303**
Admiralty, injuries occurring under admiralty jurisdiction, **Torts 251**
Alcoholic beverages, liability of persons furnishing for injury caused by, **Torts 293, 295**
Alternative liability, **Torts 28**
Animals, strict liability, **Torts 33, 34**
Arrest, **Torts 134, 173**
Assault, generally, **Torts 132**
Assumpsit, **Torts 15**
Assumption of risk, generally, **Torts 115**
Attractive nuisance doctrine, liablity to trespassing children, **Torts 188**
Authority of law, **Torts 172-174**
Automobiles, **Torts 255, 257, 258, 260**
Aviation, **Torts 40, 145**
Battery, **Torts 131, 132**

TORTS—Cont'd

Case, action on the case distinguished from trespass action, **Torts 14, 18**
Causation, **Torts 25, 26, 28-30, 77**
Charities, immunity, **Torts 351**
Chattels, interference with, generally, **Torts 146**
Children, **Torts 55, 188**
Common carriers, highest degree of care, **Torts 98**
Common law, evolution of tort causes of action, **Torts 12**
Comparative negligence, **Torts 109**
Compensatory damages, **Torts 303**
Consent, **Torts 159, 161, 162**
Consortium, **Torts 314**
Constitutional torts, generally, **Torts 295**
Contract, **Torts 47, 217, 220, 221, 331, 332, 334-336**
Contribution, **Torts 326**
Contributory negligence, generally, **Torts 105**
Conversion, interference with chattels, **Torts 150, 152**
Damages, generally, **Torts 303**
Deceit, generally, **Torts 405**
Defamation, generally, **Torts 379**
Defense and recovery of property, generally, **Torts 166, 167**
Defense of self and others, **Torts 163, 165**
Definition of tort, **Torts 1, 4**
Definition problems, **Torts 1, 4**
Discipline, privilege to, **Torts 175**
Dram shop liability, commercial vendors, **Torts 293**
Duty, generally, **Torts 47**
Emotional distress, **Torts 137-141, 286-288, 290**
Employees, **Torts 229, 231-233, 241**
Employers, **Torts 229, 233, 236-238, 241-243, 248, 251**
Enterprise liability, **Torts 29**
Environmental law, nuisance, **Torts 283**
Evolution of tort law, **Torts 12**
Fact and law, issues distinguished, **Torts 22**
False imprisonment, generally, **Torts 134**

TORTS—Cont'd
Fault, **Torts 2, 7, 8, 31**
Fault in general, **Torts 2, 20**
Federal Tort Claims Act, **Torts 343**
Goals of tort law, **Torts 5**
Governmental liability, **Torts 342**
History of tort law, **Torts 12**
How to Study Law and Take Law Exams (this index)
Immunities, generally, **Torts 341**
Indemnity, **Torts 328**
Independent contractor, **Torts 232, 237, 239-241**
Infants, **Torts 55, 188**
Infliction of emotional distress, **Torts 137-141, 286-288, 290**
Insanity, effect upon liability for negligence, **Torts 54**
Insurance Law (this index)
Intent, generally, **Torts 127**
Intoxication, **Torts 54, 293, 295**
Invasion of privacy. Privacy, infra
Invitees, duty of landowner to, **Torts 197**
Joint tortfeasors, **Torts 27, 229, 321-324, 326, 328**
Jones Act, **Torts 253**
Judge, role of, **Torts 22, 60**
Jurisprudential basis of tort law, **Torts 5**
Jury, role of, **Torts 22, 60**
Land, generally, **Torts 141, 166, 167, 177, 273**
Landlord and tenant, liability of lessors, **Torts 207, 208, 214**
Last clear chance, **Torts 108**
Legal authority, generally, **Torts 134, 172-174**
Lessors, liability of, **Torts 207, 208, 214**
Liability without fault, generally, **Torts 31, 229 255, 257, 258, 260**
Libel, generally, **Torts 384**
Licensees, owners and occupiers of land, **Torts 195, 196**
Malpractice, professional negligence, **Torts 270, 272**
Manufacturers, generally, **Torts 217**
Maritime employees, **Torts 251**

TORTS—Cont'd
Market share liability, **Torts 29**
Medical malpractice crisis, professional negligence, **Torts 272**
Mental distress, **Torts 137-141, 286-288, 290**
Minors, **Torts 55, 188**
Misrepresentation and nondisclosure, generally, **Torts 405**
Mitigation of damages, **Torts 123, 311**
Motor vehicles, **Torts 255, 257, 258, 260**
Municipal corporations, governmental immunities, **Torts 342, 343, 345, 347, 349**
Necessity, **Torts 170, 171**
Negligence, generally, **Torts 47**
Nuisance, generally, **Torts 273**
Owners and occupiers of land, generally, **Torts 177**
Prenatal harm, **Torts 291, 292**
Prima facie tort, **Torts 128**
Privacy, generally, **Torts 399**
Privileges, generally, **Torts 157**
Products liability, generally, **Torts 217**
Professional negligence, generally, **Torts 270**
Proximate cause, generally, **Torts 77**
Psychic harm, **Torts 137-141, 286-288, 290**
Real property, generally, **Torts 141, 166, 167, 177, 273**
Reasonable person, negligence, **Torts 49, 52-54, 56, 57**
Reckless conduct, **Torts 101**
Reduced chance, liability for, **Torts 30**
Res ipsa loquitur, **Torts 70**
Self defense, **Torts 163, 165**
Slander, generally, **Torts 384**
Sovereign immunity, **Torts 342, 343, 347, 349, 345**
Statutes, source of standards of care, **Torts 63**
Statutes of limitations and repose, **Torts 124**
Strict liability, generally, **Torts 31**
Suppliers of chattel, generally, **Torts 217**
Survival of tort claims, **Torts 359**
Toxic Torts (this index)

TORTS—Cont'd
Trespass to land, generally, **Torts 141**
Trespass writ, **Torts 13, 14, 18**
Trover, generally, **Torts 146**
Vicarious liability, generally, **Torts 229**
Wilful and wanton misconduct, **Torts 101**
Workers' compensation, **Torts 242**
Wrongful birth, **Torts 292**
Wrongful death, generally, **Torts 363**
Wrongful life, **Torts 292**

TOXIC SUBSTANCES
Hazardous Wastes and Toxic Substances, Law of (this index)

TOXIC TORTS
Generally, **Toxic 1-16**
Adequacy of representation, prerequisites to class action, **Toxic 279, 280**
Admissibility of scientific evidence in court, causation, **Toxic 213-222**
Agent Orange litigation, class actions, **Toxic 271-275**
Aggravation of injury, workers' compensation, **Toxic 109, 110**
AIDS, emotional distress from fear of, **Toxic 237, 238**
Alternative dispute resolution, mass toxic torts, **Toxic 316-319**
Animal toxicological studies, causation, **Toxic 210-212**
Antismoking legislation, environmental tobacco smoke, **Toxic 349-352**
Asbestos abatement, insurers as special defendants, **Toxic 150, 151**
Bankruptcy, settlement, **Toxic 308-310**
Battery, **Toxic 62, 63**
Benedectin litigation, admissibility of scientific evidence in court, **Toxic 216-218**
Blood shield statutes, products liability defenses, **Toxic 42-44**
Causation, generally, **Toxic 195-229**
CERCLA liability, **Toxic 78-97**
Certification requirement, class actions, **Toxic 275**

TOXIC TORTS—Cont'd
Choice of law, mass toxic torts, **Toxic 327-331**
Cigarette cases, preemption as defense, **Toxic 185-190**
Citizens' suits, CERCLA liability, **Toxic 95-97**
Civil conspiracy, indeterminate defendants, **Toxic 159**
Class actions, **Toxic 270-297**
Cleanups, CERCLA liability, **Toxic 81-87**
Cohort studies, causation, **Toxic 208**
Collateral estoppel, mass toxic torts, **Toxic 319-326**
Commonality, prerequisites to class action, **Toxic 278**
Consolidation, mass toxic torts, **Toxic 298-301**
Contractors, governmental, **Toxic 138-140**
Contribution claims, settlement, **Toxic 310-316**
Convergence of public law and private law, **Toxic 15, 16**
Culpable conduct, defenses, **Toxic 180-182**
Damages and injuries, generally, **Toxic 230-267**
Daubert vs. Merrell Dow Pharmaceuticals Rule, admissibility of scientific evidence in court, **Toxic 216-222**
Defenses, generally, **Toxic 87-92, 168-194**
Defined or construed, **Toxic 1-16**
DES cases, indeterminate defendants, **Toxic 160-167**
Design defect, **Toxic 21, 22**
Disclosure duty, **Toxic 32, 33**
Discovery rule, defenses, **Toxic 169-174**
Discrimination, **Toxic 124-128, 342-345**
Dual capacity, workers' compensation, **Toxic 110, 111**
Emotional distress, **Toxic 230-238**
Employers' liability, **Toxic 98-128**
Enforcement, **Toxic 79-81, 121-124**
Environmental tobacco smoke, **Toxic 332-352**
Epidemiological studies, causation, **Toxic 207-210**
Exclusivity of remedy, workers' compensation, **Toxic 104-111**
Exposure, generally, **Toxic 1-5**
Express warranty, **Toxic 27, 28**
Federal environmental cases, preemption as defense, **Toxic 184, 185**

TOXIC TORTS—Cont'd
Federal Tort Claims Act, **Toxic 132-138**
Feres doctrine, **Toxic 136-138**
Frye Doctrine, admissibility of scientific evidence in court, **Toxic 214**
Future victims, settlement, **Toxic 306-308**
Governmental entities, **Toxic 129-138**
Identifying the class as prerequisite in class action, **Toxic 276, 277**
Implied warranties, **Toxic 25-27**
Increased risk of disease, **Toxic 239-247**
Indeterminate defendants, **Toxic 154-167**
Injunctive relief, **Toxic 111, 340, 341**
Injuries and damages, generally, **Toxic 230-267**
Innocent landowner defense, **Toxic 89-92**
Insurers as special defendants, **Toxic 146-154**
Intentional misconduct of employer, workers' compensation, **Toxic 106-109**
Intergenerational torts, extent of liability, **Toxic 67-72**
Joint and several liability, tort reform measures, **Toxic 73-75**
Latency period, **Toxic 5, 6**
Learned intermediary, products liability defenses, **Toxic 41, 42**
Legal certainty versus scientific certainty, causation, **Toxic 202, 203**
Legislative punitive damages reform, **Toxic 265-267**
Lenders as special defendants, **Toxic 144-146**
Lone pine orders, causation, **Toxic 203, 204**
Manufacturing defect, **Toxic 22, 23**
Mass toxic torts, **Toxic 268-331**
Medical device cases, preemption as defense, **Toxic 192-194**
Medical monitoring, **Toxic 247-252, 305, 306**
Military service, **Toxic 136-138**
Misrepresentation claims, **Toxic 27-29**
Multidistrict litigation transfer, mass toxic torts, **Toxic 297, 298**
Negligence, generally, **Toxic 29-32**
Notice of 23(b)(3) class actions, **Toxic 293-295**

TOXIC TORTS—Cont'd

Nuisance, claims related to activities on real property, **Toxic 52-57**

Numerosity, prerequisites to class action, **Toxic 277, 278**

Occupational disease statutes, workers' compensation, **Toxic 101-104**

Occupational Safety and Health Act regulation, workers' compensation, **Toxic 111-122**

Per se negligence, **Toxic 63-65**

Pesticide cases, preemption as defense, **Toxic 190, 191**

Pollution exclusion clause, insurers as special defendants, **Toxic 152-154**

Preemption, defenses, **Toxic 182-194**

Prerequisites, class actions, **Toxic 275-280**

Probabilistic evidence, causation, **Toxic 200-202**

Products liability, generally, **Toxic 17-19**

Property damage claims, defenses, **Toxic 174, 175**

Punitive damages, **Toxic 253-267**

Quality of life, injuries and damages, **Toxic 252, 253**

Real estate brokers, claims related to activities on real property, **Toxic 58-61**

Real property, **Toxic 44-61, 89-92**

Reform measures, **Toxic 72-77, 222-224**

Reliance on expert scientific testimony, **Toxic 8-10**

Repose statutes, defenses, **Toxic 175-177**

Res judicata, defenses, **Toxic 177-180**

Restatement 2nd § 402A strict liability theories, **Toxic 19-21**

Restatement revisions, tort reform measures, **Toxic 72, 73**

RICO, **Toxic 65-67**

Savings clause, CERCLA liability, **Toxic 94, 95**

Scientific evidence, causation, **Toxic 204-213**

Sellers of products, claims against, **Toxic 17-32**

Settlements, **Toxic 92-94, 295-297, 304-319**

Smoke, environmental tobacco smoke, **Toxic 332-352**

Sophisticated user, products liability defenses, **Toxic 38-41**

Sovereign immunity, generally, **Toxic 129-132**

TOXIC TORTS—Cont'd
State criminal enforcement of workplace safety, workers' compensation, **Toxic 122-124**
State-of-the-art, products liability defenses, **Toxic 34-36**
Statutes of limitations, defenses, **Toxic 168-175**
Statutes of repose, defenses, **Toxic 175-177**
Strict liability, **Toxic 28, 29, 45-48**
Successor and predecessor corporations, **Toxic 140-144**
Theories of liability, **Toxic 17-77**
Third party defense, **Toxic 88, 89**
Tobacco smoke, environmental, **Toxic 332-352**
Toxicological studies, causation, **Toxic 210-213**
Transporters, CERCLA liability, **Toxic 81-87**
Trespass, claims related to activities on real property, **Toxic 48-51**
Trial management, mass toxic torts, **Toxic 301-304**
Typicality, prerequisites to class action, **Toxic 279**
Unavoidably unsafe products, products liability defenses, **Toxic 36-38**
Uncertainty, scientific uncertainty and causation problems, **Toxic 6-8**
Warning failure, **Toxic 23-25**
Workers' compensation, **Toxic 98-111, 337-340**
Workplace issues, environmental tobacco smoke, **Toxic 337-345**

TRADE AND INVESTMENT
International Trade and Investment (this index)

TRADEMARKS AND TRADE NAMES
Generally, **Unfair Trade 97 et seq.**
Affirmative defenses, **Unfair Trade 185-191**
Art Law (this index)
Infringing and noninfringing uses, **Unfair Trade 158 et seq.**
Product substitution or alteration, **Unfair Trade 197-210**
Remedies, **Unfair Trade 191-196**
Similar trademarks and trade names, **Unfair Trade 97 et seq.**

TRADITIONS
Comparative Legal Traditions (this index)

TRANSFERS
Generation-skipping transfer tax. **Federal Estate and Gift Taxation** (this index) generally
Partnership interest. **Federal Income Taxation of Partners and Partnerships** (this index)

TRANSPORTATION
Hazardous Wastes and Toxic Substances, Law of (this index)

TREATIES
International Environmental Law (this index)
International Human Rights (this index)
International Taxation (this index)
International Trade and Investment (this index)
Legal Research (this index)
Public International Law (this index)

TREATISES
Legal Research (this index)

TRIAL ADVOCACY
Additional emphasis techniques on direct examination, **Trial Adv 122-127**
Analogies, closing argument, **Trial Adv 256-263**
Approaching the bench, customs and practices, **Trial Adv 347**
Approach to litigation, **Trial Adv 1-10**
Arguments, **Trial Adv 2-4, 11-64, 137, 138, 181-183, 233, 234, 236-291, 270, 312**
Authentication of exhibits, **Trial Adv 159-162**
Bench trials, closing argument, **Trial Adv 282, 283**
Benefits of exhibits, **Trial Adv 155, 156**
Bias, credibility of witnesses, **Trial Adv 36-40**
Bottom line, identification of, **Trial Adv 81, 82**
Brochures, foundations for common exhibits, **Trial Adv 173**

TRIAL ADVOCACY—Cont'd

Burden of proof, closing argument, **Trial Adv 270-272**
Character evidence impeachment, cross examination, **Trial Adv 232, 233**
Chronology, deviation from on direct examination, **Trial Adv 100-105**
Circumstantial evidence, inferential arguments, **Trial Adv 46-48**
Closing argument, generally, **Trial Adv 236-291**
Common exhibits, foundations for, **Trial Adv 165-176**
Common sense, personal characteristics of effective litigators, **Trial Adv 7, 8**
Concluding direct examination, **Trial Adv 133**
Constructing arguments, **Trial Adv 11-23**
Continuing objections, **Trial Adv 302, 303**
Converse in the triangular, customs and practices, **Trial Adv 347, 348**
Courthouse etiquette, customs and practices, **Trial Adv 348**
Credibility arguments, generally, **Trial Adv 24-44**
Cross examination, generally, **Trial Adv 177-235**
Cumulative witnesses on direct examination, **Trial Adv 133-135**
Customs and practices, generally, **Trial Adv 346-350**
Definitions, **Trial Adv 16, 17, 46**
Demeanor, credibility of witnesses, **Trial Adv 41-44**
Deviation from chronology, direct examination, **Trial Adv 100-105**
Diagrams, foundations for common exhibits, **Trial Adv 166-172**
Direct examination, generally, **Trial Adv 84-153**
Distractions of client, customs and practices, **Trial Adv 348, 349**
Ditry Tricks Hall of Fame, **Trial Adv 350-353**
Effective communication techniques, closing argument, **Trial Adv 274-276**
Embryonic argument, **Trial Adv 48-53**
Emphasis technique, cross examination, **Trial Adv 212-215**
Ethical considerations, objections, **Trial Adv 298-300**
Evasive answers, responding to on cross examination, **Trial Adv 220-223**
Evidence, **Trial Adv 241, 242, 270-272, 303, 304, 312-314**

TRIAL ADVOCACY—Cont'd

Evidentiary rules, impeachment with prior inconsistent statements, **Trial Adv 205-208**
Excessive detail, opening statement pitfall, **Trial Adv 74, 75**
Excluding witnesses, **Trial Adv 293, 294**
Exhibits, generally, **Trial Adv 154-176**
Expertise, credibility of witnesses, **Trial Adv 35, 36**
Expert witnesses, **Trial Adv 332-340**
Explanations, responding to on cross examination, **Trial Adv 224-229**
Explicitness, closing argument, **Trial Adv 243-251**
Eye contact, opening statement, **Trial Adv 82**
Falsus in uno, falsus in omnibus, closing arguments, **Trial Adv 288**
Fax documents, foundations for common exhibits, **Trial Adv 173**
Fishing, unsafe questions on cross examination, **Trial Adv 199-205**
Forgoing cross examination, **Trial Adv 217, 218**
Form letters, foundations for common exhibits, **Trial Adv 173**
Formulating stories, constructing arguments, **Trial Adv 13-15**
Front load important events, deviating from chronology on direct examination, **Trial Adv 100-102**
Handwritten documents, foundations for common exhibits, **Trial Adv 172, 173**
Harmful evidence, eliciting of on direct examination, **Trial Adv 131-133**
Hearsay, foundations for common exhibits, **Trial Adv 173, 174**
Highly safe questions, cross examination, **Trial Adv 188-205**
Housekeeping tips, direct examination, **Trial Adv 140-143**
Identification, **Trial Adv 15-23, 48-50, 81, 82**
Impeachment, **Trial Adv 205-212, 232, 233**
Individual style, closing argument, **Trial Adv 237, 238**
Inferential arguments, **Trial Adv 45-56**
In limine motions, objection to, **Trial Adv 297, 298**
Inoculation technique, closing argument, **Trial Adv 255, 256, 288, 289**
Instructions to jury, generally, **Trial Adv 340-342**

TRIAL ADVOCACY—Cont'd

Integrity, personal characteristics of effective litigators, **Trial Adv 8, 9**
Introductory remarks, closing argument, **Trial Adv 238-240**
Judge-tried case, generally, **Trial Adv 318-321**
Jury and jury trial, generally, **Trial Adv 318-321**
Laying foundation, **Trial Adv 144-153, 157-163**
Leading questions, cross examination, **Trial Adv 183-185**
Legal principles, closing argument, **Trial Adv 270-274**
Lying or mistaken, credibility of witnesses, **Trial Adv 35**
Marking exhibits, **Trial Adv 157-159**
Medium safe questions, cross examination, **Trial Adv 192-199**
Misquoting witness on cross examination, **Trial Adv 234, 235**
Motion in limine, objection to, **Trial Adv 297, 298**
Motive, credibility of witnesses, **Trial Adv 36-40**
Narrative questions, direct examination, **Trial Adv 118-122**
Normative arguments, **Trial Adv 57-61, 137, 138, 269, 270**
Note-taking, customs and practices, **Trial Adv 349, 350**
O. J. Simpson, People vs., closing argument, **Trial Adv 283-291**
Objections, **Trial Adv 121, 122, 297-314**
Observing courthouse etiquette, customs and practices, **Trial Adv 348**
Offers of proof, **Trial Adv 303, 304, 313, 314**
One-item questions, cross examination, **Trial Adv 185, 186**
Opening statement, generally, **Trial Adv 65-83**
Open questions, cross examination, **Trial Adv 215, 216**
Order of closing arguments, **Trial Adv 240, 241**
Overruled objections, **Trial Adv 313**
Packing for trial, **Trial Adv 343-346**
Personal background questions, starting direct examination, **Trial Adv 105-107**
Personal characteristics of effective litigators, **Trial Adv 5-9**
Photographs, foundations for common exhibits, **Trial Adv 165, 166**
Pitfalls, opening statement, **Trial Adv 72-77**
Preemption, closing arguments, **Trial Adv 290**

TRIAL ADVOCACY—Cont'd
Preparation of witness, **Trial Adv 315-317**
Printed documents, foundations for common exhibits, **Trial Adv 173**
Prior statement of witness as provable, cross examination, **Trial Adv 188-191**
Professional exhibits, foundations for common exhibits, **Trial Adv 174-176**
Promises you cannot keep, opening statements, **Trial Adv 75-77, 285, 286**
Promptness, customs and practices, **Trial Adv 347**
Protecting witness on cross examination, **Trial Adv 233-235**
Pseudo-normative arguments, **Trial Adv 269, 270, 291**
Publishing exhibits, **Trial Adv 163, 164**
Puffing, **Trial Adv 279, 280, 285**
Rapid-fire questioning on cross examination, **Trial Adv 234**
Rationality of everyday experience, **Trial Adv 4, 5**
Real versus illustrative exhibits, **Trial Adv 154, 155**
Reason to observe or recall, credibility of witnesses, **Trial Adv 40, 41**
Redirect examination, **Trial Adv 138-140**
Refreshing recollection, direct examination, **Trial Adv 147-151**
Rules of closing argument, **Trial Adv 276-282**
Safe questions, cross examination, **Trial Adv 187-205**
Scene-setting questions, starting direct examination, **Trial Adv 107-112**
Self-confidence, personal characteristics of effective litigators, **Trial Adv 5, 6**
Sequestering witnesses, **Trial Adv 293, 294**
Signed documents, foundations for common exhibits, **Trial Adv 172, 173**
Silent arguments, generally, **Trial Adv 61-64**
Sitting, customs and practices, **Trial Adv 346**
Source credibility, **Trial Adv 33-44**
Standing, customs and practices, **Trial Adv 346**
Starting direct examination, **Trial Adv 105-112**
Stipulations, **Trial Adv 294-297**

TRIAL ADVOCACY—Cont'd
Subpoenas, **Trial Adv 342, 343**
Sustained objections, **Trial Adv 313**
Tactical considerations, objections, **Trial Adv 298-300**
Testimony, credibility of, **Trial Adv 26-44**
Theory of case, closing arguments, **Trial Adv 289**
Truth and the adversary system, **Trial Adv 9, 10**
Two-sided closing arguments, **Trial Adv 251-256, 290**
Unsafe questions, cross examination, **Trial Adv 199-205**
Use exhibits on closing argument in People vs. O. J. Simpson, **Trial Adv 284**
Verbal gestures, direct examination, **Trial Adv 141-143**
Visual aids, **Trial Adv 79**
Voir dire examination, **Trial Adv 321-332**
Vouching, rules of closing argument, **Trial Adv 280, 281**
Willingness to learn about diverse subjects, personal characteristics of effective litigators, **Trial Adv 6, 7**
Witnesses, **Trial Adv 26-44, 84-153, 233-235, 293, 294, 315-317, 330-340**

TRIAL AND PRACTICE SKILLS
Admissions, generally, **Trial & Prac 271-273**
Advice giving, office skills, **Trial & Prac 247, 248**
Agenda control, negotiation process, **Trial & Prac 293, 294**
Alternatives, **Trial & Prac 25-34**
Appellate argument, structure of, **Trial & Prac 54-57**
Appellate briefs, legal writing, **Trial & Prac 76-83**
Arguments, generally, **Trial & Prac 38-60**
Attorneys' fees, negotiating conflicts, **Trial & Prac 307, 308**
Averting disaster, last-minute concerns, **Trial & Prac 214-219**
Believable testimony, direct examination, **Trial & Prac 119-128**
Briefs, legal writing, **Trial & Prac 76-83**
Business deals and evaluating cases, negotiation of, **Trial & Prac 297-314**
Candor, negotiation process, **Trial & Prac 286-289**
Care/cure quandary, counseling, **Trial & Prac 320, 321**
Checklists, counseling, **Trial & Prac 318, 319**

TRIAL AND PRACTICE SKILLS—Cont'd

Checklists, legal writing, **Trial & Prac 89-91**
Chronology, direct examination, **Trial & Prac 106-109**
Clarity, legal writing, **Trial & Prac 64-76**
Closing argument, generally, **Trial & Prac 168-181**
Concessions, negotiation process, **Trial & Prac 289-292**
Conflicts, negotiation of, **Trial & Prac 303-314**
Confrontation
  goals and ethics of cross-examination, confrontation of witness, **Trial & Prac 143, 144**
  office skills, confrontation of client, **Trial & Prac 246**
Contracts, negotiation of, **Trial & Prac 297-303**
Costs and fees, negotiating conflicts, **Trial & Prac 307, 308**
Counseling, generally, **Trial & Prac 315-321**
Cross-examination
  direct examination, **Trial & Prac 115-118**
  goals and ethics of cross-examination, generally, **Trial & Prac 134-157**
  last-minute concerns, **Trial & Prac 209, 210**
  techniques, generally, **Trial & Prac 158-167**
Damages, negotiating conflicts, **Trial & Prac 305, 306**
Delivery
  closing argument, **Trial & Prac 179-181**
  legal arguments, **Trial & Prac 57-60**
Demeanor, generally, **Trial & Prac 182-187**
Demonstrations, use of on direct examination, **Trial & Prac 110, 111**
Depositions, generally, **Trial & Prac 256-268**
Diagrams, use of on direct examination, **Trial & Prac 110, 111**
Direct examination
  generally, **Trial & Prac 105-133**
  cross-examination, goals and ethics of, **Trial & Prac 140, 141**
  last-minute concerns, witness preparation, **Trial & Prac 208, 209**
  limitation of direct examination, goals and ethics of cross-examination, **Trial & Prac 145-147**
  problem witnesses at trial, last-minute concerns, **Trial & Prac 211, 212**

TRIAL AND PRACTICE SKILLS—Cont'd

Discovery, generally, **Trial & Prac 250-274**
Discrediting witness, goals and ethics of cross-examination, **Trial & Prac 147-157**
Dogma, paradox of, **Trial & Prac 34-37**
Drafting
  interrogatories, **Trial & Prac 270, 271**
  negotiation agreement, **Trial & Prac 294, 295**
Dress of witness, last-minute concerns, **Trial & Prac 210, 211**
Editing, legal writing, **Trial & Prac 83-91**
Ethics and goals of cross-examination, generally, **Trial & Prac 134-157**
Evasive witnesses
  cross-examination techniques, **Trial & Prac 162-166**
  last-minute concerns, **Trial & Prac 212-214**
Explicitness, closing argument, **Trial & Prac 175**
First offers, negotiation process, **Trial & Prac 289-292**
First Trial (this index)
Flexibility in defining conflict, evaluating cases, **Trial & Prac 310, 311**
Goals and ethics of cross-examination, generally, **Trial & Prac 134-157**
Impeachment, last-minute concerns, **Trial & Prac 212-214**
Interesting testimony, direct examination, **Trial & Prac 128-131**
Interrogatories, generally, **Trial & Prac 268-271**
Interviewing, office skills, **Trial & Prac 230-249**
Investigation, litigation skill of case planning, **Trial & Prac 94-102**
Jury selection, generally, **Trial & Prac 199-204**
Labels and labeling, **Trial & Prac 17-25**
Last-minute concerns, generally, **Trial & Prac 205-227**
Leading questions
  cross-examination techniques, **Trial & Prac 158-162**
  direct examination, **Trial & Prac 123-126**
  last-minute concerns, **Trial & Prac 218, 219**
Limitation of direct examination, goals and ethics of cross-examination, **Trial & Prac 145-147**

TRIAL AND PRACTICE SKILLS—Cont'd

Listening
cross-examination techniques, listening to answers, **Trial & Prac 166, 167**
office skills, **Trial & Prac 236-240**
Litigation costs, negotiating conflicts, **Trial & Prac 307, 308**
Litigation skills, generally, **Trial & Prac 93-227**
Lying witness, closing argument, **Trial & Prac 176**
Mail, negotiation process by, **Trial & Prac 293, 294**
Mistaken witness, closing argument, **Trial & Prac 176**
Narrative questions, last-minute concerns, **Trial & Prac 218, 219**
Negotiation
generally, **Trial & Prac 275-296**
business deals and evaluating cases, **Trial & Prac 297-314**
Nervous witness, last-minute concerns, **Trial & Prac 205-207**
New material, goals and ethics of cross-examination, **Trial & Prac 141-143**
Notebooks, litigation skill of case planning, **Trial & Prac 94-102**
Objections, last-minute concerns, **Trial & Prac 219-227**
Office skills, generally, **Trial & Prac 230-321**
Omission of unnecessary details, direct examination, **Trial & Prac 118, 119**
Opening statements, generally, **Trial & Prac 187-199**
Order of questions, cross-examination techniques, **Trial & Prac 166**
Paradox of dogma, **Trial & Prac 34-37**
Personal integrity, negotiation process, **Trial & Prac 282, 283**
Personalizing witness, direct examination, **Trial & Prac 126-128**
Planning
goals and ethics of cross-examination, **Trial & Prac 138-140**
litigation skills, planning case, **Trial & Prac 94-104**
negotiation, **Trial & Prac 280-282**
Policy, legal arguments, **Trial & Prac 47-49**
Precedents, legal arguments, **Trial & Prac 45-47**
Preparation of witness, last-minute concerns, **Trial & Prac 205-211**
Pretrial Litigation (this index)

TRIAL AND PRACTICE SKILLS—Cont'd

Prior inconsistent statements, last-minute concerns, **Trial & Prac 212-214**

Problem solving, **Trial & Prac 16-37**

Problem witnesses at trial, last-minute concerns, **Trial & Prac 211-214**

Research, litigation skill of case planning, **Trial & Prac 102-104**

Responding to objections, last-minute concerns, **Trial & Prac 222-224**

Teacher, lawyer as, **Trial & Prac 316-318**

Techniques of oral argument, **Trial & Prac 49-54**

Timing, negotiation process, **Trial & Prac 293, 294**

Tone of voice, cross-examination techniques, **Trial & Prac 159, 160, 166**

Tort damages, negotiating conflicts, **Trial & Prac 305, 306**

Truth, office skills, **Trial & Prac 241-246**

Tying up evidence upon presentation, direct examination, **Trial & Prac 111-114**

Unfavorable testimony, goals and ethics of cross-examination, **Trial & Prac 144-157**

Untruthful witness, closing argument, **Trial & Prac 176**

Voir dire, generally, **Trial & Prac 199-204**

Witnesses
- analyzing testimony, closing argument, **Trial & Prac 176**
- believable testimony, **Trial & Prac 119-128**
- cross-examination, supra
- direct examination, generally, **Trial & Prac 105-133**
- discrediting witness, goals and ethics of cross-examination, **Trial & Prac 147-157**
- evasive witnesses, supra
- last-minute concerns, problem witnesses at trial, **Trial & Prac 205-214**
- lying witness, closing argument, **Trial & Prac 176**
- mistaken witness, closing argument, **Trial & Prac 176**
- preparation of witness, **Trial & Prac 205-211**
- problem witnesses at trial, **Trial & Prac 211-214**
- untruthful witness, closing argument, **Trial & Prac 176**

Writing, generally, **Trial & Prac 61-91**

GENERAL INDEX

References are to Titles and Pages

TRUSTS

Wills and Trusts (this index)

TRUSTS AND TRUSTEES

Federal Estate and Gift Taxation (this index) generally

Interest on Lawyers' Trust Account (IOLTA) Funds. **Professional Responsibility** (this index)

UNCLOS (UNITED NATIONS CONVENTION ON THE LAW OF THE SEA)

International Environmental Law (this index)

UNCONTESTABILITY CLAUSE

Insurance Law (this index)

UNFAIR TRADE PRACTICES

Generally, **1 et seq.**

UNIFORM COMMERCIAL CODE

Absence of due negotiation, shipping and storing goods covered by documents of title, **UCC 334-339**

Acceptance

- buyer's remedies, **UCC 122-128**
- default by lessor, **UCC 555-565**
- finality of acceptance, **UCC 296, 297**
- improper delivery, performance of contract for sale, **UCC 92-102**
- liability of drawee and acceptor, **UCC 231-236**
- performance of contract for sale, **UCC 86-88**

Accommodation party, obligation of, **UCC 236-245**

Accrual of cause of action, **UCC 245, 246**

Altered instruments, liabilities regarding, **UCC 298-301**

Anticipatory repudiation, lease contract, **UCC 541**

Assignment of rights, contract for sale, **UCC 34-36**

Attachment of security interest, **UCC 377-386**

Bank collection process, **UCC 274-288**

UNIFORM COMMERCIAL CODE—Cont'd

Bankruptcy trustee, priority rules with regard to other conflicting interest, **UCC 470-482**
Beneficiaries of warranties, generally, **UCC 71**
Bills of lading
  negotiation, obligations of indorsers or persons negotiating, **UCC 339-341**
  shipping and storing goods covered by documents of title, **UCC 310-348**
Bulk sales, **UCC 155, 156**
Carriers
  forged documents, liability for, **UCC 347, 348**
  misdescription, liability for, **UCC 345-347**
Cashier's check, obligation of maker of, **UCC 219, 220**
Cash sale transaction, remedies, **UCC 120, 121**
Causation, defenses to warranty actions, **UCC 62, 63**
Cause of action, accrual of, **UCC 245, 246**
Certified item, priorities in customer's account, **UCC 288**
Checklist of items included in contract for sale, **UCC 36-39**
Collections, bank collection process, **UCC 274-288**
Conflict of warranties, **UCC 61, 536**
Consideration requirement, **UCC 18-21, 528**
Construction and interpretation
  lease contract, **UCC 529, 530**
  sale, contract for, **UCC 28-33**
Contracts
  lease contract, **UCC 527-530**
  liabilities of parties, **UCC 215-254**
  sale, generally, **UCC 3-39**
Contracts (this index)
Contribution rights of accommodation party, **UCC 238, 239**
Conversion liability of drawee or acceptor, **UCC 234-236**
Cumulation of warranties, **UCC 61, 536**
Default
  lease contract, **UCC 552-571**
  third parties, rights and obligations of, **UCC 488-491, 495-512**

UNIFORM COMMERCIAL CODE—Cont'd

Defenses
- accommodation party, **UCC 239-245**
- leases, defenses to warranties, **UCC 537**
- negotiable instruments, **UCC 167-213**
- warranties, **UCC 62-64, 537**

Delegation of performance, contract for sale, **UCC 34-36**

Delivery
- default by lessor, **UCC 555-560**
- excuses to bailee, **UCC 341-345**
- improper tender or delivery, **UCC 103-107**
- performance of contract for sale, **UCC 83-86, 92-102**
- shipping and storing goods covered by documents of title, **UCC 313-324**
- stoppage of delivery in transit by seller, **UCC 339**

Discharge of obligations, **UCC 246-252**

Dishonor, wrongful dishonor by payor bank, **UCC 273, 274**

Disposal of collateral, proceeds from, **UCC 462-470**

Documents of title, shipping and storing goods covered by, **UCC 310-348**

Draft, obligation of drawer of, **UCC 220-229**

Due negotiation, shipping and storing goods covered by documents of title, **UCC 326-339**

Encoding warranties, **UCC 298**

Enforcement
- accommodation party, **UCC 239**
- default, lease contract, **UCC 552, 553**
- lease contract, **UCC 543-545**

Evidence, quality of goods disputes, **UCC 108**

Exclusions
- leases, exclusion of warranties, **UCC 538, 539**
- transactions excluded from Article 9, **UCC 376, 377**
- warranties, exclusion of, **UCC 64-69, 538, 539**

Excused performance, **UCC 108-111, 341-345, 541, 542**

Final or finality
- acceptance, finality of, **UCC 296, 297, 564, 565**
- default by lessor, final acceptance, **UCC 564, 565**
- payment, finality of, **UCC 289-296**
- payor bank, final payment of item by, **UCC 283-285**

UNIFORM COMMERCIAL CODE—Cont'd

Finance leases, **UCC 540, 542, 543**
Financing process, secured transactions, **UCC 349-523**
Fitness for particular purpose, implied warranty of, **UCC 536**
Forged instruments, liabilities regarding, **UCC 298-304, 347, 348**
Formation of contract, **UCC 3-18, 527**
Form of lease contract, **UCC 528, 529**
Fraud remedies, default in lease contract, **UCC 554**
Fundamentals of secured transactions, generally, **UCC 349-352**
Funds transfers, **UCC 306-309**
Good faith purchasers, shipping and storing goods covered by documents of title, **UCC 325, 326**
Holder in due course, **UCC 178-213**
Implied warranty of merchantability, **UCC 535, 536**
Improper tender or delivery, **UCC 103-107**
Indorser of instrument, obligation of drawer of, **UCC 220-229**
Infringement, warranties against, **UCC 535**
Insolvency of buyer, remedies, **UCC 119, 120**
Inspection of goods, performance of contract for sale, **UCC 91, 92**
Installment contract, **UCC 103**
Installment lease contract, default by lessor, **UCC 561, 565**
Insurable interest, **UCC 48, 49, 531**
Intangible collateral, **UCC 455-460**
Interference, warranties against, **UCC 535**
Investment securities, **UCC 156-159, 304-306**
Irrevocable promises, finance leases, **UCC 542, 543**
Jurisdiction, perfection of security interests in multiple state transactions, **UCC 484-488**
Leases, generally, **UCC 524-571**
Legal process, priorities in customer's account, **UCC 286-288**
Letter of credit, **UCC 513-524**
Liabilities of parties, generally, **UCC 215-254**
Limitation of remedies for breach of warranty, **UCC 69-71, 539**
Lost, destroyed, or stolen instruments, **UCC 253, 254**
Merchantability, implied warranty of, **UCC 535, 536**
Misdescription, liability for, **UCC 345-347**

UNIFORM COMMERCIAL CODE—Cont'd
Modification of warranties, **UCC 64-69, 538, 539**
Multiple state transactions, perfection of security interests in, **UCC 483-488**
Negotiable instruments, **UCC 160-309**
Negotiable Instruments and Check Collection (this index)
Negotiation
  obligations of indorsers or persons negotiating, **UCC 339-341**
  shipping and storing goods covered by documents of title, **UCC 325-333**
Note, obligation of maker of, **UCC 219, 220**
Notice, **UCC 63, 64, 286-288, 553**
Parol evidence, **UCC 33, 530**
Payment for goods, performance of contract for sale, **UCC 88-90**
Payor bank and customers, relationship between, **UCC 254-285**
Perfection or nonperfection, **UCC 408-488**
Performance
  contract for sale, **UCC 79-111**
  excuse of, **UCC 108-111**
  lease contract, **UCC 540-543**
Performance, contract for sale, **UCC 34-36**
Personal Property (this index)
Presentment, finality of payment or acceptance, **UCC 289-298**
Priorities
  conflicting interest, **UCC 408-483**
  customer's account, **UCC 286-288**
  lease contract, **UCC 545-552**
Privity, leases, **UCC 539**
Quality of goods, **UCC 55-61, 65-69, 108**
Recoupment, **UCC 167-213, 239**
Rejection
  default by lessor, **UCC 555-561**
  improper delivery, performance of contract for sale, **UCC 92-102**
Remedies, generally, **UCC 111-139**
Repudiation, lease contract, **UCC 540, 541**
Retention warranties, **UCC 298**
Revocation, **UCC 122-128, 561-564**

UNIFORM COMMERCIAL CODE—Cont'd
Risk of loss, **UCC 50-54, 531-534**
Sales, generally, **UCC 1, 2**
Sales and Leases of Goods (this index)
Seals, contracts, **UCC 27, 28, 529**
Secured transactions, **UCC 349-523**
Secured Transactions (this index)
Securities as negotiable instruments, **UCC 304-306**
Security interest, **UCC 49, 50, 531**
Setoff, priorities in customer's account, **UCC 286-288**
Shipping and storing goods covered by documents of title, **UCC 310-348**
Special property, lease contract, **UCC 531**
Special property, property incidents of contract of sale, **UCC 48**
Statute of frauds, **UCC 21-27, 528**
Statute of limitations, **UCC 63, 245, 246, 554**
Stop order, priorities in customer's account, **UCC 286-288**
Stoppage of delivery in transit by seller, **UCC 339**
Substituted performance, lease contract, **UCC 541**
Suspension of payor bank's authority to pay, **UCC 267-273**
Terms of contract, **UCC 28-33, 529, 530**
Third parties
  default, rights and obligations of before or after, **UCC 488-491, 495-512**
  leases, third party beneficiaries of warranties, **UCC 539**
  rights of, **UCC 140-154**
  secured party, protection against third party claims, **UCC 386-408**
  standing to sue, default in lease contract, **UCC 554, 555**
Title, **UCC 39-47, 54, 55, 64, 530**
Torts, liabilities of parties, **UCC 215-254**
Transfer warranties, liability of transferors, **UCC 229-231**
Trustee in bankruptcy, priority rules with regard to other conflicting interest, **UCC 470-482**
Validity of lease contract, **UCC 543-545**
Warehouse receipts
  obligations of indorsers or persons negotiating, **UCC 339-341**

UNIFORM COMMERCIAL CODE—Cont'd
Warehouse receipts—Cont'd
shipping and storing goods covered by documents of title, **UCC 310-348**
Warehouses and warehousemen
excuses to bailee, **UCC 341-345**
forged documents, liability for, **UCC 347, 348**
misdescription, liability for, **UCC 345-347**
Warranty, **UCC 54-79, 297, 298, 534-540**
Wrongful dishonor, payor bank, **UCC 273, 274**

UNIFORM PROBATE CODE
Accounts of trustee, **Unif Probate 541, 542**
Adopted persons, determination of status, **Unif Probate 54-58**
Advancements, prior gifts and transactions, **Unif Probate 63-69**
Affinity, determination of status, **Unif Probate 60, 61**
After-acquired property, wills, **Unif Probate 207**
Afterborn persons, determination of status, **Unif Probate 58, 59**
Aliens or noncitizens, determination of status, **Unif Probate 61**
Ancillary administration of wills, **Unif Probate 435-443**
Antilapse, wills, **Unif Probate 210-212, 221-223**
Appointments, **Unif Probate 245-253, 327-335, 364-370**
Apportionment of estate taxes, special distribution provisions in wills, **Unif Probate 418-421**
Augmented estate calculation, **Unif Probate 85-99**
Avoidance devices, **Unif Probate 459-461**
Bonds, **Unif Probate 292, 293, 370-373, 482-484**
Capacity of testator, execution of will requirements, **Unif Probate 133, 134**
Children or minors, **Unif Probate 171-121, 465-469**
Choice of law, rules of construction applicable to wills, **Unif Probate 224, 225**
Closing estates, wills, **Unif Probate 422-430**
Compensation of personal representatives, wills, **Unif Probate 386-388**
Confidential public depository, wills, **Unif Probate 172, 173**
Conservatorship. Guardianship and conservatorship, infra

UNIFORM PROBATE CODE—Cont'd

Construction, rule of, **Unif Probate 15, 16, 208-225**
Contested wills, **Unif Probate 294-297**
Continuing jurisdiction, flexible system of administration, **Unif Probate 294**
Contractual arrangements, nonprobate transfers, **Unif Probate 501-504**
Coordination of domiciliary and ancillary proceedings, wills, **Unif Probate 441-443**
Courts, **Unif Probate 23, 24**
Creditors, **Unif Probate 321-324, 397-408, 494, 495, 516, 517**
Custodian of will, **Unif Probate 173**
Debtor heirs, prior gifts and transactions, **Unif Probate 70**
Definitions, generally, **Unif Probate 20, 232-234, 245-247, 507-510, 520-522**
Descendants, intestate succession, **Unif Probate 44-52**
Devisee lapse, **Unif Probate 177-192**
Devolution of decedents' estates and necessity of probate and administration, **Unif Probate 298-300**
Discharge of security for fiduciary performance, closing estates, **Unif Probate 429, 430**
Disclaimer of property interests, **Unif Probate 227-231**
Distributee liability, closing estates, **Unif Probate 424, 425**
Domiciliary foreign personal representative, wills, **Unif Probate 437-440**
Durable powers of attorney, **Unif Probate 461-464**
Duration of conservator, protective proceedings, **Unif Probate 496, 497**
Elective share of surviving spouse, **Unif Probate 73-113**
Estate taxes apportioned, special distribution provisions in will, **Unif Probate 418-421**
Exclusions or exemptions, **Unif Probate 96-99, 125, 265, 266**
Exculpatory provision, personal representative's duties, powers and liabilities, **Unif Probate 381-383**
Execution requirements, wills, **Unif Probate 133-140**
Exemptions, **Unif Probate 96-99, 125, 265, 266**
Expenses of personal representatives, wills, **Unif Probate 386-388**

UNIFORM PROBATE CODE—Cont'd

Expressed contrary intention of testator, **Unif Probate 185-187**
Extinction, ademption and nonademption by, **Unif Probate 196-202**
Family protections, **Unif Probate 122-126**
Financial institutions, multiple-party accounts, **Unif Probate 510-512, 517-519**
Flexible system of administration of wills, **Unif Probate 273-297**
Foreign and international will, execution requirements, **Unif Probate 140-145**
Foreign personal representative and ancillary administration, **Unif Probate 435-443**
Foreign trustee, administration of trust, **Unif Probate 544-546**
Formal closing estates proceedings, **Unif Probate 425-429**
Formality analysis, wills, **Unif Probate 128-133**
Forum non conveniens in trust litigation, **Unif Probate 536**
Fraud, **Unif Probate 16, 17, 293, 294**
Funding elective share, **Unif Probate 100-104**
Future interests, constructional rules for, **Unif Probate 218-224**
General pattern, intestate succession, **Unif Probate 31-36**
Gifts, prior gifts and transactions, **Unif Probate 63-70**
Guardianship and conservatorship, generally, **Unif Probate 445-450**
Half-blooded persons, determination of status, **Unif Probate 58**
History, **Unif Probate 2-6**
Holographic will, execution requirements, **Unif Probate 138-140**
Homestead allowance, family protections, **Unif Probate 124**
Homicide, effect of, **Unif Probate 236-241**
Honorary trusts, rule against perpetuities, **Unif Probate 270-272**
Husband and wife, **Unif Probate 37-44, 73-117, 232-236**
Improper distribution, flexible system of administration, **Unif Probate 293**
Incapacitated person, guardian of, **Unif Probate 470-477**
Incorporation by reference, wills, **Unif Probate 161-163**
Independent proceedings, wills, **Unif Probate 306-308**
Independent significance, events of, **Unif Probate 166, 167**
Influence of, **Unif Probate 9, 10**

UNIFORM PROBATE CODE—Cont'd

Informal closing procedure, **Unif Probate 422-424**
Informal probate, **Unif Probate 336-356**
In kind distribution, special distribution provisions, **Unif Probate 415-418**
Interrelationships, guardianship and conservatorship, **Unif Probate 451-453**
Intestacy, **Unif Probate 29 et seq., 279-283, 285-287**
Joinder, wills, **Unif Probate 306-308**
Jurisdiction, generally, **Unif Probate 22-24**
Limitations of antilapse protection, wills, **Unif Probate 179-182**
Lost or destroyed will, revocation by, **Unif Probate 152-154**
Minors, **Unif Probate 171-121, 465-469**
Missing person, wills, **Unif Probate 354-356**
Multiple generation class gifts, wills, **Unif Probate 216, 217**
Multiple-party accounts, nonprobate transfers, **Unif Probate 505-519**
Multiple venues, **Unif Probate 22-24**
Multistate estate, foreign personal representative and ancillary administration, **Unif Probate 435-437**
Negative testacy provision, **Unif Probate 70-72**
No contest or claim clauses in wills, **Unif Probate 173, 174**
Nonexoneration right, wills, **Unif Probate 207**
Nonmarital issue, determination of status, **Unif Probate 59**
Nonprobate transfers, **Unif Probate 500-526**
Nontestamentary contractual arrangements, nonprobate transfers, **Unif Probate 501-504**
Notice, generally, **Unif Probate 25, 26**
Operation of law, **Unif Probate 152, 234-236**
Ordinary witnessed will, execution requirements, **Unif Probate 134-137**
Overriding policies and provisions, **Unif Probate 16-21**
Ownership, **Unif Probate 512, 513, 522-525**
Passive and affidavit procedures for small estates, succession without administration, **Unif Probate 310-312**
Payment of creditors' claims, wills, **Unif Probate 405-407**
Payors, protection of, **Unif Probate 241-245**

UNIFORM PROBATE CODE—Cont'd
Perjury, **Unif Probate 17, 18, 293, 294**
Perpetuities, rule against, generally, **Unif Probate 254-272**
Physical act, revocation of wills by, **Unif Probate 148, 149**
Power of attorney, durable powers of attorney, **Unif Probate 461-464**
Powers of appointment, **Unif Probate 245-253**
Powers of trustee, **Unif Probate 542, 543**
Presentation of creditors' claims, wills, **Unif Probate 402-404**
Pretermitted children, **Unif Probate 171-121**
Pretermitted spouses, **Unif Probate 114-117**
Prior gifts and transactions, **Unif Probate 63-70**
Priority and disqualification for appointment of personal representative, **Unif Probate 364-369**
Promulgation and maintenance of Code, **Unif Probate 6-9**
Proof of death or status, overriding policies and provisions, **Unif Probate 18-20**
Protective proceedings, generally, **Unif Probate 478-499**
Purposes, **Unif Probate 15, 16**
Reformation, rule against perpetuities, **Unif Probate 262-265**
Registrar, **Unif Probate 23, 24**
Registration, **Unif Probate 520-526, 530-532**
Rejection of creditors' claims, wills, **Unif Probate 402-404**
Relational terminology for dispositive purposes, wills, **Unif Probate 212-218**
Relevant lapse problems, application to, **Unif Probate 182-184**
Removal, **Unif Probate 389-392, 496, 497**
Representation, **Unif Probate 26-28, 44-52, 217, 218, 251-253, 362-389, 435-443, 536, 537**
Revival of wills, **Unif Probate 154-161**
Revocation, **Unif Probate 147-154, 234-236**
Revocation of wills, generally, **Unif Probate 147-154**
Rules of construction applicable to wills only, **Unif Probate 175-207**
Satisfaction, ademption by, **Unif Probate 202-206**
Secured creditors' claims, wills, **Unif Probate 407, 408**
Securities, accessions regarding devises of, **Unif Probate 192-196**

UNIFORM PROBATE CODE—Cont'd

Selection of conservator, protective proceedings, **Unif Probate 482-484**
Self-proved will, execution requirements, **Unif Probate 145-147**
Separate writings, reference to, **Unif Probate 167-169**
Settlement agreements, wills, **Unif Probate 431-434**
Shares of surviving spouse, **Unif Probate 37-44**
Simultaneous death, **Unif Probate 61-63**
Special administrator, wills, **Unif Probate 393-396**
Special distribution provisions, wills, **Unif Probate 409-421**
Spouses, **Unif Probate 37-44, 73-117, 232-236**
Status, determination of, **Unif Probate 53-61**
Statute of wills, **Unif Probate 127, 128**
Subject matter jurisdiction, **Unif Probate 302, 303, 454-456, 534**
Subsequent administration, closing estates, **Unif Probate 430**
Subsequent instrument, revocation of wills by, **Unif Probate 149-151**
Substantial compliance doctrine, wills, **Unif Probate 128-133**
Succession contracts, wills, **Unif Probate 169-172**
Succession without administration, procedures for, **Unif Probate 310-325**
Successor and copersonal representatives, wills, **Unif Probate 384-386**
Summary procedure for small estates, succession without administration, **Unif Probate 312-314**
Supersession, revocation, and revival of wills compared, **Unif Probate 158-161**
Supervised administration, wills, **Unif Probate 290, 291, 357-361**
Surviving spouse, **Unif Probate 37-44, 73-113, 232-234**
Survivors and survivorship, **Unif Probate 37-44, 61-63, 73-113, 209, 210, 219-221, 232-234**
Termination, **Unif Probate 232-236, 389-392, 496, 497**
Third persons or parties, **Unif Probate 241-245, 383, 384, 388, 389, 494, 496, 540, 541**
Time limitations on probate and administration, **Unif Probate 300-302**
Title of conservator, protective proceedings, **Unif Probate 492, 493**

UNIFORM PROBATE CODE—Cont'd
Transfers, nonprobate transfers, **Unif Probate 500-526**
Trusts, generally, **Unif Probate 527, 528**
Uniform TOD Security Registration Act, **Unif Probate 520-526**
Universal succession, succession without administration, **Unif Probate 314-325**
Venue, generally, **Unif Probate 22-24**
Virtual representation, generally, **Unif Probate 26-28**
Wife and husband, **Unif Probate 37-44, 73-117, 232-236**
Wills, generally, **Unif Probate 127-174**
Worthier title, constructional rules for future interests, **Unif Probate 223**

UNITED NATIONS
Public International Law (this index)

UNITED NATIONS CONVENTION ON THE LAW OF THE SEA (UNCLOS)
International Environmental Law (this index)

UNITED STATES-CANADA
International Environmental Law (this index)

UNITED STATES/MEXICO
International Environmental Law (this index)

UNITED STATES TAX COURT
Tax Procedure and Tax Fraud (this index)

URBAN GROWTH
Land Use (this index)

VAGUENESS
First Amendment (this index)

VALUE OR VALUATION
State Constitutional Law (this index)

VALUES
Energy and Natural Resources Law (this index)

VICARIOUS LIABILITY
Medical Liability (this index)

VISAS
Immigration Law and Procedure (this index)

WAIVER OR ESTOPPEL
Insurance Law (this index)
International Business Transactions (this index)
Landlord and Tenant (this index)

WAREHOUSE RECEIPTS
Uniform Commercial Code (this index)

WAREHOUSES AND WAREHOUSEMEN
Uniform Commercial Code (this index)

WARRANTIES AND CONDITIONS
Insurance Law (this index)

WASTE OR TOXIC SUBSTANCES
Hazardous Wastes and Toxic Substances, Law of (this index)

WASTES
International Environmental Law (this index)

WATER LAW
Generally, **Water 1-4**
Abandonment, loss of water rights, **Water 176-178**
Access to water sources, **Water 180-185**
Adverse possession, loss of water rights, **Water 179, 180**
Allocation, interstate allocation, **Water 397-417**
Appurtenances, **Water 59, 185**

WATER LAW—Cont'd

Aquifers, groundwater, **Water 239-241**
Artificially created watercourses, riparian lands, **Water 27-29**
Avulsion and accretion, loss of riparian rights, **Water 68, 69**
Beneficial use, elements of appropriation, **Water 97-100**
Carrier ditch companies, water services and supply organizations, **Water 421, 422**
Changes in use, **Water 161-176**
Civil law doctrine, diffused surface waters, **Water 297-299**
Clean Water Act, federal control of water and water development, **Water 379-388**
Coastal management, **Coastal and Ocean 1 et seq.**
Common enemy doctrine, diffused surface waters, **Water 295-297**
Compact formation, interstate allocation, **Water 407-412**
Condemnation, **Water 184, 185, 230**
Conflict of laws, federal control of water and water development, **Water 365-368, 376-379**
Conjunctive use, groundwater, **Water 271-281**
Constitutional law, interstate allocation, **Water 407, 408**
Contamination, controlling groundwater contamination, **Water 285-290**
Contiguity to source, riparian lands, **Water 23**
Diffused surface waters, **Water 10, 11, 291-307**
Discharge of waste, rights of riparian proprietors, **Water 42-44**
Ditch rights to water rights, appurtenancy of, **Water 185**
Diversion, elements of appropriation, **Water 92-97**
Drainage, diffused surface waters, **Water 301-303**
Eastern United States, early development of riparian rights, **Water 18-20**
Economic effect of rules, groundwater, **Water 259-262**
Economic solutions, limits on riparian rights, **Water 55, 56**
1866 Mining Act, development of prior appropriation doctrine, **Water 79**
1870 Amendment to Mining Act, development of prior appropriation doctrine, **Water 80**
1877 Desert Land Act, development of prior appropriation doctrine, **Water 80, 81**

WATER LAW—Cont'd

Energy and Natural Resources Law (this index)
Environmental legislation, federal control of water and water development, **Water 379-392**
Equitable apportionment doctrine, interstate allocation, **Water 404-407**
European precedents, riparian rights, **Water 15-18**
Export of water, state restrictions on, **Water 415-417**
Federal and Indian reserved rights, **Water 308-345**
Federal control of water and water development, **Water 346-396**
Federal Power Act, federal control of water and water development, **Water 363-365**
Fish and Wildlife Coordination Act, federal control of water and water development, **Water 391**
Fish and wildlife protection, federal control of water and water development, **Water 368-371, 391**
Foreign and developed water, waters subject to appropriation, **Water 110-112**
Foreign waters, riparian lands, **Water 27**
Forfeiture, loss of water rights, **Water 178, 179**
Formation of compact, interstate allocation, **Water 407-412**
Grants and reservations, transfers of riparian rights, **Water 59, 60**
Gravel recovery, rights of riparian proprietors, **Water 41, 42**
Groundwater, **Water 8-10, 237-290, 325, 326**
Hawaiian Water Law, administration of hybrid systems, **Water 206-212**
Hybrid systems, **Water 7, 8, 54, 190-216**
Hydroelectric generation, rights of riparian proprietors, **Water 40, 41**
Implied rights of access, surface of waterways, **Water 230-233**
Indians, federal and Indian reserved rights, **Water 308-345**
Industrial uses, rights of riparian proprietors, **Water 35, 36**
Intent, elements of appropriation, **Water 89-92**
Intergovernmental problems, **Water 12-14**
International treaties, federal control of water and water development, **Water 392-396**
Interstate allocation, **Water 397-417**

WATER LAW—Cont'd
Irrigation, **Water 35, 36, 429-435**
Lakes, **Water 24-26, 109**
Legislation and legislature, **Water 72, 73, 412-415**
Liability rules, generally, **Water 254-259**
Loss of rights, **Water 66-73, 176-180**
Louisiana Water Law, administration of hybrid systems, **Water 212-214**
Mills, rights of riparian proprietors, **Water 39, 40**
Mining
  1866 Mining Act, development of prior appropriation doctrine, **Water 79**
  1870 Amendment to Mining Act, development of prior appropriation doctrine, **Water 80**
  Hawaiian Water Law, administration of hybrid systems, **Water 206-212**
  Louisiana Water Law, administration of hybrid systems, **Water 212-214**
  riparian proprietors, rights of, **Water 35, 36**
Modifications in hybrid systems, riparian rights, **Water 197-201**
Municipalities, **Water 36-38, 427-429, 435**
Mutual ditch and irrigation companies, water services and supply organizations, **Water 422-426**
Mutual water companies, water services and supply organizations, **Water 421**
Nature of riparian rights, **Water 34-47**
Navigable waters, **Water 45, 46, 218-224**
No harm rule, transfers and changes of water rights, **Water 161, 162**
Nonriparian uses, **Water 51-56**
Ocean management, **Coastal and Ocean 1 et seq.**
Perfection and administration of rights, prior appropriation, **Water 135-155**
Permits, groundwater, **Water 262-265**
Permit systems, **Water 56-59, 138-149**
Place of use, transfers and changes of water rights, **Water 168, 169**

WATER LAW—Cont'd

Point of diversion, transfers and changes of water rights, **Water 168**
Point of return, transfers and changes of water rights, **Water 171, 172**
Ponds, **Water 24-26, 109**
Precedents, riparian rights, **Water 15-18**
Prescription, **Water 54, 55, 69-72, 204-206**
Prior appropriation, **Water 6, 7, 74-189**
Priority, linchpin of appropriative right, **Water 101-106**
Private lands, access to water sources, **Water 182-185**
Private organizations, water services and supply organizations, **Water 420-426**
Public lands, access to water sources generally, **Water 180, 181**
Public organizations, water services and supply organizations, **Water 427-435**
Public rights, **Water 11, 12**
Public trust doctrine, rights to use surface of waterways, **Water 224-226**
Pueblo Water Rights, administration of hybrid systems, **Water 214-216**
Pumping groundwater, statutory limits on, **Water 265-271**
Purpose of use, transfers and changes of water rights, **Water 169, 170**
Quantity and quantification, **Water 319-323, 330-344**
Reasonable use doctrine, diffused surface waters, **Water 299-301**
Reasonable use limitation, riparian rights, **Water 47-51**
Recapture, extent of appropriative right, **Water 129-135**
Reciprocal rights, riparian owners, **Water 44, 45, 233-236**
Reclamation projects, federal control of water and water development, **Water 371-379**
Recognition in American West, riparian rights, **Water 20-22**
Repudiation in American West, riparian rights, **Water 20-22**
Reservations and grants, transfers of riparian rights, **Water 59, 60**
Reserved rights doctrine, federal and Indian reserved rights, **Water 308-318**
Restatement rule, limits on riparian rights, **Water 52, 53**

WATER LAW—Cont'd

Reuse, extent of appropriative right, **Water 129-135**
Rights of riparian proprietors, **Water 34-44**
Rights-of-way, access to water sources, **Water 183-185**
Riparian rights, **Water 4-6, 15-73, 192, 193, 197-201, 203, 204, 233-236, 317, 318**
Salvaged water distinguished, waters subject to appropriation, **Water 112, 113**
Services, water services and supply organizations, **Water 418-435**
Source of title rule, riparian lands, **Water 31, 32**
Springs, **Water 26, 109, 110**
State restrictions, transfers and changes of water rights, **Water 156-158**
Storage, **Water 38, 39, 185-189, 281-284**
Streams, **Water 24, 107-109, 241, 242**
Surface of waterways, **Water 44-47, 217-236**
Surface water, **Water 10, 11, 291-307**
Time of use, transfers and changes of water rights, **Water 170, 171**
Title, riparian lands, **Water 30-32**
Transbasin diversions, transfers and changes of water rights, **Water 158-161**
Transfers, **Water 59-65, 155, 156, 326-329**
Treaties, federal control of water and water development, **Water 392-396**
Trespassing appropriators, access to water sources, **Water 182, 183**
Underground streams distinguished, groundwater, **Water 241, 242**
Underground watercourses, riparian lands, **Water 26, 27**
Unity of title rule, riparian lands, **Water 30, 31**
Utilities, water services and supply organizations, **Water 420, 421**
Water services and supply organizations, **Water 418-435**
Watershed limitation, riparian lands, **Water 29, 30, 51, 52**
Waterwheels, rights of riparian proprietors, **Water 39, 40**
Wells, **Water 242-246**
Wetlands, diffused surface waters, **Water 302, 303**

WATER LAW—Cont'd

Wild and Scenic Rivers Act, federal control of water and water development, **Water 391, 392**

Withdrawals from appropriation, **Water 113-117**

WHITE COLLAR CRIME

Generally, **White Collar Crim 1-15**

Act-Of-Production Doctrine, self-incrimination privilege, **White Collar Crim 357-366**

Administrative agency investigations, **White Collar Crim 282-297**

Agents, **White Collar Crim 30-32, 373-376**

Antiracketeering, bribery and extortion, **White Collar Crim 118-131**

Antitrust conspiracies, **White Collar Crim 54-56**

Assistance of counsel, grand jury investigations, **White Collar Crim 278-281**

Attorney-client privilege, **White Collar Crim 384-395**

Attorneys

- administrative agency investigations, attorney's role, **White Collar Crim 295-297**
- assistance of counsel, grand jury investigations, **White Collar Crim 278-281**

Bankruptcy crimes, **White Collar Crim 213-222**

Banks and banking, **White Collar Crim 72, 73, 199-203**

Bank Secrecy Act, currency reporting crimes, **White Collar Crim 199-203**

Bribery and extortion, **White Collar Crim 110-131**

Collateral estoppel, parallel proceedings, **White Collar Crim 317-319**

Collective knowledge, corporate criminal liability, **White Collar Crim 27-29**

Computer crimes, **White Collar Crim 236-240**

Concealment, bankruptcy crimes, **White Collar Crim 217-220**

Conspiracy, **White Collar Crim 37-56, 144, 145**

Constitutionality of guidelines, **White Collar Crim 412-414**

Continuing investigations, administrative agency investigations, **White Collar Crim 290-293**

WHITE COLLAR CRIME—Cont'd
Corporate criminal liability, **White Collar Crim 16-36**
Corruptly, obstruction of justice, **White Collar Crim 98-101**
Currency reporting crimes, **White Collar Crim 198-212**
Defenses, **White Collar Crim 11-15, 393-395**
Delay, parallel proceedings, **White Collar Crim 303-306**
Discovery, parallel proceedings, **White Collar Crim 300-303**
Domestic financial institutions, currency reporting crimes, **White Collar Crim 203-205**
Entities, self-incrimination privilege, **White Collar Crim 369-376**
Environmental crimes, **White Collar Crim 223-235**
Evasion of taxes, **White Collar Crim 189-191**
Exceptions, exemptions, or exclusions
  attorney client privilege and work product doctrine, **White Collar Crim 392, 393**
  licenses and program exclusion, sanctions, **White Collar Crim 422-425**
  self-incrimination privilege, exception, **White Collar Crim 369-373**
False declarations, **White Collar Crim 164-180**
False oath, bankruptcy crimes, **White Collar Crim 217-220**
False returns, tax crimes, **White Collar Crim 194-197**
False statements, generally, **White Collar Crim 149-163**
Federal criminal law, **White Collar Crim 3-10**
Federal Sentencing Commission, **White Collar Crim 399-401**
Federal Sentencing Guidelines, **White Collar Crim 401-414**
Fines, **White Collar Crim 415-417**
Force, obstruction of justice, **White Collar Crim 98-101**
Forfeiture, Racketeer Influenced and Corrupt Organizations (RICO), **White Collar Crim 145-147**
Fourth Amendment, **White Collar Crim 247-257, 283-285, 378-381**
Fraud, **White Collar Crim 57-90, 216, 217, 220-222, 392, 393**
Grand jury investigations, **White Collar Crim 243-281, 308-311, 327-329**
Hobbs Act, bribery and extortion, **White Collar Crim 118-131**

WHITE COLLAR CRIME—Cont'd
In furtherance test, mail fraud, **White Collar Crim 70, 71**
Insider trading, securities fraud, **White Collar Crim 82-86**
International prosecutions, **White Collar Crim 8-10**
Interstate commerce, **White Collar Crim 119-123, 138, 139**
Joint defense agreements, attorney client privilege and work product doctrine, **White Collar Crim 393-395**
Knowledge, **White Collar Crim 27-29, 220**
Law office searches, **White Collar Crim 381**
Legitimate purpose challenges, administrative agency investigations, **White Collar Crim 288-290**
Licenses and program exclusion, sanctions, **White Collar Crim 422-425**
Mail fraud, **White Collar Crim 57-75**
Mens rea, **White Collar Crim 79-82, 225-227**
Misappropriation theory, securities fraud, **White Collar Crim 86-90**
Oath as false, bankruptcy crimes, **White Collar Crim 217-220**
Objections, grand jury investigations, **White Collar Crim 257-268**
Obstruction of justice, **White Collar Crim 91-109**
Parallel proceedings, **White Collar Crim 298-319**
Penalties, self-incrimination privilege, **White Collar Crim 336-340**
Perjury, **White Collar Crim 164-180**
Personal liability of corporate agents, **White Collar Crim 30-32**
Pinkerton rule, conspiracy, **White Collar Crim 52-54**
Preliminary to requirement, parallel proceedings, **White Collar Crim 311-313**
Public officials, **White Collar Crim 113-118, 125-128**
Punishment, **White Collar Crim 397-425**
Racketeer Influenced and Corrupt Organizations (RICO), **White Collar Crim 132-148**
Racketeering, **White Collar Crim 118-148**
Recantation, perjury and false declarations, **White Collar Crim 177-180**
Referrals, administrative agency investigations, **White Collar Crim 290-293**

WHITE COLLAR CRIME—Cont'd
Refuse Act, environmental crimes, **White Collar Crim 227, 228**
Regulatory inspections, **White Collar Crim 381-383**
Resource Conservation and Recovery Act (RCRA), environmental crimes, **White Collar Crim 231-235**
Responsible corporate officer, corporate criminal liability, **White Collar Crim 32-36**
Returns, tax crimes, **White Collar Crim 193-197**
Robbery, Hobbs Act, **White Collar Crim 123-125**
Sanctions, **White Collar Crim 397-425**
Searches, **White Collar Crim 377-383**
Secrecy violations, grand jury investigations, **White Collar Crim 268-273**
Securities fraud, **White Collar Crim 76-90**
Self-incrimination, **White Collar Crim 306-308, 320-376**
Staff misconduct, administrative agency investigations, **White Collar Crim 293-295**
State or federal prosecution, **White Collar Crim 6-8**
Subpoenas, **White Collar Crim 246, 247, 282, 283**
Tax crimes, **White Collar Crim 181-197**
Third parties, self-incrimination privilege, **White Collar Crim 366-368**
Threats, obstruction of justice, **White Collar Crim 98-101**
Travel Act, bribery and extortion, **White Collar Crim 128-131**
Water Pollution Control Act, environmental crimes, **White Collar Crim 228-230**
Wire fraud, **White Collar Crim 71, 72**
Work product doctrine, **White Collar Crim 387-392**

WILDLIFE
Energy and Natural Resources Law (this index)

WILLFULNESS
Tax Procedure and Tax Fraud (this index)

WILLS AND TRUSTS
Abatement, changes in items bequeathed, **Wills 149-151**

WILLS AND TRUSTS—Cont'd
Accounts and accounting, powers and duties of trustees, **Wills 294-299**
Accretion, changes in items bequeathed, **Wills 151-153**
Ademption, **Wills 139-142, 153-159**
Adopted children, **Wills 12, 13**
Advancements by satisfaction, beneficiary's own action or nature, **Wills 139-142**
Agency versus trust, **Wills 174-176**
Bailment versus trust, **Wills 178**
Beneficiaries, generally, **Wills 116-143, 211-243, 308-323**
Changes in wills, **Wills 80-115, 144-161**
Charitable trusts, **Wills 221-243, 232-240, 249**
Children, **Wills 12-15**
Classification, explanation of trust classification, **Wills 243-259**
Codicils, changing wills, **Wills 101-103**
Community property, summary of spousal rights, **Wills 18-20**
Conditional bequests, beneficiary's own action or nature, **Wills 135, 136**
Conservator, **Wills 177, 178**
Construction or interpretation, **Wills 65, 66, 162-164**
Contested wills, generally, **Wills 70-79**
Contracts, **Wills 130-132, 183, 184**
Custodianship versus trust, **Wills 176, 177**
Cy pre doctrine, **Wills 228-231**
Death, beneficiary's own action or nature, **Wills 119-124**
Decedents' estates, generally, **Wills 165 et seq.**
Definition of trust, **Wills 170-173**
Dependent relative revocation of will, **Wills 93-101**
Deviation, powers and duties of trustees, **Wills 268, 269**
Discretion, powers and duties of trustees, **Wills 266-268**
Diversification, powers and duties of trustees, **Wills 302-304**
Dower and curtesy, summary of spousal rights, **Wills 18-20**
Elections, beneficiary's own action or nature, **Wills 137, 138**
Elements of trust, **Wills 189-259**
Equitable changes, beneficiary's own action or nature, **Wills 136, 137**

WILLS AND TRUSTS—Cont'd

Equitable charge versus trust, **Wills 180-183**
Executors and administrators, **Wills 177, 178**
Exemptions, summary of spousal rights, **Wills 17**
Exoneration, changes in items bequeathed, **Wills 160, 161**
Explanation of trust classification, **Wills 243-259**
Family maintenance allowance, summary of spousal rights, **Wills 17, 18**
Fees, trustee fees, **Wills 327-330**
Felons, beneficiary's own action or nature, **Wills 117-119**
Fraud, contested wills, **Wills 74-77**
Guardian, **Wills 177, 178**
Heirs, generally, **Wills 1-5, 8**
Holographic wills, **Wills 61, 62**
Homestead exemption, summary of spousal rights, **Wills 17**
Honorary trusts, **Wills 240-243**
Husband and wife, superseding rights of spouse and issue, **Wills 16-37**
Illegitimate children, **Wills 14, 15**
Impartiality, powers and duties of trustees, **Wills 304, 305**
Imperfect gift versus trust, **Wills 184, 185**
Improvements, powers and duties of trustees, **Wills 265, 266**
Incapacity, contested wills, **Wills 72-74**
Incorporation by reference, revoking and changing wills, **Wills 111-113**
Indemnity of trustee, **Wills 330-332**
Integration, revoking and changing wills, **Wills 103-105**
Intent, **Wills 66-70, 82**
Interested witness, **Wills 52-61**
In terrorem clauses, beneficiary's own action or nature, **Wills 133-135**
Inter vivos trusts, **Wills 250**
Intestacy, generally, **Wills 1-15**
Investments, powers and duties of trustees, **Wills 265, 266, 281-289**
Joint action, beneficiary's own action or nature, **Wills 133-143**
Land trusts, **Wills 255-258**

WILLS AND TRUSTS—Cont'd
Leases, powers and duties of trustees, **Wills 263-265**
Legal and illegal trusts, **Wills 245-249**
Liens, **Wills 180-183**
Life insurance trusts, **Wills 255, 256**
Lost wills, **Wills 89-91**
Loyalty, powers and duties of trustees, **Wills 273-280**
Massachusetts Business Trusts, **Wills 256-258**
Modification of trust, **Wills 337-339**
Mortgages, **Wills 180-183, 263-265**
Murder, beneficiary's own action or nature, **Wills 124-129**
New York Estates, Powers and Trusts Law, **Wills 40, 41**
Nominees, powers and duties of trustees, **Wills 289-294**
Operation of law, revocation of will by, **Wills 81**
Partial revocation of will, **Wills 89**
Passive and active trusts, **Wills 244**
Per stirpes, **Wills 8-12**
Pledge, **Wills 180-183**
Post-will spouse, **Wills 22, 23**
Power of appointment versus trust, **Wills 179, 180**
Powers and duties of trustees, **Wills 261-307**
Pretermission, **Wills 23-37**
Probate, **Wills 40-51, 62-65, 82-84, 121**
Property settlement agreements, beneficiary's own action or nature, **Wills 138**
Quarantine, summary of spousal rights, **Wills 16**
Remedies of beneficiaries against trustees, **Wills 323-327**
Renunciation, beneficiary's own action or nature, **Wills 124**
Republication, revoking and changing wills, **Wills 105-111**
Res, elements of trust, **Wills 195-204**
Resulting trusts, **Wills 244, 245**
Revival, revoking and changing wills, **Wills 91-93**
Revocation, **Wills 80-115, 251**
Sales, powers and duties of trustees, **Wills 263-265**
Satisfaction, beneficiary's own action or nature, **Wills 139-142**
Setoffs, beneficiary's own action or nature, **Wills 142, 143**

WILLS AND TRUSTS—Cont'd
Sine qua non, revoking wills, **Wills 80**
Small estates, summary of spousal rights, **Wills 18**
Spendthrift trusts, **Wills 252-255**
Statute of wills, generally, **Wills 38-79**
Strict versus liberal interpretation, **Wills 65, 66**
Successive beneficiaries, **Wills 308-323**
Superseding rights of spouse and issue, **Wills 16-37**
Surviving spouse, **Wills 21, 22**
Termination of trust, **Wills 337-339**
Third parties' rights, **Wills 332-337**
Totten trusts, **Wills 258, 259**
Transfer, elements of trust, **Wills 189-195**
Trusts, generally, **Wills 169-188**
Undue influence, contested wills, **Wills 77-79**
Uniform Probate Code, **Wills 40-51, 62-65, 82-84, 121**
Uniform Probate Code (this index)
Widow or widower, **Wills 21, 22**
Witnesses, **Wills 51-56**
Writing, revocation of will by, **Wills 84-87**

WITHHOLDING
Health Care Law and Ethics (this index)
International Taxation (this index)

WITNESSES
Evidence (this index)

WOMEN
International Human Rights (this index)

WORD PROCESSING
Legal Writing (this index)

WORKERS' COMPENSATION AND EMPLOYEE PROTECTION LAWS
Generally, **Work Comp 1-23**

WORKERS' COMPENSATION AND EMPLOYEE PROTECTION LAWS—Cont'd
Abortion, Title VII of 1964 Civil Rights Act, **Work Comp 217-219**
Acts of God, ''arising out of'' concept, **Work Comp 64**
Administration, **Work Comp 110-121**
Age Discrimination Act of 1975, **Work Comp 271, 272**
Age Discrimination in Employment Act of 1967, **Work Comp 256-260**
Agricultural employees, **Work Comp 44, 45**
Alienage Discrimination and the Immigration Reform and Control Act of 1986, **Work Comp 269, 270**
Aliens, **Work Comp 49, 50**
Antidiscrimination laws, generally, **Work Comp 189-193**
''Arising out of'' concept, **Work Comp 61-70**
Assault, ''arising out of'' concept, **Work Comp 66, 67**
Assumption of risk, **Work Comp 4, 5**
Automobile insurance, **Work Comp 134, 135**
Bad faith, struggle for coverage and noncoverage, **Work Comp 37**
Casual employees, **Work Comp 44**
Charitable organizations, **Work Comp 55**
Children and minors, **Work Comp 50, 91, 92, 158; Work Comp 91, 92, 158**
Civil Rights Act of 1968, title I, **Work Comp 270**
Civil Rights Acts of 1866, 1870, and 1871, **Work Comp 244-253**
Civil Rights Attorney's Fees Awards Act, **Work Comp 263-266**
Class actions, Title VII of 1964 Civil Rights Act, **Work Comp 232-234**
Co-employees, struggle for coverage and noncoverage, **Work Comp 35, 36**
Commissions versus courts, **Work Comp 111, 112**
Common law, generally, **Work Comp 34**
Common law marriage, widow, **Work Comp 90, 91**
Compromise and settlement, **Work Comp 117, 118**
Compulsory coverage, **Work Comp 27**
Concurrent employees, **Work Comp 56**

WORKERS' COMPENSATION AND EMPLOYEE PROTECTION LAWS—Cont'd

Conflict of laws, extraterritorial problems and overlapping coverages, **Work Comp 122-124**
Constitutional law, generally, **Work Comp 24-28, 275-277**
Contagious diseases in the workplace, **Work Comp 286, 287**
Contributory negligence, **Work Comp 4**
Coverage formula, generally, **Work Comp 58-86**
Death and death benefits, **Work Comp 87-93, 108, 109**
Defenses, third party actions, **Work Comp 132**
Dependency and partial dependency, **Work Comp 87-89**
Disabilities, generally, **Work Comp 100-104**
Disaster unemployment assistance, **Work Comp 149**
Discharge from employment, **Work Comp 40, 41, 281-284**
Discrimination, generally, **Work Comp 189-193**
Disparate treatment, Title VII of 1964 Civil Rights Act, **Work Comp 198-209**
Domestic employees, **Work Comp 45**
Drugs in the workplace, **Work Comp 284**
Dual capacity employers, struggle for coverage and noncoverage, **Work Comp 36**
Education Amendments of 1972, Title IX, **Work Comp 262**
Election, **Work Comp 25, 26**
Emergencies, "in the course of" concept, **Work Comp 75, 76**
Employee Retirement Income Security Act of 1974 (ERISA), **Work Comp 278, 279**
Employer-employee relationship, generally, **Work Comp 42, 43**
Employers' Liability Acts, **Work Comp 5, 6**
Enforcement, **Work Comp 160, 161, 166-168**
Equal Pay Act of 1963, **Work Comp 253-256**
European compensation legislation, **Work Comp 6-8**
Evidence, **Work Comp 115-117**
Exclusiveness of remedy, **Work Comp 27, 28**
Executive orders, **Work Comp 274, 275**
Ex-servicemen, **Work Comp 148, 149**
Extended benefits, **Work Comp 147, 150**

WORKERS' COMPENSATION AND EMPLOYEE PROTECTION LAWS—Cont'd

Extraterritorial problems and overlapping coverages, **Work Comp 122-128**
Fair Labor Standards Act, **Work Comp 152-161**
Federal Black Lung Benefits Legislation, **Work Comp 22, 23, 169-173**
Federal Constitution, **Work Comp 275-277**
Federal construction projects, **Work Comp 280**
Federal credit laws, **Work Comp 280, 281**
Federal employees, **Work Comp 47, 48**
Federal Employees' Compensation Act, **Work Comp 13, 14**
Federal Employees' Liability Act, **Work Comp 14-16**
Federal legislation, **Work Comp 12-23**
Federal unemployment insurance programs, **Work Comp 144-149**
Fellow-servant doctrine, **Work Comp 2-4**
Fetal vulnerability rules, Title VII of 1964 Civil Rights Act, **Work Comp 219, 220**
Foreign boycott laws, **Work Comp 272**
Freedom of contract, **Work Comp 25**
Full faith and credit, extraterritorial problems and overlapping coverages, **Work Comp 124, 125**
Future of workers' compensation, **Work Comp 136-140**
General and special employees, **Work Comp 53, 54**
Germany, European compensation legislation, **Work Comp 7**
Going to and from work, "in the course of" concept, **Work Comp 72, 73**
Great Britain, European compensation legislation, **Work Comp 7, 8**
Handicap Discrimination and the Rehabilitation Act of 1973, **Work Comp 266-269**
Hearings, **Work Comp 115-117**
Heart cases, arising out of" concept, **Work Comp 67, 68**
Horseplay, "arising out of" concept, **Work Comp 67**
Hospital insurance (HI), Social Security, **Work Comp 184-186**
Illegal employments, **Work Comp 50, 51**

WORKERS' COMPENSATION AND EMPLOYEE PROTECTION LAWS—Cont'd
Imported dangers doctrine, "arising out of" concept, **Work Comp 65, 66**
Independent contractors, **Work Comp 51, 52**
Inspectors' negligence, struggle for coverage and noncoverage, **Work Comp 37**
Intentional torts of employers, struggle for coverage and noncoverage, **Work Comp 39, 40**
Intergovernmental Personnel Act of 1970, **Work Comp 270, 271**
"In the course of" concept, **Work Comp 70-79**
Intoxication, "in the course of" concept, **Work Comp 77, 78**
Jones Act, **Work Comp 16-18**
Jury service, **Work Comp 281**
Labor Management Relations Act, **Work Comp 272, 273**
Labor union liability, Title VII of 1964 Civil Rights Act, **Work Comp 225, 226**
Liberal construction of compensation acts, **Work Comp 32, 33**
Loaned employees, **Work Comp 45, 46**
Longshore and Harbor Workers' Compensation Act, **Work Comp 18-22**
Lump sum commutation, **Work Comp 117, 118**
Medical expenses, **Work Comp 94-109**
Medicare, Social Security, **Work Comp 184-186**
Migrant farm workers, **Work Comp 285, 286**
Minimum number of employees, **Work Comp 53**
Minimum wage, Fair Labor Standards Act, **Work Comp 154, 155**
Minors, **Work Comp 50, 91, 92, 158**
Mixed-purpose trip, "in the course of" concept, **Work Comp 73, 74**
Modification, **Work Comp 118, 119**
Multiple and successive injuries, **Work Comp 104-106**
National Commission on State Workmen's Compensation Laws, **Work Comp 136-138**
National Labor Relations Act, **Work Comp 279, 280**
National Workers' Compensation Standards Act proposals, **Work Comp 138**

WORKERS' COMPENSATION AND EMPLOYEE PROTECTION LAWS—Cont'd

Necessity of personal injury by accident, **Work Comp 79-82**
No-fault insurance, **Work Comp 134, 135**
Occupational disease, **Work Comp 82-86**
Occupational Safety and Health Act, **Work Comp 162-168**
Overlapping coverages, **Work Comp 122-128**
Overtime compensation, Fair Labor Standards Act, **Work Comp 155, 156**
Partial dependency, **Work Comp 87-89**
Pension contributions and benefits calculations gender-based, Title VII of 1964 Civil Rights Act, **Work Comp 220, 221**
Personal comfort doctrine, "in the course of" concept, **Work Comp 75**
Physicians, **Work Comp 38, 39, 96, 97**
Plant closings, notice of, **Work Comp 285**
Polygraph tests, **Work Comp 285**
Preexisting injury or disease, "arising out of" concept, **Work Comp 68, 69**
Pregnancy, Title VII of 1964 Civil Rights Act, **Work Comp 217-219**
Presumptive coverage, **Work Comp 26, 27**
Priorities, **Work Comp 92, 93**
Products liability, struggle for coverage and noncoverage, **Work Comp 37, 38**
Professional employees, **Work Comp 52**
Professionally developed ability tests, Title VII of 1964 Civil Rights Act, **Work Comp 222-224**
Property actions, struggle for coverage and noncoverage, **Work Comp 36**
Proximate cause, "arising out of" concept, **Work Comp 62**
Public employees, **Work Comp 46-48**
Recreation, "in the course of" concept, **Work Comp 74, 75**
Redistribution, **Work Comp 118, 119**
Rehabilitation, medical expenses, **Work Comp 95, 96**
Religious discrimination, Title VII of 1964 Civil Rights Act, **Work Comp 215, 216**

WORKERS' COMPENSATION AND EMPLOYEE PROTECTION LAWS—Cont'd
Removal, **Work Comp 121**
Reopening, **Work Comp 118, 119**
Retaliation, **Work Comp 40, 41, 224, 225**
Retirement and Survivors Insurance (OASI), **Work Comp 177-180**
Reverse discrimination, Title VII of 1964 Civil Rights Act, **Work Comp 234-242**
Review, **Work Comp 115-117**
Second injury fund, **Work Comp 106-108**
Seniority systems, Title VII of 1964 Civil Rights Act, **Work Comp 221, 222**
Sex-based wage discrimination, Fair Labor Standards Act, **Work Comp 157, 158**
Social and economic policies, **Work Comp 28-32**
Social Security, **Work Comp 174-188**
State and municipal employees, **Work Comp 46, 47**
State compensation acts, generally, **Work Comp 8-12**
State financed programs, unemployment compensation, **Work Comp 150, 151**
Statute of limitations, **Work Comp 113, 114**
Statutory actions, generally, **Work Comp 34**
Street risk doctrine, ''arising out of'' concept, **Work Comp 65**
Subcontractors, **Work Comp 54, 55**
Subrogation, **Insur 289, 290; Work Comp 132, 133**
Successive employees, **Work Comp 56, 57**
Suicides, ''in the course of'' concept, **Work Comp 78, 79**
Supplemental benefits, **Work Comp 147**
Supplemental Security Income (SSI), **Work Comp 186, 187**
Supplementary Medical insurance (SMI), Social Security, **Work Comp 184-186**
Systemic disparate treatment, Title VII of 1964 Civil Rights Act, **Work Comp 204-209**
Termination, **Work Comp 118, 119**
Third party actions, **Work Comp 129-135**
Title VI of Civil Rights Act of 1964, **Work Comp 260-262**

WORKERS' COMPENSATION AND EMPLOYEE PROTECTION LAWS—Cont'd
Title VII of 1964 Civil Rights Act, **Work Comp 194-243**
Torts, generally, **Work Comp 34**
Trade adjustment assistance, **Work Comp 149**
Unemployment compensation, generally, **Work Comp 141-151**
Unexplained accidents, "arising out of" concept, **Work Comp 69, 70**
Uninsured motorist insurance, **Work Comp 134, 135**
Unjust discharges, **Work Comp 281-284**
Veterans, generally, **Work Comp 148, 149**
Vietnam Era Veterans Readjustment Act of 1974, **Work Comp 271**
Volunteers, **Work Comp 49**
Wage discrimination, Title VII of 1964 Civil Rights Act, **Work Comp 216, 217**
Widow, **Work Comp 89-91**
Willful misconduct, "in the course of" concept, **Work Comp 76, 77**

WORLD TRADE ORGANIZATION (WTO)
International Trade and Investment (this index)

WRITING
Legal Writing (this index)

WTO (WORLD TRADE ORGANIZATION)
International Trade and Investment (this index)

ZONING
Land Use (this index)

TABLE OF NUTSHELL/AM JUR 2D CORRELATIONS

Am Jur 2d is an A-Z encyclopedic text covering every title of American law. It's the best source to consult first for quick, accurate answers to any legal problem. This table correlates the titles in the West Group Nutshell Series with the articles in Am Jur 2d.

Nutshell Series	Am Jur 2d
Accounting and Finance for Lawyers in a Nutshell	Accounts and Accounting
Administrative Law and Process in a Nutshell	Administrative Law
Admiralty in a Nutshell	Admiralty
Agency-Partnership, and the LLC	Agency; Partnership
Agency-Partnership in a Nutshell	Agency; Partnership
Agriculture Law in a Nutshell	Agriculture
AIDS Law in a Nutshell	Health § 19 et seq.
Alternative Dispute Resolution in a Nutshell	Alternative Dispute Resolution
American Indian Law in a Nutshell	Indians
Anglo-American Law in a Nutshell	Common Law
Antitrust Law and Economics in a Nutshell	Monopolies, Restraints of Trade and Unfair Trade Practices
Appellate Advocacy in a Nutshell	Appellate Review
Art Law in a Nutshell	Copyright and Literary Property

TABLE OF CORRELATIONS

Nutshell Series	Am Jur 2d
Banking and Financial Institutions Law in a Nutshell	Banks; Building and Loan Associations
Bankruptcy and Other Debtor-Creditor Law in a Nutshell	Bankruptcy
California Civil Procedure in a Nutshell	Trial, see also Cal Jur Trial
Civil Procedure in a Nutshell	Trial
Coastal and Ocean Management Law in a Nutshell	Waters
Community Property in a Nutshell	Community Property
Comparative Legal Traditions in a Nutshell	Common Law
Conflicts in a Nutshell	Conflict of Laws
Constitutional Analysis in a Nutshell	Constitutional Law
Constitutional Civil Rights in a Nutshell	Civil Rights § 5 et seq.
Constitutional Federalism in a Nutshell	Constitutional Law § 89 et seq., 246 et seq.
Constitutional Law in a Nutshell	Constitutional Law
Consumer Law in a Nutshell	Consumer and Borrower Protection; Consumer Product Warranty Acts
Contract Remedies in a Nutshell	Contracts § 724-728; Specific Performance
Contracts in a Nutshell	Contracts; Restitution and Implied Contracts
Corporations in a Nutshell	Corporations

TABLE OF CORRELATIONS

Nutshell Series	Am Jur 2d
Criminal Law in a Nutshell	Abduction and Kidnapping; Adultery and Fornication; Arrest; Arson and Related Offenses; Assault and Battery; Bail and Recognizance; Bigamy; Bribery; Burglary; Conspiracy; Counterfeiting; Criminal Law; Embezzlement; Escape, Prison Breaking and Rescue; Extortion, Blackmail, and Threats; Extradition; Forgery; Gambling; Habeas Corpus; Habitual Criminals and Subsequent Offenders; Harboring Criminals; Homicide; Incest; Indictments and Informations; Larceny; Lewdness, Indecency, and Obscenity; Mayhem and Related Offenses; Obstructing Justice; Pardon and Parole; Perjury; Prostitution; Rape; Receiving and Transporting Stolen Property; Robbery; Searches and Seizures; Sedition, Subversive Activities, and Treason; Sodomy
Criminal Procedure-Constitutional Limitations in a Nutshell	Criminal Law § 635 et seq.

TABLE OF CORRELATIONS

Nutshell Series	Am Jur 2d
Debtor-Creditor Relations in a Nutshell	Assignments for Benefit of Creditors; Composition with Creditors; Consumer and Borrower Protection; Credit Cards and Charge Accounts; Insolvency; Moneylenders and Pawnbrokers
Disability Law in a Nutshell	Americans with Disabilities Act
Elder Law in a Nutshell	Job Discrimination § 16, 17, 168-172; Social Security and Medicare
Employee Benefit Plans in a Nutshell	Employment Relationship § 77-215; Pensions and Retirement Funds
Employee Rights in a Nutshell	Employment Relationship; Federal Employers' Liability and Compensation Acts; Labor and Labor Relations; Unemployment Compensation; Wrongful Discharge
Employment Discrimination in a Nutshell	Job Discrimination
Energy and Natural Resources Law in a Nutshell	Atomic Energy; Energy; Gas and Oil; Mines and Minerals
Environmental Law in a Nutshell	Pollution Control
Estate and Gift Taxation in a Nutshell	Inheritance, Estate, and Gift Taxes
Estate Planning in a Nutshell	Estates; Wills

TABLE OF CORRELATIONS

Nutshell Series	Am Jur 2d
European Union Law in a Nutshell	Labor and Labor Relations
Evidence in a Nutshell: State and Federal Rules	Evidence; Expert and Opinion Evidence; Witnesses
Family Law in a Nutshell	Adoption; Annulment of Marriage; Birth Control; Desertion and Nonsupport; Divorce and Separation; Dower and Curtesy; Marriage; Parent and Child; Support of Persons
Federal Income Taxation Individuals in a Nutshell	Federal Taxation
Federal Income Taxation of Corporations and Stockholders in a Nutshell	Corporations § 164-175; Federal Taxation ¶ 4000 et seq.
Federal Income Taxation of Partnerships in a Nutshell	Federal Taxation ¶ 2000 et seq.
Federal Jurisdiction in a Nutshell .	Federal Courts § 560-601, 665-1226, 2266-2318
Federal Rules of Evidence in a Nutshell	Evidence
First Amendment Law in a Nutshell	Constitutional Law § 407-559
Future Interests in a Nutshell	Estates § 1, 171-187, 194-332; Life Tenants and Remaindermen
Government Contracts in a Nutshell	States, Territories and Dependencies § 73, 74
Hazardous Wastes and Toxic Substanses in a Nutshell	Pollution Control

TABLE OF CORRELATIONS

Nutshell Series	Am Jur 2d
Health Care Law and Ethics in a Nutshell	Health; Physicians, Surgeons and Other Healers § 200-301, 306, 310-377
How to Study Law and take Law Exams in a Nutshell	Attorneys at Law
Immigration Law and Procedure in a Nutshell	Aliens and Citizens
Injunctions in a Nutshell	Injunctions
Insurance Law in a Nutshell	Automobile Insurance; Insurance
Intellectual Property-Patents, Trademarks and Copyright in a Nutshell	Copyright and Literary Property
International Business Transactions in a Nutshell	Commerce § 1, 2, 5, 19, 22-26, 35, 75; Foreign Corporations; International Law
International Human Rights in a Nutshell	International Law
International Law in a Nutshell	Ambassadors and Consuls; International Law; Treaties
International Taxation in a Nutshell	Customs Duties and Import Regulations; International Law § 49
Judicial Process in a Nutshell	Process
Jurisprudence (Legal Philosophy) in a Nutshell	Common Law; Statutes
Labor Arbitration Law and Practice in a Nutshell	Labor and Labor Relations § 3352-3510
Labor Law in a Nutshell	Labor and Labor Relations

TABLE OF CORRELATIONS

Nutshell Series	Am Jur 2d
Land Use in a Nutshell	Zoning and Planning
Landlord and Tenant Law in a Nutshell	Landlord and Tenant
Law and Economics	Markets and Marketing
Legal Drafting in a Nutshell	Attorneys at Law; Prosecuting Attorneys
Legal Interviewing and Counseling in a Nutshell	Attorneys at Law; Prosecuting Attorneys
Legal Negotiation in a Nutshell	Compromise and Settlement
Legal Research in a Nutshell	Attorneys at Law; Prosecuting Attorneys
Legal Writing in a Nutshell	Attorneys at Law; Prosecuting Attorneys
Legislative Law and Process in a Nutshell	Parliamentary Law
Local Government Law in a Nutshell	Municipal Corporations, Counties, and Other Political Subdivisions
Mass Communication Law in a Nutshell	Telecommunications
Medical Liability in a Nutshell	Physicians, Surgeons and Other Healers § 200-377
Military Law in a Nutshell	Military and Civil Defense
Modern Public Land Law in a Nutshell	Public Lands
Negotiable Instruments and Check Collection in a Nutshell	Bills and Notes; Collection and Credit Agencies
Oil and Gas in a Nutshell	Gas and Oil
Personal Property in a Nutshell	Property
Pretrial Litigation in a Nutshell	Pretrial Conference and Procedure
Products Liability in a Nutshell	Products Liability

TABLE OF CORRELATIONS

Nutshell Series	Am Jur 2d
Professional Responsibility in a Nutshell	Attorneys at Law; Prosecuting Attorneys
Real Estate Finance in a Nutshell .	Vendor and Purchaser § 78, 294-312
Real Property in a Nutshell	Adjoining Landowners; Adverse Possession; Boundaries; Dedication; Deeds; Easements and Licenses; Ejectment; Homestead; Improvements; Property; Quieting Title and Determination of Adverse Claims; Real Estate Time-Sharing
Regulated Industries in a Nutshell .	Corporations
Remedies in a Nutshell	Actions § 2 et seq.; Coram Nobis and Allied Statutory Remedies; Election of Remedies
Sales and Leases of Goods in a Nutshell	Bailments; Sales
Schools, Students and Teachers in a Nutshell	Colleges and Universities; Schools
Sea in a Nutshell	Waters
Section 1983 Litigation in a Nutshell	Civil Rights § 16-288
Secured Transactions in a Nutshell	Secured Transactions
Securities Regulation in a Nutshell	Securities Regulation-Federal; Securities Regulation-State

TABLE OF CORRELATIONS

Nutshell Series	Am Jur 2d
Sentencing, Corrections and Prisoners' Rights in a Nutshell	Criminal Law § 525-631; Escape, Prison Breaking and Rescue; Federal Sentencing Guidelines; Habeas Corpus; Pardon and Parole; Penal and Correctional Institutions
Sex Discrimination in a Nutshell	Civil Rights § 84-92, 154-192, 246; Job Discrimination
Sports Law in a Nutshell	Entertainment and Sports Law
State and Local Taxation and Finance in a Nutshell	State and Local Taxation
State and Religion in a Nutshell	Constitutional Law § 415 et seq.
State Constitutional Law in a Nutshell	Constitutional Law
Study and Practice of Law in a Nutshell	Attorneys at Law; Prosecuting Attorneys
Tax Procedure and Tax Fraud in a Nutshell	Federal Tax Enforcement; State and Local Taxation
Torts in a Nutshell	Federal Tort Claims Act; Municipal, County, School, and State Tort Liability; Negligence; Torts
Toxic Torts in a Nutshell	Torts
Trial Advocacy in a Nutshell	Trial
Trial and Practice Skills in a Nutshell	Trial
Trial (Where Do I Sit? What Do I Say?) in a Nutshell	Trial

TABLE OF CORRELATIONS

Nutshell Series	Am Jur 2d
Unfair Trade Practices in a Nutshell	Monopolies, Restraints of Trade and Unfair Trade Practices
Uniform Commercial Code in a Nutshell	Commercial Code
Uniform Probate Code in a Nutshell	Descent and Distribution; Executors and Administrators; Wills
Water Law in a Nutshell	Waters
White Collar Crime in a Nutshell .	Criminal Law
Wills and Trusts in a Nutshell	Trusts; Wills
Workers' Compensation and Employee Protection Laws in a Nutshell	Workers' Compensation

TABLE OF NUTSHELL/KEY NUMBER SYSTEM CORRELATIONS

This table correlates the titles in the West Group Nutshell Series with the topics in the West Key Number Classification System, an essential aid to solving legal problems. Finding one or more Key Numbers applicable to a point of law greatly facilitates thorough case retrieval.

Nutshell Series	Key Number Topic
Accounting and Finance for Lawyers in a Nutshell.	Account
Administrative Law and Process in a Nutshell	Administrative Law and Procedure
Admiralty in a Nutshell.	Admiralty
Agency-Partnership, and the LLC .	Partnership; Principal and Agent
Agency-Partnership in a Nutshell . .	Partnership; Principal and Agent
Agriculture Law in a Nutshell.	Agriculture
AIDS Law in a Nutshell	Health and Environment § 21 et seq.
Alternative Dispute Resolution in a Nutshell	Arbitration; Labor Relations
American Indian Law in a Nutshell	Indians
Anglo-American Law in a Nutshell	Common Law
Antitrust Law and Economics in a Nutshell	Monopolies
Appellate Advocacy in a Nutshell .	Appeal and Error
Art Law in a Nutshell	Copyright and Intellectual Property § 16 et seq.

TABLE OF KEY NUMBER SYSTEM CORRELATIONS

Nutshell Series	Key Number Topic
Banking and Financial Institutions Law in a Nutshell	Banks and Banking; Building and Loan Associations
Bankruptcy and Other Debtor-Creditor Law in a Nutshell	Bankruptcy; Debtor and Creditor
California Civil Procedure in a Nutshell	Trial
Civil Procedure in a Nutshell	Federal Civil Procedure; Trial
Coastal and Ocean Management Law in a Nutshell	Waters and Water Courses
Community Property in a Nutshell	Husband & Wife § 246 et seq.
Comparative Legal Traditions in a Nutshell	Common Law
Conflicts in a Nutshell	Action; Contracts; Torts
Constitutional Analysis in a Nutshell; Constitutional Civil Rights in a Nutshell; Constitutional Federalism in a Nutshell; Constitutional Law in a Nutshell	Constitutional Law
Consumer Law in a Nutshell	Consumer Credit; Consumer Protection
Contract Remedies in a Nutshell	Contracts § 324 et seq.; Specific Performance
Contracts in a Nutshell	Contracts; Implied and Constructive Contracts
Corporations in a Nutshell	Corporations
Creditor-Debtor Relations in a Nutshell	Consumer Credit

TABLE OF KEY NUMBER SYSTEM CORRELATIONS

Nutshell Series	Key Number Topic
Criminal Law in a Nutshell	Adultery; Arrest; Arson; Assault and Battery; Bail; Bigamy; Bribery; Burglary; Conspiracy; Counterfeiting; Criminal Law; Embezzlement; Escape; Extortion and Threats; Extradition and Detainers; Forgery; Gaming; Habeas Corpus; Homicide; Incest; Indictment and Information; Larceny; Lewdness; Mayhem; Obscenity; Obstructing Justice; Pardon and Parole; Perjury; Prostitution; Rape; Receiving Stolen Goods; Robbery; Searches and Seizures; Sodomy; Treason
Criminal Procedure-Constitutional Limitations in a Nutshell	Constitutional Law
Debtor-Creditor Relations in a Nutshell	Debtor and Creditor
Disability Law in a Nutshell	Civil Rights
Elder Law in a Nutshell	Social Security and Public Welfare
Employee Benefit Plans in a Nutshell	Pensions
Employee Rights in a Nutshell	Labor Relations; Master and Servant
Employment Discrimination in a Nutshell	Civil Rights § 141 et seq.
Energy and Natural Resources Law in a Nutshell	Electricity; Gas; Mines and Minerals
Environmental Law in a Nutshell	Health and Environment

TABLE OF KEY NUMBER SYSTEM CORRELATIONS

Nutshell Series	Key Number Topic
Estate and Gift Taxation in a Nutshell	Taxation § 856 et seq.
Estate Planning in a Nutshell	Wills
European Union Law in a Nutshell.	Labor Relations
Evidence in a Nutshell: State and Federal Rules	Criminal Law; Evidence; Witnesses
Family Law in a Nutshell	Abortion and Birth Control; Adoption; Dower and Curtesy; Husband and Wife; Marriage; Parent and Child
Federal Income Taxation Individuals in a Nutshell	Internal Revenue § 3110 et seq.
Federal Income Taxation of Corporations and Stockholders in a Nutshell	Internal Revenue § 3620 et seq.
Federal Income Taxation Partnerships in a Nutshell	Internal Revenue § 3910 et seq.
Federal Jurisdiction in a Nutshell	Federal Courts § 1 et seq.
Federal Rules of Evidence in a Nutshell	Evidence
First Amendment Law in a Nutshell	Constitutional Law § 82 et seq.
Future Interests in a Nutshell	Remainders; Reversions; Wills
Government Contracts in a Nutshell	Public Contracts
Hazardous Wastes and Toxic Substanses; Health Care Law and Ethics in a Nutshell	Health and Environment
Health Care Law and Ethics in a Nutshell	Physicians and Surgeons

TABLE OF KEY NUMBER SYSTEM CORRELATIONS

Nutshell Series	Key Number Topic
How to Study Law and take Law Exams in a Nutshell	Attorney and Client
Immigration Law and Procedure in a Nutshell	Aliens
Injunctions in a Nutshell	Injunction
Insurance Law in a Nutshell	Insurance
Intellectual Property-Patents, Trademarks and Copyright in a Nutshell	Copyright and Intellectual Property; Patents; Trade Regulation
International Business Transactions in a Nutshell	Commerce; Corporations
International Human Rights in a Nutshell	International Law
International Law in a Nutshell	Ambassadors and Consuls; International Law; Treaties
International Taxation in a Nutshell	Customs Duties; Internal Revenue
Judicial Process in a Nutshell	Courts § 1 et seq.
Jurisprudence (Legal Philosophy) in a Nutshell	Common Law; Statutes
Labor Arbitration Law and Practice in a Nutshell; Labor Law in a Nutshell	Labor Relations
Land Use in a Nutshell	Zoning and Planning
Landlord and Tenant Law in a Nutshell	Landlord and Tenant
Law and Economics	Commerce
Legal Drafting in a Nutshell	Attorney and Client; District and Prosecuting Attorneys
Legal Interviewing and Counseling in a Nutshell	Attorney and Client; District and Prosecuting Attorneys
Legal Negotiation in a Nutshell	Compromise and Settlement

TABLE OF KEY NUMBER SYSTEM CORRELATIONS

Nutshell Series	Key Number Topic
Legal Research in a Nutshell	Attorney and Client; District and Prosecuting Attorneys
Legal Writing in a Nutshell	Attorney and Client; District and Prosecuting Attorneys
Legislative Law and Process in a Nutshell	Parliamentary Law; States § 27 et seq.
Local Government Law in a Nutshell	Counties; Municipal Corporations; Towns
Mass Communication Law in a Nutshell	Telecommunications
Medical Liability in a Nutshell	Physicians and Surgeons § 15 et seq.
Military Law in a Nutshell	Armed Services; Military Justice
Modern Public Land Law in a Nutshell	Public Lands
Negotiable Instruments and Check Collection in a Nutshell	Bills and Notes; Credit Reporting Agencies
Oil and Gas in a Nutshell	Gas
Personal Property in a Nutshell	Property § 3 et seq.
Pretrial Litigation in a Nutshell	Pretrial Procedure
Products Liability in a Nutshell	Products Liability
Professional Responsibility in a Nutshell	Attorney and Client; District and Prosecuting Attorneys
Real Estate Finance in a Nutshell	Mortgages
Real Property in a Nutshell	Adjoining Landowners; Adverse Possession; Boundaries; Dedication; Deeds; Easements; Ejectment; Homestead; Improvements; Property; Quieting Title

TABLE OF KEY NUMBER SYSTEM CORRELATIONS

Nutshell Series	Key Number Topic
Regulated Industries in a Nutshell .	Public Utilities
Remedies in a Nutshell	Action; Election of Remedies
Sales and Leases of Goods in a Nutshell	Bailment; Sales
Schools, Students and Teachers in a Nutshell	Colleges and Universities; Schools
Sea in a Nutshell	Admiralty
Section 1983 Litigation in a Nutshell	Civil Rights § 181 et seq.
Secured Transactions in a Nutshell.	Secured Transactions
Securities Regulation in a Nutshell.	Securities Regulation
Sentencing, Corrections and Prisoners' Rights in a Nutshell	Criminal Law; Escape; Habeas Corpus; Pardon and Parole; Prisons
Sex Discrimination in a Nutshell . .	Civil Rights § 105 et seq.
Sports Law in a Nutshell.	Theaters and Shows
State and Local Taxation and Finance in a Nutshell	Taxation
State and Religion in a Nutshell . . .	Constitutional Law § 84 et seq.
State Constitutional Law in a Nutshell	Constitutional Law § 4 et seq.
Study and Practice of Law in a Nutshell	Attorney and Client; District and Prosecuting Attorneys
Tax Procedure and Tax Fraud in a Nutshell	Internal Revenue; Taxation
Torts in a Nutshell.	Negligence; Torts
Toxic Torts in a Nutshell	Health & Environment; Torts

TABLE OF KEY NUMBER SYSTEM CORRELATIONS

Nutshell Series	Key Number Topic
Trial Advocacy in a Nutshell; Trial and Practice Skills in a Nutshell; Trial (Where Do I Sit? What Do I Say?) in a Nutshell	Trial
Unfair Trade Practices in a Nutshell	Monopolies
Uniform Commercial Code in a Nutshell	Sales; Secured Transactions
Uniform Probate Code in a Nutshell	Descent and Distribution; Executors and Administrators; Wills
Water Law in a Nutshell	Waters and Water Courses
White Collar Crime in a Nutshell	Criminal Law § 5 et seq.
Wills and Trusts in a Nutshell	Trusts; Wills
Workers' Compensation and Employee Protection Laws in a Nutshell	Workers' Compensation